Homer's Iliad
The Basel Commentary

Homer's Iliad
The Basel Commentary

Editors
Anton Bierl and Joachim Latacz

Managing Editor
Magdalene Stoevesandt

General Editor of the English Edition
S. Douglas Olson

Homer's Iliad
The Basel Commentary

Edited by
Anton Bierl and Joachim Latacz

Book XVIII

By Marina Coray

Translated by Benjamin W. Millis and Sara Strack and
edited by S. Douglas Olson

DE GRUYTER

The publication of *Homer's Iliad: The Basel Commentary* has been made possible
by the kind financial support from the following organizations:
Stavros Niarchos Foundation
Freiwillige Akademische Gesellschaft (FAG), Basel
L. & Th. La Roche Stiftung, Basel

ISBN 978-3-11-057046-5
e-ISBN (PDF) 978-3-11-057288-9
e-ISBN (EPUB) 978-3-11-057074-8

Library of Congress Control Number: 2018949501

Bibliographic information published by the Deutsche Nationalbibliothek
The Deutsche Nationalbibliothek lists this publication in the Deutsche Nationalbibliografie;
detailed bibliographic data are available in the Internet at http://dnb.dnb.de.

© 2018 Walter de Gruyter Inc., Boston/Berlin
Typesetting: Dörlemann Satz GmbH & Co. KG, Lemförde
Printing and binding: Hubert & Co. GmbH & Co. KG, Göttingen

www.degruyter.com

Table of Contents

Preface to the German Edition

Book 18 of the *Iliad* dedicates much space to Achilleus' new armor, particularly his shield. This object, fantastical in every regard, could be discussed endlessly, and much that is clever and stimulating has already been written on the topic. In the present commentary, discussion of this section takes up considerable space; the complexity of the ekphrasis and the abundance of scholarship relating to it made it useful to include overviews as guides and introductory chapters to these verses in the commentary. The presentation of different interpretations and of the many disputed issues, as well as the bibliographic references, are meant to enable the reader to engage more deeply with these topics.

As was the case for previous volumes of this commentary, the present commentary is based on the Greek text of the edition of the *Iliad* by Martin L. West (Bibliotheca Teubneriana, 1998/2000).

*

Writing and publishing this commentary would not have been possible without help and support from a variety of sources:

First and foremost, I warmly thank the project directors and editors of this commentary on the *Iliad*, Joachim Latacz and Anton Bierl, for their judicious guidance of my engagement with the text. I am also indebted to our international team of experts for valuable suggestions and corrections: Rudolf Führer, Fritz Graf, Martin Guggisberg, Irene de Jong, Michael Meier-Brügger, Sebastiaan van der Mije, René Nünlist, Jürgen von Ungern-Sternberg, Rudolf Wachter and Martin L. West. As previously, they have all provided advice, suggestions and a keen eye.

In addition, I owe warm thanks to the members of the commentary team for innumerable ideas, suggestions, conversations and encouragement at all stages of the process: Martha Krieter-Spiro, Magdalene Stoevesandt, Katharina Wesselmann and particularly Claude Brügger, who also guided me in a masterful way through the vagaries of the layout process. The long communal work of writing commentaries has fostered a deep connection between us.

I am similarly grateful for the lively exchange of ideas at the 'Rosshof', the Center for Classical Studies at the Unversity of Basel, and especially for the numerous suggestions by those who assisted me with topics beyond ancient Greek philology or who carefully read sections of the commentary. Thanks are also due the staff of the Classical Studies library at the 'Rosshof' and of the Basel University Library for their generous and straightforward provision of scholarly literature concerning Homer, as well as to the Walter de Gruyter publishing

https://doi.org/10.1515/9783110572889-001

house, and especially Katharina Legutke and Serena Pirrotta for their meticulous care during publication.

I would also like to offer here my personal thanks to the sponsors of the project: the *Schweizerischer Nationalfonds zur Förderung der wissenschaftlichen Forschung* and the *Hamburger Stiftung zur Förderung von Wissenschaft und Kultur,* as well as the following institutions in Basel: the *Freiwillige Akademische Gesellschaft*, the *Frey-Clavel-Stiftung*, the *Max Geldner-Stiftung* and the University of Basel.

My most heartfelt thanks are reserved for my husband who was prepared with unfailing patience to discuss the interpretation of challenging passages and to join me in taking delight in the wonderful world of Homeric poetry.

Basel, March 2015   Marina Coray

Preface to the English Edition

The following is the slightly revised version of the German commentary final-ized for publication in 2015, which I have corrected wherever needed and supple-mented with literature published since.

I feel much obliged to various persons and institutions who have enabled the development of this English edition:

First and foremost I sincerely thank Prof. Dr. Joachim Latacz and Prof. Dr. Anton Bierl, the two directors of the Homer Commentary, who have also tirelessly supported the translation into English. A very special thanks goes to the trans-lators Dr. Benjamin W. Millis and Dr. Sara Strack, as well as Prof. Dr. S. Douglas Olson, the general editor of the English edition, for their excellent and diligent work. They have once again performed a Herculean labour and not only created a wonderful translation of an occasionally complex text, but also carefully cor-rected omissions and errors which had been overlooked. The English edition would not have been possible without the generous financial backing by the *Stavros Niarchos Foundation*, the *Freiwillige Akademische Gesellschaft*, and the *L. & Th. La Roche Stiftung*. Also the *Walter de Gruyter* publishing house has sub-stantially contributed to the completion of this book. I owe them all the greatest debt of gratitude. Lastly, I warmly thank my colleagues, Dr. Magdalene Stoeve-sandt and Dr. Martha Krieter-Spiro, and especially my husband for their manifold support and assistance.

Basel, May 2018   Marina Coray

https://doi.org/10.1515/9783110572889-002

Notes for the Reader

1. In the commentary, four levels of explanation are distinguished graphically:
    a) The most important explanations for users of all audiences are set in regular type. Knowledge of Greek is not required here; Greek words are given in transliteration (exception: lemmata from *LfgrE*, see COM 41 [1]).
    b) More detailed explanations of the Greek text are set in medium type. These sections correspond to a standard philological commentary.
    c) Specific information on particular sub-fields of Homeric scholarship is set in small type.
    d) The 'elementary section', designed to facilitate an initial approach to the text especially for school and university students, appears beneath a dividing line at the foot of the page.

    The elementary section discusses Homeric word forms in particular, as well as prosody and meter. It is based on the '24 Rules Relating to Homeric Language', to which reference is made with the abbreviation 'R'. Particularly frequent phenomena (e.g. the lack of an augment) are not noted throughout but are instead recalled ca. every 50 verses. — Information relating to Homeric vocabulary is largely omitted; for this, the reader is referred to the specialized dictionaries of CUNLIFFE and AUTENRIETH/ KAEGI.

    Complex issues are addressed in the elementary section as well as the main commentary; they are briefly summarized in the elementary section and discussed in greater detail in the main commentary. Such passages are marked in the elementary section with an arrow (↑). In contrast, references of the type 'cf. 73n.' in the elementary section refer to notes within the elementary section itself, never to the main commentary.

2. The chapters of the *Prolegomena* volume are cited by the following abbreviations:

    CG/CH   Cast of Characters of the *Iliad*: Gods/Human Beings
    COM   Introduction: Commenting on Homer
    FOR   Formularity and Orality
    G   Grammar of Homeric Greek
    HT   History of the Text
    M   Homeric Meter (including prosody)
    MYC   Homeric-Mycenaean Word Index
    NTHS   New Trends in Homeric Scholarship

https://doi.org/10.1515/9783110572889-003

xxxᴾ   Superscript 'P' following a term refers to the definitions of terms in 'Homeric Poetics in Keywords'.

STR   Structure of the *Iliad*

In addition:

R   refers to the '24 Rules Relating to Homeric Language' in the present commentary (below, pp. 1 ff.).

3. Textual criticism

The commentary is based on the Teubner text of M.L. WEST. In some passages, the commentators favor decisions differing from that edition. In these cases, both versions of the lemma are provided; West's text is shown first in square brackets, followed by the version favored in the commentary.

4. English lemmata

The English lemmata in the commentary are taken from the translation of R. LATTIMORE. In places where the commentators favor a different rendering, both versions are of the lemma are provided; the rendering of Lattimore is shown first in square brackets, followed by the version favored in the commentary.

5. Quotations of non-English secondary literature

Quotations from secondary literature originally written in German, French or Italian are given in English translation; in such cases, the bibliographic reference is followed by the notation 'transl.' In the case of terms that are especially important or open to misinterpretation, the original is given in square brackets.

6. Formulaic language

On the model of 'Ameis-Hentze(-Cauer)', repeated verses and verse-halves are usually noted (on this, cf. COM 30). Other formulaic elements (verse beginning and verse end formulae in particular) are only highlighted to the extent necessary to convey an overall impression of the formulaic character of Homeric language.

7. Type-scenesᴾ

For each type-scene, the commentary provides at the appropriate place an 'ideal version' by compiling a cumulative, numbered list of all characteristic elements of the scene that occur in the *Iliad* and/or *Odyssey*; the numbers of the elements actually realized in the passage in question are printed in bold. Each subsequent occurrence refers back to this primary treatment and uses numbering and bold print in accord with the same principle.

8. Abbreviations

(a) Bibliographic Abbreviations
For the bibliographic abbreviations, see below pp. 277 ff.

(b) Primary literature (for the editions used, see below pp. 280 f.)

Aesch.	Aeschylus (*Ag.* = *Agamemnon, Eum.* = *Eumenides*)
'Apollod.'	Works ascribed to Apollodorus (*Bibl.* = *Bibliotheke*)
Apoll. Rhod.	Apollonius Rhodius
Arat.	Aratus (*Phaen.* = *Phaenomena*)
Certamen	*Certamen Homeri et Hesiodi*, 'Contest of Homer and Hesiod'
Chrest.	*Chrestomathia* (Proclus' summary of the 'Epic Cycle')
Cypr.	*Cypria* (in the 'Epic Cycle')
Diog. Laert.	Diogenes Laertius
Eur.	Euripides (*El.* = *Electra, Hec.* = *Hecuba*)
Eust.	Eustathius
Hdt.	Herodotus
Hes.	Hesiod (*Op.* = *Opera*, 'Works and Days'; *Th.* = *Theogony*)
'Hes.'	Works ascribed to Hesiod (*Sc.* = *Scutum*, 'Shield of Herakles', *fr.* = fragments)
hom.h.	A collective term for the Homeric hymns
h.Ap.,	Individual Homeric hymns: to Apollo,
h.Bacch.,	– to Bacchus/Dionysos,
h.Cer.,	– to Ceres/Demeter,
h.Merc.,	– to Mercury/Hermes and
h.Ven.	– to Venus/Aphrodite
Hyg.	Hyginus (*Fab.* = *Fabulae*)
Il.	*Iliad*
Il. parv.	*Ilias parva*, 'Little Iliad' (in the 'Epic Cycle')
Il. Pers.	*Iliou Persis*, 'Sack of Troy' (in the 'Epic Cycle')
Od.	*Odyssey*
Ov.	Ovid (*Met.* = *Metamorphoses*)
Pind.	Pindar (*Isthm., Nem., Ol.* = 'Isthmian, Nemean, Olympian Odes' [Victory Odes], *fr.* = fragments)
Plut.	Plutarch (*Thes.* = *Theseus*)
Schol.	scholion, scholia
schol. A (etc.)	scholion in manuscript A (etc.)
Soph.	Sophocles (*Ant.* = *Antigone, Trach.* = *Trachiniae*)
Xen.	Xenophon (*Anab.* = *Anabasis*, 'March Up-country')

(c) Other abbreviations
(Commonly used abbreviations, as well as those listed under 2 above, are not included here.)

*	reconstructed form
<	developed from
>	developed into
|	marks verse beginning and end
↑	in the elementary section, refers to the relevant lemma in the main commentary
a/b after a verse number	indicates the 1st/2nd verse half
a/b after a verse number	indicates only in the *app. crit.* an additional verse
A 1, B 1 (etc.)	indicates caesurae in the hexameter (cf. M 6)
app. crit.	*apparatus criticus* (West)
fr., frr.	fragment, fragments
Gr.	Greek
I-E	Indo-European
imper.	imperative
impf.	imperfect
Introd.	Introduction
loc.	locative
ms., mss.	manuscript, manuscripts
n.	note[1]
sc.	*scilicet*
subjunc.	subjunctive
s.v., s.vv.	*sub voce, sub vocibus*
svw.	soviel wie
t.t.	*terminus technicus*
VB	verse-beginning
VE	verse-end
VH	verse-half
v.l., vv.ll.	*varia lectio, variae lectiones*
voc.	vocative

---

1 '48n.' refers to the commentary on verse 48 in the present volume, whereas 1.162n. refers to the commentary on verse 162 in Book 1. – 'In 19.126 (see *ad loc.*)' and 'cf. 24.229 ff. (see *ad locc.*)' refer primarily to the relevant passages in the Homeric text, secondarily to one or more commentary entries relating to the relevant passages. (In the first example, the commentary entry can be found under 19.126–127; in the second, relevant information can be found under 24.229–234 and 24.229–231.)

24 Rules Relating to Homeric Language (R)

The following compilation of the characteristics of Homeric language emphasizes its *deviations* from Attic grammar. Linguistic notes are included only exceptionally (but can be found in the 'Grammar of Homeric language' [G] in the *Prolegomena* volume; references to the relevant paragraphs of that chapter are here shown in the right margin).

R1	Homeric language is an **artificial language**, characterized by:	**G**
1.1	meter (which can result in a variety of remodellings);	3
1.2	the technique of *oral poetry* (frequently repeated content is rendered in formulae, often with metrically different variants);	3
1.3	different dialects: Ionic is the basic dialect; interspersed are forms from other dialects, particularly Aeolic (so-called Aeolicisms), that often provide variants according to 1.1 and 1.2.	2

Phonology, metric, prosody

R2	**Sound change of ᾱ > η:** In the Ionic dialect, old ᾱ has changed to η; in *non-Attic* Ionic (i.e. also in Homer), this occurs also after ε, ι, ρ (1.30: πάτρης). When ᾱ is nonetheless found in Homer, it is generally:	5–8
2.1	'late', i.e. it developed *after* the Ionic-Attic sound change (1.3: ψυχάς);	
2.2	or adopted from the Aeolic poetic tradition (1.1: θεά).	
R3	**Vowel shortening:** Long vowels (esp. η) before another vowel (esp. ο/ω/α) in medial position are frequently shortened, although not consistently (e.g. gen. pl. βασιλήων rather than the metrically impossible four-syllable -έων; the related phenomenon of *quantitative metathesis* [lengthening of a second short vowel] often does *not* occur [e.g. gen. sing. βασιλῆος rather than -έως]).	39 f.
R4	**Digamma (ϝ):** The Ionic dialect of Homer no longer used the phoneme /w/ (like Engl. *will*). It is, however,	
4.1	attested in Mycenaean, as well as in some dialects still in the alphabetic period (Mycenaean *ko-wa* /korwā/, Corinthian ϙόρϝα);	19
4.2	in part deducible etymologically (e.g. Homeric κούρη – with compensatory lengthening after the disappearance of the digamma – in contrast to Attic κόρη).	27

https://doi.org/10.1515/9783110572889-004

In Addition, digamma can often be deduced in Homer on the
basis of the meter; thus in the case of

4.3   hiatus (see R 5) without elision (1.7: Ἀτρεΐδης τε (ϝ)άναξ);   22

4.4   hiatus without shortening of a long vowel at word end (1.321: τώ   21
       (ϝ)οι, cf. R 5.5);

4.5   a single consonant 'making position' (1.70: ὅς (ϝ)είδη).   24

4.6   Occasionally, digamma is no longer taken into account (1.21: υἱὸν   26
       ἐκηβόλον, originally ϝεκ-).

R 5   **Hiatus:** The clash of a vocalic word end with a vocalic word
       beginning (*hiatus* 'gaping') is avoided through:

5.1   elision: short vowels and -αι in endings of the middle voice are   30/
       elided (1.14: στέμματ' ἔχων; 1.117: βούλομ' ἐγώ; 5.33: μάρνασθ'   37
       ὁπποτέροισι), occasionally also -οι in μοι/σοι (1.170; hiatus that
       results from elision is left unchanged (1.2: ἄλγε' ἔθηκεν);

5.2   *ny ephelkystikon* (movable *ny*): only after a short vowel (ε and ι),   33
       esp. dat. pl. -σι(ν); 3rd sing. impf./aor./perf. -ε(ν); 3rd sing. and
       pl. -σι(ν); the modal particle κε(ν); the suffix -φι(ν), cf. R 11.4; the
       suffix -θε(ν), cf. R 15.1; *ny ephelkystikon* also provides metrically
       convenient variants;

5.3   contraction across word boundaries (noted as *crasis*: τἄλλα,   31
       χἠμεῖς).
       – Hiatus is admissible predominantly in the case of:

5.4   loss of digamma (cf. R 4.3);   34

5.5   so-called correption: a long vowel/diphthong at word end is   35
       shortened (1.17: Ἀτρεΐδαι τε **καὶ ἄλλοι** ἐϋκνήμιδες; 1.15
       [with synizesis: R 7]: χρυσέῳ ἀνὰ σκήπτρῳ);

5.6   metrical caesura or more generally a semantic break;   36

5.7   after words ending in -ι and 'small words' such as πρό and ὅ.   37

R 6   **Vocalic contraction** (e.g. following the loss of intervocalic /w/   43–
       [digamma], /s/ or /j/) is frequently not carried out in Homeric   45
       Greek (1.74: κέλεαι [2nd sing. mid., instead of Attic -ῃ]; 1.103:
       μένεος [gen. sing., instead of -ους]).

R 7   **Synizesis:** Occasionally, two vowels are to be read as a single   46
       syllable, especially in the case of quantitative metathesis
       (1.1: Πηληϊάδεω: R 3) but also in the gen. pl. -έων. (Synizesis is
       indicated by a sublinear curved line connecting the affected
       vowels, 1.18: θεοί.)

R 8   **Diectasis:** Contracted forms (e.g. ὁρῶντες) may be 'stretched   48
(ὁρόωντες); the metrically necessary prosodic shape of older
uncontracted forms (*ὁράοντες, ‿‿–‿) is thus artificially reconstructed. Similarly, the aor. inf. -εῖν is written -έειν (rather than
the older *-έεν).

R 9   **Change in consonant quantity** creates metrically convenient variants (which usually derive originally from different dialects: R 1.3):
9.1   τόσ(σ)ος, ποσ(σ)ί, Ὀδυσ(σ)εύς, ἔσ(σ)εσθαι, τελέσ(σ)αι; Ἀχιλ(λ)εύς;   17
ὄπ(π)ως, etc.
9.2   Variation at word beginning creates similar flexibility in π(τ)   18
όλεμος, π(τ)όλις.

R 10   **Adaptation to the meter:** Three (or more) short syllables in a   49 f.
row, or a single short between two longs (both metrically impos-
sible), are avoided by:
10.1   metrical lengthening (ἀ̄θάνατος, δῑογενής, **οὖ**ρεα rather than
ὄρεα; μένεα πν**εί**οντες rather than πνέ-);
10.2   changes in word formation (πολεμήϊος rather than πολέμιος;
ἱππιοχαίτης rather than ἱππο-).

Morphology

Homeric Greek declines in ways that sometimes vary from Attic forms or
represent additional forms:

R 11   Especially noteworthy in the case of **nouns** are:
11.1   1st declension: 68
gen. pl. -άων (1.604: Μουσάων) and -έων (1.273: βουλέων);
dat. pl. -ῃσι (2.788: θύρῃσι) and -ῃς (1.238: παλάμῃς);
gen. sing. masc. -αο (1.203: Ἀτρεΐδαο) and -εω (1.1:
Πηληϊάδεω);
11.2   2nd declension: 69
gen. sing. -οιο (1.19: Πριάμοιο);
dat. pl. -οισι (1.179: ἑτάροισι);
11.3   3rd declension: 70–
gen. sing. of *i*-stems: -ιος (2.811: πόλιος) and -ηος (16.395:   76
πόληος);
gen./dat./acc. sing. of *ēu*-stems: -ῆος, -ῆϊ, -ῆα (1.1: Ἀχιλῆος;
1.9: βασιλῆϊ; 1.23: ἱερῆα);

dat. pl. -εσσι in the case of *s*-stems and other consonant
stems (1.235: ὄρεσσι);

11.4 gen./dat. sing./pl. in -φι (1.38: ἶφι; 4.452: ὄρεσφι); often metrically   66
convenient variants (e.g. βίηφι beside βίη).

R 12 Varying **stem formation** (and thus declension) appears in the
following nouns among others:

12.1 νηῦς: gen. sing. νηός, νεός, dat. νηΐ, acc. νῆα, νέα; nom. pl. νῆες,   77
νέες, gen. νηῶν, νεῶν, dat. νηυσί, νήεσσι, νέεσσι, acc. νῆας, νέας.

12.2 πολύς, πολύ (*u*-stem) and πολλός, πολλή, πολλόν (*o/ā*-stem) are   57
both fully declined.

12.3 υἱός: gen. sing. υἱέος, υἷος, dat. υἱέϊ, υἱεῖ, υἷϊ, acc. υἱόν, υἱέα, υἷα;   53
nom. pl. υἱέες, υἱεῖς, υἷες, gen. υἱῶν, dat. υἱάσι, υἱοῖσι, acc. υἱέας,
υἷας.

12.4 Ἄρης: gen. Ἄρηος, Ἄρεος, dat. Ἄρηϊ, Ἄρεϊ, Ἄρῃ, acc. Ἄρηα, Ἄρην,   53
voc. Ἄρες, Ἆρες.

12.5 Similarly complex declensions occur in the case of γόνυ (gen.   53/
γούνατος beside γουνός, nom./acc. pl. γούνατα beside γοῦνα),   77
δόρυ (δούρατος, -τι etc. beside δουρός, -ί etc.); Ζεύς (Διός, Διΐ, Δία
beside Ζηνός, Ζηνί, Ζῆν/Ζῆνα).

R 13 Among other unusual **comparative forms** note: χερείων,   79
χειρότερος, χερειότερος (beside χείρων); ἀρείων (beside
ἀμείνων). Some omparatives and superlatives are formed from
nouns, e.g. βασιλεύτερος, βασιλεύτατος.

R 14 Varying **pronoun forms**:

14.1 Personal pronoun: 81

1st sing. gen. ἐμεῖο, ἐμέο, μεο, ἐμέθεν (very rare: μοι, e.g. 1.37)
2nd sing. gen. σεῖο, σέο, σεο, σέθεν; dat. τοι
3rd sing. gen. εἷο, ἕο, ἔθεν, ἑθεν; dat. οἷ, ἑοῖ, οἱ; acc. ἕ, ἑέ, ἑ, μιν
1st pl. nom. ἄμμες; gen. ἡμέων, ἡμείων; dat. ἧμιν, ἄμμι; acc. ἡμέας, ἄμμε
2nd pl. nom. ὕμμες; gen. ὑμέων, ὑμείων; dat. ὕμμι; acc. ὑμέας, ὕμμε
3rd pl. gen. σφείων, σφεων; dat. σφισι, σφι; acc. σφέας, σφε, σφεας, σφας
1st dual nom./acc. νώ, νῶϊ; gen./dat. νῶϊν
2nd dual nom./acc. σφώ, σφῶϊ; gen./dat. σφῶϊν
3rd dual nom./acc. σφωε; gen./dat. σφωϊν

14.2	Interrogative/indefinite pronoun:	84

gen. sing. τέο/τεο; dat. sing. τεῳ; gen. pl. τέων; correspondingly
ὅττεο, ὅτεῳ etc.

14.3	Anaphoric demonstrative pronoun (= 'article', cf. R 17):	83

the same endings as nouns (R 11.1–2); nom. pl. masc./fem. often
with an initial τ (τοί, ταί).

14.4	Possessive pronoun:	82

1st pl.   ἁμός
2nd sing./pl.   τεός   ὑμός
3rd sing./pl.   ἑός, ὅς   σφός

14.5	Relative pronoun:	83

The anaphoric demonstrative pronoun frequently functions as a
relative pronoun (14.3).

R 15	**Adverbial forms** straddle the border between morphology	66

(cases) and word formation. They can form metrically convenient
variants to the true cases:

15.1	'genitive':	-θεν (whence?, see also R 14.1), e.g. κλισίηθεν (1.391);
15.2	'dative':	-θι (where?), e.g. οἴκοθι (8.513);
15.3	'accusative':	-δε (whither?), e.g. ἀγορήνδε (1.54).

R 16   For **verbs**, the following points deserve particular attention:

16.1	Augment: frequently absent (which can lead to assimilation, e.g.	85

ἔμβαλε rather than ἐνέβαλε, κάλλιπον rather than κατέλιπον, cf.
R 20.1); used to fit the meter.

16.2	Personal endings:	86/
		93

2nd sing. -σθα (1.554: ἐθέλησθα)
1st pl. mid. -μεσθα beside -μεθα (1.140: μεταφρασόμεσθα)
3rd pl. mid. (predominantly perf.) -ἄται/-ἄτο beside -νται/-ντο
     (1.239: εἰρύαται)
3rd pl. -ν (with preceding short vowel) beside -σαν (with corre-
     sponding long vowel), esp. aor. pass. -θεν beside -θησαν (1.57:
     ἤγερθεν)
The difference from Attic forms frequently lies merely in the omission of contraction (cf. R 6) between verbal stem and ending.

16.3	Subjunctive:	89

frequently with a short vowel in the case of athematic stems
(ἴομεν from εἶμι, εἴδομεν from οἶδα); formed like the fut. ind. in
the case of σ-aorists (1.80: χώσεται). – In the 3rd sing. subjunc.,
the ending -ησι(ν) (1.408: ἐθέλησιν) is found beside -ῃ.

16.4	Infinitive:	87

Aeolic -μεν(αι) (predominantly athematic verbs) beside Ionic -ναι
(e.g. ἔμ(μ)εν and ἔμ(μ)εναι beside εἶναι);
Aeolic -ῆναι beside Ionic -εῖν (2.107: φορῆναι);
thematic -έμεν(αι) (1.547: ἀκουέμεν; *Od*. 11.380: ἀκουέμεναι);
thematic aor. -έειν (2.393: φυγέειν; 15.289: θανέειν).

16.5	Forms with -σκ- stand for repeated action in the past	60

(1.490: πωλέσκετο).

16.6	Especially noteworthy as variant forms of εἰμί are:	90

pres. ind.: 2nd sing. ἐσσι, 1st pl. εἰμεν, 3rd pl. ἔασι(ν);
impf.: 1st sing. ἦα, 3rd sing. ἦεν and ἔην, 3rd pl. ἔσαν (cf. 16.1);
fut.: 3rd sing. ἔσ(σ)εται;
part. ἐών, -όντος; for the inf., 16.4.

Syntax

R 17	**ὅ, ἥ, τό** (on the declension, R 14.3) is rarely a 'pure article' and instead generally has an older anaphoric demonstrative function.	99

R 18 **Number:**

18.1	The dual is relatively common; forms of the dual and the plural can be freely combined.	97
18.2	The plural is sometimes used simply for metrical convenience (1.45: τόξα).	

R 19	**Use of the cases:**	97
19.1	Accusative of respect is especially common (among other instances in the so-called σχῆμα καθ᾽ ὅλον καὶ κατὰ μέρος: two accusatives indicate respectively the whole and the part of something, 1.362: τί δέ **σε φρένας** ἵκετο πένθος;).	
19.2	Indications of origin, place or direction sometimes occur *with no preposition* (1.359: ἀνέδυ … ἁλός; 1.45: τόξ᾽ ὤμοισιν ἔχων; 1.322: ἔρχεσθον κλισίην).	

R 20	**Prepositions:**	
20.1	show a greater diversity of forms: ἄν (= ἀνά; with apocope, frequently with assimilation: ἂμ πεδίον, 5.87; cf. R 16.1); ἐς (= εἰς); εἰν, ἐνί, εἰνί (= ἐν); κάτ (= κατά; see on ἀνά); πάρ, παραί (= παρά); προτί, ποτί (= πρός); ξύν (= σύν); ὑπαί (= ὑπό);	59

| 20.2 | are more independent in use and position (1) with regard to | 98 |

20.2 are more independent in use and position (1) with regard to nouns (i.e. are used in a more adverbial manner), frequently also placed after them as 'postpositions' in so-called *anastrophe* (and thus often with an acute accent on the first syllable: e.g. ᾧ ἔπι, 1.162); (2) with regard to verbs (i.e. not necessarily connected to the relevant verb as a preverb, so-called *tmesis*: ἐπὶ μῦθον ἔτελλε, 1.25); this produces metrically convenient variants.

R 21 **Use of the moods:** 100
21.1 The moods and the modal particle (κε/κεν = ἄν) follow rules that are less strict than those described in grammars of Attic Greek.
21.2 The functions of the subjunctive and the future cannot always be sharply distinguished.

R 22 Characteristic Homeric **conjunctions** are: 101
22.1 conditional: αἰ (= εἰ);
22.2 temporal: εἷος/εἵως (= ἕως) 'while', ἧμος 'when', εὖτε 'when', ὄφρα 'while, until';
22.3 causal: ὅ τι, ὅ;
22.4 comparative: ἠΰτε 'like';
22.5 final: ὄφρα.

R 23 **Alternation of voice:** In the case of some verbs, the act. and 100
mid. forms are used as convenient metrical variants with no discernible difference in meaning, e.g. φάτο/ἔφη, ὀΐω/ὀΐομαι.

R 24 **Particles** are sometimes used in ways that differ from later usage: 101
24.1 ἄρα, ἄρ, ῥα, ῥ': signals or suggests that something is evident, roughly 'therefore, naturally, as is well known'; probably often used mainly for metrical reasons (especially ῥ' to avoid hiatus, cf. R 5).
24.2 ἀτάρ, αὐτάρ (metrical variants, etymologically distinct but used interchangeably in Homer with no distinction in meaning): 'but, still'; sometimes adversative (1.127: σὺ μὲν ... αὐτὰρ Ἀχαιοί), sometimes progressive (1.51: αὐτὰρ ἔπειτα), rarely apodotic (like δέ, see below).
24.3 apodotic δέ: δέ can introduce a main clause (apodosis) after a preceding dependent clause (protasis) (e.g. 1.58). Occasionally ἀλλά (e.g. 1.82), αὐτάρ (e.g. 3.290, cf. 1.133), and καί (e.g. 1.494) are used apodotically as well.

24.4 ἦ: 'really, actually'; almost exclusively in direct speech. – Weakened in the compounds ἤτοι (e.g. 1.68), ἠμὲν … ἠδέ 'on the one hand … on the other hand' and ἠδέ 'and'.

24.5 κε(ν): = ἄν (cf. R 21.1).

24.6 μέν: used not only to introduce an antithesis (with a subsequent δέ) but also commonly in its original, purely emphatic sense (≈ μήν, μάν; e.g. 1.216).

24.7 μήν, μάν: emphatic; when standing alone, almost always in negative sentences (e.g. 4.512) or with imperatives (e.g. 1.302); otherwise it strengthens other particles, esp. ἦ and καί (e.g. 2.370, 19.45).

24.8 οὐδέ/μηδέ: these connectives can occur after affirmative clauses, not only after negative ones as in Attic.

24.9 οὖν: almost always in conjunction with temporal ἐπεί or ὡς, '(when) therefore' (e.g. 1.57).

24.10 περ: stresses the preceding word; specifically concessive, esp. with participles (1.586: κηδομένη περ 'although saddened'); intensive (1.260: ἀρείοσι ἠέ περ ὑμῖν 'with even better men than you'); limitative-contrasting (1.353: τιμήν περ 'at least honor').

24.11 'epic τε': occurs in generalizing statements (e.g. 1.86, 1.218), esp. common in the 'as' part of similes (e.g. 2.90).

24.12 τοι: ethical dat. of the 2nd pers. personal pronoun fossilized as a particle (and often not clearly distinguishable from it); appeals to the special attention of the addressee, roughly 'imagine, I tell you'.

24.13 τοιγάρ: 'so then' (to be distinguished from τοι ≈ σοι; the initial element belongs to the demonstrative stem το-, cf. τώ 'therefore'); in Homer, it always introduces the answer to a request (e.g. 1.76).

Overview of the Action in Book 18

https://doi.org/10.1515/9783110572889-005

609–617   Hephaistos forges the remaining defensive arms: corselet, helmet and greaves. After they are complete, Thetis immediately departs from Olympos with the arms.

Commentary

Book 18 describes the final events of the third day of battle in the *Iliad* (i.e. of the 26th day of the action of the *Iliad* overall: STR 21 fig. 1), which is the subject of Books 11–18 (239–242n.); for the previous events of this day of battle, see the introductions in the commentaries on Books 14 and 16. At the beginning of Book 18, Patroklos has died, the battle for his corpse is at its peak, and Achilleus' armor, which had been worn by Patroklos, has fallen into the hands of the enemy (on the death of Patroklos, see the references to the commentary on Book 16 in the notes to vv. 453–456). What the Greeks fail to achieve, namely at least to rescue the corpse from Hektor and the Trojans (17.1–18.164: 148–164n.), Achilleus manages to accomplish with divine help after he receives the report of his friend's death at the beginning of Book 18; he may be without armor, but with Athene's aid Achilleus manages a terrifying appearance (arranged like an epiphany: 203–221n.) at the edge of the encampment of ships: the Trojans flee in panic, and the slain Patroklos can now be brought back to the camp and laid out for mourning (230–242). The remainder of the Book describes the events of the night between the 3rd and 4th (and final) day of battle in the *Iliad*: mourning, the Trojans' strategic consultation, the production of new weapons for Achilleus by the divine smith Hephaistos. Overall, Book 18 prepares in various ways for the conclusion of the wrath of Achilleus and his reentry in Book 19 into the military community of the Greeks, thus forming a transition to the final phase of the *Iliad*: (a) the narrator[P] repeatedly has characters[P] look back to the 'menis'-story or recapitulate earlier events ('récit spéculaire'), namely in the speeches by Thetis (74–77, 436–461: see *ad loc.* and esp. notes on 444–456) and Achilleus (98–113, 125, 324–332), on the Trojan side by Polydamas (257–260) and Hektor (293 f.), more as an intimation in the conversation between Zeus and Hera (356–368 [see *ad loc.*]); he achieves the same in an indirect manner through the design of some of the images on the shield of Achilleus (478–608n. section **B.2.b.**); (b) he has both Achilleus and Hektor resolve to fight one another (90 ff., 114 ff., 334 f. and 305 ff.), thus preparing for the duel between the two in Book 22, and he signals via his commentary on the results of the Trojan military assembly (310–313) that Trojan success in battle is at an end and that a change will take place in the trajectory of the fighting; (c) the production of Achilleus' new arms (468–617) facilitates his reengagement in combat and prepares his participation in the battle on the next day (19.424–23.4) – the first within the *Iliad* in which he takes an active part; the story of the origin of the armor and the description of its elements are elsewhere integrated within arming scenes, but in this unique case they are lifted out of the scheme and moved forward (18.369–19.3) – the arming scene follows at 19.364–398 (478n.): the narrator[P] designs a scene in which the arms, especially the shield, are made, providing a breathing

https://doi.org/10.1515/9783110572889-006

space prior to Achilleus' campaign of vengeance and allowing for reflection on the artistic achievement. – Two themes permeate the Book: (1) the arms of Achilleus: (a) the loss of his first set of armor, inherited from Peleus (21, 82–85, 130–133, 188, 197, 451–456, 460b), (b) Achilleus unarmed (134 f., 189 f., 192 f., 203–206), (c) the new armor from Hephaistos' workshop (136 f., 143 f., 147, 191, 457–460a, 466–617, see also 19.3–22); (2) the death of Achilleus: both his mother and especially he himself engage repeatedly with the topic of his mortality, in particular because his decision to exact revenge on Hektor inevitably brings his death closer (59 f., 86–93, 95 f., 98–101, 114–121a, 329–333, 432–443, 464 f., see also 19.408–423).

The following entries provide an overview of the action in Book 18:

Overview of the action (see above, p. 8 f.); within the commentary, 1–147n., 134–144n., 145–147n., 239–242n., 243–314a n., 254–309n., 315n., 343–355n., 356–368n., 369–427n., 429–461n., 468–617n. (the *hoplopoiia* as a whole), 478–608n. section **B.1.b.** (shield).

Entries on inividual **topics**:

Achilleus' death: 22–147n., esp. (a) foreshadowing: 88–93n., 95–96n., 114–126n., 328–332n., 333–342n., (b) lament for Patroklos mirroring mourning for Achilleus: 28–31n., 37–72n., (c) mortality *vs.* elevation to the divine and divine support: 117–121a n., 464–467n.

Burial rites: 336–337n., 343–355n., 352–353n.

Catalogue of Nereïds: 39–49n. (on the individual names, see nn. on the relevant verses)

Hoplopoiia, esp. Achilleus' shield: 468–617n., 478–608n. section **B.1.–B.4.**, 478–482n.

Lamentation: 23–27n., 28–31n., 37–72n., 55–60n., 56–57n., 315n., 316n., 317n., 324–342n.

Music, song and dance: 491b–496n., 493n., 494n., 495a n., 570n., 571–572n., 590–606n., 592n., 593–602n., 594n., 603–604a n., 605b–606n.

Neoanalysis: 17n., 26–27n., 37–72n., 95–96n., 130–137n., end., 453–456n., end.

Characters[P]:

Antilochos: 2n., 17n.

Charis: 382n.

Hektor: 92n., 285–309n., 286–292n., 243–314a n.

Hephaistos: 369–381n., 370–371n., 383n., 394–409n., 395–397a n., 400n.; his miraculous objects: 376n., 417–420n., 419–420n., 469n.

Hera: 119n., 168n., 356–368n.

Polydamas: 249–253n., 251–252n.

Thetis: 85n., 394–409n., 429–461n., 432–434a n., 434a n.

Poetics:

'If-not' situations[P]: 165–168n.

'récit spéculaire': 444–456n., 478–608n. section **B.2.b.**

Similes[P] and comparisons[P]: 109–110n., 161–164n., 203–221n., 207–227n., 207–214n., 219–221n., 318b–322n., 318b n., 478–608n. section **B.2.b.** (on 4b), 579–586n., 600–601n., 616–617n.

'table of contents' speech: 134–144n., 333–342n.

Type-scenes[P] and themes[P] (in alphabetical order): 'ambush' 513n.; 'arrival' and 'visit' 369–427n.; 'change of location by a deity' 65–72n.; 'delivery of a message' 1–22a n., 166–202n.; 'dressing' 414–416n.; 'return of a warrior to battle' 203–221n.; 'supplication' (457n.).

1–147 Lamentation for Patroklos

The book begins with a transition from the fight for Patroklos' corpse (1), which was portrayed in the course of Book 17 and is continued at 18.148bff., to Achilleus (2), who increasingly becomes the focus of the story again. When Achilleus last appeared, he prayed to Zeus for Patroklos' well-being and prepared to observe the battle (16.220–256: 16.255–256n.). In the battle descriptions that follow Patroklos' death (on the events leading up to the death, see the introduction in Book 16), he is portrayed as completely ignorant of Patroklos' fate (17.401b–406a); both Aias and Menelaos ensure that he is notified by Antilochos of his friend's death (17.640–642, 654f., 691f., 701, 708f.: RUTHERFORD 1982, 155). At the beginning of the scene, after mention of the external situation (18.2f.), Achilleus' thoughts and fears when faced with the distress of the Greeks come into focus, first being alluded to by the narrator (4), subsequently expanded in Achilleus' speech (6–14), and finally confirmed by Antilochos (18–21). In the narrative that follows, the space before the return to depiction of the battle (148b) is taken up with responses by the characters to the notification of the death: Achilleus is overcome by grief and sorrow for his friend (22–35a), Thetis has a terrible forboding and fears for her son (35b–64), Achilleus describes his situation to his mother (65–147). On the overall structure of these scenes, see SCHADEWALDT (1936) 1997, 151–160; EDWARDS on 1–69.

1–34 Achilleus receives the report that Patroklos has died.

1–22a 2–22 represent the conclusion of the type-scene[P] 'delivery of a message' (on which, 1.320–348a n.), containing elements (**3**) the messenger arrives (2), (**4**) finds the person in question (description of the situation at 3–15), (**5**) approaches (16–17a), (**6**) delivers the message (17b–22a); elements 1–2 (instructions and departure) precede at 17.684–701. The battle descriptions that occur at 17.702–18.1 and are inserted into the type-scene – the current Book-divisions were established only in the post-Homeric period (1n.) – serve *inter alia* to fill the time needed for Antilochos' journey from the battlefield to the encampment of ships (covering scene[P]; cf. 6.119–236n.; KURZ 1966, 162; on the technique for depicting simultaneous actions, see RICHARDSON 1990, 225–227 n. 14; RENGAKOS 1995).

1 = 11.596, 13.673; to caesura C 2 = 17.366. — **So …:** a summary of the preceding battle action between Greeks and Trojans. The VB formula 'So these' (Greek *hōs hoi men*, see below) prepares the change of scene (here the return to the messenger scene: 1–22a n.); this formula was frequently chosen as an endpoint of a Book in the – post-Homeric – division of the *Iliad* into 24 Books (16.1n. with bibliography; DE JONG on *Il.* 22.1–4) and is here preferred to a second break in the action, namely the nightfall at 239 (WEST 2011, 343; cf. 1.605–611n., 19.1–39n.). — **fire:** Comparison[P] with fire often serves to characterize heated battle (ROLLINGER 1996, 166 ff. [with Ancient Near Eastern parallels]; STOEVESANDT 2004, 414 f.), here the defence of Patroklos' body, which is in danger of being captured by the Trojans (17.722 ff.).

ὣς οἳ μέν: an inflectable VB formula (26× *Il.*, 23× *Od.*), often in combination with a verb in the impf.; μὲν … | … δ(έ) here, as frequently, links simultaneous actions, with the impf. indicating that the preceding, summarily mentioned action continues in the background (RENGAKOS 1995, 30; SEECK 1998, 139–142; cf. 1.318a n., 19.3n., 24.22n.; on the explication in the scholia [so-called παραγραφή], NÜNLIST 2009, 60). — μάρναντο: The verb, attested only in the present stem, is a metrically convenient variant of μάχεσθαι but has an archaic character (24.395n.). — δέμας πυρὸς αἰθομένοιο: The adverbial use of the acc. δέμας ('like') is attested in early epic only in the present expression (see *iterata*; CHANTR. 2.48; *LfgrE*); π. αἰ. is a VE formula (7× *Il.*, 2× *Od.*, 3× Hes.).

2 Antilochos: Nestor's son Antilochos (CH 4) is Achilleus' second-best friend after Patroklos (23.556, *Od.* 24.15 f., 24.78 f.) and is considered the fastest among the younger warriors (*Il.* 15.569 f., 23.756), a trait he shares with Achilleus (78n.); here he is chosen to serve as messenger for this very reason (17.640–642, 17.654 f., 17.691–693): JANKO on 15.568–71.

Ἀντίλοχος δ' Ἀχιλῆϊ πόδας ταχύς: The juxtaposition of the names creates a close connection between the messenger and the recipient of the message; attention immediately shifts to Achilleus (KURZ 1966, 121). πόδας ταχύς is an inflectable formula before caesura C 2 (nom./acc. sing.: 8× *Il.*, 1× 'Hes.' *fr.* 204.88 M.-W.), elsewhere often in reference to Achilleus himself (in total 5×; cf. the echoes of Ἀχιλῆα πόδας ταχύν at 13.348, 17.709, 18.358 and π. τ. … Ἀχιλῆα at 18.354, variants of the more common VE formula πόδας ὠκὺς Ἀ. [30× *Il.*]). This use of the formula highlights speed as a characteristic of *both*

---

1 οἵ: with anaphoric demonstrative function (R 17); likewise τόν (3), etc. — μάρναντο: on the unaugmented form, R 16.1. — αἰθομένοιο: on the declension, R 11.2.
2 Ἀχιλῆϊ: on the declension, R 11.3; on the single -λ-, R 9.1. — πόδας … ἄγγελος: predicative, 'as'; πόδας is acc. of respect (R 19.1).

characters (cf. EDWARDS on 1–2; ALONI 1979, 221–223). — **ἄγγελος ἦλθεν:** an inflectable phrase in various positions in the verse (24.194n.).

3–5 found …: In Homeric arrival scenes, the description of the situation (here 'delivery of a message' element 4) usually takes place from the point of view of the arriving character (1.329–333n., 2.169–171n.; cf. the type-scene[P] 'arrival' at 1.496b–502n.). But here the scene is not rendered in secondary focalization[P] to the same degree, since, contrary to common practice elsewhere, what is described is not the visible posture or occupation of the character in question (e.g. standing or sitting: 2.170n.; lying down: 19.4 [see *ad loc.*]), or actions indicating his or her mood (e.g. sighing at 24.123), but instead the narrator immediately directs attention to the thoughts (3 f. 'thinking over', Greek *phronéont'*) that make clear that he already fears what the messenger is about to report (EDWARDS on 1–69; KURZ 1966, 66; DE JONG [1987] 2004, 108 f.). The introduction 'spoke to …' (on the speech introduction formula[P], 5n.) and the rendering in direct speech notwithstanding, Achilleus' entire speech is to be read as an internal monologue, cf. the speech capping formula at 15 (PELLICCIA 1995, 128–134; KULLMANN [1999] 2002, 180–182; LÉTOUBLON 2001, 248–257, esp. 250 f.). *Inter alia*, internal monologues of this sort serve to portray a character's isolation (PELLICCIA *loc. cit.* 134 ff., esp. 141–146, 218 n. 196). They can be divided into monologues of decision (on which, 2.3–7n., 16.431–461n.; DE JONG on *Il.* 22.91–137) and monologues of deliberation, with the latter being triggered by observations, here the flight of the Greeks (6 f., cf. 17.755–761, 18.148–150): DE JONG on *Od.* 5.299–312; HENTZE 1904, 14–16; PELLICCIA 1995, 120–128 (esp. 121 f.).

3 ≈ 19.344. — **ships:** From his ship, Achilleus observes the progress of battle (cf. 11.599 ff.). – The Achaian ships had been pulled up onto the beach and arranged side by side in staggered rows in an arched semi-circle; Achilleus' ship is at the right-hand end of the encampment of ships – facing the Trojan plain and Troy itself (11.7–9): 1.12b n.; outline in HAINSWORTH on *Il.* 11.5–9 and JANKO on 13.681; on the location of the encampment of ships, see 'Appendix topographica' in the commentary to Book 14.

νεῶν ὀρθοκραιράων: on the sense and usage of the epithet[P] ('with upright horns', perhaps in reference to prow and stern), 19.344n.

4–5 Greek *thymós* sometimes denotes the seat of emotions ('mind, heart, soul', as the seat of mental processes affected by emotions), sometimes the emotions themselves; it can also be the source of intellectual processes, here *phronéont'* (2.196n., 6.72n.; *LfgrE s.v.* θυμός 1085.22 ff.; BREMMER 1983, 54 f.).

---

3 νεῶν: on the declension, R 12.1. — ὀρθοκραιράων: on the declension, R 11.1.

For discussion of whether the *thymós* also represents the self, see *LfgrE s.v.* θυμός 1085.37 ff.; BÖHME 1929, 79 f.; VOIGT 1934, 90; JAHN 1987, 20–23, 212–220, 225–232; SULLIVAN 1995, 58.

4 ≈ 2.36 (see *ad loc.*); 1st VH ≈ 10.491, *Od.* 2.116; VE ≈ *Il.* 8.454. — **τά:** on the anticipatory demonstrative function before relative clauses, G 99. — **φρονέοντ(α):** 'having in mind', in reference to future issues 'imagining', here in regard to a set of facts that may or may not have taken place (AH: 'suspecting' [transl.]; *LfgrE s.v.* 1043.4 ff.). — **ἀνὰ θυμόν:** a formula before caesura B 2 designating the seat of mental processes (2.36n., 24.518n., cf. 15n.). — **τετελεσμένα ἦεν:** an inflectable VE formula τετελεσμένος/-ον/-α + form of εἶναι (12× *Il.*, 11× *Od.*, 1× *h.Hom.*; of which 14× fut., 5× pres., 3× subjunc., 2× impf.); the hiatus is due to modification of the formula (M 14). Periphrasis of the verb via perf. part. + εἶναι stresses finality (1.212n.): the narrator is concerned with rendering palpable the intimacy between Achilleus and Patroklos by having Achilleus guess what has in fact (δή: as already told) occurred (EDWARDS 1968, 262 and on 3–4; FINKELBERG 1988, 207, 210; on δή, BAKKER 1997, 74–80, esp. 78: 'draws the hearer into the story'; CUYPERS 2005, 55–58).

5 = 11.403, 17.90, 20.343, 21.53, 21.552, 22.98, *Od.* 5.298, 5.355, 5.407, 5.464. – a formulaic verse introducing an internal monologue (3–5n.; DE JONG on *Il.* 22.98; *LfgrE s.v.* ὀχθῆσαι; USENER 1990, 86 f.). Achilleus' unease regarding the flight of the Greeks (6 f.), his fears for Patroklos (8-12) and his impatience with Patroklos' urge to fight (13 f.) are thus rendered in a far more forcefully empathetic manner than could be achieved by authorial description.

ὀχθήσας δ' ἄρα εἶπε: a VB formula (8× *Il.*, 5× *Od.*). — **μεγαλήτορα θυμόν:** an inflectable VE formula (dat./acc.: 11× *Il.*, 6× *Od.*, 1× Hes.). μεγαλήτορα ('with much energy': *LfgrE*) is a generic epithet[P] of various characters as well as of θυμός (6.283n.).

6–14 At the center of the monologue, arranged in a ring-composition[P], is the recollection of the prophecy by Achilleus' mother Thetis; the ring-composition[P] is comprised of the framing verses 4 f./15 and 2/16 f. and the speech itself, consisting of: (A) contemporary observation of the flight toward the ships (6 f.), (B) concern about impending doom (8), (C) recollection of the prophecy (9–11), (B') suspicion that concern has turned into reality (12–13a), (A') the earlier order to Patroklos to retreat to the ships (13b–14). Achilleus thus answers his initial question himself directly via recollection of the prophecy (8–11), while his fears mirror the actual events that led to Patroklos' death (internal analepsis[P]; see 13n., 14n.; AH on 12; EDWARDS on 6–14 and 12–14; HENTZE 1904, 20; LOHMANN 1970, 20 n. 23; PELLICCIA 1995, 184 ff., 193 n. 156). – Similarly at 22.450 ff., Andromache fears that Hektor has died when she hears cries

---

4 φρονέοντ(α): on the uncontracted form, R 6; on the elision, R 5.1. — δή: suggests obviousness ('indeed'). — ἦεν: = ἦν (R 16.6).

5 ἄρα (ϝ)εῖπε: on the prosody, R 4.3. — ὅν: possessive pronoun of the 3rd person (R 14.4).

and laments at the wall; like Achilleus, she is the last to learn of the calamity (SCULLY 1986, 149 f.; EDWARDS 1987, 270).

6 VB ≈ 11.404, *Od.* 5.465. — **once again:** Before sending Patroklos, Achilleus had already observed the Greeks retreating toward the ships in the face of the Trojan onslaught (16.17 f.); cf. the battle description at 15.304 ff., 360 ff., 592 ff., 653 ff., 696 ff. and STR 21 with Fig. 1. — **Achaians:** In addition to 'Danaäns' and 'Argives', 'Achaians' is one of the Homeric terms for the Greeks (1.2n.; FOR 24; LATACZ [2001] 2004, 133–136; [2011] 2014, 490–492); on the Achaians' long hair and the VE formula, 2.11n.

ᾧ μοι ἐγώ: a VB formula, 8× *Il.*, 6× *Od.*; ᾧ μοι expresses various negative emotions (1.149n.), here foreboding fear; on the spelling of ᾧ (with ι subscript), see WEST 1998, XXXVII. – τί ταρ αὖτε: In interrogative clauses, αὖτε can mark irritation on the speaker's part (BONIFAZI 2012, 244 f.); on the meaning of the reinforcing particle ταρ ('why then?') and the disputed orthography (ταρ or τ' ἄρ?), 1.8n.; WEST 1998, XXIX; *LfgrE s.v.* ταρ; REECE 2009, 217–230.

7 2nd VH ≈ 6.38. — **plain:** For discussion of the location of the battlefield in the Trojan plain, see 'Appendix topographica' in the commentary to Book 14.

κλονέονται ἀτυζόμενοι πεδίοιο: κλονέομαι, derived from κλόνος 'throng, hurly-burly' (TUCKER 1990, 102), means 'be massed together, entangled' and describes the scrum that occurs e.g. during a panic or flight (KURZ 1966, 144); here in combination with νηυσὶν ἔπι 'they crowd together in a knot toward the ships'. The basic meaning of ἀτυζόμενος is 'frightened, panicked', usually of warriors ('frightened off') or their horses ('balking'), in combination with the indication of location/direction πεδίοιο (lit. 'a little way through the plain': 2.785n., 6.38n.).

8–11 This recollection forms a contrast with the narrator[P] commentary at 17.401–411, where Achilleus' ignorance is foregrounded; he never expected that his friend Patroklos might die before him, but rather thought that he himself would die first (cf. 19.328–333 with n.): EDWARDS on 17.404–11; REINHARDT 1961, 374 ('There is a knowledgeable Achilleus, as well as a blind one, and the poet can alternate between the two' [transl.]); BURGESS 2009, 48–50; differently BARTH 1989, esp. 22 ff. Thetis' prophecy was an *ad hoc* invention by the narrator (cf. WEST 2011, 223 f.; 343) that serves to emotionalize and is designed to convey Achilleus' increasing unease: in addition to his concern for his friend, already a permanent feature in any case, during his observation of the flight the burning memory of the divine prophecy emerges and leads to a

---

6 μοι ἐγώ: on the so-called correption, R 5.5. — κάρη: Attic τὸ κάρα (R 2), 'head'; acc. of respect (R 19.1). — κομόωντες: on the epic diectasis, R 8.
7 νηυσὶν ἔπι: = ἐπὶ νηυσίν (R 20.2); on the declension of νηυσίν, R 12.1.

suspicion of the catastrophe (EDWARDS on 8–11; WILLCOCK 1977, 52; BURGESS
loc. cit. 50; cf. 16.36n. and JANKO on 16.49–50; on the 'expressive features' in
this prophecy rendered in indirect speech [esp. 10], BECK 2012, 85). – The motif
of recalling a repressed prophecy at the moment it becomes reality also occurs
in the *Odyssey*: 9.507 ff. (blinding of Polyphemos), 10.330 ff. (Odysseus' visit
to Circe), 13.172 ff. (Poseidon's threats against the Phaiakians): EDWARDS 1987,
270; additional examples: DE JONG on *Od.* 2.171–6.

8 μὴ δὴ ... τελέσωσι: a reference back to ἃ δὴ τετελεσμένα ἦεν at 4; an independent fear
clause expressing concern, 'that ... not (in any way)', cf. 1.28 (see *ad loc.*), 16.128 (see
ad loc.), *Od.* 5.356 (with AH *ad loc.*): AH; WILLCOCK; see also K.-G. 1.224 (with additional examples); SCHW. 2.317; WACKERNAGEL [1920/24] 2009, 747). — **κήδεα:** 'suffering,
sorrow', usually mourning for relatives (1.445n., 6.240–241n.), clarified as a reference
to mental suffering via the combination with θυμῷ (at VE also at 53, θυμοῦ *Od.* 8.149,
14.197) and intensified with the formula κακὰ κήδεα (after caesura C 1: also at *Od.* 1.244,
6.165, 15.344): *LfgrE s.v.* κῆδος. In Achilleus' view, this suffering is intended by the gods
(τελέσωσι θεοί).

9 διεπέφραδε: reduplicated aor. of δια-φράζω (SCHW. 1.748); the preverb διά signals separation, i.e. approximately 'explicate' (CHANTR. 2.95; *LfgrE s.v.* φράζ(ω): 'make clear'); it
is clarified by καί ... ἔειπεν (AH; cf. schol. D). — **ἔειπεν:** on the reduplicated aor., 19.76n.

10 'Dying warriors are often emphatically termed the «best» of their group' (6.7–
8n.; cf. 6.208n., 24.242n.; EDWARDS 1984), thus also Patroklos in Menelaos'
report (17.689 f.). But in Thetis' prophecy, the paraphrase 'best among the M.'
actually designates the leader of the contingent (on this use of Greek *áristos* in
general, *LfgrE s.v.* ἄριστος, 1289.49 ff.; VAN WEES 1988, 21; BARTH 1989, 5–10;
on 'Myrmidons' as a designation for Achilleus' followers, 2.684n.; CH 2 with
n. 11) and so can only refer to Patroklos, 'the son of Menoitios' (12). He originally hailed from Locrian Opus, but was raised together with Achilleus in the
house of Peleus in Phthia, from where he joined the campaign against Troy
(11.771 ff., 23.84 ff.; cf. CH 2, 16.2n.; LATACZ [1995] 2014, 309 f. n. 107; for bibliography on the friendship between the two characters, see 19.4–6a n.; *LfgrE
s.v.* Patroklos 1060.58 ff., 1069.51 ff.; FANTUZZI 2012, 187–215). But the designation as 'the best' here does evoke associations with Achilleus, of whom it is
frequently used (1.244, etc.): NAGY (1979) 1999, 32–34 (Patroklos assumed 'the
heroic identity of Achilles' [quotation: p. 34]).

---

8 μοι ... θυμῷ: σχῆμα καθ' ὅλον καὶ κατὰ μέρος, here in the dat. (R 19.1). — κήδεα: on the uncontracted form, R 6.
9 ὡς: 'as'. — ἔειπεν: = εἶπεν (↑).
10 ἔτι ζώοντος ἐμεῖο: gen. absolute; ζώοντος = ζῶντος (R 8), part. of ζώειν (= ζῆν), ἐμεῖο = ἐμοῦ
(R 14.1).

τὸν ἄριστον: On this use of the anticipatory demonstrative functioning as an article, see Basset 2006, 111; cf. 1.11n. — ἔτι ζώοντος ἐμεῖο: a shorter variant beside more common phrasings with synonym doubling (... καὶ ἐπὶ χθονὶ δερκομένοιο 1.88, ... καὶ ὁρᾷ φάος ἠελίοιο 61n.).

11 1st VH = 11.827. — **χερσὶν ὕπο:** VB χερσὶν ὕπ(ο) 9× *Il.*, 1× 'Hes.' *Sc.*; on ὑπό + dat. in the sense 'under the influence of', see Schw. 2.526; Chantr. 2.140; Aliffi 2002. — **λείψειν φάος ἠελίοιο:** ≈ 'die', also at *Od.* 11.93, Hes. *Op.* 155, *h.Ven.* 272 (on Indo-Iranian parallels, West 2007, 86 f.); contrast ὁρᾶν φάος ἠελίοιο at e.g. 18.61 (see *ad loc.*; *LfgrE s.v.* φάος 819.23 ff.). φάος ἠελίοιο is a VE formula (8× *Il.*, 10× *Od.*, 3× Hes., 4× *h.Hom.*); on its use in Homer, Foley 1991, 150–154.

12 son of Menoitios: The same formulaic patronymic paraphrase is used of Patroklos at the moment of his death by both the narrator (16.827) and Thetis in her report (18.455), in each case with a reference to his achievements in battle (used by Achilleus also at 19.24, see *ad loc.*). In the *Iliad*, Menoitios is mentioned only in his role as Patroklos' father (CH 2; see also 326n.).

ἦ μάλα δή: an emphatic combination of particles, always in character language[P]; here introducing a suspicion that is a certainty for the speaker, see 6–14n. ('certainly, surely': 6.255n.). — ἄλκιμος υἱός: an inflectable VE formula (nom./acc.), in total 15× *Il.* (of which 12× in combination with Μενοιτίου), 5× Hes., 1× *h.Merc.* (19.24n., 16.278n.); on the structure of the 2nd VH (patronymic in the gen. + adj. + υἱός/ν), 16.14n.

13 2nd VH ≈ 16.301; VE = 9.347, 9.674. — The position of Greek *schétlios* ('stubborn') as a runover word in progressive enjambment[P] adds emphasis: Achilleus rightly suspects that Patroklos has not obeyed his instructions, an action that inevitably resulted in his death (on the narrative motif 'disregarding a warning', 249–253n., 16.686–687n.). Achilleus forcefully warned his friend before he left for battle that he should return immediately after he drove the Trojans away from the ships and should not advance further toward Troy under any circumstances (16.87–96; cf. 16.83–96n.). But Patroklos continued the attack (16.372 ff., 394 ff., 462 ff., 692 ff.) after succeeding in driving the enemies away from the ships and extinguishing the burning ship (16.284–305). In the narrator commentary at 16.684–693, this behavior, which will lead to his death, is described as both 'delusional' and a result of Zeus' overpowering influence, which drove Patroklos into battle; cf. 16.652 ff. (with 16.684–691n., 16.685n. [on Patroklos' 'delusion'] and 16.688–691n. [on Zeus]).

---

11 χερσὶν ὕπο: = ὑπὸ χερσίν (R 20.2). — φάος: = φῶς (R 6). — ἠελίοιο: = ἡλίου.

12 ἦ: emphatic (R 24.4); likewise in the following verse.

13 ἀπωσάμενον: from the mid. ἀπωθέομαι 'push away from oneself'; replaces the subject acc. in the acc.-inf. construction, which is dependent on ἐκέλευον.

σχέτλιος: A term of character language[P], here with a negative connotation, 'stubborn'; on the original sense ('persistent') and the usage elsewhere, 2.112n., 24.33n. — **ἦ τ(ε):** a combination of particles in which τε adds a contrast ('and yet'): MONRO (1882) 1891, 309 ('and yet, although'); RUIJGH 796–800 ('and [yet] it is true that ...' [transl.]); EDWARDS on 17.170–172; cf. 3.56n. — **δήϊον πῦρ:** δήϊον is to be read with a shortening in the internal hiatus (◡◡–); used as an epithet of πῦρ, πόλεμος and ἀνήρ. On the adj.'s etymology and the development of its meaning ('destructive' or 'burning'), 2.415n. (with bibliography); 16.127n.; CHANTR. 1.107; on the use of πῦρ (concretely as well as metaphorically of enemy attacks), GRAZ 1965, 150 f., 327.

14 Hektor: With his instructions to retreat, Achilleus evidently implied that Patroklos was not to fight against Hektor, although without stating this explicitly. Patroklos (as Achilleus suspects) also attacked Hektor himself (16.380–383, 733 ff., 754 ff.).

νῆας ἔπ' ἂψ ἰέναι: thus the main tradition; several mss. transmit the reading ἂψ ἐπὶ νῆας ἴμεν, as at 21.297 (cf. 16.395, 17.432; on this, see *app. crit.* and LEAF), which is also preferred here by EDWARDS since ἂψ is usually placed before the preposition, although not invariably: see *LfgrE s.v.* 1786.48 ff. — **ἶφι μάχεσθαι:** a VE formula (7× *Il.*).

15–17 a return to the main action of 2–5 and a continuation of the type-scene[P] 'delivery of a message' (1–22a n.). The synchronicity, suggested linguistically, of the internal monologue and the approach of Antilochos in tears (15 f. Greek *héōs ... / tóphra ...*) may indicate that Achilleus, full of apprehension (triggered by the observation at 6 f.), spots Antilochos approaching and feels his fears to be confirmed (cf. CERRI; MONTEIL 1963, 302 f.; RICHARDSON 1990, 95 and 227 n. 16).

15 = 1.193, 11.411, 17.106, *Od.* 4.120, 5.365, 5.424; ≈ *Il.* 10.507, *Od.* 6.118; 2nd VH = *Il.* 4.163, 5.671, 6.447, 8.169, 15.163, 20.264, 7× *Od.*, 1× *h.Ap.* — A summary[P] formulaic verse[P], which here serves as a speech capping formula[P] and again hints at the way the 'speech' should be understood (cf. 5n.); on the linguistic presentation of internal monologues via the demonstrative pronoun *taúta*, BAKKER [1999] 2005, 89–91. The formulaic verse frequently introduces a change of scene or, as here, a new entrance (1.193n.).

ἕως: < *ἧος; to be read as trochaic (–◡); on the prosodic 'irregularity' and the conjectures, 1.193n. — **ὥρμαινε:** durative (background action), in contrast to the aor. in the main clause. ὁρμαίνω means 'move back and forth (in one's mind), consider' (*LfgrE*); the same process is paraphrased by φρονέοντ(α) at 4. — **κατὰ φρένα καὶ κατὰ θυμόν:**

---

14 νῆας ἔπ(ι): = ἐπὶ νῆας (R 20.2); on the declension of νῆας, R 12.1 — ἂψ: 'back'. — μηδ(έ): in Homer, connective μηδέ also occurs after affirmative clauses (R 24.8). — ἶφι: 'instrumental' (-φι: R 11.4) of the nominal root (ϝ)ίς (cf. Lat. *vis*), 'with power, with/by force, forcibly'.
15 ἕως: 'while' (R 22.2); on the prosody, ↑. — ὅ: anaphoric demonstrative (R 17).

a VE formula with various spiritual or mental processes (10× *Il.*, 11× *Od.*, 1× *h.Ap.*; of which, with ὥρμαινε 5× *Il.*, 4× *Od.*, see *iterata*), with metrically convenient synonym doubling (1.160n.); in these cases, φρήν and θυμός do not designate different aspects of these mental processes: the lexemes for the seats of mental processes are interchangeable (6.447n.).

16 1st VH = 18.381. — **ἀγαυοῦ Νέστορος υἱός:** Νέστορος υἱός is a VE formula (7× *Il.*); the combination with ἀγαυοῦ is unique but unexceptional (cf. 5.277; note also ἀγαυοῦ after caesura B 2 in total 18× in early epic). The metrical and prosodic variant of the half-verse formula καὶ Νέστορος ἀγλαὸς υἱός (1× *Il.*, 3× *Od.*) cannot be combined with the 1st VH (EDWARDS 1968, 264). – ἀγαυοῦ is a generic epithet[P] of humans and gods; the meaning is uncertain, most likely 'illustrious, noble' (3.268n.).

17 1st VH = 16.3, 18.235; ≈ 7.426, *Od.* 4.523, 24.46; 2nd VH ≈ *Il.* 2.787. — **wept warm tears:** Antilochos had set off weeping to meet Achilleus with the message (17.695–701; on men crying, 19.5–6a n.). He no longer plays a role in the subsequent scenes with Thetis (35 ff., 67 ff.) and is thus not mentioned again (silent character[P]; cf. FENIK 1974, 65 f.); he only makes an appearance again in the games in honor of Patroklos (23.301 ff.). – The description of Antilochos' arrival echoes the scene at the beginning of Book 16: Patroklos comes to Achilleus weeping, after the Achaians have come under great pressure in the battle; at the end of the scene, Achilleus lets him go into battle in his own place (EDWARDS; SEGAL 1971, 26). From a neoanalytic perspective (on which, EDWARDS pp. 16–19; BURGESS 2006; TSAGALIS 2011; cf. NTHS 10), both the connection of the characters via these two scenes and the fact that Antilochos here appears as a messenger indicate that the presentation of Patroklos is influenced by the depiction of Antilochos in older, orally transmitted versions of the mythic cycle concerning Troy, in which the latter hero fell at Memnon's hands (cf. *Od.* 4.187 f.) – as was subsequently related in the epic cycle (*Aethiopis*, Proclus *Chrest.* § 2 West; on the relationship between the Homeric epics and the cycle, see LATACZ [1985] 1996, 61; BURGESS 2001, esp. 132 ff.; WEST 2003, 5 ff.; for additional bibliography, 16.419–683n., end.): SCHADEWALDT [1952] 1965, 176; KULLMANN 1960, 316; [1977] 1992, 203; [1991] 1992, 115–118; KRISCHER 1994, 158 ff.; WILLCOCK 1997, 181 f., 187 f.; CURRIE 2006, 26 f.; a critical approach: BURGESS 1997, esp. 10 ff.; DAVIES 2016, 5–12; for possible parallels between Antilochos and Patroklos, see also 16.684–867n., end; cf. 1.307n., 19.3n. But within the *Iliad*, both the parallel of 16.3/18.17 and the fact that Antilochos stays with Achilleus and the two grieve together (32 ff.) serve to gradually introduce the new situation in which

---

16 τόφρα: 'in the meantime'. — τόφρα (ϝ)οἱ: on the prosody, R 4.3. — οἱ: = αὐτῷ (R 14.1). — ἐγγύθεν: '(up) close'.

17 φάτο: impf. of φημί; on the middle, R 23. — ἀγγελίην: on the -η- after -ι-, R 2.

the deceased friend is slowly replaced by other characters (cf. 19.392n. on Automedon): RUTHERFORD (1996) 2013, 120 f.; BOUVIER 2002, 398. — **gave ... his sorrowful message:** a transition to element 6 of the type-scene 'delivery of a message' (1–22a n.), used in place of a formulaic speech introduction (cf. the 'messenger scene' at 2.787/790: EDWARDS); the narrator renders palpable the messenger's haste both in the introduction and in the speech itself (cf. 18–21n.) and characterizes its content in advance, as does the messenger himself at 18 f.

δάκρυα θερμὰ χέων: on the inflectable half-verse formula, the formula system 'shed tears' and the epithet with δάκρυ, 16.3n.

18–21 The form of this messenger speech matches the dramatic situation: after his rapid run, the messenger arrives out of breath and in tears (cf. 17.694 ff.), and the agitated addressee already suspects the catastrophe. Without further ado, Antilochos comes to the point and in a few words reports the pertinent facts to Achilleus (schol. bT on 20–1). Since he himself was gently prepared for this errand by Menelaos, who gave him his orders at 17.685–693 (EDWARDS on 17.685–6 and 18.20–1; DE JONG [1987] 2004, 281 n. 70), Antilochos is full of empathy as he prepares Achilleus for the news of Patroklos' death (18 f.). The speech is a condensed abridgment of Menelaos' order with some literal echoes: 1. address, bad news (18 f., cf. 17.685 f.); 2. facts: death, fight over the corpse, loss of the armor to Hektor (20 f., cf. 17.689b–690a, 17.693). The report focuses entirely on Patroklos and Hektor; mention of the other characters involved (Achaians and Trojans) is avoided (20). Missing is thus a reference to the situation of the Greeks (cf. 17.687–689a, 17.690b) and especially to the originator of the message (on which, 6.269–278n.; DE JONG on *Od.* 5.1–42) and his pleas for help in retrieving the corpse (cf. 17.691 f.). In contrast, see 2.23–34n. as an example of a detailed messenger speech; on epic narrative conventions for the motif 'execution of an order', 6.86–101n., end, with bibliography.

18–19 18b–19 ≈ 17.685b–686. — **ᾧ μοι:** 6n. — **Πηλέος υἱέ:** a formula before caesura B 2 (5× *Il.*, 1× *Od.*); sometimes expanded by an adj. at VB, but here this stressed position is already occupied by the emphatic exclamation (SHIVE 1987, 117). On the short-vowel form Πηλέος, G 76. — **δαΐφρονος:** 'skilled in war', a generic epithet[P], usually of men, as here frequently of 'fathers of heroes' and thus of their sons as well (so of Achilleus at 30) (6.161–162n.). — **ἦ μάλα:** 'certainly' (cf. 12n.). — **λυγρῆς | ... ἀγγελίης:** an intensification of 17.685 f., where Antilochos himself receives the news of the catastrophe (see also 17.641 f.), via integral enjambment[P] with separation of the words (EDWARDS; BLANC 2008, 431; cf. 19.337n.). — **ἢ μὴ ὤφελλε γενέσθαι:** grammatically, ἥ refers to

---

18 λυγρῆς: on the -η- after -ρ-, R 2.
19 πεύσεαι: on the uncontracted form, R 6.

ἀγγελίης, but by metonymy also to its contents. Both the impf. ὤφελλον/ὄφελλον and the aor. ὤφελον/ὄφελον can introduce unfulfilled wishes regarding the past and present (1.353n.; ALLAN 2013, 16 ff.); on ἦ μὴ ὤφελλε + inf. for εἴθε μὴ + past ind., see SCHW. 2.346 f.; CHANTR. 2.333.

20–21 21 ≈ 17.122, 17.693. — In the various reports concerning Patroklos' death and the fight for his corpse, the despoiling of Patroklos, i.e. the loss of the armor Achilleus lent to his friend (16.40 and 64 f.), is recalled repeatedly (on the exchange of weapons motif, 16.278–283n.): in addition to the current passage, also at 17.192–197 and 210–214 by the narrator; 17.120–122, 689–693, 711–714 by Menelaos; 17.201–208, 443–450 by Zeus; 17.472 f. by Alkimedon; 18.80–85, 188–195, 333–335 by Achilleus; 18.130–137, 451–461 by Thetis. The general motif 'despoiling an opponent' (on which, 6.28n.) is given particular weight so that it can be utilized repeatedly: the narrator[P] employs it to (1) illustrate Hektor's overconfidence (17.201 ff., 22.322 ff.), (2) make it plausible that Achilleus, although he saves Patroklos' corpse, does not immediately exact revenge, i.e. to delay his return to battle and the slaying of Hektor (retardation[P]), (3) insert an elaborate ekphrasis concerning the production of new armor and its splendor (468 ff.), and (4) structure the course of the action in such a way as to create time for the military assembly the following morning (19.40 ff.; see 19.40–281n.), when Achilleus officially rejoins the military community and submits himself to Agamemnon's supreme command, while Agamemnon publicly concedes his mistakes and provides recompense (EDWARDS on 17.711 and p. 139 f.; 1987a, 57 f.; JANKO p. 311). — **Hektor ... his armor:** clarifies that it is Hektor who killed Patroklos. Only at 19.411–414 (see *ad loc.*) does Achilleus learn of the involvement of a god (Apollo), from the words of his horse Xanthos (cf. 16.786–867, 17.125–197).

κεῖται Πάτροκλος: explicative asyndetic clause (cf. 1.105n.; MAEHLER 2000, 421 f.), with a highly concise rendering of the message: 'P. is dead' (literally 'he lies there dead'); the same sentence structure at 16.541 (Sarpedon: see *ad loc.*), similarly at 5.467, 16.558 (*LfgrE s.v.*; KURZ 1966, 18). — **νέκυος ... | γυμνοῦ:** In the *Iliad*, γυμνός 'bare, denuded' is often used of corpses despoiled in battle (*LfgrE s.v.*), here lent particular stress via the enjambment; likewise at 17.122, where Menelaos pleads with Achilleus for support in the battle for the corpse, and at 17.693, where he sends Antilochos to Achilleus to request his help: an indignant and piteous appeal; cf. 22.510, also Tyrtaeus *fr.* 10.21–27 West (EDWARDS on 17.120–122). — **τά γε τεύχε(α):** τά is an anticipatory demonstrative, cf. G 99; SCHW. 2.21 f. — τεύχεα ('armor, arms') is primarily comprised of the helmet, corselet, shield and greaves, see 458–460, 466 (*LfgrE s.v.* τεῦχος). — **νέκυος ... ἀμφιμάχονται:** with gen.

---

20 δή: 4n. — ἀμφιμάχονται: Achaians and Trojans are to be understood as the subj.
21 ἀτάρ: 'but' (R 24.2). — τεύχε' ἔχει: on the hiatus, R 5.1; on the uncontracted form τεύχε(α), R 6.

'fight over (around) something/someone' in the sense 'fight to protect someone, over the possession of someone', cf. 173 ἀμυνόμενοι νέκυος πέρι (16.496n.: 'the local and metaphorical meanings ... converge'; *LfgrE s.v.* μάχομαι 55.27 ff.). — **κορυθαίολος Ἕκτωρ:** a VE formula (37× *Il.*); on the epithet (either 'shaking the helmet' or 'with gleaming helmet'), 6.116n.

22–147 In these scenes (22–35a/35b–147), the narrator[P] paints a picture of the mourning for Patroklos not only by describing Achilleus' grief but also by pointing ahead to his death, while conjuring up sorrow for Achilleus' fate via the words and gestures of other characters[P] (external prolepsis[P]; on the various interpretations of Patroklos as a stand-in for Achilleus, 16.165n.): (a) announcements in character language (59 f., 88–91, 95 f., 98, 115 f., 120 f.); (b) formulations that can evoke associations with the deceased Achilleus (22n., 23–27n., 24n., 26–27n., 28–31n., 71n.); (c) mourning by Achilleus' mother Thetis and her sisters as a representation of their mourning for Achilleus himself (37–72n., 55–60n., 56–57n.): EDWARDS on 22–31; SCHEIN 1984, 129–137; SEAFORD 1994, 166 f.; KIM 2000, 121–124; GRETHLEIN 2006, 121 f. Discussion, still on-going, has thus arisen regarding the manner in which the narrator[P] here could have utilized epic templates concerning Achilleus' death (bibliography: 37–72n., end.; RUTHERFORD [1996] 2013, 118–120; KELLY 2012, 223 f. with n. 9).

22–35a Achilleus' reaction to the message is portrayed as a climax from mute grief to a loud scream: overwhelming pain (22), silent gestures of mourning (23–27, accompanied by the laments of those around him at 28–34), moaning (33b), a loud cry of grief (35a). Initially, his grief is silent; he speaks of his pain first after the entrance of his mother (78 ff., 97 ff.), later in his speech of lament over the corpse (316 ff., 19.314 ff.): AH, *Anh.* p. 120 f.; EDWARDS on 1–69; SCHADEWALDT (1936) 1997, 152–154; KRAPP 1964, 343–345; HOLST-WARHAFT 1992, 105 f., 113 f.

On the paratactic narrative style via δέ, 1.10n.; BAKKER 1997, 62–71.

22–24a = *Od.* 24.315–317a.

22 = 17.591 (Hektor's reaction to the report that his companion Podes has died). – On the speech capping formula 'spoke' + addressee's reaction in general, 1.33n., 24.200n.; on speeches triggering emotions that in turn provide an impulse for action, 2.142n.; BARCK 1976, 145. — **the black cloud ... closed:** The image portrays the overwhelming pain of loss that envelops Achilleus and renders him benighted, as it were, and that because it is similar to expressions for dying (see below), is perhaps an indirect anticipatory reference to his death

---

22 φάτο: 17n. — τόν: on the anaphoric demonstrative function of ὅ, ἥ, τό, R 17. — ἄχεος: on the uncontracted form, R 6. — νεφέλη ἐκάλυψε: on the hiatus, R 5.6.

(22–147n.); on 'envelop' as an expression for a variety of alterations of consciousness, 2.19n., 3.442n. and 16.316n. (all with bibliography). The remaining books of the *Iliad* are governed by this emotion of Achilleus; until Hektor is killed, he is wrapped up in his 'cloud of pain', and even afterwards he can be reached only with difficulty by the cajoling of his friends (24.2b–13n., 24.3n.; SCHEIN 1984, 128 f.; collection of examples: KARSAI 1998, 42 ff.). – The Greek term *áchos* denotes mental anguish caused by external events, which initially results in feelings of powerlessness and resignation that subsequently often change into anger and aggression, triggering an impulse for action, albeit still a painful one (2.169–171n., 19.125n.); here this manifests itself in Achilleus' determination to fight Hektor at 90 ff., 98 ff., 114 ff. (see also 322 ff., 19.15 ff. [see *ad loc.*]; cf. 19.307n.). On Achilleus' *áchos*, see 62 (with n.), 436 ff. (on which, NAGY [1979] 1999, 80 f.; LATACZ [1995] 2014, 320 ['This is Achilleus' basic mood throughout the entire *Iliad*' (transl.)]).

τὸν δ᾽ ἄχεος νεφέλη ἐκάλυψε μέλαινα: A forceful description of effects of the message, in contrast to formulations such as those at 1.188 (see *ad loc.*), 2.171 (see *ad loc.*) and 14.475 (cf. 19.125 [see *ad loc.*]): it contains echoes of various formulaic expressions for the moment of death, in which darkness or night closes over the victim's eyes (for examples, 6.11n., 16.316n.), cf. esp. the formulations νεφέλη δέ μιν ἀμφεκάλυψεν | κυανέη (20.417 f.) and θανάτου δὲ/θανάτοιο μέλαν νέφος ἀμφεκάλυψεν (16.350 [see *ad loc.*], *Od.* 4.180). Additional examples of a character being suddenly enveloped by a feeling of grief after the death of *another*, as here: 11.249 f. (grief), 22.466 (horror); on other emotions enveloping the senses (φρένες), 1.103n.; μέλας also serves to describe physical pain after an injury (4.117, 4.191, 15.394; cf. νὺξ ἐκάλυψε μέλαινα for Hektor fainting after an injury at 14.438–439n.): *LfgrE s.v.* μέλας; MAWET 1979, 48; note also 2.834n. and 16.687n. on the VE formula μέλανος θανάτοιο.

23–27 Achilleus' pain manifests itself neither in an immediate response to the messenger (at 17.694-700, Antilochos also remained speechless) nor in spontaneous lamentation; the silent gestures hint at the internal tension that is not discharged until he screams at 35 (22–35a n.; AREND 1933, 56 n. 1; PETERSMANN 1973, 6 f.; LATEINER 1995, 13). These gestures, signs of pain, are also mentioned elsewhere when a character spots the corpse of someone they loved or learns of the person's death: defacing the head with dirt or ashes (Priam at 24.164; Laërtes *Od.* 24.316 f.; cf. Achilleus' horses at *Il.* 17.439 f.), rolling around on the ground (Priam at 22.414, 24.165, 24.640), tearing at the hair (Hektor's relatives at 22.77 f., 22.406, 24.711); on such self-defacement, see ANDRONIKOS 1968, 1 f.; DERDERIAN 2001, 53 f. with nn. 146 and 148; additional bibliography: 19.284–285n., 24.164n., 24.711–712n.; parallels in Ancient Near Eastern literature in WEST 1997, 340 with n. 12 (esp. Gilgamesh mourning for his friend Enkidu, and *Job* 42:6). The description of Achilleus' mourning also has similarities with the description of slain warriors (22–147n.; KURZ 1966, 40 f.; EDWARDS 1986, 86, 91 n. 12): (a) the dirt-encrusted head in the context of defeat and death, e.g. 16.638–640 of Sarpedon, 16.795 ff. of Patroklos' helmet, 22.402 f. of Hektor (RICHARDSON on *Il.* 22.401–404; DE JONG on *Il.* 22.401–404; cf. 24n. *s.v.* χαρίεν); (b) lying prostrate like a corpse (26–27n.).

23–25 the grimy dust | ... | the black ashes: The framing position of terms for the sooty-black dust (23, 25) on the 'handsome countenance' and the 'immortal tunic' results in a strong contrast within the image of the grieving Achilleus (esp. 24b–25). The scene as a whole is full of terms for 'black' (22/23/25), 'dust' (23/26) and the disfiguration of the outward appearance (Greek *éischyne* 24/27), with the darkness of pain mirrored in the gestures of mourning (BREMER 1976, 73 f.); on 'black' as the color of mourning, 24.94n.

23 = *Od.* 24.316; 1st VH = *Od.* 5.428; ≈ *Il.* 18.123, *Od.* 4.116. — **κόνιν αἰθαλόεσσαν:** corresponds to 25 μέλαιν(α) ... τέφρη ('ashes, soot', see 23.250 f.). αἰθαλόεις is derived from αἴθαλος/αἰθάλη ('smoke, soot', from αἴθω 'burn'), an epithet also of σποδός 'ashes' (*Certamen* § 9 West) and μέλαθρον (2.415, *Od.* 22.239) denoting the area blackened by the fire in the hearth; the reference is thus to sooty-black ashes (*LfgrE s.vv.* αἰθαλόεις, κόνις).

24 **χεύατο:** mid. of the root aor. ἔχε(υ)α, from *χέ(ϝ)ω (3.10n.). — **κὰκ κεφαλῆς:** '(from above) across the head', likewise at *Od.* 8.85, 23.156, 24.317 (SCHW. 2.479; CHANTR. 2.113). — **χαρίεν:** 'lovely, charming', serves to characterize an individual's external appearance (6.90n.), of Achilleus' face also at 16.798 f., in contrast to his helmet lying in the dust (at the moment of Patroklos' fall: 16.795–797), here contrasting with ἤσχυνε and κόνιν αἰθαλόεσσαν (23) and thus evoking pity. The present passage can also be compared to 22.401–403: Hektor's previously delightful head (κάρη ... | ... πάρος χαρίεν) lies in the dust (ἐν κονίῃσιν) (TREU 1955, 56 f.; LATACZ 1966, 101 f.). — **ἤσχυνε:** in a factual sense 'render ugly, deface'; only here and at 27 of a living person, elsewhere of the disfigurement of corpses (18.180, 22.75, 24.418): *LfgrE*.

25 **νεκταρέῳ:** The exact sense (literally 'nectar-like') as an attribute of garments (also at 3.385) is obscure (schol. bT; 3.385n. with bibliography; on νέκταρ, 19.38n.); suggestions: 'rubbed with oil, scented' (LEAF; EDWARDS); 'divine, of divine beauty' on analogy with ἀμβρόσιος (with reference to 16.222–224: Achilleus received his garments from Thetis: AH; EDWARDS; *contra* LEAF); 'gleaming, white' in contrast to μέλαινα τέφρη (SCHMID 1950, 35; cf. SCHADEWALDT [1936] 1997, 153 ['around the clean tunic']). — **χιτῶνι:** a soft 'undergarment' worn by men beneath a corselet or cloak (2.42n.; VAN WEES 2005, 1 f. with older bibliography; *LfgrE s.v.* χιτών). — **ἀμφίζανε:** a Homeric *hapax*[P], 'set around' or 'settled down' (in the sense 'stuck fast'): *LfgrE*; on the formation type ἵζω/ἱζάνω, RISCH 271 f.

---

23 ἀμφοτέρῃσι: on the declension, R 11.1.
24 κάκ: = κατά (with assimilation: R 20.1).

26–27 αὐτός: 'he himself', with his entire body, in contrast to the garment and individual parts of the body at 23–25 (ἀμφοτέρῃσι χερσίν, κεφαλῆς, πρόσωπον, χιτῶνι): *LfgrE s.v.* 1651.30 f. and 1652.24 f./46 ff.; cf. 1.4n. — **μέγας μεγαλωστὶ τανυσθείς | κεῖτο:** echoes the description of fallen warriors: (1) the adverb μεγαλωστί, here in reference to τανυσθείς ('across a large area', i.e. 'stretched out at length'), in early epic always found in combination with μέγας (on the formation, RISCH 366 with bibliography; in general, ANGHELINA 2007; on the iteration, SCHW. 2.700), is elsewhere used solely in reference to the dead: κεῖτο/κεῖσο μέγας μεγαλωστί at 16.776 of Kebriones (Patroklos' final victim: see *ad loc.*), *Od.* 24.40 of Achilleus. (2) Similarly, the combination of τανύω and κεῖμαι elsewhere serves to describe prostrate corpses: VE formula κεῖτο τανυσθείς (*Il.* 13.392, 16.485, 20.483), VB formula κεῖτο ταθείς (13.655, 21.119): *LfgrE s.v.* τανύω; EDWARDS; KURZ 1966, 18 f. The expression is thus probably in origin a general one used of dead warriors in battle scenes (BURGESS 2009, 84 f.; 2012, 171–176; cf. 16.485n.). 26 f. have often been suspected as interpolations (e.g. by WEST 2001, 12 n. 28, 243 f.; more cautiously, WEST 2011, 343, cf. *loc. cit.* 46 f.), since (a) the wording 'he himself lay …, the great one, stretched out at length' is less appropriate here than at 16.776 and *Od.* 24.40 (see above; *contra* DIHLE 1970, 23 f., and *LfgrE s.v.* μεγαλωστί: it is instead 16.776 and *Od.* 24.40, where τανυσθείς is missing, that are secondary, so that μεγαλωστί must be referred to κεῖτο: κεῖμαι is nowhere else linked to an adv.; see also 22n., 23–27n., 24n.); (b) the context suggests that Achilleus is standing or sitting (24 f.: dust and ashes from top to the bottom; 28–31: women surround him; 32: ἑτέρωθεν 'is naturally taken to mean «opposite Achilles, facing him»' [see *ad loc.*]; 33 and 70 f.: this would hardly be conceivable were Achilleus to lie on the ground [but see 70n., 71n.]). The question of whether the use of the expression in the present scene – as suspected by neoanalytic scholarship – should be regarded as a direct transfer from a description of the deceased Achilleus in pre-Homeric epic is scarcely answerable (doxography: DANEK 1998, 466–469; CURRIE 2006, 40 with n. 181; BURGESS 2009, 151 f. n. 35; 2012, 170–173; see also 22–147n.). — **δαΐζων:** a strongly emotionally colored verb meaning 'cut up, tear apart violently', usually in military contexts of massacres (24.393n.); similar to here at *h.Cer.* 41, of the shredding of headdresses as a pathetic gesture of mourning (*LfgrE*).

28–31 Achilleus is the focal point of a noisy, busy scene of mourning, in that the women present in his residence join in the lament – albeit with no explanation of how they know about the situation – and display typical mourning behavior of a sort repeated in the subsequent scene with Thetis and her sisters: they raise cries of grief (29/37a), crowd around the mourner (30a/37b–38), beat their chests (30b–31/50b–51a). A similar scheme occurs in other scenes of lament, although in these cases the groups that form are always single-sex: (1) for Patroklos: (a) Briseïs with female captives (19.284–302), (b) Achilleus with companions (18.314b–355, 19.4–6a, 19.303–339); (2) for Hektor: (a) Hekabe with Trojan women (22.430), Andromache with her sisters-in-law (22.473–515), Andromache, Hekabe and Helen with Trojan women (24.723–761), (b) Priam with Trojans, alternatively with his sons (22.412–429, 24.160–165); (3) for

Achilleus: (a) Thetis and her sisters (24.83–86, *Od.* 24.47–49/58 f.): DERDERIAN 2001, 35 f. with n. 81 and 53–56; GAGLIARDI 2007, 102–105; ELMER 2013, 199–202; see also 316n. Usually mourning women gather around male *dead* (cf. at 339 f. the same women around Patroklos, at *Od.* 24.58–61a Thetis and her sisters around Achilleus).

28 As 'servants' (Greek *dmōiaí*), the women captives had to do domestic work in particular in the military camp (food preparation, bathing guests, preparing beds: 24.582–583a n.; WICKERT-MICKNAT 1983, 77, 164 n. 63). That these captives mourn along with Antilochos and Achilleus, as Briseïs does later on when faced with Patroklos' body, is worth noting; the lamentation of these women is a substitute for laments by the female relatives of the deceased (19.282–302n.; on the motivation for their laments, 19.302n.). — **Achilleus and Patroklos:** Achilleus himself mentions these forays, when reminiscing about his friend, as *joint* activities, see 341 f., 24.7 f. (cf. also 9.328 f.: external repetitive analepses[P]). On Achilleus' conquests, 1.366n.; STR 23 fig. 3; on women as war booty, 6.426n.; on the fate of female captives, 1.13n., 1.31n., 6.57b–60n.; on the broader historical context, LATACZ (2001) 2004, 280–282.

ληΐσσατο: aor. of ληΐζομαι ('capture'), as also at *Od.* 1.398; a denominative from ληΐς (SCHW. 1.735; RISCH 298); on the congruence of the verb with the preceding subject, see also *Il.* 2.858, 19.310 (on the phenomenon in general, SCHW. 2.610 f.; CHANTR. 2.18 f.).

29 θυμόν: the mental seat affected by emotions ('internally, mentally'), synonymous with κῆρ at 33 (*LfgrE s.v.* θυμός 1086.10 ff., esp. 65 ff.; cf. 1.24n., 19.57n.). — **ἀκηχέμεναι:** serves as the perf. part. of ἄχνυμαι, a metrically conditioned form of the fem. (also ἀκηχεμένη at 5.364, *h.Cer.* 50) beside masc./neut. ἀκαχήμενος/-ον/-οι (always before an initial vowel: 4× *Il.*, 9× *Od.*, 1× Hes.) of ἀκάχημαι 'be distressed' (RISCH 343; CHANTR. 1.436; SCHW. 1.766); elsewhere, it usually emphasizes a continuing state of mind caused by a loss at some point in the past (*LfgrE s.v.* ἄχνυμαι, ἀκαχίζω, ἄχομαι 1772.4 ff., esp. 22 ff.). — **μεγάλ' ἴαχον:** a variable formula (μεγάλ' ἴαχον/-ε) after caesura B 1 (4× *Il.*, 1× *Od.*, 1× 'Hes.'); on the variants of the phrase μεγα(-λα) + ἰάχω, KAIMIO 1977, 20–22. μεγάλα is a designation of quantity denoting the intensity of the sound (3.221–222n., 6.207n.; WILLE 2001, 74). ἰάχω denotes a scream of special intensity, frequently in response to an event or a speech, here the report of the death (*LfgrE s.v.*); the forms ἴαχε, ἴαχον (reduplicated pres. stem, also functioning as an aor.?) are variously explained (CHANTR. 1.393; *LfgrE s.v.*; LIV 665; cf. 19.41n. with bibliography).

30 δαΐφρονα: 18–19n. — **χερσὶ δὲ πᾶσαι:** stresses the collective character of mourning, likewise and with a similar verse structure (clause beginning with subject after caesura

---

C 2 and act of mourning [predicate] in enjambment[P]) in the scene with Thetis and the Nereids at 50 f. und 65 f.

31 1st VH = 51; 2nd VH = *Od.* 18.341; ≈ *Il.* 16.805, *Od.* 11.527. — **πεπλήγοντο:** a reduplicated aor. with iterative meaning (*LfgrE s.v.* πλήσσω 1291.26; SCHW. 1.777 n. 4; LATACZ 1966, 58 f., 62; TICHY 1983, 48). — **λύθεν ... γυῖα:** The combination of a medio-pass. form of (ὑπο)λύω and γυῖα denotes in particular, in addition to the effects of fatigue or injury, a psychosomatic reaction as the consequence of violent emotions, e.g. terror and fear at 16.805 f., *Od.* 18.341, similarly *Il.* 7.215, 20.44, *Od.* 18.88 ('slacken, go limp' [so that the knees buckle]: 6.27n., 24.498n.; cf. also 16.312n.); on the use of γυῖα ['limbs'], 3.34n. — **γυῖα ἑκάστης:** an inflectable VE formula (3× *Il.*, 3× *Od.*).

32 ≈ 22.79; 2nd VH = *Od.* 16.214. — **ἑτέρωθεν:** mostly signals a change of scene or perspective (1.247a n.), here more concretely as a locative adverb (cf. 3.230, 9.666, 16.763): 'a symmetrical grouping of two partners', namely Antilochos vis-à-vis Achilleus, prostrate and grieving' (KURZ 1966, 73 n. 4 [transl.]; WEST 2001, 244: 'facing him'), see the indication of location ἀμφ' Ἀχιλῆα at 30; with athetesis of 26 f., Achilleus is standing up. — **δάκρυα λείβων:** a VE formula (3× *Il.*, 6× *Od.*); for additional versions of VE formulae for 'shed tears' (with δάκρυ χέω), 1.413n., 3.142n.; HASLAM 1976, 203–207; cf. 17n.

33 2nd VH ≈ 10.16, *Od.* 21.247. — **held the hands:** Handholding can be interpreted in various ways, depending on the context: either as a gesture of kind reassurance and encouragement (24.361n., 24.671–672n.) or as control over both the individual concerned and his or her actions (LATEINER 1995, 57; BOEGEHOLD 1999, 17 f.); here, the gesture is justified at 34 – if the verse is genuine, see *ad loc.* – by Antilochos' fear for Achilleus. At 22.412 f., the Trojans try in a similar manner to hold on to Priam to prevent him from marching straight off to the enemy camp to plead for release of his son's body (EDWARDS on 32–34).

χεῖρας ἔχων Ἀχιλῆος: cf. χεῖρας ἔχοντες/ἔχουσαι at 594, *h.Ap.* 196 (dancers hold each other by the hands); different are χειρὸς ἔχων Μενέλαον at VB in 4.154 and τὸν ... | χειρὸς ἔχων at 11.487 f., where a character, concerned for another, holds the other person by the arm or hand and takes care of him (*LfgrE s.v.* ἔχω 839.41 ff.; on additional formulations for this gesture, BARCK 1976, 141–143.). — **ἔστενε ... κῆρ:** a variant of the formulaic expression βαρὺ στενάχων (70 [see *ad loc.*], 78); not necessarily to be understood as a silent, internal moan, but as something approximating the phrase 'groan from the bottom of one's heart', cf. μέγα in the *iterata* (*LfgrE s.v.* στένω; KRAPP 1964, 31 f.; SPATAFORA 1997, 9; on κῆρ, 29n.). — **κυδάλιμον:** a generic epithet[P] of heroes and of the κῆρ ('brave, glorious'), related to κῦδος ('being singled out') (6.184n. with bibliography).

---

31 λύθεν: = ἐλύθησαν (R 16.2). — ὑπό: adverbial ('below'). — γυῖα (F)εκάστης: on the prosody, R 4.3.

32 ὀδύρετο: on the unaugmented form, R 16.1.

33 Ἀχιλῆος: cf. 28n., 29–30n. — ὅ: Achilleus is meant. — κῆρ: acc. of respect (R 19.1).

34 Suicide is also mentioned in the *Odyssey*: *Od*. 10.49 ff. Odysseus' deliberation as to whether to fling himself into the sea in his desperation or endure
the storm on the ship; 11.271–279 suicide of Epikaste, Oedipus' mother/wife;
11.543 ff. an allusion to Aias' suicide (albeit without explicit mention of it), see
Aethiopis fr. 6 West (AH, *Anh*. p. 121; EDWARDS on 32–34). *Od*. 4.539 f. is the
closest parallel for the present situation: Menelaos' death-wish after the report of Agamemnon's death. Suicide due to grief is occasionally attested for
mythological characters in post-Homeric literature: e.g. Theseus' father Aigeus
(Plut. *Thes*. 22), Niobe's husband Amphion (Ov. *Met*. 6.271 f.), Protesilaos' wife
Laodameia (Hyg. *Fab*. 243); sometimes other causes come into play (Haimon's
anger at himself: Soph. *Ant*. 1234 ff.; Deianeira's feelings of guilt: Soph. *Trach*.
1130 ff.). – Some scholars consider this verse an interpolation, since, in contrast to 32 f., the changes of subject between Achilleus (33b, 34b–35a) and
Antilochos (34a) are not signalled: WEST 2001, 244 ('suspect line'); cautiously
LEAF (with reference to the change of subject at 7.186–189; see also CHANTR.
2.359); *contra* EDWARDS on 32–34, with reference to schol. T (Antilochos' fear is
'perfectly reasonable'). Retention of the line could be supported by the fact that
without 34, although Antilochos' action at 33 could be interpreted as at most a
gesture of consolation, with the sequence 33/35 the scene would nevertheless
lose its drama; in contrast, see 22.412 f. (33n.). The 2nd VH of 33 could also be
understood as a parenthesis (thus FAESI; VAN LEEUWEN) with the function of a
conjunctive participle (see 70); for the relatively rare use of Greek *síderos* 'iron'
to denote a weapon (AH, *Anh*. p. 121 f.; LEAF), see below.

δείδιε: plpf. of the perf. δείδω 'be afraid' (6.99n.). – **ἀπαμήσειε:** The compound from
ἀμάω ('mow, reap'), aside from here also in tmesis at *Od*. 21.300 f. and Hes. *Th*. 180 f.
of the severing of limbs (*LfgrE s.v.*), is a *v.l.* (also the reading of Aristarchus, see *app.
crit.*) and the *lectio difficilior* vis-à-vis the main tradition ἀποτμήξειε ('cut off, cut into
pieces', *inter alia* of body parts: *Il*. 11.146 as a *v.l.*, *Od*. 10.440, Hes. *Th*. 188; 'cut through':
Il. 16.390; see *LfgrE s.v.* τμήγω; LEAF; VAN DER VALK 1964, 118). An imitation of the formulation λαιμὸν ἀπαμήσειε, perceived as unusual and thus occasionally rejected, occurs at Apollonius Rhodius 4.374 (RENGAKOS 1993, 99). – **σιδήρῳ:** here metonymy for
a weapon, possibly a knife; mentions of iron weapons at 23.30, *Od*. 16.294 = 19.13 (cf.
also *Il*. 4.123, 7.141) are comparable; elsewhere in Homeric epic, 'iron' usually describes
tools, while weapons are glossed χαλκός ('bronze'): *LfgrE s.v.* σίδηρος; on the issue of
the mention of bronze weapons beside iron, 6.3n., 6.48n.; on the metonymy, 1.236n.

---

34 δείδιε: 'he fears', *sc*. Ἀντίλοχος; on the form, ↑. — ἀπαμήσειε ... ὤμωξεν: Achilleus is again
the subj.

35–147 *Thetis is concerned for her son Achilleus. She departs to visit Hephaistos in order to ask for new armor.*

For the purpose of the change of scene, the narrator follows, as it were, the spread of the cry of lament away from the mourning women and the Achaian ships and toward the depths of the sea, where it reaches Thetis and her sisters (additional examples of this type of change of scene: RICHARDSON 1990, 113, 229 n. 8); from there, the narrator accompanies the sea goddesses to the encampment of ships (65–68a), and with their approach the scene is once more focused on the character of Achilleus (70 ff.). Fluid changes of setting are thus produced (DE JONG/NÜNLIST 2004, 73 f.). – Thetis appeared previously in the *Iliad* in her visit to plead with Zeus in Book 1 (1.495 ff.), when she convinced him to grant Achilleus' wish and give the Trojans the upper hand in battle, after which she withdrew to the depths of the sea (1.531 f.). The present scene between Achilleus and his mother makes reference, by means of linguistic echoes and explicit recollections (18.74b–75), to that scene in Book 1 (1.357–430a), where Thetis likewise rises from the sea (whence she had been called upon by Achilleus) to be at the side of her weeping son after he has experienced a loss (there Briseïs, here Patroklos), followed by her setting out to support his plans (gaining satisfaction or weapons): cf. esp. 1.357 f./18.35 f., 1.362 f./18.73 f., 1.409/18.76, 1.364/18.78, 1.417/18.95 and 1.420/18.136 f.; Achilleus' actions, as already in Book 1, take a decisive turn (EDWARDS on 36; CERRI on 70–137; SCHADEWALDT [1938] 1966, 132; REINHARDT 1961, 368–373; KRAPP 1964, 345 f.; TAPLIN 1992, 194 ff.; WEST 2011, 344).

35 1st VH ≈ *Od.* 9.395. – **heard:** The spatial spread of the lament to the depths of the sea and Thetis' spontaneous reaction to it (37, 63 f.) suggest its unusual intensity (cf. the effects of the lamentation by Thetis and the Nereids at *Od.* 24.48 ff.: 2.153n., 24.512n.).

σμερδαλέον ᾤμωξεν: σμερδαλέον/-έα characterizing a sound is elsewhere often used in the context of aggression (cries of attack: 19.41n., rebuke: 19.399n.), ᾤμωξεν denotes men's screams caused by pain (24.591n.). The combination marks the strong emotions of Achilleus, who is filled with both grief for his friend and anger at Hektor (91–93), and the resultant volume of his scream – the eruption of his emotions after the groaning at 33 (*LfgrE s.v.* οἰμώζω; KAIMIO 1977, 62 f.). – πότνια μήτηρ: a VE formula denoting goddesses and respected women (21× *Il.*, 13× *Od.*, 3× *h.Cer.*), used 9× of Thetis (1.357n., 6.264n.).

---

35 σμερδαλέον: 'terribly, awfully' (adv.).

36 = 1.358; 2nd VH = 17.324. — **father:** In Hesiod (*Th.* 233 f.), he is called Nereus (1.358n.; CG 20).

ἡμένη: a formulaic VB, ἧσθαι meaning 'be located, dwell' (1.358n.).

37–72 The appearance of Thetis and her sisters, the Nereids (daughters of Nereus, and occupants of the depths of the sea: CG 20), is in accord with the expected reaction to Achilleus' cry of lament – in other scenes, close associates likewise immediately take care of the grieving individual (at 22.408 ff. of Priam, 22.473 ff. of Andromache; see 28–31n.); at the same time, the scene manifests itself not merely as the lament for Patroklos but also as an anticipation of the lament for Achilleus (on this, 22–147n.; on lamentation by female relatives, 19.282–302n.; KELLY 2012, 252 f. with n. 82; on premature lamentation in the *Iliad*, 6.497–502n., 24.85n.; KELLY *loc. cit.* 229–245, 264 f.). The description contains a number of motifs typical of scenes of lament, with the Nereids acting in a manner comparable to that of the female servants in the preceding scene (cf. 28–31n.): (a) scream (29 servants; 37/71 Thetis), (b) crowding around a mourner (30 Achilleus; 37 f./65 f. Thetis), (c) collective self-flagellation (30 f. servants; 50 f. Nereids [stressed 'all together']), (d) speech introduction (51b, see *ad loc.*), (e) Thetis' statements at 54 and 59b–60 (with nn.), (f) touching or supporting the head (71, see *ad loc.*): EDWARDS on 65–69; KAKRIDIS 1949, 66 ff.; REINHARDT 1961, 368; PETERSMANN 1973, 13 f.; GRIFFIN 1980, 27 f.; SCHEIN 1984, 130–132. By means of Thetis' lament, which perhaps also arises from her knowledge of Achilleus' impending early death (in which case, cf. 24.83 ff.), the narrator unfolds the background of the hero's coming demise, before which the action of the remaining Books takes place: SCHADEWALDT (1936) 1997, 155 f.; THALMANN 1984, 50 f.; TSAGALIS 2004, 139; on the external prolepses[P] of Achilleus' death, 19.328–333n., 19.409–410n. – That the Nereids appear as a collective (37b–38, 49–51b, 52 f.) that acts like a chorus of mourning women in response to Thetis' scream already at the bottom of the sea (50 f.) and that accompanies her to the encampment of ships is striking. This sequence seems to echo the scene of Achilleus' funeral as transmitted in the *Odyssey* (24.47 ff.) and the epic cycle (*Aethiopis*, Proclus *Chrest.* § 4 West) (lamentation by Thetis and the Nereids or by the Nereids and Muses), and is regarded by some as a clear indication that the scene is modelled on one in an epic that described Achilleus' death and the mourning for him: HEUBECK on *Od.* 24.47–49; KAKRIDIS 1949, 70 ff.; KULLMANN 1960, 36 f., 332; SEAFORD 1994, 154–172, esp. 166 f.; WILLCOCK 1997, 177 f., 187 f.; WEST 2011, 46 f., 344 f.; 2013, 154; cautiously BURGESS 2009, 83–87 with bibliography; *contra* CERRI on 65–69; DIHLE 1970, 20–22; DI BENEDETTO (1994)

36 ἡμένη ἐν: on the so-called correption, R 5.5. — βένθεσσιν: on the declension, R 11.3.

1998, 309 n. 25; KELLY 2012 (esp. 246–255); DAVIES 2016, 15, 19 f.: premature lament as a generally common epic motif (see above); detailed discussion of the various positions in TSAGALIS 2008, 239–271, esp. 245 ff. (cf. 17n.). For general discussion of the motifs and narrative structures of the *Iliad* (esp. concerning the characters[P] Achilleus and Patroklos) and their links to possible epic forerunners (esp. the stories surrounding the Trojan War transmitted in the epic cycle [*Aethiopis*]), 16.419–683n., end (with bibliography); 16.684–867n., end.

37 1st VH = 24.703 (Kassandra at the sight of the deceased Hektor). — For the sequence, cf. 23–30 (28–31n.).

κώκυσέν τ' ἄρ' ἔπειτα: one of several VB formulas that denote emotional responses (3.398n.); κωκύω frequently describes a woman's cry of lament at the sight of a deceased loved one or out of concern regarding someone dear to her (19.284n.).

38 ≈ 49. — κατὰ βένθος: 'across the depths', stresses the spatial extent (cf. SCHW. 2.479) and picks up ἐν βένθεσσιν (36). On the relationship between Homeric βένθος and Ionic-Attic βάθος, *DELG* s.v. βαθύς.

39–49 The catalogue of Nereids consists of a list of 33 names, a mere three of which are expanded via (generic) epithets[P] (40, 45, 48); it is framed by repetitions, some linguistic (38 ≈ 49), some in terms of content (37/50 f.), that represent hinges between the catalogue[P] and the narrative (on this, 2.760n. [Catalogue of Ships], 16.306–357n. [androktasiē scene]). The depiction of 'all' the Nereids (38, 50) gathering around Thetis serves to illustrate the extent of the mourning, which had spread since the arrival of the bad news and even encompasses the divine plane, and to highlight the significance of the moment via the double mourning (for Patroklos and for Achilleus himself, see 37–72n.); the long list of names, which is explicitly interrupted (49), is meant to illustrate in addition the large number of people gathered around (THALMANN 1984, 11 f. and 191 n. 36; MINCHIN 1996, 17; 2001, 94; GAERTNER 2001, 302 f.; SAMMONS 2010, 9–11). The catalogue was suspected as an interpolation already in antiquity and is classified by WEST as one of the 'rhetorical expansions' (WEST 2001, 12), a view that might be supported by the succession of names, uncommonly long for Homeric catalogues, with almost no expansions (AH and AH, *Anh.* p. 123; LEAF; EDWARDS; BLÖSSNER 1991, 53 n. 191; WEST 2001, 244 f.; cf. schol. A on 39–49 with the verdict of Zenodotus). In this regard, it resembles the catalogue of Nereids in Hesiod's *Theogony* (243–262), which consists of 50 names of the daughters of Pontos' son Nereus and offers the following correspondences with the present catalogue: 43 = *Th.* 248, 45 ≈ *Th.* 250; in addition, the fol-

---

37 μιν: = αὐτήν (R 14.1). — ἀμφαγέροντο: aor. of ἀμφ-αγείρομαι 'gather around'.

lowing Nereids (aside from Thetis) are mentioned in both catalogues: Glauke, Kymodoke, Nesaie, Speio, Thoë, Aktaia, Kymothoë, Melite, Agauë, Nemertes (EDWARDS on 39–49; WACHTER 1990, 23–26; BLÖSSNER *loc. cit.* 51). The relationship between the two catalogues is a matter of dispute: the present one (a) could have been created under the influence of Hesiod (LEAF; SELLSCHOPP 1934, 59–63; NICKAU 1977, 235 f.; BLÖSSNER *loc. cit.* 52–58; WEST 2001, 245: 'a Homerid taking inspiration from the Theogony'; 2011, 344 f.; 2011a, 220 f.; cautiously BOLLING 1953, 294); (b) could have been Hesiod's model (KRAFFT 1963, 144–152; VAN DER VALK 1964, 437–439; BUTTERWORTH 1986, 41–43); or (c) both might be based on a common earlier epic model (WILLCOCK; KAKRIDIS 1949, 75 [with reference to 49: interruption of a pre-existing list]; WACHTER 1990, 24 ff. [with reference to the mix of commonalities and differences in the choice and order of the names]; BURGESS 2001, 234 n. 238; TSAGALIS 2010, 325 with n. 6; 2011, 224; cautiously EDWARDS); additional bibliography on this contentious issue in NICKAU 1977, 232 n. 7; APTHORP 1995; *LfgrE s.v.* Νηρηΐ(ς). – Within the present list of names, there is aesthetic play with many correspondences of rhythm and sound, in combination with great variety in the distribution of the Greek terms for 'and' (*te, kai, te kai*) and in the number of syllables in the names, producing continuous change in the pace of the enumeration: VB 39 ≈ 47, VE 44 ≈ 46, same verse structure at 41/44/46); assonance at VE of 46 f. and within 43 (1st VH) and 47 (2nd VH); increasing number of syllables (e.g. 39, 43, 46); asyndeton at VB and epithet with the final name (40/45/48); identical caesurae (39/43); names composed of the same elements (e.g. Amphi-, Kymo-, Kalli-, -thoë, -ménē, -áneira, -ánassa: see below on the individual verses): KRAFFT 1963, 146–148; NICKAU 1977, 234 f.; BUTTERWORTH 1986, 40–42; PERCEAU 2002, 139–141; 2015, 123–130. The speaking names are associated both with locations (coast, grottoes, islands) or attributes of the sea (its gleam, movement, force) and with the competencies of the Nereids as marine goddesses (e.g. assistance, gifts), and evoke for the audience an image of the sea in its various aspects. On the Nereids in general, WEST on *Th.* 240–264; *KlP s.v.*; *LfgrE s.v.* Νηρηΐ(ς); on additional catalogues of names, 19.238–240n.; DE JONG on *Od.* 3.412–415; EDWARDS 1980, esp. 99; KELLY 2007, 122 f.; on the mnemonic function of speaking names in catalogues, MINCHIN 2001, 82–84, 88–90; for general bibliography on catalogues in oral poetry, see catalogue[P] with n. 9; 2.494–759n. (1.).

39 Glaúkē: female equivalent of the common personal name 'Glaukos' (6.119n.), as an adjective also an epithet and a kenning (Hes. *Th.* 440) for the sea. The

---

39 ἔην: = ἦν (R 16.6); likewise in 47.

meaning ('the gray-blue' or 'the brightly gleaming') and etymology are not entirely clear (WATHELET *s.v.* Γλαῦκος [with bibliography]: 'bright and clear with a blueish reflection' [transl.]; WEST on *Th.* 244 and 440 ['the gray']; for additional bibliography, 16.34n.). — **Kymodókē:** explained at *Th.* 252 ff. as the Nereid who, together with Kymatolégē and Amphitrítē, 'calms the waves (*kýmata*)' (-*dokē* related to Greek *déchomai* 'receive' [cf. Greek *douro-dókē* and *histo-dókē*, objects that hold masts and spears, respectively]: *LfgrE s.v.*). — **Tháleia:** 'the opulent', derived from the verb *thállō* 'thrive'; as an adjective, an epithet of *daís* 'meal, feast' (*LfgrE*); in Hesiod also the name of one of the Muses (*Th.* 77, cf. Thalíē at *Th.* 909: one of the Charites).

ἔνθ' ἄρ' ἔην: ἄρ(α) here picks up what was announced at 37 f. and elaborates on it, 'so' (GRIMM 1962, 10; *LfgrE s.v.* ἄρα 1148.52 ff.); similarly at 47 ἔνθα δ᾽ ἔην, continuing the list.

40 from caesura A 4 onward ≈ Hes. *Th.* 245. — **Nēsáiē:** derived from *nêsos* 'island' (*LfgrE*); listed in Hesiod (*Th.* 249) in a systematizing fashion together with **Aktáiē** (see 41; related to *aktḗ* 'coast'); on the formation, RISCH 126. — **Speió:** related to *spéos* 'cave', hence a 'grotto nymph' (*LfgrE*); on the worship of Nereids at the coast and in caves, WEST on *Th.* 249. — **Thóē:** 'the swift'. — **Halíē:** an adjectival derivation from *hals* 'sea', also a joint attribute of the Nereids (86) and their father Nereus (141), as a nominalized adj. 'sea-goddess(es)', see 86, *Od.* 24.47/55.

Νησαίη ...: Asyndeton at VB within lists of names is not unusual, here also in 45, 48 with epithet expansions (for additional examples, WEST on *Th.* 245). — βοῶπις: a generic beauty epithet[P] of various goddesses and human women, usually of Hera; of others, aside from the present passage, also at 3.144 (likely interpolated, see *ad loc.*), 7.10 and 2× Hes., 1× *h.Hom.*; interpreted as 'large-eyed' (1.551n., 3.144n.).

41 Kymothóē: a compound with the initial element *kýma* (39n.); the final element is to be understood as either nominal (*thoós*: 'swift'), thus 'the one swift as a wave' (VON KAMPTZ 74), or verbal (*théō*: 'run'), thus 'she who runs in the waves' (GIGANTE/BONINO 1973, 114; cf. RISCH 202). — **Limnóreia:** a compound with an initial element related to *límnē* 'standing water'; the final element is obscure: derived from either *órē* ('care for/about something') or *óros* ('mountain', cf. 48n.); she is thus either the 'mistress of the marshes' (*LfgrE s.v.* Λιμνώρεια with bibliography) or 'mistress of the high seas' (*LfgrE s.v.* Νηρηΐ(ς) 375.56).

42 Melítē: related to *méli* 'honey' (*LfgrE*); at *h.Cer.* 419, the name of an Okeanid, playmate of Persephone, as well as *inter alia* the name of islands (e.g. Malta): *BNP s.v.* Melite. — **Iaira:** meaning obscure (see below). — **Amphithóē:** on the final element, 41n.; the initial element is either intensifying (EDWARDS; VON KAMPTZ 54, 74: 'the very swift'; cf. SCHW. 2.437) or spatial 'all around' (*LfgrE* *s.v.* Ἀμφιθόη: 'she who hastens all around'; cf. RISCH 202). — **Agaué:** perhaps means 'the admirable' (3.268n.); one of Kadmos' daughters, the mother of Pentheus, bears the same name (Hes. *Th.* 976).

"Ιαιρα: is linked either to the adj. ἱερός (Vedic *iṣirá-*; VON KAMPTZ 121; EDWARDS), which may originally have meant 'powerful' (cf. *DELG*, FRISK and BEEKES *s.v.*) or 'vigorous' (cf. 16.407n. [of a fish], 24.681n.), or it is an abbreviated form of a name beginning with Ἰ- (RISCH 138; cf. PETERS 1980, 194: -αιρα as an 'independent suffix' [transl.]).

43 = Hes. *Th.* 248. — **Dōtṓ:** 'the giver', likewise **Dōrís** at 45 (on the formation, RISCH 192; SCHW. 1.442); the name either refers to the gifts produced by fishing (WEST on *Th.* 244) or generally to everything the sea has to offer (including e.g. flotsam). — **Prōtṓ:** usually understood as an abbreviated form of a name in *Prōto-* (Hes. *Th.* 249 Protomedeia) and connected with *prṓtos* ('the first'), although some connect it with **prṓton* ≈ *peprōménon* ('determined by fate'): SCHULZE 1892, 22 f. n. 3; WEST on *Th.* 248; *LfgrE s.vv.* Πρωτώ, Πρωτεύς with bibliography. — **Dynaménē:** pres. part. of *dýnamai* 'be able to, be in one's power to do'. — **Phérousa:** pres. part., 'the bearer, bringer', i.e. she who brings ships to their destination (WEST on *Th.* 248 and GIGANTE/BONINO 1973, 114, with reference to *Od.* 3.300, etc.), or alternatively in reference to the gifts the sea provides to humans (*RE s.v.* Nereiden).

44 Dexaménē: aor. part. of *déchomai* 'receive' (39n.), hence e.g. 'she who receives hospitably' as a protectress of ships (*LfgrE*; WILLCOCK with reference to 398: 'she who protects'; differently EDWARDS: she who heeds prayers or sacrifices). — **Amphinómē:** fem. form of the personal name Amphinomos (*Od.* 16.394), which is usually interpreted as 'with a wealth of pastures' (Greek *nomós*; *amphí* with an intensifying force): VON KAMPTZ 55, 74; RISCH 201; EDWARDS. — **Kalliáneira:** 'she who has beautiful men' (*LfgrE*; on the formation, RISCH 138, 219).

45 ≈ Hes. *Th.* 250. – a verse constructed in accord with the 'law of increasing parts', consisting of three personal names, with the third expanded via an epithet[P] (1.145n., 19.87n.). — **Dōrís:** 43n. — **Panópē:** probably 'the all-seeing' (*LfgrE* with bibliography; EDWARDS). — **Galáteia:** perhaps derived from *gála* 'milk' (RISCH 138) in reference to the milky white sea-foam (*RE s.v.* Nereiden; EDWARDS).

ἀγακλειτή: 'very famous, magnificent', a generic epithet[P] of both men and women, as well as of ἑκατόμβη; always after caesura B 2 (5× *Il.*, 6× *Od.*, 3× Hes., 1× *h.Hom.*), cf. 6.436–437n. on the metrical-prosodic variant ἀγακλυτός.

46 Rhythmically and – especially at VE – acoustically, the verse is constructed in a manner similar to 44. — **Nemertḗs and Apseudḗs:** The adjectives ('infallible, unerring' and 'without deception, true') denote traits that in early epic characterize the 'Old Man of the Sea' – who is sometimes given different names (*Od.* 4.349/384/401/542, 17.140, Hes. *Th.* 233 ff.), cf. Hes. *Th.* 262; they are probably connected to the mantic gifts ascribed to marine divinities (WEST on *Th.* 233 and 261–262; LUTHER 1935, 41 f., 81; DÉTIENNE 1967, 30–32; cf. WEST on *Od.* 4.349. On the formation of *nēmertḗs*, 6.376n.). — **Kalliánassa:** a compound comprised of the elements 'beautiful' (cf. 44n.) and 'mistress, protectress' (VON KAMPTZ 85; RISCH 139; cf. 6.402–403n. *s.v.* Astyanax on the sense of *ánax*); meaning obscure ('she who rules in a beautiful manner'?: *LfgrE*).

47 Klyménē: 'the famous' (RISCH 54; VON KAMPTZ 242; cf. 2.742n., 19.10n. on the adj. *klytós*); in Hesiod the name of an Okeanid, the wife of Iapetos (*Th.* 351, 508). — **Iáneira and Iánassa:** Both are compounds with an obscure initial element (if the initial element were related to *[w]îphi* ['with force, powerfully', cf. Latin *vīs*], a long vowel would be expected) and a final element related to *anḗr* ('man'; cf. 44n.) and *ánax* ('ruler'; cf. 46n.), respectively: RISCH 139; VON KAMPTZ 102, 121; SCHW. 1.452.

ἔνθα δ' ἔην: beginning of a new clause, with echoes of 39 (see *ad loc.*); 39–46 show the closest correspondences with Hesiod (esp. *Th.* 244b–245, 247–250; for 46, cf. *Th.* 262): WACHTER 1990, 24–26.

48 corresponds to 45 in structure and sound (VE) (see *ad loc.*). — **Maira:** 'the glimmering', related to the verb *marmáirō* (RISCH 137; VON KAMPTZ 121; *LfgrE*); like Klymene, the name of a heroine at *Od.* 11.326. — **Ōreíthyia:** interpreted as 'she who storms at the mountain' (see below), but the original meaning is obscure (*LfgrE s.v.* Νηρηΐ(ς) 375.53 f.; perhaps like the wind storming down from the mountains toward the sea?: EDWARDS); in post-Homeric literature, this is also the name of the daughter of Erechtheus and wife of the wind god Boreas. — **Amátheia:** related to *ámathos* 'sand', probably corresponds to the Nereid Psamathe at Hes. *Th.* 260 (WEST *ad loc.*; *LfgrE s.v.* ἄμαθ(ος); RISCH 138, 174).

ἐϋπλόκαμος: 'with beautiful tresses', a generic epithet[P] of goddesses and human women; on this and other, similar epithets, 6.379–380n. — Ὠρείθυια ... Ἀμάθεια: The reading Ἀμάθεια is to be preferred to the main transmission Ἀμάθυια, since the name is probably linked to Ψαμάθη/Ψαμάθεια, while the reading with the final element -θυια has been influenced by Ὠρείθυια (WEST on *Th.* 260; WEST 2001, 245). – Ὠρείθυια is a compound of ὄρος (wth metrical lengthening) + θύω (RISCH 136; *LfgrE s.v.* Ὠρείθυια; WYATT 1969, 49 n. 14).

49 ≈ 18.38 (see *ad loc.*). — **the depth of the sea:** The phrase frames the list of names here and at 38 (on the phenomenon, 39–49n.).

ἄλλαι θ' αἴ ...: the same interruption in a list of names as at 2.649 (see *ad loc.*), Hes. *Th.* 21, 363–370 (WEST on *Th.* 21).

50–67a Thetis' speech before her assembled sisters is framed by verses that are matched in terms of content and structure: the cave (50a/65a), syntactically a new clause beginning at caesura C 2 (50b/65b; on this in general, 1.194n.), mourning by the sisters (50b–51a/65b–66a, in each case with integral enjambment[P]). The speech introduction at 51b (see *ad loc.*) and the individual motifs from the laments (54n., 55–60n.) notwithstanding, the speech does not correspond to a mourning speech in a strict sense (on the structure of laments, 19.286–339n., 24.725–745n., 24.749–750n.): (1) beginning and end are situational (52f. a request to listen with an address to bystanders / 63f. a reference to a subsequent encounter with Achilleus), (2) 61f. illustrate Thetis' concern for the living Achilleus; in addition, 56–62 are repeated in her speech to Hephaistos at 437–443: EDWARDS on 52–64; CERRI on 52–64; LOHMANN 1970, 54; PETERSMANN 1973, 13–15; TSAGALIS 2004, 137f.; 2008, 240–255, 265f.; BECK 2005, 258–260, 268; GAGLIARDI 2007, 101, 169f.

50 VE ≈ 30 (see *ad loc.*). — **cave:** on Thetis' abode in a cave in the sea off the coast of Asia Minor, 24.83n.

καί: refers to the statement in its entirety: the consequence of 37f. (AH; cf. 16.148n.). — ἀργύφεον: 'bright, white, shining', an expansion of ἄργυφος (on the etymology, 24.621n.). Elsewhere used as an epithet of sheep and garments, it here describes the play of light in the cave in the sea (CERRI; cautiously *LfgrE s.v.* ἀργύφε(ος): rather 'spacious and bright' [transl.]).

51 1st VH = 31 (see *ad loc.*); 2nd VH ≈ 18.316, 22.430, 23.17, 24.723, 24.747, 24.761. — The gesture of mourning by the assembled individuals and the speech introduction belong to the context of lamentation (28–31n., 37–72n.; ALEXIOU [1974] 2002, 13; DERDERIAN 2001, 35f.).

ἐξῆρχε γόοιο: ἐξάρχω means 'strike up, lead', of certain forms of song (e.g. a dance song [606n.], dithyramb and paian [Archil. *fr.* 120 and 121 West]), here, as in a lament, of ululation (CALAME [1977] 1997, 82f.; ZIMMERMANN 1992, 19f.); γόος usually denotes the spontaneous lamentation of relatives during a mourning ritual (in contrast to the formal θρῆνος), sometimes also outside a ritual context 'weeping, mourning' (24.160n., 24.723n.).

52–53 Thetis' concern arises particularly from her knowledge of Achilleus' impending early death (1.414–418, 1.505f.), i.e. of the fact that he will not return from Troy (18.59–62, 18.95f., 18.429–461 [esp. 440f.], 21.276–278, 24.84ff., 24.131f.): KELLY 2012, 249f.; on Greek *thymós*, 4–5n.

---

50 πλῆτο (+ gen.): 'be filled with', root aor. mid. of πίμπλημι.
52 ὄφρ(α) (+ subjunc.): final (R 22.5).
53 εἴδετ(ε): short-vowel subjunc. (R 16.3). — ἀκούουσαι, ὅσ(α): on the hiatus, R 5.6. — ἐμῷ ἔνι: on the bridging of hiatus by non-syllabic ι (*emōy éni*), M 12.2. — ἔνι: = ἐν (R 20.1), ≈ ἔνεστι.

κλῦτε: imper. 'listen!', always at VB, usually combined with an address to familiar individuals, likewise at 2.56, *Od.* 4.722, 6.239, 14.495, 15.172 (*LfgrE*); a root aor. (G 63), -ῠ- is perhaps analogous with the imper. sing. κλῦθι with metrical lengthening (CHANTR. 1.103, 379; WYATT 1969, 210; BEEKES s.v. κλύω), beside VB with κέκλῠτε (on which, 3.86n.). – **ὄφρ' εὖ πᾶσαι | εἴδετ':** a variant of the inflectable VE formula ὄφρ' εὖ εἴδω/ εἴδῃς (1.185n.); as at 38 and 50, the group's collective character is highlighted (cf. n.). – **ἐμῷ ἔνι ... θυμῷ:** 'in my heart' is stressed, but now her sisters will share in the sorrow (JAHN 1987, 229). – **κήδεα:** 'suffering, pain', usually in the sense of grieving for relatives (8n.), which is also insinuated in the present context (37–72n.). But in what follows, the focus is on Thetis' worries for her son ('distress, sorrow': *LfgrE*), see esp. the stress on 'I' via ἐμῷ ... θυμῷ, in the exclamation at 54 and via pronouns and verbs in the 1st pers. sing. in 55/57–62 (suggestion by VAN DER MIJE).

54 1st VH ≈ 22.431, *Od.* 5.299. – The cry of grieving, the pathos of which is further heightened via the doubling, unique in early epic, of *ōi moi* ('o my'), is explicated in what follows: 55–56 'child-bearer of the best' (*aristo-tókeia*), 59b–62 'sorrowful me', 'unlucky' (*dys-*); cf. Thetis' lament to Achilleus himself at 1.414/418 (SCHADEWALDT [1936] 1997, 155 f.; TSAGALIS 2004, 48, 138 f.; 2008, 266–271). The adj. *deilé* ('deplorable, miserable') is also used in laments by Briseïs in reference to herself (19.287, see *ad loc.*) and by Hekabe (22.431).

ᾤ μοι ἐγώ: 6n.; an emphatic anaphora of the interjection (FEHLING 1969, 206), with a change in rhythm due to the position in the verse. – **δυσαριστοτόκεια:** a *hapax legomenon*[P] meaning 'unfortunate bearer of a hero' (schol. D: ἐπὶ κακῷ τὸν ἄριστον τετοκυῖα; *LfgrE*: 'wretched mother of a noble son'), comprised of the nominal compound ἀριστο- τόκεια (related to τίκτω, -εια because of the VE) with the negative prefix δυσ- (RISCH 229; SCHW. 1.428 n. 4; on the prefix, 3.39n.; additional examples of such highly emotional self-designations in GRIFFFIN 1986, 41 f.).

55–60 An external analepsis[P]: Thetis describes her role during Achilleus' adolescence and at his departure for Troy. The passage contains echoes of motifs from the narrative section of laments, which are particularly recognizable in the laments of Hekabe and Andromache for Hektor in Books 22 and 24: reference to the familial relationships of the deceased, the life of the deceased with a eulogy, the future of the survivors: EDWARDS; REINER 1938, 13 f.; PATTONI 1998, 15–18; DERDERIAN 2001, 36 f.; TSAGALIS 2004, 88–90; see also 56–57n.

ἥ τ' ἐπεὶ ἄρ τέκον ... | (3 verses) | ... ὑποδέξομαι: explication of δυσαριστοτόκεια at 55–56a, with a transition from hypotaxis to parataxis in the narrative section, with similes[P] at 56/57 (ὃ δ' ἀνέδραμεν ...) and juxtaposition of the action at 57 ff. (τὸν μὲν ἐγὼ ... | ...προέηκα ...Ἴλιον εἴσω vs. τὸν δ' οὐχ ὑποδέξομαι ... | ... δόμον Πηλήϊον εἴσω): AH on 56; LEAF on 55 and on 17.658; CERRI on 57; CHANTR. 2.361; on the explicative function of relative clauses with compounds, 24.479n.

55 2nd VH from υἱόν = 4.89, 5.169, 21.546, *h.Ap.* 100; from ἀμύμονα = Hes. *Th.* 1013, 'Hes.' *frr.* 141.14, 171.6 M.-W. — **ἥ τ' ἐπεὶ ἄρ:** VB ≈ 17.658, 24.42 (ὅς), *h.Ap.* 158 (αἵ) and 4× *Il.* without ἄρ; on the use of ἐπεὶ ἄρ, 24.42–43n. — **ἀμύμονα:** conventionally interpreted 'excellent'; on the disputed etymology of this generic epithet[P], 6.22–23n.

56–62 = 437–443, likewise spoken by Thetis; the verses illustrate the conflicted emotions of the mother who has let her son go off to war: on the one hand, pride (cf. the emphatic runover word at 56); on the other, concern. The mother-son relationship is also stressed by other means in this and the subsequent scene: by the designation of Achilleus as 'son' and 'child' in the speeches to Thetis' sisters at 55, 63, 144; in the addresses at 73, 95, 128; in the narrator-text at the beginning and end of the encounter at 71 (see *ad loc.*), 138, 147; cf. the periphrastic denomination[P] of Thetis as 'mother' in the narrator-text at 35, 70 and in the address at 79 (DE JONG [1987] 2004, 190). – Already in Book 1, Thetis lamented the two central conditions of Achilleus' life: his early death and his sorrowful life (1.417, see *ad loc.*; DI BENEDETTO [1994] 1998, 306 f.).

56–57 Similes[P] involving plants serve to illustrate *inter alia* the growing and thriving of young people (in addition to the present passage, *Od.* 6.157–169 of Nausikaa, 14.175 of Telemachos; cf. *Il.* 22.86 f., *h.Cer.* 66, 187, *h.Ven.* 278, *Il. parv. fr.* 31 West [with WEST 2013, 185]; on parallels in the Hebrew Bible, WEST 1997, 242); at the same time, they show the transitoriness of human life (cf. 6.146–149n. with bibliography), e.g. in the context of a young warrior's death in battle at *Il.* 8.304 ff., 17.53 ff. (SCOTT 1974, 70 f.). In the present passage, the simile refers initially to Achilleus' thriving, but in the continuation of Thetis' speech (59 f.) there is an allusion to the early death of her son, nurtured like a plant (TSAGALIS 2004, 139; GRETHLEIN 2006, 90 f.; on this type of simile[P] in laments, see ALEXIOU [1974] 2002, 195 ff., esp. 198; on similes in character[P] speeches in general, 2.289n.; DE JONG [1987] 2004, 135 f.).

56 VE ≈ *Od.* 14.175. — **ἔξοχον ἡρώων:** ἔξοχος is commonly used in reference to achievements in battle, but other combinations with a gen. are more common (e.g. the VE formula ἔξοχον ἄλλων [12× early epic]: *LfgrE s.v.* ἔξοχος; 2.188n.; cf. the appeal to Achilleus at 11.784 ὑπείροχον ἔμμεναι ἄλλων). In the *Iliad*, only Agamemnon is also ἔξοχος ἡρώων – albeit temporarily, during the departure for battle at 2.483 (2.480–483n.); on the use and connotations of the term ἥρως, 1.4n., 6.34–35n. — **ἀνέδραμεν:** 'shot up', of a rapid increase in height, stresses the speed with which, in retrospect, the child grew in the eyes of his mother; contrast *Od.* 6.163 νέον ἔρνος ἀνερχόμενον (Odysseus to Nausikaa regarding the growth of a plant, to which she is herself then compared): LEAF; *LfgrE s.v.* δραμεῖν.

---

55 ἥ τ' ἐπεί: a contextual continuation of ἥ in the main clause 59b–60 ('epic τε': R 24.11); ἐπεί is to be connected with τέκον. — ἄρ: = ἄρα (R 24.1). — τέκον: on the unaugmented form, R 16.1.
56 ἔρνεϊ (ϝ)ῖσος: on the prosody, R 5.4.

57 VE = 9.534, 18.438. — **nurtured:** In other versions transmitted in the epic cycle, Thetis left her husband Peleus shortly after the birth of Achilleus; his upbringing was thus taken over by the centaur Cheiron (24.83n.; MARCH 1987, 23 f.).

φυτὸν ὥς: on the prosody (long scansion of the syllable before ὥς), 2.190n. — γουνῷ ἀλωῆς: γουνός is probably related etymologically to γόνυ and may mean 'elevation, hill' (*DELG*; FRISK; *contra* BEEKES), ἀλωή denotes cultivated land, such as an orchard or vineyard (*Od.* 1.193, 11.193, *h.Merc.* 207 γουνὸν ἀλωῆς οἰνοπέδοιο), that is partially enclosed (ἕρκος) (561/564, 5.90, *Od.* 24.224, *h.Merc.* 188): *LfgrE s.vv.* ἀλωή, γουνός; RICHTER 1968, 97 f. The simile stresses the care and nurturing done by the mother.

58 In this highly emotional speech, Thetis speaks from the point of view of the deeply concerned mother who has sent her son off to war and is thus responsible for his participation in the campaign (on her role in Achilleus' departure, 16.222–224n.). Elsewhere in the *Iliad*, when other characters[P] report on Achilleus' departure for Troy, the focus is on Peleus (9.252–259 Odysseus, 9.438–443 Phoinix, 11.769–790 Nestor): ANDERSEN 1990, 40 f.; LATACZ (1995) 2014, 309 f. n. 107; TSAGALIS 2004, 88 f.; contrast the version in which Peleus hid his son on the island of Skyros (*Cypr. fr.* 19 West, with WEST 2013, 103 f.). — **Ilion:** another name for Troy (1.71n.; FOR 24), hence the title '*Iliad*' (*hē Iliás* ⟨*poíēsis*⟩, 'the ⟨poem⟩ about Ilion').

νηυσὶν ἔπι προέηκα κορωνίσιν: thus the text in WEST – on analogy with the VB formula νηυσὶν ἔπι γλαφυρῇσι (12× *Il.*; cf. 304n.) – whereas others prefer to write the double compound ἐπι-προ-έηκα indicating a directional ('toward ⟨the enemy⟩') departure ('send out') with νηυσίν as an instrumental dat. (AH; LEAF with reference to the meaning of ἐπί v.: elsewhere in Homer 'at/toward the ships' [and cf. *LfgrE s.v.* νηῦς 385.53 ff.]; EDWARDS; *LfgrE s.v.* ἵημι 1154.65 ff.). – The ship epithet κορώνισιν (probably 'curved', of the prow) is always used in the dat. pl. and occurs between caesurae B 2 and C 2 immediately after νηυσὶ/νήεσσι, although here with the words separated (1.170n.; EDWARDS 1968, 266); but cf. 17.708. — Ἴλιον εἴσω: a VE formula (6× *Il.*, 2× *Od.*, 1× 'Hes.'); εἴσω is an adv. also used as a postpositive preposition (1.71n.) meaning 'toward' (*LfgrE s.v.* εἴσω) here and at 1.71, 18.493, *Od.* 19.182, 19.193.

59b–60a ≈ 89b–90a, *Od.* 19.257b–258a. – The thought of death in battle is often linked to the notion that a man will no longer return to his father or his home-

---

57 τὸν μέν: picked up again by 59 τὸν δέ to contrast the predicates; on the anaphoric demonstrative function of ὅ, ἥ, τό, R 17. — θρέψασα: aor. part. of τρέφω. — φυτὸν ὥς: = ὡς φυτόν; on the prosody, ↑. — γουνῷ: locative dat. without preposition (R 19.2).
58 νηυσὶν ἔπι: = ἐπὶ νηυσίν (R 20.2), on the declension of νηυσίν, R 12.1. — προέηκα: aor. of προΐημι 'send forth' (ἕηκα is a by-form of ἧκα).
59 μαχησόμενον: fut. part. of μαχέομαι (a by-form of μάχομαι). — αὖτις: = αὖθις.
60 δόμον ... εἴσω: ≈ εἰς δόμον. — Πηλήϊον: 'belonging to Peleus, of Peleus'.

land (2.162n., 19.329n.; on the motif 'return home', MARONITIS 2004, 64 ff.). Here the motif is varied by the mother inserting herself into the imagined homecoming scene (see also 330–332, 19.422) – even though she does not live with Peleus (57n.) – thus increasing the pathos (on Thetis' foreknowledge, 52–53n.).

οἴκαδε νοστήσαντα: an inflectable VB formula (5× *Il.*, 7× *Od.*, 1× 'Hes.'); on νοστήσαντα, 238n. — **Πηλήϊον:** on possessive adjectives in -ιος, 2.20n.

61 ≈ 24.558 (see *ad loc.*), *Od.* 4.540, 4.833, 10.498, 14.44, 20.207, *h.Ven.* 105. — **ζώει καὶ ὁρᾷ φάος ἠελίοιο:** synonym doubling with emphatic effect (cf. 1.88n.; on its function in terms of versification, 1.160n.; cf. its antithesis: τεθνᾶσι/τέθνηκε καὶ εἰν Ἀΐδαο δόμοισιν 22.52, *Od.* 4.834, etc.); the formulaic expression is expanded with μοι only here, representing maternal sympathy. On Indo-Iranian parallels for the expression 'see the sun' = 'live', WEST 2007, 86 f.; on the VE formula φ. ἠ., 11n.

62 ≈ 11.120. — *áchnymai/áchos*, a designation for the 'basic constant of human human existence', applies to Achilleus' life in particular and represents a contrast with the carefree existence of the gods (24.526n.; LATACZ [1995] 2014, 319 f.; on hypotheses regarding the acoustic or even etymological links between the word family and the personal name *Achilleus*, 16.21–22n.). But here it is set in contrast to Thetis' helplessness: although a goddess, she cannot save her human son from these actualities nor can she prevent his short life from being deprived of joy; see also 446, 461 (SLATKIN [1991] 2011, 30 ff.).

χραισμῆσαι: 'be a protector, help', cf. 11.117 (the helplessness of a hind who cannot protect her young), 16.837 (Achilleus and Patroklos): *LfgrE s.v.* — **ἰοῦσα:** concessive, 'even if I go there' (*sc.* to Achilleus at Troy); continued at 63 ἀλλ᾽ εἶμ(ι).

63 to listen: an echo of the introduction to Thetis' own lament in front of her sisters (52 f.) and a transition to Achilleus' mourning. She is unaware of the reasons for Achilleus' grief (cf. 73–77), just as she did not know the reason for his sorrow at 1.362 f. (see *ad loc.*). This need not be considered a contradiction of her mantic abilities (cf. 9–11, 95 f.): (a) it illustrates an additional aspect of her constant concern for her son, whom she instructed to keep away from battle, see 1.421 f. and 64 (KELLY 2012, 249 f. n. 72); (b) in addition, this allows the narrator to have Achilleus describe his situation himself; for the audience, 22–126 result in a staggered experience of suffering (EDWARDS; TAPLIN 1992,

---

61 ὄφρα: 'so long as'. — ζώει: epic form for ζῇ. — φάος: = φῶς (R 6). — ἠελίοιο: = ἡλίου.
62 οὐδέ τι: 'and in no way' (literally 'and not in any respect': τι is acc. of respect, R 19.1). In Homer, connective οὐδέ also occurs after affirmative clauses (R 24.8). — τι (ϝ)οι: on the prosody, R 5.4. — οἱ: = αὐτῷ (R 14.1).
63 ὄφρα (ϝ)ίδωμι: on the prosody, R 4.3. — ὄφρα (+ subjunc.): final (R 22.5). — ἠδ(έ): 'and' (R 24.4).

198 f.; on the phenomenon of 'poetic licence', schol. A on 63–64 and NÜNLIST 2009, 174 ff., esp. 176; different weighting in CERRI).

ἴδωμι: on the form (1st pers. sing. aor. subjunc.), G 89. — φίλον τέκος: an intensification vis-à-vis υἱόν at 55; always before caesura C 2 (12× *Il.*, 4× *Od.*, 1× *h.Cer.*), aside from here and *h.Cer.* 71 always used as an address (EDWARDS 1968, 266; cf. *LfgrE s.v.* τέκος); on the prosodic variants τέκος/τέκνον, 1.202n.

64 ἵκετο πένθος: On formulations for 'overcome, affect' with abstract subjects, 24.707–709n.; on πένθος 'suffering, grief' as a reaction to loss, 1.254n.; *LfgrE*. — **πτολέμοιο:** In early epic, this usually (as here) means 'fighting/battle', less commonly 'war' (2.453n.; *LfgrE s.v.* 1335.41 ff.).

65–147 The encounter between Achilleus and Thetis is framed by the arrival and departure of the other marine goddesses and contains two similarly structured speeches by Achilleus (ring-composition[P]: SCHADEWALDT [1936] 1997, 156–160; LOHMANN 1970, 141–144, esp. 142; on the speeches, 79–126n.): (A) Thetis and the Nereids rise from the sea and join Achilleus (65–71), (B) Thetis' introductory speech with a glance at the past (72–77), (C) Achilleus' first speech (78–93), (D) Thetis on the fate of Achilleus (94–96), (C') Achilleus' second speech (97–126), (B') Thetis' concluding speech with a look to the future (127–137), (A') Thetis parts from Achilleus, sends the Nereids back into the sea and departs for Olympos (138–147). Everything in this scene is focussed on mother and son: the grieving bystanders (the female servants as well as Antilochos: 30–33) are no longer mentioned, the Nereids appear only in the framing sections A/A' (on the surroundings being blocked out during divine appearances, 1.197–198n.).

65–72 The portrayal of Thetis' visit to the Myrmidons' encampment of ships resembles the scene at 24.96 ff. and contains elements of the type-scene[P] 'change of location by a deity' (24.89–102n.), here with company (65b–66a, 68): (**1**) occasion (63 f.), (**3**) departure and description of the route (65–67a), (**5**) arrival (67b–69). This is combined with elements of the type-scene[P] 'arrival' (1.496b–502n.): (**3**) description of the situation (68b–69), (**4**) the character approaches (70 f.), (**5**) she speaks (72 ff.).

65 ὣς ἄρα φωνήσασα: an inflectable VB formula (speech capping formula[P]): 24.468n. — **αἳ δὲ σὺν αὐτῇ:** on the structure of the verse, 30n.

---

64 ὅττι: = ὅ τι (cf. R 9.1 and R 14.2), refers to πένθος. — μιν: = αὐτόν (R 14.1). — ἀπὸ πτολέμοιο μένοντα: 'remaining far from ...'; the part. is temporal or concessive. — πτολέμοιο: on the πτ-, R 9.2.
65 λίπε: on the unaugmented form, R 16.1. — αἴ: on the anaphoric demonstrative function of ὅ, ἥ, τό, R 17.

66–67a was broken: on this motif, 24.96n.

κῦμα θαλάσσης: a VE formula (4× *Il.*, 1× *h.Hom.*: 24.96n.); on the collective sing. κῦμα, SCHW. 2.41; CHANTR. 2.29.

67b 2nd VH ≈ 23.215. — ἐρίβωλον: 'with large clods', an epithet of landscapes, of Τροίη (as a designation of the region 'Troad': 2.141n.) also at 9.329, 23.215; metrical-prosodic variant of ἐριβῶλαξ (on which, 1.155n., 6.314b–315n.).

68 ≈ 1st VH 24.97. — ἐπισχερώ: 'one after another, successively', as in a circular dance; also at 11.668, 23.125; on the type of formation (affixation), SCHW. 2.469; on the etymology of σχερο- (nominal formation from σχέσθαι 'join'), *DELG* and BEEKES *s.v.* ἐπισχερώ; RISCH 69, 355, 358; JANKO 1979, 21–23. — θαμειαί: predicative 'close together'; on the word formation, 19.383n.

69 2nd VH ≈ 354. — Achilleus' ship, which appears to be surounded by the remaining ships of the Myrmidons, is situated at the right edge of the encampment (3n.).

ταχὺν ἀμφ' Ἀχιλῆα: What is meant here is 'surrounding the ship of swift Achilleus' (AH); ταχύς as an epithet for Achilleus is elsewhere expanded by πόδας (variant of πόδας ὠκὺς Ἀ.: VE formula 30× *Il.*), cf. 2nd VH of 354 and the formula Ἀχιλῆα πόδας ταχύν before caesura C 2 (13.348, 17.709, 18.358, cf. 2n.).

70 βαρὺ στενάχοντι: an inflectable formula after caesura A 2 (8× *Il.*), elsewhere always masc. nom. sing. (1.364n.); only in speech introductions, with the exception of the present passage and 23.60 (KAIMIO 1977, 40 f.). — παρίστατο: likewise at 19.6, where Achilleus is grieving while lying across Patroklos' body (see *ad loc.*); differently at 1.360 and 24.126 (she sits down beside him: 1.360n.). — πότνια μήτηρ: 35n.

71 took …: The gesture is an intensification vis-à-vis that at 1.361 (caressing him, likewise at 24.127), where Thetis similarly visits her son to comfort him (AREND 1933, 29; cf. 19.7n.), although it also resembles the gesture of mourning that involves close relatives holding the head of the deceased (24.711–712n. with bibliography), reinforcing the impression that the scene is designed to evoke an image of the dead Achilleus (22–147n., 37–72n.). What posture Thetis takes when Achilleus is lying on the ground (crouching or sitting? his head in her

---

66 δακρυόεσσαι: predicative, 'in tears'. — ἴσαν: unaugmented (R 16.1) 3rd pers. pl. impf. of εἶμι. — περί: 'all around'. — σφισί: = αὐταῖς (R 14.1); dat. of advantage.

67 ῥήγνυτο: 'broke'. — ταί: anaphoric demonstrative pronoun (R 14.3). — Τροίην: on the -η- after -ι-, R 2. — ἵκοντο: on the unaugmented form (short ῐ-), R 16.1.

68 ἐπισχερώ, ἔνθα: on the so-called correption, R 5.5.

69 εἴρυντο: plpf. pass. of (ϝ)ερύω, 'were drawn ⟨onto the land⟩, were laid there'. — νέες: on the declension, R 12.1. — Ἀχιλῆα: on the declension, R 11.3; on the single -λ-, R 9.1.

71 κάρη: Attic τὸ κάρα (R 2), 'head'. — ἑοῖο: possessive pronoun of the 3rd person (R 14.4); on the declension, R 11.2.

lap?; cf. the comparable situation at 19.3–7) remains uncertain; suggestions by AH; EDWARDS; CERRI; WILLCOCK; KAKRIDIS 1949, 67; KURZ 1966, 47, 95.

κωκύσασα: see her mourning cry at 37 (with n.); here reinforced by ὀξύ, stressing the piercing, shrill volume of the sound and creating a contrast with βαρὺ στενάχοντι/ στενάχων at 70/78 of Achilleus, illustrating the deep pain that also dominates the speech that follows at 79 ff. (ARNOULD 1990, 150–153). — **κάρη λάβε παιδὸς ἑοῖο:** VE παιδὸς/υἱος ἑοῖο also at 14.266, Hes. *Th.* 496 and *Il.* 14.9, 18.138; on this periphrastic denomination[P] for Achilleus, 56–62n.; SHIVE 1987, 53 f.; FRIEDRICH 2007, 129 f.; on ἑοῖο, G 82; NUSSBAUM 1998, 97 f.; on the construction (acc. of the body part and gen. of the person), 24.465n.

72 = *Od.* 2.362, 11.472, 17.40, *h.Cer.* 247; ≈ *Il.* 5.871, 11.815, *Od.* 10.265, 10.324, 10.418, 11.154, 11.616, 16.22 (ὀλοφυρόμενος and μ' ὀλ.). — **ἔπεα πτερόεντα προσηύδα:** a speech introduction formula[P] (19.20n.).

73–77 In Thetis' speech, which contains literal echoes of her appearance in Book 1 (1.362 f.), where the implementation of the plan of revenge alluded to at 76 f. began (35–147n.), the narrator makes the tragic element of the situation particularly clear: she is at a loss (on this, 63n.), since both Achilleus' wish (1.240–244, 1.408–412; on this, 1.408n., 1.410n., 1.411n., 2.375–380n.) and her plan have been fulfilled, although this is what doomed him (79–82): EDWARDS; REINHARDT 1961, 370; NAGLER 1974, 134 n. 6: 'backfiring wish'; REICHEL 1994, 122; MURNAGHAN 1997, 27 f.; RINON 2008, 34; on this causal chain as a compositional plan, LATACZ (1995) 2014, 333 f. – For comparison with a similar conversation after the death of a friend in the epic of Gilgamesh, DI BENEDETTO (1994) 1998, 314, 316; WEST 1997, 340 f.

73 = 1.362 (see *ad loc.*); VE = 24.708, *Od.* 23.224. — On the emotive effect of the repetition of the interrogative pronoun (τί ... τί) and the difference in meaning between πένθος and ἄχος, 1.362n.; on the address τέκνον, also 6.254n., 19.8n.; on the VE (ἵκετο πένθος), 64n.

74 1st VH = 1.363 (see *ad loc.*), 16.19. — **τὰ μὲν δὴ ... τετέλεσται:** pointing ahead: τά is explained at 76 f. via an appositive in the form of an acc. and inf. (AH; FAESI; CORLU 1966, 66). An assertion introduced by μάν/μήν/μέν can serve to anticipate potential objections by the addressee (CUYPERS 2005, 46); μὲν δή stresses the *evident* execution of an action (additional examples at 24.599n.) and thus the fulfilment of the wish (ὡς ἄρα δὴ πρίν γ' ηὔχεο): 'indeed (as you see)'; on the use of δή, cf. 4 τὰ ..., ἃ δὴ τετελεσμένα ἦεν (see *ad loc.*).

---

72 ῥ(α): on the avoidance of hiatus, R 24.1, cf. R 5.1. — ὀλοφυρομένη (ϝ)έπεα: on the prosody, R 4.4. — ἔπεα: on the uncontracted form, R 6.
73 τί δέ: the particle δέ joins the two questions (connective δέ). — σε φρένας: acc. of the whole and the part (R 19.1).
74 ἐξαύδα, μὴ κεῦθε: pres. imper. as a request formulated generally. — μέν: ≈ μήν (R 24.6). — τοι: = σοι (14.1).

75 2nd VH ≈ 1.450, 3.275, *Od.* 17.239, 20.97. — **Zeus:** an emphatic runover word (likewise at 2.33, 2.70, 2.669, *Od.* 1.283, 2.217; additional examples in KELLY 2007, 168 f.); it illustrates Thetis' satisfaction at her successful intervention with Zeus (see 1.495–532, 15.72–77, and cf. 8.370–373 [Athene], 13.347–350, 15.592–602 [narrator]): EDWARDS 1992, 175. — **in the way that you ...:** Thetis makes it plain that everything has gone in accord with *Achilleus'* wishes. Although the narrator text nowhere describes a direct prayer by Achilleus to Zeus, it is mentioned by characters within the action (here, at 15.74 f. by Zeus, at 16.236 f. by Achilleus [see *ad loc.*]). On the occasion of his encounter with his mother in Book 1, Achilleus asked her to present his plea to Zeus (1.351–357, 1.393–412, 1.419–427, cf. 1.502 ff., 15.76 f.): schol. bT; differently REYNEN 1983, 68 f. (referring to 1.351, i.e. to Achilleus' plea to Thetis); on prayer postures in antiquity, 3.275n. with bibliography.

χεῖρας ἀνασχών: an inflectable VE formula χεῖρας ἀνασχών/ἀνασχεῖν/ἀνέσχον (9× *Il.*, 4× *Od.*).

76 all ... be pinned on their ... vessels: This corresponds to part of Achilleus' wish, see 1.409 f., 9.650–653, 16.61b–63 (STR 21 fig. 1; on the other part – that Agamemnon is thus made to realize his wrongdoing – 19.134–138n.; on the motif of the battle for the ships, 19.135n.) and describes the Achaian situation during the two final days of battle, after the assembly of gods at the beginning of Book 8.

πρύμνῃσιν: literally 'sterns' (cf. 19.135n.), here *pars pro toto* for 'ships'; on the difference in accent between its use as a noun (as here) and as an adj., 14.31–32n., end. — πάντας ... υἷας Ἀχαιῶν: hyperbaton serving to highlight the main point, phrased more drastically by Achilleus at 1.409 f. The inflectable VE formula υἷες Ἀχαιῶν is a collective periphrastic denomination for the Achaians, likely an ancient Semitic formulation (1.162n.; additional bibliography *LfgrE s.v.* υἱός 701.3 ff.).

77 by reason of your loss: Achilleus intended this as well, see 1.240–244; on the standing motif 'the troops miss their leader', 1.240n.; KLOSS 1994, 71 f., 74 f.

σεῦ ἐπιδευομένους: on the forms, G 81 (σεῖο) and G 61 (-δευ-). — ἀεκήλια: a Homeric *hapax*[P]; formed with α privative, with the second element from the same root as ἑκών, ἕκηλος (1.554n.), i.e. 'unwanted, unwelcome' (AH; *LfgrE* and *ChronEG* 1 *s.v.* ἀεκήλιος). The phrase ἀεκήλια ἔργα echoes ἀεικέα ἔργα ('inappropriate', cf. 1.97n., 19.133n.) as

---

75 πρίν: adverbial, 'previously, earlier'. — ηὔχεο: on the uncontracted form, R 6.
76 πρύμνῃσιν: on the declension, R 11.1. — ἀλήμεναι: aor. inf. of εἴλομαι 'be crowded together'; on the form, R 16.4. — υἷας: on the declension, R 12.3.
77 σεῦ ἐπιδευομένους: on the hiatus, R 5.1. σεῖ(ο) = σοῦ (R 14.1); ἐπιδευομένους = Attic ἐπιδεομένους. — παθέειν: aor. inf. (R 16.4). — ἀεκήλια (ϝ)έργα: on the prosody, R 4.3.

well as the adj. ἀεικέλιος, which is considered the model (sometimes merely in terms of sound) for the formation of ἀεκήλιος (RISCH 122; WEST 2001, 245).

78 = 1.364; ≈ 97, 16.20. — Here, as in most dialogues, the speech introduction formula[P] replaces the speech capping formula[P] (cf. FINGERLE 1939, 373). — On the VE formula (Greek *pódas ōkýs Achilléus*: 30× *Il.*), 1.58n.; on speed as characteristic of Achilleus, 24.138n.

τὴν δὲ ... προσέφη ...: a speech introduction formula[P] with typical structure (τὸν/τὴν δέ + participle + προσέφη(ς) + noun-epithet formula): 24.55n.; on βαρὺ στενάχων, 70n.

79–126 Achilleus' speeches at 79–93 and 98–126 are closely linked thematically and represent the focus of the scene whose center (95 f.) is formed by Thetis' statement regarding the close interlinking of the deaths of Achilleus and Hektor (65–147n.), although the second speech shows Achilleus' deeper engagement with his own actions in the past and future (see also 82b–85n.): (A) pain caused by the death of his friend and the loss of his arms to Hektor (79–84a) / a death-wish because he failed to help when Patroklos and other companions were being killed by Hektor (98–103); (B) reflection and the resultant unfulfillable wish (84b–85: the arms were a wedding gift from the gods, 86 f.: if only you had never married / 104–106: his idleness so far, 107–113 cursing the strife and anger that caused this idleness); (A') a return to the present ('but now'): his own death and revenge on Hektor for Patroklos (structured chiastically: 88–93 Achilleus–Hektor–Patroklos / 114–126 Patroklos–Hektor–Achilleus). Detailed discussion of the structures and the correspondences in terms of content: EDWARDS on 79–93; SCHADEWALDT (1936) 1997, 157–160; REINHARDT 1961, 371 f.; LOHMANN 1970, 142–144.

79–93 Achilleus' first speech is characterized by his choice of words (82b n., 85n., 93n.) and the noteworthy combination of verse and sentence construction: enjambment[P], sometimes with an emotional emphasis on significant words (81, 82, 84, 87, 89, 90), clauses starting in verse middle and continuing past VE (82b–83, 90b–92), the words of formulae separated across three verses (82–84, see 84n.): EDWARDS 1992, 175–178 and on 79–93 and 83–4. The content is characterized by extreme emotion: in his desperation, Achilleus initially concentrates on the key point ('Patroklos is dead'; on the wording, 80n., 81–82a n.), in addition to a few additional bits of information (Hektor's role, the loss of his arms), before insinuating in the closing section that he intends to take revenge on Hektor in battle; Achilleus here speaks with a view toward his mother (85 'you', 86 stressed 'you', 88 'you, too', 89 f.) and thereby shows his deep feel-

---

78 πόδας: acc. of respect (R19.1).

ings for her: 85n., 86–87n., 88n.; HEBEL 1970, 118–120; THALMANN 1984, 107 f.; GAGLIARDI 2007, 119 f.

79 τὰ μὲν ἄρ μοι Ὀλύμπιος ἐξετέλεσσεν: Achilleus approvingly picks up the key point of the preceding speech (74 f.) (catch-word technique[P]), while emphasizing the action 'see through to the end' (on the preverb ἐκ-, SCHW. 2.462: 'an «intensifying» designation for the completion, for the aim of the verbal action' [transl.]). The sing. Ὀλύμπιος always designates Zeus.

80 1st VH ≈ *Od.* 24.95; 2nd VH from caesura C 1 onward = *Il.* 17.642; ≈ 5.695, 23.556; from caesura C 2 = 17.411, 17.655. — **dear companion:** a common periphrastic denomination[P] for Patroklos, used both in direct speeches (esp. by Achilleus) and in the narrator text[P] (19.209–210n., 24.4n.; on Greek *hetaíros*, also 19.305n.). The additional mention of the name, placed emphatically at VB of 81, is an expression of extreme emotion (similarly at 114 f.), as is the continuation at 81–82a (EDWARDS 1968, 267).

ἦδος: 'joy, enjoyment', from the root of ἥδομαι and ἡδύς with psilosis (FRISK and *DELG s.v.* ἥδομαι). — φίλος ... ἑταῖρος: φίλος, although elsewhere in Homer often with a pure-ly possessive sense ('my'; cf. 1.20n.), here in the context of a lament for the loss of a friend, and with the words of the formula separated, has the affective sense 'dear' (cf. 19.345n., 24.4n.).

81–82a The statement 'X honors Y just as he honors Z' expresses exception-al esteem and justifies a particular course of action (cf. 90b ff.); the position of Z is often occupied by a close relative (24.57n.). With his choice of words, Achilleus demonstrates his close attachment to the deceased (cf. 19.319–323; on their friendship, 19.4–6a n.; DE JONG on *Il.* 22.387–90). – The head (Greek *kephalḗ*) can represent the person as a whole, sometimes with the connota-tion '(endangered) life', as at e.g. 17.242 (Aias fears for his life), sometimes with the emotionally colored meaning 'dear person', as at e.g. 18.114, *Od.* 1.343 f. (Penelope on Odysseus), or in addresses (*Il.* 23.94: Achilleus' address to the deceased Patroklos, 8.281: Agamemnon's address to Teukros): 24.276n. with bibliography; ONIANS 1951, 98.

περὶ πάντων ...: 'more than all others ...'; on περί in this sense, SCHW. 2.502; CHANTR. 2.129; a formula between caesurae B 1 and C 2 (5× *Il.*, 3× *Od.*, 2× Hes.) or at VE (1.417n.).

82b–85 In Achilleus' speech, the loss of his armor, which must be retrieved from Hektor when he takes revenge in order to expunge the shame (18.334 f.,

---

79 τά: anaphoric demonstrative (R 17). — ἄρ: = ἄρα, 'indeed' (R 24.1). — ἐξετέλεσσεν: on the -σσ-, R 9.1.
80 τί μοι τῶν ἦδος: *sc.* ἐστι; approximately 'what is in this for me?' (τῶν R 17). — ὤλεθ': = ὤλετο.
81 τόν: with the function of a relative pronoun (R 14.5). — τῖον: impf. of τίω 'honor'.

22.367 ff.), takes up more room than the death of his friend (80–82a / 82b–85 and 93): the mention of the armor forms a transition to Achilleus' own fated death (88–91): it began with the armor as a wedding gift to his parents from the gods and is a first pointer to the manufacturing of new gear (see also 20–21n.). Only in the second speech will he link the loss to his own behavior (100, 102 ff.): SCHADEWALDT (1936) 1997, 157 f.; HEBEL 1970, 118 f.; MARG (1957) 1971, 26; EDWARDS 1992, 176 f.; ZANKER 1994, 7 f.

82b τὸν ἀπώλεσα: a dramatic, asyndetic clause with explicative function (cf. 20–21n.). ἀπώλεσα is ambiguous (cf. 24.44n.) but here means 'I have lost', or at most 'I have left to perish' (expressing his failure to lend support, cf. 98b–106), rather than 'I have ruined' as a admission of guilt; the wording is perhaps influenced by 80 and the subsequent topic 'loss of the armor' (cf. 460): AH; VAN LEEUWEN on 79–82; *LfgrE s.v.* ὄλλυμι 651.3 ff.; CUNLIFFE *s.v.*; cautiously EDWARDS; GRIFFIN 1980, 163 f. with n. 41; *contra* CERRI; STALLMACH 1968, 24 with n. 55; SARISCHOULIS 2008, 222.

83 2nd VH = 10.439 (Rhesos' arms). — **πελώρια:** adj. from πέλωρ 'monster, giant', an epithet of various heroes and gods ('enormous, imposing': 3.166n.), of objects in the *Il.* only of divine arms, elsewhere of waves (*Od.* 3.290), Sisyphos' rock (11.594), Kronos' sickle (Hes. *Th.* 179); frequently in reference to the effect on others (θαῦμα ἰδέσθαι: secondary [or, in direct speech as here, tertiary] focalization[P]), in which cases also 'enormous, terrifying' (*LfgrE*; DE JONG [1987] 2004, 130). — **θαῦμα ἰδέσθαι:** a VE formula (4× *Il.*, 4× *Od.*, 5× Hes., 2× *h.Hom.*); in the *Iliad*, the object of admiration is always a divine item associated with marvelousness, in character language always from the mortal point of view (here Peleus' armor, a gift from the gods, and at 10.439 arms of Rhesos that are actually appropriate for gods; in the narrator-text: 377 [see *ad loc.*], 5.725 wheels of Hera's chariot, cf. *Od.* 8.366, 13.108): DE JONG (1987) 2004, 48 f.; PRIER 1989, 94–97, 158; HUNZINGER 1994, 7–11.

84 ≈ 16.867 (Achilleus' horses), 24.534. — **καλά:** progressive enjambment[P] with a remarkable separation of the formula due to VE 82 and 83 intervening in its midst: the phrase τεύχεα καλά is a VE formula (8× *Il.*, 2× *Od.*, 1× 'Hes.' *Sc.*), VB formula (3.89 [see *ad loc.*], 18.137) and formula before caesura B 2 (6× *Il.*, 1× *Od.*), in enjambment at 22.322 f.; 19.10 f. (19.11n.) is comparable, as are (with ἔντεα rather than τεύχεα) 10.471 f., 17.186 f. (EDWARDS). — **τὰ ... ἀγλαὰ δῶρα:** τά is anaphoric with τεύχεα at 82 and points ahead to the predicate ἀγλαὰ δῶρα, a VE formula (8× *Il.*, 6× *Od.*, 1× 'Hes.', 1× *h.Merc.*); on the etymology and usage of the epithet ('shining'), 1.23n.

---

82 ἶσον: adverbial, 'equally'. — τόν: anaphoric demonstrative (R 17).
83 δῃώσας: 'butcher, kill', Πάτροκλον is to be understood as the obj. — θαῦμα (ϝ)ιδέσθαι: on the prosody, R 4.3. — ἰδέσθαι: on the middle, R 23.
84 Πηλῆϊ: on the declension, R 11.3.

85 2nd VH ≈ *h.Ven.* 199. — With the recollection of the provenance of his armor –
originally a wedding gift from the gods to his father (17.194–196, cf. 17.202) –
Achilleus' thoughts revolve around the fatal consequences of this union of a
goddess with a mortal, which he would dearly love to undo (86 f.); it is causing
his mother pain, not least due to his own mortality (88 ff.): SCHEIN 1984, 92,
132; HEATH 1992, 390 f.; GRETHLEIN 2008, 41 f. The wording *hóte se … émbalon
euné* is an allusion to the fact that the marriage of Peleus and Thetis occurred
against Thetis' will (18.432–434), or at least at the insistence of the gods (here
and at 24.537) or of Zeus (18.431) or Hera (24.59–61) (on the different versions,
1.396–406n., 24.59–63n., each with bibliography; on repetitive external analepses[P] in general, DE JONG 2007, 36 f.; collection of examples in DE JONG [1987]
2004, 155, 277 n. 15). Given the dreary prospects (88 f.), Achilleus here stresses the negative aspects, namely the compulsory act and the union goddess/
mortal (likewise Thetis at 431–441), whereas at 24.537 he speaks in a neutral
manner from Peleus' point of view; cf. the statement regarding Aphrodite and
Anchises in the narrator-text at 2.821 in contrast to that uttered by Aphrodite
at *h.Ven.* 198 f., 241 ff. (on the motif 'goddess and mortal', FAULKNER p. 10 f.).

ἤματι τῷ, ὅτε: a VB formula, elsewhere in direct speech usually a recollection of personal experiences (2.351n., 19.60n.). — βροτοῦ ἀνέρος: The expression stresses the exceptional aspects of the union between a goddess and a mortal (*LfgrE* s.v. ἀνήρ 840.32 ff.;
see also 19.22n.; on the form βροτός, 1.272n.).

86–87 VB of 86 = 1.415, 3.40; VE of 86 = *Od.* 24.47, 24.55. — In place of the topos
'if only I had never been born' (common also in laments; for the death-wish
motif, e.g. Andromache at 22.481; similarly Helen at 3.173, 6.345–348, 24.764,
where see nn.), Achilleus phrases the wish differently by starting by association with the wedding of his parents – an event initiated by the gods: if Thetis
had been able to remain among the marine goddesses, and if Peleus had married a mortal, these divine arms would never have existed (84 f.) and Thetis
would have been spared her pain regarding her mortal son (88–91): schol. bT
on 86–7; AH on 87; EDWARDS.

ὄφελες: on the use to introduce impossible wishes, 18–19n., 6.345n. (where also on
intensification via the particle of wishing). — ἀθανάτης ἁλίῃσιν: a designation for the

---

85 ἤματι τῷ: ≈ ἐκείνῳ τῷ ἤματι (ἤματι from ἦμαρ 'day'; on the demonstrative function of ὅ, ἥ, τό,
R 17). — τῷ, ὅτε: on the hiatus, R 5.6. — ἀνέρος: = ἀνδρός; initial syllable metrically lengthened
(R 10.1). — ἔμβαλον: = ἐνέβαλον (R 16.1).
86 αἴθ' (= εἴθε) ὄφελες: past unfulfilled wish. — αὖθι: short-form for αὐτόθι '(right) there', local-
ized more closely by μετ' ἀθανάτης ἁλίῃσιν. — ἀθανάτης: initial syllable metrically lengthened
(R 10.1); on the declension, R 11.1.
87 ναίειν: imperfective 'continued to dwell'.

Nereids, likewise at *Od.* 24.47, 24.55, contrast *Il.* 24.84 ἅλιαι θεαί ('marine goddesses'). The adj. ἀθανάτης (i.e. 'immortal sea-goddesses') stands in contrast to βροτοῦ ἀνέρος at 85 and θνητὴν ... ἄκοιτιν at 87 (cf. AH; FAESI; *LfgrE* s.v. ἅλιος 1; differently *LfgrE* s.v. ἀθάνατος 203.42 ff.: as a noun with ἅλιαι as attribute); on the fem. ending of ἀθανάτης, see SCHW. 2.38. — **ἀγαγέσθαι:** on the use of ἄγομαι in the sense 'lead home as a wife', 3.72n. — **ἄκοιτιν:** a possessive compound, 'who shares the same bedstead, spouse' (formed from α copulative and κοίτη 'bedstead'): 3.138n.

88–93 With the return to reality ('but now'), Achilleus' view immediately focusses on his death; since it is obvious to him (and unpreventable: 126) that he will now fight once more and avenge his friend (90b–93), he sees clearly his death before him (89), cf. his knowledge regarding his lifespan at 9.412 f. (on external analepses[P] of his death, 19.328–333n., 19.409–410n.). He links the killing of Hektor with his own death in a formulation similar to the qualified self-cursing ('I wish to be among the dead, if I do not ...': 2.258–264n.) or to the expression 'to prefer to die than experience something or fail to achieve something' (on this motif complex, 24.224b–227n.; on the death-wish motif, also 86–87n.).

88 To immortal Thetis, the mourning for her son will be interminable; cf. Achilleus' glance at his father's suffering at 19.322–324, 19.334–337 (see *ad loc.*), 24.511.

νῦν δ' ἵνα ...: a return from wishful thinking to reality (cf. 2.82n.); on νῦν δ(έ) as an expression typical of Achilleus (likewise at 101, 114, 121: character language[P]), 1.354b–356n. Assuming an ellipsis in the thought ('but now ⟨they made you the wife of a mortal⟩, so that you too ⟨like me⟩ should have immeasurable mental anguish ...' and that 89 τόν is a relative clause: AH; LEAF; WILLCOCK; EDWARDS; CHANTR. 2.167) can in any case be avoided with SCHW. 2.326: a final clause *before* the main clause (with the main tense ὑποδέξεαι; on εἴη, cf. 7.339 f.; CHANTR. 2.271: optative) 'but now, so that for you, too ..., you will lose *that one* [sc. the son]'. — **πένθος ... μυρίον:** stresses the perpetual nature of the grief (πένθος: 1.254n., 1.362n.) and the measurelessness of her suffering; in Homeric epic, μυρίος means 'countless, immeasurable' (1.2n.; *LfgrE*). — **ἐνὶ φρεσί:** 'mentally' (approximately 'deepest suffering'), almost always (80× in early epic) after caesura B 2 (19.169–170n.).

89b–90 ≈ 59b–60 (see *ad loc.*). — **οὐδ' ἐμὲ ... ἄνωγεν:** 'does not allow me too ⟨like Patroklos⟩, prohibits me too ...' (AH; FAESI); the same phrase at 6.444 (see *ad loc.*). —

---

88 ἐνί: = ἐν (R 20.1).
89 παιδὸς ἀποφθιμένοιο: objective gen., dependent on πένθος. — ἀποφθιμένοιο: on the declension, R 11.2. — τόν: on the construction, ↑ on 88. — ὑποδέξεαι: on the uncontracted form, R 6. — αὖτις: = αὖθις.
90 ἄνωγεν: perf. with present sense, 'orders, commands'.

θυμὸς ἄνωγεν: an inflectable VE formula (11× *Il.*, 6× *Od.*, 1× Hes.); on θυμός as the subject with verbs of spurring on, etc., *LfgrE s.v.* 1084.7 ff.; 2.276n.; cf. 6.444n.

91 ζώειν οὐδ' ἄνδρεσσι μετέμμεναι: comprises both the physical existence and the sphere of activity within the community of men (similarly 11.762, but ζωοῖσιν μετέω at 22.388, 23.47, *Od.* 10.52: 'live') is different: AH; LEAF; *LfgrE s.v.* ἀνήρ 845.45 ff.; on the Aeolic forms, HOEKSTRA 1965, 146.

92 ≈ 11.433, 12.250, 16.861. — a formulation reminiscent of threats against an opponent, see *iterata* and cf. 1.205, 8.358, 10.452. — **lose his life:** Hektor's death is repeatedly announced in the *Iliad*, often in combination with the information that he will fall at the hands of Achilleus (internal prolepsis[P]); first by Zeus (15.68, 17.201–208; additional gods: 18.95 f., 18.132 f., 21.296, 22.216–221), then by the dying Patroklos (16.852–854; on which, 16.851–854n.), finally by Achilleus himself (here and at 18.114 f., 333–335); in the narrator-text: 15.612–614, 16.800, cf. 12.10 ff.: EDWARDS, Introd. 8 f.; DUCKWORTH 1933, 60 f.; MORRISON 1992, 133 n. 29, 141 n. 38; DE JONG 2007, 29; on vague allusions to it, 6.367–368n.

πρῶτος: probably with a chronological aspect 'if H. does not first', with an indeterminate anticipation of 95 f. (*LfgrE s.v.*; BALENSIEFEN 1955, 121), hardly 'Hektor first', i.e. 'before all others, primarily' (AH; LEAF; CERRI). — **ὑπὸ δουρί:** ὑπό + dat. 'under the effects of' (≈ instrumental): 2.374n., 3.436n. — **θυμὸν ὀλέσσῃ:** a variable VE formula (8× *Il.*, 1× *Od.*); on the use of θυμός as 'life, life force', 1.205n., 3.294n.

93 son of Menoitios: 12n.

Πατρόκλοιο ... Μενοιτιάδεω: with the words separated only here, elsewhere a noun-epithet formula after caesura A 3 (gen.: 5× *Il.*, 1× *Od.*; with inversion at 16.554), and a half-verse formula at 16.760 (suggestion by FÜHRER); on the gen. of the patronymic (almost always after caesura B 2, as here), G 40; on the transmission, WEST 2001, 246. — **ἔλωρα:** ἔλωρ, derived from the verb ἑλεῖν, is 'booty, plunder' ('prey': 1.4n.); the pl. is used in the manner of an action noun, thus 'the despoiling', implying also the killing, cf. the phrasing in 83 (AH; WILLCOCK; *LfgrE*). — **ἀποτείσῃ:** 'pay for'; at 22.271 likewise used threateningly toward Hektor; on the spelling τεισ- vs. τισ-, 3.28n.

94 ≈ 1.413 (see *ad loc.*), 18.428. — **τὸν δ' αὖτε προσέειπε:** a speech introduction formula in dialogues (24.217n.; on προσέειπε, 19.76n.). — **(κατὰ) δάκρυ χέουσα:** an inflectable VE

---

91 ζώειν: epic form for ζῆν. — ἄνδρεσσι: on the declension, R 11.3. — μετέμμεναι: = μετεῖναι (R 16.4). — αἴ κε: ≈ ἐάν (R 22.1, R 24.5).
92 δουρί: on the declension, R 12.5. — ἀπὸ ... ὀλέσσῃ: on the so-called tmesis, R 20.2; on the -σσ-, R 9.1.
93 Μενοιτιάδεω: on the declension, R 11.1; on the synizesis, R 7. — ἀποτείσῃ: aor. subjunc. of ἀποτίνω.
94 προσέειπε: = προσεῖπε. — κατὰ ... χέουσα: on the so-called tmesis, R 20.2. — δάκρυ: collective sing.

formula (15× *Il.*, 13× *Od.*, 1× Hes.; cf. 32n.). The 2nd VH of the speech introduction formula[P] is adapted to the current mood; contrast the noun-epithet formula at 127 (see *ad loc.*; PARRY [1928] 1971, 15; EDWARDS 1968, 268 f.; FRIEDRICH 2007, 75, 103).

95–96 Thetis clarifies to a certain extent Achilleus' fate in a few words (FRAZER 1989, 385: an 'oracular pronouncement'; cf. 16.707–709) and thereby also the vague pronouncements regarding his short life (1.352, 1.417, see *ad loc.*): Achilleus' announcement that he will not return home (i.e. he will die before Troy) but that Hektor must die first (88–93n.) is affirmed on the part of the gods by pointing out the close connection – also chronological – between the fates of the two men (REINHARDT 1961, 371; LOHMANN 1970, 144). Achilleus learns that his death is imminent again at 19.409 (from his horse Xanthos), 22.358–360 (from the dying Hektor) and 24.131 f. (from Thetis); for additional announcements, 16.36n., 19.328–333n., 19.409–410n.; on the linking of the fates of Patroklos–Hektor–Achilleus, 16.844–854n. — **lose you soon:** In the *Iliad*, the adj. *ōkýmoros* ('swift-fated' , i.e. 'dying early'), a term from character language[P], occurs only in speeches by Thetis in reference to Achilleus (also at 1.417, 1.505, 18.458): 1.417n.; SARISCHOULIS 2008, 118 f.; related to *móros* (literally 'fate'), 19.421n. — **soon after:** Thetis' statement might be taken to suggest a quick sequence of the deaths of Hektor and Achilleus (on linguistic issues, see below), which increases suspense for the external audience but does not match the content of the *Iliad* as we have it (cf. 19.408, 20.126 ff., 22.385 ff., 24.657 ff.); perhaps merely a rhetorical exaggeration (hyperbole; cf. *LfgrE s.v.* ἑτοῖμος). Nevertheless, this inconsistency has triggered a serious discussion about whether the poet of the *Iliad* adapted material from the myth of Memnon, where Achilleus falls after the killing of Memnon in the same battle (cf. the content of the *Aethiopis* in Proclus, *Chrest.* § 2–3 West): *pro:* the position of neoanalysis, see KULLMANN 1960, 37 f., 311; CURRIE 2006, 29–31; BURGESS 2009, 27–30, 85–87 (with bibliography); *contra:* EDWARDS; HÖLSCHER 1955, 394–397; REINHARDT 1961, 350; LOHMANN 1970, 145; DAVIES 2016, 21; different versions of the *Iliad* by the poet of the *Iliad*: WEST 2003, 5–8, 10; 2011, 44–47, 346; 2013, 145, 149 f.; HEITSCH 2006, 17 ff.; on the discussion, see also KELLY 2012, 260–262 (with a different explanation: erroneous information regarding the time of the death as a motif in premature laments).

τέκος: 63n. — οἳ' ἀγορεύεις: a VE formula (1× *Il.*, 5× *Od.*, 1× *h.Merc.*), '(in accord with) what you are saying there' in the sense 'since you say this' (EDWARDS: 'from what you

---

95 τέκος: = τέκνον. — ἔσσεαι: = ἔσῃ (on the uncontracted form, R 6; on the -σσ-, R 9.1).
96 τοι: = σοι (R 14.1). — μεθ' Ἕκτορα: 'after H.' in reporting the sequence (in the sense 'after Hektor's death').

say'; CHANTR. 2.238; K.-G. 2.371; cf. οἷον 2.320n., 6.166n., 24.683n.); a variant of the VE formula ὡς ἀγορεύεις (24.373n.). — **αὐτίκα:** in combination with ἔπειτα, the word is elsewhere usually placed immediately before ἔπειτα (21× of 23 examples in early epic, of which 14× VB formula) but is here to be linked with ἑτοῖμος. It does not stress the rapid succession of events so much as the fact that a situation logically results in a subsequent action, i.e. Hektor's death inevitably leads to that of Achilleus, and Achilleus' announcement at 91 ff. thus explains his designation as ὠκύ-μορος: ERREN 1970, esp. 30, 38 n. 5; *LfgrE s.v.* 1600.68 ff.; differently BONIFAZI 2012, 273, 276 ('presentational value of αὐτίκα': the speaker identifies a special moment in the action). — **ἔπειτα:** likely pointing back to 90 ff. 'then, in this case', cf. VE of 95 (EDWARDS; HÖLSCHER 1955, 395; cf. 19.112–113n.), rather than chronological 'then, subsequently' as preparation for μεθ' Ἕκτορα. — **πότμος:** 'lot' (related to πίπτω), usually 'fate of death' (cf. the combination θάνατον καὶ πότμον at 2.358–359n.): *LfgrE;* DIETRICH 1965, 270 f.; SARISCHOULIS 2008, 116–121. — **ἑτοῖμος:** 'ready' in the sense 'immediately present to one's experience' (*LfgrE s.v.,* ad loc.: 'ready at hand', 'seems to involve an element of urgently vivid exaggeration'); EDWARDS ('certain to be fulfilled'); more emphasis on the chronological aspect in AH 'is imminent' [transl.]).

97 ≈ 78, 16.48, 19.419 (see *ad loc.*), 22.14 (τόν); 1st VH (to caesura C 1) = 1.517 (see *ad loc.*), 4.30, 8.208, 15.184; ≈ 7.454, 17.18, *Od.* 4.30, 4.332, 15.325, Hes. *Th.* 558. — **μέγ' ὀχθήσας προσέφη:** hints at Achilleus' frustration and the heightened agitation in regard to events that permeates his entire speech (98–126n.), similarly in the next prophecy at 19.419 (see *ad loc.*): SCULLY 1984, 22 f.; on speeches introduced by ὀχθήσας, 16.48n.; on the verse structure, 78n.

98–126 Achilleus' impatience and agitation, which fades after its initial violent outburst only to increase again, is made clear on the level of language and image: (a) indications of time 'soon' (98), 'now' (101, 111, 114, 121); (b) idiosyncratic syntax at 101–106 and 122–124 (101–114n.; SCHEIN 1984, 134, 136 f.); (c) formulation of the future as a wish (opt. 98, 121, 124, 125) and as a fact (fut. 115, 121); (d) metaphors (102, 104, 109 f., 114): SCHADEWALDT (1936) 1997, 158–160; LOHMANN 1970, 144 f.; TAPLIN 1992, 198; on the structure of the speech, 79–126n.

98–111 Achilleus begins with an impulsive eruption, underlined by emphatic runover words at 99/100 and an asyndetic continuation at 99b of the line of thought begun at 98b (EDWARDS on 98–100: 'Every word counts heavily here'; on the rhetorical effect of the asyndetic clause, MAEHLER 2000, 422). The death-wish – *inter alia,* an element of laments (86–87n.) – initially signals his acceptance of his fate (DE JONG on *Il.* 22.365–366) but then turns into an expression of desperate helplessness via the link with the death of his friend:

---

97 μέγ(α): adv., 'very'. — πόδας: 78n.

Achilleus laments that he was not meant (Greek *ouk ... émellon*: 98–99n.) to help his friend and that he was not a support to him and his companions in battle – but he does not lament letting Patroklos go into battle (on the circumstances leading up to this, 16.48–100n., 16.60–63n.). This shows that he deeply regrets the consequences and suffers from them, also due to his awareness that he failed to fulfill certain expectations (100, 102–104) or was unable to fulfill them (98 f.; see also 324–330). His admission that he is not the best in the assembly (106) leads him to reflect on the deleterious effects of strife and especially anger (Greek *éris* and *chólos*: 107–110) and finally on the starting point of the catastrophe, the confrontation with Agamemnon (111). When he curses strife and anger more generally (107 f.), this also contains a wish that he had never fallen out with Agamemnon (see also his statement to Agamemnon at 19.56–64 with n.): EDWARDS on 98–100 and 105–106; LOHMANN 1970, 143; TAPLIN 1992, 199; VAN WEES 1992, 135; 1996, 17; ZANKER 1994, 17, 100 f.; more generally: LLOYD-JONES 1971, 22; COLLOBERT 2011, 216 f.; CAIRNS 2012, 31; FULKERSON 2013, 63 f. (feelings of guilt due to Patroklos' death); for different interpretations surrounding Achilleus' character, see also DE JONG on *Il.* 22, Introd. 16–18 (bibliography 16 n. 33).

98–99 soon ...: Achilleus picks up what was said in 96 with amplification of the content (catch-word technique[P]): Greek *autíka* with the connotation 'on the spot', a wish (Greek opt. *tethnáiēn*) rather than an assertion (AH; EDWARDS on 98–100). It is difficult to believe that the repetition of *autíka*, the impulsive outburst and the remarkably brief speech by Thetis are to be taken as indicating that Achilleus interrupts his mother (thus EDWARDS following LOHMANN 1970, 145), cf. the explicit signals in the incident with Agamemnon at 1.292/304 f. (MINCHIN 2007, 234–236; on the brevity, also 95–96n.). — **I was not to stand by my companion:** The motif 'X was unable to protect Y' elsewhere serves to heighten the pathos in battle descriptions; it occurs here in the lament of the friend who did not participate in battle and in the scene of Patroklos' death at 16.837 f. in Hektor's speech of triumph mocking his opponent (16.837n.; GRIFFIN 1980, 113–115). There are numerous examples in the *Iliad* of mutual aid among companions during battle (VAN WEES 1996, 16 f., 64–66; see also 16.363n.; on Achaian solidarity in general, 3.9n.). — **land of his fathers:** The motif 'far from home' creates pathos (2.162n.; GRIFFIN 1986, 55).

ἐπεὶ οὐκ ἄρ' ἔμελλον ... | κτεινομένῳ ἐπαμῦναι: 'since I ... was not meant to provide support when he was killed'; μέλλω denoting the 'destiny of fate', here with resultive

---

98 ἄρ(α): 'indeed', indicates obviousness (R 24.1).
99 τηλόθι (+ gen.): 'far from'. — πάτρης: on the -η- after -ρ-, R 2.

aor. inf. (*LfgrE s.v.* μέλλω 113.42 ff.; K.-G. 2.179; Basset 1979, 73, 132; Ruijgh [1985a] 1996, 601 f.). — **τηλόθι πάτρης:** a VE formula (5× *Il.*, 1× *Od.*, including μάλα τ. π. at *Il.* 24.541).

100 ἐμέο δ' ἐδέησεν: δεύω is here construed with the ablatival gen. ('he needed me, he had to do without me') + consecutive inf.: 'I failed to be ... for him' (AH; Schw. 2.92; Chantr. 2.313; *LfgrE s.v.* δεύ(ω) II: 'needed me to be his protector'). West following La Roche (1869, 101 f.) prints ἐμέο δ' ἐδέησεν; the main transmission has ἐμεῖο δὲ δῆσεν, with δ' ἔδησεν as a *v.l.* (see *app. crit.*) with an otherwise unattested contracted form in place of ἐδεύησεν (*Od.* 9.483 = 9.540): G 61; West 2001, 246; on the form, Wackernagel (1881) 1953, 219; (1887) 1979, 1802; Risch 300; Schw. 1.752 n. 3; on the question of the augment, West 1998, XXVIf.; cf. G 85. — **ἀρῆς ἀλκτῆρα:** an inflectable formula after caesura B 2 (ἀ. ἀλκτῆρα/-ες: 3× *Il.*, 3× 'Hes.'); on the noun ἀρή 'harm, ruin' (i.e. 'damage to life and property that obliges relatives to provide support or exact revenge'), 24.489n.; *LfgrE s.v.* ἀρή II 1233.46 ff. and 1234.33 ff. ἀλκτήρ is a *nomen agentis* related to ἀλέξω 'fend off, protect', denoting the role generally expected of Achilleus (*LfgrE*; Schubert 2000, 45, 78 f.).

101–114 νῦν δ' ἐπεὶ ...: The sentence starting with νῦν δ(έ) (on which, 88n.) ends with an anacoluthon, evoked by the subsequent causal clause with an inserted relative clause (101–106 ἐπεὶ οὐ νέομαι ... | οὐδέ ... γενόμην ... | ..., οἳ ... δάμεν ..., | ἀλλ' ἧμαι) as well as by the adversative main clause (106 ἀγορῇ δέ); the reflection on ἔρις and χόλος at 111 leads to the concrete circumstance and to reality (νῦν), while ἀλλὰ τὰ μὲν προτετύχθαι ... (112 f.) prepares a new beginning with νῦν δ' ... (114 ff.) (Leaf; Willcock; on the punctuation, see Allen [113 f. ἀνάγκη · | νῦν δ'] *vs.* West [parenthesis at 107–113; similarly AH; Faesi]; on parentheses in Homer, 6.242–253n.).

101 = 23.150; 2nd VH in total 16 × *Il.*, 13 × *Od.*, 1× 'Hes.' — On the thought, 59b–60a n.; on the meaning of *néomai* ('return home unharmed'), *LfgrE s.v.* νέομαι.

νῦν δ(έ): 88n. — **πατρίδα γαῖαν:** on the inflectable VE formula, 2.140n.; on the attribute φίλην in this formula [here 'my'], 16.832n.

102–103 An internal analepsis[P]: summary of the preceding fights of the Achaians, which entailed heavy losses, and especially of Hektor's *aristeia* in Books 8 and 11–17 (STR 21 fig. 1; a list of killing scenes in Singor 1991, 54 n. 113). — **light:** On this metaphor for 'savior/rescue' in dire straits, 6.6n. This is what Patroklos intended to be for the Greeks when he took the place of Achilleus (16.31 ff., esp. 39), and in the embassy in Book 9 Achilleus was asked for this kind of

---

100 ἔφθιτ(ο): root aor. mid. of φθίνω. — ἐμέο: = ἐμοῦ (R 14.1); on the synizesis, R 7.
101 ἐς: = εἰς (R 20.1).
102 οὐδέ τι: 62n. — φάος: = φῶς (R 6). — ἑτάροισιν: = ἑταίροις; on the declension, R 11.2.
103 πολέες: = πολλοί (R 12.2); predicative, 'in great numbers'. — δάμεν: = ἐδάμησαν, aor. pass. of δάμνημι (cf. R 16.2); on the unaugmented form, R 16.1; with dat. Ἕκτορι δίῳ 'by god-like Hektor'.

support (9.247–251, 301–303, see also 1.283 f.): VAN WEES 1996, 66 n. 48; on the responsibility of the leader for his men, HAUBOLD 2000, 17–46.

δάμεν Ἕκτορι δίῳ: on intransitive mid. and pass. forms of δάμνημι with the dat. of persons involved, 3.183n.; on the inflectable formula Ἕκτορι δίῳ, 24.22n.

104–113 Achilleus identifies the causes of his actions in strife and anger as universal (107 'from gods and men') forces (111, 113), without invoking the influence of divine powers as Agamemnon will do later on (cf. 19.56 ff. *vs.* 19.86 ff.). By designating strife and anger as evils afflicting *everyone*, and by naming Agamemnon as the root of his anger (111), Achilleus moves the other character concerned into view as well (111n.; cf. 19.270n.; WALSH 2005, 217–219).

104 VE = *Od.* 20.379. — **sit here:** a paraphrase for his inaction; remaining with the ships is based on Thetis' instructions at 1.421 f. (on Achilleus remaining seated since the outbreak of the disagreement, 1.349n., 2.137n., 19.344–346n.). Patroklos had already indirectly accused him of being useless because of his idleness (16.31 f.). Achilleus now acknowledges via his self-accusation that he is the reason not only for the Achaian distress, which he in fact expressly wished for (1.409 f.), but also for his own misfortune by way of Patroklos' death (KURZ 1966, 44, 56).

ἧμαι: can denote inaction without implying an actual sitting posture (cf. 2.255n., 24.542n.); cf. the description of Achilleus' boycott at 1.488 f. (αὐτὰρ ὃ μήνιε ... παρήμενος ...). — ἐτώσιον: in reference to a person only here ('useless'), elsewhere in the *Iliad* of missiles that remain 'ineffective, unsuccessful' (3.368, 5.854, 14.407, 17.633, 22.292, *Od.* 22.256, 22.273), thus also of objects or entities that remain 'unfruitful, without yield' (*Od.* 24.283 δῶρα, *h.Cer.* 309, Hes. *Th.* 182 seeds, *Op.* 402, 440 words and labors): *LfgrE.* — ἄχθος ἀρούρης: ἄρουρα literally denotes arable land, thus also soil generally; the phrase is also attested as a proverb, as well as in the version ἄχθος γῆς (*LfgrE s.v.* ἄρουρα; RICHTER 1968, 93 f.).

105 1st VH ≈ *Od.* 7.312, 20.89. — Achilleus qualifies this general self-assessment, similar to that at 1.244, via a runover word and the antithesis 'in battle; but in the assembly' at 106. In the *Iliad*, various characters[P] speak of their particular proficiencies and achievements with a certain confidence in order to impress friends or enemies (Achilleus also at 1.165 ff., 1.240 ff., 1.411 f., 16.70 ff., 19.70 ff.; additional examples in STOEVESANDT 2004, 286 n. 850). But here Achilleus' positive self-assessment serves primarily to show his deliberate (104n.) idleness in an even worse light (schol. T, b on 105–106; CERRI).

---

104 νηυσίν: on the declension, R 12.1.
105 ἐών: = ὤν (R 16.6).

τοῖος ἐὼν οἷος: a variable VB formula (1× *Il.*, 6× *Od.*), with οἷος/-ον 3× to be read as two short syllables (*ho-yoς*) (here and in the *iterata*; cf. *Il.* 13.275): CHANTR. 1.168; on οἷος (character language[P]), 24.376n. — **Ἀχαιῶν χαλκοχιτώνων:** on the VE formula and the meaning of the epithet, 1.371n.

106 The same assessment is made by others (Odysseus at 19.217–219, Patroklos' father indirectly at 11.786–789). For these two typical areas of proving one's worth, Peleus assigned Phoinix to be the teacher of his son (9.438–443). On the juxtaposition of physical and intellectual superiority, and on the proving grounds of battle and council, 1.258n., 2.370n., 19.218–219n.; JANKO on 15.281–285; PATZER 1996, 168 f.; cf. 6.77–79n. on proving oneself in battle and strategic planning.

πολέμῳ: 64n. — **τ' ... καὶ ἄλλοι:** τε produces a generalizing statement: ἄλλοι are not only the others in the Achaian army, but generally others proving themselves in battle (RUIJGH 656). Achilleus shares with them a certain competence in council (cf. 9.442 f.), but not to the same extent (cf. *LfgrE s.v.* ἄλλος 554.51 ff., esp. 555.32 ff.).

107–108 Anger (*chólos*) and the inability to resolve an argument amicably are the main traits of the two adversaries in the confrontation in Book 1 (1.6, 1.8, 1.80–83, 1.192, 1.210–224, 1.277 f., 1.282 f., 1.318 f.; cf. Agamemnon's accusation at 1.176 f. [see *ad loc.*] that Achilleus always desires confrontation and fighting, as well as Peleus' advice to his son at 9.255–258). Achilleus here identifies the evil that is found especially in anger and that must be suppressed (113), since it is only anger that he characterizes negatively (108–110, 119; on the negative evaluation, cf. 1.1 f. [1.2n.]; on the meaning of *chólos*, 1.1n., 1.9n., 1.81–82n., 19.16n.). Only later, during the public reconciliation (19.56 ff., esp. 58 and 61 ff.), will he clearly refer to the negative effects on the community of the falling out (alluded to at 102 f.) that triggered his anger: HOGAN 1981, 49–52, 54–58; VAN WEES 1992, 135. – Confrontation (Greek *éris*) as a fight against enemies or rivals is a core motif in heroic epic (on the concept in the *Iliad*, 1.8n., 1.173–187n.; on pejorative epithets with *éris*, 3.7n., 16.662n.). – On the use of the polar expression[P] 'gods and men' to designate 'the totality of beings that *actually* come into consideration' (transl.), 1.339n.; WEST 2007, 100, 124–126.

ὡς: particle of wishing with the cupitive opt. ἀπόλοιτο ('if only ... disappeared'), in contrast to relative ὡς at 111 (SCHW. 2.668; CHANTR. 2.251). — **ἐφέηκε:** aor. of ἐφίημι (+ inf.) 'drive to ...' (ἕηκα is a by-form of ἧκα); here as a gnomic aor. in the dependent clause

---

106 πολέμῳ· ἀγορῇ: on the hiatus, R 5.6. — ἀγορῇ: locative dat. without preposition (R 19.2). — τ(ε): 'epic τε' (R 24.11; ↑).

107 ἐκ: 'from the middle of'.

108 τ(ε): 'epic τε' (R 24.11); likewise 109. — πολύφρονα: *sc.* τινά or ἄνδρα. — περ: stresses the preceding word (R 24.10); here intensive: 'also, indeed'.

(Schw. 2.283; Chantr. 2.185). — **πολύφρονα:** 'very sensible, sensible in many ways' (schol. D: τὸν πάνυ σώφρονα καὶ συνετόν; *LfgrE s.v.*: 'of much good sense'), similarly at *Od.* 14.464 (of the effects of wine); on the concept, cf. 9.553 f. — **χαλεπῆναι:** denotes adversarial behavior in word and deed (24.369n.), here triggered by χόλος (see at 111 ἐχόλωσεν).

109–110 Honey is used elsewhere to characterize the pleasant effects of words (1.249n.) or wine and food (2.34n., 6.258n., 6.264n.). In Achilleus' image of dripping honey, the emphasis is on the sweet, satisfying and thus welcome pleasure anger initially produces. By taking into account the etymological relationship between *chólos* ('anger') and *cholé* ('gall') (see also 16.203n.), one can identify here a hint of the oxymoron 'sweet–bitter'; see 322 (with n.) *drimýs chólos* 'sharp anger' (Walsh 2005, 219–225). The sweetness of course lasts only for a short while, and via the additional comparison[P] with smoke, the image changes to the ominous: anger grows in the chest like smoke during a sustained fire and finally permeates everything, i.e. it takes possession of and dominates all (AH; Leaf; Moulton 1977, 108 n. 52; 1979, 285; Walsh *loc. cit.* 223 f.; Ready 2011, 42–48); cf. the etymological relationship between Greek *thymós* (113) and Sanskrit *dhumáh*, Latin *fumus* 'smoke' (Meier-Brügger 1989, 244 with n. 39); on Ancient Near Eastern parallels for the metaphor 'anger – smoke', West 1997, 387. The present two-part image is effectively different from phrases in which an affect grips a character (1.387n., 2.2n., 16.22n.) or enters the character from the outside (19.16a n., 24.5n.); on similes[P] in character language, 2.289n.; de Jong (1987) 2004, 135 f.

ἠΰτε: 'like' (2.87n.).

111 here ... Agamemnon: With this transition to the case in hand, Achilleus demonstrates insight into his own psychological processes, on the one hand, while with the formulation he brings the active role of the originator into view and shows that he considers himself blameless, on the other.

ἐχόλωσεν: causative active 'made angry', likewise at 1.78, *Od.* 8.205, 18.20, Hes. *Th.* 568, elsewhere mid.-pass. (1.78n.; *LfgrE s.v.*). — **ἄναξ ἀνδρῶν Ἀγαμέμνων:** an inflectable VE formula (nom./voc.: 1.172n.); on the combination ἄναξ ἀνδρῶν, 1.7n.

112–113 = 19.65–66 (see *ad loc.*); 1st VH of 112 (to caesura C 2) = 16.60. — In each of the *iterata*, Achilleus announces an end to his anger, first to Patroklos with words similar to here (16.60 f.: 16.60–63n.), then in the subsequent military

---

110 ἀέξεται: ≈ αὐξάνεται.
112 τά: on the anaphoric demonstrative function of ὅ, ἥ, τό, R 17. — ἐάσομεν: short-vowel aor. subjunc. (R 16.3). — περ: concessive (R 24.10).
113 ἐνί: = ἐν (R 20.1). — στήθεσσι: on the declension, R 11.3; on the plural, R 18.2.

assembly with the same words as here (19.65 f.: 19.65–66n., 19.66n.). In contrast to the latter instance, in the present passage he thereby immediately breaks off his brief look back to the disagreement with Agamemnon (111). He feels compelled, because of a much more important event, namely the death of Patroklos, to suppress his anger at Agamemnon and to face what is now most urgent, namely taking revenge for Patroklos by killing Hektor (114 ff.). But by fixating on this action, he becomes inescapably caught up in a new rage, albeit one of a different emotional quality (anger aimed at vengeance: 121b–126, 316–322, 334–337, 19.16 f.): 121–125n., 19.16a n.; WOLF (1795) 1985, 119 f. (on this, STR 12); WALSH 2005, 175–182; RINON 2008, 35.

ἀλλά: a standard way of changing the subject (16.60n.). — προτετύχθαι: 'have happened, be over' (on προτεύχω: 19.65n.). — ἀχνύμενοί περ: an inflectable phrase in different positions in the verse; frequently, as here, in the context of grief and disappointment in the face of immutable facts or powers (98 f., 102 f.), combined with aggression (114 f., 122 ff.): 19.8n. — θυμὸν ... φίλον ... δαμάσαντες: φίλος here means 'dear' with reference to 109; note also the separation of noun and attribute (1.20n., 19.66n., where also on the combination θυμὸν δαμάσαι 'master agitation'; on φίλος, also 80n. and *LfgrE s.v.* 932 f.).

114–126 After accepting that avenging his friend will cost him his own life (88–93a, 101), Achilleus lays out in a menacing tone the immediate future for his mother via 'but now' (114, 121b) and qualifies his own death with a reference to Zeus' son Herakles: (A) killing Hektor (114–115a), (B) his own death whenever the gods choose (115b–116), (C) paradigm[P] of Herakles (117–119), (B') his own death (120–121a), (A') fame gained from killing Trojans (121b–126): REINHARDT 1961, 371 f.; on the ring-composition[P], EDWARDS on 114–126; LOHMANN 1970, 142 f. Achilleus accepts death (B, B') in exchange for a course of action (A, A') he considers the only correct one, cf. 126; additional examples of such behavior in Greek literature in EDWARDS 1987, 273.

114 The encounter with Hektor will not take place until Book 22 (22.90 ff.): before setting out to this battle (19.424 ff.), Achilleus will wait for his new armor and will end his disagreement with Agamemnon before the military assembly (cf. Thetis' instructions at 18.134–137, 19.34–36); after the battle begins, he will first encounter several other warriors, since Apollo is trying to prevent the two men from meeting (cf. 20.75 ff., 375 ff., 443 f., 21.34 ff., 538 ff.): retardation[P]; BREMER 1987, 33–36.

νῦν δ(έ): 88n. — ὀλετῆρα: a Homeric *hapax*[P], a *nomen agentis* related to ὄλλυμι ('destroyer, annihilator'). — φίλης κεφαλῆς: a periphrastic denomination[P] for Patroklos (cf. 23.94). After 96/98, it is unlikely that this could describe Achilleus as well (cf.

---

114 ὄφρα (+ subjunc.): final (R 22.5). — κιχείω: aor. subjunc. of κιχάνω 'catch, seize'.

EDWARDS on 114 and 1992, 182; SCHUBERT 2000, 73 f.) – in that case, κεφαλή would be used as in 82 (see *ad loc.*) and φίλος would have the possessive sense 'own' (on which, 1.20n., 3.31n.): elsewhere in early epic, the phrase φίλη κεφαλή is attested only at 8.281, where it is an address (likewise in the post-Homeric tradition), whereas 'my head' ≈ 'I' (17.242, 18.82, *Od.* 22.463, and cf. 9.498) is elsewhere always clarified via the possessive pronoun ἐμή (*LfgrE s.v.* κεφαλή 1396.55 ff.; cf. *s.v.* φίλος 936.31 f. ['cherished, dear']; LSJ *s.v.* κεφαλή).

115–116 ≈ 22.365–366 (Achilleus' reaction to the dying Hektor's prophecy that he himself will die at the hands of Paris and Apollo). – Achilleus pushes aside the issue of his death as secondary and reacts in an altogether fatalistic manner.

Ἕκτορα. κῆρα δ' ἐγώ: The enjambment[P] of the personal name causes 'Hektor', 'death' and 'I' to stand immediately next to one another in the 1st VH of 115 (EDWARDS; cf. 24.501a n.). — **κῆρα**: 'death, doom' as the destined end of life (2.301–302n.; SARISCHOULIS 2008, 100–115). — **ἀθάνατοι θεοὶ ἄλλοι**: a VE formula (4× *Il.*, 5× *Od.*, 1× Hes.), commonly used, as here, after the mention of Zeus in the 1st VH (examples at 3.298n.).

117–121a Zeus' son **Herakles** (CH 6), the hero *par excellence*, who once conquered Troy (5.638–642, 5.648–651, 14.250 f.), is the only mortal to whom Achilleus is compared in the *Iliad* (cf. paradigm[P] with argument function[P]): he too had to die despite being under the protection of Zeus. While the *Odyssey* (11.602–604) alludes to Herakles dwelling with the gods after his death (on this, HEUBECK on *Od.* 11.601–627; cf. *h.Hom.* 15.7 f. and Hes. *Th.* 950–955 with WEST *ad loc.*), here (as at 11.601/605 ff.) he is depicted as a mortal, in accord with the way heroes are characterized in the *Iliad* (on the Dioskouroi, cf. 3.237n.); not even the sons of gods can be saved from death (*Il.* 15.110–118: Ares – Askalaphos; 16.431–461 and 16.521 f.: Zeus – Sarpedon [16.441n.]; 21.109 f.: Thetis – Achilleus; cf. the temporary rescue of Aineas at 20.326–336): GALINSKY 1972, 14 f.; PRIESS 1977, 152 f.; SCHEIN 1984, 143; 2002, 92 f.; KULLMANN 1985, 16 f.; CURRIE 2006, 34 f.; on the motif of the mortality of heroes in Ancient Near Eastern literature, WEST 1997, 341, 387; on the scattered references to the myth of Herakles in the *Iliad*, 119n., 19.95–133n., 19.133n.; WEST 2011, 30 f. – Achilleus once again employs the motif 'even X has/had to die' in the fight against Lykaon, to whom he illustrates the inescapability of death via the fates of Patroklos and himself (21.107–113; similarly, but phrased more generally, Athene at 15.139–141; cf. *Od.* 3.236–238); in post-Homeric literature, this is a motif of the *consolatio* (EDWARDS on 117–119; RICHARDSON on *Il.* 21.106–107; DAVIES 2006, 585 with n. 18; cf. schol. b and T on 117). But in the present passage, it does not serve so much to comfort as

---

115 ὁππότε: on the -ππ-, R 9.1. — κεν: = ἄν (R 24.5).
116 τελέσαι: *sc.* κῆρα. — τελέσαι ἠδ(έ): on the hiatus, R 5.6; ἠδέ 'and' (R 24.4). — ἀθάνατοι: initial syllable metrically lengthened (R 10.1).

to fend off any maternal protection (cf. 126); at least for Achilleus, comfort lies rather in the fame he plans to acquire, see 121b ff. (cf. GRETHLEIN 2006, 137).

117 οὐδὲ γὰρ οὐδέ: 'since not even'; as an introduction to a mythological paradigm also at 6.130 (see *ad loc.*). — **βίη Ἡρακλῆος:** The formulaic paraphrase of the name by means of βίη + gen. or adj. (βίη Ἡρακληείη) is also used for other heroes and may be a titulature originating in the Mycenaean period (2.658n. with bibliography; LATACZ [2001] 2010, 380 f.; on the gen., cf. Πριάμοιο βίη, 3.105n.). — **φύγε κῆρα:** 'escaped death' (see 119); the combination of κῆρα and -φυγεῖν also at 5.22, *Od.* 4.502, 4.512, 15.235, elsewhere with the addition of θανάτοιο (*Il.* 16.687, 22.202) or θάνατον καὶ κ. (17.714, etc.; examples in CLARKE 1999, 245).

118 2.VH = 2.102, 7.194, 7.200, Hes. *Op.* 69; ≈ 1.502. — **dearest:** on this expression denoting 'a god favors a human', 16.94n., 24.61n.

ὅς περ ...: a relative clause highlighting a character (thus referring to Ἡρακλῆος) with particularly outstanding qualities, here after emphatic οὐδέ (cf. 6.100n.), similarly after καί 'even' at 19.95. — **ἔσκε:** pres. stem of εἰμί expanded by -σκ-, usually durative 'was always' (3.180n. with bibliography, 16.225n.; on the formation, RIX [1976] 1992, 229). — **Διὶ Κρονίωνι:** an inflectable formula after caesura B 2 (1.502n.). — **ἄνακτι:** on ἄναξ as a title of gods, 2.102n.

119 Hera: From the moment Hera (CG 16) learns of the impending birth of a son to Zeus and the mortal Alkmene, she lets those concerned feel her anger: at 19.96–133 (see *ad loc.*) by stalling Herakles' birth, at 14.250–256 and 15.25–30 with a storm at sea (14.249–261n.); cf. the confrontation mentioned at 5.392–394. For a different version of the myth, in which Herakles is not killed by Hera, see Sophocles, *Trachiniae* 1048 ff. (story of Deinaneira and the 'robe of Nessos'; cf. *BNP s.v.* Heracles).

μοῖρ(α): literally 'share', metaphorically 'what is allotted by fate'; used here and at 120 in the sense 'fate of death' (on which, 6.487–488n.) and often, like κήρ (115/117), expanded by an additional term from the semantic field 'death' (2.352n., 24.132n.). Whereas in other passages μοῖρα is spoken of as a divine power that acts alongside another deity (at 16.849/19.410 [16.844–850n., 19.410n.] beside Apollo in the case of the deaths of Patroklos and Achilleus, at 19.87 [see *ad loc.*] beside Zeus and the Erinys in the case of Agamemnon's delusion), here Hera is the driving force (TSAGARAKIS 1977, 126); on the use of the terms μοῖρα and κήρ and on the issue of personification, see also CG 29; 24.49n.; ERBSE 1986, 275 f.; CLARKE 1999, 241, 244–246. — **ἐδάμασσε:** For additional examples of the notion that a deity 'overcomes' a human being, etc., KULLMANN 1956, 59; on the congruence of the predicate with the preceding subject, 28n. — **ἀργαλέος:**

---

117 Ἡρακλῆος: on the declension, R 11.3.
118 ὅς περ: 'the very one who' (on περ, R 24.10). — Κρονίωνι (ϝ)άνακτι: on the prosody, R 5.4.
119 ἀλλά (ϝ)ε: on the prosody, R 4.3. — ἑ: = αὐτόν (R 14.1). — ἐδάμασσε: on the -σσ-, R 9.1.

'causing hardship', *inter alia* of emotions that have negative consequences for others or for the person concerned; of Achilleus' anger at 10.107, of Zeus' anger at 15.121 f. (*LfgrE s.v.* 1188.66 ff.).

120 VB = 9.325, 19.134 (see *ad loc.*); VE = 3.101, Hes. *Op.* 745. — **I likewise, if such is the fate:** i.e., like Herakles (LEAF; WILLCOCK; EDWARDS; DIETRICH 1965, 196 with n. 3; differently AH: '[the fate] affecting all' [transl.]); both die, despite having a divine parent and being cherished by Zeus (118; Achilleus: 9.117 f., 24.472).

εἰ δή ... τέτυκται: 'if (as you have announced) ... is prepared'; refers to 96, with δή stressing how obvious this is (cf. BAKKER 1997, 75; on εἰ δή, see also WAKKER 1994, 351–357).

121–125 *kléos* (121) is literally 'what is heard about someone, repute' (on the etymology, 2.115n., 2.742n.), commonly used positively in the sense 'fame' that disseminates beyond the here and now (2.325n.); on the expression 'of good repute' in I-E poetry, WEST 2007, 406. Although Achilleus is focussed on revenge for his friend, he also sees an opportunity for putting an end to idleness by fighting (125) and for achieving fame in accord with the 'heroic code' (cf. Hektor's statements at 6.444–446 [see *ad loc.*], as well as those of Achilleus himself at 9.412–415; also Patroklos' request at 16.31 f.); in what follows, Achilleus indirectly announces that he will kill as many Trojans as possible, by describing in a drastic manner the reputation he would like to have among their surviving relatives (TAPLIN 1992, 197; PATZER 1996, 216 f.; GRETHLEIN 2006, 138 n. 309; on the epic motif of returning heroes, 19.45b–46n. with bibliography). The connection between his fame and the mourning of the Trojan women (122–124) results from Achilleus' own state of mind, his thirst for revenge that is also to be quenched by the grieving of the relatives and the presence of mourning women in his company (28 ff., 67 ff., 139 ff.); grieving for the beloved person gives rise to aggression and new anger (anger for revenge) directed at Hektor and his people (112–113n.; EDWARDS on 121–125; SCHADEWALDT [1936] 1997, 159 f.; SLATEN 1993, 352 f.; PUCCI 1998, 220). – The image of the mourning relatives is evoked elsewhere in the *Iliad* in anger as well, including in a threatening tone (5.410–415, 11.393 f., 14.499–505, 20.210–212): GRIFFIN 1980, 121–125; DERDERIAN 2001, 41–44.

121 κείσομ' ... νῦν δὲ ... ἀροίμην: the more distant future ('I will lie there') in contrast to 'now' ('I will achieve for myself'), for which he announces renewed activity (AH; on νῦν δέ, 88n.). — **κλέος ἐσθλὸν ἀροίμην:** VE ≈ 5.3, *Od.* 13.422, 'Hes.' *Sc.* 107; the combination

---

120 ἐγών (before a vowel): = ἐγώ. — τέτυκται: 3rd pers. sing. perf. pass. of τεύχω.
121 κε: = ἄν (R 24.5). — ἀροίμην: aor. opt. of ἄρνυμαι, cupitive 'I wish to gain'.

κλέος ἀρέσθαι also occurs at 5.273, 17.16, *Od.* 1.240, 14.370, 24.33, cf. also 6.446 (see *ad loc.*), while the phrase κλέος ἐσθλόν (intensification: κλέος ἄφθιτον) occurs as a formula in various positions in the verse (in total 7× *Il.*, 6× *Od.*, 1× 'Hes.'). On the different expressions for the acquisition of κλέος, *LfgrE s.v.* κλέος; on the more common phrase κῦδος ἀρέσθαι, 3.373n., 16.84n.

122–124 Achilleus imagines the reaction of unnamed enemy women to his deeds: lament and the realization that he is now bringing disaster upon them (EDWARDS). His prediction will be fulfilled, particularly after he kills Hektor (22.405–515, 24.160–168, 24.695 ff.).

122–123 2nd VH of 122 ≈ 339; 1st VH of 123 = *Od.* 4.116; ≈ *Il.* 18.23, *Od.* 5.428, 24.316. — **Dardanian woman:** The Dardanians are a people from Troy's 'metropolis' Dardania (CH 8 n. 34; 2.819n.; LATACZ 2002, 1117 n. 59).

τινα: with a collective meaning 'some', cf. the pl. γνοῖεν at 125 (AH; cf. SCHW. 2.214; CHANTR. 2.8). — **Τρωϊάδων καὶ Δαρδανίδων:** elsewhere formulaic as the masc. Τρῶες καὶ Δάρδανοι (3.456n.) / καὶ Δαρδανίωνες (7.414, 8.154). — **βαθυκόλπων:** a distinctive epithet[P] of the Trojan women in the *Iliad*, likely meaning 'with deep dress-folds' (24.215n.). — **ἀμφοτέρῃσιν ... ἀπαλάων:** a four-word verse (cf. 1.75n.) with an inflected disyllabic rhyme; increases the attention of the audience. — **ἀπαλάων:** 'delicate', of body parts frequently when they are being disfigured, here by streams of tears (19.285n.).

124 1st VH ≈ *Od.* 8.88, 11.530. — **ἀδινὰ στοναχῆσαι:** designates intense, repeated cries of mourning, elsewhere ἀ. στενάχω/στοναχίζω (19.314n.; on the transmitted variants ἀδινά/ἀδινόν, WEST 2001, 246; on στεν-/στον-, 2.95n.).

125 In the story of the *Iliad*, Achilleus missed only three days of battle (STR 22 fig. 2; cf. 19.45b–46n.). His specification of the time as 'long' (Greek *dērón*) points to his impatience concerning his absence from battle (schol. A, bT; FAESI; cf. 1.488–492); what is more, the stressed personal pronoun *egṓ* is evidence of his self-confidence and knowledge of how important he is for the success of the Achaian army (AH: 'emphasized with self-confidence' [transl.]): the fact that the fortunes of battle will shift when he ends his pause from battle will also be felt by the Trojan women with bitter realization. Cf. the similar narrator commentaries concerning the effect of Achilleus' appearance on the enemy at 18.247 f. (247b–248n.), on the Achaians at 19.45 f. (see *ad loc.*), on both parties in battle at 20.42–46.

---

123 παρειάων ἀπαλάων: on the declension, R 11.1; ablatival gen., dependent on ὁμορξαμένην, aor. mid. part. of ὁμόργνυμι ('wipe away from').

124 δάκρυ' ὀμορξαμένην: on the hiatus, R 5.1. — ἀδινά: adv., 'repeatedly, continually'. — ἐφείην (+ inf.): 'bring someone to the point of ...'; aor. opt. of ἐφίημι (cf. 121n.).

125 γνοῖεν: the subj. 'Trojan women' is to be supplied from τινα Τρωϊάδων in 122. — δηρόν: adv., 'long'.

γνοῖεν: a wish clause that is supposed to be the result of a preceding wish (see also γνῷ at 1.411 f.); cf. the chiastic arrangement of ... ἐφείην, | γνοῖεν δ' ... (AH; LEAF). — δή: stresses how obvious this is: 'speakers using dḗ assume that their addressees [...] share their physical situation (or by an easy extension, the same emotional and intellectual situation)' (BAKKER 1997, 75; cf. 4n., 74n.). — πολέμοιο: 64n.

126 2nd VH = 6.360. — After reluctantly responding (98) to his mother's tears (94) and words (95 f.) already at the outset, Achilleus finally explicitly anticipates any attempt on her side to dissuade him from the plan he announced at 88 ff. (and 114 ff.) (AH; EDWARDS; MARTIN 1989, 202; SCHUBERT 2000, 73; differently LOHMANN 1970, 143 n. 74: interpolated from 6.360).

φιλέουσά περ: 'although you mean well', a paraphrase for the maternal care that is here contrasted with the heroic ethos; see 121–125n. (cf. 6.360n.). — οὐδέ με πείσεις: a variable VE formula (6× Il., 1× Od.); the context is similar to 24.218 f. (Priam is not to be dissuaded from his plan): 24.219n.; οὐδέ here with a causal function (on the parataxis via δέ rather than hypotaxis, cf. 1.10n. s.v. ὀλέκοντο δέ).

127 = 19.28; ≈ 24.89. — On the two half-verse formulae, 19.28n.; on the speech introduction formula[P], also 1.121n., 24.372n.; on the distinctive epithet[P] of Thetis ('silver-footed'), 1.538n.

128–129 After the agitated close of the previous speech, Thetis attempts to placate Achilleus with her fundamental approval and a gnome-like statement, introduced via litotes (a kind of *captatio benevolentiae*), by ignoring his actual motivation for fighting; she has graver objections to rash action (130–133) and wants to have Achilleus at least wait for new armor (134–137): AHRENS 1937, 31, 58. Advice and requests are frequently affirmed via gnomes (on this, 6.261n.), albeit rarely in dialogues between gods and men except, as here, in scenes of great intimacy between a deity and a human being or in divine messages (LARDINOIS 2000, 658; cf. 24.130–131a n.).

128 1st VH = Od. 22.486; ≈ Il. 1.286, 8.146, 10.169, 23.626, 24.379, Od. 4.266, 18.170, 20.37, 22.486. — ναὶ δὴ ταῦτά γε, ...: the VB of a variable formulaic verse, which the speaker uses to initially signal agreement with the previous speaker before expressing his own opinion (1.286n., 24.379n.; cf. LEAF): restrictive γε prepares for ἀλλά at 130. Comparison with the formulaic verse ναὶ δὴ ταῦτά γε πάντα, (address), κατὰ μοῖραν ἔειπες (see also Od. 22.486) and with the use of ἐτήτυμον in the formulaic verse καί μοι τοῦτ' ἀγόρευσον ἐτήτυμον, ὄφρ' ἐὺ εἰδῶ (Od. 1.174 etc.) suggests punctuating after ἐτήτυμον and beginning a new clause with οὐ κακόν ἐστιν: ἐτήτυμον is to be taken as an adverb in the sense 'yes, this is spoken truly, my child' (schol. A on 128–129; FAESI; WILLCOCK) or as a

---

126 μηδέ: In Homer, connective μηδέ also occurs after affirmative clauses (R 24.8). — μηδέ μ' ἔρυκε (+ gen.): 'do not attempt to hold me back from ...' (conative). — περ: concessive (R 24.10). **127** θεά: on the form, R 2.2.

predicate adv. in the nominal clause (on this, 1.416n., 6.131n.), 'this is true' (EDWARDS); differently LEAF ('these things are verily not an ill matter') and *LfgrE s.v.* ἐτήτυμος ('truly'): ἐτήτυμον with the following οὐ κακόν ἐστιν; see also AH, Anh. 147. — **τέκνον:** 73n.

129 1st VH to caesura C 2 = 17.703. — Thetis takes up Achilleus' lament at 102–106a but sets aside Patroklos' death and especially, as Achilleus himself does as well, the fight over the corpse (cf. Antilochos' report at 20 f. and the battle description at 148 ff.). The narrator has Thetis emphasize altruistic aid for companions in distress rather than revenge (on the motif, 98–99n., 102–103n.), probably in order to prevent Achilleus from becoming ever more agitated and thus impervious to her instructions at 134 ff. (128–129n.).

τειρομένοις: 'worn down' (related to the I-E root *ter-* 'grate, drill'), i.e. mentally and physically 'exhausted' (6.85n.). — **αἰπὺν ὄλεθρον:** on the VE formula and the use of αἰπύς in a metaphorical sense ('abrupt, harsh, hard to manage'), 6.57n.

130–137 This delay, caused by the loss of the armor, is prepared for at 17.709–711 (as a seed[P]). The course of events in the *Iliad* – the loss of the first set of armor, which was presented to Achilleus' father by the gods as a wedding gift (84 f.), and the gift of the second set, newly made for him by divine workmanship – fulfills several narratological functions, as discussed at 20–21n. (on the motif of newly forged armor in the epic of Gilgamesh, WEST 1997, 387). It is a reasonable hypothesis that this version is a Homeric invention (detailed discussion in EDWARDS on 84–85 and p. 19, 140 f.; KAKRIDIS 1961, 288–290, 295 f.; CURRIE 2006, 28 f. [with older bibliography]; on the exchange of weapons motif, also 16.278–283n.): (1) this means that there are two sets of divine armor for Achilleus, whereas a second set has no place in the probable pre-Homeric myth of the contest between Odysseus and Aias (*Od.* 11.543–546); (2) vase paintings depict Thetis handing over the armor in Achilleus' homeland Phthia (on which, 19.3n.; WEST 2011, 315 [on 16.143–144]). The *Iliad*'s version of the story finds a parallel in the myth of Memnon, son of Eos, as transmitted in the *Aethiopis* (Proclus, *Chrest.* § 2 West: Memnon receives armor forged by Hephaistos); there is considerable dispute about whether the *Iliad*'s version derives from the Memnon myth or *vice versa* (19.3n.; for additional parallels, also 16.419–683n., end [with bibliography]; on the relationship *Iliad* – *Aethiopis*, 17n., 37–72n., 95–96n.).

130–131 1st VH of 131 = 16.664, 23.27. — **brazen:** *chálkeos* 'of bronze'; on the use of bronze arms in Homeric epic, 2.226n., 6.3n.

---

129 ἑτάροισιν: 102n. — ἀμυνέμεν: on the form, R 16.4.
130 τοι: = σοι (R 14.1; cf. R 24.12). — μετὰ Τρώεσσιν: 'in the midst of the Trojans'.
131 τά: anaphoric demonstrative (R 17).

ἔντεα: 'equipment, arms', a prosodic variant for τεύχεα, see 137 (6.418n.). – καλά ...
| χάλκεα μαρμαίροντα: The combinations ἔντεα καλά without an additional epithet
(7× *Il.*, 1× *Od.*) and χάλκεα μαρμαίροντα with ἔντεα in the preceding verse (see *iterata*)
are formulaic. The present asyndetic succession of epithets with enjambment[P] highlights the particularity of this armor, which must now be adequately replaced; on this
epic stylistic device, 2.42–43n.; LA ROCHE 1897, 175 ff., 181 ff. (collection of examples); K.-
G. 2.341 f.; on μαρμαίροντα ('sparkling, glittering'; usually of light reflected on metal),
3.397n. – ἔχονται: passive 'are held (back)' (EDWARDS; *LfgrE s.v.* 846.65 ff.; MUTZBAUER
1893, 77; JANKUHN 1969, 77). In Homeric usage, pl. predicates are often found with neuter pl. subjects, especially when they describe several physical objects – like ἔντεα here
(CHANTR. 2.17 f.). – κορυθαιόλος Ἕκτωρ: 20–21n.

132–133 1st VH of 132 to caesura C 2 = 17.473; from caesura C 2 = 5.103, 11.589, *Od.*
15.213. – Hektor in fact exchanged his armor for that of the slain Patroklos
during battle (17.192–197) and proudly showed himself wearing it to the Trojans
(17.183–187, 212–232). But in order not to agitate Achilleus further and to render
the wait acceptable to him, Thetis immediately directs the conversation away
from Hektor's triumph to his impending death, by stating her firm conviction
that Hektor does not have much time left to savor his victory (tertiary focalization[P]); she here links donning the captured armor with Hektor's death – as
did already the narrator at 16.799 f., Zeus at 17.198–208 (TAPLIN 1992, 187 f.; on
prolepses[P] of Hektor's death, 92n.).

αὐτὸς ἔχων: a formulaic combination (VB 4× *Il.*, 1× Hes. *Th.*, 2× *Il.* before caesura C 1);
here it serves, in combination with ὤμοισιν, to further highlight Hektor as the bearer
of the captured armor (before the foil μετὰ Τρώεσσιν): '⟨now⟩ he himself having in his
possession' (cf. *LfgrE s.v.* αὐτός 1646.47 ff., esp. 71 f.; elsewhere it usually means 'keeping for oneself': 2.233n., 24.280n.). – φημί: rhetorical reinforcement of an assertion
(*LfgrE s.v.* 892.3 ff.: 'I declare [as my conviction]'). – ἐπαγλαΐεσθαι: a fut. form of ἐπ-
αγλαΐζομαι in place of the Ionic-Attic contracted form in the main transmission (RISCH
352 [who explains the form via analogy]; WEST 1998, XXXI with bibliography; cf. SCHW.
1.785). ἀγλαΐζομαι is derived from ἀγλαός ('shining': 1.23n.), transmitted elsewhere in
Homeric epic only at 10.331 as the simplex of this same form and used synonymously
with ἀγάλλομαι (132); in post-Homeric literature, poetic vocabulary: Eust. 1135.7; DELG
s.v. ἀγλαός; *LfgrE s.v.* ἀγλαΐζομαι ('take great joy in'); HAINSWORTH on *Il.* 10.331 ('will
pride yourself upon').

134–144 The instructions directed to her son (134 ff.) and sisters (140 ff.) prepare for the further action of the book, which branches out into two strands
(a so-called 'table of contents' speech, see DE JONG on *Od.* 1.81–95): (1) Thetis'

---

132 ὤμοισιν: on the declension, R 11.2; locative dat. without preposition (R 19.2). – οὐδέ (ϝ)ε: on
the prosody, R 4.3. – ἑ: = αὐτόν (R 14.1).
133 δηρόν: 125n. – ἐγγύθεν: 'near'.

visit to Hephaistos' smithy (369–613), again prepared for at the close of the scene in 146–148a; (2) the continuation of battle with Achilleus' indirect help (148b–244) and its consequences in both camps (245–314a: Trojan assembly; 314b–355 lament over Patroklos' body): KURZ 1966, 110; KRISCHER 1971, 111 and 119. Thetis tells her son to wait (134 f.) and tries to make the delay palatable to him by clearly delimiting it with specifications of time at 136. After the arms are complete, she will retun as quickly as possible and rejoin Achilleus at the next sunrise (18.614–19.3; cf. schol. A on 136).

134 ἀλλὰ σύ: a VB formula, ἀλλά marks the transition from argument to request (1.127n., 2.360n.). – **μή πω καταδύσεο μῶλον ἄρηος:** δύνω here in the sense 'enter an area, a sphere of influence'; in combination with words for (the thick of) battle – elsewhere μάχην, πόλεμον, ὅμιλον – 'throw oneself into the fight' (6.185n.; *LfgrE s.v.* 359.10 ff.). μῶλον ἄρηος ('the labor of battle') here suits the mother's apprehensive mood; on this VE formula and the etymology and development of the sense of μῶλον ('labor, effort' → 'battle'), 2.401n.; on the metonymic use of Ἄρης/ἄρης (of both the god and his sphere of influence), CG 28; 2.381n., 2.440n. – (κατα)δύσεο is an imper. of the thematic s-aor. δύσετο (19.36n.), but a negated aor. imper. rather than aor. subjunc. is rare in early epic, only here and 4.410, *Od.* 24.248 (μὴ ... ἔνθεο), also *Il.* 16.200 (μὴ ... λελαθέσθω). An explanation for this phrasing has been sought in comparable Vedic phrases (negation + injunctive: WACKERNAGEL [1920/24] 2009, 274–276; CHANTR. 2.231 f.), on the one hand, and in the influence of half-verse formulae with -δύσετο before caesura C 2 and various VE formulae (17 of 31 examples in early epic: ROTH [1970–1974] 1990, 44; SMITH 1979, 47 f.), on the other; detailed discussion in STEPHENS 1983, 71–78.

135 ≈ 190. – **πρίν γ' ... ἐν ὀφθαλμοῖσιν ἴδηαι:** The finite verb form and the addition ἐν ὀφθαλμοῖσιν stress the importance of autopsy (CHANTR. 2.264 f.). (ἐν) ὀφθαλμοῖσιν ἴδηαι is an inflectable VE formula (5× *Il.*, 1× *Od.*, 3× *h.Hom.*, of which 5× in total without ἐν); the original meaning of the preposition ἐν is disputed: either an indication of 'what is or happens in someone's field of view', i.e. 'before their eyes' (AH [transl.]), or the notion that an event is an image in the eye (cf. 24.294n.; on additional formulaic combinations of ὀφθαλμοῖσιν with roots for 'see', NUSSBAUM 2002, 184 ff.).

136 2nd VH = *Od.* 23.362; ≈ *Il.* 22.135, *Od.* 12.429. – **νέομαι:** pres. tense with fut. sense (*LfgrE s.v.* 326.26 ff. with bibliography; SCHW. 2.273).

---

134 μέν: ≈ μήν (R 24.6). — μή πω: 'not yet', specified more closely by πρίν γε (135), thus 'not ... before ...'. — ἄρηος: on the declension, R 12.4.
135 δεῦρο: 'hither'. — ἴδηαι: uncontracted (R 6) 2nd pers. sing. aor. mid. subjunc.; on the middle, R 23; prospective subjunc., in Homer also without a modal particle (R 21.1).
136 ἠῶθεν: 'at daybreak, early', from ἠώς 'dawn'; on the formation of the word, R 15.1. — νέομαι: on the synizesis, R 7. — ἠελίῳ: = ἡλίῳ.

137 ≈ 617; VE = 15.214. — **Hephaistos:** The divine smith, like other gods, here receives the title 'lord' (*[w]ánax*: 2.102n.; cf. 1.7n.; on Hephaistos, CG 15; *BNP s.v.* Hephaestus; ERBSE 1986, 76).

τεύχεα καλά: a formulaic phrase in various positions in the verse (84n.; cf. 130–131n.).

138–145 Via a speech capping[P] and speech introduction formula[P], the narrator has Thetis make two successive speeches to different addressees in order to conclude the encounter between mother and son (138, cf. 70–72) and to return to the Nereids in the manner of a ring-composition (139–145, cf. 65–69): 65–147n.; cf. DE JONG on *Od.* 5.21–42 (on the device 'two consecutive speeches by one speaker'). These contain the instructions to convey the sad message to their father (140–142a). On the narratological function of the two speeches, 134–144n.

138 1st VH to caesura C 2 ≈ 8.432, 21.415, 21.468. — **ὣς ἄρα φωνήσασα:** 65n. — **πάλιν τράπεθ᾽ υἱὸς ἑοῖο:** πάλιν here means 'away', i.e. 'turned away/aside from ...', likewise at 20.439, similarly *Od.* 7.143 (*LfgrE s.v.* πάλιν). — **υἱὸς ἑοῖο:** a prosodic variant of παιδὸς ἑοῖο, see 71n.

139 **ἁλίῃσι:** adjectival (i.e. 'sisters of the sea'), contrast 86–87n.

140 2nd VH = *Od.* 4.435; ≈ *Il.* 21.125. — **κόλπον:** 'fold of the sea' 'as an enveloping element' (*LfgrE* [transl.]; cf. 6.136n.).

141 the ancient of the sea: Nereus, the father of Thetis and the Nereids (36n.), who inhabits a cave in the sea (50 [with n.], 65 f.).

δώματα πατρός: a VE formula (1× *Il.*, 5× *Od.*, 3× Hes., 4× *h.Hom.*); sing. and pl. of δῶμα are usually employed *metri gratia* with no difference in meaning (ELLENDT [1861] 1979, 62 f.; DÜNTZER [1864] 1979, 94; *LfgrE s.v.*).

142 I ...: The announcement here, and the repetition in the narrator-text at 146/148a, serves in particular to impress Thetis' visit to Olympos on the mind of the external audience, since this strand of the action will not be picked up again until 369 ff. (134–144n.). The visit to Olympos is structured in a manner parallel to Thetis' departure to visit Zeus at 1.420 ff. (35–147n.); other passages in Homeric epic link Hephaistos with the island of Lemnos (1.593n.): WEST 2011, 292 f., 346 f. On Mt. Olympos as the abode of the gods, 1.18n.

---

137 Ἡφαίστοιο (ϝ)άνακτος: on the prosody, R 4.3.
138 υἱός: on the declension, R 12.3. — ἑοῖο: possessive pronoun of the 3rd person (R 14.4).
139 μετηύδα: 3rd pers. sing. impf. of μετ-αυδάω (+ dat. pl.) 'speak among'.
140 εὐρέα κόλπον: acc. of direction without preposition (R 19.2).
141 ὀψόμεναι: final, 'in order to see, call on'. — δώματα: on the plural, R 18.2.
142 καί (ϝ)οι: on the prosody, R 4.4. — οἱ: = αὐτῷ (R 14.1). — ἐς: = εἰς (R 20.1).

ἀγορεῦσαι: Zenodotus' reading, with imperatival inf. rather than the transmitted elided imper. ἀγορεύσατ(ε), is preferred by WEST as the *lectio difficilior* (WEST 2001, 247). In contrast to the imper. (δῦτε 140), the imperatival inf. connotes a somewhat indirect instruction, the implementation of which is left to the addressee and which in the present passage points to conventional patterns of social behavior, corresponding to instructions to a messenger ('conventional social procedures': ALLAN 2010, 215–225, esp. 218 ff.; see also 16.87n.; additional examples with a change from imper. to imperatival inf. in SCHW. 2.381; CHANTR. 2.316). — **μακρὸν Ὄλυμπον:** an inflectable VE formula (11× *Il.*, 4× *Od.*, 3× Hes., 3× *h.Hom.*), usually in the acc. (cf. 1.402n.), 2× in the nom.

143 While Thetis presents it to her son as a matter of course that she will bring new armor from Hephaistos (136 f.) – probably so as not to raise any doubts regarding the success of her mission and to prevent him from throwing himself into battle with makeshift equipment – her words to her sisters are more nuanced: the god stands in her debt (394 ff.), but she has no power over him and will have to beg; cf. 457 ff. (schol. bT on 143–144).

Ἥφαιστον κλυτοτέχνην: a formula between caesurae A 3 and C 2 (nom./acc.: 3× *Il.*, 1× *Od.*, 1× *h.Hom.*), with distinctive epithet[P] ('famed for his artistry'). — **αἴ κ' ἐθέλῃσιν:** 'in the hope that he is ready' (WAKKER 1994, 365–368, 374; cf. 1.408n., 1.420n., 6.94n.); an inflectable VE formula (8× *Il.*, 6× *Od.*, 1× Hes. *Th.*, 1× *h.Merc.*); on the range of meaning for ἐθέλω, 1.112n.; on the subjunc. ending -ῃσι (without ι subscript), G 89; WEST 1998, XXXI.

144 armor: The exceptional aesthetic quality of the armor is anticipated (see also at 466 f.), and its imposing appearance is stressed repeatedly during the handing over and the departure for battle: 617, 19.10 f., 19, 21 f., 369–383, 398 (cf. 19.374–383n.).

κλυτὰ τεύχεα παμφανόωντα: κλυτὰ τεύχεα is a common phrase in various positions in the verse (19.10n.; after caesura B 1, as here: 6× *Il.*, 1× *Od.*). The epithet παμφανόωντα, common with terms for 'armor' (τεύχεα, ἔντεα), as well as of men in armor, but also with other items (δίφρος, λέβης, ἐνώπια), usually occurs at VE (15 examples out of a total of 19 in early epic), although the present combination is found here alone (cf. 130–131n.). — **παμφανόωντα:** reduplicated φαίνω, although the prefix παμ- may have been understood as the neuter of πᾶς (2.458n.).

145–147 The departure of the goddesses, announced in the speech, is described explicitly (the Nereids again act as a collective: cf. 37–72n.): the mourning scene surrounding Achilleus is dissolved, the action in the Myrmidon camp comes to a halt; this prepares for a change of scene (see 148 with n.). 146 f. and

---

143 αἰ: = εἰ (R 22.1). — κ(ε): = ἄν (R 24.5). — ἐθέλῃσιν: 3rd pers. sing. pres. subjunc. (R 16.3).
144 υἱεῖ: on the declension, R 12.3. — δόμεναι: = Attic δοῦναι (R 16.4). — παμφανόωντα: on the epic diectasis, R 8.

148a, containing the reference to Thetis' departure, are element (**1**) of the type-scene 'arrival' (on which, 1.496b–502n.), the other elements of which follow at 369 ff.; Thetis' journey takes place in the background, while the narrator returns to the battle (148–242; see *ad loc.*): AREND 1933, 32 n. 1, 36.

145 ὣς ἔφαθ', αἳ δ(έ): a speech capping formula[P] (3× *Il.*, 6× *Od.*, cf. 19.74n.) with the speech capping scheme 'spoke' + addressee's response (1.33n.). — **κῦμα θαλάσσης:** a formula before caesura C 2 (3× *Il.*, 1× *Od.*); see 66–67a n.

146 ἣ …: On the verse structure (anaphoric pronoun at VB and noun-epithet formula at VE), see BAKKER 1997, 92, 198 f. — **θεὰ Θέτις ἀργυρόπεζα:** 127n.

147 ὄφρα φίλῳ παιδὶ … ἐνείκαι: The final clause with opt. as an indication of indirect discourse is in secondary focalization[P]; cf. Thetis' announcement at 143 f. (DE JONG [1987] 2004, 111, 268 n. 32; RICHARDSON 1990, 149, 235 n. 17 [collection of examples]). — **κλυτὰ τεύχε(α):** a formula after caesura C 1 (10× *Il.*, 1× *Od.*, 4× 'Hes.'), cf. 144n.

148–242 In the battle for the corpse of Patroklos, the Achaians were hard pressed. The rescue succeeds only when Achilleus intervenes at the request of the divine messenger Iris and, with Athene's help, reveals himself to the Trojans as a terrifying apparition. The day ends with the retrieval of the corpse.

The narrator directs attention away from Thetis and back to events on the battlefield, last mentioned at the beginning of the Book (1, 6 ff., 20 f.), by detailing the fight for the corpse and its recovery (148b–242), followed by a report on events after sunset in both the Trojan and the Greek camps (243–314a/314b–368: covering scene[P]; schol. bT on 148; SCHADEWALDT [1938] 1966, 77). The change of scene at 148 to the battle might appear somewhat abrupt (schol. bT on 148), but it is indirectly prepared for by (a) Achilleus' urge to fight against the Trojans (114 f., 121 ff.), (b) Thetis' reference to Hektor's triumph (130 ff.) and (c) her instructions that Achilleus is not allowed to throw himself into battle on this same day (134 ff.).

148–164 Picking up from the events in the battle at the end of Book 17: Menelaos and Meriones (CH 4) had begun to carry the corpse off the battlefield under the protection of the two Aiantes (CH 3) and had been particularly hard pressed by Aineias and Hektor (17.717–754), who routed many Greeks (17.758–761, 18.148b–150). Achilleus also observed their flight to the ships (6 f.). But in the present

---

145–146 ἔφαθ': = ἔφατο (17n.). — αἵ: anaphoric demonstrative (R 17); likewise ἥ in 146, in apposition to θεὰ Θέτις ἀργυρόπεζα. — Οὔλυμπόνδε: initial syllable metrically lengthened (R 10.1); on the suffix -δε, R 15.3.
147 ἤϊεν: = Attic ᾖει 'went'. — ὄφρα: final (R 22.5). — ἐνείκαι: opt. from aor. ἤνεικα ≈ Attic ἤνεγκον.

description, neither Menelaos and Meriones nor Aineias are mentioned. These differences in the situation, considered 'inconsistencies' by some scholars (AH, *Anh.* p. 115–117) vis-à-vis the portrayal at the end of Book 17, can be explained by the preceding scenes (2–147) functioning as a covering scene[P] for the Greek flight, which is not described in detail, the attempted recovery and the pursuit by the Trojans (on this Homeric narrative technique, DE JONG 2007, 30 f.). The narrator now directs attention toward Hektor (149, 154, 155 f., 158b–160, 164; cf. 175 ff.), who has in the meantime caused the situation to escalate: recovery of the corpse is in doubt (151–164; cf. schol. bT on 151–152), since the Trojans have 'once again' caught up with the group that surrounds it (153), while Hektor persists in trying to drag it away (VAN LEEUWEN; EDWARDS; KURZ 1966, 164; on corpses as part of the booty, PATZER 1996, 176–178; on resuming interrupted battle descriptions, 16.102–123n.).

148 ≈ 15.405. — **πόδες φέρον:** a formula before caesura C 2 (5× *Il.*, 1× *Od.*); the same wording with subsequent bridging of a change in location (imper. here and at 147) via descriptions of different scenes is used at 15.405 and 17.700 (by Patroklos and Antilochos, the arrival at 16.2 ff. and 18.2 ff.; cf. the change of scene at *Od.* 15.555/16.11 ff.). — **αὐτὰρ Ἀχαιοί:** an inflectable VE formula, only *Il.* (12× nom., 7× acc., 2× dat., 1× gen.); here it serves, together with τὴν μὲν …, to link two *concurrent* storylines, clarified by the statement at 146 f. repeated at 148a in the manner of a summary[P] (cf. 1n.); on changes of scene after caesura C 2, 1.194n., 24.3n. (on αὐτάρ …), 16.124n.

149 2nd VH = 1.242 (see *ad loc.*), 17.428, 17.616. — **θεσπεσίῳ:** literally 'divine', used metaphorically of noise 'with an overwhelming effect, tremendous' (2.457n.). — **ἀλαλητῷ:** an onomatopoetic term for battle cries, here (and at 21.10) the anxious cries of those fleeing, cf. 17.759 (2.149n.). Elsewhere, μεγάλῳ serves as an epithet (14.393, *Od.* 24.463, Hes. *Th.* 686), combined with θεσπεσίῳ only here and at 'Hes.' *Sc.* 382 f. — **ὑφ' Ἕκτορος:** literally 'under the influence of …' (SCHW. 2.528 f.; cf. 3.61n., 6.73n.). — **Ἕκτορος ἀνδροφόνοιο:** a noun-epithet formula at VE (8× *Il.*, 1× 'Hes.') and VB (3× *Il.*), always in the gen.; on its use in contrast to the metrically equivalent Ἕκτορος ἱπποδάμοιο, 24.509n.; DE JONG on *Il.* 22.161. Here perhaps used contextually: the battle reaches its climax; after the killing, Hektor jeopardizes the retrieval of the body (163–165): DI BENEDETTO (1994) 1998, 138.

---

148 τήν: Thetis (146) is meant; on the anaphoric demonstrative function of ὅ, ἥ, τό, R 17. — ἄρ(α): 'thus (as a result)' (R 24.1). — Οὔλυμπόνδε: 145–146n. — φέρον: on the unaugmented form, R 16.1. — αὐτάρ: 'but' (R 24.2).
149 θεσπεσίῳ ἀλαλητῷ: on the hiatus, R 5.6. — ἀλαλητῷ ὑφ': on the so-called correption, R 5.5. — ἀνδροφόνοιο: on the declension, R 11.2.

150 ≈ 15.233, 23.2; 2nd VH ≈ 24.346. – **ships ... Hellespont:** i.e. to the Greek camp, which is surrounded by the ships pulled up onto the beach like a fortress (1.12b n.) and has for the last two days been fortified in addition with a wall and ditch (cf. 7.436 ff.); on the structures, see Appendix to Book 14. Book 17 closes with a report of the fleeing warriors trying to reach the area behind the ditch (17.760 f.); the fight for the corpse takes place in the vicinity of the ships (172) at the ditch (198, 215 f., 228 f.) (cf. 148–164n.). – In Homeric epic, 'Hellespont' perhaps refers not only to the Dardanelles but also to a part of the north-east Aegean near their southern entrance (24.544–545n.).

ἵκοντο: on the aor. and related contextual issues, AH, *Anh.* 115 f.; FAESI; EDWARDS on 148–150 ('conative') and 148–164; cf. 148–164n.

151–152 How the battle can be concluded successfully remains undetermined for several verses due to a delay via description of attack and defense ('thrice', 155 ff.) and a simile (alluding to a possible defeat: 161 ff.); only with the resumption of the contrary to fact construction at 165 ff. – phrased positively from Hektor's vantage point ('and he would have dragged it away') – is it continued in an 'if-not' situationᴾ (AH; FAESI; WILLCOCK; NESSELRATH 1992, 14; cf. 165–168n.). – **henchman:** Greek *therápōn* designates a man who, although subordinate to another, is personally free ('battle companion, aide': 24.396n.). In contrast to *hétaros/hetaíros* (80 [see *ad loc.*], 98), the term brings into focus the subordinate relationship (24.4n.): Patroklos serves as Achilleus' charioteer (16.20n., end). Patroklos is also referred to as Achilleus' *therápōn* elsewhere: in the narrator-text at 16.165 (athetized by WEST), 16.653 (Zeus' thoughts), 17.271, 17.388; in direct speeches at 16.244 (Achilleus' prayer, athetized by WEST), 17.164 (Glaukos), 23.90 (Patroklos' spirit quoting Peleus): *LfgrE s.v.* θεράπων.

Πάτροκλόν περ: stresses the contrast with 150: the fleeing Achaians were able to save themselves but not the body (EDWARDS; DENNISTON 483). — ἐϋκνήμιδες Ἀχαιοί: an inflectable VE formula (31× *Il.*, 5× *Od.*, 1× Hes., of which 19× nom., 18× acc.); on the realia ('greaves'), 613n. — ἐκ βελέων: ἐκ 'outside of', i.e. 'out of range of' (CHANTR. 2.99). — νέκυν: 'the dead man', in apposition to Πάτροκλον (cf. 24.35n.). — θεράποντ' Ἀχιλῆος: this combination only here, probably echoing the VE formula θεράποντες Ἄρηος (on which, 2.110n.): EDWARDS.

---

150 νῆας ... Ἑλλήσποντον: acc. of direction without preposition (R 19.2). — νῆας: on the declension, R 12.1. — ἵκοντο: on the unaugmented form (short ῐ-), R 16.1.
151–152 οὐδέ κε ... | ...ἐρύσαντο: The contrary to fact (κε = ἄν: R 24.5) is picked up again in 165, the contextually related dependent clause follows in 166 f. εἰ μὴ ... | ... ἦλθε. — οὐδέ: In Homer, connective οὐδέ also occurs after affirmative clauses (R 24.8). — βελέων: on the uncontracted form, R 6. — Ἀχιλῆος: on the declension, R 11.3, R 3; on the single -λ-, R 9.1.

153 2nd VH from caesura C 1 ≈ 2.466, 9.708, 13.684, 17.400, 17.644, *Od.* 3.324, 4.20, 14.267, 17.436. — **αὖτις γὰρ δή:** signals the resumption of the interrupted description of the battle for the corpse (BONIFAZI 2012, 270 n. 15: 'presentational αὖτις ... «here we are»'); on δή ('of course'), CUYPERS 2005, 56. — **λαός:** the '(male) people at arms' (1.10n., 24.1n.), here a technical military term: 'footsoldiers' (*vs.* ἵπποι).

154 1st VH to caesura C 1 = 5.704; ≈ 3.314, 7.47, 11.200, 15.244; 2nd VH from caesura C 1 ≈ 4.253, 13.330, 17.281. — Filling an entire verse with the designation of a person signals their significance for the action going forward (1.36n.; cf. 155–165, 175b–177); Hektor is explicitly singled out from the crowd of Trojan attackers (153). — **flame:** The comparison to a flame (*phlogí eíkelos*) is repeatedly used to characterize Hektor during a dangerous attack (also at 13.53 f., 13.688, 17.88, 20.423), also 1× of Idomeneus (13.330) and – with slightly altered wording – of the Trojans overall (13.39). The warlike aura of a hero is described via comparisons with fire also elsewhere (particularly that of Achilleus: 205–206n.): FRÄNKEL 1921, 50 f.; SCOTT 1974, 67; TSAGARAKIS 1982, 138 f.; ROLLINGER 1996, 160 ff. (with Ancient Near Eastern parallels); WEST 2007, 494 (with I-E parallels).

155 Three times: A typical number[P], the triple attempt is a motif typical of battle scenes (6.435n. with bibliography). The motif 'three times X, three times Y' (155–158), elsewhere often continued with 'but the fourth time' (5.436 ff., 16.702 ff., 16.784 ff., 21.176 ff., 22.165/208, *Od.* 21.125 ff.: KIRK on 5.436–439; DE JONG on *Od.* 21.125–128), is here combined with an 'if-not' situation[P] (165 ff., see *ad loc.*). — **caught him:** The Trojans have already managed several times to grab the corpse and pull on it (17.125 ff., 277 ff., 288 ff., 384–397, cf. 17.229 ff.); tugging at the foot of a corpse is a typical motif in Homeric battle descriptions, see 536–537n., 539–540n.

τρὶς μέν: formulaic VB (16× early epic), usually followed by τρὶς δέ (here at 157) in the same or the following verse (10× *Il.*, 4× *Od.*): KELLY 2007, 194–197. — **φαίδιμος Ἕκτωρ:** a VE formula (29× *Il.*); the generic epithet[P] φαίδιμος probably has a purely ornamental sense ('radiant, magnificent', perhaps in reference to the armor: 6.144n., 16.577n.).

156 1st VH ≈ 176. — **μεμαώς:** part. of μέμονα ('strive for, have the urge to'); μέμονα is often linked with an inf. meaning 'fight' (cf. 6.120n.) or 'kill' and, in the context of war, denotes a 'forceful, aggressive drive' (*LfgrE s.v.* 122.58 ff. [transl.]). — **μέγα:** 'loud', like-

---

153 αὖτις: = αὖθις. — κίχον: 'caught, reached', unaugmented (R 16.1) aor. of κιχάνω. — λαός: λᾱϝός, = Attic-Ionic λεώς (cf. R 3). — ἵπποι: 'team of horses'.
154 φλογὶ (ϝ)είκελος: on the prosody, R 5.4. — ἀλκήν: acc. of respect (R 19.1).
155 μιν: = αὐτόν (R 14.1). — μιν ... ποδῶν λάβε: 'got hold of him by the foot' (gen. of the body part grasped). — μετόπισθε: 'from behind'.
156 ἑλκέμεναι: on the form, R 16.4. — Τρώεσσιν: on the declension, R 11.3. — ὁμόκλα: unaugmented (R 16.1) 3rd pers. sing. impf. of ὁμοκλάω.

wise at 160 (cf. 29n.). — **ὁμόκλα:** 'shouted loudly at'; describes a 'cry of encouragement' (KRAPP 1964, 84–86 [transl.]) and is intensified with μέγα only here; on its wider use and etymology, 6.54n.

157 ≈ 7.164, 8.262. — **the two Aiantes:** CH 3; their efforts during the defense of the corpse are mentioned several times in the preceding battle description: 17.718 f., 732 f., 746 f., 752 f. (148–163n.).

θοῦριν: 'impetuous', adj. related to θορεῖν 'leap' (FRISK; LfgrE); as an epithet of ἀλκή elsewhere usually in the VE formula θούριδος ἀλκῆς (16.270n.: 21× Il., 1× Od.). — **ἐπιειμένοι ἀλκήν:** an inflectable VE formula (3× Il., 2× Od.); on ἐπιειμένος ('dressed in') with an abstract, 1.149n.; on ἀλκή ('fighting spirit'), 3.45n., 19.36n.

158a ἀπεστυφέλιξαν: 'push away from (with blows)', sc. Hektor (LfgrE s.v. στυφελίζω; cf. 1.581n.).

158b–160 A vivid description of Hektor's attack: his halt does not signify a termination of the attack but serves to intensify his cry to battle (LfgrE s.v. ἰάχω 1114.18 ff.; KRAPP 1964, 77; KURZ 1966, 82–85, esp. 84, 145). Hektor's repeated battle cries (Greek mégā iáchōn) on the opposing side balance the cries of fear from the fleeing Achaians (149). The motifs of the battle cry and the flame emanating from the warrior reappear, in extended form, during Achilleus' appearance at 217 ff. (EDWARDS).

ἔμπεδον … | ἄλλοτ' ἐπαΐξασκε …, ἄλλοτε δ' αὖτε | στάσκε: The repeated ἄλλοτε, the adv. ἔμπεδον ('persistently, repeatedly': LfgrE) and the iterative forms ἐπαΐξασκε and στάσκε (G 60; SCHW. 1.711) reinforce the image of the repeated attack. On the anaphora after the bucolic diaeresis, 24.10n. — **ἀλκὶ πεποιθώς:** a VE formula (5× Il., 1× Od.) with the dat. sing. of the root noun ἀλκ- (cf. ἀλκή at 157n.); with the exception of the present passage, always in comparisons of a warrior with lions or wild boars. On πεποιθώς 'trusting in', 6.505n. — **κατὰ μόθον:** 'through the fray', a formula before caesura C 2 (3× Il., 1× 'Hes.'): LfgrE. — **μέγα ἰάχων:** The digamma in ἰάχω often lengthens the preceding final syllable of the adv. in -ᾰ (*-ᾰ ϝιϝαχ-; examples in CHANTR. 1.139 f.; on the present phrase and its variants, 29n.). — **οὐ … πάμπαν:** 'not at all' (παν-παν, see 1.422n.); on the metrical usefulness of this 'expanded form', 19.334n.

161–164 The narrator's use of a simile[P] follows from the battle description at the end of Book 17, where similes abound: 17.725 ff. (dogs: attackers), 737 ff. (conflagration: battle), 742 ff. (mules: bearers of the corpse), 747 ff. (mountain: the two Aiantes), 755 ff. (flock of birds: fleeing Achaians): SCOTT 1974, 45; 2009, 152 f. Here the narrator uses the simile to characterize the futile attempt by

---

157 δύ' Αἴαντες: on the hiatus, R 5.1. — θοῦριν(ν) ἐπιειμένοι: on the prosody, M 4.6 (note also the caesura: M 8).
159–160 ἐπαΐξασκε … | στάσκε: iterative (-σκ-: R 16.5) of ἐπαΐσσω ('rushed ahead') or ἵσταμαι ('stood still'). — κατὰ (μ)μόθον: on the prosody, M 4.6. — μέγα (ϝ)ι(ϝ)άχων: on the prosody, R 4.3.

the two Aiantes to rescue the corpse from Hektor (cf. the bracketed position of Greek *apó sṓmatos* and *apó nekroú* at 1st VH 161 and 2nd VH 164) as well as to prepare for the 'if-not' situation[P] (165 ff.): the hungry lion illustrates Hektor's fighting strength, energy and tenacity – he cannot be separated from his prey – while the shepherds show the helplessness of the two defenders in a hopeless situation (KRISCHER 1971, 72; SCHNAPP-GOURBEILLON 1981, 40 f.; SCOTT 2009, 153; on lion similes[P] and comparisons[P], 3.23n., 24.41b–44n.). In similes, shepherds are often shown carrying out the difficult task of protecting the flocks, e.g. in inclement weather (3.10 ff., 4.275 ff.) or, as here, during dangerous encounters with wild animals, in which they are not infrequently defeated (5.136 ff., 15.586 f., 15.632 f., 16.352 ff., 17.61 ff., 18.577 ff. [Achilleus' shield]): 3.11n.; RICHTER 1968, 37; HAUBOLD 2000, 18 ff.; on the motif of the helpless shepherd in Ancient Near Eastern literature, WEST 1997, 219, 388.

161–162 lion: On the presence of lions in Greece and Asia Minor in the Archaic period, 3.23n.

161 σώματος: the animal just killed by the lion ('dead body, cadaver'); in contrast, the deceased Patroklos is here designated νέκυς/νεκρός ('deceased person, corpse') (152 [see *ad loc.*], 158, 164, 173); on the meaning of σῶμα in Homer, 3.23n. — **αἴθωνα:** As a designation of color in animals, this means 'reddish-brown' (EDGEWORTH 1983, 35, 39 f.; cf. 19.243–244n.).

162 1st VH = Hes. *Th.* 26. — **πεινάοντα:** in the *Iliad* only of lions (3.25n.). — **δίεσθαι:** transitive 'chase off'; the inf. (proparoxytone: schol. A) is sometimes used with the function of an aor. (*LIV* 107 with n. 3; cf. CHANTR. 1.293), as it is here, parallel with δειδίξασθαι (*LfgrE s.v.* δί(ημι), δί(ω)).

163 ≈ 13.201. — **Αἴαντε:** This dual is generally used in the *Iliad* to denote the homonymous sons of Telamon and Oïleus, but originally it probably designated the two sons of Telamon, Aias and Teukros (2.406n. [with bibliography]; NAPPI 2002; WEST 2011, 144, 270). — **κορυστά:** derived from κόρυς, used only as an epithet of the two Aiantes (see the *iteratum*) and in the VE formula ἄνδρα κορυστήν (4.457, 8.256, 16.603), i.e. literally 'helmet-wearing, helmeted', thus generally 'armed' (*LfgrE s.v.* κορυστής; cf. 6.198b–199n. *s.v.* χαλκοκορυστήν).

164 Ἕκτορα Πριαμίδην: an inflectable VB formula, only in the *Iliad* (7× nom., 3× dat., 5× acc.). — **δειδίξασθαι:** δειδίσσομαι (Attic δεδίττομαι) is a deverbative from δείδω/

---

161 τι: acc. of respect (R 19.1), strengthens οὐ: 'not in any respect, in no way, not at all'.
162 μέγα: adv., 'very'. — πεινάοντα: on the uncontracted form, R 6.
163 ῥα: = ἄρα (R 24.1). — τόν: anaphoric demonstrative (R 17), to which Ἕκτορα Πριαμίδην (164) is in apposition. — ἐδύναντο δύω Αἴαντε κορυστά: a plural in combination with three duals (R 18.1). On the hiatus δύω Αἴαντε, R 5.6.
164 Πριαμίδην: initial syllable metrically lengthened (R 10.1).

δέδοικα with a factitive meaning 'intimidate', here with ἀπό 'scare off, frighten away' (FRISK and *DELG* s.v. δείδω).

165–168 Highlighting of the dramatic situation via an 'if-not' situation[P]; used by the narrator to (a) heighten suspense, (b) hint at a possible alternative storyline (the consequences of which are illustrated vividly in Iris' messenger speech at 175 ff.), (c) prepare for the turning point in the battle (on the use of the narrative device, 2.155–156n., 6.73–76n.; GRETHLEIN 2006, 281 f.).

165 = 3.373. — **καί νύ κεν:** a frequent introduction to an 'if-not' situation, followed by a dependent clause with εἰ μή (166): 2.155–156n.; on νυ (with 'temporal force' [transl.]) RUIJGH 1957, 59. — **ἄσπετον ἤρετο κῦδος:** On the thematic aor. of ἄρνυμαι ('obtain'), the formulaic combination with κῦδος and the adj. ἄσπετος ('unspeakable' > weakened 'large, great'), 3.373n.; on κῦδος (designating the elation felt after a successful deed – usually a military one – and the prestige gained via the success), also 19.204n.; DE JONG on *Il.* 22.205–207.

166–202 An abbreviated and much modified form of the type-scene[P] 'delivery of a message', the composition of which, containing the unprepared-for appearance of the divine messenger Iris (CG 38), reflects urgent haste (for the complete form of the scene, 1.320–348a n.); only now is the Achaian message to Achilleus delivered in full, namely that his help is needed in the battle for the corpse (cf. 18–21n.). The integration of the scene into the 'if-not' situation[P] causes the omission of element 4 (description of the situation) as well as – somewhat in contradiction to the 'continuity of time' principle[P] – the rearrangement of elements 1–3: (**3**) arrival (166–167a), (**2**) departure (167b), (**1**) issuing of orders (167c–168), (**5**) the messenger approaches (169), (**6**) carries out her orders (170–202). The scene is also noteworthy in other respects: (a) Iris is not travelling as Zeus' messenger (168n., 184 ff.); (b) she does not initially make herself known (170–180n.); (c) Achilleus nonetheless recognizes her immediately (182n.); (d) the wording of Hera's orders remains obscure (167n.); (e) Achilleus does not act immediately but instead asks questions (181–195n.); (f) Iris must clarify the message (197 ff.); overall, and in contrast to other scenes between deities and humans, the present scene shows a certain informal directness between the interlocutors and thus has something of the appearance of a dialogue between confidants – a sign of Achilleus' proximity to the gods (SCHEIN 1984, 94; ERBSE 1986, 58 f.; TURKELTAUB 2007, 70–72; on the course of the conversation, see also BECK 2012, 12 f.); on epic narrative conventions for messenger speeches, see 2.23–34n., 2.28–32n.

---

165 κεν: = ἄν (R 24.5.). — εἴρυσσεν: aor. of (ϝ)ερύω 'tug, drag'; on the -σσ-, R 9.1.

166–167 Iris: On the role of Iris – personification of the rainbow and messenger of the gods – *LfgrE s.v.*; ERBSE 1986, 54–65; KELLY 2007, 322–324; on Iris' epithets[P], 24.77n. — **Peleus' son:** Iris reveals herself only to him, while his surroundings remain unmentioned – as is frequently the case in divine appearances; on this in general, 1.197–198n., 24.169–170n.; on designating Achilleus by a variant of his patronymic (in Book 18 here and at 226, 261, 267 *Pēléiōn*, 170 and 316 *Pēléidēs*; 221 f. *Aiakídēs* [with an initial vowel] after his grandfather), 1.1n.; LATACZ (1995) 2014, 304 n. 87. — **to arm:** *thōréssesthai* denotes not only donning armor (thus at 189, see 191) but also mental preparation for battle, working oneself up into a battle-lust (*LfgrE s.v.* θωρήσσω). This brief allusion to the instructions creates the impression that Thetis' command is being circumvented and that Achilleus is being ordered to join battle against Hektor (cf. Achilleus' reaction at 188); Iris' speeches (170 f., 198 f.) also clarify only gradually how Achilleus is supposed to keep the corpse from being captured by the Trojans, namely by simply appearing at the ditch (REINHARDT 1961, 167 f.).

166 ποδήνεμος ὠκέα Ἶρις: a VE formula (9× *Il.*, 1× *h.Ap.*); on the variants of the VE formula, ποδήνεμος ('with feet quick as the wind') and the form ὠκέα (shortening of the diphthong in internal hiatus), 2.786n., 24.77n. (*s.v.* ἀελλόπος).

167 = 11.715. — **ἄγγελος ἦλθε:** 2n. — **θωρήσσεσθαι:** inf. as a command after ἄγγελος ἦλθε, which takes the place of a verb of speaking (SCHW. 2.374; cf. 24.118n.), cf. the imperatival formulations of the direct speech at 170 f., 178, 198; similar renderings in indirect and direct speech at 4.301 ff., 20.365 ff., 23.204 f., 23.854 ff. (DE JONG [1987] 2004, 117, 270 n. 47).

168 2nd VH ≈ 1.195. — **Zeus ... Hera:** In Homeric epic, Iris is usually a messenger from Zeus, and she is sent by Hera only here (3.121n.; *LfgrE s.v.* Ἶρις); at 1.195 ff., Hera similarly guides Achilleus' actions in an indirect manner (there via Athene) onto the right track (on the relationship Hera – Achilleus, 19.407–417n.). – Zeus had prohibited the gods from intervening in the battle in any manner under threat of punishment (8.7 ff.) and had, via the divine messenger, guaranteed Hektor victory on this day until sunset (11.185–194, 11.200–209; cf. the revelation of his plan to Hera at 8.473–476, 15.61–77); even after Patroklos' death, he continued to support the Trojans from his seat on Mt. Ida (17.206, 17.593–596), while at the same time wishing for the rescue of the body (17.268 ff., cf. 17.545 f., 17.645–650). Against this background, the narrator has Hera act in favor of the Achaians, at first secretly but soon openly (cf. 239 f. and Zeus' rebuke at 356 ff.). The secrecy of the instructions, also mentioned by Iris

---

166 ὠκέα (F)ἶρις: on the prosody, R 4.3.
168 κρύβδα (+ gen.): 'hidden from ...'. — πρὸ ... ἧκε: on the so-called tmesis, R 20.2. — μιν: = αὐτήν (R 14.1). — Ἥρη: on the -η after -ρ-, R 2.

(184–186), perhaps contributes to the characterization of Hera as well: malice (cf. 19.97n.) or mistrust toward her spouse (EDWARDS *ad loc.* and 1987, 273 f.; SCHADEWALDT [1938] 1966, 116 f.).

169 ἀγχοῦ δ' ἱσταμένη: an inflectable VB formula (18× *Il.*, 6× *Od.*, 2× *h.Cer.*), always with a verb of speaking in the 2nd VH; often used, as here, in element 5 of the type-scene 'delivery of a message' (2.172n.). — **ἔπεα πτερόεντα προσηύδα:** 72n.

170–180 The messenger speech is characterized by urgent haste in view of the circumstances: Iris begins and ends with an emotional appeal (170–171a / 178–180), which she justifies via a description of the situation (171b–177; cf. esp. 173–176 with 151–158a, 165). Contrary to his first impulse (90 ff., 114 f.), Achilleus' principal aim is supposed to be protecting Patroklos (171, 178b–179) rather than revenge. But the lack of certain information (the identity of the individual who sent the instructions – contrast 2.26n. – a concrete course of action) necessitates clarification (181–195n.): DE JONG (1987) 2004, 75, 79, 181; on the lack of a specified sender, cf. 6.269–278n.

170 ≈ 1.146. — **son of Peleus:** 166–167n.; he is also termed 'most terrifying' (*ekpaglótatos*, literally 'before whom one should be the most terrified': 1.146n.). The rationale for this address is revealed in the instructions that follow at 199, and this is in fact the effect Achilleus' appearance will have (218, 222–231). An appeal to no longer mourn passively is perhaps also implied, see esp. 178 (LEAF; EDWARDS; CERRI; *LfgrE s.v.* ἔκπαγλος).

ὄρσεο: This request is made regardless of whether the addressee is standing, sitting or lying down; the stress is on the haste with which the action is to be performed (*LfgrE s.v.* ὄρνυμι 799 f.54 ff.; on the formation and orthography, 19.139n.). — **Πηλεΐδη:** 166n.

171 Πατρόκλῳ ἐπάμυνον: ἐπαμύνω 'come to help' is used with a dat. of person (see 99) or absolutely; only ἀμύνομαι 'fight for' is used with a gen. (here a *v.l.*) (sometimes with περί), see 173 (LEAF). (ἐπ)αμύνω is a common catchword in battle paraeneses (FINGERLE 1939, 125). — **εἵνεκα:** on the metrical lengthening, 1.174n. — **φύλοπις αἰνή:** an inflectable VE formula (nom./acc.; in total 11× *Il.*, 1× *Od.*, 2× Hes., 1× *h.Hom.*); on φύλοπις and its epithets, 6.1n.

172 VE = 11.530 VB. — **in front of the ships:** 150n.

ἕστηκε: 'is underway', see 153 ff.; ἵσταμαι is used with an abstract subject only rarely (e.g. at 13.333 νεῖκος): *LfgrE s.v.* ἵστημαι 1241.42 f. — **οἳ δ(έ):** anticipatory demonstrative (G 99): the reference is to the Trojans and Achaians, who at 173–175 are divided into οἳ

---

169 ἱσταμένη (Ϝ)έπεα: on the prosody, R 4.4; on the uncontracted form ἔπεα, R 6.
170 ὄρσεο: thematic aor. imper. of ὄρνυμαι 'rouse oneself, set out'; on the uncontracted form, R 6.
171 Πατρόκλῳ ἐπάμυνον: 'Hurry to Patroklos' aid!'; on the hiatus, R 5.6.

μὲν ἀμυνόμενοι ... and οἳ δὲ ...| ... ἐπιθύουσι, with Τρῶες in apposition and a change in the construction. — **ὀλέκουσιν**: 'destroy'; the κ-present of ὄλλυμι stresses a successful execution of the action (1.10n.).

173 νέκυος ... τεθνηῶτος: pleonasm in accord with the pl. version νεκύων κατατεθνηώτων (VE formula: 3× *Il.*, 5× *Od.*): *LfgrE s.v.* νέκυς. On the form τεθνηῶτος, G 95, CHANTR. 1.430 f.

174 2nd VH = 3.305 (see *ad loc.*), 8.499, 12.115, 13.724, 23.64; ≈ 23.297, 'Hes.' *fr.* 136.8 M.-W. (restored), *h.Ven.* 280. — **ἠνεμόεσσαν**: on the use and etymology of this geographical epithet ('windy', related to ἄνεμος), 2.606n., 3.305n.

175a ἐπιθύουσι: a compound from ἰθύω (in addition to the present passage, also *Od.* 16.297, *h.Merc.* 475) meaning 'push forward, advance', with inf. 'be intent on' (*LfgrE*).

175b–177 Iris skillfully directs attention to Hektor, who is Achilleus' prime target (cf. 90 ff., 114 f.). The disfigurement of enemy corpses is a common practice and is threatened or carried out via a number of variants, with severing the head also at 11.145–147, 11.259–261, 13.202–205, 14.496–500, 17.39 (24.22n. with bibliography; EDWARDS on 176–177; DE JONG on *Il.* 22.337–354). In regard to Patroklos, the narrator lists a variety of supposed plans by Hektor: at 16.836, to leave him to the vultures (see *ad loc.*), at 17.125–127, to decapitate him and throw him to the dogs (in contrast, see Glaukos' suggestion at 17.159–163); the fact that Iris here insinuates more drastic intentions (tertiary focalization[P]: DE JONG [1987] 2004, 169 f.) serves, together with 178–180, to stir up Achilleus (cf. his own announcements at 333 ff. and 22.335 f.): SEGAL 1971, 22–25; ANDERSEN 1990, 31; MORRISON 1992, 84 f. and 141 n. 33, 142 n. 47; on Ancient Near Eastern parallels for the display of (parts of) bodies, GRIFFIN 1980, 45 f.; WEST 1997, 388.

In contrast to the main tradition, Zenodotus' text (HT 10) at VE of 174 had αἰπὺ θέλοντες, 175 was missing and 176 f. were placed after 155 (narrator-text, with μεμαώς rather than μέμονα) (schol. A on 174; see also EDWARDS on 155–156 and RENGAKOS 1993, 62 f.), which would deprive Iris' speech of its urgency (see above).

175b φαίδιμος Ἕκτωρ: 155n.

176 1st VH ≈ 156. — **μέμονεν**: 156n. — **θυμὸς ἄνωγεν**: 89b–90n.

177 VE = 13.202; ≈ 3.371. — **πῆξαι ἀνά ...**: 'impale on ...': aor. of πήγνυμι 'fasten' (*LfgrE*); ἀνά with dat. (locative) denotes a position of rest, 'at the top of' (SCHW. 2.441). — **σκολόπεσσι**: a term, used only in the pl., for the stakes used as defensive fortifications

---

173 νέκυος πέρι: = περὶ νέκυος (R 20.2). — τεθνηῶτος: = τεθνεῶτος (↑).
174 δὲ (ϝ)ερύσσασθαι: on the prosody, R 4.3; on the -σσ-, R 9.1. — προτὶ (ϝ)ίλιον: on the prosody, R 5.4. — προτί: = πρός (R 20.1). — ἠνεμόεσσαν: initial syllable metrically lengthened (R 10.1; ↑).
176 ἐλκέμεναι: 156n. — δέ (ϝ)ε: on the prosody, R 4.3. — ἑ: = αὐτόν (R 14.1). — ἄνωγεν: perf. with present sense, 'orders, bids'.

in combination with a wall, elsewhere in the *Iliad* only of the fortification of the encampment of ships (7.441, 8.343, etc.), at *Od.* 7.45 of the city of the Phaiakians (IAKOVIDES 1977, 218 f.); some scholars connect the present passage with the fortifications of the city of Troy ('palisades': AH; LEAF; cf. LATACZ [2001] 2004, 28 f.), others also posit a poetic plural (*LfgrE s.v.* σκόλο(ψ)). — **ἁπαλῆς:** 'delicate' in the sense 'vulnerable' (19.285n.); its position next to ταμόνθ' stresses the savagery of the act.

178 VB = 6.331, 9.247, *Od.* 18.13. — **Up, then ...:** Achilleus will obey this order at 203; on lying down as a signal of his psychological pain (see 27) and inactivity (cf. also 461), 2.688n., 19.4–6a n. (cf. the paraenesis at Callinus *fr.* 1 West). — **shame:** The noun *sébas*, a *hapax*[P] in the *Iliad*, and verbs derived from it are synonymous with *aidós/aidéomai*, both terms designating a consideration for social norms and an aversion to criticism, cf. at 180 *lôbē* 'shame, ignominy' (6.167n., 6.442n.); in Menelaos' appeal to the Achaians at 17.254 f., the same warning is introduced by the verb *nemesizésthō* ('one shall disapprove'); on this word family, 3.156n., 24.463n.). In both the *Odyssey* (5× in a formula in the 2nd VH) and the Homeric hymns, *sébas* is a term for reverent wonder in encounters with a human being or divine apparition (*LfgrE*).

ἀλλ(ά): On ἀλλά with the imper., 134n. — **ἄνα, μηδ' ἔτι κεῖσο:** a rhetorical polar expression[P] with the adv. ἄνα employed as an imperative ('Up!'; on this, SCHW. 2.421, 424) and the imper. of κεῖμαι (on the form, SCHW. 1.668, 679; CHANTR. 1.474 f.) with μηδ' ἔτι ('and lie no more': SCHW. 2.564): TZAMALI 1997, 133. — **σέβας ... ἱκέσθω:** 64n.

179 = 17.255; 2.VH ≈ 13.233. — **dogs:** On this macabre image, 1.5n.; the motif of fear that a corpse might become prey for dogs is present from the beginning of the *Iliad*, see 1.4n., 2.393n., 24.22n.; RICHARDSON on *Il.* 22.41–42; DE JONG on *Il.* 22.337–354; on this motif in reference to Patroklos, cf. the appeals at 17.254 f. and 17.556–559, as well as 175b–177n.; in reference to the Trojans, see Polydamas' warning at 271.

μέλπηθρα: a deverbative from μέλπω ('sing, dance'), with a suffix denoting an instrument, means or location (RISCH 41, 43); in early epic only in the *Iliad*, of slain warriors left to the dogs (see *iterata*). This is perhaps based on a notion of 'playthings' in reference to ball games, with the dogs scrapping over the corpse (cf. 17.558 κύνες ἑλκήσουσιν) (LASER 1987, 90; different interpretations: notion of a dancing chorus of dogs surrounding the body parts ['«occasions» or «instruments for choral performance»']: *LfgrE*). In any case, this is a highly pathetic paraphrase for the otherwise usual terms ἑλώρια/ἕλωρ (1.4, *Od.* 24.292), κύρμα (*Il.* 17.272, *Od.* 15.480) or ἕλωρ καὶ κύρμα (*Od.* 3.271, 5.473).

---

178 μηδ(έ): in Homer, connective μηδέ also occurs after affirmative clauses (R 24.8.). — σε θυμόν: acc. of the whole and the part (R 19.1.). — ἱκέσθω: 3rd pers. imper.
179 Πάτροκλον ... γενέσθαι: acc./inf. construction dependent on σέβας ('have shame lest ...'). — Τρῳῆσι: on the declension, R 11.1.

180 Disfigurement of the corpse would prevent an appropriate burial (19.26n., 24.22n.).

λώβη: 'shame', i.e. loss of τιμή (1.232n., 19.208n.; on the semantic field 'shame' in battle appeals, STOEVESANDT 2004, 301 f. with n. 900). — **ᾐσχυμμένος:** 'disfigured'; αἰσχύνω of a corpse also at 22.75, 24.418, with ἀεικίζω used elsewhere (19.26n., 24.22n.); on the form, CHANTR. 1.422 and 433. — **αἴ κεν ... ἔλθῃ:** is variously interpreted: (1) the most likely meaning 'when the corpse ... returns', i.e. 'is brought back', cf. 17.161/163 (AH; FAESI; WILLCOCK; CERRI; *LfgrE s.v.* ἐλθεῖν 538.75 f. and cf. *s.v.* νέκυς); (2) 'when the corpse ... departs' (Eust. 1137.2: ἔστι δὲ τὸ ἔλθοι ἀντὶ τοῦ ἀπέλθοι γλυκέως καὶ ἀφελῶς ἐπὶ νεκροῦ ὡσεὶ καὶ ἐμψύχου φρασθέν); (3) 'when he ... joins the dead', with νέκῦς as an acc. pl. (< *-υνς: CHANTR. 1.221 f.; LEAF with reference to 15.251 [where however νέκυας καὶ δῶμ' Ἀΐδαο]; VAN LEEUWEN; SCHNAUFER 1970, 149 f.; cf. EDWARDS: 'The last interpretation gives the best meaning [so Leaf], the second is the most natural'; on the arrival of slain warriors in the underworld, see BREMMER 1983, 83 f.). — Syntax and context support interpretation (1) as well as understanding the form νέκῦς as nom. sing. (as at *Il.* 22.386, 23.160, 23.190), i.e. as a reference to Patroklos, rather than as acc. pl. (on the morphology of νέκῦς, MARTÍNEZ GARCÍA 1996, 108–129, 245–248; *contra* BEEKES/CUYPERS 2003, 485–488): (a) elsewhere in early epic, νέκῦς as acc. pl. is syntactically unequivocally identifiable as an obj. (with predicate in the 3rd pers. pl.: 7.420, *Od.* 24.417; νέκυας occurs more frequently: 5× *Il.*, 4× *Od.*); (b) from Patroklos' death to the present passage, the term νέκυς is always used to signify his body (*Il.* 17.121, 127, etc., then esp. 724, 735, 746, 18.20, 152, 173 [in total 9× acc., 3× gen.]), likewise with sing. forms of νεκρός (13× acc., 3× gen., 1× dat.; see esp. 158, 164); (c) the objective of the speech, namely to prevent Achilleus from dallying, fits best with interpretation (1): Iris suggests that the body can be retrieved, and at 178b–180 combines the threat of disfigurement of the deceased with a loss of honor to Achilleus in order to urge him on to immediate action; once the corpse is mutilated, visible to all, Achilleus will be the subject of criticism by the Achaians and shame, cf. the similar appeal to Menelaos at 17.556 ff. (CERRI; SEGAL 1971, 24 f.). The importance of intactness for burial is also illustrated in the case of Hektor's body, which Achilleus carefully makes right for its return (24.582 ff.).

181–195 A character[P] usually executes an order immediately and without objection (1.345n., 2.182–183n.), if sometimes reluctantly, e.g. at 1.201 ff. (Achilleus with Athene), *Od.* 5.116 ff. (Kalypso with Hermes). Although Achilleus is prepared to intervene in battle (cf. double motivation[P] and 1.55n.), he is held back by both the loss of his armor and Thetis' prohibition (188 ff. with repetition of isolated words from 130 ff.). He thus demands to know that the messenger

---

180 σοὶ λώβη: *sc.* ἔσται. — λώβη, αἴ: on the hiatus, R 5.6. — αἴ κέν: ≈ ἐάν (R 22.1, R 24.5). — τι: acc. of respect, 'in some regard, somehow' (R 19.1). — ᾐσχυμμένος: 'disfigured', perf. pass. part. of αἰσχύνω.

is legitimate and will only obey the orders once a concrete course of action is articulated (203 ff.).

181 ≈ 1.121 (see *ad loc.*). — Within this dialogue, the narrator changes the formulae of reply, cf. 183/196 (τὸν δ' αὖτε προσέειπε), 187 (τὴν δ' ἀπαμειβόμενος προσέφη): cf. FRIEDRICH 2007, 69 ff.; on the use of the different formulae, 1.121n., 24.372n.; on the VE formula ποδάρκης δῖος Ἀχιλλεύς (21× *Il.*), the etymology of the epithet ποδάρκης and formulae for 'swift-footed Achilleus', 1.121n., 24.668n.

182 VB = 15.206 (Poseidon to Iris). — On Achilleus' short speeches, see EDWARDS on 20.428–429: 'When upset, Akhilleus is often sparing with words', cf. 1.216–218, 20.425–427, 20.429, 21.150 f., 23.707/753, 24.139 f. (a list of one-verse speeches in *Il.* and *Od.* in DE JONG on *Od.* 7.342). — **Divine Iris:** In contrast to other mortals, Achilleus the demi-god is able to recognize gods immediately upon their appearance, without them having to introduce themselves (cf. 1.199 f. [see *ad loc.*], 22.15 after a deception [21.599 ff.]): TURKELTAUB 2007, 69–71 with n. 68.

τίς ταρ: 'who then?', cf. 6n.

183 = 196; 1st VH = 94 (see *ad loc.*); 2nd VH = 166 (see *ad loc.*).

184–186 The information supplied at 168 (see *ad loc.*) by the narrator[P] is repeated and expanded on in reverse sequence, since it is significant to the character[P] (for additional examples, 6.386–389n.). On the character plane, the intimate, seemingly conspiratorial comment at 185 f. supports the call to action: Hera considers rapid action sufficiently important to risk bypassing Zeus (cf. schol. bT on 185).

184 2nd VH = Hes. *Th.* 328; ≈ *Od.* 11.580; VE ≈ *Od.* 15.26. — **Διὸς κυδρὴ παράκοιτις:** a replacement for the formulae for Hera that are elsewhere common in this verse position (θεὰ λευκώλενος Ἥρη / βοῶπις πότνια Ἥρη: 1.55n., 1.551n.), leaving the goddess' name emphasized at VB (FRIEDRICH 2007, 97). — **κυδρή:** 'venerable', an epithet of goddesses (sometimes in the superlative; in total 4× Hera, 2× Leto, 2× Demeter, 2× Athene, 1× each Persephone, Dike, Hekate); on the etymology and meaning, cf. κύδιστος at 1.122n. — **παράκοιτις:** 'she who shares the bed, wife'; on the formation of the word, cf. 3.138n. (ἄκοιτις).

185 **ὑψίζυγος:** an epithet of Zeus, always used in the same verse position and constituting a formula before caesura C 2 in combination with Κρονίδης (3× *Il.*, 2× Hes.), *Il.* 4.166, Hes. *Op.* 18, 'Hes.' *fr.* 343.9 M.-W.) before VE αἰθέρι ναίων. Semantically obscure: the second element (ζυγόν literally 'yoke') means either 'rowing bench', as in other compounds (likewise the pl. ζυγά at *Od.* 9.99, 13.21), in which case it refers to Zeus' elevated position,

---

183 προσέειπε: = προσεῖπε. — ὠκέα (ϝ)ἶρις: 166n.
184 προέηκε: aor. of προΐημι 'send (out, forth)' (ἕηκα is a by-form of ἧκα).
185 οὐδ' οἶδε: on the elision, R 4.6 (in contrast, cf. 192n.); on οὐδέ after an affirmative clause, R 24.8. — Κρονίδης: 'son of Kronos' = Zeus.

i.e. 'who sits on the topmost thwart, who steers the ship' or rather 'who sits high above, who sits enthroned' (cf. *Il.* 20.155; also WEST 1997, 114 with reference to Ancient Near Eastern expressions for the supreme god, 'who sits on high'), or 'balance beam, balance arm', although this meaning is attested only in post-Homeric texts ('who holds aloft the scales'); for discussion for/against and bibliography, *LfgrE s.v.* — **οὐδέ τις ἄλλος:** an inflectable VE formula (m./f.: 4× *Il.*, 9× *Od.*, 1× *h.Cer.*); here it stresses the conspiratorial element.

186 Olympos: on the snow-capped peaks of Olympos and the abode of the gods, 1.18n.

οἳ Ὄλυμπον ... ἀμφινέμονται: cf. the shorter VE formula οἳ Ὄλυμπον ἔχουσι(ν), 24.427n. — **ἀγάννιφον:** 'thickly covered with snow', an epithet of Olympos (cf. νιφόεις at 616, *h.Hom.* 15.7, 5× Hes. *Th.*); a compound comprised of intensive ἀγα- + *(σ)νίφος (1.420n.; G 16); for a collection of all the epithets of the place, *LfgrE s.v.* Ὄλυμπος 670.64 ff.

187 = 1.215, 24.138; ≈ 9× *Il.* (on this, 1.84n.); on the 1st VH, 24.64n., on the 2nd VH, 24.138n.

188 πῶς ταρ: 6n. — **μῶλον:** 'battle', frequently in combination with ἄρηος (134n.), without the addition also at 17.397, *Od.* 18.233, 'Hes.' *Sc.* 257. — **ἐκεῖνοι:** sc. the opponents; points to 'things not under the control of the speaker, thus things farther away' (transl.) (SCHW. 2.208).

189 μήτηρ ... φίλη: Forms of μήτηρ and φίλη ('my mother') elsewhere usually occur adjoining one another (1.351, 1.572, 1.585, 9.555, 21.276, *Od.* 2.88, 2.373, 15.127, *h.Ven.* 115, Hes. *Th.* 932), similarly separated only at *Od.* 21.103; on the separation, 1.20n. (παῖδα ... φίλην). The striking word order and metrical structure of the verse – all spondees except for the 2nd metron, a rare phenomenon in Homeric epic (4× *Il.*, 1× *Od.*: DEE 2004, 489) – lend weight to both the prohibition and the authority behind it; see also 216.

190 ≈ 135 (see *ad loc.*).

191 στεῦτο: an athematic epic verb, only in the 3rd pers. sing., frequently in combination with the fut. inf.; it means 'makes/made clear that', here in reference to the conversation with Thetis 'she promised that' (LEAF; *LfgrE s.v.* στεῦται). — **Ἡφαίστοιο πάρ' οἰσέμεν:** The main tradition shows an unusual structure with the metrical caesurae A 3, B 2 and C 2, with caesura B 2 bridged rhetorically by the phrase Ἡφαίστοιο πάρ' (cf. M 6 n. 10; 4.97 is similar) – hence the *v.l.* with the unique compound παροίσεμεν (LEAF; WILLCOCK;

---

186 ἀθανάτων: initial syllable metrically lengthened (R 10.1).

187 πόδας: acc. of respect (R 19.1).

188 τεύχε' ἐκεῖνοι: on the hiatus, R 5.1; on the uncontracted form, R 6.

189 πρίν: adv., but in 190 a conjunction ('earlier ..., | before').

190 ὀφθαλμοῖσιν: on the declension, R 11.2. — ἴδωμαι: prospective subjunc., in Homer also without a modal particle (R 21.1); on the middle, R 23.

191 Ἡφαίστοιο πάρ(α): = παρ' Ἡφαίστου (R 11.2, R 20.1). — οἰσέμεν: fut. inf. of φέρω; on the form, R 16.4.

EDWARDS) – but accords with Thetis' statement at 137 (cf. FAESI). – **ἔντεα καλά:** a formulaic phrase in various verse positions (130–131n.).

192–195 Ancient interpreters sought a rational basis for explaining Achilleus' inability to wear Patroklos' armor, e.g. his build (schol. bT, A on 192; cf. AH), but his statement can be explained on narratological grounds: it provides a *post hoc* justification for new armor, especially a set made by divine hands, that is equivalent to what Hektor will be wearing in their duel (EDWARDS).

192 ἄλλου δ᾽ οὔ τεο οἶδα τέο … δύω: Although the contents of the verse are clear, there are difficulties in syntax and transmission (WEST 2001, 247 f.; on the gen. τεο, G 84): (1) the gen. ἄλλου … τεο can be explained as attraction of the case to τέο (inverse attraction: AH; FAESI; EDWARDS; WILLCOCK; differently LEAF: dependent on οἶδα; undecided, CHANTR. 2.292); (2) the interrogative pronoun τέο is variously interpreted: (a) it is used instead of an expected relative pronoun ('I know no other whose armor…'): AH; EDWARDS; MONTEIL 1963, 5 f.; post-Homeric examples for this usage in K.-G. 2.517 f.; SCHW. 2.644; (b) it introduces an indirect question, in which case the indefinite pronoun τεο would be redundant ('I do not know who else's arms …'): WILLCOCK; *LfgrE s.v.* οἶδα 542.29 ff. and 544.4 f.; (c) it introduces a direct rather than an indirect question ('I know not – whose arms can I wear?'): LEAF; there may be a contamination of (a) and (b): WEST *loc. cit.* 247; on the closeness of a relative clause and a dependent interrogative clause, see SCHW. 2.643; CHANTR. 2.167, 238, 293; MONTEIL 1963, 72 f.; (3) the modal particle ἄν transmitted in the manuscripts (see *app. crit.*) is athetized by several editors since it is unusual in deliberative questions (BECHTEL in ROBERT 1901, 345; VAN LEEUWEN; WEST *loc. cit.* 248. – **κλυτὰ τεύχεα:** a common phrase, e.g. as a formula after caesura C 1 (10× *Il.*, 1× *Od.*, 4× 'Hes.' *Sc.*: 19.10n.); on τεύχεα/ἔντεα, 130–131n.

193 Aias: Telamon's son Aias is considered the second best Achaian warrior after Achilleus, and is the 'bastion of the Achaians' (CH 3; 2.557n., 2.768n. with bibliography, 6.5n., 16.102–123n.). The shield is the characteristic element of his armor (11.526 f., cf. Soph. *Ai.* 19, 574 ff.), which Aias also uses to protect Patroklos' body (17.132 ff., cf. 17.746 ff.). According to the description at 7.219–224, it consists of seven layers of cow hide (Greek *heptabóeios*) and an eighth layer of metal and appears to be otherwise exceptional as well, since its shape and size were already highlighted repeatedly (7.219 = 11.485 = 17.128 'tower-like'; cf. 7.245, 7.266, 8.267–272, 13.709–711): *LfgrE s.v.* σάκος; KIRK on 7.219–223; JANKO on 13.159–161.

σάκος: with reference to Aias' 'tower-like' (see above) shield always in the meaning, perhaps original, 'long shield'; the term ἀσπίς, sometimes used synonymously with σάκος, is never applied to Aias' shield (TRÜMPY 1950, 30; on the two terms, 458n.). –

---

192 τεο … τέο: = τινός … τίνος (R 14.2.; on the syntax, ↑). – τεο (ϝ)οἶδα: on the prosody, R 4.3.
193 μὴ Αἴαντος: on the hiatus, R 5.7. – Τελαμωνιάδαο: on the declension, R 11.1.

Τελαμωνιάδαο: a variant of the patronymic in the gen. (VE 7× *Il.*, 1× *Od.*, of which 7× with Αἴαντος before caesura B 1), cf. the VE formula Τελαμώνιος Αἴας (2.528n.; on the formation of the patronymic, RISCH 148).

194 foremost: on the warriors in the front row of the fighting, 3.16–17n.

ἔλπομ(αι): parenthetical only here, 'I think, I assume' (for which οἴω/οἴομαι is used elsewhere); here it probably carries the additional connotation 'hope', as often elsewhere as well (*LfgrE*). — **ἐνὶ πρώτοισιν ὁμιλεῖ:** a variant of the variable formula ἐνὶ/ μετὰ πρώτοισι + form of μάχεσθαι (6× *Il.*); in military contexts, ὁμιλεῖ denotes contact with the enemy in massed combat (*LfgrE*; TRÜMPY 1950, 146 f.; LATACZ 1977, 229).

195 2nd VH = 8.476, 17.120, 17.182; ≈ 24.16, etc. (see *ad loc.*). — **περί:** 'around' in a metaphorical sense (of a prize being fought over *vel sim.*), likewise at 3.137, 15.416, 17.120 f., 17.182, 18.265, 23.659 (K.-G. 1.493; SCHW. 2.502; CHANTR. 2.128).

196 = 183; 1st VH = 94 (see *ad loc.*); 2nd VH = 166 (see *ad loc.*).

197 1st VH = 8.32, 8.463. — **we also know well:** an emphatic speech introduction with which the speaker recognizes the legitimacy of an objection while at the same time preparing a rejoinder, see 198 f. 'But ...' (cf. 19.421n.); on the conversational tone of the present scene, 166–202n.

νυ: 'indeed' (19.95–96n.). — **κλυτὰ τεύχε(α):** 192n. — **ἔχονται:** passive, 'be held (back)' (130–131n.), i.e. with the result that others possess it, see 188 (cf. catch-word technique[P]).

198–199 199 to 200 Τρῶες ≈ 11.799 f., 16.41 f.; 2nd VH from 199 to 200 Τρῶες = 14.78 f. — An echo of the description of earlier events on the same day (STR 21 Fig. 1): after the Achaian leaders were wounded, Patroklos followed Nestor's advice and asked Achilleus that he, Patroklos, enter battle wearing Achilleus' armor in order to terrorize the Trojans and provide relief to the Achaians (16.38–45). Now Achilleus is supposed to achieve the same results by facing the enemy without armor. The desired result will follow, see 222 ff., 246 ff. (cf. Achilleus' impact in his new armor at 20.44 ff., 22.131 ff.). — **ditch:** dug around the encampment of ships in addition to a wall (150n.; 16.369n.).

αὔτως: 'thus (as you are)', i.e. without armor (*LfgrE s.v.* 1683.6 ff.; BONIFAZI 2012, 286 n. 55). — **φάνηθι:** 'Show yourself!'; a form of the imper. pass. in -ηθι attested only here in Homeric epic (SCHW. 1.758, 800). — **αἴ κε:** 143n. — **ὑποδδείσαντες:** 'becoming scared';

---

194 καὶ αὐτὸς ὅ: 'he himself', i.e. 'he for his part' (anaphoric demonstrative ὅ: R 17). — ἔλπομ(αι): on the elision, R 5.1. — ἐνί: = ἐν (R 20.1).
195 δηϊόων: absolute, 'rage murderously, cause a bloodbath'; on the epic diectasis, R 8.
196 = 183 (see *ad loc.*).
197 ἴδμεν: = ἴσμεν. — ὅ: = ὅτι 'that' (cf. R 22.3). — τοι: = σοι (R 14.1). — ἔχονται: in Homeric Greek, a neut. pl. subj. can take a pl. predicate.
199 αἰ: = εἰ (R 22.1). — κε: = ἄν (R 24.5). — ὑποδδείσαντες: < ὑποδ(ϝ)είσαντες, on the prosody, R 4.5. — ἀπόσχωνται (+ gen.): 'desist from, leave off'.

ὑπό amplifies the ingressive aspect of the aor. (CHANTR. 2.138; on the form, G 24). — **πολέμοιο**: 64n.

200–201 = 11.800–801, 16.42–43. — These verses, not transmitted by all manuscripts in the present passage, are probably to be considered a concordance interpolation on the basis of the context (AH; LEAF; APTHORP 1996, 141–144; WEST 2001, 13 with n. 31; *contra* EDWARDS: would constitute an unusually short speech), since the focus of the scene (165 ff.) is solely on rescuing the body (165–167, 171, 178 f., 194 f.; see also 231b ff.); detailed discussion of the manuscripts and papyri in APTHORP *loc. cit.* 144–148. – For issues of content (breathing pause, gnomic expression) and language (including 'sons of the Achaians'), 16.42–43n.

202 = 8.425, 11.210, 24.188; ≈ 5.133, *Od.* 1.319, 6.41, 15.43, 15.454. – **ἣ ...:** on the verse structure, 146n. – **ἣ μὲν ἄρ᾿ ὣς εἰποῦσ(α):** a variable VB formula (8× *Il.*, 4× *Od.*). – **πόδας ὠκέα ῏Ιρις:** a VE formula (9× *Il.*, 1× Hes.); cf. 166n.

203–221 Achilleus' first appearance before the Trojans in the *Iliad* is designed in a particularly effective manner and resembles the epiphany of a god, especially the similar appearance of Apollo in support of the Trojans at 15.307–322. Because of the divine support for Achilleus in terms of both his equipment (203–206) and his battle cry, the Trojans are so terrified that their fear persists even after the battle is over (222–229, 247 f.); the corpse is rescued (231–236): LORD (1967) 1994, 188 f.; BREMER 1976, 80 f.; SCHEIN 1984, 138; BIERL 2004, 49; CONSTANTINIDOU 2010, 98 f.; cf. 203–204n., 205–206n.; on the terrifying effect of epiphanies, see RICHARDSON on *h.Cer.* 188–90; GRIFFIN 1980, 151–156. A similarly effective appearance before the enemy is reported of Gilgamesh (WEST 1997, 340; SZLEZÁK 2004, 20; additional parallels in Ancient Near Eastern and I-E literature in NAGLER 1974, 140 n. 15; GRIFFIN *loc. cit.* 38 f.; CLARKE 2006, 263 f.). – The narrator illustrates the effects of the appearance via two similes[P] that, like the gathering of Achaian troops in Book 2 (2.455–458/459–466, see nn.), are designed to convey both optical and acoustic impressions (on the linking of multiple similes in general, see 2.144–149n., 2.455–483n.). Particular weight is put on fire and gleaming (206, 211, 214, 225–227), with the narrator using the jet of fire at 206 to provide a variation on the more common motif of the gleam of weapons (KRISCHER 1971, 38; cf. 6.513n., 19.374–383n.), and this emphasis is adapted to representing Achilleus' appearance as an epiphany

---

200 υἱες: on the declension, R 12.3.
201 τειρόμενοι · ὀλίγη: on the hiatus, R 5.6. — τ(ε): 'epic τε' (R 24.11).
202 ἥ: anaphoric demonstrative (R 17), in apposition to ὠκέα ῏Ιρις. — εἰποῦσ(α): on the elision, R 5.1. — πόδας: acc. of respect (R 19.1). — ὠκέα (ϝ)ῖρις: on the prosody, R 4.3.

(205–206n.); in this way, the narrator unfolds a series of light phenomena that accompany Achilleus' presence from this point until Hektor's death (citations at 19.17n.), while the description of the overwhelming effect of gleam and battle cry is used to prepare the moment at which Achilleus, equipped with his new armor, will enter battle together with the Achaians (19.362 ff., 19.397 ff.): EDWARDS on 203–206 and 219–221; GRIFFIN *loc. cit.* 37 f.; BONNAFÉ 1984, 35–37; SCHEIN 1984, 137 f. On the motif of the besieged city found in both similes, and on possible associations with Troy, see 207–227n., 219–221n. – The overall sequence shows similarities with the theme[P] 'return of a warrior to battle' (FENIK 1968, 22 f.): (**1**) the warrior joins battle (215 f.: only at the ditch), (**2**) simile (207–214, 219–221, (**4**) a strong reaction by the opposing side (218, 222–229); element 3 (killing enemies) is varied (230 f.), since Achilleus is unarmed.

203–204 rose up: Achilleus' rising, announced already in the Catalogue of Ships at 2.694 and also mentioned by Hektor (305) and Zeus (357–258a) in what follows, initiates his renewed engagement in battle and thus the turning point of the action of the *Iliad*: like a trumpet blast (219), his cry (217) acts as a prelude to the coming *furioso*, and after a night of mourning his dead friend (354 f., 19.4–6), he can barely be restrained from his lust for battle when he sees his new armor (19.12 ff.) (2.694n.; KURZ 1966, 41 f. and 76 f.). — **Athene:** Athene, who supports the Achaian side (CG 8), as does Hera, frequently acts in conjunction with the latter (1.195n.) and appears on multiple occasions as Achilleus' protectress (19.342n.). But her intervention here occurs unexpectedly and unprepared for (cf. 185 f.): whether she has been briefed by Hera or rushes to help due to her own observations is left open by the narrator (perhaps to avoid distracting from events surrounding Achilleus: EDWARDS on 203–206; ERBSE 1986, 145; on divine intervention in general, 1.43–52n.). — **aegis:** The function and appearance vary depending on context; it frequently appears as a type of shield or protective cloak, fringed with tassels (2.446b–454n. with bibliography, 2.447–449n., 2.448n., 24.20n.). Usually worn by Zeus (cf. 1.202n.), but occasionally also by Athene and Apollo (KEIL 1998, 97 with n. 11), it allows a deity to instill courage (e.g. Athene in the Achaians at 2.446 ff.) or cause fear in a warring party (e.g. Apollo in the Achaians on Zeus' orders at 15.229 f./320 ff., Zeus in the Achaians at 17.593 ff., likewise Athene in the suitors at *Od.* 22.297 ff.). Only in the present passage is it donned by a living mortal, on the one hand for protection (cf. also *Il.* 24.20: Patroklos' body), on the other hand in order to lend a preternatural air to his appearance (CERRI; HEATH 2005, 126).

---

203 αὐτάρ: 'but' (R 24.2). — ὦρτο: root aor. of ὄρνυμαι 'rise'.
204 ἰφθίμοισι: on the declension, R 11.2. — βάλ(ε): on the unaugmented form, R 16.1.

αὐτὰρ Ἀχιλλεύς: a VB formula (5× *Il.*), also a VE formula (17× *Il.*); on the use of this phrase, 24.3n. — διΐφιλος: a generic epithet[P] (17× *Il.*), always between caesurae B 2 and C 2 (1.74n.); on the meaning ('beloved to Zeus') and formation of the initial element διῒ- (I-E dat. in *-ei*), see 24.472n. — ἀμφὶ ... | ὤμοις ἰφθίμοισι βάλ(ε): an echo of arming scenes, with integral enjambment[P] and separation of the formula ἀμφὶ δ' ἄρ' ὤμοισιν βάλετ(ο) (6× *Il.*), cf. 2.45n. and esp. 5.738 (Athene arms for battle); this adapts the phrase to the particular situation (Athene arms Achilleus). In early epic, ἴφθιμος ('powerful, strong') is an epithet of creatures and their body parts, commonly the head (EDWARDS on 203–206; cf. 1.3n.). — αἰγίδα θυσανόεσσαν: a VE formula (5× *Il.*); θυσανόεις ('fitted with tassels') is a distinctive epithet[P] with αἰγίς (*LfgrE*).

205–206 a golden cloud: The trait 'golden' is characteristic of items belonging to the gods; thus e.g. the embellishments of the aegis, or the aegis itself, are golden (2.448n., 24.21n.; on gold and the gods in I-E literature, see WEST 2007, 153 f.). Clouds are elsewhere employed by the gods to impede others' vision, for protection on the battlefield or to confuse fighters (cf. esp. Apollo's appearance at 15.308 and JANKO on 15.308–311; for additional examples, see *LfgrE* s.vv. νέφος, νεφέλη) and, on Olympos, to conceal events (golden clouds: 13.523, 14.343 f./350 f. [14.343n.], *h.Ap.* 98). Here the golden cloud, draped about the hero's head like a kind of nimbus, creates a terrifying aura. — **flame:** In a similar manner, Athene supports Diomedes when he departs for battle at the beginning of Book 5 by making flames blaze from his helmet, shield and armor (the two passages are also designed in a linguistically analogous manner by virtue of a framing verb 'let burn' [Greek *dáie*] at 206/227 and 5.4/7 and a simile at 207–214 and 5.5 f.), although in Achilleus' case, since he has no armor of his own at the moment, the flames emanate from his body: DI BENEDETTO (1994) 1998, 226; on the relationship Achilleus – Diomedes, 6.96–101n.; on I-E parallels for a flame emanating from the hero's body, WEST 2007, 456, 463; on light and radiance as signs of an epiphany, RICHARDSON on *h.Cer.* 188–90; BIERL 2004, 51 with n. 31; cf. 203–221n. – In the case of other heroes, fighting power is characterized via comparisons or similes involving fire, cf. 154n., 2.455–458n., 19.374–383n.

ἀμφὶ ... νέφος ἔστεφε: The cloud prompts an association with a kind of casing for the head in the manner of a supernatural helmet, while ἔστεφε evokes a wreath (*LfgrE* s.vv. νέφος, στέφω). — δῖα θεάων: a VE formula used to describe various goddesses

---

205 ἀμφὶ ... ἔστεφε: 'she wrapped around ...'. — δέ (ϝ)οι: on the prosody, R 4.3. — οἱ κεφαλῇ: σχῆμα καθ᾽ ὅλον καὶ κατὰ μέρος, here in the dat. (R 19.1); οἱ = αὐτῷ (R 14.1). — θεάων: on the declension, R 11.1, cf. R 6.
206 δαῖε: transitive impf. 'let burn, blaze continuously'. — παμφανόωσαν: on the epic diectasis, R 8.

(19.6b n.). – **ἐκ δ' αὐτοῦ:** probably 'from him', i.e. from his head, cf. 214 and 225–227 (AH; VAN LEEUWEN; LEAF; EDWARDS; BREMER 1976, 79 f.), rather than 'from it', i.e. the cloud (schol. AT; WILLCOCK). As in the description of Diomedes, the body part and the casing appear as one to the onlooker observing from a distance, cf. 5.4 *vs.* 5.7. – **φλόγα παμφανόωσαν:** likewise at 21.349; cf. 144n.

207–227 Two similes[P] – both against the background of a besieged city – illustrate the effects of Achilleus' appearance before the enemy (203–221n.): the first (207–214: a signal fire) conveys the optical impression of the flames and golden cloud, the second (219–221: war trumpet) the acoustic impression of his battle cries. The description of the observations occurs in reverse order vis-à-vis the description of the phenomena (cf. 'continuity of thought' principle[P]): (A) visual matters, originating with Athene (205–214); (B) acoustic matters, originating with Achilleus with Athene's support (217–221); (B') 'they heard' (222–224); (A') 'they saw', with reference to Athene (225–227): cf. *LfgrE s.v.* ὀπός II. The motif of the besieged city here may evoke various associations: (a) with the encampment of ships besieged by the Trojans, which is to be freed from the pressure of the siege with Achilleus' help (LYNN-GEORGE 1988, 221 f.); (b) with beleaguered Troy, the existence of which is once again in acute danger, now that Achilleus has appeared, cf. Polydamas' advice in the Trojan assembly that follows at 254–266 (EDWARDS on 207–214; WHITMAN 1958, 137; MOULTON 1977, 106 f., 111; HUBBARD 1981, 60; on the various similes that involve fire and take their starting point from a city, and on their links to Troy, see EDWARDS on 17.736–741; GRETHLEIN 2006, 265–267). But based on the Achaian situation, there might also be a change in perspective between the first (optical) and second (acoustic) simile: 207 ff. a signal for the Trojans: Achilleus as support in defending the encampment of ships (cf. 207–214n.); 219 ff. a signal for the Achaians: Achilleus supporting the attack (cf. 219–221n.; MOULTON *loc. cit.* 107 n. 51). – That the image of the simile derives from the same sphere as the context – as is the case with the two present similes – is comparatively rare; additional examples at 7.208–210 and 13.298–303 (warriors departing for battle are compared to Ares and Phobos), 14.147–152 (Poseidon's battle cry is as loud as that of nine or ten thousand men), 16.589–592 (Trojans retreat a distance equal to a spear throw): 14.147–152n. with bibliography.

207–214 The first simile[P] addresses the flame above Achilleus' head and sketches the image of an island where signal fires directed at neighboring areas are lit during a defensive battle; the beacons are visible day and night due to the columns of smoke and radiating light and are meant to summon help from afar (LEAF on 207; EDWARDS on 207; FRÄNKEL 1921, 50, 52 n. 1). This fire simile illustrates the narrative via associations that touch on a variety of issues (EDWARDS on 207–214; GRAZ 1965, 197 f.; ELLIGER 1975, 101 f.): (1) it stresses that the phenomenon is visible from afar (VE 207/214, VB 208, 212 f.); (2) the smoke and the beacons are an expression of hope for support on the part of the besieged; the simile thus underlines that the Achaians now, with Achilleus' appearance – in contrast to previously (100 ff.) – can expect support in the guise of a 'defender against evil' (213) (cf. the fire simile at 19.375–380 [see *ad loc.*]); (3) fire signals also imply danger for the attackers: in the simile, from those who were summoned to reinforce the besieged; in the actual situation, probably as a manifestation of Achilleus' destructiveness and fighting prowess (WHITMAN 1958, 137 f.; GRAZ *loc. cit.* 199, 265; SCOTT 1974, 114); (4) the indications of time 'the whole day' and 'with the setting of the sun' (209 f.) might reflect the length of the eventful third day of battle at 11.1–18.242 (EDWARDS; cf. FRÄNKEL *loc. cit.* 99; on the course of this day, 239–242n.).

207–212 ὡς δ᾽ ὅτε ... ἵκηται | ..., τὴν δήϊοι ἀμφιμάχωνται, | οἳ δὲ ... κρίνωνται ... | ..., ἅμα δ᾽ ἠελίῳ καταδύντι | ... φλεγέθουσιν ... | γίνεται: In Homeric similes in which the 'as' part consists of several clauses (with changes of subject), as here, a transition from hypotaxis (with subjunc.) to parataxis (with ind.) frequently occurs: 2.147–148n.; EDWARDS, Introd. 38; CHANTR. 2.355 f.

207 ≈ 21.522. — The smoke (*kapnós*) comes from the signal fires (210–211n.), the shining of which is widely visible at sunset; during the day, the rising smoke in particular is visible from afar (LEAF; WILLCOCK on 210–212; CERRI on 207–214).

ὡς δ᾽ ὅτε: a common introduction to similes (VB formula: 21× *Il.*, 9× *Od.*), with the ind. or, as here, the subjunc. (2.147–148n.; on the subjunc., RUIJGH 630–634; CHANTR. 2.253). — αἰθέρ᾽ ἵκηται: a variable VE formula (19.379n.); in Homer, αἰθήρ denotes the sky as the sphere of wind and clouds (2.412n.).

208 far away: seen from the point of view of an observer who perceives the smoke from across the sea (cf. 212 f.): AH.

τηλόθεν: 'from afar' (*LfgrE*). — δήϊοι: substantive 'enemies'; on the disputed basic meaning ('hostile, destructive' or 'burning, blazing'?), 2.415n. — ἀμφιμάχωνται: 20–21n.

209 ≈ 2.385; 1st VH = 1.472, *Od.* 3.486, 15.184. — οἳ δὲ ... κρίνωνται: thus WEST and others, following Heyne, for an indication of change of subject (the reference is to the defenders of the city) rather than the transmitted relative clause οἵ τε (see *app. crit.*); ἄστεος ἐκ σφετέρου (210) means 'out of their city' (AH; LEAF; CHANTR. 2.355 f.; in contrast, with

---

207–209 ὡς δ᾽ ὅτε ... ἵκηται | ... | ... κρίνωνται: In generalizing (iterative) comparative and temporal clauses in Homer, the subjunc. commonly occurs by itself (cf. R 21.1).

207 ἄστεος: = ἄστεως.

208 τήν: with the function of a relative pronoun (R 14.5). — δήϊοι ἀμφιμάχωνται: on the so-called correption, R 5.5.

209 οἵ: on the demonstrative function of ὅ, ἥ, τό, R 17. — πανημέριοι: The Greek adj. is to be rendered adverbially in English: 'the whole day long'. — ἄρηϊ: on the declension, R 12.4.

no change of subject: Schw. 2.463 and Chantr. 2.99: 'far from their city'). The sentence structure is rendered even clearer with the *v.l.* κρίνονται preferred by some editors (ind.: transition to parataxis). — **στυγερῷ:** 'horrifying, loathsome'; an epithet with words denoting battle, death, etc. (2.385n.; *LfgrE*); on negative epithets with terms for battle, 6.1n. — **κρίνωνται ἄρηϊ:** 'engage in battle'; κρίνεσθαι contains a notion of separation and qualitative differentiation; ἄρηϊ can be understood as either a locative or an instrumental dat. (2.385n.; on the metonymic use of Ἄρης/ἄρης, 134n.).

210–211 signal | fires (Greek *pyrsói*): i.e. beacons to transmit information (*LfgrE* s.v. πυρσ(ός)); cf. Sinon's fire signal for the Achaians to take Troy by storm (*Il. parv. fr.* 14 West; *Il. Pers.*, Proclus *Chrest.* § 2 West) or the spread of the news that Troy fell (at Aesch. *Ag.* 281 ff.); on the transmission of news in antiquity by means of fires, see Diels (1914) 1924, 77 ff.; *KlP* s.v. Nachrichtenwesen; *BNP* s.v. Telegraphy.

210 2nd VH = 1.592, 19.207, *Od.* 16.366. — **ἡελίῳ καταδύντι:** an inflectable VE formula (ἅμα δ' + dat., ἐς + acc.: in total 6× *Il.*, 10× *Od.*, 1× Hes. *Th.*, 1× *h.Merc.*).

211 τε ... δ(έ): used in place of τε ... τε, it here shifts the emphasis somewhat to the second part, cf. 5.359, 9.519, 23.277 (Ruijgh 205 with n. 114; cf. K.-G. 2.244; Denniston 513 with n. 2). — **φλεγέθουσιν:** 'flare (up), burn' (cf. φλόγα at 206), an expansion of φλέγω, here in order to produce a metrically suitable form (G 60; *LfgrE*; on the suffix -εθ-, 2.303–304n.). — **ἐπήτριμοι:** literally 'in rows, in succession' (on the etymology, 19.226n.), here perhaps rather 'close together' (of a chronological succession, AH).

212 a four-word verse (122–123n.). — **γίνεται:** to be linked with ὑψόσε ('upward'), i.e. approximately 'spreads upward, rises' (AH; *LfgrE* s.v. γίγνομαι 150.67 ff.; on the form γίνεται, West 2001, 248). — **περικτιόνεσσιν ἰδέσθαι:** 'for those living in the surrounding areas to see', i.e. 'so that those living in the surrounding areas could see it' (on περικτιόνεσσιν, 19.104n.).

213 αἴ κέν πως: 'in the hope that'; elsewhere always in direct speech (6× *Il.*), here conveying the hope of the defenders mentioned in the simile (Wakker 1994, 366 n. 3). — **ἀρῆς ἀλκτῆρες:** 100n.

214 ≈ 19.379. — **σέλας:** Like αὐγή (211), this denotes the glow of the fire, but perhaps stresses the divine origin of that glow somewhat more, cf. 8.75 f., 19.374/379, *Od.* 18.353–355,

---

210 σφετέρου, ἅμα: on the hiatus, R 5.6. σφέτερος is the possessive pronoun of the 3rd pers. pl. — ἠελίῳ: = ἡλίῳ.
211 τε: 'epic τε' (R 24.11).
212 γίνεται: = γίγνεται. — ἀΐσσουσα: 'moving swiftly', from ἀΐσσω. — περικτιόνεσσιν: on the declension, R 11.3. — ἰδέσθαι: on the middle, R 23.
213 αἰ: = εἰ (R 22.1). — κεν: = ἄν (R 24.5). — νηυσίν: on the declension, R 12.1.
214 Ἀχιλλῆος: on the declension, R 11.3, R 3. — ἵκανεν: on the unaugmented form (short ἵ-), R 16.1.

Hes. *Th.* 867, *h.Cer.* 189 (GRAZ 1965, 311 f. ['religious connotation' (transl.)]; CIANI 1974, 15 f.; cf. *DELG s.v.* σέλας). — **αἰθέρ' ἵκανεν:** 207n.

215 wall ... ditch: in the space between wall and ditch, cf. 8.213 f., 9.66 f., 9.87 (HAINSWORTH on *Il.* 9.67; MANNSPERGER 1995, 346 f., 349; 1998, 294; cf. 198–199n.).

στῆ ... ἰών: picked up again by 217 ἔνθα στάς, stressing movement and thus Achilleus' action; contrast ἧμαι (104).

216 mother: At 134 f., Thetis gave him an unequivocal order not to join the fighting, a ban he also reported to Iris (189 f.).

πυκινὴν ... ἐφετμήν: ἐφετμή (related to ἐφίεμαι) means 'orders, command'; combined with an epithet only here: πυκινός (literally 'dense, compact'; on the metaphorical use with mental processes, 2.55n.) here has the connotation either 'prudent, deliberate' or ('compressed' →) 'massive' (*LfgrE s.v.* 1632.49 ff. and 1633.9). — **ὠπίζετ(ο):** a verb derived from ὄπις ('gaze') and meaning 'have in mind, take into consideration, heed'; almost always used in reference to deities (FRISK, *DELG*, BEEKES *s.v.* ὄπις; BURKERT [1981] 2001, 100 f.).

217–218 1st VH of 217 ≈ 5.784 (Hera), 11.10 (Eris); 2nd VH of 218 ≈ 10.523. — **shouted ... | ... gave cry:** Although Achilleus' cry is amplified by Athene, in what follows the narrator only mentions Achilleus when stressing the superhuman intensity of his voice or illustrating its effects on the enemy (219–223a, 228 f., esp. VE 221/222, 228); nothing comparable is said about Hektor's battle cries at 159 f. – The loudest human voice in the *Iliad* is that of Stentor, in whose guise Hera drives the Achaians into battle (5.784–786, see KIRK *ad loc.*). Gods also produce battle cries elsewhere to spur men on or scare them off: 11.10–12 Eris, 14.147 ff. Poseidon, 15.321 f. Apollo, 20.48–55 Athene and Ares; 5.859 ff. is different: Ares' cry at being wounded (WILLE 2001, 28; cf. 14.147–152n.).

ἤϋσ(ε): like ἴαχε (cf. 160, 228), frequently denotes the loud war cries of a warrior in battle (*LfgrE s.v.* (ἀύω), αὔω). — **Παλλὰς Ἀθήνη:** a VE formula (23× *Il.*, 18× *Od.*, 4× Hes., 1× *Cypr.*); on the disputed interpretation of Παλλάς, 1.200n. — **φθέγξατ(ο):** 'made a noise, made their presence known (by calling)' (*LfgrE*). The cries of gods are generally louder than those of human beings (KRAPP 1964, 136 ff.). — **κυδοιμόν:** denotes the chaos and confusion of the masses in battle when panic takes hold of them (TRÜMPY 1950, 158 f.;

215–216 ἐπὶ τάφρον: to be taken with στῆ. — τείχεος: on the uncontracted form, R 6. — οὐδ(έ): In Homer, connective οὐδέ also occurs after affirmative clauses (R 24.8). — ἐς: = εἰς (R 20.1). — ἐς ... | μίσγετο: 'intermingled ...'.
217 ἀπάτερθε: 'separately, apart, by oneself'.
218 ἀτάρ: 'but' (R 24.2), likewise 223. — Τρώεσσιν ἐν: = ἐν Τρώεσσιν (R 20.2). — ὧρσε: Achilleus is the subj.

KAIMIO 1977, 33: 'noisy confusion and tumult'). This is described repeatedly in what follows: 223a, 225a, 229–231a (see nn.).

219–221 The second simile[P], which involves war trumpets, underlines the over-powering volume of Achilleus' battle cry on the battlefield, in much the same way that the intensity of Stentor's voice (5.786) and the shouting by Ares and Poseidon (5.860 f., 14.148–151a) are illustrated by a comparison (on the repetition in the simile of words from the context [219/221, likewise at 207/214], EDWARDS, Introd. 27 f. and 31; on similes for volume, KAIMIO 1977, 90 ff.). In the present simile of a trumpet sounding during the siege of a city (219n.), who the signal originates from is not stated explicitly (on the wording, 220n.): (a) the defenders of the besieged city, as a variation of the fire signals in the simile at 207 ff.? (AH; WILLCOCK; FRÄNKEL 1921, 50; KRAPP 1964, 338 n. 2); or (b) the besiegers, as a signal for attack, with a change of emphasis from defense (fire: signalling for outside help) to attack? (EDWARDS on 220; CERRI; MOULTON 1977, 107 n. 51; cf. 207–227n.); in both cases, an association of the besieged city with Troy suggests itself. It is evident that (1) the image characterizes Achilleus' battle cry, which is meant to stand in for his attack and affects the enemies accordingly: human beings and animals interpret the cry as a signal of danger (222–224 [222n.], 228 f.); (2) on the planes of both simile and narrative, the acoustic signal initiates a new phase in battle, cf. 230 ff. and the Trojan debate at 254 ff. (EDWARDS on 222; WILAMOWITZ 1916, 168 f.; KRAPP 1964, 337 ff.).

219 1st VH ≈ 221. — **trumpet** (Greek *sálpinx*): No musical instruments are mentioned in Homeric battle descriptions in the context of the transmission of signals; communication on the battlefield takes place via shouting (cf. 2.408n., 16.76–78). In early epic, the *sálpinx*, a kind of trumpet, occurs only in the present simile, as well as indirectly in the description of the noise at the beginning of the battle of gods at 21.388, where the cognate verb is used metaphorically (*esálpinxen ... ouranós*: 'the heaven trumpeted'; cf. RICHARDSON *ad loc.*); at the same time, the *sálpinx* is mentioned repeatedly in post-Homeric literature as an instrument for signalling (e.g. Aesch. *Eum.* 567 f., Xen. *Anab.* 4.4.22), while in pictorial representations, it occurs in black-figure vase paintings (*BNP s.v.* Musical instruments; WEST 1992, 118–121; LANDELS 1999, 78–81; HOLMES 2008; on early attestations of trumpet-like wind instruments in the Mediterranean, see also SHEAR 2000, 221 f. n. 10). The lack of signalling instruments in battle descriptions in the Homeric epics is explained by some scholars as the result of the narrator's penchant for archaizing (schol. A, T, b, D; LEAF; EDWARDS on 219–221; KRAPP 1964, 57 f.; WEGNER 1968, 18 f.; WILLE 2001, 46–48).

---

219 τ(ε): 'epic τε' (R 24.11). — φωνή, ὅτε: on the hiatus, R 5.6.

ὡς δ' ὅτ': a common introduction to similes (207n.), here with ellipsis of the verb γίγνεται, see 221; similarly 2.394 f. (see *ad loc.*; EDWARDS; differently AH, CERRI: indef. ὀτέ). — **ἀριζήλη:** a determinative compound meaning 'very clearly' (RISCH 107, 213, 216); used in early epic only here (and at 221) of a sound, in order to characterize the volume (222, but cf. *Od.* 12.453 ἀριζήλως εἰρημένα 'things said clearly'), elsewhere of sight. It frequently denotes a phenomenon that suggests a divine presence or causes a premonition; cf. 224b (KAIMIO 1977, 34 f.). — **φωνή, ... ἴαχε:** a description of the trumpet signal, with the term for '(human) voice' or the sounds produced by an animal (φωνή is used metaphorically of a musical instrument only here: *LfgrE* s.v.) in combination with ἴαχε 'shouted' (cf. 160, 228); the latter is to be understood as a gnomic aor. (LEAF; RUIJGH 490 n. 5; on the form, 29n.).

220 2nd VH = 16.591 (athetized by WEST). — **ἄστυ περιπλομένων δηίων ὕπο:** The formulation has called for discussion on several grounds: (1) περιπλομένων: the aor. part. of περιπέλομαι is used only here in early epic in reference to persons (+ acc.: 'move around something'), elsewhere it is intransitive as part of an inflectable VE formula with ἐνιαυτός (6× early epic). In addition, its connection to the prepositional expression δηίων ὕπο is unusual (*LfgrE* s.v. περιπέλομαι; LEAF; WILLCOCK; EDWARDS thus suggests connecting ἄστυ περιπλομένων as an attribute with σάλπιγξ ['the trumpet of those surrounding a city']). (2) Who the trumpet signal originates from is unclear (LEAF; cf. also 219–221n.): perhaps from the surrounding enemies ('ἴαχε ὑπό is sounded *by* the besiegers'; thus EDWARDS; CERRI on 219–221; MOULTON 1977, 107 with n. 51; cf. FAESI) rather than from the besieged ('ὕπο, *by reason of* death-dealing foe-men'; thus AH, cf. AH on *Od.* 19.48 [ὑπό 'of concomitant or contributory causes' (transl.)] and AH, *Anh.* 5; WILLCOCK; KRAPP 1964, 338 n. 2; cf. WILAMOWITZ 1916, 168 f. n. 3; on ὑπό meaning 'under the influence of', SCHW. 2.528 f.). – On δηίων, 208n. — **θυμοραϊστέων:** used only in the *Iliad* and otherwise only in the formula θάνατος χύτο θυμοραϊστής (13.544, 16.414/580); a compound from θυμός 'breath of life, life force' (cf. *LfgrE* s.v. θυμός 1080 f.) and the *nomen agentis* of ῥαίω 'smash, destroy' with a more recent formation in -της (on the older formations with a concrete meaning, cf. 476–477n.), i.e. 'destroying life' (*LfgrE* s.v.; cf. θυμοφθόρος 6.169n.).

221 1st VH ≈ 219. — **Aiakides:** Aiakos, son of Zeus, is the father of Peleus and grandfather of Achilleus (CH 2; cf. 166–167n.).

Αἰακίδαο: 16× *Il.*, 2× *Od.* at VE (3× *Il.* before caesura B 2); a metrical-prosodic variant of Πηλεΐωνος in 226 (cf. 1.1n., 2.860n.; FRIEDRICH 2007, 129).

222–229 The battle cry and spurt of fire startle and terrify the enemy, causing their attack on the Achaians to end abruptly (cf. 148b–150): the horses balk (223b–224), and warriors and charioteers panic (225a, 229), with fatal conse-

---

220 δηίων ὕπο: = ὑπὸ δηίων (R 20.2). — θυμοραϊστέων: on the synizesis, R 7.
221 ἀριζήλη φωνὴ γένετ(ο): ἀριζήλη predicative, with γένετο as copula ('rang out, resounded'). — Αἰακίδαο: on the declension, R 11.1.

quences (230 f.). On the connection of horse and warrior in I-E literature, see WEST 2007, 465, 467 f. – The motif 'three times X, three times Y' (228 f., cf. 155–158) initiates the return to the battle description (cf. 155n.).

222 heard: signals secondary focalization[P] (DE JONG [1987] 2004, 127): not only do the Trojans and their horses hear the cry, they understand its significance, cf. 223 f., 229 (*LfgrE s.v.* ἄϊον). — **brazen voice:** The metal elsewhere used especially for weapons (cf. 130–131n.) here metaphorically represents strength and hardness (cf. 2.490 with n.), much like the characterization 'bronze-voiced' (Stentor at 5.785, the dog Kerberos at Hes. *Th.* 311). It thus initially indicates the piercing intensity of Achilleus' cry – especially after the image of the trumpet – which continues unabated, cf. 225 f. 'the unflagging fire' above his head (KRAPP 1964, 22: 'powerful intensity' [transl.]; FORD 1992, 193 f.). In addition, the metaphor allows his cry to be associated with having the effect of a weapon (HEATH 2005, 125: 'his voice is not that of a man, but of a weapon'; *LfgrE s.v.* χάλκε(ι)ος and cf. *s.v.* σάλπιγξ; on the battle cry of I-E heroes, GRIFFIN 1980, 39 with n. 98; WEST 2007, 457).

ὄπα: 'voice'; a root noun with the deduced nom. *ὄψ or *ὤψ, cf. Latin *vōx* (*LfgrE s.v.* ὀπός II with bibliography).

223 1st VH = 5.29, 16.280. — The same terms (*orínthē thymós*) describe the effect of Diomedes' attack, which is supported by Athene, and Patroklos' appearance in Achilleus' armor (see *iterata*). *orínō* means 'move, agitate', e.g. concretely of masses of water, secondarily also to describe an emotion that presages an action: the panic of human beings and animals, triggered by visual as well as acoustic signals, leads to unthinking flight (2.142n., 3.395n.; *LfgrE s.v.* ὀρίνω; on *thymós*, 4–5n.). The description often mentions – as here – that 'all' so affected are seized by it (2.143n.).

ὀρίνθη θυμός: elsewhere formulated with the active in formulaic phrases with θυμὸν ὀριν- (3.395n., 24.467n.). — καλλίτριχες ἵπποι: an inflectable VE formula (nom./acc. pl.: 11× *Il.*, 3× *Od.*, 1× *h.Hom.*, 1× 'Hes.'); on horse epithets, 2.383n.

224 The horses stop pursuing the Achaians without the charioteers taking any action. – There is no horse-riding in Homeric epic, only driving two-wheeled chariots used in battle especially for flight and pursuit (2.384n., 24.14n. [both with bibliography]; BUCHHOLZ 2010, 29–38; RAAFLAUB 2011, 18–20, 24). —

---

222 οἳ δ(έ): refers to the Trojans, anaphoric (R 17) with Τρώεσσιν 218. — ἄϊον (ϝ)όπα: on the prosody, R 4.5. — χάλκεον: here two-termination, refers to the fem. ὄπα.
224 ἄψ: 'back'. — τρόπεον: frequentative of τρέπω; on the uncontracted form, R 6. — τρόπεον(ν), ὄσσοντο: on the prosody, M 4.6; but cf. M 8 (caesura).

their hearts saw: an authorial interpretation of the events just mentioned (on which, RICHARDSON 1990, 148 f. [collection of examples, 235]).

ὄχεα: *plurale tantum* for 'chariot', τὸ ὄχος is literally 'the thing that drives', from the same root as Latin *vehere*, Engl. *wagon* (*LfgrE s.v.* ὄχεα); additional terms for 'war chariot': 2.775b n. (ἅρμα), 6.232n. (ἵπποι), 3.262n. (δίφρος). — **ὄσσοντο:** In contrast to ἴδον at 225, the word means 'see in the mind's eye', of evil prospects 'foresee' (here of animal sensitivity), and can be clarified by the addition of θυμῷ ('internally, mentally'), as here (*Od.* 18.154, Hes. *Th.* 551, cf. (προτι)ὄσσετο θυμός *Od.* 10.374, 14.219: *LfgrE*).

225 ἡνίοχοι: literally 'holder of reins', a term for charioteers (19.401n.). — **ἔκπληγεν:** The compound ἐκ-πλήσσω ('strike out of') is only used in a metaphorical sense of the expulsion of the φρένες due to sudden, violent confusion, thus at 13.394 and 16.403 ἐκ ... πλήγη φρένας (16.403–404a n.: 'he was robbed of his wits [from fright]', likewise of the charioteer); in the present passage it is elliptical (without φρένας) 'they lost control (from fright)' (post-Homeric ἐκπλήττομαι 'be given a fright') and implies that they were no longer able to respond adequately (*LfgrE s.v.* πλήσσω 1293.6 ff.; on the form πλήγ-, ALLAN 2003, 134). — **ἀκάματον πῦρ:** a VE formula (7× *Il.*, 2× *Od.*), prosodic variant of θεσπιδαὲς πῦρ; ἀκάματος is an epithet of both πῦρ and certain body parts (16.122–123n.).

226 2nd VH = 17.214, 19.75. — **δεινόν:** to be taken adverbially with δαιόμενον in 227 (AH; WILLCOCK; EDWARDS: 'more effective'; *LfgrE*; GRAZ 1965, 166) or (more likely) as a runover word with πῦρ at 225 (EDWARDS: 'more natural in Homeric style'). — **μεγαθύμου Πηλεΐωνος:** Whether the use of the epithet μεγάθυμος ('with great passion, high-spirited') beside 223 f. (θυμός/θυμῷ) lends a bit more weight to the mention of Achilleus (EDWARDS; cf. 19.75n.) – in contrast to the VE formula Πηληϊάδεω Ἀχιλῆος (on which, 1.1n.) – cannot be decided (FOR 39). On the patronymic, 221n.

227 δαιόμενον· ... **ἔδαιε** ... **Ἀθήνη:** Cf. 206. Word repetition for the purpose of explaining or complementing a participial statement is a common epic stylistic feature (cf. 19.376n.); the intransitive mid.-pass. is frequently followed, as here, by an active formulation with the agent specified (JANKUHN 1969, 109 f.). — **θεὰ γλαυκῶπις Ἀθήνη:** On the VE formula and the distinctive epithet (likely 'with bright/shining eyes'), 1.206n.

228 Three times: 155n.

μέγαλ' ἴαχε: 29n. — **δῖος Ἀχιλλεύς:** a VE formula (55× *Il.*); the generic epithet[P] δῖος is 'an expression of the greatest excellence' (1.7n., 1.141n.).

229 2nd VH = 6.227; ≈ 3.451, 11.220, 17.14. — **ἐκυκήθησαν:** κυκάω denotes the mixing of liquids, metaphorically in battle the arising of disorder and great confusion among humans and animals (11.129, 20.489: horses can no longer be guided): *LfgrE* ('be thrown

---

225 ἔκπληγεν: = ἐξεπλάγησαν (R 16.2). — ἐπεὶ (ϝ)ίδον: on the prosody, R 4.4; on the unaugmented form, R 16.1. — ἀκάματον: initial syllable metrically lengthened (R 10.1).
227 ἔδαιε: 206n. — θεά: on the form, R 2.2.

into confusion'). – **κλειτοί τ' ἐπίκουροι:** an inflectable VE formula (7× *Il.*, 1× Hes.); in combination with Τρῶες it serves to denote the Trojan party (6.111n., 6.227n.).

230–231a perished | upon their own chariots and spears: The depiction of the general confusion and panicked flight leading to fatal accidents may be imprecise and unrealistic, as some scholars have insisted since antiquity (cf. schol. A on 230–231; LEAF), but it serves primarily to illustrate the consequences of Achilleus' appearance: (1) no orderly retreat but a panic, during which the Trojans, without direct contact with the enemy, end up beneath their own chariots or run through by their own weapons when falling; (2) dead opponents, even though Achilleus, bereft of his weapons, cannot intervene directly – an amplification when compared to Patroklos' attack at the ditch in 16.372–379 (AH; WILLCOCK; EDWARDS on 228–231; *LfgrE s.v.* ὄχεα 898.51 ff.; ALBRACHT [1886] 2005, 48; VAN DER VALK 1964, 58 f.; cf. 222n.; on the description of the flight, see also 16.278–418n.). – **twelve:** a typical number[P] (LORENZ 1984; HAWKE 2008, 47, 59); groups of twelve nameless warriors who are killed or captured also occur at 10.488, 10.560, 15.746, 18.336 (likewise at 21.27, 23.22, 23.175, 23.181): WALTZ 1933, 22, 36 [collection of examples of the number twelve]; LORENZ *loc. cit.* 272; SINGOR 1991, 36; I-E parallels, WEST 2007, 481). That slain opponents remain nameless is rare in Homeric epic, and usually occurs when they are described as a group (for additional examples, PAGANI 2008, 416 n. 252).

καὶ τότ(ε): 'also then', i.e. during the chaos (229 ἐκυκήθησαν), although there was no longer any fighting, since the Achaians were taking care of the corpse (231b ff.): FAESI; LEAF. – φῶτες ἄριστοι: an inflectable VE formula (nom.: here; acc.: 6.188, *Od.* 4.530, 4.778). – ἀμφί ...: zeugma with ὀχέεσσι and ἔγχεσιν: an indication of location 'around their chariots and lances' in the sense 'at, near ...', as a description of the general chaos (somewhat differently, AH; FAESI; LEAF: the second element to be taken more concretely, in the sense of pierced by their own lances). Additional examples of zeugma with terms for 'team' and 'arms': 3.327, 5.356 (cf. the list of examples in VAN LEEUWEN on 4.282). – ὀχέεσσι: dat. pl. (G 70) of ὄχεα (224n.).

231b–238 The narrator[P] directs attention away from the chaos of the fleeing Trojans and toward the Achaians, while gradually narrowing the circle of characters[P]: starting with the Achaians laying out the corpse (231b–233a), via the mourning companions, i.e. the Myrmidons (233b–234a), to the weeping Achilleus (234b–235a) and his grief when faced with the deceased (237 f.); the focus is on the emotions of the characters (232 'gladly', 234 'mourning', 235 'letting warm tears fall', each at VB), whereas the actual process of retrieval,

---

230 δυώδεκα: a metrical variant beside δώδεκα and δυοκαίδεκα.

with the laying out and the convoy to the encampment of ships, is referred to only briefly (233 f.): EDWARDS on 231–238; DI BENEDETTO (1994) 1998, 234 f. In the description of Achilleus' first encounter with his dead friend, his lament – as was the case with the arrival of the death message (22–35a n.) – is effectively delayed: Achilleus sheds tears but remains speechless; what is shown are his thoughts, in which the pain regarding his own actions is hinted at (237 f.). The first speech of lamentation in the Achaian camp (316 ff.) is retarded[P] by the assembly scene in the Trojan camp (243–314a): EDWARDS on 237–238; DE JONG (1987) 2004, 121 f.

231b αὐτὰρ Ἀχαιοί: 148n.

232 ἀσπασίως: 'in a welcome manner, relieved' (19.72n.). – **ὕπεκ βελέων ἐρύσαντες:** picking up 151 f. in the manner of a ring-composition[P] (see *ad loc.*), and a positive conclusion to the situation that initially seemed hopeless. On the orthography of ὕπεκ (compound, accent), see WEST 1998, XVIIIf.

233 1st VH ≈ *Od.* 24.44; 2nd VH = *Il.* 23.695; ≈ 24.123. – **his own companions:** The reference is to the Myrmidons, as whose leader Patroklos entered this battle (cf. 16.268 ff.).

λεχέεσσι: dat. pl. (G 70) of λέχος 'bedstead', also 'death bed' (352), here 'bier' (cf. 236): 24.589–590n.

234 1st VH = 23.14; ≈ 13.658, *Od.* 4.17, 13.27. – **mourning:** The Greek verb *mýromai* (a term for joint mourning for a deceased person: 19.6a n.) sets off the general mourning for Patroklos, which continues in what follows throughout the so-called 'prothesis', i.e. the laying out of the corpse: 314 ff., 354 f.; on the next day, 19.4–6, 19.212 f., 23.9 ff.; on the day following, 23.109 ff. (19.5–6a n., 19.211–213a n., 24.664–667n., end).

ποδώκης ... Ἀχιλλεύς: a variation of a number of noun-epithet formulae for 'swift-footed Achilleus' at VE (similarly at 20.89): (1) formulae in the gen. (ποδώκεος Αἰακίδαο) and dat./acc. (ποδώκεϊ/-α Πηλεΐωνι/-α) – nom. ποδώκης in addition to the present passage only of Dolon (10.316) and Atalante (3× 'Hes.'); (2) the nom. formula with the distinctive epithet ποδάρκης (π. δῖος Ἀχιλλεύς 181n.): 1.121n., 2.860n., 24.458n. with bibliography, 24.668n.; cf. 78n. (on πόδας ὠκὺς Ἀ.)

235 1st VH = 17 (see *ad loc.*). – **steadfast companion:** The inflectable VE formula (Greek *pistón hetáiron*, nom./acc.: 7× *Il.*, 1× *Od.*, 1× 'Hes.') is otherwise employed in direct speech or in a speech introduction, and stresses a warrior's

---

231 σφοῖς: possessive pronoun of the 3rd person (R 14.4).
233 κάτθεσαν: = κατάθεσαν (with apocope, cf. R 20.1); on the unaugmented form, R 16.1. – λεχέεσσι: on the plural, R 18.2. – ἀμφέσταν: = ἀμφέστησαν (R 16.2).
234 μετὰ δέ σφι ... εἵπετ(ο): 'joined them'; σφι = αὐτοῖς (R 14.1).

reliability and loyalty (cf. 16.147). Aside from the speech introduction formulae (17.500, *Od.* 15.539), the formula is a periphrastic denomination[P] for slain fighters, for the deceased Patroklos also at *Il.* 17.557 and 18.460. In the present passage, its use as an acc. obj. with Greek *eíside* ('saw, spotted') is an indication that 237 f. are an expression of Achilleus' thoughts, which go through his head when he sees the body (secondary focalization[P], cf. 231b–238n., 236n.): ROISMAN 1984, 23–25, 29; *LfgrE s.v.* πιστός.

236 2nd VH = 19.283, 19.292; ≈ 19.211, 22.72. — **φέρτρῳ:** 'bier', a derivation from φέρω; it corresponds to λέχος at 233. A Homeric *hapax*[P], it is only rarely attested in post-Homeric literature (*LfgrE*; SCHW. 1.532). — **δεδαϊγμένον:** The emotionally colored verb δαΐζω ('shred') is frequently used in direct speech (in addition to the *iterata*, e.g. 2.416, 16.840, 19.203, 319, 24.393) or different types of secondary focalization[P] (as here, see 235n., 19.283) (19.203n., 24.393n., 14.20n.). — **ὀξέϊ χαλκῷ:** on the VE formula and the metonymic use of χαλκός (literally 'bronze') for 'weapon', 1.236n., 6.3n., 24.393n.

237 2nd VH = 4.297, 5.219, 9.384, 12.119; ≈ 5.794. — **with horses and chariot:** Internal analepsis[P]: Achilleus sent his friend, who as a charioteer (cf. 17.427, 17.439, 23.280) did not have his own horses and chariot at his disposal, into battle not only with his own, i.e. Achilleus', armor (16.63 ff., 16.130 ff.) but also with his own team of immortal horses (16.145 ff.); he will later reproach them for not bringing his friend back from battle (19.400–403 [see *ad loc.*]).

ἔπεμπε: impf. with the function of an aor. (confective, i.e. completed; cf. SCHW. 2.259); the impf. stresses the sustained effects of the action that will only be concluded with the attainment of its goal (VB 238) (*LfgrE* with bibliography; SCHW. 2.277).

238 never again …: implies Achilleus' pain; the contrast is with the typical motif of joy at the return of a warrior from battle (6.480–481n., 24.705n.). The narrator uses wording similar to that employed elsewhere in Book 18 by Achilleus and Thetis in reference to Achilleus' own fate (neither his mother nor his father will welcome their son home again: 59 f./440 f. Thetis, 89 f./330 f. Achilleus; cf. *Od.* 19.257 f. Penelope referring to Odysseus), thus signalling the close connection between the two friends and their respective destinies (GRETHLEIN 2006, 221 with n. 252; on the notion of dying as a failure to return home, 59b–60a n.).

νοστήσαντα: The verb νοστέω, attested in early epic only in the fut. and aor., means 'escape unscathed', often specifically 'return home' (cf. the VB formula οἴκαδε νοστήσ- 59b–60a n.), and is sometimes linked, as here, with δέχομαι ('receive') (5.157 f., 17.207 f., 18.59 f., 89 f., 330 f., 440 f., *Od.* 19.257 f.): *LfgrE s.v.* (νοστέω) νοστήσω, νοστῆσαι;

---

237 τόν: with the function of a relative pronoun (R 14.5). — ῥ': = ἄρα (R 24.1). — ἤτοι: R 24.4. — ὄχεσφιν: on the form, R 11.4.
238 ἐς: = εἰς (R 20.1). — πόλεμον(ν), οὐδ': on the prosody, M 4.6; but cf. M 8 (caesura). — οὐδ(έ): also after affirmative clauses (R 24.8); here with an adversative connotation ('but not').

MARONITIS 2004, 64–69. The part. often occurs elsewhere in the *Iliad* at VE in the formula μάχης ἐκ νοστήσαντι/-α (24.705n.); in the present passage, the enjambment[P] ἐς πόλεμον creates a kind of antithesis between VB and VE: a suspenseful link between the departure for battle (cf. 64n.) and the return, focussing in each case on Achilleus' actions.

239–242 The end of fighting on the third day of battle in the *Iliad*, which began in Book 11 with Agamemnon's *aristeia* (11.15 ff.) and led to Hektor's triumph, as Zeus promised he would have until sunset on this day (11.186–194/200–209, cf. 17.206–208); the remaining narrative until the end of Book 18 is occupied by events taking place after sunset (on the human plane: the military assembly and evening meal at 245–314a, lament at 314b–355; on the divine plane: conversation between Zeus and Hera at 356–368, Thetis visiting Hephaistos and the manufacture of the armor at 369–617; cf. 134–144n.). Of the four days of battle described in the *Iliad*, the present one – in accord with the significance of events – occupies the most space, with the narrator explicitly marking the structure of the day (11.1 f., 11.84–90, 16.777–780 [see *ad loc.*: turning point of the action], 18.241): STR 21 with fig. 1 and STR 22 fig. 2; EDWARDS on 239–242 and 314–355; LATACZ 1977, 101–110, 113; REICHEL 1990, 136 f.; RENGAKOS 1995, 10 ff.; RAAFLAUB 2005, 241–244; cf. the principle of elaborate narration[P]. What is more, the portrayal of this day of battle closes with a special version of the motif 'night concludes the fighting' (on which, 2.387n.): the end of the second day of battle also occurred at a moment auspicious for the Achaians, contrary to the will of the Trojans, who had the upper hand (8.485–488, cf. their assembly at 8.489 ff.); now Hera acts in favor of the Achaians and against the Trojans (cf. 367) by prematurely ending Hektor's day of triumph (240n.; OWEN 1946, 183 f.; SCHEIN 1984, 138 f.; cf. 168n.; on Hera's intervention in favor of the Achaians, cf. 19.407–417n.).

Linguistically, the change of scene is elaborately designed, with chiasmus in 239 (noun + epithet), 241 (subject + predicate, μέν – δέ), 242 (noun + epithet, καί), VB 242 and VE 243 (noun + epithet κρατερῆς), and with a deceleration of the narrative flow via synonyms and epithets (suggestion by FÜHRER).

239 1st VH ≈ 484, Hes. *Th.* 956, *h.Hom.* 31.7. — **ἠέλιον:** In indications of time, this denotes the heavenly body in its orbit (cf. 484, 16.777–779), esp. at sunset (210n., 241n.): CG 38; *LfgrE*. This process is located on the divine plane at 239 f. and is described from a human point of view at 241 f. (CLARKE 1999, 273 f.); in contrast to WEST, some editors therefore capitalize Ἥλιος, understanding it as a personification (thus also ERBSE 1986, 47; on the issue of so-called personification, see CG 28: 'confluence of anthropomorphic and non-anthropomorphic action ... in the space of a few lines'). — **ἀκάμαντα:** 'untiring'; an

---

239 ἠέλιον: = ἥλιον; likewise the nom. in 241.

adj. formed in the manner of a pres. act. part., comprised of α privative and a derivation of the root καμ-/καμα (cf. ἀκάματος 225 and κάματος 'fatigue, weariness'): RISCH 27, 211; FRISK and *DELG s.v.* κάμνω; a generic epithet[P] with ἠέλιος (see *iterata*, in addition 1× each of Spercheios and σῦς: *LfgrE*), here perhaps used contextually vis-à-vis 240, the forced end to the day's labors (EDWARDS on 239–242; on I-E parallels for the untiring course of the sun, see WEST 2007, 211). — **βοῶπις πότνια Ἥρη:** a noun-epithet formula in the 2nd VH (14× *Il.*, 3× *h.Ap.*); on the hiatus in the ancient VE formula π. Ἥ., 1.551n. The choice between this formula and the prosodically identical θεὰ λευκώλενος Ἥρη is perhaps contextual: β. is used in the context of 'opposition and conflict' (BECK 1986, 484, 487; THOMAS 2002, 3–7; FRIEDRICH 2007, 78 f.); on the generic epithet[P] βοῶπις (literally 'ox-eyed', interpreted as 'large-eyed'), 1.551n., 3.144n., 14.159n.).

240 The interference in the regular course of the sun is unique in the *Iliad*, and the only comparable passage is *Od.* 23.241 ff. (Athene delays dawn as a favor to Odysseus and Penelope); on the motif of the course of day and night being altered, see ERBSE 1986, 47 f.; cf. the narrative motifs THOMPSON D1546.1 ('Magic object controls sun'), D2146.1.2 ('Day magically shortened') and D2146.2.2 ('Night magically lengthened'). Elsewhere, gods intervene in battle by temporarily enveloping warriors in darkness or fog (examples in FENIK 1968, 52 f.; cf. 3.380b–381n.). – The narrator awakens the audience's attention via the forced sunset and underlines the significant aspect of this day's end: the time of Hektor's triumph has passed (239–242n.), Achilleus will be armed on the following dawn (136 f.), Hektor's life is coming to an end (EDWARDS on 239–242; OWEN 1946, 183; ROBERT 1950, 28; LOUDEN 2006, 138, 302 n. 45). — **Ocean:** a circular stream surrounding the earth (1.423n.).

νέεσθαι: means 'return home, go back', namely to where the sun usually rises again from (see *Od.* 3.1).

241–243 A hinge passage with the end of battle and the branching out of the action into the two camps: Achaians at 241b–242/314b–355, Trojans at 243–314a (239–242n.).

241 1st VH ≈ *h.Merc.* 68. — **ἠέλιος ... δῖοι Ἀχαιοί:** a chiastically structured verse with ἠέλιος placed at VB, as in 239 (see *ad loc.*); by contrast, cf. the VB formulae for 'sunset' δύσετο δ᾽/τ᾽ ἠ. (1× *Il.*, 9× *Od.*), δύη τ᾽ ἠ. (3× *Il.*) and ἦμος δ᾽ ἠέλιος κατέδυ (1× *Il.*, 6× *Od.*: 1.475n.): EDWARDS on 239–242. On the various ways of saying 'sunset' in *Il.* and *Od.*, see KELLY 2007, 349–351 and DE JONG on *Od.* 1.423. – δῖοι Ἀχαιοί is a VE formula (5× *Il.*, 2× *Od.*); on the generic epithet[P], 229n.

---

240 Ὠκεανοῖο: on the declension, R 11.2. — ἀέκοντα: < ἀϝέκοντα, = ἄκοντα. — νέεσθαι: on the uncontracted form, R 6.

242 ≈ 13.635; 1st VH = *Od.* 16.268. — a chiastically structured verse with synonym doubling of terms for 'battle' (on which, 1.492n.). — **φυλόπιδος κρατερῆς:** on φύλοπις (a term for 'fighting, battle' with largely negative connotations), 6.1n.; on κρατερός as an epithet with terms from this semantic field ('forceful, powerful'), 2.40n. – φύλοπις and πόλεμος are combined with other epithets also at 4.15, 4.82, 13.635, *Od.* 11.314, 24.475, Hes. *Op.* 161, 'Hes.' *Sc.* 23, *fr.* 195.23 M.-W., *h.Cer.* 266. — **ὁμοιΐοο πτολέμοιο:** a VE formula (6× *Il.*, 2× *Od.*); the adj. ὁμοίϊος means 'jointly' in the sense 'involving all, sparing none' and is also an epithet of γῆρας, θάνατος and νεῖκος (*LfgrE*; on the aspiration, WEST 1998, XVII). The reconstructed ancient gen. ending in -οο rather than the contraction in -ου as transmitted by all mss. allows metrical lengthening of ὁμοίϊου to be avoided (WEST *loc. cit.* XXXIIIf., but on the issue, see G 45 n. 24 and G 18; also 2.518n., 6.61n., each with bibliography; on the development of the gen. ending, see WILLI 2008, esp. 261–266).

***243–314a** After the inauspicious outcome of the battle, the Trojans deliberate about the strategy for the following day in a military assembly. Influenced by the goddess Athene, they disregard Polydamas' advice to withdraw behind the city walls and instead follow the plan of their leader Hektor to maintain their camp in the open field outside the city.*

The final Trojan military assembly described in the *Iliad*, which gathers spontaneously after the fright caused by Achilleus' appearance, and which proceeds informally in comparison to other assemblies (245–248n.). This is (a) the counterpart to the assembly of the Trojans, likewise held in the open field, which Hektor convened at the end of the last day of battle that proved successful for the Trojans, and which unanimously approved Hektor's suggestion that they spend the night outside the city (8.489–542, cf. esp. 8.530f. with 18.277 f./303 f., 8.542 with 18.310; cf. the Trojan assembly within the city at 7.345–379); (b) the equivalent of the Achaian assembly on the following morning, when the Achaians, roused from their battle-weariness by Achilleus' call, will invoke their unity and solidarity in battle under his command (19.40–277, cf. esp. 18.310 and 19.74 f.): schol. bT on 245–249; AREND 1933, 119 f.; KURZ 1966, 48; TSAGARAKIS 1982, 100–102; BANNERT 1987, 19; MACKIE 1996, 24 f.; RUZÉ 1997, 38; ELMER 2013, 139 f. In the present assembly with a speech (254–283 Polydamas [CH 9]), a speech of rebuttal (285–309 Hektor) and general agreement with the second speech (310), literal repetitions stress the core of the disagreement (catch-word technique[P]), namely where to camp and where to continue fighting on the next day (277 f. *vs.* 303 f./306); the narrator leaves no doubt about whose advice is better (253, 311–313: narrator commentary with

---

242 πτολέμοιο: on the πτ-, R 9.2.

proleptic[P] character [310–313n.]; on the parallel structure of the two speeches, 254–309n.). – Scholarly assessments of Hektor's actions in the present scene range from criticism (boundless overconfidence: SCHADEWALDT [1936] 1997, 161–164; EDWARDS) to the strongest possible defense (ERBSE [1978] 1979; PRALON 1995); for additional bibliography on the assessment of Hektor, 285–309n. On the one hand, the embedding of the scene very clearly illustrates Hektor's outsize self-confidence: it is framed by the portrayal of (a) Achilleus' mourning for his friend and his resolve to avenge him in a fight against Hektor (234–238, 316–355); (b) Thetis' efforts to procure new armor for Achilleus (128–147, 369–617); (c) Achilleus' more realistic self-assessment (101–111/115–121, 19.56–64); (d) Achilleus' openness to advice that slows down his urge to act rashly (for his own benefit: 134–137/188–201; for the benefit of the Achaians: 19.155 ff./216 ff./275; cf. Hektor's characterization at 13.726 ff.): EDWARDS on 243–314, 284–309 and 314–55; SEGAL 1971, 27 f. Scenes (a) and (b) illustrate that Hektor is deceiving himself, since he underestimates the threat emanating from Achilleus (on Hektor's tendency toward overconfidence, see 16.830–842n. and 16.837–842n.); Hektor's delusion is also shown by his disregard of the time limit set on the divine support he receives (until the end of the day: 11.206–209). In the end, he will recognize his errors (22.99 ff.: DE JONG on *Il.* 22.99–110 and *Introd.* 15). On the other hand, Hektor's perseverance in his disastrous offensive strategy is understandable, given his assessment of the situation and his self-image as the protector of Troy; it is also consistent with his code of honor: on this, see esp. 285–309n., also 249–253n. (the relationship between Hektor and Polydamas).

243 1st VH = 8.55, 11.56, 20.3; 2nd VH = 16.447 (see *ad loc.*). — As at the end of the previous day of battle (8.489 ff.), the Trojan troops remain in the plain and do not retreat to the city.

ἑτέρωθεν: 'on the other side/hand', always before caesura B 2 (28× *Il.*, 5× *Od.*, 3× Hes., 1× *h.Cer.*), commonly after a preceding personal or ethnic name (1.247a n.); it signals a change in perspective, here underlined by the chiastic arrangement of the genitives with κρατερῆς at VB 242 / VE 243 (on the 'presentational functions' of αὖτε, BONIFAZI 2012, 218–235). — **κρατερῆς ὑσμίνης**: an inflectable VE formula denoting 'battle conducted with force and fury' (2.40n.; gen.: 2× *Il.*, 16.645 in verse middle); ὑσμίνη is an archaic term for 'fight', often used, as here, synonymously with πόλεμος and φύλοψ (242); based on its etymology (related to the I-E root *Hi̯eu̯dʰ- 'be set in motion': *LIV* 225 f. n. 1), it probably originally denoted the action of fighting, the 'fray of battle' (*LfgrE s.v.*; *DELG s.v.*; TRÜMPY 1950, 162–165; LATACZ 1977, 138).

---

243 αὖθ': = αὖτε, with elision (R 5.1) and assimilation of the aspiration. — κρατερῆς: on the -η- after -ρ-, R 2; likewise for ἀγορήν in 245.

244 2nd VH = 8.402, 8.416, 24.14, *Od.* 3.478. — **χωρήσαντες:** χωρέω means 'make way, retreat', elsewhere in the *Iliad* usually of the retreat by a party under pressure from the enemy, here conditioned by the end of day (239–241) although preceded by a mass panic (222 ff., cf. 246 ff.): *LfgrE*; KURZ 1966, 146. By contrast, the previous day ended with Greek flight (8.342–347). — **ὑφ' ἅρμασιν:** The locative dat. (in the *iterata* with ζεύγνυμι [24.14n.] and γυιόω) probably occurs here in place of the metrically impossible ablatival gen. ἁρμάτων, cf. the phrase for unharnessing (λύειν) horses common elsewhere: ὑπὸ ζυγοῦ/ζυγόφιν (8.543, 24.576, *Od.* 4.39), ὑπ' ὄχεσφι (*Il.* 23.7), ἐξ ὀχέων (5.369, 776, 8.50, 13.35), ὑπὲξ ὀχέων (8.504) (EDWARDS; MONRO [1882] 1891, 182; CHANTR. 2.140; cf. SCHW. 2.525; differently AH, FAESI, LEAF: attributive with ἵππους). — **ὠκέας ἵππους:** an inflectable VE formula with correspondences in other I-E languages (3.263n.).

245–248 The narrator repeatedly characterizes this spontaneous consultation, convened by no one in particular, as an 'assembly' (Greek *agoré, agéronto* at 245 f., cf. *agoreúein, agorésato* 'speak [publicly]' at 249, 253, 310: FINGERLE 1939, 299, 302) and justifies its procedural particularities as due to the Trojans' emotional state, caused by the terrifying appearance of Achilleus (on the Homeric assembly, 1.54n., 19.40–281n., each with bibliography). The disquiet and confusion portrayed (no consideration given to eating, standing rather than sitting, shivering: EDWARDS on 246–248; GRIFFIN 1980, 14) is also reflected in the narrative flow and verse structure (rapid changes of subject, short sentences, enjambment[P], contrasts with 243 f.: BAKKER 1997, 153).

245 2nd VH ≈ 24.2, *Od.* 19.321. — **ἀγορήν:** 'assembly' or 'place of assembly' (1.54n.; RUZÉ 1997, 26), here in a *figura etymologica* with ἀγέροντο the 'assembly' in the open field (AH; CERRI; cf. 2.788n.). — **πάρος:** with an inf. (elsewhere always aor.) 'before' (*LfgrE* s.v. 992.14 ff. (with bibliography).

246–247a Participants in an assembly are usually seated (1.54n.); the deviation from the norm – justified by fear – is highlighted via the rhetorical polar expression[P] 'standing upright' *vs.* 'sitting down' and its position at VB.

ὀρθῶν ... ἑσταότων: The syntagma 'standing upright' is also attested in Indo-Iranian languages (SCHMITT 1967, 251 f.). — **οὐδέ τις ἔτλη:** a VE formula (6× *Il.*, 3× *Od.*, 1× *h.Hom.*).

247b–248 from caesura C 2 = 19.45b–46, 20.42b–43. — Achilleus' boycott of battle gave the Trojans a period of superiority, the end of which is now signalled by

244 ὠκέας: on the uncontracted form, R 6.
245 ἐς: = εἰς (R 20.1). — ἀγέροντο: (summarizing) aor. of ἀγείρομαι; on the unaugmented form, R 16.1. — δόρποιο: on the declension, R 11.2.
246 ὀρθῶν ἑσταότων: ὀρθῶν predicative with ἑσταότων (= ἑστώτων, perf. of ἵσταμαι, cf. R 6). — οὐδ(έ): in Homer, connective οὐδέ also occurs after affirmative clauses (R 24.8).
247 ἔχε: = εἶχε (R 16.1). — οὕνεκ(α): crasis for οὗ ἕνεκα (R 5.3), 'because'.
248 δηρόν: adv., 'long'.

his appearance. The indication of time 'long' (Greek *dērón*) for the duration of three days of battle (cf. 125n.) can be explained via secondary focalization[P]: these are the thoughts of the alarmed Trojans (EDWARDS on 246–248; DE JONG [1987] 2004, 112, 233, 268 n. 34; cf. 19.45b–46n. [where also on the epic motif of the returning hero]).

ἐξεφάνη· ... ἀλεγεινῆς: In the present passage, the compound ἐκ-φαίνομαι ('appear, come to the fore') – elsewhere, aside from the *iterata*, in similes concerning natural phenomena (8.557 stars, 16.299 mountain peaks; act. ἐκφαίνω 19.104 [Eileithyia] and Hes. *Th.* 689 [Zeus]) – underlines Achilleus' overwhelming, epiphany-like appearance (cf. 203–221n.); on the emphatic integral enjambment[P], as well as on μάχη having an epithet with a predominantly negative connotation, 19.45b–46n. – δηρὸν δέ: an addition joined paratactically, probably with the sense 'after he ... for a long time' (FAESI; CLASSEN [1851–1857] 1867, 23 f.; cf. CHANTR. 2.354: 'he who had ... ' (transl.); on the parataxis via δέ rather than hypotaxis, 1.10n. *s.v.* ὀλέκοντο δέ; for the scholarly debate since Nicanor [HT 15] on the punctuation [semicolon *vs.* full stop] and the related issue regarding the focalization of δηρὸν ... ἀλεγεινῆς, see NÜNLIST 2003, 65 f.; 2009, 128 f.).

249–253 Polydamas (CH 9), who makes an appearance only on the third day of battle in the *Iliad*, was already introduced as a Trojan lieutenant (11.56 f.) and as Hektor's advisor (12.60–80, 12.210–229, 13.723–747) and battle companion (14.423 ff.), and he corresponds to the type of one who offers a warning. Others of this type are (a) on the Trojan side: Antenor, a member of the council of elders (7.348 ff.: CH 9), and the seer Helenos (CH 8; 6.75–76n.); (b) on the Achaian side: Nestor (e.g. 1.254 ff., 9.93 ff.: CH 3), Odysseus (e.g. 2.183 ff., 2.278 ff., 14.95 ff., 19.155 ff., 19.216 ff.: 3.191–224n.), Achilleus' mentor Phoinix (9.434 ff.: CH 5) and the seer Kalchas (1.68 ff.: 1.69–73n.); (c) in the *Odyssey*: Halitherses and Mentor (REINHARDT 1961, 272 f.; NICOLAI 1993, 333–335; DE JONG on *Od.* 2.157–160). – Polydamas' tactical advice is heeded by Hektor to the benefit of the Trojans (12.80 ff., 13.748 ff.), but his warnings against excessive boldness toward the Achaians are rejected, as here (12.230 ff., 18.285 ff.: anticipation of scenes[P]). The present scene, containing his final appearance in the *Iliad*, shows him for the first time as a speaker in the assembly; to this end, he is introduced further between two speech introduction formulae[P] (249n., 253n.) and is legitimized as an advisor: he is Hektor's contemporary and opposite, highly qualified in consultations (on the belated introduction of characters[P], RICHARDSON 1990, 44, 215 n. 13). This marks the significance of his speech and serves to direct audience expectations: his advice is important for Hektor's future and thus Troy's fate, especially at this point – i.e. the end of the day of triumph promised Hektor (cf. 22.99 ff.): EDWARDS on 249–253; HAINSWORTH on *Il.* 12.60; DE JONG on *Il.* 22.100–103; *LfgrE s.v.* Πουλυδάμας with bibliography; SCHADEWALDT [1938] 1966, 104–109; REINHARDT 1961, 272–277; REDFIELD (1975)

1994, 143–153; Schein 1984, 183–185; Schofield (1986) 2001, 239–242; de Jong (1987) 2004, 199; Taplin 1992, 156–160; Reichel 1994, 175–182; Mackie 1996, 33 ff.; on the relationship between Polydamas and Hektor, also 251–252n.; on the parallel structure of the Hektor–Polydamas scenes, Lohmann 1970, 178–182 ('an overarching composition' [transl.]); Dickson 1995, 133–141; on the rhetorical qualities of Polydamas' speeches, Dentice 2012, 243–260; on the advisor scenes with Polydamas and Helenos, Bannert 1988, 71–81.

249 ≈ 7.347, *Od.* 22.461; 1st VH to caesura C 2 ≈ *Od.* 1.367, 15.502. — a speech introduction formula[P], usually at the beginning of assemblies (3× *Il.*, 5× *Od.*); the subject and its epithet (or appositive) is arranged around the central caesura B 1 (1.571n.). Here the direct speech only follows after the formulaic verse at 253 (see *ad loc.*); on expanded speech introduction formulae[P], 249–253n.; cf. 2.790n., 19.404n. — **First ... was:** The first speaker in an assembly is often the person who convened it (cf. Hektor at 8.489/493 ff.) or an experienced advisor (e.g. the Trojan Antenor at 7.347 ff.: CH 9): Ruzé 1997, 53. In the field, the role is occupied by Polydamas; he is introduced as the son of Panthoös (VB 250; cf. Bakker 1997, 170 f.), who, like Antenor, is a member of the Trojan council of elders, whose members no longer participate in battle due to their advanced age (3.146–151a).

πεπνυμένος: 'intelligent, clever'; part. of πέπνυμαι ('be conscious' > 'be sensible, intelligent': *LIV* 489), used as a generic epithet[P] of heralds, advisors and capable young speakers (3.148n., 24.377n.). In the present passage, there are indications that it is used contextually: (1) the additional characterization at 250, 252 f.; (2) the contrast with the neutral speech introduction at 12.60, 12.210, 13.725; (3) the use of the metrically equivalent epithet ἐγχεσπάλος in the battle situation at 14.449 (Edwards).

250 ≈ *Od.* 24.452. — The Greek figure of speech 'look forward and backward' (*hórā próssō kai opíssō*) describes Polydamas' special skill of diligently taking into consideration all relevant points, maintaining an overview, and using his experience to draw conclusions regarding future issues from circumstances as they change (see 257–265 and 268–271, as well as 12.63–66, 12.71–77, 12.217–225, 13.736–744); on the proverbial saying, 1.343n., 3.109–110n.; Edwards; *LfgrE* s.vv. ὀπίσ(σ)ω, πρόσ(σ)ω; additional bibliography in Pralon 1995, 237 f. n. 8. The addition 'alone' (Greek *óios*) identifies him as the most important Trojan analyst, comparable to the situation of Hektor, who is the 'sole' protector of

---

249 τοῖσι: 'among them' (R 19.2); on the anaphoric demonstrative function of ὅ, ἥ, τό, R 17; on the declension, R 11.2. — Πουλυδάμας: initial syllable metrically lengthened (R 10.1).
250 Πανθοΐδης: 'son of Panthoös'. — οἶος: 'alone'. — ὅρα: unaugmented (R 16.1) 3rd pers. sing. impf. of ὁράω. — πρόσσω ... ὀπίσσω: on the -σσ-, R 9.1. — καὶ ὀπίσσω: on the correction, R 5.5.

Troy (suggestion by DE JONG; on Hektor see 6.402–403n., 24.499n.; DE JONG on *Il.* 22.506–7).

Πανθοΐδης: on the position of the patronymic in progressive enjambment[P], 2.576–577a n. ('ostentatiously highlights his descent'), 24.687–688n.

251–252 Polydamas' role as Hektor's advisor and his designation as 'companion' (Greek *hetaîros* 251), stressing the close relationship between the two men (cf. 343n.), lets the pair of characters Polydamas–Hektor appear analogous to the pair Patroklos–Achilleus; the latter shows the arrangement, common in Homeric epic, 'older advisor – younger addressee', cf. 11.786 ff. (on this, 1.259n., 3.108–110n., 19.218–219n.), whereas here the same age combined with a difference in skills makes Polydamas Hektor's alter ego, as it were (REINHARDT 1961, 272–276: 'Hektor's counterpart' [quotation p. 276 (transl.)]; REDFIELD [1975] 1994, 143–153; THALMANN 1984, 180 f.; SCHOFIELD [1986] 2001, 240; BANNERT 1988, 81 n. 24; PRALON 1995, 238 f.; CLARK 2010, 137 ff.; additional bibliography, 249–253n.; cf. DE JONG on *Il.* 22.100–103). Narratologically, the contemporaneity serves to make Polydamas' intelligence appear to be a special talent (cf. 13.730–734, as well as 1.247b–252n. [linking rhetorical skill with advanced age]) and gives Hektor great leeway in whether or not to follow his contemporary's advice, cf. Polydamas' commentary at 12.211–214, 13.726–728 (EDWARDS). — **words ... spear:** tools in the assembly and in battle, respectively (on this, 1.258n. with bibliography); corresponds to the juxtaposition at 106 (Achilleus' self-assessment; see *ad loc.*). Hektor's merits as a warrior are undisputed (e.g. 5.602, 7.237 ff., 9.351 ff., 12.462 ff., 14.388 ff.: 6.402–403n.; on Polydamas' achievements as warrior, see STOEVESANDT 2004, 175 f.); the mention of his deficits in advising, which Polydamas says are god-given, remains uncontradicted (13.726–735, 748: JANKO on 13.726–729 and 15.281–285; for passages where Hektor is the addressee of paraeneses and advice, 6.75–80n.).

ἦεν: 4n. — **ἔγχεϊ:** on the metonymic use (in the sense 'in battle'), BAKKER [1991] 2005, 20.

253 a speech introduction formula[P] verse for a piece of advice, esp. in assemblies, frequently with a speaker considered an expert (9× *Il.*, 6× *Od.*): FINGERLE 1939, 299; DE JONG on *Od.* 2.157–160; KELLY 2007, 72, 375 f.

---

251 ἦεν: = ἦν (R 16.6). — ἰῇ: = μιᾷ; '(in) one and the same (night)'.
252 ἄρ: = ἄρα (R 24.1). — πολλόν: adverbial acc., 'by far' (on the declension, R 12.2). — ἐνίκα: here 'was superior (via special abilities)'.
253 σφιν: = αὐτοῖς (R 14.1). — ἐΰ: = εὖ.— φρονέων: on the uncontracted form, R 6. — μετέειπεν: = μετεῖπεν (cf. 9n.).

ὅ: in reference to Polydamas (249 f.), anaphoric with ὃ γάρ (250) and ὃ μέν (252). — **σφιν**
ἐΰ φρονέων: 'well-reasoning, sensible', i.e. 'having in mind what is appropriate for
the situation'; σφιν is to be taken with μετέειπεν (1.73n.; *LfgrE s.v.* φρονέω 1041.53 ff.). —
ἀγορήσατο καὶ μετέειπεν: a VE formula (9× *Il.*, 15× *Od.*) with synonym doubling (on
which, 1.160n., 2.39n.): denominative ἀγοράομαι meaning 'speak in the assembly'
(1.73n.), μετ-ειπεῖν for speeches addressed to a collective (cf. 19.55n., 19.76n.).

254–309 The two speeches in the assembly (254–283 and 285–309) are closely
coordinated in content and structure (parallel formᴾ; LOHMANN 1970, 30–32,
119 f., 188, 201; EDWARDS on 253–283 and 284–309; on the motifs in speeches in
the *Iliad* at the end of the fighting day, esp. in the case of Hektor at 8.497 ff., see
KELLY 2007, 352–354 ['night instruction | morning prediction']):

(I) Polydamas (254–283):

Part (1) in ring-compositionᴾ:

(A/A') demand for retreat (254–256/266);

(B) justification via analysis of the situation (earlier – now):
  (a) Achillleus' anger has thus far given the Trojans an advantage in battle
  (257–260),
  (b) from now on, Achilleus will attack Troy (261–265);

Part (2) *two* options for action (C) *vs.* (D):

(C) remaining in the plain:
  (a) during the night (267–268a), (b) tomorrow (268b–270a),
  (c) consequence: the Trojans are pushed back, many are killed and eaten
  by animals (270b–271);

(D) retreat to the city: introduction (273),
  (a) during the night (274–276), (b) tomorrow (277–278a),
  (c) consequence: Achilleus will be beaten back, perhaps even killed and
  eaten by animals (278b–283).

(II) Hektor (285–309):

Part (1) in ring-compositionᴾ:

(A/A') rejection of the recommendation to retreat (285 f./293–296);

(B) justification via analysis of the situation (earlier – now):
  (a) in the past, Troy was wealthy (287–289),
  (b) now her resources are dwindling (290–292);

Part (2) *one* appeal to action (C), with a different assessment of the situation:

(C) remaining in the plain: introduction (297),
  (a) now, i.e. during the night (298–302), (b) tomorrow (303 f.),
  (c) consequence: confrontation between Hektor and Achilleus in battle
  (305–309).

Polydamas' conjectures regarding the further course of the battle (262b–265, 268–271, 278–283a) will be fulfilled toward the end of Book 21 and in Book 22 (Reichel 1994, 180).

254 2nd VH from caesura C 2 = 23.894, *Od.* 17.400. — ἀμφί: 'from/toward both sides', adverbial with φράζεσθε ('consider!, be careful!': cf. 24.354n.), amplified by μάλα: the consequences of *both* options for action (255 f.) must be considered closely (267 ff. and 274 ff.): AH; Leaf; Fritz 2005, 95, 101. — φίλοι: an address to a larger group of addressees, suggesting familiarity (2.56n., 2.299n.); in contrast to the opening speeches in the preceding assembly (7.348 f., 8.497), brief and unembellished due to the urgency of the situation.

255 2nd VH ≈ 11.723, *Od.* 9.151, 9.306, 9.436, 12.7, 16.368. — **into the city:** Already at 12.215 ff., Polydamas advised retreating from the ships to the city, likewise on the basis of the interpretation of a portent (12.217 ff.) and likewise to no avail (12.238 ff.): anticipation of scenes[P]; his concern now is not only for the safety of the troops (268–272) but especially for the city (261–265), and in exchange for this he is willing to give up the advantage won in battle thus far. – Recommendations of careful, defensive action addressed to Hektor are also found elsewhere: 15.721 ff. (the Trojan elders), 6.433 ff. (see *ad loc.*) and 22.56 f., 84 f. (pleas from relatives). The motif 'advocating for retreat' also occurs on the Achaian side: as a suggestion to abandon the war and return home (2.114 ff. [the so-called *Peira*: 2.73–75n.], 2.236 ff., 9.21 ff., 14.74 ff.), on the one hand, as advice to retreat before the enemy in battle, on the other (5.243 ff., 7.109 ff., 8.139 ff., 15.294 ff., 17.622 f.); on the motif, Stoevesandt 2004, 289 n. 863; Kelly 2007, 164 f.; Pagani 2008, 366–372; Rinon 2008, 98 ff. This provides the narrator with opportunities to bring possible alternatives to the storyline into focus (cf. 1.169–171n.; Morrison 1992, 60 ff.; also 166–202n.). — **divine dawn:** Greek ēṓ dían is a formulaic phrase (13× early epic, of which a VE formula 3× *Il.*, 6× *Od.*); on I-E parallels, Schmitt 1967, 172–175; West 2007, 218 f.; cf. 2.48n.

ἄστυδε: For the inhabitants of a city, ἄστυ is perhaps the more emotional term in comparison with πόλις (24.327n.); in Polydamas' speech, also 266, 274 vs. 265, 281, in Hektor's speech, 286 vs. 288. — μὴ ... ἠῶ δῖαν: Verses with a dactylic 1st VH and only spondees in the 2nd VH are rare in Homeric epic (8× *Il.* [see 41, 404], 5× *Od.*: Dee 2004, 488 f.); here the rhythm perhaps underlines the content (contrasting movement and lingering). – ἠῶ is a contracted from *ἠόα (G 45).

256 VB to caesura A 4 = 2.473, 2.812, 3.133, 7.66, 20.217. — **plain beside the ships:** in the vicinity of the battlefield (7n.; Appendix to Book 14).

---

255 ἄστυδε: on the suffix, R 15.3. — μίμνειν: formal (reduplicated pres.) and metrical variant of μένειν. — ἠῶ: 'dawn' (↑; Attic ἕω, cf. R 3).
256 νηυσίν: on the declension, R 12.1. — τείχεος: on the uncontracted form, R 6. — εἰμέν: = ἐσμέν (R 16.6).

ἑκάς: 'far (from)', intensified by ἀπό only here; aside from the adverbial use, used elsewhere as a preposition + gen. (SCHW. 2.538; CHANTR. 2.147 f.); ἑκὰς δ᾽ ἀπὸ τείχεος stresses the distance to the walls of Troy and the refuge they offer.

257 Achilleus' anger is the theme of the *Iliad* starting in Book 1 (*mḗnis, mēníō*: 1.1–12a n., 1.1n., 1.247a n., 19.75n.). Only thanks to Achilleus' boycott of battle were the Trojans presented with the opportunity to remain outside the city walls (5.788–791; on the motif 'boycott of battle by an enraged hero', 6.326n.). Both the Achaians (1.282–284, 9.352–355, 11.798–801, see also Hera's rebuke at 5.787–791) and the Trojans (16.278–283, 18.261, see also Apollo's call to battle at 4.509–513) are aware of the significance of Achilleus' superior strength in fighting for the course of the battle (VAN WEES 1992, 139 f.; cf. 6.99n.). Polydamas tries to prepare the Trojans for the turning point in the course of the battle and for the resulting danger by suggesting via his wording an end to Achilleus' boycott (cf. also 265, 268 f.), although he – in contrast to the audience – can only guess and does not know for certain that Achilleus will again participate in battle after this, cf. Hektor's reply at 305 (TAPLIN 1992, 158 n. 3; cf. paralepsis[P] and 'transference': DE JONG on *Od.* p. xviii); at the same time, his guess is highly plausible coming after Patroklos' death. The fact that Polydamas and the Trojans are generally familiar with the reason for Achilleus' boycott of the fighting, i.e. his quarrel with Agamemnon, can be explained e.g. via the scene in the Aias–Hektor duel in Book 7, where Aias in his speech of challenge attributes Achilleus' absence from battle to his anger at Agamemnon (7.229 f., see also 4.512 f., 16.281 f.). — **this man:** A periphrastic denomination[P] for Achilleus. Polydamas uses the deictic pronoun *hoútos* ('this one') to point to Achilleus' appearance, just experienced by everyone present, which still reverberates, see 246–248 (AH; FAESI; cf. BAKKER [1999] 2005, 77 ff.). In addition, in direct speech the designation *hoútos anḗr* ('this man') is frequently used with a pejorative tone, e.g. of an enemy who is reluctantly recognized, usually of 'present or still visible individuals' (*LfgrE s.v.* ἀνήρ 857.62 ff. and 858.46 ff. [transl.]; CHANTR. 2.169). At 13.746 f., Polydamas finds clearer words for Achilleus ('a man insatiate of fighting'; on paraphrases for Achilleus in general, 24.204n.).

ὄφρα ...: an asyndetic explanatory clause (AH; cf. 20–21n.). — Ἀγαμέμνονι ... δίῳ: elsewhere an inflectable VE formula (4× *Il.*, 1× *Od.*, 1× 'Hes.': 2.221–222a n.) and formula before caesura B 2 (2× *Il.*, 1× 'Hes.'); aside from the present passage and *Od.* 11.168 (Odysseus), always in narrator[P] text. On the generic epithet[P] δῖος, 228n.

---

257 ὄφρα: 'while, so long as' (R 22.2), correlative with τόφρα (258).

259–260 Polydamas acts as a diplomatically skilled speaker by pretending in a rhetorical *captatio benevolentiae* that he has until this point agreed with Hektor's optimistic assessment of the possibility of realizing their aim in battle (but see 249–253n. for his earlier appeals for caution); during the previous two days in battle, the latter repeatedly spread optimism regarding a possible victory (cf. esp. 8.498–528, 15.497–500, 15.718–720). In what follows, he explicitly grounds his advice for caution in the current, changed situation (261 ff.). His statements also illustrate the effects of Achilleus' wish (the Achaians are to be attacked at their ships: 76n.) from the enemy point of view: the proximity to the ships lifts the mood among the Trojans.

χαίρεσκον ... ἰαύων, | ἐλπόμενος: Only ἐλπόμενος and not the part. ἰαύων ('spend the night': 19.71a n.) is to be connected with χαίρεσκον (χαίρω 'rejoice', as an emotional feeling: *LfgrE*) (in contrast AH: the topic [ἰαύων] and the reason [ἐλπόμενος] for the joy; CHANTR. 2.322 [transl.]: 'to camp near the ship in the hope that ...'; PRALON 1995, 239), since the iterative sense (cf. G 60) is not quite appropriate: the Trojans have only spent one night outside (STR 21, fig. 1; cf. LEAF; WILLCOCK). ἔλπομαι ('expect, reckon with') in combination with χαίρω is an emphatic expression of an optimistic attitude (*LfgrE s.vv.* ἔλπομαι and χαίρω, esp. 1093.1 ff.; LATACZ 1966, 74 [transl.]: 'the entire time that I was lying by the ships I rejoiced again and again at the thought of us taking the ships'). The statement illustrates the mood prevalent among the Trojans since they were able to set up camp near the ships the previous night: optimism and anticipation regarding the hoped-for victory and booty (260). — θοῆς ἐπὶ νηυσίν: an inflectable formulaic expression after caesura B 2; a designation for the Achaian encampment of ships (24.1n.; cf. 19.160n.). — ἐλπόμενος ... ἀμφιελίσσας: a four-word verse that points emphatically to the reasons for joy (BASSETT 1919, 223 f.; cf. 1.75n.). — ἀμφιελίσσας: an epithet of ships, always used at VE, meaning 'curved on both sides' (in reference to the hull): 2.165n.; CASSON 1971, 45 with n. 17.

261 1st VH = 1.555, *Od.* 24.353; ≈ *Il.* 9.244, 10.538, *h.Ap.* 70. — Polydamas apparently takes it as certain that the fears he mentioned earlier, namely that Achilleus would rejoin battle when needed (13.746 f.), will come to pass *now* (262 ff.).

ποδώκεα Πηλείωνα: on the inflectable VE formula (12× *Il.*) and its variants, 234n., 24.458n.

---

258 δέ: 'apodotic δέ' (R 24.3). — ῥηΐτεροι: comparative of ῥηΐδιος (= Attic ῥᾴδιος); personal construction (ῥ. πολεμίζειν ἦσαν) with transitive πολεμίζειν 'fight against'.
259 χαίρεσκον: iterative (-σκ-: R 16.5; ↑). — θοῆς: on the declension, R 11.1.
260 νῆας(ς) αἱρησέμεν: on the prosody, M 4.6 (note also the caesura: M 8); on the declension of νηῦς, R 12.1. — αἱρησέμεν: fut. inf. (R 16.4); ἡμᾶς is to be understood as the subj. acc.
261 δείδοικα: = δέδοικα (δείδοικα < *δεδϝοικα: R 4.2).

262 1st VH = *Od.* 15.212; ≈ *Il.* 15.94. — Achilleus joining the battle will drive movement in the opposite direction, namely away from the plain and toward the city (265); the Trojans should anticipate this (255 f., 266).

οἶος …, οὐκ ἐθελήσει: The subordinate clause, introduced by relative οἶος, does not substantiate the statement at 261 (Polydamas' fear) but rather the following main clause (Achilleus' future actions in battle), likewise *Od.* 15.212 (AH; EDWARDS; *LfgrE s.v.* οἶος 605.22 ff.; cautiously, LEAF; MONTEIL 1963, 192 f.; on οὐκ ἐθελήσει ['will not be inclined to'], *LfgrE s.v.* 417.20 ff.). — ἐκείνου: a demonstrative pronoun used in character language[P]; it can signal spatial distance, as here: 'of him over there' (3.391n.; SCHW. 2.209 f.; CHANTR. 2.169 f.; temporal: 2.330n.). In contrast to 257 (οὗτος, see *ad loc.*), the speaker here expresses a greater distance from Achilleus, which perhaps also suggests a certain respect; 11.653 f. is similar, see also 5.790 (distance from anger: 9.678, 14.368 (see *ad loc.*), 20.106): cf. BONIFAZI 2012, 60 f. — ὑπέρβιος: means 'overpowering' (on the formation, RISCH 187, 189); it serves to characterize characters[P] as an epithet with θυμός (also *Od.* 15.212 [Nestor]), with ἦτορ (Hes. *Th.* 139 [Cyclopes], 898 [son of Zeus]), with ὕβρις (*Od.* 1.368, 4.321, 16.410 [the suitors]), and with ἄχθος (Hes. *Op.* 692): *LfgrE.* In the present passage, it describes Achilleus' passion (*LfgrE s.v.* θυμός 1081.51 ff.; BÖHME 1929, 70 f. n. 1: 'pride'; PRALON 1995, 239: 'vital energy' [transl.]).

263 Τρῶες καὶ Ἀχαιοί: an inflectable VE formula (nom., gen. and acc. pl.: 9× *Il.*).

264 ἐν μέσῳ, ἀμφότεροι: This indication of location, in combination with the emphatic addition 'both', creates a contrast to the movement to be expected from Achilleus – namely straight against the city (262 f., 265). — μένος ἄρηος δατέονται: a unique expression, comparable to *Od.* 16.269 μένος κρίνηται ἄρηος (see also 209). δατέομαι means 'divide out (among each other)' (objects are especially war booty, inheritance, land and food), μένος means 'urge, drive, aggressive energy' (1.103n.); μένος ἄρηος δατέονται is thus 'divide the drive to fight among each other', i.e. 'measure forces against, compete in battle' (*LfgrE s.vv.* δατέομαι, μένος 140.31 f., cf. *s.v.* Ἄρης 1261.15 ff. and 209n.).

265 ≈ *Od.* 11.403, 24.113. — **for the sake of our city:** The first of a series of statements by various characters[P] who fear that Achilleus will soon conquer Troy: 20.29 f. Zeus, 21.308–310 the river god Skamandros, 21.515–517 Apollo, 22.56 ff. Priam, 24.728 f. Andromache (cf. Agenor 21.583 f.); in addition, see Achilleus' spontaneous impulse at 22.378–392 after killing Hektor, which he suppresses,

---

263 πεδίῳ, ὅθι: on the hiatus, R 5.6. — ὅθι: 'where' (cf. R 15.2). — περ: stresses the preceding word (R 24.10).
264 ἀμφότεροι: 'both (sides, armies)'. — ἄρηος: initial syllable metrically lengthened (R 10.1); on the declension, R 12.4.
265 πτόλιος: on the declension, R 11.3; on the πτ-, R 9.2. — μαχήσεται: fut. of μαχέομαι (a by-form of μάχομαι). — ἠδέ: 'and' (R 24.4).

and 21.544 f. in narrator-text ('if-not' situation[P]): SCHADEWALDT (1938) 1966, 156 f. n. 4; on the repeated prolepses[P] of Troy's conquest, 2.12n., 6.447–449n.; DE JONG on *Il.* 22.56–76. — **women:** Polydamas refers indirectly to the fate looming over the women – in addition to Helen, all the other women from the conquered city will also be war booty (cf. 28n.) – thus transitioning to the paraenetic section at 266 ff., where he attempts to commit the Trojans to his tactics for protecting the city and its women; on this motif, cf. the Trojans battle paraeneses at 5.485 f., 15.496–499, 17.223–228, and Hektor's commands at the end of the previous day of battle at 8.520 f. (cf. STOEVESANDT 2004, 292).

περί: 195n. — **πτόλιος:** beside ἄστυ at 266; on this, 255n.

266 1st VH ≈ *Od.* 24.358. — **ἀλλ' ἴομεν:** a VB formula (5× *Il.*, 6× *Od.*); on its expansion with προτὶ ἄστυ and on the verse structure (three complete sentences in *one* verse as a rare phenomenon in the *Iliad*), HIGBIE 1990, 95 f.; on ἀλλά, 134n. — **πιθέσθε:** on the sentence structure, cf. SCHW. 2.633 ('emphatic asyndeton of imperatives' [transl.]); for the accent on the imper. (an older paroxytone), schol. T; WACKERNAGEL (1925) 1953, 864–866. — **ὧδε:** pointing back to 262 ff., as a conclusion to the exhortation (VAN LEEUWEN; EDWARDS: 'That's the way it will be!' [with reference to 272]): with the statement ὧδε γὰρ ἔσται, Polydamas conclusively visualizes the analysis of the situation he presented, before turning to detailed analysis of the two options for action (differently AH; FAESI; LOHMANN 1970, 31, 120; PRALON 1995, 239 with n. 16: pointing ahead to 267 ff.); on backward pointing/anaphoric ὅδε, ὧδε, K.-G. 1.646 f.; CHANTR. 2.168.

267–283 Polydamas analyzes the options for action and their consequences on the basis of his fundamental assessment of Achilleus' behavior (261–265), while linking them closely in terms of content and via literal repetitions (254–309n.): 'swift-footed son of Peleus' at VE 261/267, 'night' 267/274, 'tomorrow' and 'in arms' 269/277, flight to Troy 270–271a / return to the encampment of ships 280a, 'dogs will eat many' 271b / 'will eat him (should he try to enter the city)' 283b; also 262b–263a/278b–279a and 265/279b. – The description of option (C) (remaining in the plain) contains formulations (esp. 269–271) similar to 19.71 f., Achilleus' confident speech before the military assembly on the following day.

267–268 To Polydamas' mind, only the sunset protected the Trojans from a worse fate (on the motif 'night concludes the fighting', 2.387n.); he is unaware that Achilleus did not yet have the means to become truly dangerous. On the pre-

---

266 ἴομεν: short-vowel subjunc. (R 16.3). — προτὶ (ϝ)άστυ: on the prosody, R 5.4. — προτί: = πρός (R 20.1).

267 ἀπέπαυσε: 'stopped, interrupted'.

268 ἀμβροσίη: on the -η after -ι-, R 2. — ἀμβροσίη· εἰ: on the hiatus, R 5.6. — ἄμμε: = ἡμᾶς (R 14.1). — κιχήσεται: fut. of κιχάνω 'catch (up to), come across'. — ἐόντας: = ὄντας (R 16.6).

vious day, in contrast, the onset of night protected the Greeks, since it prevented Hektor's assault on the encampment of ships (8.487–501, where see
also for Zeus' prophecy regarding the course of battle on the day now ending:
8.473–476; on the motif of night falling at the moment of greatest crisis, see
BIERL 2012, 143, 169 f.). — **immortal:** The adjective *ambrósios* (in the Greek
line 268, in Lattimore 267) means 'associated with the immortals, divine', and
as an epithet of the night is usually understood 'divine gift' or 'giving vitality'
(2.57n.). On the character plane, it can signal Polydamas' relief at the end of
the day (secondary focalization[P]), while being on the narrator plane an echo of
239–242 (suggestion by DE JONG).

ποδώκεα Πηλεΐωνα: 261n. — ἀμβροσίη: on the etymology (derivation from ἄμβροτος),
24.341n., G 15; elsewhere in the nom. VE formula ἀμβροσίη νύξ (3× *Od.*), on the formula
system in the acc., 2.57n.

269–270 σὺν τεύχεσιν: a formulaic phrase after caesura B 1 (25× *Il.*, 1× *Od.*); τεύχεα comprises armor and offensive weapons, σὺν τ. is thus approximately 'fully armed' (for battle): 3.29n. — εὖ νυ: Aside from here, the phrase is found at VB (4× *Il.*, 1× *Od.*), always
in combination with the verb 'know' (cf. 197n.); the particle νυ is not so much temporal as intensifying in exclamations, requests or questions (Schw. 2.571; RUIJGH 1957,
59 ff., on εὖ νυ, 61; cf. 19.95–96n.). — εὖ ... αὐτόν | γνώσεται: on the meaning 'get to
know (someone's physical strength)', 3.53n. — τις: with a collective meaning 'some' (cf.
122–123n.). — ἀσπασίως: 'glad, relieved'; in a similar context at 7.118, 11.327, 19.72 (see
ad loc.); cf. ἀσπάσιοι 21.606 f. There is a certain tension between ἀσπασίως δ' ἀφίξεται
Ἴλιον and 259 χαίρεσκον ... ἐπὶ νηυσὶν ἰαύων. — Ἴλιον ἱρήν: on the inflectable VE formula (21× *Il.*, 2× *Od.*) and on ἱερός as a generic epithet[P] of cities, 1.38n.; WEST on *Od.* 1.2;
on ἱερός with other terms, 24.681n.

271 2nd VH ≈ 22.42. — **vultures ...:** on the motif, 179n.; Polydamas employs it
twice: here as a warning to the Trojans regarding the heavy losses Achilleus
will inflict on them (cf. schol. A, bT), and at 283 in the confident conclusion
to his speech, in which there is a threatening overtone against Achilleus, cf.
278 ff. (SEGAL 1971, 26–28; GRIFFIN 1980, 115).

γῦπες ἔδονται: a variable VE formula (γ. ἔδονται/ἔδοιεν): 4× *Il.*, 1× *Od.*

272 The statement – perhaps proverbial – represents the wish that what was just
described should not come to pass, cf. 22.454: Andromache hopes that the concerns just expressed will not come true (VAN LEEUWEN and EDWARDS: '*absit
omen*'). The phrase 'far from the ear' is variously interpreted, but it most likely

---

270 ἀφίξεται Ἴλιον: originally (ϝ)ίλιον (R 4.6). — ἱρήν: = ἱεράν.
271 κε: = ἄν (R 24.5).
272 Τρώων: dependent on πολλούς (271). — αἲ γάρ: = εἰ γάρ (cf. R 22.1), εἴθε. — οὔατος: = ὠτός
(gen. sing. of οὖς 'ear').

means 'may I never hear that my fears are coming to pass' (thus AH; similarly FAESI; EDWARDS; CERRI; PRALON 1995, 240 n. 19; WILLE 2001, 60; DE JONG on *Il.* 22.454) and is not a wish that what was said remain unheard, i.e. be unspoken, as it were (thus VAN LEEUWEN; LEAF [with reservations]; WILLCOCK; FRONTISI-DUCROUX 1986, 36 f., with reference to 4.363; cf. *LfgrE s.v.* γίγνομαι 152.7 f.: '*sc.* my rash words' [transl.]).

The verse is suspected by some as an interpolation because of: (a) the runover word Τρώων that is seemingly unnecessary (after 268, 270) (but see e.g. 2.13/30/67, 5.94, 10.222, 10.232, 11.121, 17.753), (b) a use of ὧδε deemed unusual ('thus, as I said above', i.e. 'what was said': AH; FAESI; differently CERRI: purely deictic, in combination with a gesture of distance away from the ears), rendering the formulation less clear in comparison to 22.454 (αἲ γὰρ ἀπ' οὔατος εἴη ἐμοῦ ἔπος): LEAF; BEKKER 1872, 31; EDWARDS 1968, 274 f.; WEST 2001, 12 n. 28 ('rhetorical expansion'); but see 266n. on backward pointing ὧδε.

273 Polydamas reprises his appeals at 266 ('follow me!'), but here seeks to win the approval of his audience for his favored option by phrasing his argument in terms of a conditional clause (*ei d' an emoís epéessi pithṓmetha*: 'should we follow my words') and by showing solidarity via 'we' (likewise at 274, 277–279, contrast 269–271), thus invoking the brotherhood of arms (WACKERNAGEL [1920/24] 2009, 62 f.; TABACHOVITZ 1951, 80 f.; SCHW. 2.246; cf. *LfgrE s.v.* πείθω 1097.29 ff.). In contrast, Hektor's speech, especially its second part, is more emotional and is dominated by commands (297 ff., with the exception of 297b and 304: 297n.). — **it hurts us:** implies the painful realization by all concerned that retreat is necessary, the earlier successes in battle notwithstanding; cf. Agamemnon's plainer words in a similar context at 7.109–111 (AH; *LfgrE s.v.* κήδω 1401.29 f.; MAWET 1979, 366).

εἰ δ' ἂν … πιθώμεθα: a prospective subjunc. (expression of a certain expectation) introducing the second variant, in contrast to the neutral fut. ind. of the first variant (268 εἰ … κιχήσεται); the change in mood could indicate that the speaker considers it quite possible that the Trojans will accept his argument (cf. 1.135–137n.; CHANTR. 2.281; WAKKER 1994, 209 f.). — **ἐμοῖς ἐπέεσσι:** < *ἐμοῖσι ϝέπεσσι (WEST 1998, XXXIII; cf. G 69–70). — **κήδομενοί περ:** an inflectable VE formula (6× *Il.*, 4× *Od.*, 1× *h.Ven.*).

274–276 Polydamas' speech focuses on the safety of both the troops and the city. His list of selected locations and bulwarks especially evokes the protection they grant (see the epithets with 'gates' and esp. 'door leaves' at 275) and the safety of the community, which is easier to defend under cover of the walls (very differently Hektor at 288 ff.); on the towers of the city walls, 3.149n.; on the gates, 2.788n. Polydamas does not merely demand retreat and flight in the

---

273 εἰ δ' ἂν: = ἐὰν δέ. — ἐπέεσσι: on the declension, R 11.3 and ↑. — περ: concessive (R 24.10).

face of Achilleus' impending reentry into battle, but presents a defensive strategy for the night (274) and the following morning (277 f.): namely gathering 'in the place of assembly' (*agorḗ*), so that on the following morning the troops are fully armed at once and can fend off the enemy with full force (EDWARDS; CERRI; LYNN-GEORGE 1988, 222; SCULLY 1990, 49 f.; HAMMER 2002, 47).

274 σθένος ἕξομεν: σθένος 'strength' is here variously interpreted: (a) as 'strength of the army, military force', in the sense 'the troops'; this usage could be based on phrases such as πύλας καὶ τεῖχος Ἀχαιῶν | ῥηξόμεθα σθένεϊ μεγάλῳ (12.223 f.) and Ἀργεῖοι δέ κε κῦδος ἕλον ... | κάρτεϊ καὶ σθένεϊ σφετέρῳ (17.321 f.), but is attested only in post-Homeric literature, e.g. Soph. *Ai.* 438; in this case, ἔχω means 'hold back, hold (in one location)': schol. bT on 274; AH; FAESI; WILLCOCK; *LfgrE* s.vv. σθένος and ἔχω 839.77 ff.; MADER 1970, 105; cautiously EDWARDS on 274–276; LSJ s.v. σθένος; (b) as physical strength: LEAF ('we will keep (husband) our strength (by resting) in the agora'); PRALON 1995, 240 n. 20 ('«we will maintain and preserve our strength», i.e. our ability to fight' [transl.]). Interpretation (a) fits what follows, where the troops occur as part of the means of defense listed later, whereas (b) is perhaps more easily integrated with the statement 'we (= the army) will preserve our strength, the towers ... will preserve the city'.

275 2nd VH ≈ 21.535, *Od.* 2.344, 22.128, 23.42. — **σανίδες τ' ἐπὶ τῆς ἀραρυῖαι:** σανίς ('board') in the pl. denotes the door leaves set into the gates, which were secured with crossbeams and bolts (12.453–456 [Achaian encampment of ships], 21.531–538 [Troy]). πύλαι here are thus the gate posts (*LfgrE* s.vv. ἀραρίσκω 1183.25 ff. and σανίς; HAINSWORTH on *Il.* 12.455–456; FERNÁNDEZ-GALIANO on *Od.* 21.137; IAKOVIDES 1977, 219; WILLETTS 1977; ROUGIER-BLANC 2005, 150).

276 1st VH ≈ 13.613. — The four-word verse (122–123n.) with spondeic VE and an asyndetic series of epithets with an increasing number of syllables (on which, 130–131n.), together with an accumulation of words in -αι at 275 f., underlines the significance of the terms chosen to describe the quality and functionality of the city gates (EDWARDS on 274–276). — **εὔξεστοι:** an epithet with items made of wood, usually after caesura B 2 (24.271n. [where also on the word formation]). — **ἐζευγμέναι:** ζεύγνυμι is used elsewhere in early epic only of animals yoked to a wagon, here in a metaphorical sense of the joined, i.e. closed leaves of the door (*LfgrE* s.v.; AH; LEAF).

277–283 At the conclusion of part (2) (254–309n.), Polydamas uses paraenetic motifs to highlight his favored tactics of defense and attrition: he points to the defensive strength of the warriors on the bulwark (277b–278a), utters threats

---

274 νύκτα μέν: 'throughout the night', the temporal continuation is 277 πρωὶ δ(έ). — εἰν: = ἐν (R 20.1). — ἕξομεν, ἄστυ: on the prosody, R 4.6 (no account is taken of ϝ); contrast 266 (with n.).
275 ἐπὶ τῆς ... ἀραρυῖαι: 'joined to them (sc. the πύλαι)'; on the anaphoric demonstrative function of ὅ, ἥ, τό, R 17; on the declension of τῆς, R 11.1.
276 εὔξεστοι ἐζευγμέναι: on the hiatus, R 5.6. — εἰρύσσονται: fut. of ἔρυμαι 'protect'; initial syllable metrically lengthened (R 10.1); on the -σσ-, R 9.1.

against the enemy (278b–279) and spreads confidence (280–283): the enemy will not obtain his goal (283); he briefly sketches the battle movements he hopes to realize with his tactics (278–280: Achilleus' assault from the direction of the ships – fended off at the wall – return to the ships). In comparison, Hektor's speech as a whole appears more emotional (on the conclusion of the speech, 303–309n.). – Linguistically, there are echoes of Hektor's speech on the preceding day of battle, when he announced his attack on the ships (esp. 277/8.530 f., 278b–279/8.532 f.).

277 = 8.530, 18.303; 2nd VH = 11.49, 11.725, 12.77. — **πρωΐ:** 'early, before the time' (*prō* + loc. ending -*i*: Schw. 1.622; 2.505; on the accent, *LfgrE*). — **ὑπηοῖοι:** predicate adj., a compound of ὑπό + an adj. derived from ἠώς: 'toward daybreak' (Risch 129; Schw. 2.532; West on Hes. *Op.* 548). — **σὺν τεύχεσι:** 269–270n.; echoes of 269 (of the attacker).

278 2nd VH ≈ 1st VH of 306. — The warriors take their positions on the platforms of the towers that also serve as lookout points (3.149n.).

ἄλγιον: a comparative derived from ἄλγος 'pain', used in early epic only in the neut. sing. and with a weakened comparative meaning (AH: 'all the worse'; Mawet 1979, 243–247: 'so much for that' [transl.]). — **αἴ κ' ἐθέλησιν:** an inflectable VE formula (143n.), here with threatening overtones ('should he feel the urge, if he so desires'): *LfgrE* s.v. ἐθέλω 414.51 ff., esp. 68 f.

279 1st VH = 10.337.

280–281 he wears out ... | ... his horses: The audience knows that Achilleus' horses are exceptional: the best among the Achaian horses (2.769 f.), the offspring of the wind god Zephyros and thus as fast as the wind and immortal, given to his father Peleus by the gods (16.149 ff., 16.866 f.), capable of human emotions (see their mourning for Patroklos at 17.426 ff.); in the battle for Patroklos' corpse, they were led into battle by Automedon (CH 4) and Alkimedon (17.474 ff.): 2.770n., 19.399n., 19.400n.

280 ἂψ πάλιν εἶσ' ἐπὶ νῆας: an emphatic asyndetic clause, representing a strong contrast with ἐλθὼν ἐκ νηῶν at VB 279 (AH; cf. 20–21n.). — **ἐριαύχενας ἵππους:** an inflectable VE formula (nom./acc. pl.: 5× *Il.*); the possessive compound ἐ. is a distinctive epithet[P] of horses, likely meaning 'holding the neck high, with high neck', in reference to their proud demeanor (ἐρι- < *seri* 'above, on high': Willi 1999, esp. 96f; cf. *LfgrE* s.v. ἐριαύχην).

---

278 ἂμ πύργους: 'up on the towers' (ἄμ = ἀνά: R 20.1). — τῷ: refers to Achilleus, anaphoric (R 17) with αὐτόν (269). — αἴ κ(ε): ≈ ἐάν (R 22.1, R 24.5). — ἐθέλησιν: 3rd pers. sing. pres. subjunc. (R 16.3).
279 νηῶν: on the declension, R 12.1. — ἄμμι: = ἡμῖν (R 14.1).
280 ἄψ: 'back'. — εἶσ': = εἶσι (R 5.1) 'will go'. — κ(ε): = ἄν (R 24.5).

281 ἄσῃ: an aor. subjunc. of the defective verb ἄμεναι 'sate', usually used in a metaphorical sense of satiation with an activity (esp. fighting and mourning: 19.307n., 19.402n.), here with παντοίου δρόμου in the sense 'make weary of running to and fro, tire via running to and fro'. — **ὑπὸ πτόλιν:** an indication of location with acc. of spatial extent (FRITZ 2005, 333, 335; cf. SCHW. 2.530; CHANTR. 2.144); it means approximately 'along under the walls of the city, below at the walls of the city', i.e. 'before the city' (cf. 2.216n.), and is the antithesis of εἴσω at 282 (AH). — **ἠλασκάζων:** a derivation from ἠλάσκω ('swarm here and there, roam about', cf. 2.470 of flies, 13.104 of hinds), which in turn is derived from ἀλάομαι ('wander [about]') (RISCH 272, 298; on -σκ-, G 60); h.Ap. 142 (νήσους τε καὶ ἀνέρας ἠλάσκαζες [of Apollo]) is also similar to the present passage in terms of the indication of location, Od. 9.457 is different (ἐμὸν μένος ἠλασκάζει: pejorative 'skulk about before'): LfgrE s.v. ἠλάσκω; TRÜMPY 1950, 226. The part. elaborates further παντοίου δρόμου and illustrates futile, ineffective attacks (as an antithesis of εἴσω ἐφορμηθῆναι at 282), i.e. intensive/expressive 'wander about, chase about (in vain)' (AH; CHANTR. 1.338: 'run randomly' [transl.]; TRÜMPY loc. cit. 'roam about'; somewhat differently, LEAF [suffix -άζω is pejorative] and EDWARDS [ἠ. with 'contempt of some kind']).

282 οὔ μιν θυμὸς ... ἐάσει: θυμός as an active subject is elsewhere often the driving force of an inner impulse (2.276n. with bibliography), but here, with ἐάω and a preceding pregnant negative, it is the mental authority that inhibits: 'his θυμός will not let him dare, not drive him that far', i.e. 'will restrain him' (LfgrE s.v. ἐάω 384.16 f. and 385.11 ff.; see also VAN LEEUWEN; FAESI; BÖHME 1929, 77 f., esp. 78 n. 3; PELLICCIA 1995, 239 n. 238). The formulation is probably to be understood with reference to 262 as a qualification of the warning of Achilleus' drive to fight, in the sense 'however great his θ. is, it will not let him ...' (AH and EDWARDS).

283 2nd VH ≈ 22.89, Od. 2.11, 21.363. — With the statement 'X will not come about, first Y will happen', Polydamas portrays his defensive strategy as a promising one; in his formulation, scenario Y is sketched as a rhetorical figure to stress the improbability of scenario X (24.550–551n.; KELLY 2007, 191 f.). — **dogs:** a reprise of 271 (see ad loc.); on dogs as scavengers, 179n.; on 'fast' as an ornamental epithet of dogs, 3.26n.

ἐκπέρσει: The preverb ἐκ- expresses completeness: 'destroy utterly, raze' (SCHW. 2.462; CHANTR. 2.97). — **ἀργοί:** On the meaning 'fast' (cf. 578 πόδας ἀργοί, 24.211 ἀργίποδας), 1.50n., 24.211n.; RUSSO on Od. 17.292; see also 19.400n. on the horse name Ποδάργη.

284 = 12.230, 17.169; 1st VH (with slight variants) 17× Il., 9× Od., 1× 'Hes.', 1× h.Hom.; 2nd VH 10× Il. — hypódra idṓn, always in speech introduction for-

---

281 πτόλιν: on the πτ-, R 9.2.
282 μιν: = αὐτόν (R 14.1).
283 ἐκπέρσει: sc. πτόλιν (281); fut. of ἐκπέρθω. — πρίν: adverbial 'before, beforehand'.
284 ὑπόδρα (ϝ)ιδών: on the prosody, R 4.3.

mulae[P], (literally 'looking at from beneath') signals the speaker's outrage at the breaking of social norms (1.148n., 2.245n.; CAIRNS 2003, 42–44); of Hektor here and at 12.230 in reaction to Polydamas advising caution (toward Achilleus and the Achaians), which incenses him (a similar situation at 5.251, 14.82 [see *ad loc.*]), and at 17.169 toward the ally Glaukos, who accused him of cowardice.

ὑπόδρα: on the word formation (root compound with zero-grade final element -δρα < *dr̥k, cf. δέρκομαι 'gaze'), 24.559n. — **κορυθαίόλος Ἕκτωρ: 20–21n.**

285–309 Because of the vigorous rejection of the suggestion (285 f., 295), the uncompromising dictation of the decision (296 f., 303 f.) and his confident appearance (293 f., 306 ff.), some scholars stress the arrogance and overconfidence in Hektor's reply (schol. bT on 285, 293–294 and 296; EDWARDS on 243–314, 284–309 and 309; SCHADEWALDT [1936] 1997, 161–164; [1938] 1966, 106; [1956] 1970, 28–31; ALDEN 2000, 277–281; ELMER 2013, 139; on the difference in the manner of achieving a consensus in the Achaian [esp. in Book 1] and the Trojan military assemblies, see MACKIE 1996, 132 f.; HAMMER 2002, 156 f.). But his attitude could be attributed to the successes of the two previous days of battle (STR 21 fig. 1; cf. 239–242n.), as well as to the high expectations he faces as the individual chiefly responsible for defending the city (STOEVESANDT 2004, 281, 285 f.; on Hektor's code of honor, cf. his disagreement with Andromache at 6.407–496n., 6.441–446n., 6.459–463n.). He views his main goal, conclusively driving away the enemy (see also 8.526–528, 15.494–499) and reversing the long-standing siege of the city in the face of dwindling resources (288 ff.), as hampered by the suggested retreat, cf. 287 and already 15.719 ff. (REDFIELD [1975] 1994, 128, 152 f.; CARLIER 1984, 170 n. 156; SCHMITT 1990, 184 f. and 301 n. 603; SCULLY 1990, 117–119; PRALON 1995, 241 f.). His personal error consists of (a) not having fully understood that Zeus' promise of victory stipulates that his guaranteed success will last until he reaches the ships and until sunset (11.206–209 *vs.* 18.293 f.; cf. 22.301–303): EDWARDS on 293–295; REINHARDT 1961, 179 f., 274 f.; TAPLIN 1992, 159 f.; PRALON *loc. cit.* 241; STOEVESANDT *loc. cit.* 219 f., 341 f.; DE JONG on *Il.* 22., *Introd.* 15; CAIRNS 2012, 33–49; (b) pushing for a continuation of offensive combat (303 ff.) against the advice he received, and betting on his chances for victory in the duel against Achilleus – unlikely given their relative power (308 f.; likewise at 16.859–861; but cf. Achilleus' recollection of a direct encounter at 9.354 f.) without developing further tactics to secure and strengthen the troops in the face of impending danger (cf. 22.101–107): 308b n.; EDWARDS on 308; CARLIER *loc. cit.* 199 with n. 307; SCHOFIELD (1986) 2001, 242; DE ROMILLY 1997, 98; RUZÉ 1997, 86; STOEVESANDT *loc. cit.* 220. – On the structure of the speech, 254–309n.

285 = 12.231; ≈ 7.357 (Paris on Antenor's advice); 1st VH ≈ 13.751; VE = *Od.* 8.236; ≈ *Il.* 12.173. — **no longer:** The statement implies that under normal circumstances Polydamas' advice is perfectly welcome, but that he has now crossed a boundary and there is no longer any agreement between the two men (cf. AH and KIRK on 7.357; also WILSON 1987, 196 ff. [on *oukéti*]). Hektor's rejection of Polydamas' advice is anticipated at 12.211–214/231 ff. – in a much less dangerous situation (anticipation of scenes[P]).

Πουλυδάμα: on the vocative form, WEST 1998, XXXIVf. — ταῦτ(α): in reference to earlier statements usually pejorative in character language (DE JONG [1987] 2004, 287 n. 25).

286–292 Hektor, who is actually considered the protector of Troy (285–309n.), here ignores the aspect of safety the previous speaker connected with his picture of the city (274–276) and stresses the state of being besieged (286 f.) and its negative consequences via the contrast of 'earlier' and 'now' (schol. bT on 286–287): the city's erstwhile famed wealth (288) has been spent on the payment and upkeep of foreign auxiliary troops (cf. 17.220–226, 18.300 f.); should the defensive strategy continue, these can hardly be maintained as allies any longer (cf. at 5.472 ff. and 17.144 ff. the criticism of the Lykians Sarpedon and Glaukos [CH 10]): EDWARDS on 290–292; REDFIELD (1975) 1994, 152 f.; LYNN-GEORGE 1988, 222; VAN WEES 1992, 39 f. and 380 n. 11; on the auxiliary troops, 2.130–133n., 2.803, 2.816–877n. (with overview).

286–287 VB of 286 = 12.235, 14.96. — **had your glut:** In the context of war, the motif 'have one's fill of battle' is often used elsewhere (with the verbs *koréssasthai* and *ásasthai*: 281n.; LATACZ 1966, 181 ff.): either in the sense of satiating oneself with fighting and blood (esp. 'insatiable in fighting') or – much like 281 – as a signal that the warrior is flagging in the sense 'be fed up with battle'. In the present passage, the motif of satiation is in accord with 281 (fatigue from running around the city) in reference to crowding together where the defenders fight exclusively downward from the platforms of the towers. — **outworks:** 274–276n., 278n.

ἀλήμεναι ... | ... ἐελμένοι: The mid.-pass. εἴλομαι ('crowd together') is frequently used in descriptions of Troy's beleaguered state (24.662–663n.; of the Achaian encampment of ships at 76, 294); the process always occurs as a result of retreat from battle due to enemy predominance. Following Polydamas' advice (254 f.) would lead once again to

---

285 μέν: ≈ μήν (R 24.6). — φίλα: predicative, to be connected with οὐκέτ(ι): ≈ 'no longer acceptable to me'.
286 κέλεαι: on the uncontracted form, R 6. — κατὰ (ϝ)άστυ (ϝ)αλήμεναι: on the prosody, R 4.3. — ἀλήμεναι: aor. inf. of εἴλομαι 'crowd together' (on the form, R 16.4). — αὖτις: = αὖθις; with ἰέναι 'go back'. — ἰόντας: *sc.* ἡμᾶς.

this situation (ἀλήμεναι ... αὖτις ἰόντας). – **ἦ οὔ πω κεκόρησθε:** ἦ 'really?, actually?' frequently introduces a rhetorical question (19.56n.). κορέσασθαι ('sate oneself') is used in the perf. only here and at *Od.* 8.98, 14.456, 23.350, Hes. *Op.* 593 (*LfgrE*: 'do you have enough yet?') and is connected with a perf. part. only here, elsewhere with a pres. part. The two verb forms in the perf. stress the prevailing situation: being fed up and crowded.

288–292 The mention of Troy's earlier, legendary wealth serves repeatedly in the *Iliad* as a contrast to the present time of war, see 9.401 ff., 22.156, 24.543 ff. (2.797n., 24.543n.; AH on 288 and 290; DE JONG on *Il.* 22.156). It is noteworthy that in the present passage, this contrast between 'in the past' and 'now' is drawn exclusively from the point of view of economic consequences (similarly by Achilleus at 9.402 f.) and that Hektor draws on the loss of wealth and material possessions as arguments in favor of more offensive combat; see the Greek terms 'much ..., much ...' (2nd VH 289), 'treasures ... have vanished' (290), 'many possessions' (Greek in hyperbaton at VB 291/292), 'sold' (291).

288 2nd VH ≈ 18.342, 18.490, 20.217, *h.Ap.* 42. – **Πριάμοιο πόλιν:** an inflectable formula before caesura C 1 (5× *Il.*, 3× *Od.*); a periphrastic denomination[P] for Troy with the generally less emotional term πόλις (as opposed to ἄστυ: cf. 255n.) was perhaps chosen here with a view to the perspective of outsiders (but see 1.19n.). – **μέροπες ἄνθρωποι:** elsewhere a VE formula in the gen. pl. (7× *Il.*, 2× *Od.*, 6×. Hes., 2× *h.Hom.*); the short in *longum* is thus to be ascribed to inflection of the formula (M 14). The etymology and meaning of the epithet[P] μέροπες are obscure (1.250n.; RUSSO on *Od.* 20.49).

289 2nd VH ≈ 10.315 (Dolon). — a four-word verse (122–123n.); on gold and 'bronze' (*chalkós*) as markers of wealth, 2.226n., 6.3n., 6.48n.; *LfgrE s.v.* χαλκός, esp. 1123.30 ff.

πολύχρυσον πολύχαλκον: Wealth is frequently highlighted via a combination of compounds with emphatic doubling of πολυ-: cf. πολυκτήμων πολυλήϊος (5.613) and πολύρρηνες πολυβοῦται (9.154/296, 'Hes.' *fr.* 240.3 M.-W.) for individuals, πολυσημάντωρ πολυδέγμων (*h.Cer.* 31) for Hades' power, also πολύμητις ... πολυμήχανον (*h.Merc.* 319): FEHLING 1969, 247; on I-E parallels, DURANTE 1976, 152; WEST 2007, 110; on additional emphatic doublings of compound elements, 3.40n. In the present passage, see also the repetition of the sounds πρι- and πολ- at 288 f. – πολύχρυσον is elsewhere an epithet of the city of Mycenae (*Il.* 7.180, 11.46, *Od.* 3.305: HAINSWORTH on *Il.* 11.46) as well as of the goddess Aphrodite (VE formula 8× Hes., 2× *h.Ven.*), πολύχαλκον of the city of Sidon (*Od.* 15.425) and of οὐρανός (*Il.* 5.504, *Od.* 3.2).

---

287 κεκόρησθε (ϝ)ε(ϝ)ελμένοι: on the prosody, R 4.3. — ἐελμένοι: perf. part. of εἴλομαι. — ἔνδοθι: = ἔνδον (on the suffix, R 15.2), + gen. 'within'.
288 πρίν: adverbial 'beforehand, earlier'. — μέν: prepares for δὲ δή in 290/291. — μέροπες ἄνθρωποι: on the prosody, ↑.
289 μυθέσκοντο: iterative (-σκ-: R 16.5); here, with predicative adjectives, 'call'.

290 ἐξαπόλωλε: an emphatic double compound with the preverb ἐκ- as at 283 (see *ad loc.*; SCHW. 2.462); with gen.: 'have been completely eradicated from, have disappeared from'. — **κειμήλια:** 'treasures', related to κεῖμαι 'lie in storage' (6.47n.).

291–292 291 ≈ 3.401 (see *ad loc.*); 2nd VH of 291 = *h.Ap.* 179; 2nd VH of 292 ≈ *Od.* 1.62. — **Phrygia | ... Maionia:** In the *Iliad*, Phrygians and Maionians are close partners of the Trojans and provide allied contingents (24.544–545n.). Phrygia is located in northwest Asia Minor and extends to the river Sangarios in the east; Maionia corresponds approximately to Lydia (2.862n., 2.864n., 2.866n.; *BNP* s.vv. Phryges and Maeonia). – On the possible historical background for this redistribution of wealth from Troy to Phrygia and Maionia in the Homeric period, see SHEAR 2000, 97; JABLONKA/ROSE 2004, 624–627; BRYCE 2006, 141 f. — **Zeus:** Human misfortune or suffering, the causes of which are unknown, is in principle frequently ascribed to Zeus (cf. Jörgensen's principle[P]), and the Achaians, like Hektor here, also sometimes blame him for their losses in the war (19.273b–274n., cf. 24.525 ff. [see *ad loc.*] and 24.543 ff. [24.534–548n.]). Hektor speaks of Zeus' anger, but mentions no reason for it (TSAGARAKIS 1977, 18 f.). He seems to deduce the divine anger from the fact that the war has been dragging on for a long time and is linked with significant losses for Troy, leading to a critical situation. In this regard, he focusses especially on the time before the quarrel between Achilleus and Agamemnon, the consequences of which in fact provided the Trojans with an advantage and some relief (cf. Polydamas at 257–260); he himself had recently enjoyed Zeus' support in battle, a situation he believes he will be able to exploit further (293 ff.).

ἐρατεινήν: a generic epithet[P] (19.347n.), e.g. for various geographical designations (2.532n.). — **περνάμεν(α):** on the basic meaning of the verb πέρνημι ('export'), 24.752n. — **μέγας ... Ζεύς:** μέγας is an epithet of various gods ('powerful'), the phrase is formulaic in the gen. (Διὸς μεγάλου/-οιο: 2.134, 5.907, 6.304 [with n.], etc.), here likely used pregnantly, cf. also Hes. *Th.* 479 Ζῆνα μέγαν. — **ὠδύσατο:** used almost exclusively in reference to the anger of gods at mortals (*LfgrE* s.v. ὀδύσ(σ)ασθαι).

293 ≈ 2.205. — The invocation of Zeus' current support is used by Hektor (1) to lift the morale of his people and strengthen the case for the offensive strategy he favors, as in his battle paraeneses (8.175 f., 11.288 f., 13.153 f., 15.488–493, 15.719–725) (on the topos of divine support in battle paraeneses, see STOEVESANDT 2004, 278–281; for a collection of examples of Zeus' support for the Trojan side, see REICHEL 1994, 158–174); (2) to make Polydamas' advice appear absurd (sim-

---

291 Φρυγίην καὶ Μηονίην: acc. of direction without a preposition (R 19.2), to be connected with ἵκει in 292.
293 ὅτε περ: 'but since' (on περ, R 24.10). — ἀγκυλομήτεω: on the declension, R 11.1; on the synizesis, R 7.

ilarly at 12.235 f.): rather than the expected continuation in the main clause (e.g. 'you suggest retreat'), what follows at 295 is a violent rebuke that reveals his outrage (AH; EDWARDS). But this shows the dramatic irony[P]: Zeus' support was granted only for one day, which is now ending (285–309n.).

Κρόνου πάϊς ἀγκυλομήτεω: a VE formula (7× *Il.*, 1× *Od.*; also the inflectable VE formula Κρόνος ἀγκυλομήτης: 1× *Il.*, 5× Hes., 2× *h.Ven.*). On the etymology and meaning of the epithet ἀγκυλομήτης ('of crooked counsel'), 2.205n.; on additional formulae for 'Zeus' after caesura B 2, 16.88n., 24.88n.

294 2nd VH ≈ 1.409. — Internal analepsis[P]: Hektor makes reference to his successes on the day of battle that has just ended (STR 21 fig. 1). The Achaians crowded together between the encampment of the ships and the sea corresponds to Achilleus' original wish, see 1.409 f. (see *ad loc.*; also 76n.).

κῦδος ἀρέσθ(αι): elsewhere (aside from the present passage and 16.88) a VE formula (6× *Il.*, 1× *Od.*, 1× 'Hes.'), here at VB with an indication of location following and in a chiastic arrangement vis-à-vis the 2nd VH. On the phrase, 165n.; cf. κῦδος ἔδωκεν 19.204n. — **θαλάσσῃ τ' ἔλσαι:** dat. of destination (SCHW. 2.139 ['push toward the sea']; CHANTR. 2.68), cf. 1.409 κατὰ πρύμνας τε καὶ ἀμφ' ἅλα ἔλσαι.

295 Hektor calls Polydamas a *nḗpios*: the term serves to characterize a person who fails to recognize the truth and is unable to assess a situation objectively ('fool!'); as an address in the sing. it appears also at 16.833 (Hektor to Patroklos), 21.99 (Achilleus to Lykaon), 22.333 (Achilleus to Hektor), Hes. *Op.* 286/397/633 (Hesiod to Perses), otherwise often in narrator commentary (2.38n.; KELLY 2007, 205–208; see also 16.46–47n.). The narrator[P] indirectly qualifies the character's[P] statement with his comments at 249 f., 253 and esp. 311 f. (see *ad loc.*). — **our people:** The term *dḗmos*, designating the inhabitants of a community, is frequently used in reference to those attending a public assembly, as here (likewise at 500, *Od.* 2.239, 8.157, 15.468): 2.198n.; *LfgrE s.v.* δῆμος 276.27 ff.

μηκέτι ... φαῖν(ε): φαίνω here in the sense 'state, utter', cf. 3.212 (see *ad loc.*), 14.127 (*LfgrE s.v.* 808.7 ff.); the negative pres. imper. (rather than the aor. subjunc.) signals that the action is not to be continued, i.e. 'do not say ⟨any more⟩' (cf. 6.68–69n.). It is combined with ταῦτα νοήματα 'these thoughts' as a *nomen rei actae* (sc. the plan for retreat), see also 285 with n.

296 VE = 17.449. — **οὐ γάρ ..., οὐ γὰρ ἐάσω:** on the anaphora after the bucolic diaeresis, 24.10–12n. οὐ ... ἐάσω 'I will not permit it' (*LfgrE s.v.* 384.49); on the function of the fut., CHRISTENSEN 2010, 562 f. — **οὐ ... ἐπιπείσεται:** a rejection of the appeal πιθέσθε μοι at

---

294 νηυσί: on the declension, R 12.1. — τ' ἔλσαι: originally (ϝ)έλσαι (aor. inf. of εἰλέω 'push, crowd together'), but the digamma is no longer taken into account (R 4.6).
295 ἐνί: = ἐν (R 20.1).

266: both phrases occur in the concluding verse of part (1) of the respective speeches (EDWARDS; cf. 254–309n.); the positively worded antithesis follows at 297.

297 = 2.139, 9.26, 9.704, 12.75, 14.74, 14.370, 15.294, *Od.* 13.179; ≈ *Od.* 12.213, *h.Ap.* 486. — A formulaic verse introducing a request in assembly speeches and scenes of counsel (imperatives at 298 f., 301) after the situation has been analyzed; the appeal 'let us all follow' is usually successful (2.139n.). In contrast, cf. Polydamas' more restrained phrasing at 273 (see *ad loc.*) and the future forms at 274 ff.

298–299 ≈ 7.370–371; 2nd VH of 298 = 7.380, 11.730. — **δόρπον:** 'evening meal' (19.208n.). — **κατὰ στρατόν:** a variable formula before caesura C 2 (1.10n.). — **ἐν τελέεσσιν:** τέλος with the concrete meaning 'division, squad' (in addition to the *iterata*, cf. 10.56, 10.470); from the root τλῆναι (I-E *telh₂- 'pick up, take upon oneself': *DELG s.v.* τέλος; *LIV* 622 f.), with the original meaning 'duty one undertakes' (cf. the Mycenaean term /telestas/ for a person tasked with a particular duty: *DMic s.v.* te-re-ta). As a military technical term, it perhaps developed from 'the notion of «bringing up, putting up» men' (transl.) (cf. 'levy', 'raising troops'): *LfgrE*; somewhat differently, LEUKART 1994, 192 n. 164a ('developed from the use of τέλος as «service ... of providing men fit for military service»' [transl.]). — **φυλακῆς μνήσασθε:** φυλακή ('guard') is used in Homeric epic only as a technical military term, usually as an action noun; μιμνήσκομαι means 'turn one's thoughts toward, recollect' (*LfgrE s.vv.*). The phrase is comparable to formulations in calls to battle (μ. χάρμης, ἀλκῆς: 19.147–148n.). — **ἐγρήγορθε:** 2nd pers. pl. perf. act. imper. of intr. ἐγείρομαι ('stay awake!'), related to the I-E root *h₂ger- LIV* 245 f.; a new attempt at explaining the form (*ἐγρήγορσ-τε > ἐγρήγορθε [rst > rht > ρθ]) is made by HACKSTEIN 2002, 246–248. — **ἕκαστος:** on ἕ. as a distributive apposition, 2.775b n.; K.-G. 1.286.

300–302 Hektor also gives instructions to prepare the evening meal in the open field during the assembly at the end of the preceding day of battle (8.505–507). But here his thoughts are still occupied with the city's economic straits, which require that a blow be struck to mend the situation (287–292). He thus addresses the vanishing goods once more and tries, via demagogic formulations and suggestive allusions, to discredit those who agree with Polydamas and to win the sympathy of the crowd. On thef basis of the vague phrases and imprecise accusations, several warnings and insinuations can be identified (cf. LEAF: '300–02 are very obscure in thought and expression'): (1) the request for solidarity with the entire collective as a muted criticism of unsupportive behavior (301n.); (2) his statements overall as (a) a warning that the strategy of bar-

---

297 ἄγεθ': = ἄγετε, originally imper. of ἄγω, ossified as a particle in requests in combination with an imper. or subjunc.: 'come on!'. — ἐγὼ (ϝ)είπω: on the prosody, R 4.4.
299 ἐγρήγορθε (ϝ)έκαστος: on the prosody, R 4.3.

ricading oneself in will inevitably result in the end in the loss of all remaining property to the Achaians (cf. 302), and thus an implicit accusation that Polydamas' advice will ultimately lead to the conquest and looting of the city (AH; CERRI); (b) an insinuation – obviously absurd – that certain people were hoping this might happen, since their wealth oppressed them and they wanted to be rid of it (CAUER [1895] 1923, 689 n. 17); differently schol. bT on 300–301; FAESI; WILLCOCK; EDWARDS: an accusation directed against Polydamas and like-minded persons that the suggestion and agreement to retreat resulted merely from fear for their own property.

300 ὑπερφιάλως ἀνιάζει: 'feels excessively harassed'; ὑπερφίαλος perhaps originally meant 'exceeding the (rim of the) pot', i.e. not staying within appropriate limits (on φιάλη 'pot, jar': 3.106n.; or perhaps like ὑπερ-φυής and Latin *super-bus* related to the I-E root **bʰū-* 'grow, increase': BEEKES *s.v.*); together with ἀνιάζει ('feel disturbed, harassed': *LfgrE s.v.*), it stresses the barb against any partisans of Polydamas (AH).

301 The compound *kata-dēmo-borḗsai* means literally 'consume the people' (see below), but is here reinterpreted in an ironic manner by turning on its head the otherwise common accusation that kings are freeloaders who consume their people (on this, 1.231n.; cf. 24.262n.): the property of the wealthy is now to be consumed by the people rather than the people themselves being consumed (EDWARDS on 300–302; on linguistic issues, see below). This play with the metaphor is stressed via a four-word verse (1.75n.).

λαοῖσι: '(the) people', in military contexts in the *Iliad* usually 'men-at-arms', warriors' (1.10n., 24.1n.). — καταδημοβορῆσαι: A *hapax legomenon*[P], in formal terms coined in accord with the verb-noun compound δημο-βόρος 'consuming the people' (1.231n.), but semantically δῆμος must be the subject, and the property mentioned in 300 the object, thus either 'so that the people consume them' or 'so that they are consumed by the people' (although the basis for the passive formation, *δημό-βορος 'consumed by/among the people', is attested only in post-Homeric texts: RISCH 198). In view of its semantic reinterpretation, the verb has an explicit/ironic element; κατά stresses the completeness and amplifies this effect (*LfgrE*; on δῆμος, 2.198n.).

303–309 Concluding section with paraenesis: echoing 277 f. literally, Hektor turns against Polydamas' stonewalling tactics and successfully (see 310) strengthens the confidence and willingness of the initially frightened Trojans

---

300 κτεάτεσσιν: Attic ≈ κτήμασιν; causal dat.
301 δότω: 3rd pers. sing. aor. imper. of δίδωμι.
302 τῶν: anaphoric demonstrative (R 17) referring to λαοῖσι (301); partitive gen. dependent on τινα. — ἐπαυρέμεν: aor. inf. of ἐπαυρίσκω 'have the use of, enjoy' (on the form, R 16.4), with τινα as the subject-acc.; the obj. is to be supplied from 300 (κτεάτεσσιν). — περ: stresses the preceding word (R 24.10).

to fight by (1) invoking a sense of community among the fighters, as on the previous evening (303 f. = 8.530 f.), (2) directly attacking Polydamas' reading of the situation (305n.), (3) uttering threats against the enemy (306a), (4) stressing, as on the previous evening, his own readiness to face the most powerful individual enemy in battle (306b–308: Achilleus; cf. 8.530–534: Diomedes): schol. bT on 307–308; AH and LEAF on 303; PRALON 1995, 242 f.; for comparison of Hektor's two speeches in Books 8 and 18, see DI BENEDETTO (1994) 1998, 205–208; KELLY 2007, 360 f.

303 = 277 (see *ad loc.*).

304 = 8.531. — **νηυσὶν ἔπι γλαφυρῇσιν:** an inflectable VB formula (28× *Il.*, 1× *Od.*: 16.18n.); on the ship epithet γλαφυρός, 2.454n. — **ἐγείρομεν ὀξὺν ἄρηα:** on the VE formula, the metaphor (rousing battle) and the metonymic use of Ἄρης/ἄρης, 134n., 2.381n.

305 a reference back to 261 ff. Hektor uses his formulation to insinuate that Polydamas' interpretation of Achilleus' appearance (cf. 257n.) is not compelling (EDWARDS). The scepticism may be only a pretense intended to quell the Trojans' panic and preserve their will to fight; even Hektor seems to expect to encounter Achilleus in the next battle (306 ff.). On the narrative composition of Achilleus' appearance, 203–221n.; on the epic motif of the reappearing hero, 19.45b–46n.

εἰ δ' ἐτεόν: a formulaic phrase (at VB 4× *Il.*, 7× *Od.*: 14.125n.); ἐτεόν is here, as normally, used adverbially ('actually, in fact': 2.300n.; *LfgrE*; LUTHER 1935, 54; LEVET 1976, 176; SNELL 1978, 96 f.). — **παρὰ ναῦφιν:** a variable formula before caesura B 2 (ἀπὸ/παρὰ v.: 5× *Il.*, 1× *Od.*), with ablatival gen. in -φι(ν) ('from the [direction of the] ships'): 2.794n.; THOMPSON 1998, 224; on the suffix, 16.139–140n. (with bibliography). — **ἀνέστη:** 'he arose (from his passivity)', an echo of 2.694 τάχα δ' ἀνστήσεσθαι ἔμελλεν (narrator commentary; see *ad loc.*), picked up again at 358 ἀνστήσασ' Ἀχιλῆα (Zeus to Hera): *LfgrE s.v.* ἵστημι 1242.58 ff.; on what occurred, see 215/217 with 215n. — **δῖος Ἀχιλλεύς:** 228n.

306–308a a literal borrowing from the previous speech (1st VH 306 and VB 308 ≈ 278; cf. catch-word technique[P]). Whereas elsewhere in the *Iliad*, the advice to retreat from the enemy for tactical reasons is neither unusual nor necessarily dishonorable (cf. 255n.), Hektor here, by pointedly propounding his personal intent with the juxtaposition 'flee' *vs.* 'resist', creates the impression that retreat would equal flight; on the linguistic composition, see the stressed personal pronoun *egṓ ge* at VE in 306, the predicates at VB in 307/308 and the rhetorical polar expression[P] 'not to flee – to stand up and face' (general bib-

---

304 νηυσὶν ἔπι: = ἐπὶ νηυσίν (R 20.2). — γλαφυρῇσιν: on the declension, R 11.1. — ἐγείρομεν: short-vowel subjunc. (R 16.3). — ἄρηα: on the declension, R 12.4.
305 ναῦφιν: on the form, R 11.4.

liography on this: 3.59n., end.). On Hektor's 'heroic code', cf. 6.441–446 (see *ad loc.*), 22.106 ff. (cf. DE JONG on *Il.* 22.106–108). – After Achilleus' statement of his determination (88 ff., 114 ff.: 88–93n.), the audience must now assume that the coming day will lead to a direct encounter between the two men in battle (but see 114n.). But during this encounter, Hektor will consider retreat (22.99 ff.) and will ultimately turn to flee (22.136 ff.).

306 1st VH ≈ 2nd VH of 278 (see *ad loc.*) — **αἴ κ' ἐθέλησι:** used on analogy with 278 (see *ad loc.*), thus ἄμμι μάχεσθαι is to be supplied mentally (schol. bT; FAESI; EDWARDS).

307 ≈ 11.590. — **δυσηχέος:** an adj. with a negative connotation but an otherwise obscure meaning (related to ἠχέω [i.e. 'ringing terribly'] or ἄχος?), in Homer exclusively with πόλεμος (πολέμοιο δ. formula before caesura C 2: 7× *Il.*) and θάνατος (3× *Il.*): 16.442n.; on the (predominantly pejorative) epithets[P] with terms for 'battle, war', 6.1n., end., 6.330n. — **ἄντην:** 'in the face, directly' (19.15n.), with ἴσταμαι 'stand up and face'.

308b ≈ 13.486. — **he ... or ... I:** Dramatic irony[P] (cf. Hektor facing Achilleus at 22.130, 253, 256 f.): it has already been announced repeatedly that Hektor will die at Achilleus' hands (92n.). In order to encourage his audience, Hektor here testifies to his readiness for the duel, although he phrases the possibility of victory more cautiously than he did on the evening before the fight against Diomedes (8.532–534): DI BENEDETTO (1994) 1998, 206 f. – On the motif 'either A will overcome me/us or I/we will overcome A' and similar formulations in direct speeches, DE JONG on *Il.* 22.108–110; MACKIE 1996, 63, 108 f.; for I-E parallels, WEST 2007, 476 f.

ἤ κε φέρησι ... ἤ κε φεροίμην: an indirect double question with ellipsis of a statement of wanting to know, cf. 8.532 f. ('⟨and we will see⟩ whether he ... or whether I'), and a change of mood (similarly at 16.648–651, 22.244–246, *Od.* 4.692, 12.156 f.); there is also word play[P] (on which, cf. *Il.* 11.410, 22.253): EDWARDS; DE JONG on *Il.* 22.244–246; cf. K.-G. 2.534 n. 16. Both the nuance of the meaning in the change in mood and the tone of the statement are matters of dispute (cf. 24.586n. with bibliography): (1) prospective subjunc. beside potential opt. (expectation *vs.* possibility), the tone interpreted as (a) measured/confident (CHANTR. 2.211 and cf. 2.295; DUCKWORTH 1933, 71; PRALON 1995, 243 n. 34) or (b) boastful/defiant (LEAF); (2) prospective subjunc. beside cupitive opt. (expectation *vs.* wish: AH *ad loc.* and *Anh.* 153 f.; *LfgrE s.v.* φέρω 850.25 ff.), with κε marking the favored but less likely variant (EDWARDS; cf. κε with cupitive opt. at 6.281–282a n.); (3) no difference in meaning between the moods (cf. 22.243 ff., where Athene tries to instil courage into Hektor: Achilleus' victory [subjunc. κεν ... φέρηται] there must not appear more likely than his defeat [opt. κεν ... δαμείη]); in that case, the present passage

---

306 cf. 278n. — τῷ: anaphoric (R 17). — ἔσσεται: = ἔσται (R 16.6). — μιν: = αὐτόν (R 14.1.).
307 δυσηχέος: on the uncontracted form, R 6.
308 κε: = ἄν (R 24.5). — φέρησι: 3rd pers. sing. subjunc. (R 16.3).

would be comparable to 13.486 and 22.253, where in each case both verbs are used in the potential opt. Cf. the *v.l.* φέροιτο (Tabachowitz 1951, 51 f.); in favor of this view are the gnomes at 309. – On the subjunc. ending -ησι (without ι subscr.), West 1998, XXXI. — **μέγα κράτος:** a formula after caesura B 2 (6× *Il.*, 1× *h.Cer.*); in reference to the actual situation in battle, κράτος means 'supremacy, predominance', the combination μ. κ. φέρω/φέρομαι 'be victorious' (*LfgrE s.v.* κράτος 1527.64 ff., esp. 1528.11 ff.).

309 A concluding gnome that serves to underline the paraenesis at 303 ff. and to encourage (himself): the god of battle is nonpartisan, luck in battle can change (similarly Paris at 6.339 [see *ad loc.*]; cf. 3.439 f., *Od.* 11.537), a victory over Achilleus is also possible (AH; Ahrens 1937, 31); on I-E parallels in terms of syntax and content, Watkins [1976] 1994, 256 f.; 1995, 326–329; West 2007, 111; on gnomes at the end of speeches, 1.218n., as an affirmation of advice and requests, 6.261n. – The name Enyalios (originally the god of the duel) is attested already on Linear B tablets and is later interpreted as an epithet of Ares (2.651n., CG 6; Latacz [2001] 2010, 381 f.). The wording became proverbial (as an appeal to fight against a superior enemy), cf. Archilochus *fr.* 110 West and Aristotle *Rhet.* 1395a16, also Latin *communis Mars belli* in Livy (Edwards; Hölscher 1939, 41 n. 1).

An asyndetic explanatory clause (Ruijgh 765, 767; cf. 1.105n., 19.90n.). — **ξυνός:** 'together', in early epic also with γαῖα (15.193), κακόν (16.262), δαῖτες and θόωκοι ('Hes.' *fr.* 1.6 M.-W.), i.e. with items and circumstances in which all can share in the same manner (cf. *Il.* 12.422 ἐπιξύνῳ ἐν ἀρούρῃ and 1.124, 23.809 ξυνήϊα); in the present context, used of the god of battle and meaning approximately 'nonpartisan' (*LfgrE*; Edwards). — **κτενέοντα κατέκτα:** κτενέοντα is the fut. part. of κτείνω (cf. 6.409n., G 62; West 1998, XXXII), i.e. 'the one who is preparing to kill' (Chantr. 2.201; Wackernagel [1920/24] 2009, 262 f.; on the use of the fut. part. in early epic in general, 19.120n.; Classen [1851–1857] 1867, 78–80). For additional examples for the play with sound (here with the consonants k and t) and words (here with reciprocal action), Edwards, Introd. 57–59; for parallels esp. for the word play[P] with verb and object, Fehling 1969, 231.

310–313 Concluding narrator[P] commentary (on which in general, 2.38n., 6.234–236n.; Edwards, Introd. 4 f.), at 311 on the participants in the assembly (echoing Hektor's reproach to Polydamas at 295 and 12.234) and at 312b/313b on the two speakers (echoing Polydamas' assessment at 12.212); here with a proleptic character (prepared for in 249–253 [see *ad loc.*]): internal prolepsis[P], fulfilled in Books 20–21 (see also 22.99 ff.). For additional passages with the Trojans behaving naïvely, 2.872n.

---

309 καί: 'also', refers to κτενέοντα. — τε: 'epic τε' (R 24.11). — κατέκτα: root aor. (3rd pers. sing.) of κατακτείνω; gnomic aor.

310 = 8.542. — **κελάδησαν:** a denominative related to κέλαδος ('noise') meaning 'clamor, cheer'; as a description of acclamations, it is used only for Trojan assemblies (here and at 8.542), elsewhere of the Achaians as spectators of contests (23.869) and of natural phenomena (κελάδων of rivers at 576, 21.16, of wind *Od.* 2.421): *LfgrE s.v.* κελάδων, κελαδῆσαι; TICHY 1983, 196 f.; ELMER 2013, 33 f. It highlights the noise associated with exuberant cheering, while the formulations more common in the context 'assembly', (μέγα ἐπ)ιάχω and (ἐπ)αινέω (312), describe shouts of approval (KRAPP 1964, 99–103; MACKIE 1996, 93 f.; for a collection of examples of 'approval, agreement', BARCK 1976, 145; ELMER *loc. cit.* 30–38). The noisy cheering in the assembly might be an additional indication of the Trojans' rather undisciplined and careless behavior (cf. 3.8–9n. with bibliography); see also *Od.* 24.463–469.

311 fools: on *népioi,* 295n.; as narrator[P] commentary, this characterization indicates that those concerned will perish as a result of their misjudgment, not in the sense of a reproving assessment but as a pointer toward the tragic element in the fate of the characters[P] (16.46–47n. with bibliography; EDWARDS; RICHARDSON 1990, 161 f.). A deity robbing someone of their senses (*phrénes*) or damaging them is a common formulation for justifying mistakes based on (temporarily) clouded judgement (6.234n., 19.137n.); here the narrator[P] uses it to make plausible the fact that everyone without exception (see 313) now enthusiastically agrees with Hektor's offensive strategy, even though they were all quite frightened at the beginning of the assembly (245–248, see *ad loc.*), and thus to guide the action in the desired direction (schol. bT on 312–313a; ELMER 2013, 141–145). — **Athene:** She generally acts in favor of the Achaian side in the war (203–204n.; *LfgrE s.v.* Ἀθηναίη 214.3 ff.).

Παλλὰς Ἀθήνη: 217–218n.

312 ἐπήνησαν: a common expression for statements of consent in an assembly ('agree, applaud'); only here with a dat. obj. (*LfgrE s.v.* αἰνέω), showing the Trojan focus on the person of Hektor (ELMER 2013, 23, 140 f.). — **κακὰ μητιόωντι:** VE ≈ 15.27, *Od.* 1.234. μητιάομαι is a deverbative from μῆτις (RISCH 321), the term designating practical intelligence and planning, strategic thinking (2.169n.; on the epic diectasis, G 48; on the change of voice, G 100); κακὰ μ. together with 313 (ἐσθλὴν φράζετο βουλήν) forms the antithesis 'make a good *vs.* a bad suggestion' (literally 'ponder bad things' *vs.* 'devise a good counsel/plan') and is another pointer by the narrator[P] at the characters' tragic actions, see 311n. (*LfgrE s.v.* μητιάομαι; DE JONG [1987] 2004, 138; BERTOLÍN CEBRIÁN 1996, 201).

---

310 ἀγόρευ', ἐπί: on the hiatus, R 5.1. — ἐπὶ ... κελάδησαν: on the so-called tmesis, R 20.2.
311 ἐκ ... εἵλετο: σφεων (= αὐτῶν: R 14.1) is dependent on the verb; on the so-called tmesis, R 20.2. — σφεͷων: on the synizesis, R 7.
312 μητιόωντι: on the epic diectasis, R 8.

314a to caesura C 2 = 7.380 (athetized by WEST); ≈ 11.730; 1st VH = *h.Cer.* 511. —
The curt reference to the execution of Hektor's orders implies the end of the
assembly (on dissolving Homeric assemblies, 1.305n.). Contrary to epic narrative convention, according to which the execution of an order is repeated almost literally (6.86–101n.), the narrator[P] restricts himself to the first order (298)
while omitting both the other two (299) and the addition at 300–302 (provoca-
tion of the preceding speaker: see *ad loc.*; DE JONG [1987] 2004, 210). This, as
well as the fast change of scene at 314b, underlines the contrast in mood between the two camps: among the Trojans, euphoric cheering reigns during the
preparation of the evening meal; among the Achaians, mourning and lament
for Patroklos (OWEN 1946, 185; RICHARDSON 1990, 116, 226).

314b–355 *Achilleus and the Myrmidons prepare Patroklos' corpse to be laid out*
(prothesis) and perform laments throughout the night.

314b a change of scene to the camp of the Achaians, who spend the entire night
lamenting Patroklos (picking up from 231 ff.: 231b–238n.); the Trojans reappear
only at their departure for battle at 20.3 ff. (239–242n.; EDWARDS on 314–355; DI
BENEDETTO [1994] 1997, 235 with n. 16).

αὐτὰρ Ἀχαιοί: 148n.

315 ≈ 355; 2nd VH ≈ *Od.* 9.467. — The scene that follows initiates the lament by
the side of Patroklos' body, which has been laid out, where Achilleus delivers an initial speech of mourning. The scene is framed by verses with literal repetitions (315/354 f.); the action described there is picked up again and
continued after the divine scenes at 356–19.3 (ring-composition[P]; VAN OTTERLO
1948, 68; TSAGALIS 2004, 148; KELLY 2007, 356; on variations in verse structure, EDWARDS 1968, 277; on the four-word verse, 1.75n.): (a) the lengthy lament
('the entire night') on the following morning during Thetis' arrival at 19.4–6a
(19.5–6a n.), likewise the following night at 23.217–232; (b) the joining in the
lament by those present as a response to the individual speech of mourning (at
315b/355b; on echoes of the formulaic verse, see below) on the next day before
the departure for battle at 19.301/338 after the speeches of mourning by Briseïs
(19.286–300) and Achilleus (19.314–337), similarly in the evening (23.17–23).

ἀνεστενάχοντο γοῶντες: echoes the formulaic designation of the responsion after a
preceding mourning speech ἐπὶ δὲ στενάχοντο + subj. (19.301n., 24.720b–722n., 24.722n.,
each with bibliography). ἀναστενάχω/ἀναστοναχίζω means literally 'groan', cf. 10.9 f.

---

314 αὐτάρ: 'but' (R 24.2).
315 παννύχιοι: predicative adj., 'the whole night through'. — ἀνεστενάχοντο: on the middle,
R 23.

(KRAPP 1964, 31; cf. 19.314n.), with an obj. here and at 23.211 'mourn for someone' (cf. 19.301n.), while the prefix may also stress the intensity (TSAGALIS 2004, 66 f.: 'to groan aloud over someone'); γοάω designates the ritual lament (24.160n.). The process of mourning is frequently expressed via synonyms, cf. ὀδυρόμενος στεναχίζω at *Od.* 1.243, 9.13, 11.214, 16.195 and the emphatic synonym doublings at 6.373, 24.48 with nn. (KAIMIO 1977, 82).

316 = 23.17; 2nd VH = 22.430, 24.747 (see *ad loc.*); ≈ 18.51 (see *ad loc.*), 24.723, 24.761. — A formulaic verse for introducing a lament (24.723n., see also 51n.): in addition to the present passage and 23.17, the variable VE formula *(ex-)êrche góoio* (7× *Il.*) always introduces a speech of mourning by a woman speaking to a group of women: Thetis (51), Hekabe lamenting Hektor (22.430, 24.747), Andromache (24.723) and Helen (24.761). But here Achilleus, as the person closest to the deceased, opens the lament and, in what follows (see 354 f., also 19.4–6a, 19.303 f./338, 23.9–18, 23.108 f., 23.153 f.), will be surrounded by a group of men (contrast 28–31 [see *ad loc.*]): ALEXIOU [1974] 2002, 13 f.; DERDERIAN 2001, 35 f. and 56; GAGLIARDI 2007, 103 f. n. 43; cf. 19.303n. The direct speech, Achilleus' first 'public' one, i.e. a speech of mourning accompanied by a group of mourners, occurs only after an additional speech introduction formula[P] (323) naming the said group (an expanded speech introduction formula[P]: 249n.); his mood is first called to mind via both the portrayal of his mourning behavior (groaning at 318a, 323a: KAIMIO 1977, 98 f.; gesture: 317) and a simile (318b–322 [see *ad loc.*]) (TSAGALIS 2004, 60 f.; BECK 2005, 261–263). – On a similar composition in the Epic of Gilgamesh (Gilgamesh mourns his friend Enkidu), see DI BENEDETTO (1994) 1998, 313–315; WEST 1997, 341–343.

Πηλεΐδης: a periphrastic denomination[P] via patronymic (166n.). — **ἀδινοῦ:** 'repeated, sustained' (cf. 124n.).

317 = 23.18. — One Homeric gesture of mourning is relatives touching the deceased, esp. embracing him (19.4 f. and 19.284 f. Achilleus and Briseïs with Patroklos) and touching or holding his head as a sign of affection (23.136 Achilleus with Patroklos; 24.712 and 24.724 Andromache and Hekabe with Hektor; cf. also 71 [see *ad loc.*]): 19.284–285n., 24.711–712n., each with bibliography; on pictorial representations, HUBER 2001, 204 f. The gesture in the present passage, together with the characterization of Achilleus' hands as 'man-killing', prepares for the subsequent speech, the main topics of which are honoring promises and

---

316 τοῖσι: 'among them' (R 19.2); on the anaphoric demonstrative function of ὅ, ἥ, τό, R 17; on the declension, R 11.2. — ἀδινοῦ ἐξῆρχε: on the hiatus, R 5.6. — γόοιο: on the declension, R 11.2.
317 ἐπ' ... θέμενος: on the so-called tmesis, R 20.2. — στήθεσσιν: on the declension, R 11.3; on the plural, R 18.2.

exacting revenge (324–327, 334–337: 324–342n.), cf. also 23.18–23 during the fulfilment of the promise after Hektor has been killed, and 24.478 f. in the *hikesia* scene between Priam and Achilleus (see *ad loc.*): HAMPE 1952, 20 f.; TSAGALIS 2008, 243; slightly differently, CAMEROTTO 2009, 110 f. ('manslaughtering' as a reference to Achilleus' impending *aristeia*); on Gilgamesh's comparable gesture, see WEST 1997, 342.

ἀνδροφόνους: a generic epithet[P] derived from I-E poetic language, in early epic usually in a gen. formula of Hektor (13×: 1.242n., 6.498n., 24.509n.); also 3× of Achilleus' hands, 2× of Ares, 1× each of Lykurgos (6.134n.), Herakles' lance and a poison (*LfgrE*).

318a ≈ 21.417. — **πυκνὰ ... στενάχων:** a variant of the formula βαρὺ στενάχων at 323, with πυκ(ι)νά designating the chronologically 'dense', i.e. continuously repeated, sounds of lamentation; likewise at 21.417; 10.9 (πυκίν' ... ἀνεστονάχιζ(ε)) is similar, 124 with ἀδινά στ. is comparable (see *ad loc.*; *LfgrE s.v.* πυκινός 1630.64 ff.; KRAPP 1964, 30 f.; KAIMIO 1977, 52).

318b–322 Although lion similes usually illustrate the energy, aggression and courage of an animal or warrior (3.23n., 24.41b–44n., each with bibliography), in the present simile[P] these traits are connected to pain and grief but also to anger, i.e. emotions triggered by a loss (SEGAL 1971, 50: 'it condenses the combination of violence and tenderness into a single vivid image'). The image of the lion whose young, left behind hidden in the bushes, have been taken is framed by terms for Achilleus' lamentation (318a, 323); it illustrates both his current situation and mood and his relationship with his friend, in which he has the role of a protector (see 326 f., as well as 23.222–225 [Achilleus mourns for Patroklos like a father for his son]): (a) he had to let his friend enter battle on his own, was unable to protect him and thus has lost him (320b and 324–327, 333; also 98 f., 102 ff.); (b) he feels pain and anger, combined with the urge for revenge (320n.): pain at 320 (*áchnutai*) and 316/318a/323, as well as 22; anger (*chólos* and *cholōthéis*) at 322b and 333–337; (c) he will search for the perpetrator on the battlefield and pursue him (321–322a and 334 f.; cf. 20.75 ff., 20.423 ff., 22.188 ff.): schol. bT on 318–322; EDWARDS; FRÄNKEL 1921, 93; MOULTON 1977, 105 f.; SCHNAPP-GOURBEILLON 1981, 87 f.; DE JONG (1987) 2004, 127, 272 n. 81; LONSDALE 1990, 93 f.; CLARKE 1995, 155 f.; MILLS 2000, 8–10; STOEVESANDT 2004, 259–261; on the proleptic function of similes, DUCKWORTH 1933, 14 f.; SCHADEWALDT (1938) 1966, 156 n. 2; EDWARDS, Introd. 31 f.; on similes with parent-child motifs in the context of Achilleus, 16.7–11n.; DE JONG on *Il.* 22, Introd. 24). – The mourning Gilgamesh is likewise compared *inter alia* to a lion whose cubs have been taken, with his inner agitation portrayed via the animal's external restlessness (WEST 1997, 342 f., with reference to similar animal comparisons in the Hebrew Bible); for discussion of potential Ancient Near Eastern models for the present Homeric simile, 319n.; EDWARDS (direct influence inconclusive: 'a parallel creation is very probable'); ALDEN 2005, 340–342; CURRIE 2012, 550 f., 568 ff.; cf. NTHS 54–57.

318b = 17.109; ≈ 15.275. — **lion:** It has been a matter of discussion since antiquity whether the reference is in fact to a male lion with a mane (the adj. *ēygéneios* means 'with handsome facial hair') or – in opposition to the grammatical gender at 318–320 – to a lioness, since the mother takes care of the litter and since 'lion' and 'lioness' are not yet lexically distinct in early epic (cf. 21.483 f. Artemis as a lion). But in the present simile, as in other animal similes with parent animals protecting and defending their young (9.323 f., 12.167–170, 16.259–265, 17.133–136 [Aias defends Patroklos' corpse as a lion does his cub]), it is not the gender of the animal that is significant but the species; the narrator[P] specifies the female parent animal only in the context of caring for the brood (5.554 f., 17.4 f. [Menelaos circles the deceased Patroklos like a primiparous cow does its heifer]) or of lacking the physical means to protect its young (11.113–119, 16.353–354): schol. A on 318 and on 17.134–136; *LfgrE s.v.* λέων; EDWARDS on 17.133–136; FRÄNKEL 1921, 92 f.; on the vacillating transmission of gender in the lion simile in the Epic of Gilgamesh, WEST 1997, 342 with n. 17; ALDEN 2005, 340 n. 42; on female animals in Homeric similes in general, LONSDALE 1990, 28–30. – In Ancient Near Eastern and archaic art, pronounced facial hair and mane are a common characteristic of lions (EDWARDS, Introd. 36 n. 43; *BNP s.v.* Lion).

ὥς τε: a common introduction to comparisons and similes (2.289n. with bibliography). — **λίς:** an epic term for λέων, in early epic nom./acc. sing., always before caesura C 2 (5× *Il.*, 1× 'Hes.'); the grammatical gender is always masc. (cf. *iterata* and 'Hes.' *Sc.* 172): *LfgrE s.v.* λέων; LSJ *s.v.* λίς. — **ἠϋγένειος:** a generic epithet[P] of lions (*iterata, Od.* 4.456) and of Pan (*h.Pan* 39); a compound with ἐϋ-/ἠϋ-, the second element related to γένειον ('chin, cheek') and γενειάδες ('chin-beard'), i.e. 'with handsome facial hair' (cf. ἠϋκόμος of women at 1.36n.); in the case of lions, this refers to facial hair or whiskers (*LfgrE*; JANKO on 15.271–276; cautiously, EDWARDS on 17.106–109) or to the mane (CERRI; WEST on *Od.* 4.456), see schol. A and T.

319 Nowhere else in Homeric hunting similes does a hunter take lion cubs. Mention of this incident – probably to be thought of as a chance find by a hunter (VAN LEEUWEN; *LfgrE s.v.* σκύμνος; ALDEN 2005, 339 n. 37) – is thus sometimes considered to have been influenced by Ancient Near Eastern mod-

---

318b ὥς: 'like'. — τε: 'epic τε' (R 24.11), likewise 319 (θ'), 320, 321. — τε (λ)λίς: on the prosody, M 4.6. — ἠϋγένειος: = ἐϋ-, initial syllable metrically lengthened (R 10.1).

319 ῥα: = ἄρα (R 24.1). — ὑπὸ ... ἁρπάσῃ: generalizing subjunc. without a modal particle (R 21.1); on the so-called tmesis, R 20.2. — σκύμνους: 'the (animal) young'. — ἁρπάσῃ ἀνήρ: on the correption, R 5.5. — ἀνήρ: initial syllable metrically lengthened (R 10.1).

els or practices (Epic of Gilgamesh; capture of lion cubs to raise them for royal exhibition matches) that must have been familiar to the audience to some extent (ALDEN *loc. cit.* 342); at the same time, lions were present in Greece and Asia Minor during the Mycenaean period and likely until the Archaic period (3.23n. with bibliography). The narrator[P] likely chose the hunter's chance find deliberately: the implicit comparison of Hektor with the hunter is appropriate inasmuch as Hektor, when killing Patroklos (16.806–821), was able to exploit a 'favorable opportunity' (STOEVESANDT 2004, 261 [transl.]). Whether the motif of the deer hunt in a simile in Book 22 should be understood in reference to the present passage (thus LONSDALE 1990, 93 f.) is less certain: during the encounter between Achilleus and Hektor on the battlefield, Hektor is compared *inter alia* to a fawn (22.189–193) that is tracked down by a hunting dog (Achilleus).

ᾧ ῥά θ' ... ἁρπάσῃ: Simple comparisons[P] (here 318) are frequently expanded to similes[P] via appositives or relative clauses (2.145n.; EDWARDS, Introd. 26); on the transition from hypotaxis with a subjunc. to parataxis with an ind. (320 f.), 207–212n. – **ἐλαφηβόλος ... ἀνήρ:** Like σκύμνος, ἐλαφηβόλος is a Homeric *hapax legomenon*[P]; of a deer hunter only here, elsewhere a designation for Artemis (*h.Hom.* 27.2, 'Hes.' *fr.* 23(a).21 M.-W.): *LfgrE* and LSJ *s.v.* ἐλαφηβόλος. On designations for occupations and functions by means of gender terms (ἀνήρ, γυνή) and appositives, 2.474n.; on the epic terms for 'hunter' (e.g. phrases with ἀνήρ + θηρητήρ at 12.170, 21.574, θηρήτωρ 9.544, θηρευτής 12.41, 'Hes.' *Sc.* 303, 388), see BUCHHOLZ et al. 1973, 6 f. – **ὑπὸ ... ἁρπάσῃ:** means 'steal'; beside the indication of location ὕλης ἐκ πυκινῆς at 320, ὑπό here has an aspect of motion (*LfgrE s.v.* 1343.63 f. and 1344.3 ff.; cf. 16.353n. [ὕπεκ]) and perhaps an additional connotation of secrecy (AH; on this nuance of ὑπο-, 513n. [ὑπεθωρήσσοντο]; SCHW. 2.524; *LfgrE s.v.* ὑποκλοπέομαι; FERNÁNDEZ-GALIANO on *Od.* 22.38).

320 1st VH ≈ *Od.* 6.128. – **anguished:** The word family *áchnymai/áchos* denotes psychological pain combined with feelings of helplessness, anger and aggression (321 f./334 ff.). This mood is applied to animals only in the present simile, otherwise it is fundamental to human life and especially that of Achilleus (thus Thetis at 62: cf. 22, 112): 22n., 62n.; much the same applies to 'anger', *chólos* (322b/337b, also 90 ff., 108 ff., 114 ff., cf. 19.15b–16, 19.367 f.: 107–108n.). This amplifies the intensity of the image: 'The lion and Achilles are merging' (HEATH 2005, 140); on so-called imagery interaction in similes, 2.87n., 24.42–43n. (each with bibliography); LONSDALE 1990, 132–135; PELLICCIA 1995, 90 n. 150.

---

320 ὅ: anaphoric demonstrative (R 17). – ὕστερος: predicative, 'later' *sc.* than the theft by the hunter.

321 ἄγκε(α): 'mountain gorges', mentioned in Homeric epic only in similes (e.g. 22.190), usually as the abode of wild animals (*LfgrE*). — **ἐπῆλθε:** Similes frequently have aor. forms beside pres. ones (here at 320, 322; for additional examples, CHANTR. 2.186; see also 16.299–300n. [on the gnomic aor.]). — **μετ' ... ἴχνι(α):** to be connected with either ἐρευνῶν ('searching for': EDWARDS; SCHW. 2.486; CHANTR. 2.119; FRITZ 2005, 213) or ἐπῆλθε ('following the tracks'), clarified by the part. ἐρευνῶν (AH; *LfgrE s.v.* ἐρευνάω: 'abs. or *sc.* ἴχνια' [transl.], cf. *Od.* 19.436).

322 2nd VH ≈ 17.67. — **εἴ ποθεν ἐξεύροι:** 'whether ... somewhere' (namely based on the tracks); the dependent interrogative clause with the opt., as with verbs of attempting, deliberation, etc., assumes a wish on the part of the lion (SCHW. 2.687; LEAF). — **μάλα:** emphatic at the beginning of the sentence (*LfgrE s.v.* 22.27 ff.). — **δριμύς:** means 'sharp, piercing', the etymology is obscure (FRISK, *DELG s.v.*); in early epic, the word is used in the context of overwhelming emotions (*Od.* 24.319 μένος, with physical effects: HEUBECK on *Od.* 24.318–319; 'Hes.' *Sc.* 457 ἄχος), as well as in a comparison of the pain after an injury with labor pains that run through the body like missiles (*Il.* 11.269–271: βέλος ὀξὺ ... | δριμύ ... | ... πικρὰς ὠδῖνας), then of μάχη ('violent': 15.696, 3× Hes.), and in post-Homeric literature also of things that have negative effects on the sense of taste or the eyes ('bitter, spicy, acrid') and as the antithesis of γλυκύς (*LfgrE* and LSJ *s.v.*). On δριμὺς χόλος, cf. Achilleus' description of the χόλος that initially works like sweet honey (109–110n.). — **χόλος αἱρεῖ:** for similar formulations, 3.446 [with n. *ad loc.*] ἵμερος αἱρεῖ, 17.67 δέος αἱρεῖ.

323 1st VH = 9.16; 2nd VH ≈ *Od.* 8.201, 16.354, 18.35. — **βαρὺ στενάχων:** 70n.

324–342 Achilleus' speech – the only direct speech in this scene – is exceptional in terms of structure and content when compared with other laments in the *Iliad*, which are usually tripartite with a ring-composition[P] structure (19.286–339n., 24.725–745n., 24.749–750n.; on their motifs in particular, see DERDERIAN 2001, 36 f.). The present speech contains two parts (324–332/333–342) – marked by an exclamation (324) and an address (333) – that share the close linking of Patroklos' death with that of Achilleus himself (esp. 329–333): (1) remembering things past (Patroklos in the 3rd pers. at 326 f.) and a lament for their two predestined deaths before Troy ('us both' at 329): (a) hoped for return home at 324–327, (b) gnome at 328, (c) death in a foreign land at 329–332; (2) turning to the deceased, an announcement of avenging and honoring the deceased (Patroklos in the 2nd person; on the composition, 333–342n.): (a) an address to the deceased and an account of the situation at 333; (b) a promise

---

321 ἄγκε' ἐπῆλθε ... ἴχνι' ἐρευνῶν: on the hiatus (twice), R 5.1. — ἄγκε(α): on the uncontracted form, R 6. — μετ(ά): 'after' in the sense 'in the direction of, behind'. — ἀνέρος: = ἀνδρός; initial syllable metrically lengthened (R 10.1).

323 ὥς: = οὕτως. — μετεφώνεε: on the uncontracted form, R 6. — Μυρμιδόνεσσιν: on the declension, R 11.3.

to take revenge on Hektor and the Trojans at 334–337; (c) an announcement of continuous lamentation beside the corpse by the women captives at 338–342 (LOHMANN 1970, 66 f. n. 112, 103 n. 18; TSAGALIS 2004, 143–148; BECK 2005, 262 f.; on the great weight given to revenge in this speech of mourning, see WAGNER-HASEL 2000, 89 f.; DERDERIAN 2001, 34 n. 76, 41, 55 f.).

324–327 External completive analepsis[P]: the farewell scene in the house of Peleus prior to the campaign against Troy has already been described twice: by Odysseus at 9.252–259 (warnings by Achilleus' father) and in detail by Nestor at 11.765–791 (advice of the two fathers), according to whom Patroklos' father Menoitios highlighted the virtues of the two friends (11.786–789: intelligence *vs.* physical strength); on Achilleus' departure for Troy, see also 58n. Here Achilleus merely mentions the promise 'given on that day' that he was unable to keep, an allusion likely meant not for the bystanders but primarily for Achilleus himself. The speech overall begins like a kind of soliloquy ('Ah me. It was an empty word I cast forth …' 324), whereas in other speeches of mourning in the *Iliad*, the deceased is addressed at the beginning, see 19.287, 315, 22.431, 477, 24.725, 748, 762 (on the question of different addressees of laments, see PELLICCIA 1995, 154 f. n. 87). The narrator[P] uses this first mention of the promise (principle of 'ad hoc narration'[P]) to show the extent to which Achilleus feels responsible for his friend and, by having Achilleus repeat the content of the promise precisely, makes clear the speaker's desperation regarding the catastrophe (HEBEL 1970, 120 f.). On statements of wishes that remain unfulfilled in laments, ALEXIOU (1974) 2002, 178; TSAGALIS 2004, 42–44; on references to the farewell scene scattered throughout the *Iliad*, LATACZ (1995) 2014, 309 f. n. 107; on warriors' recollections of farewell scenes in general, 6.207–210n.

324 ὦ πόποι: a word of character language[P], expressing (usually disagreeable) surprise and displeasure (1.254n.; KELLY 2007, 220–223), here regarding the uselessness of the promise given in the past. — **ἅλιον ἔπος ἔκβαλον:** a vivid expression probably based on a missile (not) missing its target: (οὐχ) ἅ. βέλος 6× *Il.*, always with a form of βαλεῖν ('strike') in the context (NÜNLIST 1998, 148 f. with reference to Pind. *Ol.* 9.11 f.). Elsewhere of words: οὐδ'/οὐχ' ἅλιον ἔπος at 24.92/224 of divine orders that remain unfulfilled, also ἅ. μῦθον ὑπέστημεν (5.715) of a promise, ἅ. πέλει ὅρκιον of an oath (4.158); *LfgrE s.v.* ἅλιος 2, cf. also 1.201n. on ἔπεα πτερόεντα ('flying stably and thus accurately'). The etymology of ἅ. is obscure: perhaps a derivation from ἅλς (by analogy with ἠέριος, αἰθέριος), marking the missile that (originally in the context of fishing?) misses and falls into the water (SCHW. 1.461; *DELG s.v.* ἅλιος; SNELL [1964] 1966, 65). ἔκβαλον reveals the impulsiveness of the past statement, cf. *Od.* 4.503 (AH). — **ἤματι κείνῳ:** a VE formula

324 ἦ: 'indeed, in fact' (R 24.4). — ῥ(α): on the avoidance of hiatus, R 24.1. — ἅλιον (ϝ)έπος: on the prosody, R 4.5. — ἤματι: from ἦμαρ 'day'. — κείνῳ: = ἐκείνῳ.

(5× *Il.*, 2× Hes.), aside from the present passage always in narrator-text (elsewhere in character language ἤματι τῷ, ὅτε: 85n.); usually (with the exception of 2.37, 21.517) in reference to an action in the past; Achilleus highlights the irretrievable past (DE JONG [1987] 2004, 235 f.).

325 in his halls: The expression *en megároisin* is often used with an emotional connotation in the sense 'at home' (24.208b–209a n.). — **the hero Menoitios:** The designation *hḗrōs* occurs as a generic epithet[P] or periphrastic denomination[P] of various major and minor characters and marks them as 'belonging to a grand past' (6.34–35n.; on Menoitios, 12n.).

326 The town of Opous in East Lokris (called Opoeis in the *Iliad*) is Patroklos' *original* hometown (2.531n.). But after he struck dead a playmate in anger when he was a child, his father Menoitios brought him to Achilleus' father Peleus in Phthia, who raised him together with Achilleus (23.84–90), and from there he went to war together with Achilleus (11.769–790: taking leave from the fathers in Phthia; on this, see LATACZ [1995] 2014, 309 n. 107): CH 2; on the motif 'exile after a killing', 24.480–484n. The statement 'back to Opous' is thus striking (esp. after 11.769–771). At the same time, a return to Opous is not necessarily denied forever: the killing (23.87 f.) could be redressed by payment of blood money, cf. 9.632–636, 18.497–501 (LEAF; cf. NÜNLIST 2009a, 628 f.). But the formulation can perhaps also be explained by the narrator[P] picking up and combining two narrative motifs at 326 f. in order to elevate Patroklos, with both motifs focussing on 'homeland': (1) in the promise to return him home to his father, the combination of 'die far from home' with the notion that someone will not return home to their father (59b–60a n., 24.86n.); (2) in the portrayal of Patroklos as the destroyer of Troy, the motif 'a felicitous return home after the destruction of Troy' (cf. 327 and the formulaic 2.113 [see *ad loc.*]); in this, he juxtaposes the chain of associations Achilleus–Peleus–Phthia (e.g. 59 f., 101, 330 f.) with the corresponding one Patroklos–Menoitios–Opous.

φῆν δέ: a quotation formula at VB for introducing indirect speech (FÜHRER 1967, 86 f., with a collection of examples). — περικλυτόν: a generic epithet[P] with various characters[P], with regard to Patroklos only here (on κλυτός, 19.10n.); probably to be understood as predicative with ἀπάξειν, as a result of the successes mentioned in 327 (schol. bT; AH; EDWARDS on 324–327); for additional expressions for the notion 'widely spread fame', 6.111n.

---

325 θαρσύνων: conative ('attempting to give courage'). — μεγάροισιν: on the declension, R 11.2; on the pl., R 18.2.
326 φῆν: unaugmented (R 16.1) 1st pers. sing. imper. of φημί. — δέ (ϝ)οι: on the prosody, R 4.3. — οἱ: = αὐτῷ (R 14.1). — ἀπάξειν: 'bring back, return' (away from Troy).

327 2nd VH ≈ *Od.* 5.40, 13.138. — **his share of war spoils:** Booty, a motif not without importance even for Achilleus' participation in military campaigns, largely consists of cattle (1.154–157n.), tripods and cauldrons, gold and bronze – as well as women, who must then serve as slaves (28n.), e.g. 9.135–140 (*LfgrE s.v.* ληΐς; Nowag 1983, 26 f.). On Patroklos' share of the booty, see Achilleus' promise at 24.595.

Ἴλιον ἐκπέρσαντα: an inflectable VB formula (8× *Il.*: 2.113n., 2.133n.). — λαχόντα ... αἶσαν: i.e. after he has received the share (αἶσα) each warrior is entitled to from the joint booty, which is distributed equitably, in contrast to the γέρας for the leaders; cf. 9.367, *Od.* 14.232 f. (*LfgrE s.v.* λαγχάνω; on the procedure for allotting the spoils, 1.118–129n.).

328–332 Achilleus summarizes his experiences by means of a gnome (328): Zeus takes no account of human plans. The narrator[P] had already signalled to the audience the limits to which human wishes and plans can be satisfied, given the will of Zeus; he did this during Patroklos' departure for battle at 16.252, when Zeus reacted to Achilleus' prayer, and at 16.688 by means of a similar gnome (a similar notion in reference to Hektor at 10.104 f.; cf. *Od.* 22.51): Ahrens 1937, 31; Hebel 1970, 121; Rutherford 1982, 156; Lardinois 2000, 645. Achilleus himself has been aware of his own destiny for some time (1.352n., 9.410 ff.: brief life), but was convinced, until he received the report of Patroklos' death, that he would die before his friend (cf. 333) and that the latter would return home unharmed (19.328 ff.): cf. 8–11n., 19.328–333n. He now realizes that, due to predetermined fate, he will be unable to honor his promise, cf. the stressed position of 'both' (Greek *amphō*) and 'here' (Greek *autoú*) at the VB of 329/330.

328 ἄνδρεσσι: a generalizing statement with the use of ἄνδρες, since the starting point is represented by battle and luck in war (*LfgrE s.v.* ἀνήρ 834.38 ff.).

329 **stain:** one of the paraphrases involving the term 'earth' (*gáia*) for 'die' (similarly 11.394 of the slain lying on the ground unburied), it facilitates the formulation of the *joint* scene of the death ('same soil'); cf. 'bite the dust' (2.418n.), 'claw the ground with the hand' (11.425, etc.), 'go underground' (332n., 333n.).

πέπρωται: related to πορεῖν (I-E root *perh₃- 'provide, allocate': *LIV* 474 f.); in reference to human beings, the perf. is used in the context of predestined death, cf. ὁπποτέρῳ θανάτοιο τέλος πεπρωμένον ἐστίν (3.309) and θανάτου δέ οἱ αἶσα πέπρωται (*Cypr. fr.* 9 West), both with subj. and dat. obj., in the present passage in an impersonal construc-

---

327 ἐκπέρσαντα: aor. part. of ἐκπέρθω 'destroy utterly'.
328 ἄνδρεσσι: = ἀνδράσι (cf. R 11.3).
329 ἄμφω ... πέπρωται ... ἐρεῦσαι: impersonal πέπρωται ('it is destined') with acc./inf. construction ἄμφω ('both of us') ... ἐρεῦσαι (related to ἐρεύθω 'redden', *sc.* 'with our blood').

tion with acc.-inf. ('it is fated that both of us ...'), in contrast to the personal construction ἄνδρα ... πεπρωμένον αἴσῃ (16.441 [see *ad loc.*] = 22.179): *LfgrE s.v.* πορεῖν; DIETRICH 1965, 265; SARISCHOULIS 2008, 38.

330–332 A commonly used motif that presents dying as a failure to return home or to one's father (326n.), it is varied, for increased pathos, by the additional mention of his mother (likewise at 19.422) and framed by an indication of location 'here' (*autoú* at 330/332) and reference to the fate shared with his friend (329 'the same soil' / 333 'follow you underground'): TSAGALIS 2004, 78, 80.

330 1st VH = 2.237, 19.330, *Od.* 18.226. — **Τροίη:** The reference is to the region 'Troad' (cf. 2.141n.).

331 2nd VH = 7.125, 9.438, 11.772. — **in his great house:** 325n.

ἱππηλάτα: an epithet[P] with heroes of the older generation, usually combined formulaically with γέρων (19.311n.). On the nom. in -ᾰ and the meaning ('charioteer'), 2.336n. *s.v.* ἱππότα.

332 1st VH = 16.34; VE from caesura C 2 = 16.629, *Od.* 13.427, 15.31; ≈ 11.549 — **earth:** The phrase 'the earth holds someone' is a paraphrase for 'someone is dead' (cf. 2.699 and *iterata*), cf. his soul travels 'under the earth' (333n.) into Hades (*LfgrE s.v.* γαῖα 110.60 ff.; CERRI; SACKS 1987, 73 ff.; CLARKE 1999, 180 f.).

333–342 The second part of Achilleus' speech of mourning brings his dead friend to the foreground (cf. the frequent use of forms of 'you', and of 'your' in 333–335, 337–339 and 'we' in 341 f., in contrast to the first part of the speech with 'I', 'me' in 324, 326, 330 and 'the two of us' at 329), but also the revenge and retribution that are mandatory for Achilleus, since his friend was killed before him. He thus lists the future events, important from his point of view and all of which will come true (a type of 'table of contents' speech, on which see DE JONG on *Od.* 1.81–95), in reverse chronological order in contrast to the narrative[P] (cf. epic regression[P]): (a) Achilleus' own death (333b: external prolepsis[P]); (b) Patroklos' funeral (334a: Book 23, esp. 23.110b–257a); (c) the killing of Hektor and the despoiling and defacing of his body (334b–335: Books 22–24); (d) the capture of twelve Trojan warriors who will be killed at the funeral (336 f.: 21.26–32, 23.175 f./180 f.); (e) the lament by captive women beside the laid out corpse (339–342: 19.282–302). The preparations necessary for carrying this out will be suggested by Thetis (reconciliation with Agamemnon and the troops, preparations for battle: 19.34–36n.).

---

330 αὐτοῦ: adv., 'on the spot, here' (likewise in 332). — ἐνί: = ἐν (R 20.1). — Τροίη: on the -η after -ι-, R 2. — Τροίη, ἐπεί: on the hiatus, R 5.6.
331 ἱππηλάτα: nom. sing. (↑).

333 Patroklos: The address to the deceased is usually placed at the beginning of a speech of mourning (324–327n.; on the comparable structure of Gilgamesh's speech of mourning, see WEST 1997, 343). — **underground:** a variant of the expression 'go into Hades/into the house of Hades', cf. *Od.* 20.81, *h.Cer.* 431 (6.19n. with bibliography; cf. 3.322n.); see also 332n.

νῦν δ': a return to reality (cf. 88n.).

334 not ... till: The expression 'not ... until' largely belongs to character language[P], where it is used in announcements, threats, etc., that are usually fulfilled – as the ones mentioned here are over the course of the following two days (cf. 333–342n. and STR 21 fig. 1), with Achilleus explicitly pointing out the fulfillment of the promises to his friend (23.20–23, 23.180–183): KELLY 2007, 339–341; on the motif of delayed burial, 19.23b–27n.; on burial customs in Homeric epic, 24.37b n. (necessary speed), 24.38n. (cremation). — **armor:** The reference is to Achilleus' own armor that Hektor took off the slain Patroklos and has since been wearing in battle, cf. 131 f., 22.322 f. (cf. 20–21n., 82b–85n.). The lack of any indication of this in the present passage (likewise at 22.331, 22.368 f.) has sometimes been criticized as an inaccuracy on the part of the poet (schol. bT on 334–335; AH; LEAF; EDWARDS), but is understandable given that the fact is secondary at this highly emotional moment: what is important is the despoiling and mistreatment of the slain Hektor in order to avenge and honor Achilleus' dead friend (cf. the threatening speech at 17.39: revenge by means of capturing the enemy's 'head and armor'; also 13.202 f.). It remains unclear to what extent the lack of reference to the exchange of arms as well as different versions of Hektor's actions after killing Patroklos (has the captured armor brought to Troy: 17.130 f.; dons it in place of his own armor, to Zeus' displeasure: 17.186–197 and 17.198–208; offers half as a price to whoever captures Patroklos' body: 17.231 f.) are remnants of different phases of the formation of the *Iliad* (thus WEST 2011, 331 [on 17.122] and 332 f. [on 17.186–228]: Hektor's exchange of weapons is secondary and thus sometimes omitted).

οὔ ..., πρὶν Ἕκτορος ... ἐνεῖκαι: In Homer, πρίν is usually construed with an inf. even after a negative main clause (SCHW. 2.654 f.; CHANTR. 2.315; cf. 1.97–100n.). — **κτερίω:** fut. of κτερίζω ('solemnly inter'), a linguistically more recent variant of κτερεΐζω (24.38n.; CLARKE 1999, 184; on the accent, WEST 1998, XXXI). — **Ἕκτορος:** The unusual position of the gen. with enjambment in the following verse (τεύχεα καὶ κεφαλήν) adds

---

333 σέ(ο): = σοῦ (R 14.1); comparative gen., dependent on ὕστερος ('later than you').
334 πρὶν ..., πρίν: The first πρίν is an adv., the second a conjunction with the inf. ἐνεῖκαι (from ἔνεικα ≈ Attic ἤνεγκον): 'earlier ..., before'. — πρὶν(ν) Ἕκτορος: on the prosody, M 4.6.

emphasis, cf. 16.840 f. (EDWARDS 1968, 278; on this, ROSÉN 1984, 93: gen. with an ablatival function rather than a possessive gen.: 'from Hektor bring here | armor and head').

335 head: The motif of maltreating a dead opponent, mentioned in the two preceding scenes, is developed further: on the character[P] plane on analogy with Hektor's intentions toward Patroklos (18.175 ff., see also 17.126: 175b–177n.), i.e. revenge in accord with 'an eye for an eye'; on the narrator[P] plane as a reminiscence of the earlier Trojan assembly during which Polydamas described the lot of the fallen (271/283) and Hektor announced his willingness to face Achilleus in a duel (306b–308; see also the allusion to Hektor's misjudgement at 310–313). Although the narrator[P] has Achilleus maltreat Hektor's body (22.395–404, 23.24–26, 24.14–21), he does not mutilate it, allowing it to be returned intact to Priam for a dignified burial (24.582–595): EDWARDS; SEGAL 1971, 28, 65; for prolepses[P] of Hektor's death, 92n.

μεγαθύμου σεῖο φονῆος: μεγάθυμος ('with great passion, in high spirits') is a generic epithet[P] of various heroes and peoples (1.123n., 19.75n.), including Hektor (15.440) and Patroklos (killing scene at 16.818), but mostly with personal names and only rarely with appellatives. In early epic, the gen. μεγαθύμου always occurs between caesurae B 1 and C 2, frequently with a patronymic or personal name following (*LfgrE s.v.* μεγάθυμος; HOEKSTRA 1965, 24); here it probably refers to φονῆος, i.e. to Hektor (VAN LEEUWEN; WILLCOCK; *LfgrE s.v.* μεγάθυμος) – a homage to the opponent that also increases the value of the revenge – rather than to σεῖο, i.e. Patroklos – as an element of praise of the dead in a speech of mourning (LEAF; preferred by EDWARDS). On the main transmission σεῖο (objective gen. of the personal pronoun rather than the possessive pronoun σοῖο), 24.486n.; LEAF.

336–337 = 23.22 f. — Achilleus' promise to kill twelve Trojans at the funeral illustrates his extraordinary state of mind, which mingles grief, anger and the desire to take excessive revenge on the enemy (cf. also 23.175 ff.). The remarkable aspect of his plan is that the killing is supposed to take place not during fighting on the battlefield, as in other instances of revenge for a slain friend or relative (killing the perpetrator or a random enemy: 16.398n.; on Achilleus, see 19.214 [see *ad loc.*], 21.97–135; the death of Hektor in Book 22, esp. 22.260–272), but during Patroklos' funeral 'before the pyre'. The personal ritual is meant to be both a visible demonstration of his revenge for the killing of his friend and an honor to the latter, as well as relieving Achilleus' grief and anger (337 'my anger over your slaying', 21.28 'compensation' [Greek *poiné*: 3.290n.]):

---

335 σεῖο: gen. sing. of the personal pronoun (= σοῦ: R 14.1). — φονῆος: on the declension, R 11.3.
336 πυρῆς: on the -η- after -ρ-, R 2.
337 σέθεν: = σοῦ (R 14.1, cf. R 15.1). — σέθεν κταμένοιο: causal gen., dependent on χολωθείς. — κταμένοιο: aor. mid. part. (with pass. sense) of κτείνω; on the declension, R 11.2.

RICHARDSON on *Il.* 23.166–176; GARLAND (1982) 1984, 12–14; HUGHES 1991, 49–56, 70 ('ritual revenge'); KITTS 2008, 229–237 (with an outline of the ritually conditioned elements in the description in Book 23). This killing of human beings during a burial ritual is unique in Homeric epic but is not explicitly judged by the narrator[P] (23.176 'evil thoughts' only refers to the point of view of the perpetrator or victims: DE JONG [1987] 2004, 138); this act likely serves to show Achilleus' limitless thirst for revenge, much as in his treatment of Hektor's corpse (on which, 24.22n.), and is to be viewed as a contrasting foil to his sympathy for Priam in Book 24. Comparable to the present ritual to some extent is the killing of Priam's daughter Polyxena during Achilleus' burial – mentioned in post-Homeric literature (e.g. *Il. Pers.*, Procl. *Chrest.* § 4 West; Eur. *Hec.*); on human sacrifice in Greek mythology, see *BNP s.v.* Human sacrifices; HUGHES *loc. cit.* 60–65, 71–92; HERMARY/LEGUILLOUX 2004, 129–131. To what extent the narrator[P] here introduces knowledge of actual human sacrifice in the context of burial rituals remains unclear; for discussion of possible evidence for human sacrifice in Greece, and on the comparison of the portrayal in Book 23 with burials in Lefkandi on the island of Euboea, RICHARDSON on *Il.* 23.166–176; ANDRONIKOS 1968, 27–29, 82–84; BLOME 1991, 46–50; HUGHES *loc. cit.* 65–70; BURKERT 1994, 97 f.; ANTONACCIO 1995; HERMARY/LEGUILLOUX *loc. cit.* 131 f.; KITTS *loc. cit.* 219–225; on pictorial representations of the killing scene in the *Iliad*, see STEUERNAGEL 1998, 19–28; on a possible parallel in the annals of Assurbanipal (7th cent. B.C.), BURKERT *loc. cit.* 98 n. 7; ROLLINGER 1996, 182–184. — **burning pyre:** on the cremation customary in Homeric epic, 24.38n., 24.777–804n. — **twelve:** 230–231a n.; this is also a typical number[P] of sacrificial animals, and can signal completeness: cf. 6.93n.; GRAZIOSI/HAUBOLD on 6.93–94. — **my anger:** cf. 112–113n.; on this typical element in the context of revenge for the death of a kinsman, WALSH 2005, 175–186.

ἀποδειροτομήσω: The compound (ἀπο-)δειροτομέω (only here and at Hes. *Th.* 280 [Medusa] with the prefix ἀπο-) meaning 'slaughter' is derived from δείρη ('throat') and τάμνω ('cut off') (on the formation, RISCH 181, 218, 309; SCHW. 1.644) and in the *Iliad* is always used with Achilleus as the subject. Outside the context of fighting (21.89, 555, *Od.* 22.349, Hes. *Th.* 280), it designates the killing of sacrificial animals ('slaughter in a ritual fashion': *Il.* 23.174, *Od.* 11.35, *h.Merc.* 405), of a group of human beings only here: *LfgrE s.v.* δειροτομέω. — Τρώων ἀγλαὰ τέκνα: corresponds to the killing scene at 23.175/181 Τρώων ... υἱέας ἐσθλούς. The combination Τρώων τέκνα is elsewhere used only in the formulaic verses 6.95/276/310, 17.223 (Τρώων ... νήπια τέκνα), the phrase ἀγλαὰ τέκνα in various positions in the verse, including before caesura B 2 (2× *Il.*, 1× *Od.*, 1× 'Hes.') and as a VE formula (7× early epic: 2.871n.); aside from the present passage, it is always an indication of the genealogical origin of characters[P]. The expression Τρώων ἀγλαὰ τέκνα is, on the one hand, a reference to the youth of those doomed to die (see 21.27

κούρους) – cf. the sacrificial animals that must be 'without blemish' (1.66n.) – but on the other hand also a definition of their origin (see the women in 339). Cf. the inflectable VE formula υἷες Ἀχαιῶν (1.162n., 24.495n.) and *Od.* 11.547 (παῖδες δὲ Τρώων), 24.38 (Τρώων καὶ Ἀχαιῶν υἷες): *LfgrE s.v.* τέκνον; on the epithet ἀγλαός 'gleaming, radiant', cf. the inflectable VE formulae ἀγλαός/φαίδιμος υἱός (on this, 6.144n.; CIANI 1974, 105).

338 κορωνίσι: a ship epithet meaning 'curved' and 'towering'; on the etymology and its verse position, 1.170n.; παρὰ νηυσὶ κ. is a formula between caesurae A 4 and C 2 (8× *Il.*; also without κ. 31× *Il.*, 2× *Od.*). — **κείσεαι:** 'lie there', of the deceased (cf. 20–21n.); of the laid out, as yet unburied Patroklos, as here, also 19.9, 32, 212, 319, 22.386, 23.210 (*LfgrE s.v.* κεῖμαι). On the sequence of events before the burial in Book 23, 333–342n. — **αὔτως:** 'thus (as you are)', i.e. unburied (*LfgrE s.v.* 1683.6 ff.; BONIFAZI 2012, 286 n. 55).

339–342 The enemy's women are supposed not only to cry because of their dead relatives (121–125n.), but also to strike up laments day and night for a slain opponent until his funeral (cf. 19.302n.); on the lament by the captive women and on Achilleus' forays into Troy's hinterland, 28n.

339 2nd VH ≈ 122 (see *ad loc.*). — **ἀμφὶ δέ σε:** local 'around you', cf. *Od.* 10.486 (AH; SCHW. 2.439; CHANTR. 2.88).

340 ≈ 24.745, *Od.* 11.183 = 13.338 = 16.39. — **νύκτας τε καὶ ἤματα:** on the polar expression[P] (notion of an uninterrupted process) and the inflectable formula after caesura A 4, 24.745n. — **δάκρυ χέουσαι:** 94n.

341 2nd VH = 'Hes.' *fr.* 280.1 M.-W.; from caesura C 2 = *Il.* 5.297, 7.140. — The emotional conclusion of the speech: via his memory of the laborious but successful *joint* forays (*autói kamómestha* and dual *pérthonte* at 342), Achilleus expresses deep connection with his deceased friend (on the memories of the mourning Achilleus, 19.314n., 24.6–8n.).

καμόμεσθα: κάμνω in the mid. (here and at *Od.* 9.130) means 'procure, prepare something with difficulty' (*LfgrE*).

342 2nd VH = 490, 20.217. — **πιείρας:** an I-E feminine form of πίων (19.179–180n.); *inter alia* an epithet of regions and of agricultural land ('fertile'), here of cities and the surrounding countryside ('wealthy'): *LfgrE s.v.* πίων. — **πόλις:** on πόλῑς as an acc. pl. (< *-ινς), CHANTR. 1.217 f.; WEST 1998, XXXIV. — **μερόπων ἀνθρώπων:** 288n.

343–355 The beginning of the burial ritual (on which, 24.580–595n. with bibliography; ALEXIOU [1974] 2002, 5 f.) with washing, anointing, enshrouding and

---

338 τόφρα: 'in the meantime'. — νηυσί: on the declension, R 12.1. — κείσεαι: on the uncontracted form, R 6.
340 ἤματα: from τὸ ἦμαρ 'day'. — δάκρυ: collective sing.
341 τάς: functions like a relative pronoun (R 14.5). — καμόμεσθα: on the form, R 16.2. — βίηφι: on the form, 11.4. — δουρί: on the declension, R 12.5.
342 πέρθοντε: nom. dual of the pres. part. of πέρθω 'destroy, sack'.

laying out ('prothesis') the corpse, accompanied by laments that continue until the interment (354 f., 19.4–39, 19.282–339, 23.4 ff., interrupted by the military assembly [19.40–281] and the subsequent battle [19.356 ff.]); for additional descriptions of such processes, 16.667–673/679–683 (Sarpedon), 24.587–590 (Hektor), *Od.* 24.44 f., 67 f. (Achilleus). In the present scene, the description of readying the body closely follows the type-scene[P] 'bath' (request 343–345; preparations for ablution 346–349; carrying out the tasks of washing, anointing, dressing 350–353), with the detailed description of the preparation of hot washing water (cf. the triple mention of the tripod at 344, 346, 348) marking the zealous diligence and affection for the person cared for (cf. 22.442 ff. Andromache for Hektor, *Od.* 8.433 ff. Arete for Odysseus, 10.358 ff. Kirke for Odysseus): DE JONG on *Od.* 8.433–469; AREND 1933, 124 f. with n. 1; EDWARDS 1986, 86–88; GRETHLEIN 2007, 28 f.; on the realia of bathing scenes in Homeric epic, see LASER 1983, 138–148.

343 companions: The Greek term *hétaroi/hetaíroi* denotes both 'comrades (in arms)' in general and a leader's close confidantes or friends in particular (19.305n., 24.4n.), who are 'often regarded as equivalent to brothers or other close relatives' (24.793n.) and who, in the male community of the military camp, also see to a variety of domestic tasks (19.316n.; WICKERT-MICKNAT 1982, 52 f.). In contrast to the bathing scenes (cf. 346n.) and the preparation of Hektor's corpse in the Myrmidon camp (24.587 f.), it is not women but the 'comrades' of Achilleus and the deceased who here assume the tasks of cleaning and dressing the body – so too, perhaps, in Achilleus' funeral at *Od.* 24.43–45 (WICKERT-MICKNAT *loc. cit.* 57 f.). Very special treatment is given to Zeus' slain son Sarpedon – he is washed, anointed and dressed for burial by Apollo (*Il.* 16.666–683).

ὡς εἰπών: an inflectable VB formula (nom. masc./fem., acc.), mostly in the nom. (in total 74× *Il.*, 42× *Od.*, 3× Hes., 11× *h.Hom.*). — δῖος Ἀχιλλεύς: 228n.

344–345 ≈ 23.40 f.; 344 ≈ 22.443, 23.40, *Od.* 8.434; VE = 5× *Il.*, 7× *Od.*, 1× 'Hes.', 2× *h.Hom.*; 2nd VH of 345 = *Il.* 7.425, 14.7; ≈ 13.640. — **cauldron:** Cooking pots were set up over the fire on three legs (*trípos*) usually made from bronze (19.243–244n.; *BNP s.v.* Tripod; *LfgrE s.v.* τρίπος).

The request to prepare the corpse is merely rendered summarily in indirect speech, with one issue highlighted (στῆσαι τρίποδα); it is not the wording of the request that is im-

---

343 ἑτάροισιν: = ἑταίροις (on the declension, R 11.2). — ἐκέκλετο (+ dat.): reduplicated aor. of κέλομαι 'exhort, urge'.
344 τρίποδα (μ)μέγαν: on the prosody, M 4.6. — ὄφρα: final (R 22.5).
345 λούσειαν ἄπο: = ἀπο-λούσειαν (R 20.2).

portant but its execution (DE JONG [1987] 2004, 116 f.; on the brevity of indirect speeches, cf. 19.128–130n.). The subordinate clause ὄφρα ... | ... λούσειαν can here be understood both as a continuation of the indirect speech and as narrator[P] commentary on the request (DE JONG *loc. cit.* 114 with 269 n. 39; BECK 2012, 64 f. ['free indirect speech']); final clauses with an opt. indicating indirect speech can contain the unspoken thoughts of a character[P] (secondary focalization[P]), illustrating the purpose of an action to the audience (24.583b–585n.). The phrase ὄφρα τάχιστα frequently occurs in direct speech (10× from a total 19× early epic, usually after a request), with indirect speech, as here, also at 23.196–198, *Od.* 3.174 f., cf. *Il.* 9.620 f. (see also *LfgrE s.v.* τάχιστα 341.9 ff.). — **ἀμφὶ πυρί:** 'around the fire', so that the fire burns between the tripod's legs (EDWARDS; GRAZ 1965, 255 n. 1; cf. SCHW. 2.438). — **Πάτροκλον ... βρότον:** a double acc., i.e. of the person and the thing, dependent on ἀπο-λούσειαν ('wash off, away'); cf. 16.667 f. (SCHW. 2.83; CHANTR. 2.43; *LfgrE s.v.* λοέσσαι). The etymology of βρότος is obscure (related to Sanskrit *mūrtá-* 'coagulated'?: *DELG*, Frisk and BEEKES *s.v.*); it means 'crust (of blood)' and in early epic is always used in the context of washing as a term for coagulated blood, in the *Iliad* always with explanatory αἱματόεντα (also at 14.7, 23.41): *LfgrE s.v.* βρότ(ος). See also the formulaic combination ἔναρα βροτόεντα (9× early epic).

346–348 ≈ *Od.* 8.435–437 (bathing scene).

346 λοετροχόον: literally 'pouring bathwater', attested in Mycenaean as a designation for female servants who assist with bathing (with metathesis /lewotro-/ > λο(ϝ)ετρο-: MYC; *DMic s.v.* re-wo-to-ro-ko-wo; RISCH 42 with n. 38a; on this chore as women's work, cf. 22.442–444, *Od.* 3.464, 4.49, 8.433 ff., 10.358 ff. etc.: 24.582–583a n.; LASER 1983, 142–144); in early epic also at *Od.* 20.297 of the person responsible, here and at *Od.* 8.435 as an epithet for a tripod, thus approximately 'bathwater cauldron' (*LfgrE s.v.* λοετροχόος). — **πυρὶ κηλέῳ:** a VE formula (4× *Il.*, 2× *Od.*, 1× Hes. *Th.*); κηλέω (attested in early epic only in the dat. sing. as an epithet of πυρί) is an adjectival formation related to καίω, i.e. 'burning' (< *κηϝ-αλέος: FRISK *s.v.*; RISCH 104 [modernized from *κηαλέωι?]).

348 ἄμφεπε: 'engage with someone/something, take case of someone/something', commonly used of persons, with 'fire' as the subj. also 16.124, *Od.* 8.437 (*LfgrE s.v.* ἕπω).

349 = *Od.* 10.360. — **αὐτὰρ ἐπεὶ δή:** a common phrase for introducing dependent clauses (16.187n.). — **ἤνοπι χαλκῷ:** χαλκός ('copper, bronze') is here used via metonymy for 'pot', elsewhere usually for 'weapon' (*LfgrE s.v.*; cf. 1.236n., 6.3n.). The compound ἦν-οψ is attested in early epic only in this combination in the dat. sing.; in addition to the cooking pot, also at 16.408 for a fishing hook (see *ad loc.*). The meaning is generally thought

---

346 οἵ: anaphoric demonstrative (R 17). — λοετροχόον: on the uncontracted form, R 6. — κηλέῳ: on the synizesis, R 7.

347 ἐν ... ἔχεαν: 3rd pers. pl. aor. of ἐν-χέω; on the so-called tmesis, R 20.2. — ὑπό: adverbial ('underneath').

348 γάστρην: 'belly (of a cauldron)'.

349 αὐτάρ: 'but, indeed' (progressive: R 24.2). — ζέσσεν: aor. of ζέω 'boil, seethe' (on the -σσ-, R 9.1). — ἐνί: = ἐν (R 20.1). — ἐνὶ (ϝ)ήνοπι: on the prosody, R 4.3.

to be 'glossy', cf. the VE formulae αἴθοπι χ. (522n.) and νώροπι χ. (16.130n.) for elements of armor and weapons. But the etymology of the initial element is obscure, with only the initial digamma being deducible from the three attestations (*ϝην-: Frisk and *DELG s.v.*; Chantr. 1.152; cf. G 20 and 21).

350 ≈ *Od.* 3.466; 2nd VH ≈ *Il.* 10.577, 14.171, *Od.* 19.505. — **olive oil:** on the use of olive oil to care for the body of both the living and the dead, 2.44n., 14.172n., 24.587–588n.

καὶ τότε δή: a VB formula (10× *Il.*, 27× *Od.*, 4× *Hes.*, 1× *h.Ap.*); sometimes at the beginning of a sentence and sometimes, as here, after a preceding temporal clause (in which case καί is apodotic; cf. Bakker 1997, 79). — λίπ’ ἐλαίῳ: a VE formula (3× *Il.*, 5× *Od.*, 1× Hes. *Op.*). The adverb λίπα ('extensively', literally 'fat'; for the etymology, *DELG s.v.*) always occurs in combination with an aor. of ἀλείφω or χρίω and always in the context of ablutions (14.171n.).

351 The preparation of the body is evidently done with a special ointment made from animal or vegetable fat that is designed to carefully protect the wounds from signs of decomposition, allowing the funeral to be delayed until the fulfilment of the promise; cf. Achilleus' concern regarding the effects of fly larvae in the deceased's wounds at 19.23 ff. (Andronikos 1968, 4 f., 25; Laser 1983, 160–162; on Greek *aleíphatos*, see MYC). Nine is a typical number[P] that in Homeric epic is used in particular of time spans (cf. 1.53n.; Blom 1936, 255–258; Germain 1954, 13 f. [collection of examples, 99 f.]) and that here is meant to underline the quality and effectiveness of the ointment.

ὠτειλάς: usually designates fatal injuries or wounds on corpses (19.25n.). — ἐννεώροιο: a *hapax*[P] in the *Iliad* ('nine year'); in the *Odyssey*, it describes animals (10.19, 10.390), the twins Otos and Ephialtes (11.311) and Minos' reign on Crete (19.178 f.; see Russo on *Od.* 19.179). On the formation of the compound from the numeral ἐννέα and ὥρη ('season'), see Schw. 1.590 f.; Risch 189; West 2001, 248.

352–353 The treatment of Hektor's body after the washing and anointing is similar: he is dressed in a shroud, laid out on a blanket and covered with a second blanket (Greek *pháros*); see 24.580 f., 24.587 f. (24.588n.). Patroklos' body is wrapped with particular care from head to toe in a soft cloth and likewise covered with a blanket, the 'white' color of which highlights the diligent cleansing and treatment of the corpse (cf. *LfgrE s.v.* λευκός). In this way, he is laid out for the lament (354 f.) until the time of his funeral (the so-called 'prothesis': 19.5–6a n., 24.589–590n.).

---

350 καί: apodotic (cf. R 24.3). — λοῦσαν: The obj. is to be supplied from 345 (Πάτροκλον); likewise with the following transitive verbs. — λίπ(α): on the elision, R 5.1.
351 ἐν … πλῆσαν ἀλείφατος: 'they filled with ointment' (on the so-called tmesis, R 20.2); ἀλείφατος gen. sing. of ἄλειφαρ. — ἐννεώροιο: on the synizesis, R 7.

352 ≈ 23.254 (container with Patroklos' bones). — **λεχέεσσι:** 233n.; here it designates the
ritual bier for laying out the corpse. — **δέ:** On δέ in third position after the combination
prep. + noun, 24.273–274n. (end.). — **ἑανῷ λιτί:** The phrase designates a soft, simple
piece of cloth that can easily be wrapped around the entire body (CERRI): (1) ἑανός is
an epithet with terms for clothing (5.734, 8.385 with πέπλος; 18.613 with κασσίτερος, a
material used for greaves) and is distinct from ἑᾱνός, a term for a female garment (on
which, 3.385n., 14.178n.); the etymology and meaning are obscure, and interpretations
range from 'soft' or 'supple' to 'gleaming': *LfgrE s.v.* ἑανός. (2) λίς is used here as a noun
designating a simple, smooth, unembellished cloth (cf. neut. pl. λῖτα: cloths for covering a wagon [8.441], a table [*Od.* 1.130], chairs [10.353: at the bottom λῖτα, covered
by πορφύρεα, on which 24.645n.]), in folk etymology connected with λίνον 'linen' and
interpreted as 'sheet'; in origin an adj. with the basic meaning 'smooth' (*Od.* 12.79 of
rocks, likewise the derivative feminine λισσή at 3.293, 10.4; cf. *DMic s.vv. ri-ta and pa-wo*:
ri-ta pa-we-a /*līta pʰarweha*/), etymologically related to λεῖος (FRISK, *DELG*, BEEKES *s.v.*
λίς; BECHTEL 1914, 217 f.).

353 1st VH = 23.169. — **ἐς ... ἐκ:** 'from ... to'; on the expression cf. 22.397, *Od.* 7.87, in the
reverse order ἐκ ... ἐς *Il.* 16.640 (with the prepositional clauses separated), 20.137 (SCHW.
2.459; CHANTR. 2.103). — **φάρεϊ:** a cloak-like cape as part of male dress (2.43n.), in funer-
ary rituals the blanket for the corpse (cf. 24.580, 588 for Hektor, *Od.* 2.97, etc. for Laërtes):
LfgrE; BUCHHOLZ 2012, 89 f.

354–355 1st VH of 354 = 7.476; 2nd VH of 354 ≈ 69; 355 ≈ 315. — A concluding summary of the nocturnal lament, with repetition of the temporal indication 'the
entire night' (*pannýchioi*, here and at 315 [see *ad loc.*]). The subsequent change
of perspective away from the group of human beings to the divine couple is
stressed by the names placed directly adjacent one another (355 f. *Myrmidónes
Pátroklon ... | Zéus d' Hérēn*).

παννύχιοι μέν ... | Ζεὺς δ(έ): 1n. — **πόδας ταχὺν ... Ἀχιλῆα:** on the formula, 2n., 69n.

356–368 *Zeus and Hera discuss Hera's interference on behalf of the Achaians.*

The brief scene, beginning abruptly, between the married couple Zeus and
Hera takes place after sunset (239–242n.), as do both the action in the two
military camps and Thetis' visit to Hephaistos. The narrative[P] shifts from the
human plane to the divine until the end of the Book, and various earlier individual events are thus concluded: (a) by returning to Hera's high-handed in-

---

352 λεχέεσσι: on the declension, R 11.3; on the plural, R 18.2.
353 ἐς: = εἰς (R 20.1). — καθύπερθε: 'over, across', *sc.* κάλυψαν (see 352), i.e., they wrapped him
in a second cloth.
354 παννύχιοι: 315n. — πόδας: acc. of respect (R 19.1). — Ἀχιλῆα: on the declension, R 11.3; on
the single -λ-, R 9.1.

tervention to mobilize Achilleus (357–358a n.), the narrator[P] again points to the end of Achilleus' passivity and transitions to the preparations for his reentry into battle, namely the production of new armor; (b) the dialogue illustrates after the fact that Zeus was aware of Hera's clandestine action and allowed it to happen; he himself also wished for Patroklos' corpse to be rescued (17.268–273, 545 f., 648–650), and the destruction of Troy is a settled matter for him as well (15.64–71): Zeus' support for Hektor and the Trojans has reached its end; (c) his mocking/provocative remark regarding Hera's partisanship in favor of the Achaians (358b–359) and her irritated, opinionated reply (362–367), with which she defends her actions against the Trojans, represent the final engagement in the quarrel between the two spouses (cf. 368n.), in which Zeus' promise to Thetis, namely to weaken the Achaians for a certain amount of time and strengthen the Trojans in battle, again and again provided a trigger for confrontation (1.518–523, 1.539–567 [with 1.541–543n.], 8.461–483, 15.13–78; cf. 4.24–64a, esp. 31–36, 57–61; contrast Zeus' speech in the divine assembly on the following morning at 20.22–25): EDWARDS; OWEN 1946, 180 f. and 186; ERBSE 1986, 58 f. and 202; SCHÄFER 1990, 108 f.

This scene was the subject of discussion already in antiquity: according to schol. bT on 356, Zenodoros doubted its authenticity on the basis of the content (on this, NICKAU 1977, 152; NÜNLIST 2009, 62, 160, 279–281; for additional discussion, see AH, *Anh.* 126 and 155; BLÖSSNER 1991, 58–61 [the relationship of 361–367 to *Od.* 20.45–48]); but see above on its function and contextual embedding.

356 ≈ 16.432; 2nd VH = *h.Hom.* 12.3; ≈ *h.Ven.* 40. — A speech introduction formula[P] that intimates the change of scene by naming both interlocutors in the 1st VH – the form of the speech introduction formula is compressed from the couple's dialogue in Book 16 (16.431 f.); the apposition in the 2nd VH prepares for Hera's justification at 364–366 (see *ad loc.*; EDWARDS *ad loc.* and 1970, 15 f.). An indication of the location of this dialogue between the divine couple is lacking, since changes of location by deities frequently remain unmentioned and are implied (gap[P]). Also similar to the present passage is the conversation between the two that preceded the death of Sarpedon (16.431–461): while 15.78 f. mentions Hera's trip to Olympos, at 16.431 ff. she appears together with Zeus, who since 11.181 ff. has been observing the battlefield from Mt. Ida (16.431–432n.); now, after the battle has ended, Olympos should probably be envisaged as the location.

προσέειπε: 9n. — **ἄλοχον:** a possessive compound meaning 'who shares the same bed, spouse' (< *ἄ-λοχ- with α *copulativum*): 19.298n.

---

356 προσέειπε: = προσεῖπε (cf. 9n.).

357–358a An internal repetitive analepsis[P]: Zeus comments on the events before sunset (165 ff.), when Hera arranged without his consent for Achilleus to become active again (203: 203–204n.) even though his honor was not yet restored (cf. Thetis' plea at 1.509 f. and Zeus' plan at 15.72–87).

ἔπρηξας … | ἀνστήσασ(α): πρήσσω elsewhere usually appears with an object (gen. or acc.), with a part. also at *Od.* 14.197 (οὔ τι διαπρήξαιμι λέγων, slightly differently at *Il.* 9.326 ἤματα … διέπρησσον πολεμίζων): *LfgrE* s.v. πρήσσω; in the present passage, the use of the part. is comparable to the use with verbs of striving (CHANTR. 2.328: 'you have arrived at your desired end by rousing…, you have succeeded in rousing' [transl.]). On ἀνστήσασ(α), 305n. — **καὶ ἔπειτα:** refers to the preceding aor. ἔπρηξας (likewise at *Od.* 8.519 f. τολμήσαντα | νικῆσαι κ. ἔ.) that is placed at the beginning of the sentence in an emphatic manner: Hera's intention, already noticed frequently, is to obtain her own aim: 'you have (once again) achieved (what you wanted)' (AH; LEAF; EDWARDS). — **βοῶπι πότνια Ἥρη:** a noun-epithet formula, usually in the nom. (239n.), as an address only at 8.471 and 15.49. The final syllable of βοῶπι in the *longum* can be explained as resulting from inflection of the formula (M 14) in which, in place of the nom. that can exceptionally be used for the voc., the voc. form is used (cf. SCHW. 2.63 [an attribute is possible in the voc. or nom.] and *app. crit.*; somewhat differently WACKERNAGEL [1878] 1979, 1534 f. [nom. form was replaced by the voc. form in the post-Homeric period]; on the metrical/prosodic particularities with voc. forms, cf. 2.8n., 19.400n., 24.88n.); for discussion regarding the original length of the final syllable of βο-ωπῖ (cf. the *v.l.* βοῶπις), 1.551n.; WACKERNAGEL (1914) 1953, 1171; CHANTR. 1.208. — **Ἀχιλῆα πόδας ταχύν:** a formula between caesurae A 4 and C 2 (13.348, 17.709); on the formulae for Achilleus with πόδας ταχύς (here and at 354), 2n., 69n.

358b–359 A mocking/exaggerated and slightly provocative justification of Hera's solicitous behavior toward the Achaians (on which, 239–242n., end; 1.55n.); at the same time, as the father of Dardanos and great-grandfather of Tros, the founder of Troy (20.215–240), Zeus is in fact the ancestor of the opposing party (EDWARDS). On mother-child comparisons for a goddess' solicitous behavior, see 4.130 f. and 23.782 f. (Athene toward Menelaos and Odysseus: FRÄNKEL 1921, 12, 91 f.); cf. 19.342 f. (Zeus ironically on Athene and her protégé Achilleus). — **Achaians:** 6n.

ἦ ῥά νυ: 'really then', emphatic (6.215n.) and here with an ironic overtone, introducing the unusual explanation, which is stressed via enjambment (EDWARDS).

---

357 ἔπρηξας: 2nd pers. sing. aor. of πρήσσω (Attic πράττω). — καὶ ἔπειτα: on the correption, R 5.5.
358 ἀνστήσασ': = ἀναστήσασα (R 20.1; on the elision, R 5.1). — Ἀχιλῆα πόδας ταχύν: 354n. — ἦ: emphatic (R 24.4). — ῥα: = ἄρα (R 24.1). — σεῖο: = σοῦ (R 14.1), with ἐξ αὐτῆς, 'from you yourself'.
359 κάρη κομόωντες: 6n.

360 = 1.551 (see *ad loc.*), 4.50, 16.439, 20.309; 1st VH = 127 (see *ad loc.*). — **βοῶπις πότνια Ἥρη:** 239n.

361 = 1.552, 4.25, 8.462, 14.330, 16.440; 2nd VH = 8.209 (Poseidon to Hera). — The formulaic verse is always used in speeches by Hera in which she criticizes her husband (14.330n., 16.440n.).

αἰνότατε Κρονίδη: an expression of outrage; in general, αἰνός is common in addresses to gods (16.440n.). — **μῦθον ἔειπες:** a variable VE formula (1.552n.); on ἔειπες, 9n.

362–367 A conclusion *a minore ad maius*, see esp. 362 f. and 364 (AH; cf. 2.292–294n.); Athene argues in a similar fashion at *Od.* 20.45–47. Hera insists on her prerogative to act on her anger at the Trojans – likely based on her disrespectful treatment in the Judgement of Paris (see CG 16; 2.155–181n., 24.27–30n.) – as human beings are apt to do (SCHADEWALDT [1938] 1966, 147; VAN WEES 1992, 112).

362 2nd VH from caesura C 2 ≈ 19.22. — **καὶ μέν:** introduces the generalizing statement (καί with τις ... βροτός: 'even a mortal') and prepares the contrast at 364 πῶς δὴ ἐγώ γ', ... θεάων ... ἀρίστη (DENNISTON 390; RUIJGH 749). — **δή:** The speaker suggests, via the use of the particle here and at 364, that the opinions she states are obvious and surely shared by the addressee (4n., 6.98n.). — **πού ... μέλλει:** μέλλει + inf. in the sense 'it is very likely that', frequently combined with που underlining the subjective tone ('I do think'), as here: 2.116n., 24.488n.; BASSET 1979, 82 f., 110 f.; BAKKER (1997) 2005, 99. — **βροτὸς ἀνδρί:** a syntactic splitting of the inflectable formula after caesura C 1 (9× early epic: 19.22n.; for a similar situation, cf. 2n.). βροτός ('mortal') denotes the human being, inferior and limited in his means in comparison to a god (cf. 364), and one whose shortcoming are listed in addition in the relative clause that follows at 363 (θνητός: mortality; οὐ τόσα μήδεα: limited action strategies); ἀνήρ is here a generic term inclining toward the meaning 'human (being)' (*LfgrE* s.vv. ἀνήρ 844.4 ff., esp. 26 ff., and βροτός; WACKERNAGEL [1920/24] 2009, 758). — **ἀνδρὶ τελέσσαι:** means 'realize for a person, put into action', a neutral wording that is only substantiated at 367 with κοτεσσαμένη κακὰ ῥάψαι (FAESI; WILLCOCK); on the notion and the wording, cf. 1.81 f. (see *ad loc.*).

363 = *Od.* 20.46. — **ὅς περ ...:** The relative clause with περ amplifies the conclusion *a minore ad maius* by listing the characteristic traits of the βροτός: 'even a human being, despite ...' (the antithesis follows at 364: 'the greatest among the goddesses'): RUIJGH 446; cf. BAKKER 1988, 79 f.; similarly at 19.95 (see *ad loc.*) — **οὐ τόσα μήδεα:** The comparison is not explicitly brought to a conclusion, but is unequivocal from the context (364 ff.): 'not as many plans, *sc.* as me'; on the comparison οὐ τόσ(σ)ον/τόσ(σ)α – ὅσ(σ)ον/ὅσ(σ)α,

---

360 τόν: on the anaphoric demonstrative function of ὅ, ἥ, τό, R 17.
361 Κρονίδη: 'son of Kronos' = Zeus. — ποῖον: predicative, 'as what kind of a ...'. — ἔειπες: = εἶπες (9n.)
362 μέν: ≈ μήν (R 24.6). — τελέσσαι: on the -σσ-, R 9.1.
363 μήδεα (ϝ)οῖδεν: on the prosody, R 4.3; on the uncontracted form, R 6.

see KELLY 2007, 329–331. — μήδεα οἶδεν: a variable VE formula (μήδεα εἰδώς/οἶδ-/ἴδμεν, μήδε᾽ ἰδυι-: 4× *Il.*, 4× *Od.*, 11× Hes., 2× *h.Hom.*) denoting the strategic intelligence of extraordinary human beings (3.202n.) and esp. of Zeus (24.88n.; *LfgrE s.v.* μήδεα).

364 The formulation *theáōn … arístē* corresponds to the characterization of Zeus as *áristos* ('the best, greatest') and stresses Hera's own status in the world of gods (cf. 19.95–96n.): her outstanding position both by birth (4.59: Kronos' eldest daughter; cf. CG 26) and by her marriage to the ruler of the gods (KIRK on 4.58–61; *LfgrE s.v.* γενεή 127.14 f.).

ἔμμεν: on the use of the Aeolic inf. form, G 87; WACHTER 2007, 319.

365–366 = 4.60–61 (athetized by WEST); 2nd VH of 366 ≈ 12.242, 14.94, *Od.* 7.23, Hes. *Th.* 506. — ἀμφότερον: in apposition to the clause γενεῇ τε καὶ οὕνεκα …, 'both', i.e. 'what applies on both grounds' (3.179n.; SCHW. 2.617). — τε καί: connects sentence parts that are closely linked in content (reasons for Hera's social standing) but in different syntactic constructions (19.336n.). — παράκοιτις: 184n.

367 The verb *rháptein* literally means 'sew together', a common metaphor for joining separate parts (individual elements of a plan) into a meaningful whole (also with the objects 'murder' [*Od.* 16.379] and 'death' [16.421 f.]; cf. *Od.* 3.118, 16.423 and the noun *kakorraphíē* at *Il.* 15.16, *Od.* 2.236, 12.26); in post-Homeric texts, it occurs in the designation of the singer as a rhapsode (a skilful assembling of a song recital): *LfgrE s.vv.* ἀρτύνω 1366.63 ff. and ῥάπτω; MÜLLER 1974, 241–243; NAGY 1996, 61 f., 66–69; CLARKE 1999, 251 f. with n. 49.; on comparable metaphors from the sphere of textiles ('weave/spin a trick on someone' or 'weave someone's destiny'), see 6.187n. and 3.212n., as well as 24.209b–210n.; on Hera's anger, 362–367n.

ὄφελον: denotes something unfulfillable/unfulfilled in the past ('I should have [had]'): 18–19n. — κοτεσσαμένη: κοτέω denotes persistent aversion as an inner attitude (cf. κότος 'wrath': 1.81–82n., 2.222b–223n.; WALSH 2005, 53 f.).

368 = 5.274, 5.431, 7.464, 8.212, 13.81, 16.101, 21.514, as well as 16× *Od.* — The speech capping formula[P] implies a reference to a lengthier dialogue with speeches of similar content (summary[P]); at the same time, it prepares for a change of scene to events happening concurrently, here a return to 146–148 (DE JONG [1987]

---

364 πῶς δὴ ἐγώ γ(ε): continued by οὐκ ὄφελον in 367. — θεάων: on the form, R 2.2; cf. R 6. — ἔμμεν: = εἶναι (R 16.4).

365 γενεῇ: causal dat., 'because of my birth, origin'; on the -ῃ after -ε-, R 2. — οὕνεκα: crasis for οὗ ἕνεκα (R 5.3), 'because'.

366 ἀθανάτοισιν: initial syllable metrically lengthened (R 10.1); on the declension, R 11.2.

367 Τρώεσσι: on the declension, R 11.3. — κοτεσσαμένη: ingressive 'having taken to anger/wrath'; on the -σσ-, R 9.1; on the middle, R 23.

368 ἀγόρευον: on the unaugmented form, R 16.1.

2004, 206, 287 n. 28; RICHARDSON 1990, 31 f.; KELLY 2007, 226–228; see also 1n., 239–242n., 16.101n.).

369–467 *Thetis reaches Olympos, finds Hephaistos at work and is received in a friendly manner, first by Hephaistos' wife, then by the god himself. The divine smith immediately satisfies her plea for new armor for her son.*

The scene of Thetis' reception in Hephaistos' house is comprised of conversations between hosts and guest, as well as a detailed description of the divine smith's work and several items he has made from different metals (cf. principle of elaborate narration[P]); at the same time, the portrayal of the manufacturing of Achilleus' new armor is prepared for in several steps: (1) an introduction to the location (369–371), the divine smith and his working methods (372–380, 410–413), his wife, his past and his connections with Thetis (382–409); (2) repeated references to his exceptional artistic skill (370, 373–380, 389 f., 393b, 400 f., 417–420, 462b); (3) a recapitulation in the dialogue between Thetis and Hephaistos of the events on the human plane (424–467). In addition, the scene contains reminiscences of Book 1: (a) Thetis as supplicant on Olympos on behalf of her son (1.497 ff.); (b) fulfillment of her plea on the basis of the principle *do ut des* (394 ff., cf. 1.396 ff. [see *ad loc.*]); (c) Hephaistos' awkward appearance and helpful actions (1.571–600 [see *ad loc.*]): MARG (1957) 1971, 24 f., 39–41; REINHARDT 1961, 391–394.

369–427 With Thetis' arrival, the type-scene[P] 'arrival' interrupted at 148 is first continued (for element 1, see 146 f.: 134–144n., 145–147n., 239–242n.; for additional examples of scenes that introduce a break in the time span between departure and arrival, see 1–22a n., 6.119–236n.): (**2**) the character arrives (369–371); as frequently elsewhere, this is expanded by a description of the locality (on this, 6.242–253n., 24.440–485n.); (**3**) she finds the character who is being sought; a description of the situation: busy at work (372–380); (**4**) she approaches (381; see *ad loc.*); element **5** (she speaks [428 ff.]) is retarded[P] via the transition to the type-scene[P] 'visit' (on which, 24.477–478n.; cf. AREND 1933, 34–37; on the combination of the type-scenes 'arrival' and 'visit', see the additional examples in DE JONG on *Od.* 1.96–324); here, a new character enters the scene – the wife of the character in question: (**2**) she spots the recent arrival and (**3**) rushes to meet her (382 f.), (**4**) grasps her by the hand and welcomes her (384–388a; so too Hephaistos at 423–427), (**5**) she leads the guest into the house (388b) and (**6**) offers her a seat (389 f.); (**9**) those present start a conversation (424 ff.); the food and drink (elements 7 and 8) is announced (387, 408) but not described; instead, the encounter between Thetis and Hephaistos is prepared for via a conversation between the spouses, after which the divine smith puts aside his work (391–427n.): AREND 1933, 36 f.; EDWARDS 1975, 62 f.; for critical remarks on this, TSAGARAKIS 1982, 52–54. The appearance of Hephaistos' wife Charis creates a scene of domestic harmony which presents a strong contrast to both the preceding argument between the couple Zeus–Hera and the lament in the Achaian camp, and provides a moment of pause and respite before the following scenes (production of the armor and preparations for battle on the following day): EDWARDS on 369–467; CERRI p. 25 f.; OWEN 1946, 186–189; REINHARDT 1961, 394–398; HEIDEN 2008, 225 f.

369–381 The divine smith Hephaistos, son of Zeus and Hera (CG 15), has a physical defect (370–371n.), on the one hand, but is equipped with special skills (373–377n.) and expertise (380, likewise at 482), on the other (this is made apparent in a similar manner during his first occurrence in the *Iliad* [1.599 f. vs. 1.571, 1.607 f.]). Disabled limbs are indeed a serious defect in a world where physical integrity is important and where speed and mobility in particular are considered military virtues (cf. 2.217n. on Thersites). But the *Odyssey*, in the poem of the singer Demodokos about Ares and Aprodite, outlines how the slow, limping Hephaistos wins via *téchnē* against the swift Ares (*Od.* 8.329–333); cf. the narrative motif 'outward appearance versus inner quality' in the case of human characters[P] (on this, DE JONG on *Od.* 18.1–158; BERNSDORFF 1992, 25–40, 73–85; cf. 2.211–224n., 2.216n., 2.217n. on the human outsider Thersites, who is portrayed in a wholly negative manner). Among the Olympian gods, characterized by physical perfection, Hephaistos occupies the role of an outsider (e.g. 1.597–600 [1.586–594n. with bibliography], 20.32–37), given that he is a god with crippled feet (371) and a resultant limping gait (397a, 411, 417), as well as less than handsome in appearance (also 411, 415); his 'physical deformity is a narrative symbol for the social marginality' of the god, who due to his skills is nevertheless an irreplaceable, esteemed craftsman and is considered the terrifying master of fire (GRAF 1990, 69–71 [quotation p. 71, transl.]); see also *BNP s.vv.* Hephaestus and Disability; DELCOURT [1957] 1982, 110 ff.; DETIENNE/VERNANT [1974] 1978, 257–260; BURKERT [1977] 1985, 168; ERBSE 1986, 76–80). Hephaistos' limping is explained in a variety of ways (cf. 395–397a n.): as (a) a congenital defect (396 f.), (b) a consequence of the fall from Olympos described at 1.590 ff. (EDWARDS on 394–409; RINON 2008, 129); (c) an affliction that is characteristic of a smith (*LfgrE s.v.* "Ηφαιστος 950.65 ff.; ERBSE 1986, 79 n. 25); the character of the smith is generally an element of I-E myths, in which he also sometimes suffers from a physical handicap (MALTEN 1912, 336 f.; BOWRA 1952, 150–153; WEST 2007, 154–157, esp. 156 with n. 123), and the Homeric scenes with Hephaistos share several motifs with the description of the Ugaritic divine smith Kothar in particular (WEST 1997, 57, 384, 388 f.).

369 on Hephaistos' abode on Mt. Olympos, 142n.; on the VE, 127n.

ἵκανε: an impf. functioning as an aor. (SCHW. 2.259).

370–371 In this description of a locality (see 369–427n., element 2) via an asyndetic series of epithets (on this epic stylistic element, 130–131n.) and a four-word verse (on its epexegetic function, BASSETT 1919, 224 f.), Hephaistos is introduced at the very beginning of the scene as the creator of objects of special quality (additional divine residences made by him: 1.606–608, 14.166 f., 20.10–12); on the appreciation of craft skills in Homeric epic, 6.313–317n.; cf. *HE s.v.* handicraft. — **imperishable:** Objects belonging to gods or made by them, especially those from Hephaistos' workshop, are in the narrator's mind always indestructible (on the adj. *áphthitos*, 2.46n. [Agamemnon's scepter], as well as 2.447n. [aegis], 14.238n. [Hera's throne]). — **built in bronze:** Metal as a building material for the house is a sign of the elaborate furnishings, the wealth and splendor (gold, silver), and the solidity and durability (bronze) of divine abodes, likewise of Poseidon's palace (13.21 f.), in the case of iron thresholds or floors in divine palaces (1.426n., 14.173n. [both on χαλκοβατὲς δῶ]), and perhaps of the gleaming doors (i.e. with metal fittings?) of the gods' chambers (14.169n.); see also the impressive/phantastical palace of Alkinoös, the king of the Phaiakians (*Od.* 7.86–94, 13.4), the comparison of Menelaos' palace with that of Zeus (4.72–75), and the iron walls around the island of the wind god Aiolos (10.1–4): HAINSWORTH on *Od.* 7.81–132; *LfgrE s.v.* χάλκε(ι)ος 1110.35 ff.; WEILER 2001, 75 f. (where also on possible reminiscences in ancient comments regarding temple architecture); ROUGIER-BLANC 2005, 38 f., 144; D'ACUNTO 2010, 150–152. Like the adj. *asteróeis* (see below), 'of bronze' is occasionally used as an epithet with 'sky', in part to mark its 'indestructibility and durability' (*LfgrE s.v.* οὐρανός 869.15 ff. [transl.]). — **god of the dragging footsteps:** Vase paintings from the 6th cent. depict Hephaistos riding a mule, his feet twisted backward, i.e. with clubbed feet that cause his limp (397, 411, 417): *LIMC s.v.* Hephaistos 628, 652 f.; BROMMER 1978, 11, 16, 145 f. with pl. 10 f.

ἀστερόεντα: In early epic, with the exception of the present passage and 16.134 (Achilleus' corselet), the adj. is always used as an epithet of 'sky' (6.108n.). As in the case of the corselet with metal elements, here in the case of Hephaistos' house with components of bronze the adj. is most likely used in the sense 'sparkling (like the starry sky)' (schol. b and T; cf. 16.134n.; on the comparison 'shining like a star', 6.295n.,

---

369 δόμον: acc. of direction with no preposition (R 19.2).
370 μεταπρεπέ᾽ ἀθανάτοισιν: on the hiatus, R 5.1; on the uncontracted form μεταπρεπέ(α), R 6; on ἀθανάτοισιν, 366n.
371 ῥ᾽: = ἄρα (R 24.1). — ποιήσατο: on the unaugmented form, R 16.1.

6.401n., 19.381b–382n.), perhaps in reference to the reflection of the fire in Hephaistos' workshop on the metal fittings on the walls (*LfgrE s.v.* ἀστερόεις; differently AH, LEAF: 'starry', describing actual embellishment with stars or star-shaped ornaments; undecided, EDWARDS). — **μεταπρεπέ' ἀθανάτοισιν:** 'standing out among ...', similarly at 6.477 (παῖδ' ... ἀριπρεπέα Τρώεσσιν), in the present passage with δόμον in an abbreviated expression in which ἀθανάτοισιν ≈ ἀθανάτων δόμοις (*comparatio compendiaria*); on the locative alone in the case of plural terms for persons, SCHW. 2.155; CHANTR. 2.80. — **Κυλλοποδίων:** 'with twisted feet, club-footed' is a soubriquet of Hephaistos only in the *Iliad* (also 20.270, 21.331; more commonly Ἀμφιγυήεις, see 383); a compound with the final element ποδ- and the suffix -ων for forming an anthroponym (RISCH 56 f.), the initial element is probably from the same root as πέλομαι (**kʷelh₁-* 'make a turn'): MEIER-BRÜGGER 1990; for older explanations, see *DELG s.v.* κυλλός; on the possessive compound (also ἀργυρό-πεζα), RISCH 184.

372 found ...: The depiction of the situation in element (3) of the type-scene[P] 'arrival' (369–427n.) is described, as usual, in secondary focalization[P] from the point of view of the arriving character (3–5n.) and here serves to prepare for what is to come: depicted are (a) Hephaistos absorbed in his characteristic activity, which is also important to Thetis, illustrated by visible, physical effects (372a sweating, cf. 414 f.), being in motion (372b) and busyness with the aim of completing projects (373a, cf. 378 f.); (b) the production process for one of his objects (373b–379): AH, *Anh.* 136 f.

ἰδρώοντα: ἰδρώω is a denominative from ἰδρώς (CHANTR. 1.365 f.; RISCH 330); sweating is elsewhere ascribed particularly to warriors and participants in a contest, to gods only here and at 4.27 (Hera stresses by way of exaggeration how much she exerted herself; see KIRK on 4.26–28; *LfgrE*), inasmuch as their life and actions are usually designated 'light, easy' (3.381n., 6.138n., 24.526n.). — **φύσας:** a nominal formation in -σᾰ with an obscure etymology (onomatopoetic?: FRISK, *DELG* and BEEKES *s.v.* φῦσα); a term for bellows made from two leather pouches, used in the *Iliad* only in Book 18 and only in the pl. (372, 409, 412, 468, 470, cf. Hdt. 1.68), literally probably 'jet of air, wind' (cf. *h.Merc.* 114, of a jet of fire): *LfgrE* and LSJ *s.v.* φῦσα; FORBES 1967, 13, 15.

373–377 The special abilities of the divine smith are shown and acknowledged via an example in a climax (VE 377): capability (373), artistic/technical ability (375), magical skills (376).

373 twenty: a typical number[P] denoting a large amount, here emphasizing the superhuman output of the divine smith (WALTZ 1933, 10, 37 [collection of exam-

---

372 τόν: on the anaphoric demonstrative function of ὅ, ἥ, τό, R 17. — ἰδρώοντα, (ϝ)ελισσόμενον: on the prosody, R 4.3. — ἐλισσόμενον: 'turning here and there'.
373 ἐείκοσι: = εἴκοσι (↑). — ἔτευχεν: durative, 'was in the process of producing'.

ples]; REINHARDT 1961, 488 f.; on specifications of larger numbers in Homer, see HAWKE 2008, 43–46, 59 f.); on the tripod, 344–345n.

τρίποδας ... ἐείκοσι πάντας: πᾶς in the pl. in conjunction with numerals means 'a whole, full', i.e. here 'a full twenty tripods' (*LfgrE s.v.* 1017.35 ff.); on the prothetic vowel in ἐείκοσι, G 25; SCHW. 1.412 and 591; CHANTR. 1.182.

374 [dwelling] hall: The term *mégaron* designates (1) the central room ('hall') of the Homeric house, namely the room where social and work activities took place, as here, and (2) the house in general ('dwelling'); *LfgrE s.v.* μέγαρον (64.30 f.); additional bibliography: 24.208b–209a n.

ἐϋσταθέος μεγάροιο: a VE formula (1× *Il.*, 6× *Od.*); ἐϋσταθής ('well put up, well built') used elsewhere in early epic only in the *Odyssey* as an epithet of μέγαρον and θάλαμος. On the formation (derived from the aor. pass. ἐστάθην?), SCHW. 2.513; RISCH 82; *DELG s.v.* στάθμη.

375 golden wheels: Hephaistos' tripods are unique in Homeric epic due to this special equipment (on the attribute 'golden', 205–206n.): the only comparable wheeled utensil is a basket Helen received as a present from the Egyptian city of Thebes that serves as a storage place for her yarn and spindle (*Od.* 4.130–132). For archaeological evidence of Geometric wheeled tripods, see WEST on *Od.* 4.131–132; BROMMER 1942, 368; WILLEMSEN 1957, 2; MAASS 1978, 18 with n. 43; CANCIANI 1984, 37 f.; D'ACUNTO 2010, 153 f.

κύκλα: a plural formation from κύκλος denoting a complete group of wheels in the sense 'a set of wheels' (collective or 'comprehensive' pl., also at 5.722 on a war chariot) in contrast to κύκλοι 'circles' at 11.33 (EICHNER 1985, 141 f.). — **ἑκάστῳ:** a distributive appositive with σφι, i.e. referring contextually to the tripods (373 τρίποδας) (AH; similarly WILLCOCK; cf. 2.775b n., 19.339n.). — **πυθμένι:** denotes the lowest part or area of an object, tree or the sea ('foot, ground, bottom'; cf. English *bottom*, Latin *fundus*: FRISK, *DELG* and *LfgrE s.v.*), here the lower section of the legs as the base of a tripod (WILLCOCK). For the formulation ὑπὸ κύκλα ... πυθμένι θῆκεν, cf. *Od.* 4.131 τάλαρόν θ' ὑπόκυκλον ('a basket with wheels underneath').

376 2nd VH ≈ 7.298. — Not only do the tripods have wheels to facilitate moving them (375), they actually move of their own accord. *autómatos* ('aiming [any-

---

374 ἑστάμεναι: = ἑστάναι (cf. R 16.4); final inf. — περὶ τοῖχον: 'all around against the walls'. — ἐϋσταθέος: on the uncontracted form, R 6. — μεγάροιο: on the declension, R 11.2.

375 σφ(ι): = αὐτοῖς (R 14.1). — ὑπὸ ... πυθμένι θῆκεν: 'he placed ... under the bottom'. — κύκλα (ϝ)εκάστῳ: on the prosody, R 4.3.

376–377 ὄφρα (ϝ)οι: on the prosody, R 4.3; likewise θαῦμα (ϝ)ιδέσθαι. — ὄφρα: final (R 22.5). — οἱ: = αὐτῷ (R 14.1; here dat. of advantage). — οἱ αὐτόματοι: on the correction, R 5.5. — δυσαίατ' ... | ... νεοίατο: = δύσαιντο, νέοιντο: 3rd pers. pl. opt. mid. (R 16.2). — ἀγῶνα: acc. of direction without preposition (R 19.2). — ἠδ(έ): 'and' (R 24.4). — αὖτις: = αὖθις. — ἰδέσθαι: on the middle, R 23.

where] on its own, moving itself') is used in Homer to describe, in addition to individuals, only the self-opening gates of heaven (5.749 = 8.393). Other objects from Hephaistos' workshop also show evidence of his quasi-magical abilities: his self-activatng golden servants (417 ff.), his automatic bellows (469 f.), Zeus' aegis (15.308–310: 203–204n.), the insuperable latch on the door of Hera's chamber (14.166–168: 14.168n.), Alkinoös' gold and silver watchdogs (*Od.* 7.91–94), the trap set for Ares and Aphrodite (8.272 ff., esp. 8.296–298): 417–420n.; *LfgrE s.v.* Ἥφαιστος 949.68 ff.; DELCOURT (1957) 1982, 51–56; KOKOLAKIS 1980, 103–107; FARAONE 1987, 257–261; on the phenomenon of automatons, cf. the narrative motifs 'magic self-moving vehicle', 'automatic objects' and 'magic automata' in THOMPSON D1523, D1600, D1620, in addition to A141 f. (see also Aristotle, *Politics* 1.4 [1253b 35–37] on automata, like these tripods, that rendered slave labor unnecessary); on the magical abilities of other mythological figues with knowledge of metallurgy, see LEAF on 418; WATHELET 2000, 174 f.; BIERL 2012, 127 f. with n. 69; *BNP s.vv.* Telchines and Daktyloi Idaioi. — **into the …:** The reference is to Zeus' palace, where the gods gather for common meals, as described e.g. in Book 1 (1.493–495/533 ff., esp. 596–604; cf. 4.1, 15.84 f.).

ὄφρα οἱ … δυσαίατ(ο): like νεοίατο at 377, an opt. as an indication of indirect discourse in a final clause in secondary focalization[P] (147n.); on δύνω + acc. 'enter a sphere', 6.185n. — **αὐτόματοι:** a compound with a verbal final element -μα-τος, associated with the same root as μέμονα (on the verbal adj., RISCH 19, 210 f.), i.e. 'hastening (somewhere) oneself, under one's own volition' (FRISK and *DELG s.v.*). — **θεῖον … ἀγῶνα:** 'meeting place of the gods'; on the meaning of ἀγών ('assembly, gathering place'), 19.42n.; JANKO on 15.426–428. – The version θεῖον κατὰ δῶμα νέοιντο, which was transmitted in several mss. according to schol. AT on 376, and which perhaps omitted 377 (see *app. crit.*), is erroneous on morphological grounds (unhomeric -οιντο) (LEAF; EDWARDS; VAN DER VALK 1964, 614 f.; APTHORP 1980, 117 n. 125: 'the scholium probably is seriously corrupt').

377 θαῦμα ἰδέσθαι: a VE formula, in the *Iliad* always of divine objects with miraculous properties (83n.); in the present passage, this refers not only to appearance but also to functionality (BECHERT 1964, 143 f.; HUNZINGER 1994, 19 f.). The formula usually represents the point of view of a mortal observer, here that of the narrator (likewise at 5.725, cf. 549) and at the same time in the type-scene[P] 'arrival' (372n.), which is in secondary focalization, that of Thetis (DE JONG [1987] 2004, 49 and 259 n. 22).

378 τόσσον μὲν … δ(έ): τόσσον is used adverbially; the formulation with the sense 'thus far …, but' points to a deviation from a stated condition (likewise at 22.322/324, 23.454 f.,

---

378 οἵ: anaphoric demonstrative (R 17), refers to τρίποδας in 373. — ἤτοι: R 24.4. — τόσσον: on the -σσ-, R 9.1. — ἔχον: on the unaugmented form, R 16.1. — οὔατα: = ὦτα (pl. of οὖς), here 'handle' (↑).

similarly at 4.130/132: AH; LEAF), here their completion (ἔχον τέλος: 'had an end', i.e. 'were completed'); cf. the impf. forms ἔτευχεν (373), ἤρτυε, κόπτε (379) and ὄφρ' ... ἐπονεῖτο (380) for the work still in progress (*LfgrE s.vv.* τέλος 389.30, τόσ(σ)ος 587.26 ff.; GUNDERT 1983, 141 f.). — **οὔατα:** literally 'ears' (cf. 272), here as at 11.633 a designation for the ring-shaped handles of vessels; cf. τρίποδ' ὠτώεντα at 23.264, 23.513, Hes. *Op.* 657; see also MYC *s.v.* οὖς (Mycenaean adjective formations indicating the number of handles).

379 VE from caesura C 2 = *Od.* 8.274. — for examples of handle ornaments on Geometric tripods (from Olympia), MAASS 1978, 15–20, 39–47, 67 f.

δαιδάλεα: 'elaborately embellished'; in Books 18 and 19, Hephaistos' creations are repeatedly described with terms from the word family δαιδαλ- (390 a chair, 400 ornaments for goddesses), esp. Achilleus' new armor (the shield at 479, 482, 19.380, the helmet at 612, and the new armor in its entirety at 19.13, 19.19); on the word family, 19.13n. with bibliography — **προσέκειτο:** The form, only here in early epic, is to be understood as a plpf. pass. of προστίθημι ('were attached, fixed', cf. 375 ὑπὸ ... θῆκεν): AH. — **τά ῥ' ἤρτυε, κόπτε δὲ δεσμούς:** a glance at his current project, attaching already forged handles to the twenty tripods: ἀρτύ(ν)ω with a direct obj. means 'prepare, set out in an orderly fashion' (schol. bT: ἡτοίμαζε; *LfgrE s.v.* ἀρτύνω 1366.21 ff. 'he had set out', with reference to SCHW. 2.298 f. ['a functional pluperfect' (transl.)]); κόπτω is here 'shape by hammering, forge', likewise at *Od.* 8.274 (*LfgrE s.v.* κόπτω). This final step is representative of the entire production process (see 373). — **δεσμούς:** 'fixture, support' to attach the handle loops: rivets (schol. bT: τοὺς ἥλους; *LfgrE s.v.* δεσμός and EDWARDS; D'ACUNTO 2010, 154), perhaps also additional parts such as clamps and tabs that are used to attach the handle loop to the cauldron wall (cf. the example of a wrought Geometric tripod in MAASS 1978, 64, 67, and the additional examples in pl. 1–6, 19–25, 35–39, 43).

380 2nd VH = 1.608, 18.482, 20.12, *Od.* 7.92, 'Hes.' *fr.* 141.5 M.-W., *Nost. fr.* 6.2 West (with the exception of the last passage, always of Hephaistos). — **πραπίδεσσιν:** a designation of the seat of mental authority comparable with φρένες (literally 'diaphragm', 'lungs' or 'chest, thorax': 24.514n.); in the formula ἰδυίῃσι π. in Homeric epic, it serves to stress Hephaistos' 'expert knowledge' of smithing (cf. *h.Merc.* 49 πραπίδεσσιν ἑῇσι of Hermes inventing the lyre, here beside his physical action in 372 f. (369–381n.; SULLIVAN 1987, 185 f.; cf. *LfgrE s.v.* οἶδα 551.1 ff.; similar, but with slightly different weighting, FRONTISI-DUCROUX 2002, 475–480: 'visionary heart', as an expression of creative imagination).

381 1st VH = 18.16; 2nd VH = 18.127 (see *ad loc.*). — The verse is missing from a number of mss. and several papyri and is regarded as an interpolation by some scholars (see *app. crit.*; APTHORP 1980, 137–140, 154 f., with older bibliography; WEST 2001, 12 n. 28

---

379 ῥ': = ἄρα (R 24.1).
380 ὄφρ(α): 'while' (R 22.2). — ἐπονεῖτο (ϝ)ιδυίῃσι: on the prosody, R 4.3. — ἰδυίῃσι: fem. part. of οἶδα; on the -η- after -ι-, R 2; on the declension, R 11.1. — πραπίδεσσιν: on the declension, R 11.3.
381 cf. 16n. — θεά: on the form, R 2.2.

['rhetorical expansions']). There are admittedly arguments for retaining it: (a) the parallelism in the composition of the present arrival scene with that at the beginning of Book 18 (1/368 transitional verse, 2/369 arrival, 3–15/372–380 finding the person sought and a description of the situation, 16–17a/381 approach: 1–22a n.); (b) linking Thetis' movements via 369 (ἵκανε … Θέτις ἀργυρόπεζα) and 381 (ἦλθε … Θέτις ἀργυρόπεζα) after the description of the situation in 372–379. The objections are that (a) is an uncompelling argument in favor of authenticity, since individual elements can be omitted from type-scenes; moreover, the passage – (b) notwithstanding – is linguistically and contextually unproblematic also without 381, while a later insertion of the verse is more easily explained (concordance interpolation) than later athetizing (APTHORP *loc. cit.* 138 f. and 154 f.): (a) temporal ὄφρα is frequently, but not always, combined with τόφρα (e.g. 61 f., 5.788 f., 9.352 f.: LEAF), the combination at 380/382 ὄφρ(α) …, | τὴν δέ is thus not impossible linguistically (apodotic δέ, R 24.3); (b) Hephaistos, absorbed in his work (380), does not notice Thetis, nor does she address him (he is only informed of her arrival at 391 ff.); instead, his wife welcomes the guest (382 ff.). *Contra* is EDWARDS *ad loc.* and 1975, 62 f.: 381 marks the switch from one type-scene to the next and is a replacement for element (1) of the type-scene[P] 'visit' (24.477–478n.: the arriving guest waits at the door), cf. 369–427n.

382 Charis: With the surprise introduction of a new character[P], the narrative changes almost unnoticed to a description of a domestic scene: the unexpected guest is greeted by the hostess and led inside, while the master of the house, engrossed in his work, will receive the guest only later (414–427) (elements 2–5 of the type-scene[P] 'visit': 369–427n.; EDWARDS on 369–467; REECE 1993, 17 f.). Elsewhere in early epic, Charis is used as a name only in the plural (*Chárites*) as a collective term for a group of goddesses frequently associated with Aphrodite (5.338, *Od.* 8.364–366, 18.193 f., *h.Ven.* 61–63, *Cypr. fr.* 5 West) who embody the attraction important for marriage; in Hesiod (*Th.* 945 f.), Hephaistos' wife bears the name Aglaia and is considered the youngest of the Charites (CG 33; 14.267–268n. with bibliography; *LfgrE* s.v. Χάρις, Χάριτες; cf. CG 30; WEST on Hes. *Th.* 64). In a different version of the myth, known from the *Odyssey*, in the poem of the singer Demodokos (*Od.* 8.266 ff.), Aphrodite is Hephaistos' wife – albeit a faithless one (on this version, see DE JONG on *Od.* 8.266–366; WEST [2001] 2011, 323 f.; 2011a, 292 f. [on 14.231–82]); as a supporter of the Trojan party, she would be rather inappropriate in the present scene. The name Charis, used here by the narrator[P], evokes associations that fit with the visitation scene: the noun *cháris* means 'effect or service providing joy', hence 'grace, beauty, gentleness, goodwill', and can denote both an effect em-

---

382 τήν: anaphoric demonstrative (R 17), refers to Thetis (381 or 369). — δὲ (ϝ)ίδε: on the prosody, R 4.3. — προμολοῦσα: fem. aor. part. of προβλώσκω 'come forth'.

anating from a person and the rendering of a (reciprocal) service (*LfgrE s.v.* χάρις; LATACZ 1966, 85–98); Charis thus represents (a) beauty and attractiveness (VB 383), matching the divine smith who, although not without physical defect (415, 417, 421 f.; see 370–371n. on his afflictions), creates magnificent and effective artworks; (b) the gentleness with which the hostess meets the visitor; (c) the joyful readiness, prevailing in the house of Hephaistos, to be helpful and to offer a reciprocal good deed unconditionally (cf. 394–409, 426, 463–467): EDWARDS; CERRI; MARG (1957) 1971, 40; PRIESS 1977, 75; ROCCHI 1979, 6 f.; HOHENDAHL-ZOETELIEF 1980, 122 f.; ERBSE 1986, 38–40; on the relationship Hephaistos–Aphrodite/Charis, see also BURKERT (1960) 2001, 107 f. and WEST 2011, 293 (on 14.231–282): Charis as a substitute for Aphrodite; differently PÖTSCHER 2001, 20–23: Hephaistos–Charis as the more ancient version of the myth. — **veil:** Charis wears as an ornamental headdress a veil falling down from the crown of her head across her shoulders and back, as routinely in public by honorable women, although it also contributed to an attractive appearance (3.141n., 14.184n.); its frequently mentioned luster is due to the treatment of the fabric with oil (on this treatment of textiles, 6.295n., 14.185n.).

προμολοῦσα: a metrically convenient replacement for προελθοῦσα (*LfgrE s.v.* βλώσκω); on the preverb προ- ('forward, forth, toward'), SCHW. 2.505. — **λιπαροκρήδεμνος:** a *hapax*[P] in the *Iliad* and an epithet of goddesses (elsewhere only at *h.Cer.* 25, 438, 459, *Cypr. fr.* 6.4 West; also in the additional verse *Il.* 16.867a), in contrast to the metrically equivalent καλλικρήδεμνος as an epithet of human wives (*Od.* 4.623) and the gen. version λιπαροπλοκάμοιο of the head (*LfgrE*; cf. 19.126–127n.). κρήδεμνο-, the second element of the possessive compound (on which, cf. the VE formula λιπαρὰ κρήδεμνα 5× *Od.*), is a combination of κάρη-/κρη- with a derivation from δέω, thus literally 'headband', in Homeric epic the designation for women's veils (14.184n.).

383 2nd VH = 1.607, 18.393, 18.462, 18.587, 18.590, *Od.* 8.300, 8.349, 8.357, Hes. *Th.* 571, 579, 'Hes.' *fr.* 209.3 M.-W. — **ὤπυιε:** means 'have someone as a wife' and implies the formal status of the woman (*LfgrE*; 14.267–268n.). — **περικλυτὸς Ἀμφιγυήεις:** a VE formula (see *iterata*, also ἀγακλυτὸς Ἀ. at Hes. *Th.* 945 and κλυτὸς Ἀ. at 614 and 2× Hes.). Ἀμφιγυήεις is a distinctive epithet[P] of Hephaistos; with the exception of 14.239, in early epic always after (ἀγα/περι-)κλυτός (on which, 326n.) and likely a metrical expansion related to ἀμφίγυος 'curved on both sides' (14.26n.). The original meaning was perhaps 'who has a thing curved on both sides' in reference to a tool, later re- or misinterpreted as 'bow-legged' (1.607n.; cf. 370–371n. on the metrically equivalent Κυλλοποδίων with an initial consonant); alternatively, 'ambidextrous' might be the original sense (AH on *Od.* 8.300; VERDENIUS on Hes. *Op.* 70; WEST 2011, 99 [on 1.607], with reference

---

383 τήν: with the function of a relative pronoun (R 14.5).

to the Ugaritic divine smith Kothar), cf. ἐγ-γυαλ-ίζω 'give (into the hand?)' (*LfgrE s.v.* ἐγγυαλίζω; *DELG s.v.* *γύη).

384 = 6.253, 6.406, 14.232, 18.423, 19.7, *Od.* 2.302, 8.291, 11.247, 15.530; ≈ *Od.* 10.280; 2nd VH (speech introduction formula[P]) another 11× *Il.*, 21× *Od.*, 2× *h.Ven.* — a formulaic verse with a greeting gesture and an introduction to warm or urgent speeches (19.7n.; HENTZE 1902, 329 f., 347).

ἐν ... οἱ φῦ χειρί: 'grasped her firmly by the hand'; οἱ ... χειρί is a double dat. (σχῆμα καθ᾽ ὅλον καὶ μέρος) with χειρί as a locative dat. of destination, thus literally 'grew onto her hand' (19.7n.). — **ἔκ τ᾽ ὀνόμαζεν:** 'and addressed her by name' (see 385); due to the formulaic use of the phrase, its original meaning ('call (out) someone's name') is no longer evident in many passages (1.361n.; *LfgrE s.v.* ὀνομάζω 715.19 ff.).

385–386 = 424–425 (greeting by Hephaistos); ≈ *Od.* 5.87–88; 2nd VH of 386 ≈ *Il.* 16.796, 24.642. — **Why:** Together with her sisters, Thetis dwells in the sea with her father and does not appear to be among the gods on Olympos with any frequency (35 f., 140 ff., 24.74 ff.). She provides the answer only to Hephaistos (424 ff.), who like Charis is surprised by her visit. The narrator highlights the exceptional element of this situation via astonished questions by both hosts (suggestion by DE JONG). — **We honour you and love you:** a respectful address to a guest (see *iterata* and cf. 14.210, *Od.* 19.191, 19.254); the linking of terms from the word families of *aidós* ('respect'; cf. 394n.) and *philótēs* ('friendship') occurs frequently in early epic in the context of guest and host (24.111n.).

τίπτε: = τί ποτε 'why then?, what then?'; can signal a reproach or disconcertment, but in the present greeting is merely an expression of slight wonder regarding an unusual visit, likewise at 424, *Od.* 5.87, similarly at *Il.* 23.94, *Od.* 4.810 (*LfgrE*). — **Θέτι τανύπεπλε:** The short final syllable of the voc. Θέτι in the *longum* is to be explained either by the adaptation of an – unattested – nom. formula *Θέτις τανύπεπλος (WEST 2011, 350 f.; cf. M 14; 357–358a n., 2.8n., 19.400n.) or as a metrical licence, especially given that the voc. is placed at a caesura, as at 24.88 (cf. 24.88n. with bibliography; M 8); on the position before caesura A 4, see also 405 (Θέτις τε) and 407 (Θέτῑ). – τανύπεπλος ('with long robe') is an epithet of divine and human women and a possessive compound from *τανύς 'elongated, thin' (3.228n.). — **ἡμέτερον δῶ:** a VE formula (3× *Il.*, 3× *Od.*), a variant of the VE formulae χαλκοβατὲς δῶ (4× *Il.*, 2× *Od.*) and ὑψερεφὲς δῶ (3× *Od.*); on this, and on the etymology of δῶ (related to δόμος, δῶμα), 1.426n. — **αἰδοίη τε φίλη τε:** a variable phrase (at VB see *iterata*, also in verse middle 2× *Il.*, 1× *Od.* and at VE 2× *Od.*, 1× *h.Hom.*

---

384 ἐν ... φῦ (from ἐμφύομαι), ἐκ ... ὀνόμαζεν: so-called tmesis (R 20.2). — ἄρα (ϝ)οι ... χειρὶ (ϝ)έπος: on the prosody, R 4.3. — οἱ: = αὐτῇ (R 14.1). — ἔφατ(ο): impf. of φημί; on the mid., R 23.
385 τανύπεπλε, ἱκάνεις: on the hiatus, R 5.6. — δῶ: acc. of direction without a preposition (R 19.2).
386 μέν: ≈ μήν (R 24.6). — τι: acc. of respect (R 19.1), strengthens οὐ: 'not in any respect, in no way, not at all'.

29); αἰδοῖος is here 'who is shown αἰδώς, venerable' (*LfgrE s.v.* 268.25 ff., esp. 69 ff.), φίλος a designation of a socially close individual, especially in a guest–host relationship (*LfgrE s.v.* 944.48 ff. and 945.4 ff.; cf. 3.207n. [φιλέω], 3.354n. [φιλότης]). — **πάρος:** 'before, earlier', also employed with a present tense verb, meaning 'otherwise, usually', i.e. 'you don't do this normally (regularly)': *LfgrE s.v.* 987.6 ff. and 989.22 ff.; on the '«habitual» present', see Rijksbaron 1988, 238 (somewhat differently, Wackernagel [1920/24] 2009, 68, 203: πάρος as a reference to past actions rendered via a pres. form that is in fact timeless: 'formerly/thus far, you did not do this regularly'). — **θαμίζεις:** derived from θαμά ('in close succession, frequently'), a designation of actions that are repeated regularly (*LfgrE*).

387 = *Od.* 5.91; 2nd VH = 9.517. — **entertainment:** Charis does not expect an immediate answer to her question, but rather offers a meal first (cf. Hephaistos at 408 f.); entertaining guests with food and drink is an integral part of guest-friendship and generally takes place immediately upon arrival (e.g. 6.172 ff., 11.777 ff.): 6.173–177n.; cf. 369–427n. (elements 7 and 8 of the type-scene[P] 'visit'); Edwards on 387; Cerri on 408.

προτέρω: 'onward, forward', i.e. here: 'in (the house)', similarly in the case of the arrival of guests at 9.191/199, *Od.* 4.36 (see also πρόσω ἄγε at 388): *LfgrE s.v.* προτέρω; Reece 1993, 20 f. — **ξείνια:** ξείνιον/ξεινήϊον is a term encompassing everything involved in guest-friendship and the reception of a guest into the house (food and drink, accommodation, guest-gift); ξ. παρατίθημι denotes serving food and drink (likewise at 11.779, 18.408, *Od.* 5.91, 9.517, 15.188, cf. 4.33): Scheid-Tissinier 1994, 138–142; *LfgrE*; cf. 3.207n. — **θείω:** On the form, cf. ἀποθείομαι 409n.

388 ὣς ἄρα φωνήσασα: 65n. — δῖα θεάων: 205–206n.

389 1st VH ≈ 5.36; 2nd VH = *Od.* 7.162, 10.314, 10.366, *h.Ven.* 165. — Thetis is treated as befits a guest: the noun *thrónos*, attested already in Mycenaean (*DMic s.vv. to-no* and *to-ro-no-wo-ko*), designates the most elegant seat in Homeric society: on the one hand, the chair in the *mégaron* reserved as a seat of honor for the master of the house or for male guests, on the other, the seats of gods and goddesses (14.238n. [with bibliography], 24.515–516n.; *LfgrE s.v.* θρόνος; Laser 1968, 41; Reece 1993, 21 f.; Otto 2012, 27 f.). The epithet 'fitted with silver nails' (of 'chair' and 'sword': 2.45n.) indicates embellishment with silver nails or rivets (Laser 1968, 38 f.; cf. *LfgrE s.vv.* ἄργυρος and ἀργύρεος; on the archaeological evidence for chairs with this type of decoration [esp. from Cyprus], see

---

387 ἔπεο: imper. of ἕπομαι (cf. R 6). — τοι: = σοι (R 14.1). — προτέρω, ἵνα: on the hiatus, R 5.6; likewise πρόσω ἄγε in 388. — πάρ ... θείω: πάρ = παρά (R 20.1), on the so-called tmesis, R 20.2; θείω: aor. subjunc. of τίθημι. — ξείνια: = ξένια (ξειν- < *ξενϝ: R 4.2).

388 ἄγε: on the unaugmented form, R 16.1. — θεάων: on the declension, R 11.1.

389 καθεῖσεν: 'had her sit, take a place' (transitive aor. act. of καθίζω/καθέζω).

LORIMER 1950, 273 f.; STUBBINGS 1962, 533; KARAGEORGHIS 1968, 100 f.; 1976, 176; OTTO 2012, 24 ff.; see also ELES 2002, 77–82, 241–245 with fig. 115 and pl. II–XIII [bronze decorations on an 8th-cent. throne from Italy]).

θρόνου ἀργυροήλου: an inflectable VE formula (1× *Il.*, 5× *Od.*, 1× *h.Ven.*).

390 = *Od.* 10.315, 10.367; ≈ 1.131; 2nd VH = 4.136; ≈ *Il.* 14.240, *Od.* 19.57. — **footstool:** A comfortable seat is often paired with a footstool (Greek *thrḗnys*, Mycenaean *ta-ra-nu*, see *DMic*) designed to facilitate sitting and/or keep the feet off the dirty ground during a meal; on this and the archaeological evidence and pictorial representations, 14.239–240n.; OTTO 2012, 42.

καλοῦ δαιδαλέου: an inflectable VB formula (6× *Il.*, 3× *Od.*); the θρόνος – surely made by Hephaistos' hands – is marked out as a particularly elaborate piece of furniture via the progressive enjambment[P] and the series of epithets (on this epic stylistic element, 130–131n.; on δαιδάλεος, 379n.; on the epithets with θρόνος, *LfgrE s.v.* θρόνος). — **ποσίν:** 'for the feet' (*LfgrE s.v.* 1521.40).

391–427 The usual procedure of the type-scene[P] 'visit' is expanded via a conversation between the spouses (391–409) that serves to provide information regarding the visitor (for Hephaistos: Thetis' presence; for the audience: the Hephaistos–Thetis relationship). The narrator[P] subsequently directs attention first to Hephaistos diligently finishing his work (410–413), preparing an appropriate reception for Thetis (414 ff.) and proceeding from the workshop to the house (416 f., 421 f.) in order to also greet the guest (423–427), and then, in the following conversation, to Thetis' mood and her appearance as a supplicant (424–426, 428–461). Hephaistos' attachment to Thetis and his attitude toward his work and his tools are given great weight and create an expectation in the audience that the request for new armor will reach an open mind (394–409n.; AREND 1933, 36 f.).

391 Ἥφαιστον κλυτοτέχνην: 143n. — **εἶπέ τε μῦθον:** a VE formula (3× *Il.*, 2× *Od.*, 5× *h.Hom.*), a less common form of a short speech introduction formula (in contrast, e.g. φώνησέν τε at 24.193n.).

392 A one-verse speech (182n.), fitting with the urgency of the request (schol. bT). — **πρόμολ' ὧδε:** understood in two ways (on προμολεῖν 'come here', 382n.): (a) 'come here without ado!' (from the workshop), on the basis of the modal meaning of ὧδε in most Homeric passages: 'so' in the sense 'just like that, without further ado', with a temporal component 'immediately, straightaway' (schol. A [μηδὲν ὑπερθέμενος] and bT; LSJ *s.v.* I 2:

---

390 δαιδαλέου, ὑπό: on the hiatus, R 5.6. — ὑπό: adverbial ('underneath'). — ἦεν: = ἦν (R 16.6).
391 κέκλετο: reduplicated aor. of κέλομαι; the action of the verb is contemporary with that of εἶπέ τε μῦθον ('she called over, summoned, by ...').
392 πρόμολ(ε): aor. imper. 'come here!' (*sc.* from the workshop), cf. 382n. — σεῖο: = σοῦ (R 14.1).

'come forth, just as thou art'; AH ['accompanied by an inviting gesture' (transl.)]; LEHRS [1833] 1882, 71–73, 370–374; CERRI; cf. 2.439n.); (b) 'come over here!': ὧδε with a local function, as commonly later, esp. in Attic tragedy and comedy (LEAF and EDWARDS, with reference to the use of the verse by Plato when planning to burn his youthful poems, see Diog. Laert. 3.5 [Ἥφαιστε, πρόμολ᾽ ὧδε Πλάτων νύ τι σεῖο χατίζει]; BEKKER 1872, 38). (a) has more support, in that the request has a certain urgency (immediately, without first finishing the tripods, cf. 378 f.) and Hephaistos' response also makes reference to a time frame (408 f. σὺ μὲν νῦν ... | ὄφρ᾽ ἂν ἐγώ ['entertain her until I have tidied everything away!']). — **νύ:** here with 'causal force' (RUIJGH 1957, 60 [transl.], but cf. 165n.). — **τι σεῖο χατίζει:** 'needs you in a particular matter, is in need of your assistance with something'; on χατίζω (+ gen. 'need, rely on'), see *LfgrE* s.v.; KLOSS 1994, 130–138; cf. 6.463n. [χήτει].

393 = 18.462; ≈ *Od.* 8.357; 2nd VH = 383 (see *ad loc.*). — **τὴν δ᾽ ἠμείβετ᾽ ἔπειτα:** a VB formula (19.28n.).

394–409 In a speech divided into two parts of different length, Hephaistos responds first to the information regarding Thetis' arrival (392b: 394–407), second to Charis' request (392a: 408 f.): cf. 'continuity of thought' principle[P]. Part (1) consists of a ring-composition[P], in the outer rings of which Hephaistos' rescue by Thetis is mentioned, while the center describes his work as a smith (cf. EDWARDS): (A) Arrival of the revered, powerful goddess (394); (B) her assistance in rescuing him after his mother Hera rejected him (395–397a); (C) Eurynome and Thetis prevented suffering (397b–398); (D) Eurynome, daughter of Okeanos (399); (E) for nine years, Hephaistos forged elaborate ornaments for the two (400–402a); (D') Okeanos' stream shields his hiding place (402b–403a); (C') Thetis and Eurynome were the only ones to be informed (403b–405a); (B') they rescued him (405b); (A') arrival of the goddess to whom he owes a debt (406 f.). The secondarily focalized[P] narrative of an episode from Hephaistos' life has a key function[P]: it illustrates his attachment to Thetis, in whose debt he deems himself to be, and provides the reason for his willingness to help her (426) before knowing the contents of her plea; it clarifies for the audience already at this point that Thetis' pleading will be successful and that Achilleus will receive new armor without a problem (HOHENDAHL-ZOETELIEF 1980, 122–124; ERBSE 1986, 79 f.; WEST 2011, 351). – The present story of Hephaistos' fall and rescue contains motifs that also occur in other stories about gods in the *Iliad* and especially in the myth, transmitted in post-Homeric texts, of Dionysos' move to Olympos (on the stylistic elements of the narrative section, 395–405n.): (a) Thetis as an assistant to other gods: 1.393 ff. and 1.503 ff. Zeus, 6.135 ff. Dionysos (SLATKIN [1991] 2011, 52–71); (b) the forcible fall from Olympos: among others, Hephaistos at 1.590 ff. (additional examples at 395–397a n.); (c) refuge in a hiding place in Okeanos: 6.135 f. Dionysos (WILLCOCK [1964] 2001, 443 f.); on the contents of the fragmentary hymn to

Dionysos, see WEST (2001) 2011; 2003a, 26–31 (text with English translation); on the linking of Hephaistos and Dionysos in myth, see also 400n. It is thus unclear whether the poet of the *Iliad* (a) drew on traditional material regarding Hephaistos for the entire story or (b) adapted common motifs for the present passage, creating a version of Hephaistos' fall in which Thetis could play a major role (favoring (a): KULLMANN 1956, 12; MASCIADRI 2008, 282–293; RINON 2008, 133 f. and 190 n. 31; WEST 2011, 292 f.; on Thetis as 'cosmic power', see SLATKIN *loc. cit.* 54–56, 70 f.; favoring (b) WILLCOCK *loc. cit.* 445; 1977, 44 n. 16; BRASWELL 1971, 20 f.; ERBSE 1986, 80; on this kind of *ad hoc* invention, see also 1.262–270n., 1.396–406n., 6.218–221n., 19.95–133n., 24.599–620n., point (2) with bibliography). What is more, the present version shows similarities with the narrative patterns of myths that involve the exposure of children (DELCOURT [1957] 1982, 41–43; BINDER 1964, 128 f.; HUYS 1995, 40 f., 62, 167): (a) reasons for the exposure; (b) circumstances of the exposure (individual carrying out the deed, location); (c) rescue (by a deity or human being), adoption and maturing of the foundling, who shows extraordinary abilities; (d) return and rehabilitation (cf. 400n.); on this narrative pattern and its literary forms in general, BINDER *loc. cit.* 125–250; HUYS *loc. cit.* 27–46, 377–394; cf. also *BNP s.v.* Exposure, myths and legends of.

394 The designation of Thetis as *deinḗ te kai aidoíē* is a variation of the adjectival phrase *aidóiē te phílē te* in Charis' address (385–386n.): *deinós* means 'powerful, tremendous' (*LfgrE s.v.* δεινός 236.67; on its use in reference to deities, 6.379–380n.), *aidoíos* 'awe-inspiring, venerable' (in the context of obligations also at 14.210, *Od.* 19.254, cf. *Il.* 24.111 [with n.]; on the word family of *aidṓs*, 1.23n., 6.441–442n.); on the combination of these adjectives in Homer, CAIRNS 1993, 87–95. Hephaistos speaks of Thetis with the greatest respect and awe, as a deity who could potentially be dangerous – she has opposed other, no less powerful gods (1.398 ff.), for example – and whose claim to reverence he accepts.

ἦ ῥά νυ: an emphatic beginning to a speech (6.215n.).

395–405 The narrative part of the passage contains two stylistic elements of spoken language that point to an oral background (cf. 6.394–399n.; MINCHIN 1995; ALLAN 2009, 142 f.): a) ring-composition[P] at 395/405 (ἥ μ' ἐσάωσ' ... / ... αἵ μ' ἐσάωσαν), 398/405 (Εὐρυνόμη τε Θέτις θ' / Θέτις τε καὶ Εὐρυνόμη), 399/402 ἀψορρόου Ὠκεανοῖο / ῥόος Ὠκεανοῖο); (b) 398 f. epanalepsis of the name Eurynome after the mention of Thetis (with progressive enjambment[P]), facilitating the addition of new information (Εὐρυνόμη ... | Εὐρυνόμη, θυγάτηρ ...), here the genealogy (on which, 398n.); on the structure of 399, cf. *Od.* 6.17=6.213, 7.58, 'Hes.' *Sc.* 3.

---

394 ἦ ῥα: 'indeed' (R 24.4, ↑).

395–397a Hephaistos' own mother, Hera, rid herself of the apparently crippled child (370–371n.) by banning him from her sight (396 f.: 'who wanted to hide me'), i.e. by throwing him off Mount Olympos or getting others to do so (395: 'great fall'). The present version of Hephaistos' fall from Olympos explains his limping as a congenital defect, as at *Od.* 8.310–312, *h.Ap.* 317–320 and in the hymn to Dionysos at *h.Hom.* 1 *fr.* C 10 f. West (370–371n.; *LfgrE s.v.* ἠπεδανός); on the exposure of disabled children in ancient Greece, see *BNP s.v.* Child exposure; SCHMIDT 1983/84, 133–145, 151. Another version of his fall from Olympos with a different background is alluded to by Hephaistos in Book 1 of the *Iliad* (1.590–594: see *ad loc.* and 1.591n.): Zeus flings him off Olympos as a punishment, after which he took refuge on the island of Lemnos. In the *Iliad*, Zeus is repeatedly described as throwing gods from Olympos, either as punishment or in order to demonstrate his physical superiority (cf. 8.13, 14.256–258, 15.21–24, 19.126–131 [19.129–130n., 19.131n.]): MARG (1957) 1971, 41 f. n. 58; PRIESS 1977, 66–68; ERBSE 1986, 78 f.). For the story of Hephaistos' fall from Olympos, the narrator[P] thus employs two versions as required: here the exposure of a child by Hera and the rescue by the marine goddesses as a characterization of Thetis (394–409n., 396n.); in Book 1, the punishment by Zeus as an illustration of his position of power (1.586–594n.).

395 ἥ μ' ἐσάωσ(ε): Together with αἵ μ' ἐσάωσαν at VE of 405, this forms the frame of the episode linking Hephaistos to Thetis; elsewhere in early epic with a god as the object only at 14.259 (Nyx rescues her son Hypnos): *LfgrE s.v.* σαόω.

396 [brazen-faced] dog-eyed: In addition to 'dog/bitch', the adj. 'with the eyes of a dog' is a common term of reproach in Homeric epic and is often used in reference to shameless behavior (1.159n., 6.344n.). Here, in the context of a mother–child relationship, it underlines Hera's blatant heartlessness as a mother, while by way of contrast Thetis' care as (foster) mother, helpful in every sense, is highlighted (RINON 2008, 130–132).

ἰότητι: In early epic, this usually denotes the will of gods (19.9b n.). — κυνώπιδος: κυνῶπις is the fem. of κυνῶπης ('dog-eyed, looking in a dog-like manner'), also at 3.180, *Od.* 4.145 (Helen), 8.319 (Aphrodite), 11.424 (Klytaimestra): 1.159n. — ἥ μ' ἐθέλησεν: The relative clause refers to the content of ἰότητι (PORZIG 1942, 71, 86) and explains the use of the reproach κυνῶπις; the aor. is ingressive (*LfgrE s.v.* 414.31 ff.).

397b ≈ 9.321, 13.670, 16.55, *Od.* 13.263, 15.487; cf. *Od.* 1.4, 13.90. — The 'if-not' situation[P] (on which, 165–168n.) serves as a rhetorical means to augment the value of Thetis' actions (DE JONG [1987] 2004, 78).

---

395 ἐσάωσ(ε): = ἔσωσε (R 6).
397 ἐόντα: = ὄντα (R 16.6).

τότ᾿ ἄν: In contrast to the elsewhere common ἔνθα κεν or καί νύ κεν, this introduction to the 'if-not' situation[P] stresses the temporal distance (2.155–156n.; LOUDEN 1993, 183 n. 6). – **πάθον ἄλγεα:** ἄλγεα denotes comprehensively Hephaistos' physical and mental pain and the overall circumstances, resulting from being banished far from the community of gods, that caused it (cf. 6.450–454n.); the sing. ἄλγος at 395 is the concrete pain caused by the fall (MAWET 1979, 184). On formulaic phrases for 'suffering pain', see *LfgrE s.v.* πάσχω; MAWET *loc. cit.* 176 ff.; PUCCI (1982) 1998, 13 f.

398 2nd VH ≈ 6.136 (Dionysos, pursued by Lykurgos, finds refuge with Thetis in the sea; see *ad loc.*). – **Eurynomē:** mentioned only here in Homeric epic; in Hesiod's *Theogony* she is listed in the catalogue of Okeanids (*Th.* 358) and as one of Zeus' wives and the mother of the Charites (*Th.* 907 ff.) (*BNP s.vv.* Eurynome and Oceanids; WEST on Hes. *Th.* 881–1020; on the identical role played by Thetis and Eurynome in the myth of Dionysos, see the version of the epic poet Eumelus, *fr.* 27 West = schol. D on *Il.* 6.131). Her name contains the same second element as that of the Nereid Amphi-nómē (44n.) and thus means approximately 'with broad grazing grounds' (VON KAMPTZ 74; RISCH 201). At 399, the narrator[P] has Hephaistos refer to her origins (a four-word verse [on which, 1.75n.] entirely filled by designations for a single character [on which, 1.36n.]); it appears that she plays a quite important role for him. Some scholars explain this in terms of a familial relationship: according to Hes. *Th.* 907 f. [Eurynome as the mother of the Charites] and *Th.* 945 f. [one of the Charites as Hephaistos' wife]), she is Hephaistos' mother-in-law (schol. T on 398–399; EDWARDS on 397–399; see also on Charis, 382n.).

ὑπεδέξατο κόλπῳ: a VE formula with κόλπος as a term for the female bosom and the folds of the garment enveloping it, imparting a sense of security to the child, while vis-à-vis the marine goddesses Eurynome and Thetis, the meaning 'marine gulf, bay' may also play a role (6.136n.; cf. 140n.); on the congruence of the predicate with the neighboring subject, 28n.

399 2nd VH = *Od.* 20.65, Hes. *Th.* 776. – **bends back in a circle:** The adj. *apsórroos* is a distinctive epithet[P] of *Ōkeanós* (see *iterata*) and since antiquity has usually been understood 'flowing back (to the starting point)' (on the different ancient explanations as 'flowing back', 'fast-flowing' or 'backward flowing' [of the tides], see SCHMIDT 1976, 134 f.). This refers to the notion of Okeanos as a circular stream that flows around the disc of the earth, imagined as circular in shape, to pour back into itself (cf. the edge of the shield at 607 f., also Hes. *Th.* 790 f., 'Hes.' *Sc.* 314 f.): *LfgrE s.v.* Ὠκεανός (with bibliography); LESKY 1947, 59, 66; for additional information on this notion, 14.200n. with bibliography; WEST on Hes. *Th.* 133.

ἀψορρόου Ὠκεανοῖο: a variant of the VE formula βαθυρρόου Ὠκεανοῖο (7.422, 14.311, *Od.* 11.13, 19.434, also *h.Merc.* 185). The formation of the compound ἀψόρροος is uncertain (for discussion and bibliography, Kelly 2007a): the initial element ἄψ means 'back', namely to the starting point (cf. *LfgrE s.v.* ἄψ 1782.4 ff.); the final element -ρροος is derived from ῥέω (as in the case of βαθύ-ρροος, etc.) and expanded via the compounding vowel -ο- (Schw. 1.632) on analogy with the adj. ἄψ-ορρος ('returning': *DELG s.v.* ἄψ; Frisk *s.v.* ἄψορρος; Forssman 1980, 185 ff. [on ἔρρω]). For a possible connection with Babylonian Apsu (water), see West 1997, 148 ('a reinterpretation') and, skeptically, Kelly 2007a, 282 with n. 13; 2008, 283 n. 79.

400 nine years: A typical number[P] (351n.): periods of nine years often mark storylines that progress in an undifferentiated fashion, with decisive events occurring after they are complete (2.326–329n.). In the present case, this is Hephaistos' return to Olympos and the community of gods, which is implied but not reported in the *Iliad* (on the motif [nine years of exclusion from the community of gods, return in the tenth year], cf. Hes. *Th.* 801–804). It remains unmentioned here as well, since it is irrelevant to Hephaistos' relationship with Thetis. According to post-Homeric sources, Hephaistos sent Hera a throne – supposedly a present – that bound her; since no one else could free her and he himself refused to do so, he was plied with wine by Dionysos and brought to Mt. Olympos to unfasten Hera (394–409n.; on the various post-Homeric sources, see Burkert [1960] 2001, 108 n. 9; Erbse 1986, 80–85; West [2001] 2011, 316 f.; on pictorial representations of Hephaistos' return, 370–371n.).

χάλκευον: A derivation from χαλκεύς (only here in early epic), it means – transitively and irrespective of the metal worked – 'forge' (*LfgrE*; on χαλκός 'bronze', 2.226n., 6.3n.). The position of χάλκευον leads to an unusual 2nd VH from a metrical point of view: word end with a spondee and lengthening by position before caesura C 2 (contrary to 'Wernicke's Law': M 10.3; Edwards). — **δαίδαλα:** the elaborately made ornaments mentioned at 401 (cf. 379n.).

401 = *h.Ven.* 163. — An accumulation of technical terms for female ornaments (see *h.Ven.* 162 f.), the meaning of which – with the exception of the last – was a cause for disagreement already among ancient scholars (schol. A, bT, D), and none of which can be unequivocally associated with any particular type of ornament even on the basis of later attestations (four Iliadic *hapax legomena*[P], see below); the terms probably encompass various types of embellishments and underline the exclusivity of these small works of art (Greek *daídala* 400) from the early (or even initial?) period of Hephaistos' service as goldsmith (cf. Lorimer 1950, 512 n. 3; Keil 1998, 20, 47; for archaeological finds of Geometric and Archaic ornaments, see Higgins [1961] 1980, 94 ff.; Deppert-Lippitz 1985, 54 ff.). – (a) Greek *pórpai* denotes pins or fibula for

---

400 τῆσι πάρ': = παρὰ τῆσι (R 20.2); on the declension, R 11.1; on the anaphoric demonstrative function of ὅ, ἥ, τό, R 17. — εἰνάετες: adv., 'for nine years' (Ionic εἰνα- < *ἔνϝα-: R 4.2).

fastening garments, which were applied either in the middle of the chest or to the side beneath the shoulder, at the clavicle; on their mode of use and on archaeological finds of dress pins and fibulae, 14.180n. – (b) The Greek terms *hélikes* and *kálykes* denote spiral-shaped and blossom-, bud- or rosette-shaped ornaments (see below). Among the objects Hephaistos made for the goddesses, one would expect, in addition to dress-pins and necklaces, were most likely also ornaments for their ears, arms (bands for the upper or lower arm), hair and fingers (cf. the gifts for Penelope at *Od.* 18.293 ff.). In the case of the *iteratum* in the hymn to Aphrodite (*h.Ven.* 162 f.: ornaments and garments Anchises removes from the goddess Aphrodite), the two terms are usually interpreted as spiral-shaped arm bands (*hélikes*) and earrings in the shape of buds or blossoms with rosettes (*kálykes*), in accord with the goddess' jewelry in pictorial representations, but sometimes also as rosette-shaped links of necklaces (FAULKNER on *h.Ven.* 87); earrings with vegetal elements are mentioned as female adornments elsewhere in early epic (*Il.* 14.182 f., *Od.* 18.297 f., *h.Hom.* 6.8 f.). For archaeological finds of ear-ornaments, 14.182n. and 14.183n.; *BNP s.v.* Ear Ornaments; on armbands, BIELEFELD 1968, 58 f.; DESPINI 1996, 43 f.; on finds of spiral-shaped ornaments, also HIGGINS (1961) 1980, 97, 102, 105. – (c) In early epic, there are two terms for neck ornaments: *hórmos*, used here, designates a longer necklace (cf. *h.Ap.* 103 f., *h.Hom.* 6.10 f.), with beads or pendants of various materials threaded onto (precious) metal wire; with the exception of the present passage, the material mentioned is always gold, sometimes with amber in addition (*Od.* 15.460, 18.296), and its characteristics are color (*h.Ven.* 88 f.) and luster (*h.Ven.* 88 f. like the moon, *Od.* 18.295 f. like the sun). In contrast, *ísthmion* designates an ornament that tightly encircles the neck (*Od.* 18.300): *LfgrE s.v.* ὅρμος I; BIELEFELD 1968, 5 f., 66; BLANCK 1974, 1–7, 55 ff.; DESPINI 1996, 36 ff.

πόρπας: a Homeric *hapax*[P], perhaps like περόνη related to πείρω 'pierce' (FRISK and *DELG s.v.* πείρω; *contra* BEEKES *s.v.* πόρπη); this is one of the Homeric terms for dress-pins, although the exact association with a type (pin or fibula) and the difference between a περόνη and an ἐνετή (on which, 14.180n.) are uncertain (schol. D; *LfgrE s.v.* πόρπη ['clasp']; BIELEFELD 1968, 6–8; FAULKNER on *h.Ven.* 163 ['pin']). — **γναμπτάς:** a verbal adj., 'crooked, bent', used of manufactured objects; in addition to the ἕλικαι, also at *Od.* 4.369 = 12.332 (fishing hook), 18.294 (part of a fibula): *LfgrE*; cf. 24.359n. — **ἕλικας κάλυκάς τε:** The terms only allow conclusions regarding the shape of the ornaments (LEAF; BIELEFELD 1968, 6. 66 f.; FAULKNER on *h.Ven.* 87): ἕλιξ is associated with the same root as εἰλέω (cf. the denominative ἑλίσσω 'turn, twist') and probably means 'spiral' (FRISK, *DELG* and BEEKES *s.v.* ἕλιξ; cf. 1.98n. [ἑλικώπιδα]); in early epic, it is used only here and at *h.Ven.* 87, 163 as a designation for female ornaments (with the epithet (ἐπι)γναμπτάς), at 'Hes.' *Sc.* 295 for vines, in later attestations for a variety of spiral-shaped objects (*LfgrE s.v.* ἕλι(ξ) I; LSJ *s.v.* ἕλιξ (B)). – κάλυξ (a Homeric *hapax*[P] of obscure etymology) as a term for jewelry is always used in onomatopoetic combination with ἕλικας, elsewhere in reference to flowers (*h.Cer.* 427, *Cypr. fr.* 5.5 f. West), in later attestations also as a term for the seed-capsule of a variety of plants; it probably means 'bud, blossom' (*LfgrE* and LSJ *s.v.* κάλυξ; RENEHAN 1982, 83; cf. RICHARDSON on *h.Cer.* 8 [καλυκώπιδι]). – **ὅρμους:** probably derived from εἴρω 'thread (on a string)' (related to the root *ser-, Latin *sero*), cf. the syntactic linking of ὅρμος and perf. ἔερτο or ἐερμένος at *Od.* 15.460, 18.296, *h.Ap.* 103 f. (*LfgrE s.vv.* ὅρμος I, εἴρω II).

402 cave: Elsewhere in the *Iliad*, caves serve as dwellings only for marine deities, such as Thetis, who during the time of the action of the *Iliad* lives in one beneath the sea off the coast of Asia Minor (24.83n.), and her father Nereus (36, 50, 24.83), in the *Odyssey* for Kalypso, Polyphemos and Scylla, and at Hes. *Th.* 297 for Echidna, while Poseidon uses a cave as a submarine horse-stable (*Il.* 13.32 ff.): *LfgrE s.v.* σπέος; on the sea as a habitat of gods, ELLIGER 1975, 69 f. — **stream of Ocean:** Although he is included in the genealogy at 399 (see *ad loc.*), Okeanos here functions as the geographical space of the action on the divine plane; the image of the river is illustrated by the *figura etymologica* 'the flow flowed' (*rhóos rhéen*) at 402 f., as well as by a combination of optical and acoustic phenomena (403 roaring and foaming water). On this juxtaposition, cf. CG 28: 'confluence of anthropomorphic and non-anthropomorphic action'.

ἐν σπῆϊ γλαφυρῷ: on the formula (3× VB, 3× in verse middle), 24.83n. — **δὲ ῥόος:** an apparent short in the *longum* before caesura C 1 (cf. M 8), to be explained by ῥόος (a verbal substantive related to ῥέω < *sreu̯-; cf. the compounds with -ρροος at 399n.) originally having an initial /s/ that remains prosodically relevant: G 16; M 13.2. — **ῥόος Ὠκεανοῖο:** an inflectable VE formula (nom./acc.: 2× *Il.*, 2× *Od.*, 1× Hes. *Op.*); cf. the variant Ὠκεανοῖο ῥοάων 3.5n.

403 1st VH ≈ 5.599, 21.325. — **μορμύρων:** an onomatopoetic verb (cf. Latin *murmurare*) rendering the sound of water in motion, always in combination with ἀφρῷ of rivers rushing down with foam (see the *iterata*, also *Od.* 12.238 ἀναμορμύρεσκε): KRAPP 1964, 176 ('a mixture of optical and acoustic impressions' [transl.]); TICHY 1983, 277–279; cf. *LfgrE s.v.* ἀφρός. — **ἄσπετος:** 'unspeakably (large)' (*LfgrE*); here ῥέεν ἄσπετος of the streams of Okeanos means 'flowed mightily'. Given the imitation at *h.Ven.* 237 (τοῦ δ' ἤτοι φωνὴ ῥέει ἄσπετος of the immortal Tithonos), it was perhaps later also understood as 'lowed endlessly, incessantly' (*LfgrE s.v.* 1423.45 ff. and 1424 f.69 ff.; FAULKNER on *h.Ven.* 237). — **οὐδέ τις ἄλλος:** an inflectable VE formula (m./f.: 4× *Il.*, 9× *Od.*, 1× *h.Cer.*).

402–403 σπῆϊ: dat. of τὸ σπέος 'cave'. — περὶ ... | ... ῥέεν: unaugmented (R 16.1), uncontracted (R 6) impf. of περι-ρέω; on the so-called tmesis, R 20.2. — δὲ ῥόος: on the prosody, ↑. — οὐδέ: In Homer, connective οὐδέ also occurs after affirmative clauses (R 24.8).

404 ≈ *Od.* 7.247, *h.Cer.* 45, *Od.* 9.521 = 'Hes.' *fr.* 204.117 M.-W. = *h.Merc.* 144 = *h. Ven.* 35 ≈ *Od.* 5.32; 2nd VH = *h.Ven.* 149. — **among the gods or among mortal men:** The formulaic polar expression[P] (here with emphasis on the first term: KEMMER 1903, 80 f.; cf. 1.548n.; for I-E parallels, WEST 2007, 100) and the affirmative statement that follows (405), which picks up on the statement that precedes and varies it, emphasize the mystery of this exile and the exceptional position of the two goddesses (*LfgrE s.v.* ἄνθρωπος 883.58 ff.).

εἴδεεν: on the form, WEST 1998, XXXIII. — **θνητῶν ἀνθρώπων:** an inflectable VE formula, sometimes expanded to καταθνητ- ἀνθρώπ- (7× *Il.*, 11× *Od.*, 23× Hes., 20× *h.Hom.*), cf. 1.339n.

405 ἀλλά: After οὐδέ τις ἄλλος *vel sim.*, this means 'no other but' (24.699n.). — **ἴσαν:** 3rd pers. pl. plpf. (≈ impf.) of οἶδα (< *ϝίδ-σαν), only here and at *Od.* 4.772 = 13.170 = 23.152 (SCHW. 1.776 f.).

406–407 Closing of the ring-composition[P] with a return to 394 (A/A': 394–409n.) and the conclusion of the story: Hephaistos acknowledges his obligation to Thetis.

406 2nd VH from caesura C 2 ≈ 9.197, 11.409, 23.308. — **τώ:** 'so', adv. with the old instrumental ending -ω (19.61n.). — **χρεώ:** always in synizesis, an indeclinable epic noun meaning 'distress, need'; used like χρή (cf. VE νῦν σε μάλα χρή 13.463, 16.492 [see *ad loc.*], 22.268): *LfgrE s.vv.* χρεώ and χρή; TICHY 1981, 195–201.

407 Θέτι: on the dat. in -ῑ (< *Θέτι-ι), G 45 and 74; on the heteroclisis, G 53; cf. 24.18n. — **καλλιπλοκάμῳ:** 'with beautiful tresses', a generic epithet[P] usually of goddesses, of mortal women only at 592 (Ariadne) and 'Hes.' *fr.* 129.18 M.-W. (Stheneboia): *LfgrE*; on the semantic field, 6.379–380n. — **ζωάγρια:** formed from ζωὸν ἀγρεῖν with the suffix -ιο-, probably originally 'booty from capturing a *live* human being' (cf. ζωγρέω 'capture alive', 6.46n.), here (and at *Od.* 8.462 ζωάγρι᾽ ὀφέλλεις) approximately 'reward for saving a life, rescue-reward' (schol. D: τὰ ζωῆς χαριστήρια; on post-Homeric usage [gratitude for saving a life], LSJ *s.v.*); comparable compounds are ἀνδράγρια (14.509n.: 'booty from capturing and killing a human being'), βοάγρια (12.22, *Od.* 16.296) and μοιχάγρια (*Od.* 8.332): BECHTEL 1914, 43; FRISK and *DELG s.v.* ζωάγρια.

408 entertainment: 387n.

---

404 εἴδεεν: unaugmented (R 16.1) 3rd pers. sing. plpf. (≈ impf.) of οἶδα.
405 Εὐρυνόμη (ϝ)ίσαν: on the prosody, 4.4; on the form ἴσαν, ↑. — ἐσάωσαν: 395n.
406 ἥ: anaphoric demonstrative (R 17), refers to Θέτις in 405. — ἡμέτερον δόμον: acc. of direction without a preposition (R 19.2). — χρεώ: *sc.* ἐστι (+ acc./inf. construction με ... τίνειν), 'there is a need to ...'; on the synizesis, R 7.
407 πάντα: predicative, 'entire, complete'.
408 οἱ: = αὐτῇ (R 14.1). — ξεινήϊα: 387n.

ἀλλὰ σὺ μέν: At the end of speeches, ἀλλά with an imper. marks the transition from the argument to instructions for action (1.127n., 2.72n.); the VB formula ἀλλὰ σὺ μέν (14× *Il.*, 3× *Od.*) is here continued with the subsidiary clause ὄφρ' ἂν ἐγώ, elsewhere often with a paratactic continuation via δέ/αὐτάρ (e.g. 1.127, 1.522 f., 6.279 f., 17.479 f., 22.222, *Od.* 19.44): DENNISTON 379; the speaker guides the addressee more firmly toward the continuation of the first-mentioned action (cf. BAKKER 1997, 83–85). — **ξεινήϊα:** 387n.

409 φύσας: 372n. — **ἀποθείομαι:** like καταθείομαι (22.111), a new formation for the original *-θήομαι (likewise θείομεν for *θήομεν [3× *Il.*, 2× *Od.*] beside θέωμεν [*Od.* 24.485] with quantitative metathesis): G 40 with n. 21 and G 89; SCHW. 1.741; CHANTR. 1.459. — **ὅπλα τε πάντα:** VE = 412: emphasis on the care with which the divine smith treats his tools. In early epic, ὅπλα usually, as here, means 'tool, implement', esp. as a term for equipment on ships (esp. *Od.* 10.404, 10.424, 12.410), but also for a smith's equipment (in addition to the present passage, *Od.* 3.433), less commonly for weapons (*LfgrE*; cf. 19.21n.).

410 He spoke, and: a speech capping formula[P] with which the speaker immediately proceeds to put into practice what was said; see 412 f. (19.238–240n., 24.228n.). — **[took the] stood up from:** Together with 416b and 421b–422, this corresponds to element (3) of the type-scene[P] 'visit' (resident gets up [here *anéstē*] and/or hurries to meet visitor): 369–427n.; cf. 24.477–478n.; *LfgrE* s.v. ἵστημι 1241.69 f.

ἀκμοθέτοιο: a term for the anvil mount ('anvil block'), cf. 476, *Od.* 8.274 (FORBES 1967, 14 f.), and a compound ἀκμο-θε-το- from ἄκμων and τίθημι (RISCH 211, 217 f.; FRISK s.v. ἄκμων; *LfgrE* s.v. ἀκμοθέτοιο). — **πέλωρ:** The noun means 'monster, something of monstrous size' and denotes a creature with a visually conspicuous form that appears frightening, as e.g. the Gorgon (5.741, *Od.* 11.634), Polyphemos (9.257, 9.428), Skylla (12.87), Typhoeus (Hes. *Th.* 845, 856) or gigantic or terrifying animals (e.g. *Il.* 12.202 [cf. 2.321n.], *Od.* 10.219); cf. the adj. πελώριος for Hades (*Il.* 5.395), Ares (7.208) and the giant Aias (3.229n.). πέλωρ here probably refers to Hephaistos' enormous and conspicuous appearance, unusual for a god, with the combination of his thin legs (411n.), powerful, hairy chest (415n.) and lumbering gait (411, 417, 421): AH; FAESI on 411; EDWARDS; PIZZANI 2000, 532 ff.; *LfgrE*; cf. 3.166n. It might also evoke the sinister aura surrounding the divine smith rising to his full height. — **ἄητον:** a *hapax legomenon*[P] of unknown etymology, the meaning of which has been disputed since antiquity (*LfgrE* s.v. ἄητος, αἴητος; SABBADINI 1967); it is explained e.g. as derived from ἄημι (i.e. 'wheezing'): AH *ad loc.* and *Anh.* p. 157 f. with reference to 1.600 [see *ad loc.*] and to 21.395); *LfgrE*; cautiously SABBADINI *loc. cit.* 82 ff.; cf. LEAF on 21.395; WILLCOCK ('the heavily breathing, monstrous figure'); EDWARDS. According to other scholars, it is equivalent to the similarly obscure adj. ἄητος (21.395), although the latter fits better with ἄμεναι, ἄσαι (i.e. 'insa-

---

409 ὄφρα: 'to, up to' (R 22.2). — ἀποθείομαι: short-vowel aor. subjunc. (R 16.3) of ἀποτίθεμαι 'put away, tidy away'.
410 ἦ: 3rd pers. sing. impf. of ἠμί 'say'.

tiable, indefatigable'): FRISK *s.vv.* ἄητος and αἴητος; SCHW. 1.502 n. 6 (≈ ἄατος); on the relationship with Mycenaean *a-ja-me-no* PALMER 1963, 339 ('craftsman'?); *DMic s.v.* n. 7; undecided *DELG*; BEEKES *s.v.* ἄητος (all suggestions are phonetically impossible).

411 = 20.37 (Hephaistos goes into battle); ≈ 417. — **limping:** 369–381n., 395–397a n.

ῥώοντο: An epic word (in early epic only 3rd pers. pl. impf. and aor.) of obscure etymology: either related to the I-E root **serh₃-* 'come at' (*LIV* 535) or a deverbative of ῥέω (like πλώω in relation to πλέω: *LfgrE* ['make wave motions']; cf. FRISK; RISCH 330; sceptical *DELG*). It denotes 'fast, busy movement' (KURZ 1966, 139 [transl.]) and is elsewhere usually used with persons as subjects, describing a group of individuals who move eagerly and in concert with one another (servants working: 417, *Od.* 20.107; troops *Il.* 11.50 and leaders 16.166; dancers: 24.616 [see *ad loc.*], *Od.* 24.69, Hes. *Th.* 8, *h.Ven.* 261, *h.Merc.* 505; the Gorgons 'Hes.' *Sc.* 230); of a person's body parts that move enthusiastically, much as in the present passage, at *Od.* 23.3 (Eurykleia's γούνατα), also of hair (χαῖται) at *Il.* 1.529 (see *ad loc.*), 23.367. — ἀραιαί: means 'thin, narrow', i.e. probably without much muscle, feeble (schol. D), so that he has his servants support him when he walks (417, 421); of body parts also at 5.425 (Aphrodite's hand), 16.161 (wolves' tongues; see *ad loc.*). The etymology is obscure (*LfgrE*; WHITE 2002, 328 f.); because of the hiatus (likewise at 5.425), some assume an initial ϝ- (CHANTR. 1.151; BEEKES *s.v.*; on the rough breathing, WEST 1998, XVII).

412 φύσας: 372n. — ὅπλα τε πάντα: 409n.

413 silver strongbox: The noun *lárnax* ('chest, box') here denotes Hephaistos' toolbox, at 24.795 Hektor's urn (see *ad loc.*); for archaeological evidence for this type of chest-like container, see LASER 1968, 70–82; BRÜMMER 1985, 12–14, 23–94; on silver as a material of objects from the world of the gods, 1.37n.

414–420 on the paratactic narrative style via δέ, 1.10n.; BAKKER 1997, 62–71.

414–416 A greatly shortened form of the type-scene[P] 'dressing', containing elements (**1**) undergarment and (**4**) staff (rather than a weapon) at 416 (cf. 2.42–47n.), in combination with the preceding bodily ablutions (for this combination, 14.170–186n.). Hephaistos was perhaps working with a bare chest (415), cf. depictions on Attic vases with the working Hephaistos dressed in a short chiton or with a cloth tied around his waist (*LIMC s.v.* Hephaistos 650 f.; BROMMER 1978, 20 fig. 9).

---

411 χωλεύων: logically refers to Hephaistos (see 391–393) rather than πέλωρ, likewise 417 (*constructio ad sensum*). — ὑπό: adv., 'below'.
412 ῥ': = ἄρα (R 24.1). — ἀπάνευθε: a compound preposition (basis: ἄνευ) with gen., 'away from'.
413 ἐς: = εἰς (R 20.1). — ἀργυρέην: on the -η- after -ε-, R 2. — τοῖς: with the function of a relative pronoun (R 14.5); refers to ὅπλα (412).

414 sponge: Cleaning with a sponge (*spóngos* is a *hapax*[P] in the *Iliad*), rather than bathing, here serves to quickly clean off sweat and probably also soot (cf. 372; see the mere wiping of dust at 23.739); in the *Odyssey*, sponges are used to clean tables and chairs (*Od.* 1.111 f., 20.151 f., 22.438 f., 22.452 f.): STUBBINGS 1962, 527; LASER 1983, 148.

ἀμφὶ πρόσωπα ... ἀπομόργνυ: ἀμφί is adverbial, πρόσωπα the obj. of ἀπομόργνυ, parallel with ἄμφω χεῖρ' ... | αὐχένα τε ... καὶ στήθεα, cf. *Od.* 19.200 (WILLCOCK; CHANTR. 2.86; *LfgrE s.v.* ὀμόργνυμι; FRITZ 2005, 97), thus 'the face on both sides' (differently AH; FAESI; *LfgrE s.v.* ἀμφί 665.15 ff.: ἀμφί is the preposition 'on both sides of the face', i.e. the cheeks).

415 1st VH = *Od.* 8.136. — λαχνήεντα: literally 'shaggy, ragged', elsewhere in early epic an epithet of the Centaurs (2.743n.: 'a connotation of things wild and uncivilized'), a 'bristly' pig skin (9.548) and a roof, probably made of reeds (24.451 [see *ad loc.*]); on the etymology (derived from λάχνη 'fuzz' [at 2.219 a term for Thersites' sparse hair, at *Od.* 11.320 for the first beard of young men, at *Il.* 10.134 for the woolen fabric of a cloak]), see FRISK and *DELG s.v.* λάχνη. Achilleus and others also have hairy chests, a sign of strength (1.189n. [στήθεσσιν λασίοισι]; cf. 2.851n.), but here the formulation is probably meant to underline Hephaistos' appearance, which is unusual for the world of gods (cf. 369–381n., 410n.).

416 stick: The stick (Greek *sképtron*) serves to help Hephaistos walk, although here he receives additional support as well (417 ff.): *LfgrE s.v.* σκῆπτρον; BUCHHOLZ 2012, 257 f.; on the various other functions and meanings of *sképtra*, 1.14–15n., 1.234n., 2.101–108n.; BUCHHOLZ *loc. cit.* 260 ff.

δῦ δὲ ..., ἕλε δὲ ..., βῆ δέ: The tricolon illustrates the extent to which Hephaistos is hurrying, χωλεύων at VB 417 the retarding of his progress (suggestion by FÜHRER). — δῦ δὲ χιτῶν(α): a very brief formulation, in contrast to that at 2.42 f., 5.736, 8.387, 10.21, 10.131, 23.739; on χιτών, 25n.

417–420 The golden robot-like servants, surely products of the divine smith's workshop, attest to his extraordinary skill as a prelude to the smithing work to come: they resemble living creatures (418) and can move of their own accord (417, 421), think and speak (419 f.) – one of the rare passages in Homeric epic with fantastical or fairytale-like narrative motifs (for other magical objects from Hephaistos' workshop, 376n; on fantastical narrative motifs in Homer, 6.152–211n., point (2); 19.404–418n.). The closest parallels for the artificial servants are: (1) in the *Odyssey*, objects from the land of the Phaiakians: (a)

---

414 πρόσωπα: on the plural, R 18.2 (likewise στήθεα 415). — ἄμφω χεῖρ(ε): dual (R 18.1). — ἀπομόργνυ: unaugmented (R 16.1) impf. of ἀπ-ομόργνυμι, 'wiped away'.
415 δῦ: unaugmented (R 16.1) root aor. of δύομαι.
416 θύραζε: 'out the door'; on the form, R 15.3 (-ζε < *-σδε).

the gold and silver watchdogs and the golden torch-bearers in the palace of Alkinoös, which are likewise works of Hephaistos (*Od.* 7.91–94, 100–102), but which are not shown in motion and are thus also considered statues (DE JONG on *Od.* 7.81–135, end and on 7.91–94; FARAONE 1987); (b) the Phaiakian ships, which are endowed with a mind (Greek *phrénes*) and which reach their destination without help, a present from Poseidon (8.556–563, cf. *Il.* 18.419; on this, JAHN 1987, 42 n. 46); (2) the figure of Pandora, as transmitted in Hesiod, who was made by Hephaistos and endowed by the gods with a variety of abilities (Hes. *Th.* 571–590 and *Op.* 60–82, cf. *Il.* 18.420): EDWARDS; on the comparison with archaeological evidence of statues and figurines/statuettes dating to the 9th/8th cent. B.C., CRIELAARD 1995, 214–217.

417 ≈ 411 (see *ad loc.*). — **ἀμφίπολοι:** a term for female servants attested already in Mycenaean, literally 'who move around (someone)', elsewhere in early epic usually particularly close personal servants of noble women (3.143n.), also of the caretaker of the elderly Laërtes at *Od.* 1.189–193, 24.365–367. — **ὑπὸ … ῥώοντο ἄνακτι:** Echoes of 411 (see *ad loc.*): the artificial servants move beneath Hephaistos in concert with one another and with his legs, i.e. as his support, cf. 421 ὕπαιθα ἄνακτος ἐποίπνυον (NAGLER 1974, 90 f.).

418 A four-word verse (1.75n.) describing the external appearance of the servants: gold is typical of objects associated with the gods (205–206n.); the similarity to living nature points to the particular artistic quality of the statue-like objects, cf. the description of depictions at 548 f. (on the shield), Hes. *Th.* 584 (on Pandora's headband; see WEST *ad loc.*), 'Hes.' *Sc.* 194, 198, 244: LfgrE s.v. ζωός; HIMMELMANN 1969, 23–25; FRONTISI-DUCROUX [1975] 2000, 73–77.

νεήνισιν: The fem. form νεῆνις ('young woman') beside masc. νεηνίης (3× *Od.*) is found in early epic only here and at *Od.* 7.20: LfgrE. — **εἰοικυῖαι:** a unique form of the fem. perf. part. rather than εἰκυῖα (cf. 3.386, 4.78 etc.), formed on analogy with ἐοικώς, the initial sound εἰ- perhaps due to metrical lengthening (CHANTR. 2.424; WYATT 1969, 114 f.).

χρύσειαι: on the form of the material adj. (χρύσ-ειος/-εος), 24.21n.

419–420 ≈ Hes. *Op.* 61–62. — **intelligence … speech … | … strength:** signals that these artifical objects are not statues or mere mechanical automata like the tripods (cf. 376 with n.): *nóos* ('mind, intelligence') points in particular to mental capacities similar to those of human beings (LfgrE s.v. νόος, esp. 428.9 ff.;

---

417 ὑπὸ … ἄνακτι: 'underneath the master', i.e. supporting him. — ῥώοντο (ϝ)άνακτι: on the prosody, R 4.3.
418 ζωῆσι: fem. dat. pl. (R 11.1) of the adj. ζωός 'living'.
419 τῆς: = ταῖς (R 11.1, R 17). — ἐν μὲν … ἐστὶ …, ἐν δέ: on the so-called tmesis, R 20.2.
420 ἀθανάτων: initial syllable metrically lengthened (R 10.1). — θεῶν ἄπο: = ἀπὸ θεῶν (R 20.2). — ἄπο (ϝ)έργα (ϝ)ίσασιν: on the prosody, R 4.3.

PELLICCIA 1995, 104 f., with reference to *Od.* 10.239 f. [the companions of Odysseus turned into pigs] and 10.494 f. [the soul of the seer Teiresias in Hades]), and *audḗ* is the term for the human voice and the ability to speak (19.407n., 19.418n.); they thus have 'a faculty for mental activities' (JAHN 1987, 65 [transl.]; SULLIVAN 1989, 160; 1995, 21) and, as indicated by *sthénos*, also physical strength or life force (likewise at Hes. *Op.* 62: *LfgrE s.v.* σθένος). — **gods:** It is striking that it is not Hephaistos himself who has endowed his creations with special abilities, but the gods as a whole, which might point to the influence of traditional narratives from the myth of Pandora, see Hes. *Op.* 60–82 (EDWARDS on 420–422; somewhat differently, WEST on Hes. *Op.* 61–62; [1995] 2011, 194 f.; BLÖSSNER 1991, 62 f.: 419 f. developed in imitation of Hes. *Op.* 60–64; *contra* VERDENIUS on Hes. *Op.* 60 and 62); on the motif 'gifts from the gods', esp. *Od.* 20.70–72, Hes. *Op.* 72–80 and in general 3.54–55n.; WEST on Hes. *Op.* 63.

τῆς ἐν μὲν ..., ἐν δέ: an asyndetic explanatory clause (20–21n.) further explaining ζωῆσι ... εἰοικυῖαι (418), with emphasis on the 'mental' faculties of the artificial servants via the anaphora of ἐν (cf. 483n.) and the formula μετὰ φρεσίν. — **ἐστὶ ... | ... ἴσασιν:** The pres. likely describes the timeless enduring existence of these divine creatures, cf. the immortal and ageless gods at *Od.* 7.94 (NÜNLIST 2009, 191 n. 19). — **μετὰ φρεσίν:** a formula between caesurae B 2 and C 2 (with or without -v: 11× *Il.*, 8× *Od.*, 6× Hes., 6× *h.Hom.*; cf. the prosodic variant with ἐνί 88n.): JAHN 1987, 267; on φρένες as the seat of mental impulses, 1.24n., 19.169–170n.; *LfgrE s.v.* φρένες 1022.29 ff. Elsewhere, νόος is located ἐν(ì) στήθεσσι(ν) (3.63, 4.309, 9.554, etc.) and ἐν θυμῷ *Od.* 14.490 (*LfgrE s.v.* νόος 423.60 ff.). — **θεῶν ἄπο ἔργα ἴσασιν:** a formulaic phrase after caesura B 2, which imparts the information that 'gods are the originators of a skill or trait': cf. θ. ἄ. μήδεα εἰδώς (*Od.* 6.12, 'Hes.' *fr.* 136.12 M.-W.) and θ. ἄ. κάλλος ἔχουσα/ἔχοντα (*Od.* 8.475, *h.Ven.* 77, 'Hes.' *fr.* 171.4 M.-W., cf. *Od.* 6.18, 'Hes.' *fr.* 215.1 M.-W.): *LfgrE s.v.* ἀπό 1084.11 ff.; in terms of content, ἔργα ἴσασιν also corresponds to the inflectable VE formula ἔργ' εἰδυῖα (< *ἔργα ἰδυῖα) in the description of women versed in particular skills (19.245n.).

421 ὕπαιθα ἄνακτος ἐποίπνυον: picks up 417 (see *ad loc.*; AH): ποιπνύω, a reduplicated intensive form related to πνέ(ϝ)ω, means literally 'wheeze, puff' (1.600n., 24.475–476n.), here approximately in the sense 'hurry up, be busy' (*LfgrE*; TICHY 1983, 334–337); ὕπαιθα here means 'from underneath', i.e. supporting him from the side beneath the arms; it is elsewhere used of (flight) movements 'away from under' (21.493, 22.141: *LfgrE*; EDWARDS on 420–422). — **ἔρρων:** ἔρρω means 'walk (away)', perhaps derived from the I-E root *ṷert- 'turn around' (cf. Latin *vertor*: *LIV* 691 f.; FORSSMAN 1980, 188–198). Elsewhere in early epic, the verb belongs to character language[P], frequently in the imper. with aggressive overtones (24.239–240n.), although the part. is used in the same sense as ἰών (on the present passage, cf. *Od.* 3.469, 17.70, 21.243); elsewhere, it occurs frequently in

---

421 ὕπαιθα (ϝ)άνακτος: on the prosody, R 4.3. — ὃ ἔρρων: on the hiatus, R 5.7; ὅ is an anaphoric demonstrative pronoun (R 17), refers to Hephaistos (410–417a).

speeches characterized by slight impatience regarding the labors associated with movement (*Il.* 8.239 and 9.364 the journey to Troy, *Od.* 4.367 roaming on a deserted island):
LfgrE; thus FORSSMAN *loc. cit.* 190: here with the connotation 'move with difficulty'; cf.
schol. D and schol. T (ἐπαχθῶς διὰ τὴν χώλωσιν βαδίζων).

422 2nd VH ≈ 11.645, *Od.* 7.169. — **Thetis:** She had been led into the house and
asked to sit down by Charis, cf. 387–390. — **shining:** probably due to embellishment with metal fittings, cf. 389 (see *ad loc.*; *LfgrE s.v.* φαεινός).

423–425 = 384–386 (see *ad locc.*). — A return to the type-scene[P] 'visit' via the
repetition of element **4** (369–427n.).

426–427 = 14.195 f., *Od.* 5.89 f. — The formulation used in scenes featuring gods
serves to initiate a conversation via a polite inquiry regarding the issue at hand
and via the signalling of good will (MARTIN 1989, 190).

426 αὔδα ... φρονέεις: on this polite invitation to speak and on φρονεῖν ('have in mind')
with the connotation 'want', 14.195–196n. — θυμὸς ἄνωγεν: 89b–90n.

427 Although the absence of the verse from several mss. and three out of four papyri might
be explained as a copying error due to double τελέσαι, the verse is probably interpolated from 14.195 f., where it better matches the context (a so-called concordance interpolation); with the precondition, fulfillment of the request is promised only conditionally,
and the commitment is thus weakened – which fits Aphrodite's situation at 14.190 ff.,
but here somewhat contradicts Hephaistos' unconditional gratitude at 406 f. (EDWARDS
on 424–427; APTHORP 1980, 140 f.; WEST 2001, 13 n. 31, 248). – On εἰ ('if only'), on the
reference of γε (with τελέσαι?) and on τετελεσμένον ('realizable, doable'), 14.195–196n.;
on the VE formula, 4n.

428 = 1.413; 1st VH = 18.127 (see *ad loc.*); 2nd VH = 18.94 (see *ad loc.*).

429–461 Thetis' speech is comprised of two parts: (1) a recapitulation of events
thus far, including episodes preceding the action of the *Iliad* (429–456), and
(2) a plea for new armor for her son (457–461); cf. the comparable structure
of Achilleus' speech at 1.365–412 (see *ad loc.*, 1.366–396n., 1.370–392n.). In
contrast to normal pleas – comprised of: address (here VB 429), performative
verb (here 457), legitimation of the plea, and the plea itself (1.17–21n., 24.486–
506n.) – and contrary to expectations after 394 ff., Thetis does not legitimize
her plea with a reference to her services to the addressee (this is anticipated
in Hephaistos' speech to Charis at 395–405; similarly in Book 1 in Achilleus'

---

422 ἔνθα ... περ: περ stresses ἔνθα, '⟨to there,⟩ where Thetis was indeed ⟨sitting⟩' (R 24.10).
423–425: 384–386n.
426 ἄνωγεν: present perf., 'orders, bids'.
427 τετελεσμένον: ≈ τελεστός 'realizable'.
428 κατὰ ... χέουσα: on the so-called tmesis, R 20.2. — δάκρυ: collective sing.

speech at 1.394–406, but Thetis alludes to it before Zeus at 1.503 f.: 1.502–511n., 1.503n.); instead, she justifies her plea with a description of the suffering both she herself and her son have suffered, thus appealing not to Hephaistos' gratitude but to his compassion (HEBEL 1970, 76–80; DE JONG [1987] 2004, 216–218; MINCHIN 2007, 204 f.; on the motif 'recollection of [previous] sufferings' in pleas, see FINGERLE 1939, 199 f.; CROTTY 1994, 70–75; cf. 24.486–506n.). This narrative part (1) can be divided into: (A) the story of (a) Thetis' marriage to Peleus, (b) the birth and youth of her son until his departure for Troy (429–441: external analepsis^P), which is told entirely from her own perspective (cf. the accumulation of verb forms and personal pronouns in the 1st pers.) and the tone of which is characterized by an emotional beginning (on which, 429–431n.), by literal repetitions of her speech of mourning before her sisters (55–62) and by echoes of Achilleus' speech of mourning to Thetis (esp. 84–87); this part serves as a *captatio benevolentiae* (cf. 431n.). (B) The chronologically structured summary of those events in the *Iliad* that brought suffering to her son and led to her visit (444–456 [see *ad loc.*]: internal analepsis^P from Books 1–18) as reasons why he should receive help, introduced by a confession of her own powerlessness (442 f.). Part (2) consists of the introduction (457), the plea proper (458–460a: new armor), the factual justification (460b–461a: loss of the old armor via Patroklos' death) and an emotional conclusion (461b [see *ad loc.*]).

429–431 The emotional start to the speech has correspondences in direct speeches in the *Odyssey* that feature extended narrative passages in which the speaker first stresses *inter alia* the immeasurably large number of afflictions endured (a so-called 'emotional preamble': DE JONG on *Od.* 3.103–117), cf. esp. *Od.* 7.241–243, 9.3–15, 19.165–171.

429 1st VH ≈ 13.446; 2nd VH ≈ 1.566, 5.877, 8.451. — ἦ ἄρα δή: 'really?'; for ἦ, 19.56n. (initiates a rhetorical question).

430 1st VH ≈ *Od.* 8.368; 2nd VH ≈ *Il.* 5.156, *Od.* 11.369, Hes. *Op.* 49, 95. — ἐνὶ φρεσὶν ᾗσιν: serves to stress the mental component of the suffering (cf. 52–53n.) and to amplify the description of the emotion (cf. JAHN 1987, 241 ff.). — κήδεα: 'suffering, sorrow' (8n., 52–53n.), here especially with regard to Thetis' suffering from the transitoriness of her mortal son, who is the product of her forced marriage to a mortal (432–435, 440, 442 f.).

---

429 ἦ ἄρα: R 24.4; on the hiatus, R 5.6. — τις, ὅσαι θεαί: ≈ τις θεῶν, ὅσαι.
430–432 τοσσάδ(ε) ..., | ὅσσ(α) ... | ... δάμασσεν: on the -σσ-, R 9.1. — ἐμοὶ ἐκ πασέων ... | ἐκ ... μ' ἀλλάων: 'me beyond all/others'; on the declension of πασέων and ἀλλάων, R 11.1, on the synizesis, R 7.
430 ἐνί: = ἐν (R 20.1). — ᾗσιν: possessive pronoun of the 3rd person (R 14.4).

431 1st VH ≈ *Od.* 4.723; 2nd VH = *Il.* 2.375, 24.241; ≈ *Od.* 4.722. — With the emphasis on her role as a victim, Thetis creates commonalities between herself as suppliant and the addressee: in the same way that Hephaistos was at the mercy of Hera's power and in need of help (395–398), she is subject to Zeus' power; see also 432 'he gave me', 436 'he has given me' (cf. HEBEL 1970, 76 f.; THALMANN 1984, 107; RINON 2008, 135).

ἄλγε(α): 397b n.; corresponds to κήδεα (430) and ἄλλα (435).

432–434a In her description of the marriage, Thetis emphatically stresses both her strong aversion to marriage to a mortal and Zeus' role as the pitiless matchmaker (cf. Achilleus' formulation at 85–87 [85n.]; Hera's version at 24.59–63 with n. is different [a solicitous matchmaker]). No reason for Zeus acting contrary to Thetis' interest is provided; in post-Homeric transmission, there are two versions: (a) in order to please Hera, Thetis removed herself from a relationship with Zeus, provoking his anger (*Cypr. fr.* 2 West, 'Hes.' *fr.* 210 M.-W.); the fact that, in the present passage, Thetis omits Hera's role while putting Zeus in the foreground could be explained by Hephaistos' experiences and the aim of the speech (see 431n.); (b) Zeus abstained from a relationship with Thetis since it was foretold that her son would be stronger than his father, and he accordingly married her to a mortal (Pind. *Isthm.* 8.26–48). It is impossible to tell whether the narrator was familiar with both versions or only one of them – namely version (a), likely the more ancient of the two; for discussion, see 1.396–406n., 1.541–543n.; EDWARDS on 429–35; MARCH 1987, 8–11, 23; WEST 2013, 69 f.; with a different orientation (namely version (b) being older): LESKY (1956) 1966, 401–404; SLATKIN (1991) 2011, 52 ff. (esp. 53 f., 62–64, 79–81).

432 sisters of the sea: the Nereids, cf. 37 ff. (CG 20).

ἁλιάων: 86–87n. — μ(ε) ... ἀνδρὶ δάμασσεν: causative δάμνημι + dat. (as at 22.176, 22.270 f.); for its use in a sexual context, cf. *Od.* 3.269, Hes. *Th.* 453, 1000, 1006 (*LfgrE s.v.* δάμνημι 214.15 ff., 215.16 ff.; see also 102–103n., 3.301n.). In addition to the patronymic at the VB of 433, the term 'man' (ἀνδρί), repeated in the same position in the verse at 433, underlines the fact that Peleus is mortal and the son of another mortal (AH; *LfgrE s.v.* ἀνήρ 840.41 ff.; cf. 85n., 86–87n.).

433 Αἰακίδη Πηλῆϊ: The patronymic Αἰακίδης is elsewhere usually used for Achilleus, Aiakos' grandson (221n.); for Peleus as 'son of Aiakos', as here, also 16.15 and 21.189. In comparison to the sequence personal name–patronymic (e.g. 93, 154, 164, 193), placing the patronymic first is considered more poetic (16.15n.). — εὐνήν: literally 'bed(stead)'

---

432 μέν: ≈ μήν (R 24.6).
433 Πηλῆϊ: on the declension, R 11.3. — ἀνέρος: = ἀνδρός; initial syllable metrically lengthened (R 10.1).

(see 85), here with a sexual connotation 'sexual intercourse', in the sense of an action noun (*LfgrE* 787.49 ff.; cf. 3.445n., 19.176n.).

434a In other versions, Thetis tries to escape the liaison with Peleus by turning into wild animals or fire and is defeated by him in wrestling (Pind. *Nem.* 3.35 f., 4.62–65, 'Apollod.' *Bibl.* 3.13.5: WEST 2013, 70 f.; for depictions in vase painting, see *LIMC s.v.* Thetis); her strong aversion to the relationship as described here could allude to this motif, which finds no mention elsewhere in Homeric epic (EDWARDS on 429–435; GRIFFIN 1977, 41; MARCH 1987, 11–23; *contra* LESKY [1956] 1966, 405 f.; KULLMANN 1960, 230). In any case, the narrator avoids any explicit linking of Achilleus' mother with fighting in the shape of an animal, instead emphasizing a different issue: Thetis portrays herself as a defenseless victim (cf. 431n.) and shows how much she is suffering from having been married to a *mortal* and having given birth to a *mortal* son (433–443, see Hephaistos' reply at 464 f.; note also the speeches by Thetis at 54 ff. and Achilleus at 85 ff.): schol. A; HEATH 1992, 389; cf. SLATKIN (1991) 2011, 69–71.

πολλὰ μάλ' οὐκ ἐθέλουσα: an intensification vis-à-vis the inflectable VB formula πολλ' ἀεκαζομένη (4× early epic) and the phrases πολλ' ἀέκων (2× *Il.*) and μάλ' οὐκ ἔθελεν (*h.Ven.* 25), cf. οὐκ ἐθέλουσα/ἐθέλων in similar contexts at *Il.* 6.165, *Od.* 5.155. – πολλὰ μάλ(α) is a VB formula (8× *Il.*, 5× *Od.*, 1× *h.Hom.*, 1× Hes.).

434b–435a Aging often occurs, in addition to mortality, as the second element of the human condition in formulations that stress the contrast to the existence of the gods, who are 'im-mortal' and 'non-aging' (e.g. 8.539, 12.323, 17.444, *Od.* 5.136, 5.218, 7.257, 23.336, Hes. *Th.* 949, *h.Cer.* 242, 260, *h.Ap.* 193: *LfgrE s.vv.* ἀγήραος, γῆρας; PREISSHOFEN 1977, 6; WEST 2007, 128; GARCIA 2013, 161 f.). The mention of the circumstances of Peleus' life might suggest associations with the myth of Tithonos (the immortal but nonetheless aging husband of Eos [CG 38]), which is only transmitted in the *Hymn to Aphrodite* (cautiously EDWARDS on 429–435; CERRI; on Tithonos, see FAULKNER on *h.Ven.* 218–238; cf. 3.151–152n.), but whether this is actually intended remains dubious. – **old age:** Achilleus comments explicitly on the sad situation of the lonely, elderly Peleus (see 19.334–337 with nn.). – **in his halls:** 325n.; Thetis in turn dwells in a cave in the sea during the time of the action of the *Iliad*, see 35 ff. (50n.).

γήραϊ λυγρῷ: a VE formula (4× *Il.*); on the epithets with γῆρας, see *LfgrE s.v.* – ἀρημένος: an Iliadic *hapax*[P], in the *Odyssey* combined with the datives δύῃ 'misery, hardship' (*Od.* 18.53, 18.81) and ὕπνῳ καὶ καμάτῳ (6.2), as well as with γήραι ὕπο λιπαρῷ

---

434 πολλά: adv.; 'manifold, very', together with μάλα 'altogether, completely'. – ἐθέλουσα. ὅ: on the hiatus, R 5.6.
435 ἐνί: = ἐν (R 20.1). – ἐνὶ (μ)μεγάροις: on the prosody, M 4.6; on the pl., R 18.2.

(11.136 = 23.283); it means approximately 'impaired, weakened' (cf. schol. bT on 434–435: βεβλαμμένος). The etymology is uncertain: ἀρημένος, the perf. pass. part. of a defective verb, is commonly associated with ἀρή ('damage, ruin': 24.489n.) (BECHTEL 1914, 60 f.; FRISK and BEEKES s.v. ἀρή; CHANTR. 1.422, 436; *LfgrE*; RISCH 342).

435b ἄλλα: refers to ἄλγε(α) at 431; to be understood either as a nominal clause (*sc.* ἐστι) or as Ζεὺς ἄ. ἔδωκεν (LEAF; FAESI and WILLCOCK: Zeus is the subject also at 436).

436–440 ἐπεί μοι δῶκε ... | (3 verses) | ... ὑποδέξομαι: an explanation of the ἄλλα ἄλγεα; on the sentence structure, 55–60n.

436 2nd VH = 7.199, *Od.* 3.28. — **son:** A periphrastic denomination[P]: Thetis does not mention Achilleus by name – in contrast to Peleus (433), Agamemnon (445), Patroklos (451), Apollo (454) and Hektor (456) – since to her, he is above all else her 'son' and dominates her worried thoughts (see 458 and 56–62n.); in the case of other people, individual names have no importance to her (444n., 448b–449n.): DE JONG (1987) 2004, 217.

τραφέμεν: on the intransitive use of the strong aor. (ἔ)τραφον ('grow up'), CHANTR. 1.390; *LfgrE* s.v. τρέφω.

437–443 = 56–62 (see *ad loc.*; for bibliography, also 50–67a n.).

441 Some scholars consider this verse, missing from some papyri and one ms. (see *app. crit.*; schol. A), a concordance interpolation (from 56–62): the image appears rather inappropriate after Thetis' explicitly hostile comments regarding her marriage, while in the case of literal repetitions, the narrator frequently omits verses that seem ill-fitting or unnecessary (e.g. 444 f. *vs.* 16.56–59, 6.269–278n., 14.301–311n.): APTHORP 1980, 142–145; WEST 2001, 13, 154 f.; see also HT 17 and 25; *contra* EDWARDS: more likely omitted by a 'literal-minded scholar-editor'; on the motif (dying in war represented as not returning home to the father), 59b–60a n.

443 Thetis' helplessness in issues concerning her son is contrasted sharply with her role as a powerful, helpful goddess in Hephaistos' speech (esp. at 394–398, 405): on the intentions of the two speeches, 394–409n. and 429–461n.

444–456 Part (B) of Thetis' legitimization of her plea contains, in brief form, the events of the action of the *Iliad* so far, especially from Books 1, 8, 9 and 16 (on the structure of the speech in its entirety, 429–461n.): (a) Agamemnon taking Briseïs and Achilleus' sorrow (444–446a); (b) Trojan superiority and Achaian distress (446b–448a); (c) the embassy with an offer of gifts for Achilleus (448b–449); (d) Achilleus' refusal and the sending out of Patroklos (in Achilleus' armor) and the Myrmidons (450–452); (e) the battle at the Skaian Gate (453);

---

436 δῶκε: *sc.* Ζεύς; with acc./inf. construction υἱὸν γενέσθαί τε τραφέμεν τε; on the form τραφέμεν (Attic ≈ τραφῆναι), R 16.4.
437–443: 56–62n.

(f) Patroklos' death at the hands of Apollo and fame for Hektor (454–456). A recapitulation of multiple events by one character[P] is rare in the *Iliad*, see esp. 1.365–392 (1.365–412n.), but by contrast more frequent in the *Odyssey* (7.241–297, 17.108–149, 23.310–341, 24.121–190): REICHEL 1990, 134 f.; 1994, 82 f. In the present passage, it reflects as a secondary story[P] the *menis* plot at the point of its completion (see 112–113n., 19.40–281n.; a so-called 'récit spéculaire' or 'mirror-story': EDWARDS; CERRI; on the term, see DE JONG [1985] 2001, 478–480), comparable to Odysseus' report of his journey home at *Od.* 23.310–341 (on which, DE JONG *ad loc.*), while on the character[P] plane it serves to support the plea factually and emotionally (argument function[P]). The fact that several issues key to the *menis* plot are missing (the reason for Agamemnon' hostile act; her own plea to Zeus as desired by Achilleus; Patroklos' pleading for the beleaguered Achaians) can be explained by the purpose of the speech: Thetis is not concerned with a detailed retelling of the action but rather with stirring the addressee emotionally via information about the background to her request (arousing compassion) and with motivating him to help (429–461n.); Achilleus' suffering (446a n.) and his view on issues is thus foregrounded and also intimated by the narrator[P] via literal echoes of Achilleus' own comments (cf. 444–446 with 9.344, 9.367 f., 16.52–59; 450 with 1.341): SCHADEWALDT (1938) 1966, 130 n. 1; HEBEL 1970, 77–79; DE JONG (1987) 2004, 216–218; DI BENEDETTO (1994) 1998, 57–59, 78 f.; cf. 1.370–392n. (focalization on Achilleus' part). The passage has been wrongly suspected as an interpolation by numerous scholars since Aristarchus (schol. A on 444–456; AH, *Anh.* 137–139), who considered it a long, unnecessary and repetitive internal analepsis[P] that also shows contextual inconsistencies in terms of the *Iliad* (esp. 448–453, but see nn.), but all these issues can be explained via the above-mentioned intention of the speech (schol. bT; CAUER [1895] 1923, 357–359, esp. 358; SCHADEWALDT [1938] 1966, 113 n. 1; EDWARDS; SCODEL 1999, 62 f.; on the scholia, LÜHRS 1992, 120–123; NÜNLIST 2009, 46 f.).

444 ≈ 16.56. — **girl:** The reference is to Briseïs (CH 2); on the impersonal formulation, 436n.; cf. 19.58n. — **honor:** the leaders' share of the booty, awarded as a sign of recognition for special achievements; it is of great significance for them as a status symbol (1.118–129n., 1.162–168n.).

κούρην: an asyndetic continuation from ἄχνυται with explanatory details (cf. 1.105n., 19.90n. [end]). — ἔξελον: denotes the selection of a particularly honorable part of the

---

444 κούρην: on the form, R 2, R 4.2. — ἄρα (ϝ)οι: on the prosody, R 4.3; ἄρα 'as generally known, indeed' (R 24.1). — οἱ: = αὐτῷ (R 14.1). — ἔξελον: from ἐξ-αιρέω 'select'; on the unaugmented form, R 16.1 (likewise ἕλετο in 445). — υἷες: on the declension, R 12.3.

war booty for a figure of authority (*LfgrE s.v.* αἱρέω 364.4 ff.); contrast ἕλετο at 445n. —
υἷες Ἀχαιῶν: 76n.

445 = 16.58; 2nd VH = 9.368. — **ἂψ ἐκ χειρῶν ἕλετο:** ἐκ χειρῶν is metaphorical for the
violent removal of Briseïs (likewise at 9.344, 16.58), ἂψ with its original meaning 'away'
is intensive (16.54n., 16.58–59n.); beside the mid. ἕλετο ('took for himself'), it illustrates
the ruthless, egotistical character of Agamemnon's actions (on the meaning of the mid.,
ALLAN 2003, 112–114 with n. 198). — **κρείων Ἀγαμέμνων:** a VE formula (40× *Il.*, 1× *Od.*,
1× *Il. Pers.*): κρείων is a generic epithet[P] that means 'ruler' (1.102n.).

446a 1st VH (to ἀχέων) ≈ 2.694 (see *ad loc.*). — Achilleus' reaction to the taking
of Briseïs is described solely with regard to the mental pain the loss caused
him (on the formulation *phrénas éphthien*, cf. the metaphor 'eating his heart
out' at 6.201–202n., 19.58n.; on *achéōn*, see below and 62n.); his withdrawal
from battle is not mentioned explicitly, in contrast to its consequences for the
Achaians (446b–448a). The employment of vocabulary from this context (cf.
1.491 f. [see below] and *achéōn* at 2.694: 1.488–492n., 2.694n.) perhaps shows
that the *narrator* reminds the audience of the anger directed at Agamemnon
(cf. 1.488, 2.688 f.), whereas he has the *speaker* emphasize the suffering caused
by the loss – all with the aim of stirring compassion.

ἀχέων: a denominative from ἄχος beside the metrical variant ἀχεύων at 461 (24.128n.);
ἄχος is a term for mental pain that is immediately succeeded by anger and aggression,
cf. Achilleus' comments on his response to the taking of his γέρας at 9.646 f. (aggression)
and 16.52/55 (pain): 22n., 62n.; see also 1.103n., 1.188n., 2.169–171n. — **φρένας ἔφθιεν:**
Likewise with regard to Achilleus, cf. φθινύθεσκε φίλον κῆρ at 1.491 (see *ad loc.*; on the
semantic interchangeability of φρένες with other lexemes from the semantic field soul/
spirit, 1.24n.; JAHN 1987, 205 f.; on additional comparable formulations, JAHN *loc. cit.*
12). – ἔφθιεν (in early epic only here) is a thematic aor. of φθίνω, here probably with an
impf. sense (LEAF; CHANTR. 1.393; ANZIFEROWA 1983, 21 ff.; *LfgrE s.v.* φθίνω).

446b–447 but meanwhile the Trojans | pinned the Achaians ...: 76n.

αὐτὰρ Ἀχαιούς: 148n.

448b–449 448b = 9.574 (myth of Meleagros); 2nd VH of 449 ≈ 9.121, 'Hes.' *fr.*
22.6 M.-W. — **the elders:** The term *gérontes* designates members of the elite,

---

445 τήν: anaphoric demonstrative (R 17), picks up κούρην (likewise τῆς in 446).
446 ἤτοι: R 24.4. — ὅ: anaphoric demonstrative (R 17) referring to Achilleus, likewise τόν in
448. — τῆς: causal gen. with ἀχέων.
447 ἐείλεον: impf. of εἰλέω, 'crowd together, lock in'. — οὐδέ: In Homer, connective οὐδέ also
occurs after affirmative clauses (R 24.8). — θύραζε: 'outside' (cf. 416n.), i.e. out of the encampment of ships.
448 εἴων: 3rd pers. pl. impf. of ἐάω; *sc.* Ἀχαιούς from 446. — δὲ (λ)λίσσοντο: on the prosody,
M 4.6 (note also the caesura: M 8).

irrespective of age: the participants in the embassy in Book 9 were Odysseus and Aias (CH 3), accompanied by Phoinix, Achilleus' mentor and adviser (CH 5), and commissioned by Agamemnon on the basis of a decision in the 'council of elders' at 9.89–181 (on this, 1.144n., 2.53n.). — **gifts:** refers to the detailed enumeration of the gifts promised by Agamemnon at 9.260–299.

λίσσοντο: in the *Iliad*, of urgent, insistent pleas (1.15n.). — περικλυτά: 326n. — ὀνόμαζον: in reference to objects always of the listing of gifts (9.515, cf. ὀνομήνω 9.121, and *Od.* 24.339), in which case approximately 'name one by one' (*LfgrE*).

450–452 This compressed version might create the impression that Achilleus immediately compensated for his negative reply to the embassy by sending Patroklos forth. This is the result of Thetis' speech-intention; the events of the battle in *Iliad* Books 11–15, revealing the effects of Achilleus' battle boycott and leading to Patroklos' pleading with Achilleus (11.790 ff., 15.390 ff.), are neither relevant nor conducive to her concerns: she immediately focuses on the next action of significance to Achilleus, namely his readiness, despite everything, to provide support to the Achaians (CERRI; HEBEL 1970, 78; DI BENEDETTO [1994] 1998, 58 f. with n. 6). On the reason for Achilleus' refusal (lack of a personal apology from Agamemnon), 16.72b–73n.; on his change of heart, 16.83–96n.

450 ἔνθ(α): connective, in combination with ἔπειτα it leads to the next topic in the report (*LfgrE s.v.* 589.51 ff.). — αὐτὸς μέν: to be associated with ἀμῦναι (AH); it forms a contrast with αὐτὰρ ὃ Πάτροκλον ... ἔσσεν, | πέμπε δέ μιν at 451 f. (*LfgrE s.v.* αὐτός 1658.66 ff.), cf. 16.239 f. αὐτὸς μὲν γὰρ ἐγὼ μενέω ... | ἀλλ᾽ ἕταρον πέμπω. — λοιγὸν ἀμῦναι: an inflectable VE formula (14× *Il.*: 1.67n.); on Achilleus' refusal to do so, see esp. 1.341, 16.32, 16.80 f.

451 The exchange of armor took place at 16.130–144 after Patroklos' pleading (expressed at 16.40–42, granted at 16.64–69), originally a suggestion by Nestor (11.798): 16.36–45n.; on the motif of the exchange of armor, 16.278–283n.

452 2nd VH ≈ 9.483, 16.38 (see *ad loc.*). — πέμπε: 237n. — πόλεμόνδε: acc. with enclitic particle -δε (1.54n *s.v.* ἀγορήνδε; G 66). — λαόν: in the *Iliad*, usually 'people at arms, servicemen' (153n.). — ὄπασσεν: literally 'make follow' (etymologically related to ἕπομαι: 19.238–240n.), in the sense 'send, give along' frequently amplified by ἅμα, as here (*LfgrE*).

---

450 ἠναίνετο: impf. of ἀναίνομαι, thus durative ('refused').
451 ὅ: anaphoric demonstrative (R 17). — περὶ ... ἔσσεν: aor. of περι-έννυμι ('dress someone') with acc. of the person and of the object, thus 'had P. put on'; on the so-called tmesis, R 20.2; on the -σσ-, R 9.1. — τὰ (ϝ)ὰ τεύχεα (ϝ)έσσεν: on the prosody, R 5.4; ἅ is the possessive pronoun of the 3rd person (R 14.4), Achilleus' own arms are meant.
452 μιν: = αὐτόν (R 14.1). — πόλεμόνδε: on the suffix -δε, R 15.3.

453–456 The summary of the events in the battle of the preceding day largely
matches what happens in Book 16 (cf. 16.684–867n.), with the topics not rendered accurately in Thetis' short version serving especially to heroize the deceased, namely the temporal and spatial dimensions (453n.), the accentuation
of Apollo's role and the omission of Patroklos' initial wounding by the Trojan
Euphorbos (454n.); contrast Patroklos' own description at 16.844–850 (see *ad
loc.*; DE JONG [1987] 2004, 217; DI BENEDETTO [1994] 1998, 59 f.; REICHEL 1994,
150; on differences in renditions of events by different characters[P] in general,
DE JONG *loc. cit.* 159 f.). The commonalities with Achilleus' fate stand out more
clearly in this manner, namely the death at the Skaian Gate at the hands of
Apollo and a mortal (Hektor and Paris, respectively: 22.359 f., see also 21.277 f.:
19.409–410n.); for discussion of a possible transfer of the motif from the traditional stock of stories about Achilleus to the character[P] of Patroklos (neoanalysis), see 1.307n., 16.684–867n., end; BURGESS 2001, 74 f. (with older bibliography).

453 2nd VH ≈ 3.149, 22.360. — The summarizing account (cf. summary[P]) is wholly aligned with Patroklos' *aristeia* (16.257 ff.): over the course of the day, he
led the battle away from the Achaian encampment of ships and toward the
walls of Troy and – contrary to Achilleus' orders – attempted to storm the city
(16.684 ff.). At the Skaian Gate, leading to the battlefield and the plain of the
Skamandros (on the location, 3.145n. and appendix to Book 14), and the location of key scenes in the *Iliad* (3.145 ff., 6.237 ff., 22.5 ff.), fate overtook Patroklos
in the shape of Apollo and Hektor (16.700 f., 16.712).

μάρναντο: 1n. — περί: local (SCHW. 2.501; CHANTR. 2.129; but cf. the metaphorical use
at 265 'fight over').

454 An 'if-not' situation[P] as a means to increase pathos via the marked contrast
with the VB of 456 (HEBEL 1970, 78 f.; cf. 165–168n.); its employment recalls
the battle description in the narrator-text, according to which Patroklos would
have taken the city walls if not for Apollo's intervention (16.698–701 with n.;
LOUDEN 1993, 194 f.). — **Apollo:** Achilleus emphatically warned his friend
about the gods, especially Apollo (16.93 ff.); although the latter did not himself
kill Patroklos, he did play a crucial role in the death by (a) preventing Patroklos
from taking Troy (16.698–711), (b) urging Hektor against him (16.712–730), and
(c) rendering Patroklos unfit for battle (16.786–806a), so that he could easi-

---

453 ἦμαρ: = ἡμέραν. — πύλῃσιν: always plural, here in reference to a single gate, as frequently
(the pl. refers to the gate's two wings, cf. Lat. *fores*).
454 κεν: = ἄν (R 24.5). — αὐτῆμαρ: 'still on the same day'. — ἔπραθον: thematic aor. of πέρθω
'conquer, destroy'.

ly fall victim to the Trojan Euphorbos (16.806b–817) and especially Hektor (16.818–828): 16.784–867n., 16.793–804n., 16.844–850n.; STOEVESANDT 2004, 214–219; on the abbreviated version and the stress on Apollo's role, cf. the speech to Achilleus by the horse Xanthos at 19.413 f. (19.411–414n., 19.413n.); on Apollo's role in the *Iliad* in general, 16.94n. with bibliography.

καί νύ κεν … ἔπραθον, εἰ μὴ Ἀπόλλων: an abbreviated version of 16.698–701 (ἔνθά κεν … ἕλον … | … | εἰ μὴ Ἀπόλλων); on καί νύ κεν, 165n.

455–456 456 = 19.414 (see *ad loc.*); 2nd VH ≈ 12.255, 12.437, 15.327, 16.730. — Thetis' paraphrase (*pollá kaká rhéxanta*) is not to be understood as criticism of Patroklos but as praise, in the sense 'after he caused great damage ⟨to the enemy⟩' (cf. *LfgrE s.v.* κακός 1285.71 ff.), see the concrete formulation in the passage concerned in the narrator-text (16.827): 'who killed many'. On the paraphrasis for Patroklos via his patronymic, 12n. — **in the first ranks:** 194n. — **Hektor:** Cf. the killing (16.828 ff.) and spoliation (17.107–131) by Hektor.

κῦδος ἔδωκεν: an inflectable VE formula (7× *Il.*); on κῦδος, 165n.

457 = *Od.* 3.92, 4.322. — **knees:** Touching the knees is a common gesture for supplicants (1.500n., 6.45n.), as well as an element of the theme^P 'supplication' (approach of the supplicant – gesture of supplication – speech by the supplicant – reaction by the addressee: 1.500–531n., 24.477–571n.). But here the formulation is to be understood as a metaphorical expression with no actual contact taking place (see below for bibliography); the entire description of Thetis' visit contains no reference to her appearing as a supplicant, and the comparison of the present scene with e.g. Thetis' pleading before Zeus in Book 1 (1.500 ff.) reveals numerous differences, see esp. 1.500–513 (1.502–511n.): Thetis is not considered a supplicant but rather welcomed and entertained as a guest (387 ff., 408), the addressee of the plea approaches the pleading individual and sits beside her (422 f.), he recalls her earlier services without prompting (395 ff.) and shows his readiness to meet her request even before her plea (406 f., 426); see also the speech introduction formulae at 428 *vs.* 1.502 and the structure of the speech at 429–461n.; on the overall composition of the scene, 369–427n.

---

455 κακὰ (ϝ)ρέξαντα: on the prosody, R 4.5.
456 ἔκταν(ε): thematic aor. of (ἀπο)κτείνω. — ἐνί: = ἐν (R 20.1). — προμάχοισι: on the declension, R 11.2.
457 τούνεκα: 'therefore'. — γούναθ': = γούνατα; acc. of direction without a preposition (R 19.2); on the declension, R 12.5. — ἱκάνομαι: on the mid., R 23. — αἰ: = εἰ (R 22.1). — κ(ε): = ἄν (R 24.5). — ἐθέλῃσθα: 2nd pers. sing. subjunc. (on the ending, R 16.2).

τὰ σὰ γούναθ' ἱκάνομαι: metaphorical phrasing alluding to the gesture of pleading rather than the performative verb 'plead', cf. the use of γουνάζομαι and γουνοῦμαι in the weakened sense 'plead urgently' (*LfgrE s.vv.*; contrast *Il.* 22.338 λίσσομ' ὑπὲρ ... γούνων); on the formulation, see the *iterata* and also (σά τε) γούναθ' ἱκάνω at *Od.* 5.449, 7.147, 13.231; elsewhere in Homeric epic frequently the concrete γούνων/γούνατα λαβεῖν or ἅπτεσθαι (1.500n.; *LfgrE s.vv.* γόνυ 174.54 ff. and ἱκάνω 1175.41 ff.; NAIDEN 2006, 68, 321 f.; differently LÉTOUBLON 2011, 299: referring to the gesture actually performed, and replacing a description of it). — **αἴ κ' ἐθέλῃσθα:** 143n.; on ἐθέλῃσθα, G 89.

458–460 Thetis mentions only the defensive weapons shield, helmet, greaves and corselet, and only these are described in the smithing work that following (478 ff., 609–613). Achilleus also has as an offensive weapon the lance he inherited from his father, which was a gift from the gods (16.140 ff., 19.387 ff.: 16.130–144n., 19.387–391n.), but the sword, which Patroklos took (16.135), should also need replacing. Why it remains unmentioned in Book 18, although Achilleus arms himself with it for battle (19.372 f.), has been the subject of speculation since antiquity; suggested explanations include the following: (a) via Thetis, Nereus gave his grandson a sword made by Hephaistos (schol. T on 460); (b) Patroklos did not take *Achilleus'* sword (Eust. 1153.4 ff.); (c) Hephaistos never forges offensive weapons (DELCOURT [1957] 1982, 50 f.); (d) this is a consequence of the fact that the sword was of less significance to Greek heroes than e.g. Germanic ones, and that especially for Achilleus the lance was more important (EDWARDS on 609–613; on the lance, cf. 19.372n., 19.387n.; on the particular weapons of individual heroes in I-E myths, see WEST 2007, 460–462); (e) pure chance (CERRI on 458–460). In any case, the focus of the concerned mother is on the protection of her son (see also her insistent warning at 134 ff.); Hephaistos in turn comments on their limited protective effect (464–467 [see *ad loc.*]). For a basic account of the motif of a new set of armor for Achilleus, 130–137n.

458 short-lived: As in her plea to Zeus (1.505), Thetis refers to the aspect that dominates her son's existence aside from his mortality, namely his *early* death; on the formulation, 95–96n.

†**υἱεῖ ἐμῷ ὠκυμόρῳ†:** metrically problematic; two solutions have been considered: (a) the main tradition is to be pronounced with synaloepha (G 32) ἐμῷ ὠκυμόρῳ and with disregard of the *iota* subscript (cf. schol. A and bT), which is unusual in Homeric epic (see M 13.4); (b) rather than υἱεῖ ἐμῷ (as at 144), the dat. form υἷι is to be read (see *vv.ll.* in the *app. crit.*) and is to be pronounced υἷ' ἐμῷ with elision of the -ι, an otherwise rather poorly attested phenomenon (cf. 3.349n.): LEAF; WEST 2001, 248 f.; GUILLEUX 2001, 76 f.; in general on formulations for 'Achilleus' in the dat. sing. that fill the 1st VH, see SHIVE

---

458 υἱεῖ: on the declension, R 12.3; on the prosody, ↑. — δόμεν: = δοῦναι, on the ending, R 16.4.

1987, 86. — **ἀσπίδα:** used only here as a designation for Achilleus' new shield, which is exclusively labeled σάκος in what follows (478, 481, 608 f., 19.373, 19.379, 20.259–261, 20.268, etc.: *LfgrE s.v.* σάκος 66.41 ff.; CERRI). Both terms, as general designations of shields, are often used interchangeably in Homer, while apparently not being entirely synonymous ('σάκος is more poetic and more heroic': *LfgrE s.v.* ἀσπίς 1427.38 f. [transl.]; SCHMIDT 2006, 441; cf. 3.335n.); on this and on attempts to assign the terms to original shield types (long shield and round shield), 3.347n.; TRÜMPY 1950, 20–36; *LfgrE s.v.* ἀσπίς 1427.26 ff. — **τρυφάλειαν:** one of the terms for 'helmet', used as a metrical variant beside κόρυς (611); on the etymology (literally 'provided with four φάλοι [metal plates?]'), 3.372n., 19.380b–381a n.; on helmet types, 611–612n.

459 ≈ 3.331, 11.17, 16.131, 19.369 (arming scenes). — on the components of greaves and ankle protectors, 613n., 3.331n.

460 corselet: on the two types of breastplates in the *Iliad*, 610n., 3.332–333n. — **was lost:** Hektor took the armor off the dead man and had it brought to Troy (17.125–131). — **his steadfast companion:** 235n.

ὅ: assimilated grammatically to θώρηχ' but referring contextually to all elements of armor listed, cf. the *v.l.* ἅ and schol. bT (AH; LEAF). The formulation was perhaps chosen with a view to the killing scene in which Apollo loosens Patroklos' corselet (16.804, 16.815), causing the latter to be gravely wounded immediately afterward (16.806 f., 16.820 f.): FAESI.

461 Thetis concludes with the topic that characterizes her account of her son (*achéuōn:* see *áchnytai* at 442 f., *achnéōn* at 446 [on the term, 62n.]), and points out his state of psychological suffering: the image picks up on the scene at 70–138, where Thetis encountered Achilleus prostrate with grief (cf. Iris' exhortation to Achilleus at 178), and is in turn picked up upon Thetis' return at 19.4 (EDWARDS on 457–461; KURZ 1966, 41; DE JONG [1987] 2004, 217; cf. 178n., 19.4–6a n.6a n.).

West suspects the verse as an interpolation: WEST 2001, 12 with n. 28 ('rhetorical expansions') and 244 n. 4 ('a curiously inorganic one appended at the end of Thetis' appeal'); it nonetheless matches the tenor and objective of the speech (compassion for her son: see above and 429–461n.). — **Τρωσὶ δαμείς:** similarly of Patroklos at 17.2; on the dat., 102–103n. — **θυμὸν ἀχεύων:** VE = 5.869, 23.566, *Od.* 21.318, Hes. *Op.* 399; on ἀχεύων, MAWET 1979, 345–347 ('lasting state of mind' [transl.]); cf. 446a n.; on the combination with θυμός, 29n.

462 = 393 (see *ad loc.*).

---

460 θώρηχ': = θώρηκα (= θώρακα: R 2). — **ὅ:** with the function of a relative pronoun (R 14.5); the relative clause is the obj. of ἀπώλεσε. — οἱ: = αὐτῷ (R 14.1).
461 δαμείς: aor. pass. part. of δάμνημι. — ὅ: anaphoric demonstrative (R 17), *sc.* Ἀχιλλεύς. — θυμόν: acc. of respect (R 19.1).

463 = *Od.* 13.362, 16.436, 24.357; ≈ *Il.* 19.29; 1st VH to caesura C 2 ≈ *Od.* 4.825, *h.Ven.* 193. —
on the negative pres. imper. and the formula μετὰ φρεσὶ σῇσι (after caesura C 2), 19.29n.
and 419–420n.

464–467 By formulating a comparative wish, a speaker can affirm the certainty
of an event about to occur (Y) by juxtaposing an unattainable wish (X) ('if only
X were to be/happen just as Y will'), cf. the similar formulations at 8.538–541
= 13.825–828, 22.346–348, *Od.* 9.523–925, 15.156–159, (EDWARDS on 463–467;
DE JONG on *Il.* 22.346–348; COMBELLACK 1981, esp. 117; NAGY 1990, 296; KELLY
2007, 366 f. ['impossible wishes']; VAN ERP 2012). Hephaistos thus elegantly
addresses the two main themes of Thetis' speech, her grief in the face of her
son's imminent death and her request for new weapons: in affirmation of his
encouragement (463), Hephaistos portrays the fulfillment of her wish as an
event Y certain to occur (new weapons) and makes it parallel to his – admit-
tedly unattainable – wish X (to save Achilleus from death), for which he expresses his deep sympathies to Thetis (VAN ERP *loc. cit.* 542; cf. schol. bT on
464–465; NICKAU 1977, 238 n. 22; on the 'likelihood of fulfillment' of prolepses[P] in divine speeches, 1.212–213n.). Much like the context of the subsequent
arming scene, where Achilleus departs for battle shining like the sun-god in
his new armor, while at the same time his death is foretold (19.397 ff.), so too
here the tragic element inherent in the situation is intimated by the association of the inevitable death with the weapons made by the divine smith; what
stands out is not primarily the protection the divine armor will afford (but on
the shield, see 20.259 ff., 21.164 f., 22.289 ff. and on the greaves, 21.590 ff.) but
its aesthetic effect (EDWARDS Introd. 139; MARG [1957] 1971, 46 f.; SCHEIN 1984,
140; AUBRIOT 2001, 23 f.; RINON 2008, 136 f.; cf. 19.404–418n., end; on antic-
ipations of Achilleus' death, 95–96n.). – Although the motif of the impene-
trability of divine armor is sometimes hinted at in the *Iliad* (16.793 ff. [16.793–
804n.], 20.264 ff., 22.322 ff.), Achilleus' invulnerability (and his vulnerable
heel) as attested in post-Homeric literature is mentioned nowhere; instead, he
is considered vulnerable at 23.568–570 (EDWARDS on 20.264–267; DE JONG on
Il. 22.322; KAKRIDIS 1961, 291–293; GRIFFIN 1977, 40; BURGESS 2009, 9–15; WEST
2013, 150 f.). – Up to this point, Hephaistos has not apppeared sympathetic to
any particular party in the war (see his reticence at 1.574 f. [with note *ad loc.*]);
he has merely rescued the son of his Trojan priest from the battlefield (5.9–24;
on the typical motifs in this scene, KIRK on 5.9–26 and 5.23–4). But on the next
day of battle he will join the fight on the side of the Achaians (20.36, 20.73 f.)

---

463 τοι: = σοι (R 14.1). — μελόντων: 3rd pers. pl. imper.; in Homeric Greek, a neut. pl. subj. can
also take a pl. verb.

and, particularly at the request of Hera, will use fire to aid Achilleus against the river god Skamandros (21.328 ff.): CH 15; HIRSCHBERGER 2008, 18.

464–465 θανάτοιο ... | νόσφιν ἀποκρύψαι: θανάτοιο νόσφιν means 'far from death', with νόσφιν as a postpositive preposition (AH; cf. 2.346b–347n.), the complete phrase is thus 'hide far from death, conceal from death' (*LfgrE s.v.* νόσφι(ν)): a unique formulation for deliverance from death, elsewhere in Homeric epic frequently rendered by phrases with ἐκ θανάτοιο ἐκλύω/-ομαι, σῴζω, etc. (16.442n.; CLARKE 1999, 245 f.). Here it was probably chosen with reference to the defensive weapons, cf. 8.272 (σάκεϊ κρύπτασκε), 13.405 (κρύφθη ... ὑπ' ἀσπίδι), 14.372 f. (κορύθεσσιν | κρύψαντες): *LfgrE s.v.* κρύπτω. — **θανάτοιο δυσηχέος:** likewise at 16.442 (see *ad loc.*), 22.180; on the epithet, 307n. — **ὅτε ... ἱκάνοι:** either assimilation of the mood to the opt. in the wish-clause (LEAF: 'the event, though certain, is included by the speaker in the same category of pure imagination as the wish'; EDWARDS on 463–467; SCHW. 2.649; WAKKER 1994, 186) or a potential opt. (the point in time is uncertain) after the cupitive in the main clause (SCHW. 2.330; similarly CHANTR. 2.260). — **μόρος:** '(allotted) fate', frequently in the sense 'death', cf. 458 (19.421n.; SARISCHOULIS 2008, 77 f.).

466–467 2nd VH of 466 ≈ 9.135, 9.277; 1st VH of 467 = *Od.* 9.352. — The announcement of beautiful, admirable arms is picked up multiple times in the narrator[P]-text: in the description of the manufacture of the arms (479, 482, 549, 612), where at 549 the narrator[P] himself will be the first admirer of Hephaistos' work of art (DE JONG [1987] 2004, 49), and subsequently in descriptions of the responses of those who look at them (19.12–19, 19.21 f., 19.369 ff. [Greeks] and 20.44 ff., 22.25 ff., 22.134 ff. [Trojans]: 19.12–19n.).

τεύχεα καλά: a formula before caesura B 2 (84n.). — **παρέσσεται:** 'will be present, available', an expression for the promising of gifts, as at 1.213 (Athene), 9.135/277 (Agamemnon): RENGAKOS 1993, 63 f. (with reference to imitations in Apoll. Rhod.). — **τις ... | ἀνθρώπων πολέων:** collective τις (cf. 122–123n.): 'some among men, the numerous' (cf. LEAF). — **αὖτε:** 'later' (*LfgrE s.v.* 1584.20 ff.; cf. BONIFAZI 2012, 220 f.). — **ὅς κεν ἴδηται:** likewise at 14.416, 17.93, 17.100; θαυμάσσεται, ὅς κεν ἴδηται is an intensification of the VE formula θαῦμα ἰδέσθαι (83n.).

---

464 αἲ γάρ: = εἰ γάρ (cf. R 22.1), εἴθε. — μιν: = αὐτόν (R 14.1); likewise 465. — ὧδε: 'thus (certainly)', prepares for ὡς in 466.
465 ἀποκρύψαι, ὅτε: on the hiatus, R 5.6.
466 ὡς: 'as'. — οἱ: = αὐτῷ (R 14.1). — παρέσσεται: on the form, R 16.6. — οἷα: refers to τεύχεα καλά: 'such beautiful arms that ...'.
467 πολέων: on the declension, R 12.2. — θαυμάσσεται, ἴδηται: on the mid., R 23. — κεν: = ἄν (R 24.5).

468–617 *The production of Achilleus' armor.*

    I. The manufacture of the armor (*hoplopoiïa*: 468–613):
        A. Preparations for the manufacture (468–477)
        B. The shield (478–608):
            1. The creation of the shield:
                a. Preliminary remarks concerning the description
                b. The structure of the text
            2. The finished product:
                a. The shape of the product (archaeological aspects)
                b. The pictorial program and its links to the poem as a whole
            3. The linguistic depiction
            4. The function of the shield scene within the poem as a whole and its poetological significance
            5. Line-by-line commentary
        C. The remaining parts of the armor: corselet, helmet, greaves (609–613)
    II. Thetis receives the armor (614–617)

In this final scene of Book 18, 'the production of Achilleus' armor', the *embellishment* of the shield occupies the most space: first, the narrator names the *metals* employed in the smithing (474 f. [see *ad loc.*]; for the decoration of the shield, see esp. 517, 549, 562 f., 565, 574, 577) as well as the *tools* (476 f.). He then describes the manufacture of the *body of the shield* (478–482) and the labor of the artisan Hephaistos as it constantly progresses in relation to the shield's pictorial *embellishment* (483–608: section **B.1.b.**). At the same time, he places little emphasis on either the specifically *technical elements* of the smith's craft (476–477n.) or the actual *feasibility* and *usability* of this metal shield in battle. He also provides no specific information regarding the *placement* of the pictorial decoration on the body of the shield – with the exception of Okeanos on its rim (607 f.). Bearing this in mind, the much discussed question of *the details of the actual appearance of the shield* does not seem particularly productive. The reason is to be found in the purpose for the description of the shield aimed at by the narrator within the poem as a whole: it is evidently not the narrator's ambition to illustrate a masterpiece of craftsmanship as faithfully as possible with his words, but to have an extraordinary shield made for his extraordinary hero – based in fact on inspiring models presented by contemporary artifacts – which transcends the possibilities of an *actual* shield in its pictorial decoration (section **B.2.a.**). To this end, the narrator has the divine smith, in the manner of a poet, compose images on the shield with characters and scenes that reflect the motifs and story arcs of the frame of the verbal artwork that is the *Iliad* ('récit spéculaire', 'mise en abyme': see argument function[P], end). This precise aim – the interaction of visual art and poetry –

is served by the artifice of employing a linguistic retracing of the *genesis* of the artwork in place of a static *description* of the (completed) artwork via constant repetition of verbs of making (including Greek *poíei/poíēse* 'he made', which is used in equal measure of hand-craft and word-craft, cf. 'poetry' [478n.]). The main task of interpretation is thus to identify the function of the ekphrasis 'description of the manufacture of the shield', initially in regard to the *bearer* of the shield (sections **B.1.a.** and **B.2.b.**) but then, going further, especially in regard to the *poetological significance* of the scene of making the shield (sections **B.3.** and **B.4.**).

A. 468–477 *Preparations for the so-called* hoplopoiia *('arms-making' 478–613): In his smithy, Hephaistos readies the furnace and prepares the materials and his tools (various metals as well as an anvil, hammer, tongs).*

468 ≈ 4.292, 4.364, *Od.* 17.254. — The formulaic expression signals the beginning of movement and the change of scene (KURZ 1966, 103 f.; cf. 1.428n.). — **and left her there:** Thetis is entertained by Charis within the house (422n.).

ὣς εἰπών: 343n. — φύσας: 372n.

469 toward the fire: Hephaistos had removed the bellows from the furnace (412). — **gave them their orders for working:** Hephaistos' bellows are automata that work on his command and regulate the airflow in accord with his wishes (472 f.), much like the tripods that move independently (375–377): LEAF; PELLICCIA 1995, 51 n. 81; on Hephaistos' magical implements and the motif of helpful objects, 376n., 417–420n.

470 twenty: 373n.

φῦσαι ... ἐφύσων: φυσάω is derived from φῦσα (i.e. *figura etymologica* at VB and VE; cf. FEHLING 1969, 158; TZAMALI 1996, 482, with Greek and Sanskrit examples) and is used for both the noisy blowing to fan a fire (see also at 23.218) and the snorting of animals (16.506). – The verse as a whole displays an onomatopoetic composition via the aspirates φ-, χ-, -φ- and the final syllables -σαι, -σιν, -σι, -σων (BECKER 1995, 90). — χοάνοισιν: a Homeric *hapax*[P] and a derivative of χέω, thus frequently interpreted as 'crucible, furnace' or as a designation for the depression into which molten metal was poured (schol. T and D; LSJ *s.v.* χοανεύω; RISCH 98 f.; MADER 1970, 237 n. 3; WEST on Hes. *Th.* 863 ἐν ἐϋτρήτοις ['well pierced'] χοάνοισι: a crucible or furnace with ventilation holes; cf. on the adj. αὐτο-χόωνος [23.826] *LfgrE s.v.*; RICHARDSON on *Il.* 23.826 ['self-moulded' or 'self-

---

468 τήν: refers to Thetis, anaphoric with τὴν δ(έ) 462, which for its part points back to 428; on the anaphoric demonstrative function of ὅ, ἥ, τό, R 17. — λίπεν ... βῆ: on the unaugmented forms, R 16.1. — αὐτοῦ: adv., 'on the spot, there'.
469 ἐς: = εἰς (R 20.1). — τε (ϝ)εργάζεσθαι: on the prosody, R 4.3.
470 χοάνοισιν: on the declension, R 11.2. — ἐείκοσι: 373n. — πᾶσαι ἐφύσων: on the correption, R 5.5.

cast']; FORBES 1967, 31 ['solid cast']); at the same time, it can here also be a term for the nozzles or pipes through which air from the bellows was conducted toward the fire, cf. Attic χοάνη, χώνη 'funnel, cone' (EDWARDS). — ἐείκοσι πᾶσαι: 373n.

471 A four-word verse (1.75n.). — **παντοίην εὔπρηστον ἀϋτμήν:** describes the varied (in intensity and direction) stream of air that makes the fire burn as desired (472 f.): the *hapax legomenon*[P] εὔπρηστον likely means 'well blown' (schol. D: εὐφύσητον; BUTTMANN [1818] 1825, 105; GRAZ 1965, 225; cf. *LfgrE s.vv.* παντοῖος and πρηστήρ); it is a verbal adj. related to πρήθω, which can mean *inter alia* 'blow' (1.481) as well as 'cause to increase, swell up' and 'kindle' (2.415n.; *LfgrE s.v.* πρήθω; cf. πρηστήρ Hes. *Th.* 846 in the context of wind- and fire-storms). — **ἀϋτμήν:** a designation for a movement of air, here comparable to the 'blowing' of the winds (*Od.* 3.289, 11.400), elsewhere usually of breath (*Il.* 9.609, 10.89, 23.765) or the scorching heat of a fire (21.366 f., *Od.* 9.389 etc.), as well as of the fragrance of Hera's oil spreading through the air (*Il.* 14.174): *LfgrE s.v.*; GRAZ 1965, 308 f.

472 ἄλλοτε μὲν ..., ἄλλοτε δ' αὖτε: 'now ..., and now' (on the verse construction, see 159 [158b–160n.], 24.10 [see *ad loc.*], *Od.* 4.102, 11.303, 16.209); the subj. of παρέμμεναι ('be there, be available') is to be thought of as either ἀϋτμή (AH; FAESI) or more likely the bellows (*LfgrE s.v.* εἰμί 456.69 f.). Although the brachylogical formulation with ἄλλοτε δ' αὖτε is somewhat vague, it suggests, together with the continuation at 473, gradations in the air-supply (see παντοίην), perhaps depending on the metal being worked and the point Hephaistos' work has reached, i.e. either 'be available to the industrious smith, now this way and now that, just as Hephaistos wished' (cf. AH on 473; EDWARDS on 468–473) or 'now available to the industrious smith, now again ⟨not⟩' (LA ROCHE; BEKKER 1872, 36 f.; LEAF; WILLCOCK).

473 ὅππως ... ἐθέλοι ... ἄνοιτο: 'depending on how', with an iterative opt. (AH). ἄνοιτο is the pres. opt. of thematic ἄν(ϝ)ομαι (beside ἄνυμαι) but with short-vowel ἄν- (contrast the long-vowel pres. at 10.251, *Od.* 2.58, 17.537), i.e. without lasting effect of the ϝ (CHANTR. 1.161; SOLMSEN 1901, 92 f.; on the *v.l.* with opt. ἄνυτο/ἀνῦτο in place of ἀνῦῖτο [preferred by LEAF; SCHW. 1.696 n. 10], cf. 24.665n. on the discussion regarding the chronology of the contraction υι > ῡ). The mid. means 'approach the end, come to an end', with the subject ἔργον ('and as the labor drew to a close', i.e. depending on the stage of the work), *Od.* 5.243 (θοῶς δὲ οἱ ἤνυτο ἔργον) is similar, of time at *Il.* 10.251 (νὺξ ἄνεται): LEAF; *LfgrE s.v.* ἄνυμαι.

474–475 A list of the raw materials employed: *chalkós* is the term commonly used in Homeric epic for bronze, the alloy used for arms (2.226n., 6.3n.; *LfgrE*

---

471 παντοίην: on the -η- after -ι-, R 2. — ἐξανιεῖσαι: fem. pres. part. of ἐξ-αν-ίημι 'send out, give off toward the top'.
472 παρέμμεναι: = παρεῖναι (R 16.4); final inf., on the construction, ↑.
473 ὅππως: on the -ππ-, R 9.1. — καὶ (ϝ)έργον: on the prosody, R 4.4.
474 ἀτειρέα: on the uncontracted form, R 6.
475 αὐτάρ: 'but' (R 24.2).

s.v. χαλκός with bibliography), esp. in combination with the adj. 'indestructible, hard' (*ateirḗs*, see below; BECKER 1995, 93). But in the present passage, it must designate a raw material other than the metals tin, gold and silver, and is thus copper, which is used in combination with tin (*kassíteros*) to produce bronze; the same may be true at 9.365, where *chalkós* is described as 'reddish' (*erythrós; LfgrE s.v.* χαλκός 1122.4 ff.; FORBES 1967, 21 f.; MÜLLER 1974, 118; see also GRAY 1954, 1 n. 4). According to the description that follows, the softer metals, gold, silver and tin, are used for the decoration both of the shield and of several parts of Achilleus' armor, thus achieving a range of color effects (cf. Agamemnon's arms at 11.24–40): (a) gold is used as a prize in competition (507), for figures (516 f., 577), the field during plowing (548 f.), the vineyard (562) and the dancers' daggers (597 f.) as well as on Achilleus' crest (611 f.); (b) silver is used for the fastening straps of the daggers (598) and the stakes in the vineyard (563), as well as on the shield strap (480); (c) tin is used for the enclosure of the vineyard (564 f.) and, in addition to gold, for the cows' hides (574), as well as on Achilleus' greaves (613): *LfgrE s.vv.* κασσίτερος and χρυσός; GRAY *loc. cit.* 1, 3–5, 12; FITTSCHEN 1973, 5 f.; (d) in addition, dark effects could be achieved by alloying copper, tin, gold and silver to obtain bronze with a black patina, the so-called *Corinthium aes* (GIUMLIA-MAIR/CRADDOCK 1993, 20 f.; cf. 564n.). On the above-mentioned metals in Homeric epic and on their processing in antiquity in general, see GRAY 1954; FORBES *loc. cit.* 15–29; MÜLLER *loc. cit.* 116 ff.; on greaves and swords embellished with silver, 3.331n., 3.334n.; on gold and silver on divine weapons, 1.37n., 2.448n., 24.21n.; on the use of precious metals on weapons in general, BUCHHOLZ 2012, 202–206.

χαλκὸν ... ἀτειρέα: separation of an inflectable formula used elsewhere to designate weapons (acc. in the verse middle: 2× *Il.*, nom. at VE: 3× *Il.*): 19.233a n.; on the phenomenon, FOR). on ἀτειρής ('hard, indestructible, uncrushable'), 3.60n. — **κασσίτερον:** on the various theories regarding the origin of the word, FREEMAN 1999. — **χρυσὸν τιμῆντα:** on the contracted form of the adj. τιμή(ϝ)εις ('precious') beside uncontracted χρ. ... τιμήεντος/τιμήεντα (*Od.* 8.393, 11.327), G 43 f.; CHANTR. 1.32; SCHW. 1.527 with n. 2; WACHTER 2012, 72 f., 78. — **αὐτὰρ ἔπειτα:** a formula at VB, VE and after caesura A 3: a typical paratactic clause connection (24.273–274n.).

476–477 476 ≈ *Od.* 8.274. — A list of smith's tools, in which the different processes employed for the various metals play no role: the narrator sketches Hephaistos' actions by naming materials and tools with a view to the vivid, atmospheric mood of a forging scene rather than technical detail (cf. schol. bT on 476–477

---

476 θῆκεν: unaugmented (R 16.1) 3rd pers. sing. aor. of τίθημι. — γέντο: R 16.1 and ↑.
477 κρατερόν(ν), ἑτέρηφι: on the prosody, ↑ (note also the caesura: M 8); with ἑτέρηφι *sc.* χειρί (↑); on the ending -φι, R 11.4. — πυράγρην: on the -η- after -ρ-, R 2.

and schol. A on 483; CERRI on 468–477; STUBBINGS 1962a, 536; BECKER 1995, 94 f.), perhaps influenced by consideration of contemporary ironworking (cf. 6.3n.); the 'ponderous hammer' is suitable for forging red-hot iron, whereas gold, silver, copper and bronze were beaten cold with a light-weight hammer for peening (GRAY 1954, 12 f.; FORBES 1967, 14 f., 35; FITTSCHEN 1973, 6; CANCIANI 1984, 99 f.; BNP *s.v.* Metallurgy; see also WEST on *Od.* 3.432–433 [a goldsmith's tools]).

θῆκεν ... ἀκμοθέτῳ ... ἄκμονα: on the repetition of the word stem, 470n.; ἄκμων, a term for 'stone' attested in several I-E languages (FRISK; *DELG*; BEEKES *s.v.* with bibliography), in Greek denotes the anvil (originally an appropriated dressed stone: FORBES 1967, 14 f.); on ἀκμό-θετον, 410n. — **γέντο:** means 'he grasped', likewise at 8.43 = 13.25, 13.241; an isolated athematic form with aorist function, likely related to the same root as γέμω 'be full' (CHANTR. 1.297, 384; *LfgrE s.v.* γέντο I; FRISK, *DELG*, BEEKES *s.v.* γέντο; *LIV* 186). — **χειρί | ... , ἑτέρηφι δέ:** an antithesis not formally designated as such in the first element (*LfgrE s.v.* ἕτερος 757.54 ff.; also 24.528n.). Whereas elsewhere in Greek epic the left hand (subplot) is usually mentioned before the right (continued main plot), the situation appears reversed in the present context (hammer in the right hand, tongs in the left), see also *Od.* 19.480 f. χείρ' ... λάβε δεξιτερῆφι, | τῇ δ' ἑτέρη (WEST on Hes. *Th.* 179; *LfgrE s.v.* σκαιός). — **ῥαιστῆρα κρατερόν:** ῥαιστήρ (only here in early epic) is a *nomen agentis* related to ῥαίω 'shatter' as a designation for a forge hammer (cf. 220n.); it is thus originally masc., but the main transmission probably has κρατερήν for metrical reasons (on κρατερόν(ν), ἑτέρηφι, see *smtero- with G 16). By contrast, σφῦρα at *Od.* 3.434 designates a goldsmith's hammer (*LfgrE s.v.* ῥαιστήρ; CANCIANI 1984, 99–101). — **πυράγρην:** a verb-noun compound, the second element derived from ἀγρέω ('grasp, seize') (*LfgrE s.v.*; FRISK *s.v.* ἄγρα; RISCH 207).

B. 478–608 *Beginning of the* hoplopoiia *proper: Hephaistos forges Achilleus' shield.*

B.1.a. Preliminary remarks concerning the description

When describing objects, the narrator[P] usually prefers a dynamic description of the production process over a merely descriptive rendering of their finished state (1.234–239n., 24.266–274n.); while such descriptions occur predominantly in external analepses[P] (2.101–108n.), the production process in the case of Achilleus' shield is part of the main action itself (see Introduction on 468–617). In combination with 474–477 (preparation of materials and tools), the image of the divine smith at work is maintained until near the end of the Book (614) by repeatedly recalling the production process by means of brief interjections, even during the detailed description of images on the shield (section **B.1.b.**), avoiding the impression of a mere object description (thus already LESSING 1766, chap. 18 f.; WILLENBROCK [1944] 1969, 58 f.). Because of this composition, Book 18 in its entirety was designated in antiquity as *hoplopoiía* ('arms production'; Eust. 1127.16). In the context of the *Iliad*, the description of Achilleus' arms is the counterpart to the description of Agamemnon's arms before his *aristeia* (11.15 ff., esp. 19–28 corselet, 32–40 shield) that marked the beginning of this third, fateful day of battle (cf. STR 21, fig. 1; on the positioning of the *hoplopoiia*, also 478n.). – The passage concerning Achilleus' shield is the longest object description in Homeric epic. The narrator[P] uses it to qualify the bearer of the shield and to increase expectations before his *aristeia* (the more extensive the description, the more significant the following action in which the object is put to use): WILLENBROCK *loc. cit.* 61 ff.; MÜLLER 1968, 157 f.; AUBRIOT 1999, 9–12; MINCHIN 1999, 63 f.; 2001, 128–131; PURVES 2010, 47; cf. principle of elaborate narration[P] and retardation[P]; 2.101–108n., 2.447–449n., 24.266–274n. In addition, it provides an opportunity for the narrator[P] to display his virtuosity and poetic creativity (DE JONG 2011; sections **B.2.b.–B.4.**). The bibliography regarding the shield of Achilleus is extensive: fundamental are MARG [1957] 1971, 38 f.; EDWARDS; BECKER 1995; for detailed bibliographies, see FITTSCHEN 1977, 25–27; ARPAIA 2010 (for the years 1945–2008, arranged thematically); see also NTHS 61; more recent bibliography: FRANCIS 2009, 2012; WEBB 2009; DE JONG 2011; SCHEID-TISSINIER 2011; CARRUESCO 2016; for additional bibliography on scenes discussed most extensively, 498–501n., 506–508n., 509–540n., 556b–557n., 558–560n., 570n., 590–606n., 590n., 592n., 604b–605a n.

B.1.b. The structure of the text
The structure of the passage is characterized by the recurrent formulations 'on top of that, he created/made/placed XY' (483, 490, 541, 550, 561, 573, 587, 590, 607; on the different Greek verbs, 478n.); the narrator[P] uses this to lend the text a rhythmic aspect (refrain composition[P]: EDWARDS p. 206; GÄRTNER 1976, 51–53; WIRBELAUER 1996, 144 f. and 147–155; MOOG 2001, 11, 16), to repeatedly recall the act of creation, and via the formulation to capture in a single verse the artist, the artwork and the imagery (BECKER 1995, 42 f., 102, 107: '*ars et artifex, opus,* and *res ipsae*'; NÜNLIST 1998, 84 f.).
Section (1): the body of the shield (478–482: 'he made' [Greek *póiei*] 478/482);
Section (2): the pictorial decoration on the body of the shield (483–608):

    (I) 483–489   cosmic phenomena: earth, sky, sea, heavenly bodies (483 'on it, he created ...' [*en men ... éteux*']);
    (II) 490–606   scenes on earth, structured by introductory verses that specify the scenery:
        (A) 490–540 two cities (490 'on it, he made ...' [*en de ... poíēse*]):
            (A1)   in one ('city at peace'), a wedding celebration (491–496) and dispute arbitration in the *agorḗ* (497–508);

    (A2)   the other ('city at war') under siege (509–540: description of the situation [509–512], ambush with theft of cattle [513–529], battle [530–540]);

(B) 541–572 agricultural labor (3× 'on it, he placed' [*en d' etíthei*]):

    (B1)   541–549 plowing a fallow field;

    (B2)   550–560 cutting a field of grain;

    (B3)   561–572 harvest in a vineyard;

(C) 573–589 herds of animals (2× 'on it, he made ...' [*en de ... poíēse*]):

    (C1)   573–586 herd of cattle attacked by lions;

    (C2)   587–589 sheep meadow;

(D) 590–606 dance ('on it, he composed ...' [*en de ... poíkille*]);

(III) 607–608 Okeanos at the outer shield edge ('on it, he placed' [*en d' etíthei*]).

In terms of the composition of the content of the text, the principle of ring-composition[P] can be identified both in the delimitation of the entire passage from the context (478/609) and within the passage itself in the arrangement of individual recurrent motifs: cosmic phenomena in (I) and (III) (483–489n., 607–608n.); dance and spectators in (A 1) and (D), the first and last scenes on earth (590–606n.); animal herds and battle in (A 2) and (C 1) (REDFIELD [1975] 1994, 188, with emphasis on the switch between *nature* and *culture*; TAPLIN [1980] 2001, 348–356). There have also been various, not always entirely convincing attempts to discover more subtle structures in the composition of the content: multiple ring-compositions[P] (GÄRTNER 1976, 52f.; STANLEY 1993, 9–13; MOOG 2001, 11 with n. 42; HEIDEN 2008, 216–222 [in addition to a circular movement within the images]); scenes in groups of two and three (WIRBELAUER 1996, 154f. with n. 45); a diptych principle within the images, i.e. 'two possibilities from a single unit' (CAVALLERO 2003, 190f. [transl.]); structuring in accord with 'spatial frames' (TSAGALIS 2012, 425–429, 440).

B.2.a. The shape of the product: archaeological aspects (see also 479b–480n., 481n.)

Two types of shield are described in Homeric epic: (a) the larger long shield that covers the body down to the ankles (6.117–118n. [*s.v.* σφυρὰ τύπτε καὶ αὐχένα]) and is attested in archaeological finds already from the early Mycenaean period; (b) the smaller, more manageable round shield, which is attested from the 13th cent. onward (3.347n.), was still common in the Geometric period and was well known to the narrator (2.388–389n.; on the archaeological evidence for shields, see BORCHHARDT 1977, 1–56; SHEAR 2000, 30–42; FRANZ 2002, 48–51; BUCHHOLZ 2010, 209–213; also CERRI 39–42; additional bibliography in EDWARDS 200 f.). At the same time, descriptions of arms do not always distinguish clearly between round and long shields (either due to an amalgamation within the epic tradition of elements of different date and origin or because of the poetic fantasy employed by the narrator to describe shields depending on the situation: 6.117–118n. [s.v. ἀσπίδος ὀμφαλοέσσης]; RAAFLAUB 2011, esp. 10–14; on the two Greek terms for shield, 458n.). The lack of explicit indications of the form of Achilleus' shield notwithstanding (the shield boss of round shields [19.360n.] is also left unmentioned), the fact that the circular stream Okeanos surrounds the entire object suggests a round shape analogous to the disc of the earth, as perhaps do the comparison of the shield to the moon at 19.374 (see *ad loc.*) and the presence of round shapes and circular movements in several of the images (FITTSCHEN 1973, 7 with n. 31; SIMON 1995, 127 f., 130; MOOG 2001, 15 f.; differently SHEAR 2000, 31, 33: the greatest hero of the Greeks needs a large, representative shield that cannot be smaller than Aias' long shield).

Possible sources of inspiration for decorating circular areas are found in actual objects, e.g. Cretan bronze shields of Near Eastern influence or Phoenician silver and bronze bowls from Cyprus (concentric rings filled with figurative representations, including a town under attack, rural scenes, animals, round dances); these kinds of objects could have served as models for the narrator, cf. the laudatory mention of a Phoenician silver krater at 23.741–749 (RICHARDSON *ad loc.*) as well as *Od.* 4.615–619 = 15.115–119 (EDWARDS p. 203–205; HELBIG [1884] 1887, 409–415; FITTSCHEN 1973, 7–10 with fig. 1–4; D'ACUNTO 2010, 162–166; WEST 2011, 18; on the Cretan bronze shields, KUNZE 1931; on the Phoenician metal bowls, MARKOE 1985; additional bibliography in D'ACUNTO *loc. cit.* 193–198). It is thus assumed that, in terms of the composition of the imagery, the narrator[P] was inspired by contemporary Cypriot and Cretan art rather than by Mycenaean models and, in terms of the motifs, by Geometric vase painting (for discussion and older bibliography, SCHADEWALDT [1938] 1965, 357–361; FITTSCHEN 1973, 5–17; CRIELAARD 1995, 217–224; D'ACUNTO 2010, 155 ff., esp. 192 f.; also HAINSWORTH on *Il.* 11.20 [Agamemnon's Cypriot corselet]; WEST 1997, 99–101 [on Phoenician models in art]; SNODGRASS 1998, 40–44, 64 f., 161 f.; and CARRUESCO 2016 [on Geometric vase paintings, see also 593–602n., 594n.]; differently SHEAR 2000, 30–33; 2004, 59 f., 145 n. 476 [the decoration of the shield is influenced by Mycenaean art]). The techniques employed in making these images are not described anywhere in the text (see also 476–477n.), leaving it open whether or not the imagery was supposed to be imagined as inlays of different metals (so-called damascening) modeled on *Mycenaean* 'metal paintings' (*pro*: SIMON 1995, 129 f.; *contra*: FITTSCHEN 1973, 6).

Fundamentally, it is not to be assumed that the narrator[P] aimed at describing a 'real' shield that could actually be reproduced, and it is doubtful that he was even attempting to convey a notion of the arrangement of scenes on the shield (on which, also 497–508n., end, 509–540n.; for indications of the spatial arrangement in the individual images, see ELLIGER 1975, 32–43). Instead, he elicits a fantastical marvel with certain links to reality, a shield exceptionally designed in every sense by the divine smith himself, destined for the greatest hero among the Greeks (cf. the tower-like shield of the greater Aias at 7.219 ff.); what is more important is the overall impression it creates, as well as the effect of each individual scene and their contextual meanings, especially with regard to the action of the *Iliad*, see below **B.2.b.** (MARG [1957] 1971, 30; GÄRTNER 1976, 48 f., 55; TAPLIN [1980] 2001, 345; AUBRIOT 1999, 11 f.; OTTO 2009, 179–184; PURVES 2010, 50–52).

There have nonetheless been numerous suggestions and attempts to reconstruct the al- location of images to concentric rings (cf. the archaeological finds), which draw on the linguistic structure of the text (section **B.1.b.**) and the 'five layers' mentioned at 481 (see *ad loc.*) for their arguments: it is usually assumed that (a) the narrator[P] starts his description with the center of the shield (483 f.), since at the end (607 f.) its outermost edge is taken up by Okeanos (GÄRTNER 1976, 47 f., 55); and that (b) the innermost ring or circle surrounding the shield boss depicts the earth, sky, sea and heavenly bodies, encircled by a ring with the two cities. But there are differing views regarding the overall number of rings as well as the placement of the three agricultural scenes, the two scenes with animal herds and the depiction of the ring dance across an additional two or three rings (see e.g. VAN LEEUWEN on 483–608; WILLCOCK on 478–608 and fig. p. 270; EDWARDS p. 207 and on 483; FITTSCHEN 1973, 3 f., 9 f. and pl. III; REDFIELD [1975] 1994, 187 f.; HUBBARD 1992, 27–35; GIULIANI 2003, 39 f.; HEIDEN 2008, 216–218; on ancient depictions of shield scenes in the *Tabulae Iliacae*, SQUIRE 2011, 303–370).

B.2.b. The pictorial program and its links to the poem as a whole
Comparison of the pictorial program of the present shield with that of other shields illustrates its uniqueness and raises questions concerning the meaning of the imagery with regard to the bearer of the shield (TAPLIN [1980] 2001, 342–345): other shields are commonly decorated with terrifying figures such as Gorgo and personifications of 'fear' and 'terror' (11.32–40 Agamemnon's shield, 5.738–742 Zeus' *aegis* worn by Athene), demonstrating the usual apotropaic function of the shields' embellishment (cf. the design of Achilleus' shield at Euripides *El.* 442–486), which also dominates on the pseudo-Hesiodic shield of Herakles (on this, SCHADEWALDT [1938] 1965, 362 f.; REINHARDT 1961, 408 f.). By contrast, the imagery on Achilleus' shield shows representatives of cosmic order, such as the sky, Okeanos and the heavenly bodies with their eternal course, in addition to various motifs from everyday life, which are sometimes shown multiple times with variations (festivities, music and dance: 491b–496n., 494n., 570n., 590–606n., 605b–606n.; rural life: 541–572n., 573–589n.; dispute, war and death: 497–508n., 509–540n., 513n., 579–586n.). Within these scenes placed on the shield are depicted both sexes and all age groups, from children to the elderly; the mul-

tiple dancing scenes in particular present an occasion in which large parts of a community can participate, be it as a dancer or a spectator (492–496, 567–572, 593–604). Joint planning and action by all for the benefit of the community is picked out multiple times and sometimes contrasted with strife, raids and war (see esp. 490–540n., 550–556a n., 558–560n., 590–606n.; cf. EDWARDS 208 f.). Many scholars rightly emphasize that the images are not designed to provide a comprehensive reflection of the world – much has been left out (SCHADEWALDT *loc. cit.* 376; REINHARDT *loc. cit.* 401 f.) – but are rather to be viewed with reference to the *Iliad*. There are nonetheless differing notions concerning the interpretation of the images: (1) the creation of the shield and its imagery is understood as an allegory for cosmogony (the dominant interpretation in antiquity: HARDIE 1985, 15 ff.); (2) the images show an alternative world to that in the *Iliad* (MARG [1957] 1971, 35 ff. [with an emphasis on the joy in this world]; REINHARDT *loc. cit.* 401–411 [functioning aristocracy *vs.* warring world of the heroes]); (3) they exist in a relationship of tension vis-à-vis Achilleus, the bearer of the shield, who in his desire for exacting revenge (80 ff.) will consciously advance toward the end of his life bearing his new arms (19.397 ff.; EDWARDS 208 f.; SCHEIN 1984, 142; BYRE 1992, 40 ff.; DUBEL 1995, 254 ff.; see also 556b–557n. on the *basileús* in the image of the grain harvest), although there is perhaps also an anticipation of the readiness for reconciliation Achilleus will display in Books 23 (esp. 23.490 ff., 23.540 ff., 23.887 ff.) and 24 (498–501n.); (4) they reflect certain parts of the action of the *Iliad* by picking up (4a) central themes and (4b) motifs from similes (ANDERSEN 1976, esp. 7; TAPLIN [1980] 2001, 356–364 [with stress on contrasting images of peace]; AUBRIOT 1999, 14 ff.; ALDEN 2000, 53 ff.; HEIDEN 2008, 77 f., 222–229; on Helen's weaving, cf. 3.126n.). The understanding of individual images and the special aspects of this object description are most productively aided by (3) and (4); this ekphrasis is a type of *mise en abyme* (*récit spéculaire*) in the sense of 'a text-within-text that functions as microcosm or mirror of the text itself' (the definition in MARTIN 2000, 63; on the term, see also argument function[P] with n. 8); overall, the scene offers a reflection on the process of artistic creation, as can also be gleaned from scenes depicting singers in the *Iliad* (9.186–189) and especially the *Odyssey* (esp. 8.266 ff.; cf. NTHS 60–62).

On (4a): Themes from the action of the *Iliad* show especially the images of two cities (II A: 490–540n., end), sometimes with obvious reference to Achilleus' situation: strife and the possibility of public reconciliation, a dispute regarding the acceptance of compensation (498–501n., 506–508n., 510n. [*s.v.* δίχα ... ἥνδανε βουλή], 511n.), a city under siege, the besieged act outside the city walls, a battle and fight over the fallen (509–540n., 514–515n., 520–529n., 536–537n., 539–540n.), an ambush (513n.); perhaps also the wedding celebration as a contrast with the relationship of Paris and Helen (ANDERSEN 1976, 11) or of Achilleus and Briseïs (suggestion by BIERL) or as an allusion to the wedding of Peleus and Thetis, which started everything (HUBBARD 1992, 29). It is striking that the images of cities, as well as those that depict agricultural labor or dance and music, reveal the functioning of communities and sometimes the joy within them, see esp. 556 f., 567 f., 603 f. (EDWARDS p. 208 f.; going further, ULF 1990, 172 f.: 'an appeal by the poet to put community before individual aims and interests' [quotation p. 173; transl.]).

On (4b): Motifs from similes[P] in the *Iliad* occur especially in images involving agriculture and animal herds: plowing (541–549n., 547n.), reaping (550–556a n.), the helplessness of herdsmen (526n.), their attempts to defend their herds against predators (579–586n., 579n. [lions], 583n.), dogs acting as herdsmen's helpers (578n., 585–586n.). What is more, the typified, non-individualized images of the shield, when taken together, reveal a special form of simile by retarding[P] the action in a similar manner and by guiding the audience's gaze away from the heroic world of the past and toward the more familiar everyday (MARG [1957] 1971, 34; REDFIELD [1975] 1994, 186–189; EDWARDS 1987, 278; LONSDALE 1990a, 8–11; GIULIANI 2003, 44 f.; SCOTT 2009, 1–10; going further, PRIMAVESI 2002, 205–207: 'court scene' [497–508] and 'city at war' [509–540] as a species of 'similes for decisive situations' in the action of the *Iliad* [quotation p. 205; transl.]).

B.3. The linguistic depiction
Linguistically, the shield passage is characterized by numerous *hapax legomena*[P] as well as by limited formularity in the language (WIRBELAUER 1996, 144–146 [list of passages in n. 9 and 10]). In addition, in keeping with an object description, the distribution of verbal aspects differs markedly from narrative passages, with a significantly higher proportion (86.3%) of forms in the imperfect (durative) and perfect (state) in comparison to forms in the aorist (PRIMAVESI 2002, 195–199); on the one hand, this predominance shows the 'situational, non-narrative character of the text' (PRIMAVESI *loc. cit.* 195 [transl.]), while on the other hand it matches both the scenic descriptions and the actions that are captured on the shield and thus not completed (BECKER 1995, 109: 'the imperfect could represent the necessary incompleteness of a depicted action frozen in a metallic representation'). The description of the shield nevertheless does not appear merely static and descriptive, since it is designed dynamically and narratively in two respects, first via the incorporation of the process of creation (section **B.1.b.**), second via the composition of vivid scenes; in this way, it corresponds to an ekphrasis matching the understanding of ancient literary theory, i.e. a descriptive text 'that illustrates vividly what is communicated' (GRAF 1995, 144 [transl.]; WEBB 2009, 8 f., 28 f., 70). The narrator[P] achieves this (a) by describing movement (in all scenes aside from 587–589 [see *ad loc.*]), sounds (493, 495, 502, 506, 530, 569–572, 575 f., 580, 586, 606 [see *ad locc.*]) and the tactile properties of 'real' materials (504 polished

stones, 595 f. linen garments), (b) by inserting narrative elements, namely secondary focalization[P] (501, 510–512, 524, 526, 547; indirect speech, 499 f.), comparisons[P] (591 f., 600 f. [see *ad locc.*]) and indications of pace specifying the progression of time (525–534 [see *ad loc.*], cf. 573–586n.), and (c) by repeatedly inserting explanatory interpretations of situations or actions described (497–508n., 509–540n., 525–534n., 547n.; EDWARDS 207 f.; FRIEDRICH 1975, 50 f.; BECKER 1995, 96–150 [with detailed commentary]; OTTO 2009, 186 f.; FRANCIS 2009, 8–13; 2012, 128–133; DE JONG 2011, 5–7). He thus sometimes almost creates a story[P] and overall achieves a very high degree of vividness (*enárgeia*, Latin *evidentia*), i.e. 'the power of the text to create visual images and to turn listeners into spectators' (GRAF *loc. cit.* 145 [transl.]; WEBB 2009, 8; also HEFFERNAN 1993, 21 f.; BECKER 1995, 113); for discussion of ekphrasis and 'vividness' in antiquity, see *BNP s.v.* Ekphrasis; GRAF 1995; FRANCIS 2009, 3; 2012, 114 f., 118–126; OTTO 2009, 45–134 (on Homer, 174–189); WEBB 2009, 70–74, 87 ff. (ancient sources, 197 ff.); SCHMITT 2011. None of the figures depicted is identified by name, with the exception of the gods Ares and Athene (516–519) and the constellations of stars (486–489); instead, they remain generic types in terms of their activities, comparable to the characters in similes[P] (BECKER 1995, 118 n. 217: 'The shield does not bring *kleos* [...] as epic song can do'); similarly, the story arc is described in a generalizing fashion, and the outcome of events usually remains unknown (GIULIANI 2003, 42–44).

The interpretation of many scenes remains disputed in certain aspects even today (497–508n., 510n., 541–572n., 558–560n., 560n., 570n., 573–589n., 589n., 590n., 592n., 593–602n., 594n.; see also 604b–605a n.). Some of these can no longer be fully explained because of temporal distance (esp. 498–501n., 501n., 506–508n.), others were perhaps deliberately left ambiguous by the narrator[P], creating space for interpretation (see also 485n., 505n., 533n., 556b–557n., 565n.) – similar to how images can be ambiguous and offer the possibility of reflection.

B.4. The function of the shield scene within the poem as a whole and its poetological significance
Within the *Iliad*, this extensive ekphrasis serves to single out the shield bearer and to prepare his *aristeia* (section **B.1.a.**), on the one hand, and to reflect issues at the heart of the poem, such as strife and harmony (section **B.2.b.**), on the other. Moreover, this process of producing a work of art illustrates the way in which the divine artisan and the narrator[P] almost merge in the creation of the images. Scholarly discussion regarding the two artists reveals the following tendencies in emphasis (DE JONG 2011, esp. 1, 4 f., 9 f. [additional bibliography 11 f. n. 4–7]): (1) Hephaistos takes the foreground as a superhuman creator of (a) a marvellous work of art with actual moving figures, similar to the tripods and the golden

maid-servants (375–377, 417–420), or at least of (b) imagery that can create this impression in the observer (FORD 1992, 168–171 [with reference to 19.21 f.]); (2) the narrator[P] frequently blends description with narrative and does this (a) out of an exuberant pleasure in creating a tale or (b) with subtle objectives and, in this way and via the blending of his own creative act with that of the god, creates the impression that both are generating a work of art simultaneously – one the shield, the other the ekphrasis. When taking into account the effects of shield and ekphrasis on possible spectators or audiences (on which, FOWLER 1991, 28–31), the most plausible is (2b) (DE JONG *loc. cit.*; cf. FRONTISI-DUCROUX 2002, 470 ff.): only the narrator[P] himself serves as an admirer of the shield (549, cf. his remarks concerning the artistic qualities of the depiction at 491, 518, 548, 588, 597), whereas he makes none of the characters[P] react explicitly to its pictorial decoration, neither Thetis (615 ff.) nor Achilleus (19.16–19 [with nn.]: initial anger and aggression, followed by joy at the sight of the complete armor; differently on this, STANLEY 1993, 25: a response specifically to the images]; see also 19.10 f./21 f.: beauty of the weapons as a whole), nor indeed the Myrmidons, Greeks or Trojans; the only effect of the shield involves its gleam (19.373–380; on this, see 19.12–19n., 19.374–383n., 19.375–380a n.; differently SCULLY 2003, esp. 43 ff.). By contrast, the narrator[P] imparts lasting effects to the pictorial decoration with regard to the *audience* by concluding the *hoplopoiia* in the space of a few verses after describing the shield (609–617n.); he thus depicts in Hephaistos an artist in the midst of the creative process, in which he himself has a share and participates (DE JONG *loc. cit.* 5, 9–11); the *hoplopoiia*, and the description of the manufacture of the shield in particular, can thus be seen as a kind of indirect self-representation of the poet as artist (DE JONG *loc. cit.* 11; cf. EDWARDS 209; MARG [1957] 1971, 38 f.; BECKER 1995, 149 f.; on this, also 604b–605a n.; NTHS 60–62; on the term *metalepsis*, also DE JONG 2009; EISEN/VON MÖLLENDORFF 2013; for older bibliography, see argument function[P] n. 8).

B.5. Line-by-line commentary

478–482 A brief, summary description of the making of the shield, the embellishment of which will be described in detail in what follows (cf. 3.328–329n., 6.156–159n.), highlighted via repetitions in the manner of a ring-composition[P] of the verb 'he made' (Greek *póiei* 478/482) and the stem *daidal-* ('skillful, artistic' 479/482), which proclaims the artistic qualities of the shield (*sákos* 478/481; EDWARDS; BECKER 1995, 96–98; PERCEAU 2002, 181). 468–482 in combination with the preceding scene between Hephaistos and Thetis comprise the essential elements of an object description: size (478b), quality (479a, 482), shape (479b–480), material and composition (474 f., 481a), the maker and the story of the production (369–478): MINCHIN 1999, 62 f.; 2001, 106–112, 128 f.; cf. 19.387–391n. (Achilleus' lance). The subsequent description of detail (483–608), which starts unexpectedly and is exceptionally long, was thus – wrongly – athetized by Zenodotus (HT 10; schol. A on 483); in contrast, see MARG (1957) 1971; REINHARDT 1961, 398–400; APTHORP 1980, 187 f. n. 119; NÜNLIST 2009, 207; on the function of this ekphrasis, 478–608n. section **B.4.**

478 2nd VH = 3.335 (see *ad loc.*), 16.136, 18.609, 19.373 (see *ad loc.*), 'Hes.' *Sc.* 319. – In Book 18, the formulaic 2nd VH marks the beginning and conclusion of the manufacture of the shield; elsewhere, it is part of arming scenes (see *iterata*). These sometimes contain digressions concerning individual weapons and their origins (e.g. 11.19 ff., 19.387 ff.: cf. 19.364b–391n., 19.369–371n., 19.387–391n.), whereas in the case of Achilleus' weapons, the story of their origin is separated from the arming scene (cf. 19.368 and 19.383 and the references back to their production) and was composed in a special manner (REINHARDT 1961, 40 f., 410 f.; PATZER 1972, 40; LÉTOUBLON 1999, 215–219; PERCEAU 2002, 118).

ποίει: Hephaistos' activities are described by a variety of verbs that do not distinguish among the technical processes involved in the work; the different verbs instead serve to structure the text (478–608n. section **B.1.b.**): (1) impf. ποίει as a summary description of the production process as a whole (478, 482, see also 608 σάκεος πύκα ποιητοῖο), with the impf. circumscribing the frame for the details that follow (cf. RIJKSBARON [1984] 2002, 11); (2a) aor. ποίησε for details of decoration (490, 573, 587); (2b) δαιδάλλων (479), ἐτίθει (541, 550, 561, 607) and ποίκιλλε (590) for details of decoration; (2c) aor. τεῦξε for details of decoration (483: the spheres of the cosmos), as well as for the concluding statement concerning the production of the shield (609) and the remaining armor (610 f., 613); plpf. pass. τέτυκτο/τετεύχατο for details of decoration (549/574); (3) κάμε for the completion of the forging as a whole (614, see *ad loc.*): ECKSTEIN 1974, 5–9; for additional bibliography, see *LfgrE s.vv.* ποιέω, τεύχω; on the tenses, see DE JONG 2011, 6 f.; on the poetological use of craft-related terms such as ποιέω (attested in post-Homeric texts) and τεύχω (*Od.* 24.197 τεύξουσι ... ἀοιδήν), BECKER 1995, 96 n. 169; NÜNLIST 1998, 85 f. – πρώτιστα: adv. 'at the beginning, at the very first' (always before caesura B 2: 4× *Il.*, 6× *Od.*, 4× Hes., 4× *h.Hom.*); on the intensified form, G 80; RISCH 95; *LfgrE s.v.* πρῶτος with bibliography. – σάκος: 458n. (*s. v.* ἀσπίδα).

479b–480 1st VH of 480 ≈ 3.126 (see *ad loc.*); 2nd VH of 480 ≈ 598. – The description leaves some aspects unclear (for interpretations, see EDWARDS; HELBIG [1884] 1887, 385 f.; *LfgrE s.v.* ἄντυξ [with older bibliography]: 'The blending of reality and fantasy in the case of the shield [...] precludes further conclusions

---

478 ποίει: on the unaugmented form, R 16.1.
479 περί: adv., 'all around'.
480 μαρμαρέην: on the -η- after -ε-, R 2.

regarding the technical execution' [transl.]). *ántyx* is the term for the outer-most 'rim' of a shield (6.117–118n.; also for the upper 'edge' of a chariot seat: 16.406n.); it is described with three adjectives, two of which point to metal as the material (*phaeinḗ* 'shimmering' and *marmaréē* 'sparkling', see below; on the asyndetic series of epithets, 130–131n.), while the third adj., *tríplax*, means 'triple' and probably describes three layers of material, and thus the thickness of the rim, by analogy with *díplax* 'in two layers' (of textiles: 3.126n.), i.e. the reinforcement of the area where – on 'real' shields – the layers of hide are at-tached (WILLCOCK; *LfgrE s.v.* τρίπλαξ; FRANZ 2002, 49 f.; cf. 481n.), rather than three decorative bands at the outer edge of the shield (EDWARDS *ad loc.* and on 607–608, with reference to a Cretan bronze shield [p. 204 and FITTSCHEN 1973, 8]; SHEAR 2000, 31). The first interpretation better matches this introductory passage concerning the body of the shield and its basic structure (478–608n. section **B.1.b.**); the decoration follows at 483 ff. — **shield strap ... of silver:** The shield was carried by a leather strap (*telamṓn*), as was the sword, in order to re-lieve the shield arm; the two straps were placed across the right and left shoul-ders, respectively, and crossed over one another at the chest (14.404–406n.; cf. 2.45n., 2.388–389n.); 'of silver' likely refers to embellishment with silver fittings, similar to Agamemnon's carrying strap (11.38–40) or 'golden' in the case of Herakles' (*Od.* 11.610–614): BORCHHARDT 1977, 4; FOLTINY 1980, 239 f.; SHEAR 2000, 37; FRANZ 2002, 48 f., 50 with n. 190; BUCHHOLZ 2012, 192 ff.

πάντοσε: 'in all directions'; understood by some as a reference to the round shape of the shield (LA ROCHE, with reference to the VE formula ἀσπίδα πάντοσ' ἐΐσην [on which, 3.347n.]; AH; cf. 478–608n. section **B.2.a.**). — **δαιδάλλων:** elaborates ποίει (478; cf. 482) and prepares for the description of the multifold embellishments, similar to Odysseus' bed at *Od.* 23.200 (HEUBECK *ad loc.*; ECKSTEIN 1974, 8 f.; on the word family δαιδαλ- in reference to Achilleus' arms, 379n.). — **φαεινήν:** a generic epithet[P], usually of metal objects (*LfgrE*). — **μαρμαρέην:** 'sparkling, glittering'; of metal (cf. 617 μαρμαίροντα), the surface of the sea and textiles (3.126n.; cf. 3.397n.). — **ἐκ:** adv., '(coming) out from', i.e. 'attached to it', cf. 598 (AH; SCHW. 2.422).

481 five folds: The shields described in Homeric epic usually consist of several layers of leather, sometimes reinforced by a layer of bronze or a bronze rim (7.219–223, 7.245–248, 12.294–297, 13.803 f., etc.); these layers are thought of as concentrically stacked circles that decrease in diameter, so that the shield ends up thinner at the rim, with the outer edge reinforced by metal, cf. 20.275 f. (*LfgrE s.v.* πτύξ; EDWARDS p. 201 f.; on the archaeological evidence, HELBIG

---

481 αὐτοῦ ... σάκεος: 'of the shield itself'; on the uncontracted form σάκεος, R 6. — ἔσαν: = ἦσαν (R 16.6).

[1884] 1887, 318 f.; 1977, 2–4; FRANZ 2002, 49 f.). The present passage might give the impression that, in the case of this exceptional shield (cf. 466 f., 19.375–380), the narrator used epic exaggeration and had in mind five metal layers, analogous to leather ones (*ptýches*; cf. the poetic exaggeration of Aias' tower shield, made from seven layers of leather and one of metal, at 7.219 ff.), but he leaves open the role played by the metals listed at the beginning (EDWARDS p. 201 f.; CERRI p. 30; FITTSCHEN 1973, 6 f.; D'ACUNTO 2010, 160–162). Over the course of the subsequent battle description, the five layers are specifically described (20.270–272: two of bronze, two of tin, one of gold; but some scholars consider these verses an interpolation: WEST 2001, 12 n. 28).

ἐν αὐτῷ: picked up with anaphora by the VB ἐν μέν (483 [see *ad loc.*]) and ἐν δέ (490, 541, 550, 561, 573, 587, 590, 607), a repeated reference to the surface of the shield and thus to the '*opus ipsum*' (BECKER 1995, 102; PERCEAU 2002, 112 f.).

482 2nd VH = 380 (see *ad loc.*). — **δαίδαλα:** 379n.

483–489 The narrator[P] begins with a catalogue[P] of the eternal foundations of the world: the spatial spheres, visible to human beings, the earth, sky and sea, and perhaps as indicators of the progress of time, the sun, moon and constellations of stars, cf. the use of the constellations and heavenly bodies listed here in the description of a tapestry showing an image of the evening sky at Euripides *Ion* 1149–1158, esp. 1155 f. (485–489n.; EDWARDS; SCHADEWALDT [1938] 1965, 364; TAPLIN [1980] 2001, 348; differently LYNN-GEORGE 1988, 176 f.: no indicator of the progress of time; on the interpretations of earth, sky, sea and sun as the four elements, see CERRI; HUBBARD 1992, 29). All in all, the section that concludes with a mention of the circular stream Okeanos (489) sketches an image of the universal world, a poetic account of the world order in its cosmic dimension, and presents the framework for the subsequent individual scenes on the shield (see also the shield rim with Okeanos at 607). The extent to which this describes actual pictorial representations in the center of the shield remains open (478–608n. section **B.2.a.**).

483 ≈ *Od.* 12.404, 14.302, Hes. *Th.* 427; 2nd VH ≈ Hes. *Th.* 847. — **earth ... sky ... sea's water:** the three 'major spheres of the visible world' (SCHADEWALDT [1938] 1965, 364 [transl.]), cf. the division of the world among the gods at 15.189–193 and Hekate's share in the earth, sea and sky at Hes. *Th.* 413 f. (see also the *iterata* and *Od.* 5.293 f. = 9.68 f. = 12.314 f.); two-part sequences of terms are more common (earth – sea or sky – earth): *LfgrE s.vv.* θάλασσα, οὐρανός; SCHMIDT

---

482 πολλὰ (ϝ)ιδυίῃσι: on the prosody, R 4.3. — ἰδυίῃσι: fem. part. of οἶδα; on the declension, R 11.1. — πραπίδεσσιν: on the declension, R 11.3.
483 ἐν: adverbial, 'on top'.

1981, 3–15; possible models in Ancient Near Eastern literature: SCHMIDT *loc. cit.* 19–23; on Babylonian models for the sequence earth – sky – sea, WENSKUS 1990, 36. Since it is unclear how the pictorial representation of this triad is to be thought of, especially given the absence of relevant contemporary archaeological evidence (GÄRTNER 1976, 55; SCHMIDT *loc. cit.* 23 f.: by way of symbols), the verse has also been interpreted as a summarizing introduction to the pictorial representations, the actual description of which follows in 484–608 (EDWARDS; CERRI; FITTSCHEN 1973, 10). But the list of objects 'created' by Hephaistos that continues seamlessly at 484 presents a linguistic problem, as does the fact that *thálassa* denotes the 'sea' encircled by land and cannot be equated with the circular stream Okeanos (489, 607; LESKY 1947, 58 f.; TAPLIN [1980] 2001, 348 n. 13; SCHMIDT *loc. cit.* 24 n. 88; SIMON 1995, 128).

ἐν … ἐν … ἐν: a triple anaphora emphasizing the terms, as at 535 (see *ad loc.*), 5.740 (description of the *aegis*), 14.216 (Aphrodite's band): FEHLING 1969, 196; on I-E parallels, WEST 2007, 108 f.; cf. 24.10–12n.

484 1st VH ≈ 239 (see *ad loc.*), Hes. *Th.* 956, *h.Hom.* 31.7. — In the present passage, the attributes 'tireless' and 'full' refer to the regular, rhythmically recurrent visible luminosity of sun and moon as an expression of cosmic order: the sun is 'tireless' especially with regard to its recurrent daily run (cf. 239n. *s.v.* ἀκάμαντα; on I-E parallels, WEST 2007, 211), here perhaps also in reference to its never-waning luminosity – much like the moon (CERRI, with reference to the VE formula 'untiring fire' [on which, 225n.]; on formulations for the shining of the moon, see KOPP 1939, 184–186).

485–489 The selection of the constellations Pleiades, Hyades, Orion and 'the Bear' can be explained in the first instance by their optical effect, since they are representative constellations in specific areas of the northern sky: the Pleiades and the Hyades in the ecliptic, i.e. in the area through which the sun appears to be moving over the course of the year, Orion somewhat more to the south, Ursa Major in the area of the Arctic circle (WENSKUS 1990, 35–37; on the possible influence of Babylonian astronomy on this list, *loc. cit.* 22–24; HUNGER/PINGREE 1999, 67 f.). In addition, they might have been selected on the basis of their function in calendars concerning shipping and especially the agricultural year; according to Hesiod, the visibility of the Pleiades and the Hyades during the course of the year was thought to indicate the dates for reaping and harvesting as well as for plowing and sowing (for more information on this, 486n.; cf. plowing and reaping on the shield at 541–560). Their selection has thus been interpreted as pointing to the period of time between

484 ἠέλιον: = ἥλιον. — πλήθουσαν: from πλήθω 'be full'.

May and November (PHILLIPS 1980) or to these two terminal points in the agricultural year (HANNAH 1994; *HE s.v.* Seasons); cf. DICKS 1970, 34; on changes in the position of constellations across time since antiquity due to the movement of the earth's axis, HAINSWORTH on *Od.* 5.272–277; KIDD on Arat. *Phaen.* 39; DICKS *loc. cit.* 15 f.

485 2nd VH = Hes. *Th.* 382. — **τείρεα:** likely a variant of τέρας, 'divine signs' (with metrical lengthening?: EDWARDS; *LfgrE s.v.* τέρας with bibliography); it denotes esp. miraculous signs in various guises (cf. 6.183n.), including celestial phenomena as divine signs to human beings (4.75–77 shooting star, 17.547–550 rainbow), here constellations with specific significance for human beings (EDWARDS). — **τά τ' οὐρανὸς ἐστεφάνωται:** τά is an internal acc., 'with which the sky has adorned itself' (SCHW. 2.80; RAMELLI 1996, 247; on the middle, ALLAN 2003, 88 ff.). In early epic, στεφανόω is almost always attested in the middle-passive (8× VE ἐστεφάνωται/-το, 1× στεφάνωσαν), usually in descriptions of masses (cloud, sea, crowd of spectators) surrounding an object (15.153, *Od.* 10.195, *h.Ven.* 120; cf. 'Hes.' *Sc.* 204) or of a pictorial decoration arranged in circles (*Il.* 5.739) – an arrangement that is further clarified via ἀμφί or περί; this addition is absent both from Agamemnon's shield, in the center of which the Gorgon's head is depicted (11.36 f. τῇ δ' ἐπὶ μὲν Γοργὼ ... ἐστεφάνωτο | ... περὶ δὲ Δεῖμός τε Φόβος τε; on this, RAMELLI 1996, 246 f.) and from descriptions of the sky here and at Hes. *Th.* 382. There is accordingly dispute as to whether the present passage contains the association '(as) with a wreath' (thus AH; LEAF; WILLCOCK; CERRI; *LfgrE s.v.* οὐρανός 870.47 ff.; WORTHEN 1988; undecided, *LfgrE s.v.* στεφανόω; *contra*, RAMELLI 1996) and to what extent this indicates the arrangement of the pictorial decoration (e.g. EDWARDS: '[stars] which the sky [...] has hung up as a wreath ⟨around the earth; or around his head⟩'; *LfgrE s.v.* οὐρανός 870.47 ff.: 'with which the sky is adorned/has adorned itself as with a wreath' [transl.]). While in other descriptions that concern the arrangement of imagery on the surface of an object, the surface of the object is mentioned explicitly (*Il.* 5.738 f.: [αἰγίδα] ... ἥν πέρι; 11.32/36: [ἀσπίδα] τῇ δ' ἐπί), here the sky itself is adorned this way: 'the world represented and the visual image are conflated in the language of description' (BECKER 1995, 104).

486 ≈ Hes. *Op.* 615. — **Pleiades:** a cluster of stars in the constellation Taurus; in myth, they were identified as the seven daughters of Atlas (cf. Hes. *Op.* 383), who were pursued by the hunter Orion and placed by Zeus in the sky (schol. D = 'Epic Cycle' *fr.* 2 Davies [p. 74]; cf. WEST 2013, 209–211), where even as a constellation they flee from Orion and toward Okeanos (cf. Hes. *Op.* 619 f. with WEST *ad loc.*). In combination with other constellations, the Pleiades served as a guide for seafarers (*Od.* 5.271–275: Odysseus' nocturnal journey on a raft), as

---

485 τὰ τείρεα πάντα, τά: the first τά is demonstrative (cf. R 17), looking forward to the relative clause, the second has the function of a relative pronoun (R 14.5). — πάντα: predicative, 'altogether'. — τ(ε): 'epic τε' (R 24.11).
486 θ': = τε.

well as as chronological markers for agriculture and seafaring: their appearance, i.e. their earliest visible rise at dawn just before sunrise, the so-called heliacal rising (in antiquity in the middle of May, after having been invisible since the beginning of April: WENSKUS 1990, 25), signalled the beginning of reaping season (Hes. *Op.* 383 f.), while their setting, i.e. their early setting at dawn, the so-called cosmical setting (beginning of November), signalled the start of plowing time for the new seed (Hes. *Op.* 384, 614–617) and the beginning of the stormy season, during which ships remained on land for the winter (Hes. *Op.* 618–623): WEST on Hes. *Op.* 383–384 and on 619; HAINSWORTH on *Od.* 5.272–277; KIDD on Arat. *Phaen.* 254–267 and on 265; *KlP s.v.* Pleiaden; *BNP s.v.* Pleiades; DICKS 1970, 36. — **Hyades:** the star cluster between the Pleiades and Orion, forming the head of the constellation Taurus (KIDD on Arat. *Phaen.* 167–178). In early epic, the Hyades are mentioned only here and at Hes. *Op.* 615 f. together with the Pleiades, in the latter passage explicitly as the signal for the start of plowing and of the stormy season (see above); their name is interpreted as derived from either *hýein* ('to rain'), i.e. 'rain stars', or *hŷs* ('pig'; FRISK *s.v.* Ὑάδες; KIDD on Arat. *Phaen.* 173; WEST 2007, 353 n. 46). The Hyades were interpreted *inter alia* as a sow with piglets (cf. Latin *Suculae*), as daughters of Atlas and sisters of the Pleiades (the number varying between two and seven; five names at 'Hes.' *fr.* 291 M.-W.), as nurses of Dionysos who were turned into stars by Zeus, and as the sisters of Hyas mourning their dead brother (schol. D; *KlP s.v.* Hyaden and *BNP s.v.* Hyades). — **strength of Orion:** In early epic, Orion is (1) the name of a constellation in the vicinity of both the 'Dog Star' Sirius (= 'the dog of Orion': 22.29 with DE JONG *ad loc.*) and the Pleiades, and is named together with the latter in reference to seafaring (*Od.* 5.274, Hes. *Op.* 619) and agriculture (Hes. *Op.* 598, 615; see above); the first appearance of the constellation (its so-called heliacal rising *ca.* June 20) signals the time for threshing and winnowing grain (Hes. *Op.* 597–611): WEST on Hes. *Op.* 598 and 615; KIDD on Arat. *Phaen.* 322–325; (2) a mythical hunter of gigantic stature (*Od.* 11.572–575, cf. 11.309 f.) who was killed by Artemis (5.121–124) and turned into a star, according to post-Homeric sources (*KlP* and *BNP s.v.* Orion). The formulation 'the strength of Orion', a periphrastic denomination[P] similar to e.g. 'the power of Herakles' (see below), probably alludes to the mythical character of the hunter, as does the remark regarding the constellation 'the Bear' at 488 (see *ad loc.*; BUCHHOLZ 1871, 37; KOPP 1939, 195).

Πληϊάδας: an epic-Ionic form, Attic Πλειάδες, also transmitted as Πελειάδες 'doves' as the result of an interpretation in accord with folk etymology ('Hes.' *fr.* 288–290 M.-W.); sometimes connected with πλέ(ϝ)ω, but the etymology is unknown, as is the reason for the coexistence of Πλει- and Πληϊ- (FRISK and *DELG s.v.* Πλειάδες; *LfgrE s.vv.* Πληϊάδες and πέλεια; KIDD on Arat. *Phaen.* 254–267; WYATT 1969, 189). — σθένος Ὠρίωνος:

likewise at VE at Hes. *Op.* 598, 615 and in an expanded version at 619. The paraphrase is comparable to the combination 'genitive of a personal name + βίη' (117n.) or μένος (16.189n.), see μέγα σθένος Ἰδομενῆος (13.248, 'Hes.' *fr.* 204.56 M.-W.), Ἠετίωνος (*Il.* 23.827), Ὠκεανοῖο (607, 21.195): *LfgrE s.v.* σθένος; on the etymology of Ὠρίων (a contracted form of Ὠαρίων attested in later poetry; the ι is metrically lengthened), see *LfgrE s.v.*

487–489 = *Od.* 5.273–275. — The constellation 'the Bear' (*Árktos*) is mentioned elsewhere in early epic only in the *Odyssey*, where it helps Odysseus steer during his journey on the raft. It is associated with the story of Kallisto, daughter of Lykaon of Arcadia, a hunting partner of Artemis, who according to myth was seduced by Zeus, turned into a bear by Artemis and ultimately changed into a star by Zeus ('Hes.' *fr.* 163 M.-W.; for additional sources and the various versions of the myth, *BNP s.v.* Callisto). The reference probably is to the constellation 'the Great Bear' (standard astronomical name Ursa Major), visible year round in the northern sky in the vicinity of the North Star, whose seven brightest stars are also known as the 'Big Dipper' (British English 'Plough'; German and other languages '(Big) Wagon'; Latin *Septentriones*), see 487 with n.; according to ancient sources, the constellation 'the Little Bear' was first named by Thales of Miletus (schol. D on 487; *LfgrE s.v.* ἄρκτος; HAINSWORTH on *Od.* 5.272–277; BUCHHOLZ 1871, 38 f.; FINKELBERG 2004, 231–233), but on issues with the identification, 488–489n.

The fact that these verses are identical with *Od.* 5.273–275 led to discussion concerning which passage was older and thus served as the model for the other (e.g. USENER 1990, 119–122 [*Iliad*]; BLÖSSNER 1991, 63–66 [*Odyssey*], with older bibliography *loc. cit.* 66 n. 255). But the explanations regarding the characteristics of the constellation could also derive from an earlier epic tradition adopted into lists of constellations matching the relevant context – agriculture or navigation (HAINSWORTH on *Od.* 5.272–277; DANEK 1998, 128 f.; cf. 485–489n.).

487 give also the name of ...: a formulaic phrase in which the narrator presents a second designation citing 'anonymous spokesmen', whereby he creates a link to the present moment of the audience, note also the present tense forms 'turns', 'observes secretly' and 'participates' at 488 f. (24.316n.; DE JONG on *Od.* 5.273).

Ἄρκτον ... Ἅμαξαν: ἄρκτος is related to the designation for 'bear' attested also in other I-E languages and was also used, probably as an inherited term (WEST 2007, 351 f.), as the name of the constellation in Sanskrit (masc. pl. ŕkṣāḥ); Greek sometimes uses the by-form ἄρκος, albeit not in reference to the constellation (SCHERER 1953, 131–134; BEEKES *s.v.* ἄρκτος; see also *ChronEG* 5 *s.v.*). The designation of the constellation as 'Wagon' is presumably adopted from Babylonian: GIŠ.MAR.GÍD.DA, Akkadian *eriq(q)u*

---

487 καλέουσιν: '(people) call it, it is called' (↑); on the uncontracted form, R 6.

('wagon, heavy transport wagon') is the 'Great Wagon' (SCHERER *loc. cit.* 139; WENSKUS 1990, 21; HUNGER/PINGREE 1999, 68; WEST *loc. cit.*; cf. *CAD s.v. eriqqu*, esp. p. 297). An adaptation of *eriq(q)u* via folk etymology has thus been taken to be the explanation for the name of the constellation Ἄρκτος/Ἄρκος (SZEMERÉNYI 1962, 191 f.; HAINSWORTH on *Od.* 5.273; KIDD on Arat. *Phaen.* 27), although 'Bear' is not attested for the constellation in the Ancient Near East. On the smooth breathing on ἄμαξα, WEST 1998, XVII. — **ἐπίκλησιν καλέουσιν:** a variable VE formula (likewise at 22.29, 22.506, *Od.* 5.273, Hes. *Th.* 207, with the words separated at *Il.* 7.138 f.); ἐπίκλησις is used in early epic only in the adverbial acc., usually meaning 'a secondary or informal name' (*LfgrE s.v.*; CHANTR. 2.48).

488–489 Observable particularities of 'the Bear' in comparison to other constellations: (1) 'it observes Orion' indicates both the position of the two constellations in the northern sky, with the head of Ursa Major pointing toward Orion, and their mythological background, in that the hunter Orion appears together with animals also in descriptions of the underworld, cf. *Od.* 11.572 f. (EDWARDS on 487–489; BUCHHOLZ 1871, 37 f.; with a more far-reaching interpretation, NAGY [1979] 1999, 202; 1990, 253); the relative positions of the constellations are elsewhere repeatedly described as 'flight' and 'pursuit' (WEST on Hes. *Op.* 620; KIDD on Arat. *Phaen.* 322–325); (2) it turns in one place – the constellation is later also known as *Helíkē* 'the one who turns' (SCHERER 1953, 133; KIDD on Arat. *Phaen.* 37) – and (3) it is the only constellation not to descend into Okeanos, i.e.: the constellation found in the vicinity of the North Star at no point disappears from the horizon, but remains visible year round – in contrast to the others listed. Homer's knowledge of constellations has been the subject of critical comment since antiquity, since (2) and (3) also apply to other constellations, most notably Ursa Minor, so that the formulation 'she alone never plunged' was perceived as problematic ('she alone' [*óiē*] in reference to 'all' [*pánta*] at 485 would be factually incorrect). There has thus been repeated discussion of the extent to which Homer's description matches the constellations Ursa Major or Ursa Minor or whether he is in fact subsuming several or indeed all circumpolar constellations under the term *Arktos* (CERRI; BUCHHOLZ 1871, 38 f.; KOPP 1939, 200; SCHMIDT 1976, 147–151; FINKELBERG 2004, esp. 233 f., 237–239, 242). But the statement 'alone' is suitable and unproblematic with regard to the constellations *mentioned by name* (schol. bT on 489 [with ERBSE *ad loc.*]; HAINSWORTH on *Od.* 5.275; DICKS 1970, 31; RADT 2006, 52 f. [on 23–36]). — **the wash of the Ocean:** The appearance and disappearance of heavenly bodies at the horizon is described as diving into and

---

488 τ(ε): 2× 'epic τε' (R 24.11). — αὐτοῦ: adv., 'on the spot, in the very place'.
489 οἴη: 'alone, is the only one who'. — Ὠκεανοῖο: on the declension, R 11.2.

emerging from Okeanos, which flows around the disk of the earth as a circular stream (399n.; HAINSWORTH on *Od.* 5.275); 'the harvest star' (Sirius) and the goddess of the moon Selene thus shine forth after bathing in Okeanos (*Il.* 5.6, *h.Hom.* 32.7 f.), of the sun, cf. *Il.* 7.422 f., 8.485, *Od.* 3.1 (*LfgrE s.v.* Ὠκεανός; on I-E parallels, WEST 2007, 212).

ἤ τ' ... καί τ' ... | **... δ(έ):** καί and δέ have a coordinating function (likewise τε at 487), τε (488) a generalizing one (RUIJGH 672, 765; cf. 16.9n.). — **δοκεύει:** means 'observe, spy on someone' (for the right moment to act), e.g. 8.340 in a hunting simile of a dog pursuing its prey, here conversely of hunter and animal, approximately 'without losing sight of'; also of a warrior watching an opponent's movements in order to strike back at the right moment (13.545, 16.313, similarly 'Hes.' *Sc.* 333, 425), during a chariot race (*Il.* 23.325: the charioteer intently watches the man ahead), of Kronos and the hellhound waiting for possible victims (Hes. *Th.* 466, 772): *LfgrE.* — **ἄμμορος:** on the possessive compound (α privative + μόρος: 'without a share in'), 6.408n. — **λοετρῶν:** on the sound elements, 346n.

490–540 Hephaistos designs images of two cities: these display social interactions among the inhabitants that are fundamental to the continued existence and functioning of the community, namely the union of families in weddings and the prevention of strife and violence in their midst via public arbitration, i.e. processes that are embedded and instititutionally anchored within the community of the *pólis* (EDWARDS on 490–508: 'The blessings of ordered communal life'), on the one hand, while showing the joint resistance of all inhabitants of a besieged city and their actions against the attackers, on the other (the so-called 'city at peace' [491b–508] and the 'city at war' [509–540]; on the designations, cf. schol. bT on 490). These are depicted as processes in which the entire community of the relevant *pólis* participates in one way or another, with the women sometimes awarded greater emphasis (492, 495b–496) and sometimes the men (497 ff., 502 ff., 519b ff.). On the image of the *pólis* in Homeric epic and its relationship to the lived reality of the audience, RAAFLAUB 1993, 49–59; 2005, 259–261; HÖLKESKAMP 2002, 327–333; HAUBOLD 2005, 27–33; see also *LfgrE s.v.* πόλις 1349.38–1351.49. All actions are left hanging: the brides are still on their way from their parents' homes to those of the grooms', the resolution of the dispute and the outcome of the battle between the besieged and the attackers remain open. This fits with (a) the description of a work of art, (b) the impartial portrayal of the scenes as universal events that cannot be assigned to a specific group of people, comparable to similes, (c) the current situation in the action of the *Iliad* (LYNN-GEORGE 1988, 132–136; BECKER 1995, 123 f.; BUCHAN 2012, 84 f.; on incomplete actions in pictorial art, SIMON 1995, 126 f.; on the almost distant description of the 'city at war', GIULIANI 2003, 43 f.).

490–491a 1st VH of 490 ≈ 573, 587; 2nd VH of 490 = 342, 20.217. — **in all their beauty:** an emphasis on aesthetics via progressive enjambment[P] of the adjective *kālós* (on which, 19.11n.), which can refer both to the cities as such and to the visual artwork (BECKER 1995, 107 f.).

πόλις: acc. pl. (342n.) — μερόπων ἀνθρώπων: 288n. — ἐν τῇ μέν: continued at 509 τὴν δ' ἑτέρην πόλιν.

491b–496 The description of the wedding celebration highlights movement (492–493a procession, 494a dance), lighting effects (493a), sound (493b song, 495a music) and the effect on the spectators (495b–496), creating the image of a lively wedding celebration in the minds of the audience (similarly 'Hes.' *Sc.* 272–285a): BECKER 1995, 108–110. Mention is made of activities in which accompaniment by music and dance are key: the wedding processions, in which the brides, by torchlight and accompanied by wedding songs, are led through the city from their homes to the grooms' houses (the so-called *nymphagōgíai*), and the feasts that usually took place in the house of the father of the bride (*Il.* 24.63, *Od.* 4.17–19, 23.133–136): WEGNER 1968, 33. The image with occasions for creating community shows the point in time when the union of the couple, and thus of two families, is staged as a public spectacle, cf. 495 f. (WICKERT-MICKNAT 1982, 96), as well as a joint celebration (cf. *Od.* 4.3–19, esp. 15 ff.: a wedding celebration for the daughter and son of Menelaos). On feasts during weddings and as communal occasions within the *pólis*, see SCHMITT PANTEL *et al.* 2004, 233, 239 ff.; on Greek wedding customs and the sequence of events at a *gámos* in general, see SMITH 2011, 88, 90–93; on descriptions of these customs in Homeric epic, see WICKERT-MICKNAT 1982, 89–99; WEST on *Od.* 1.275–278: Homeric wedding customs as an 'amalgamation' of customs derived from various periods and places (cf. 6.117–118n.). – The plural forms 'wedding celebrations ... feasts ... brides' (*gámoi, eilapínai, nýmphas*) suggest an image with multiple celebrations, which could be interpreted as a summary depiction of weddings taking place within a community during the favored time for this activity (cf. the name of the Attic month *Gamēliṓn*; CERRI; WICKERT-MICKNAT 1982, 9) or as a linguistic signal that *one* wedding is depicted and is to be understood as a representative of the type (AH; LEAF; cf. MARG [1957] 1971, 32: 'In Archaic expression, plurality conveys the typical' [transl.]).

491b γάμοι ... εἰλαπίναι: The depicted celebrations contain the elements 'wedding ceremony' (γάμος, elsewhere also used in a more narrow sense for the wedding feast: *LfgrE*

---

490 ἐν: 483n.
491b τῇ: on the anaphoric demonstrative function of ὅ, ἥ, τό, R 17. — ῥα: = ἄρα (R 24.1). — ἔσαν: 481n.

s.v.; WICKERT-MICKNAT 1982, 95 f. with n. 535 and 538) and 'wedding feast' (εἰλαπίνη, a designation for feasts on a variety of occasions 'as a set social institution' [transl.]: *LfgrE s.v.*), cf. the juxtaposition of γάμος and εἰλαπίνη at *Od.* 1.226, 11.415; on the plural, 491b–496n.; CHANTR. 2.32.

492 ≈ *Od.* 19.48; 2nd VH = 23.290; VE ≈ *Il.* 13.341. — **νύμφας:** The etymology is unknown, and the meaning ranges from 'bride' (e.g. here, in contrast to the generic term γυναῖκες 495) to 'newlywed' and 'young woman' (*LfgrE*; WICKERT-MICKNAT 1982, 114 f.). — **θαλάμων:** the designation for a private retreat in the house ('chamber'), used *inter alia* for the women's quarters (14.166n.) or the bedroom (esp. of couples; of adult children in their parents' house, as here, also at e.g. 9.473, 9.475, *Od.* 1.425, 2.5, 7.7): 6.316n.; *LfgrE*. — **ὑπο:** here denoting the accompanying circumstances ('accompanied by'): SCHW. 2.529; CHANTR. 2.143; FRITZ 2005, 348 f.

493 2nd VH = 'Hes.' *Sc.* 274. — **bride song:** The word *hyménaios* denotes the wedding song with its ritual cry *hymḗn ō hyménaie* that accompanies the bride on her way to the groom's house and, in post-Homeric literature, the bridal song perfomed by a chorus of young women (*Hyménaios* is attested first in Pindar as the personification of the song as a wedding god); this song, perfomed when a girl leaves her family, is perhaps to be considered antiphonal, similar to the lament for the dead (*BNP s.v.* Hymenaios; WEGNER 1968, 33 f.; CALAME [1977] 1997, 83–85; WEST 1992, 21 f.; TSAGALIS 2004, 82–85; PAPADOPOULOU 2011, 415–417). Other songs mentioned in Homeric epic in conjunction with a rite are the paean (song for Apollo: 1.473n.; song of victory: DE JONG on *Il.* 22.391–4), the *thrḗnos* (dirge: 24.720b–722n.) and the Linos-song (570n.), in addition to girls' choruses in the context of the cult for Artemis (16.183n.): WEGNER 1968, 32–35; DALBY 1998, esp. 196–205.

ἡγίνεον: an intensive form related to ἄγω ('escort, accompany'), here describing the procession accompanying the bride, elsewhere often used to denote repeated actions, e.g. 24.784, *Od.* 10.104, 14.105 (but see the *iteratum* 'Hes.' *Sc.* 274 ἤγοντ' ἀνδρὶ γυναῖκα): *LfgrE s.v.* ἀγινέω; on the mid. ἄγεσθαι meaning 'wed', *LfgrE s.v.* ἄγω 121.30 ff. — **ἄστυ:** 255n. — **πολὺς δ' ὑμέναιος ὀρώρει:** a variation of the formula πολὺς δ' ὀρυμαγδὸς ὀρώρει (4× *Il.*, 1× *Od.*, 1× 'Hes.': 2.810n.). πολύς ('many[fold]': *LfgrE s.v.* 1413.7 ff.) denotes the intensity of the songs due to the number of singers (KAIMIO 1977, 32) and the much-repeated cries of joy (GRANDOLINI 1996, 60). ὑμέναιος – attested in early epic only here and in the *iteratum*, later in lyric and tragic poets (LSJ *s.v.*) – is derived from ὑμήν, the ritual wedding cry itself, the etymology of which is disputed (*DELG, ChronEG* 5 and BEEKES *s.v.* ὑμήν).

---

492 δαΐδων ὕπο: = ὑπὸ δαΐδων (R 20.2). — λαμπομενάων: on the declension, R 11.1.
493 ἡγίνεον(ν) ἀνά: on the prosody, M 4.6; on the uncontracted form, R 6; on the synizesis, R 7. — ἀνὰ (ϝ)άστυ: 'across town'; on the prosody, R 4.3. — ὀρώρει: 3rd pers. sing. plpf. of ὄρνυμαι 'arise, emerge' (on the unaugmented form, R 16.1).

494 young men ... dance: Youthful dancers also occur in the wedding celebrations in the house of Menelaos (*Od.* 4.17–19; see also 23.133 f.); they occur in additional scenes on Achilleus' shield during the harvest in the vineyard (*Il.* 567–572) and in the final scene on the dancing ground (593 f., 599–606; on which, 593–602n.). The dance performances during the games organized by Alkinoös, king of the Phaiakians, after the feast are described in detail (*Od.* 8.256–265, 8.370–380; on this, Bierl 2012a, 122 f.). For literary sources and pictorial depictions of dance, see Tölle 1964, 54–86, esp. 80 ff.; Wegner 1968, 40–68 (esp. 40 f. and 60–65 on groups of dancing men); Shapiro *et al.* 2004, 301–303, 312–314; *HE s.v.* 'Dance'; for additional bibliography on 'dance', see *LfgrE s.v.* χορός.

κοῦροι δ' ὀρχηστῆρες: The second term clarifies the first, cf. the combination of generic and functional terms at 17.726 κούρων θηρητήρων, 24.347 κούρῳ αἰσυιητῆρι (on the phenomenon in general, 2.474n.); on κοῦροι as dancers, see *Od.* 8.262–264. ὀρχηστήρ (more commonly ὀρχηστής) is a *nomen agentis* related to ὀρχέομαι 'dance, move in the manner of a dancer'; the etymology is uncertain (for the hypotheses, Beekes *s.v.* ὀρχέομαι; on the suffix -τήρ, Risch 28–30; Chantraine 1933, 322 f.; on the usage of the word group ὀρχε-, *LfgrE s.vv.* ὀρχέομαι and ὀρχηστής; Wegner 1968, 40–42). – ἐδίνεον: a derivation from δίνη 'whirl, vortex'; it is used both transitively (19.268n.) and intransitively, here meaning either 'turn (around one's own axis), whirl about', cf. 605 f. (= *Od.* 4.18 f.) of two acrobats (*LfgrE s.v.* δινέω; Wegner 1968, 43), or of movement in a circle (Tölle 1964, 59; Kurz 1966, 136 f.); on this, see Naerebout 1997, 282 n. 653: '*din-* refers to circular movement around a fixed point describing a circuit of *any size*, down to turning on the spot'.

495a flutes ... lyres: The wind instrument consisting of two tubes (plural *auloí*) is mentioned elsewhere in early epic only at 10.13 (in addition to Pan flutes: music in the Trojan camp) and at *h.Merc.* 452; on the origin and form, Wegner 1968, 19–22; West 1992, 81–107; *BNP s.v.* Musical instruments. – In the *Iliad*, the *phórminx* is linked to Apollo (1.603, 24.63 [wedding of Peleus and Thetis]) and Achilleus (9.186/194); it is used to provide accompaniment for singers (see 569 f., 9.189, *Od.* 1.155 f. and 22.332 ff. Phemios, 8.67 ff. and 261 ff. Demodokos) and during dancing (*Il.* 18.569 ff., *Od.* 4.18 ff., 8.248 ff., 23.133 ff.); on the different types of string instruments (including *phórminx, kítharis*), 1.603n.; *LfgrE s.v.* φόρμιγξ (both with bibliography); Schuol 2006, 143–146; Hagel 2008.

βοὴν ἔχον: a periphrasis for 'sounded', cf. καναχὴν ἔχειν at 16.105 and 16.794 (metal of a helmet), *h.Ap.* 185 (φόρμιγξ): 16.104–105n.; it denotes a persistent sound (LSJ *s.v.* ἔχω; Krapp 1964, 203; differently Buchan 2012, 84: it denotes a sound 'frozen' in pictorial

---

494 τοῖσιν: anaphoric, referring to κοῦροι (R 17); on the declension, R 11.2.

representation). βοή is used only here in early epic of a musical instrument, elsewhere of human shouts and cries (*LfgrE s.v.*).

495b–496 in the meantime | the women ... admired them: The narrator repeatedly highlights impressive aspects by mentioning spectators (e.g. at 497, 603 f.) or even by assigning them emotions, as here (admiration), much in the same way that – according to Hephaistos' announcement – the observer will marvel at the work of art being made, see 466 f. (with n.; AREND 1933, 147). The women of the city as admiring spectators point to the presentations of song, accompanying instruments and dance as a unified spectacle that is part of the character of the celebration (WICKERT-MICKNAT 1982, 30 f.; PRIER 1989, 86 f.; BECKER 1995, 109 f.; GRANDOLINI 1996, 60; differently LEAF p. 608 and SMITH 2011, 93: the reference is specifically to the mothers of the grooms, who await the brides at their doors).

αἱ δὲ γυναῖκες: likewise at 559, *Od.* 11.225, 20.161; on the appearance of new characters after caesura C 2, 1.194n. — προθύροισιν: πρόθυρον denotes the area of a door or gate (24.323n.), here the entrance area with a view across the public space of the street (ROUGIER-BLANC 2005, 123 f.).

497–508 In the context of the so-called 'trial scene', the narrator[P] lists the characters (497 f., 503 f.) and objects (505, 507) depicted and provides an explanation of the situation by describing the occasion (497b–499a), the – imaginary – statements by the characters (499b–500 [indirect speeches], 502 [noisy involvement by the public], 506b [verdicts]) and their intentions to act (501, 506, 508) – as can be deduced from the situation – conjuring up an extremely lively scene in the mind of the audience (DE JONG [1987] 2004, 118; LYNN-GEORGE 1988, 182–184; PELLICCIA 1992, 91 f.; BECKER 1995, 111–113; PALMISCIANO 2010, 53 f.; cf. 478–608n. section **B.3.**, on the *enárgeia* of the ekphrasis). The function of certain characters and the course of the proceedings, which were surely familiar to the contemporary audience, are only alluded to, leading to varying interpretations. The following is evident: people are gathered in the marketplace, where a dispute between two men regarding compensation payments for the killing of a man is playing out; one man addresses the people concerning payment, the other concerning acceptance of the compensation (497–500); the people noisily support one side or the other, and the heralds keep order (502 f.). The arbitration of the dispute somehow involves a *hístōr* and a group of *gérontes* (sitting in a circle). These deliver a verdict one by one, in as much as they are in competition, since a prize has been set (503b–508); the outcome of the legal dispute remains open. But much is disputed concerning the legal matter and the course of the proceedings: (1) What is the contentious issue (498–501n.)? (2) What is the function of (a) the *hístōr* (501n.), (b) the *géron*-

tes (502–503n.), (c) the people? In particular: who judges the competition and thus the dispute (506–508n.)? (3) Who provides the two talents of gold as prize money (506–508n.)? A summary of the issues of legal history: THÜR 2007, 183–186. – It is worth noting that here the compensation for a killing is not negotiated as a purely private matter (thus e.g. at *Od.* 13.258 ff., 15.272 ff.) but rather as a public dispute (see 497a, 500a), with the opposing parties prepared to accept arbitration of the dispute (501), and that there is an orderly procedure for it (503–505) in which different suggestions for resolving the issue are presented and weighed against one another in a competitive fashion (506, 508): TAPLIN (1980) 2001, 349 ('the stable justice of a civilized city'); HÖLKESKAMP 1997, 10 f.; 2002, 315–318; GAGARIN 2008, 15 f.; SCODEL 2008, 86–92; for comparison with the course of other civil or military assemblies (on which, 1.54n.), see VAN WEES 1992, 34 ff. – Although the 'trial scene' described can hardly be imagined as an actual pictorial representation (HEFFERNAN 1993, 13; BECKER *loc. cit.* 113; see also 478–608n. section **B.2.a.**), it has been suggested that these images be viewed as a frieze-like sequence or 'episodic' form (STANSBURY-O'DONNELL 1995, 322–324; cf. FITTSCHEN 1973, 12 f. on verses 510 ff.): image (1) dispute (497–503a), image (2) trial in the presence of the *gérontes* (503b–508): LEAF p. 607 f.; EDWARDS on 501; somewhat differently, WIRBELAUER 1996, 158, 162–167: two independent images with different kinds of arbitration, namely via the *hístōr* (497–503a) and via the group of *gérontes* (503b–508).

497 market place: The *agoré*, literally 'assembly place' (cf. 274), is also a place of public administration of justice with an audience (16.387n.), see 11.806 f., 16.387 (simile), *Od.* 12.439 f. (comparison), Hes. *Op.* 28 ff., *Th.* 84 ff.

λαοί: λαός is a term for 'people' attested already in Mycenaean. 'The plural λαοί denotes a multitude of persons who belong together [...]; the sing. λαός, by contrast, stresses the collective whole': 24.1n.; in the *Iliad*, the word frequently denotes, because of the context, 'the (male) people at arms', in the plural 'warriors' (in what follows, see 509, 519, 523 [1.10n.]). In the present passage, it is the (male) people assembled, namely (a) in the pl. as subj. (λαοί here and at 502), i.e. the two parties consisting of a multitude of men and (b) in the sing. as obj. (λαόν 503), i.e. as an undifferentiated (noisy) crowd as a whole; (c) δῆμος (500n.) designates the (administrative and legal) collective of city residents, who are addressed by the parties in the dispute (CASEWITZ 1992, 198). — **νεῖκος:** 'dispute, verbal confrontation', here as at *Od.* 12.440, Hes. *Th.* 87 and *Op.* 29 ff. a legal dispute (*LfgrE*). νεῖκος, here with ὠρώρει in integral enjambment[p], is elsewhere combined with ὄρωρε in a variable VE formula (9× *Il.*, 3× *Od.*: 3.87n.).

---

497 εἰν: = ἐν (R 20.1). — ἀγορῇ ἔσαν: on the hiatus, R 5.6; on ἔσαν, 481n.

498–501 After someone has been killed, the victim's relatives are entitled to blood revenge (e.g. *Od.* 3.196–198); the perpetrator can evade this through exile (e.g. 15.272–276; on Patroklos, see 326n.) or can buy his life via the payment of blood money (*Il.* 9.632–636): 24.480–484n. In the depicted dispute over compensation for a killing, the two opposing parties are mentioned first, namely (A) the perpetrator or his representative and (B) a representative of the victim's family, in addition to a *hístōr*. Due to linguistic ambiguities (esp. 499 f.), there are two fundamentally divergent interpretations of the dispute (bibliography of the discussion: AH, *Anh.* p. 162; EDWARDS on 497–508 and 498–500; HOMMEL 1969, 11 f. n. 1–5; WESTBROOK 1992, 54 f. n. 3–4; JANIK 2000, 9–14; also 499n., 500n.): (1) an argument regarding whether or not the accused has already paid compensation (*quaestio facti*), i.e. (A) claims to have paid in full, (B) denies having received anything; the court of arbitration is concerned with the presentation of evidence (schol. bT on 497–498 and 499–500, schol. D on 497; AH *ad loc.* and *Anh.* p. 162; WILLCOCK; CERRI on 499b–500; WOLFF 1946, 36 f.; 1961, 32 f.; HOMMEL 1969; PRIMMER 1970, 11–13; THÜR 1996; 2007, 187–190; TAUSEND 2001; CANTARELLA 2005; PELLOSO 2012, 112–115 with n. 24, 127 f. n. 62; somewhat differently, JANIK *loc. cit.* 15: a price has been determined for reparations but has not yet been paid, perhaps because the family affected suddenly asks for more than the perpetrator is prepared to pay; (2) a confrontation centering on whether the family affected is obliged to accept material compensation or whether they may refuse it and insist on actual revenge, i.e. the killing of the perpetrator (*quaestio iuris*), i.e. (A) insists on satisfying all claims via payment of compensation, (B) refuses to accept blood money, i.e. insists on affecting revenge; the court is meant to mediate between the two or even decide which redress (blood money or revenge) is appropriate for the killing (LEAF p. 610–612; EDWARDS on 498–500 [following WESTBROOK 1992]; *LfgrE s.v.* ποινή; PFLÜGER 1942; BENVENISTE 1969, 240–242; ANDERSEN 1976, 12–14; WESTBROOK 1992 [with a more far-reaching interpretation: a decision regarding the amount of compensation based on an assessment of the killing as deliberate or not]; VAN WEES 1992, 370 n. 143; SCHEID-TISSINIER 1994a, 201 ff.; 2011, 59–61; WIRBELAUER 1996, 157 f.; NAGY [1997] 2003, 72–82; PRIMAVESI 2002, 199 f.; cautiously, WILSON 2002, 159–161). On the function of the *gérontes* being in competition, see 506–508n. Linguistically, both interpretations are possible (HOMMEL *loc. cit.* 15 f.; see 499n., 500n.), but factually objections can be raised against both: to (1), that a public hearing, with impassioned partisanship by those present, regarding whether (complete) payment had been made or not seems hardly plausible, since such a payment would surely have been made in the presence of witnesses, who are not summoned here unless 500a is read this way (LEAF; KÖSTLER [1946] 1950, 67 f.; SCHEID-TISSINIER 2011, 60 f.; ELMER

2013, 183); to (2), that there is no entitlement to material recompensation and thus no reason for a public dispute with a verdict by a court of arbitration, should the victim's family want to exact blood revenge (CERRI; HOMMEL *loc. cit.* 16; CARLIER 1984, 175 n. 179; CANTARELLA 2005, 342 f.). Taking into account possible links to the action of the *Iliad*, there is much to be said for interpretation (2); this offers a closer connection to the conflict situations and to the willingness of the opponants to reconcile in the action of the *Iliad*: (a) regarding the refusal of material compensation in Books 1 and 9, it becomes evident that this offer to restore honor need not be accepted automatically, but can be refused – contrary to Aias' suggestion at 9.632 f. – (see also 7.381–404), except in cases with religious counter-arguments (as in that of the priest Chryses); (b) regarding Achilleus' current situation, namely his as yet unresolved argument with Agamemnon and his thirst for vengeance on Hektor, preparation for the possibility of a settlement can be glimpsed (in the subsequent Book 19, Achilleus will end the strife), as can a readiness to reconcile with the father of his slain enemy (in Book 24, Achilleus will accept Priam's ransom for the body of Hektor): EDWARDS; ANDERSEN *loc. cit.* 14–16; MACDOWELL 1978, 20; VAN WEES *loc. cit.* 370 n. 143; LOWENSTAM 1993, 100–103; NAGY *loc. cit.* 82–87; ALDEN 2000, 55–60 (esp. 56 n. 23); PRIMAVESI *loc. cit.* 200 f.; SCODEL 2008, 88, 92; ELMER *loc. cit.* 129 f., 183–187).

498 ἐνείκεον: an epexegetic repetition of the word stem νεικ- (497) denoting verbal confrontations (*LfgrE*), the contents of which are laid out in 499b and 500b via parallel structures (*Parison*): FEHLING 1969, 165, 323. — **ποινῆς:** a designation for 'compensation' in both material and concrete form (3.290n.: 'penalty' or 'revenge'; WILSON 2002, 61 ff.; SCODEL 2008, 75–93).

499 ηὔχετο πάντ' ἀποδοῦναι: εὔχομαι means 'provide official information regarding oneself' (6.211n.), on the one hand, and is used to denote the act of swearing an oath, on the other (3.296n.; thus THÜR 2007, 189–191: 'was prepared to swear' [transl.]), and is used only here in Homeric epic in a legal context, i.e. approximately 'claim' (MUELLNER 1976, 53–66, 98 f., 100–106). Since the aor. inf. does not necessarily have a temporal meaning (3.28n. *s.v.* τείσασθαι; CHANTR. 2.307 ff.; cf. RIJKSBARON [1984] 2002, 109) and thus can refer to both past and future action, the statement can be rendered in two basic ways (CORLU 1966, 331–336; for discussion of the content, 498–501n.): 'he claimed to have given' (REYNEN 1983, 122–124; PELLOSO 2012, 127 n. 62) or 'he claimed to give', i.e. 'to be willing to give' (PFLÜGER 1942, 141–144; CORLU *loc. cit.* 334–336; PERPILLOU 1972, 178 f.; MUELLNER *loc. cit.*, 102–106 [both with reference to the comparable use of εὔχομαι

---

498 ὠρώρει: 'had erupted, reigned' (493n.). — εἵνεκα: initial syllable metrically lengthened (R 10.1).
499 ἀποφθιμένου. ὅ: on the hiatus, R 5.5.

in Mycenaean tablets from Pylos: PY Ep 704, Eb 297, see *DMic s.v. e-u-ke-to-qe*]; AUBRIOT-SÉVIN 1992, 203–207; WESTBROOK 1992, 73 f.: 'is claiming the right to pay the ransom (ποινή) in full (πάντα)'; cautiously, CHANTR. 2.310 and 2.335 n. 1).

500 δήμῳ: denotes both the territory of a community and its inhabitants ('population'), see e.g. 3.50 (see *ad loc.*; 1.10n., 2.198n.), and is attested already in Mycenaean as a term for local administrative units as well as legal collectives (*DMic. s.v. da-mo*); in the present passage and at 295 (see *ad loc.*), it denotes the participants in an assembly whose assent is being competed for, i.e. it highlights the public nature of the process (HÖLKESKAMP 2002, 317; cf. 497n.). — **πιφαύσκων:** a reduplicated σκ- pres., related to the same root as φάος (< φαϝ-), which here carries the causal meaning 'make shine, illuminate'; it is frequently combined with expressions of speaking, in which case it means 'clarify, expound', see esp. 10.202, 21.99, *Od.* 11.442 f., 12.165 (*LfgrE s.v.*; *DELG s.v.* φάε; MUELLNER 1976, 104 f.). — **ἀναίνετο μηδὲν ἑλέσθαι:** Three issues are disputed in the interpretation of this phrase: (1) in early epic, ἀναίνομαι (a) usually means 'refuse' (with an inf. also at 450, 23.204) or 'reject someone/something, decline', (b) occasionally means also 'deny something' (9.116 absolutely, *Od.* 14.149 f. with acc./inf.: ἀναίνεαι οὐδ' ἔτι φῇσθα | κεῖνον ἐλεύσεσθαι): *LfgrE s.v.* ἀναίνομαι; (2) the negative μηδέν (rather than οὐδέν) is either (a) interpreted as a reference to a statement of intent (LEAF) or (b) explained with reference to the formulation of an oath (WILLCOCK; cf. 19.261n.); (3) as at 499 (see *ad loc.*), the aor. inf. can denote either (a) future or (b) past actions. This results in two understandings of the phrase corresponding to the two interpretations of the scene as a whole listed at 498–501n., namely (a) 'he refused to accept something' (thus *LfgrE s.v.* αἱρέω 359.27 ff. [with reference to *Il.* 9.679]; CHANTR. 2.235 f. n. 1; CORLU 1966, 332 f.; MUELLNER *loc. cit.* 105 f.; ELMER 2013, 184 f.: ἀναίνομαι as 'the negation of socially constructive speech') or (b) 'he denied having accepted anything'; on a pleonastic negative after a negative term, see CHANTR. 2.335; SCHW. 2.598. Linguistically, interpretation (a) – and thus interpretation (2) at 498–501n. – seems somewhat more plausible. – ἑλέσθαι is a unique expression for accepting ποινή (and ἄποινα), elsewhere δέχομαι is used (for examples, MUELLNER *loc. cit.* 102 n. 11; on the vocabulary, also WILSON 2002, 22–25).

501 1st VH ≈ *Od.* 3.344. — **arbitrator:** The noun *hístōr* is a *nomen agentis* (**wid-tōr*) related to *oída/ísmen* ('know') and means literally 'one who (has seen and thus) knows; knowledgeable one, expert' (*DELG s.v.* οἶδα; FRISK and BEEKES *s.v.* ἵστωρ; differently, FLOYD 1990). In the present passage, it is not used with the meaning 'witness' (thus schol. bT; SCHUBERT 2000, 56; CANTARELLA 2005, 343; on this usage of *hístōr*, which is attested only in post-Homeric texts, see LEUMANN 1950, 277 f.; SCHEID-TISSINIER 1994a, 189 ff.), but rather of an 'expert' appearing as an 'adjudicator' (*LfgrE*; BENVENISTE 1969, 174 f.), perhaps one versed in mediation (EDWARDS: '«one who sees and knows ⟨what is right⟩»',

---

500 μηδέν: 'something' (↑).
501 ἱέσθην: 3rd pers. dual impf. of ἵεμαι 'desire'. — ἐπὶ (ϝ)ίστορι: on the hiatus, R 5.4. — ἐπί: 'by'.

or perhaps [...] «one familiar with the facts»'; SCHADEWALDT [1938] 1965, 483 n. 2; WIRBELAUER 1996, 159–161). The only other example in the *Iliad* (23.486) is when Agamemnon is appointed *hístōr* after two competitors in the chariot race get into an argument (and want to enter into a type of bet) over who is ahead and will win; as a figure of authority and an 'expert, adjudicator', he is supposed to clarify who the winner is; additional examples in early epic are Hes. *Op.* 792 (*hístora phôta* 'a knowledgeable man') and *h.Hom.* 32.2 (*hístores ōdês* as a designation for the Muses). In the present passage, there also are two arguing parties seeking a solution with the help of a *hístōr*, but neither his actual function nor his relationship to the group of *gérontes* ('elders') at 503 ff. is described, and both are accordingly disputed: he is either one of them or an authority figure advised by them (EDWARDS; HOMMEL 1969, 17–25; see also 506–508n.). *hístōr* is thus interpreted as a designation for (a) that member of the group of *gérontes* whose verdict over the course of the competition (506–508) is considered the best by the crowd and/or by the parties to the argument (PFLÜGER 1942, 148; WOLFF 1946, 37–40; MACDOWELL 1978, 20 f.; WESTBROOK 1992, 75 n. 69; SCHEID-TISSINIER 1994a, 206 f.; NAGY [1997] 2003, 85 f.; RUZÉ 1997, 92), (b) the committee's chairman, who hears the verdicts of the *gérontes* and as an 'adjudicator' determines the best one on the basis of the pleas of the two parties (AH; SCHADEWALDT [1938] 1965, 482 f. n. 2; HOMMEL *loc. cit.* 17–32, esp. 26 ff.; CARLIER 1984, 176; CERRI), or (c) the president of the court, who is not involved in the verdict (KÖSTLER [1946] 1950, 70–72), or the guarantor and guardian of the proceedings (THÜR 1996, 68 ff. [with reference to an oath]). A different approach to interpretation is advocated by WIRBELAUER 1996, 161 f. and 166–168: 501–508 show two distinct arbitration proceedings following different procedures, the one administered by an 'expert' (*hístōr*), the other by an advisory committee of 'elders' (*gérontes*). — **decision:** The original meaning of *peírar* is unclear; in early epic it means (1) 'boundary' (always in the pl., esp. of the edges of the earth), metaphorically 'destination, end', (2) 'cord, (end of a) rope', metaphorically 'fate' (*LfgrE*; cf. 6.143n.). In the present passage, meaning (1) is to be assumed, but in addition various nuances are presumed for *peírar helésthai*: (a) 'receive the verdict', i.e. reach the goal and conclude the argument (*LfgrE s.v.* πεῖραρ; AH; KÖSTLER [1946] 1950, 70); (b) 'receive the concluding verdict and thus the binding decision regarding compensation payments', i.e. *peírar* 'both in the sense of a terminus and of a «determination»' (BERGREN 1975, 43–45 [quotation p. 45]); (c) 'have a limit imposed', i.e. the upper limit to the compensation, be it in the form of blood vengeance or blood money (EDWARDS on 498–500 and 501; WESTBROOK 1992, 75 f.; ELMER 2013, 186).

502–503 Much as in the assembly scenes (cf. the military assemblies at 1.22 f. and 2.97), the heralds provide order and space to allow the consultation to proceed; on the 'heralds" function of providing order within the assembly, 1.54n., 2.50–52n., cf. 19.79–84n., end; on the use of *erḗtyein* (conative in the pres. stem) 'halt', 2.75n. The designation for the members of the advisory committee, *gérontes*, is a technical term for members of the elite serving on the council, who are also sometimes called *basilḗes* (2.53 f./86): 1.144n., 2.53n.; SCHULZ 2011, 9 ff.; cf. 448b–449n.

λαοὶ … | … λαόν: 497n. — ἐπήπυον: ἠπύω means literally 'produce a sound', transitive 'call someone' (*Od.* 9.399, 10.83: *LfgrE s.v.*), with ἐπ- (meaning 'toward': SCHW. 2.466) 'call out (approvingly) to someone', like ἐπ-ευφήμησαν at 1.22 (see *ad loc.*). — ἀμφὶς ἀρωγοί: 'both sides as helpers', i.e. one side supporting one party, the other side the other (AH). ἀμφίς is a metrically convenient by-form of ἀμφί (SCHW. 1.405). — οἱ δὲ γέροντες: 495b–496n.

504 The *gérontes* sitting on specially prepared ('polished') stone seats arranged in a circle (*kýklos*) can be interpreted as a signal of the special significance of this council of elders, as well as of its institutional status (GSCHNITZER 1983, 155 f.; SCHULZ 2011, 41 f.); for archaeological discussion regarding the *kýklos*, see VENERI 1984, esp. 354 ff.; LONGO 2010; for structuring an *agorḗ* with rows of stone seats (likewise at *Od.* 8.6), 1.54n., 2.99n.; HÖLKESKAMP 2002, 320. — **sacred:** The epithet 'sacred' (*hierós*) marks the sphere of law and administration of justice under the protection of Zeus and Themis (1.238–239n.), as well as the location where these are practiced, cf. the designation of the threshing floor as 'sacred' at 5.499–501 (LEAF; EDWARDS; *LfgrE s.v.* ἱερός 1141.52 ff.); on the identification of an office as 'sacred', 24.681n.

εἵατ(ο): on the spelling εἵ- (rather than ἥ-), 2.137n. — ξεστοῖσι: 'smoothed, polished'; an epithet of objects made from wood or stone, of stone seats also at *Od.* 3.406, 8.6 (*LfgrE*).

505 In public assemblies, the speakers hold a staff (*skḗptron*) in their hands (1.54n., 2.278b–279n.) – it is sometimes said explicitly that a herald signals the right to speak by handing it over (cf. 23.567 f., *Od.* 2.37 f.) – particularly speakers administering justice (11.568–571). It is unclear whether a single 'public' staff is handed to each speaker in turn (in which case the pl. here is analogous to the gen. pl. *kērýkōn*: LEAF; CARLIER 1984, 191 n. 255; WIRBELAUER 1996, 165; BUCHHOLZ 2012, 261) or whether each dignitary carries a staff fitting his sta-

---

504 εἵατ(ο): = ἧντο, 3rd pers. pl. plpf. (≈ impf.) of ἧμαι (on the ending, R 16.2). — ἱερῷ ἐνί: on the bridging of hiatus by non-syllabic ι (*hierōy enî*), M 12.2. — ἐνί: = ἐν (R 20.1).
505 ἔχον: on the unaugmented form, R 16.1.

tus as a sign of his authority, cf. Agamemnon's personal *sképtron* at *Il.* 2.101 ff. (*LfgrE s.v.* σκῆπτρον 147.23 ff., esp. 40 ff.: here the staffs maintained by the *pólis* heralds are handed to the *gérontes* on this occasion; MacDowell 1978, 20; Schulz 2011, 72 f.; additional bibliography: 1.234n.; *LfgrE s.v.* σκῆπτρον 146.23 ff.; cf. West on *Od.* 2.37). That the formulation 'is subject to the requirements of the imagery' (Wirbelauer *loc. cit.* 165 n. 83 [transl.]) cannot be ruled out: all *gérontes* are visible with a staff in their hands at the same time, but are to be thought of as acting successively. — **who lift their voices:** The etymology of the adj. *ēeró-phōnos* is not entirely clear (see below), but it does clearly refer to the power of the heralds' voices, a basic precondition for their office (cf. their distinctive epithet[P] *ligý-phthongos* 'clear-voiced': 2.50n.).

ἠεροφώνων: a *hapax legomenon*[P]; the initial element is disputed: either ἠερο- related to ἀήρ 'fog, air' (e.g. ἠερο-φοῖτις 19.87n.), in which case approximately 'whose voices sound through the fog/air' (i.e. are loud), or a misspelling for ἱερο-φώνων (see *v.l.* in the *app. crit.*) comparable to Vedic *vácam iṣirám* ('powerful voice'), in which case 'with strong, powerful voice' (Schulze 1892, 211 f.; West 2001, 249 f.; Wachter 2008, 121 [ἠερο- is perhaps an early itacistic misunderstanding for ἱερο-]; undecided, *DELG s.v.*; Kaimio 1977, 77 f.).

506–508 The interpretation of the proceedings is dependent on the issues of the matter under dispute in 499 f. (cf. 498–501n.); the verdict of the '*gérontes*' is thus considered a suggestion for a judgement (type of compensation) or the substantiation of a judgement (from the assessment of evidence) or even an oath formula for the parties involved in the dispute (on this, Sommerstein/ Bayliss 2013, 61 f.). The following aspects of the proceedings are worth noting: (1) a competition is taking place in which the best candidate gains not only social prestige but also payment of a prize – perhaps donated by the two parties as a fee for the legal action (thus AH; Leaf p. 612 f.; Edwards; Wolff 1946, 43; Pelloso 2012, 115 n. 24); parallels in language and motif (arbitration of a dispute, competition) occur in Book 23, esp. in the context of the chariot race (cf. 506/508 with 23.574/579 f., and 507 with 23.269/273/614, also 501 with 23.486); on this agonistic element in the present 'trial scene', see Hommel 1969, 22 f.; Wirbelauer 1996, 166 n. 87; cf. Lentini 2006, 169 ff.; (2) the dispute is to be settled not by a single *basileús* who elsewhere acts as a guardian of jurisprudence appointed by Zeus (see e.g. 9.98 f., 16.542, *Od.* 19.109 ff., Hes. *Th.* 81 ff., *Op.* 38 ff.: 1.238–239n.), but instead a group of equals offers suggestions for resolving the argument (Hölkeskamp 2002, 315 f.: '*gérontes*' as 'mediators and arbitrators'). It is unclear who ultimately evaluates the protagonists and allots the prize and to what extent the declarations of the people taking sides (502 f.), which are apparently taken into account in some form (500a), influence the evaluation of the case presented: (a) either the 'expert' (*hístōr*, see 501n.) determines the best verdict (CARLIER 1984, 172 ff.; 2006, 106 f.; VAN WEES 1992, 34, 327 f. n. 34: the *basileús* functions as a *hístōr*), or (b) the people do (EDWARDS; WOLFF 1946, 40–42, with reference to the Germanic *Thing*; ULF 1990, 170 f.; GAGARIN 2008, 16–18; ELMER 2013, 185, 269 f. n. 24 f.), or (c) the consensus between the disputing parties and/or all 'elders' is decisive, codetermined by the mood prevailing among the people (HOMMEL 1969, 27 ff.; SCHEID-TISSINIER 1994a, 205; JANIK 2000, 15–17).

506 The sequence of events (rise with a staff in hand – step forward – speak) corresponds to the conventions of a Homeric assembly (2.278b–279n.).

τοῖσιν ... ἤϊσσον: ἀΐσσω denotes a quick movement, as at 3.216 ἀναΐσσω is the leaping up of speakers in a consultative assembly (see *ad loc.*), and here characterizes agitation or – more likely – the speed with which one speaker succeeds another (KURZ 1966, 73 n. 3); the subject is γέροντες (503), τοῖσιν as dat. of accompaniment points to the σκῆπτρα (FAESI; AH; WILLCOCK; CHANTR. 2.75; *LfgrE s.v.* σκῆπτρον 147.37 ff.; differently LEAF and EDWARDS: the disputing parties are the subj. ['to these elders then they dashed'], with a change of subj. in the 2nd VH). — ἀμοιβηδίς: 'alternately', refers to actions executed by several characters in turn (*Od.* 18.310, *h.Cer.* 326): *LfgrE*. — ἐδίκαζον: in Homeric epic means 'make decisions' (1.542 [see *ad loc.*] and 8.431 of Zeus) and is also used in the context of settling arguments (in addition to the present passage, 23.574/579: on fairness in winning a chariot race; *Od.* 11.547: over the armor of the slain Achilleus); in the present passage, it denotes an act of speaking (see 508 δίκην ... εἴποι): 'make a suggestion that could lead to a decision' (*LfgrE*; EDWARDS; cf. PRIMMER 1970, 10 f.; GAGARIN 2008, 16 f.; SCHEID-TISSINIER 2011, 63; PELLOSO 2012, 128 f. n. 63; differently THÜR 1996, 64 ff.; 2007, 187 ff.: formulate oath formulae).

507 2nd VH = 23.269, 23.614; ≈ 9.122, 9.264. — **two talents of gold:** The same sum is offered as the fourth prize in the chariot race at 23.269/614, also at *Od.* 4.526 as a special payment for a guard; gold is also found, in addition to other goods, in lists of gifts or ransom payments (7 talents of gold: *Od.* 9.202, 24.274; 10 talents of gold: *Il.* 9.122, 9.264, 19.247, 24.232, *Od.* 4.129). The weight of a Homeric talent cannot be determined precisely (probably less than the historically attested 25kg or more), see 19.247n., 24.232n.; *LfgrE s.v.* τάλαντον.

ἐν μέσσοισι: 'in their midst'; on the construction, *LfgrE s.v.* μέσ(σ)ος 163.15 ff.

508 the straightest: The formulation recalls the common image of 'straight' (and 'crooked') judgements (*díkai, thémistes*), cf. in particular Hes. *Th.* 85 f., *Op.* 9, 35 f., 225 f., 'Hes.' *fr.* 286 M.-W., *h.Cer.* 152, as well as *Il.* 16.387, Hes. *Op.* 219, etc.; on hypotheses regarding its origin (line of border stones? guide-line?),

---

508 τῷ: demonstrative, anticipatory (R 17). — δόμεν: final-consecutive inf.; on the form, R 16.4. — μετὰ τοῖσι: 'among them', i.e. the γέροντες. — ἰθύντατα (Ϝ)είποι: on the hiatus, R 4.3.

on the various Greek phrases and on the etymology of *díkē* ('verdict, judgement'), 16.387n.; *LfgrE* (with bibliography) and *DELG s.v.* δίκη; BENVENISTE
1969, 109 f.; JANIK 2000, 9–11, 20–22; PELLOSO 2012, 108 f. with n. 11 and 12;
for additional bibliography, SULLIVAN 1995, 174 n. 1; on the usage of *díkē*, also
16.388n., 19.179–180n.

ὅς ... ἰθύντατα εἴποι: is similar to the hexameter inscription on the Dipylon oino-
choë (dated to ca. 740 BC), which was offered as a prize, a sign of agonistic culture
also in dance (see *Od.* 8.250–253, 258–260); the text (*CEG* 432): ὃς νῦν ὀρχεστῶν πάντων
ἀταλότατα παίζει | etc. (G 2; HEUBECK 1979, 116–118; POWELL 1988, 69–74, esp. 69 n. 14;
1991, 158–163; EDWARDS; LATACZ 2008, 68: 'Who now among all the dancers here dances
most fluidly' [transl.]). In the present passage, the opt. as an indication of indirect discourse is a sign of secondary focalization[P] by the part of the audience in particular that
is supposed to award the prize (DE JONG [1987] 2004, 111 and 268 n. 31; cf. NÜNLIST 2002,
452).

509–540 The presentation of regarding the so-called 'city at war' – like the 'trial scene' in the 'city at peace' (497–508n.) – contains a combination of (a) a
description of what is meant to be thought of as depicted (with information
regarding the placement of figures: 509, 515 f., 521, 523, 525, 533) and (b) explanations of the situation, repeatedly interspersed with narrative passages
(BECKER 1995, 116–124, esp. 121 on 530–534: 'The images are fully dramatized,
turned into stories'; PRIMAVESI 2002, 201–205, taking into account the frequency of aor. forms in 525–527/530–534 [see *ad loc.*]; on the structuring in accord
with narratological aspects, 513n.). (a) The following are formulated in a du-
rative/descriptive manner (Greek impf.): (A) a city is under siege (509–510a),
women, children and the elderly are standing on top of the city walls (514 f.),
the warriors are leaving the town (516–519); (B) the city-folk lay in wait at the
river (521–523); (C) a raid on herds and their two herdsmen (525–526a, 528 f.);
(D) a battle between the city-folk and the besiegers (533–540); (b) the following
verses are explanatory, substantiating and transitional: 510b–513 (situation),
520/524/526b (character thoughts), 527, 530–532 (transition to a new action).
The structure of this passage is to be understood 'not as instruction for the
reconstruction of *images* [...] but solely as a representation of virtual images in
the text' (PRIMAVESI *loc. cit.* 204 [transl.]; see also 478–608n. section **B.2.a.**).
This visualizes different processes within a war that are presented again and
again in the *Iliad* as well: besieging a city (with discord among the army of
besiegers: 510n. [*s.v.* δίχα ... ἥνδανε βουλή]), escape and attack by the besieged
(with women, the elderly and children holding out in the city), a military assembly, ambush, mass fighting in an open field battle, fighting over the bodies
of the slain on the battlefield (511n., 514–515n., 539–540n.; ALDEN 2000, 65–
67); also raids and forays against a fortified settlement, as well as cattle raids,

a common motif in I-E heroic epic, represented in the *Iliad* by Achilleus' raids in the vicinity of Troy intended to feed the troops (1.163 ff., 6.414 ff., 9.328 ff., 20.91 ff.; also e.g. 1.154 ff., 9.547 ff., 11.671 ff., *Od.* 21.15 ff.): 1.154–157n. (with bibliography), 1.366n., 6.424n.; LONSDALE 1990, 119–121; PRITCHETT 1991, 320–322; WEST 2007, 451–454. On the present representation, see also SCHADEWALDT (1938) 1965, 365 f. (transl.): the narrator aims to trace 'not so much the uniform process of a specific military undertaking. He instead picks out fundamental phases, and in a fluid succession of phases develops all the faces of past warfare' (in contrast, cf. the portrayal of siege and battle on the pseudo-Hesiodic shield of Herakles at 'Hes.' *Sc.* 237–269).

509 two forces of armed men: This does not indicate that two different armies are besieging the city at the same time, but rather renders the pictorial representation of a siege as familiar from Phoenician bowls: attackers are visible on both sides of a city (EDWARDS; SCHADEWALDT [1938] 1965, 483 n. 1; see also schol. A; on depictions of cities under siege in Mycenaean and Ancient Near Eastern art, see FITTSCHEN 1973, 12 with 10 f., fig. 3 f. and pl. VIIIa/b; SIMON 1995, 130 f.; WIRBELAUER 1996, 149 with n. 21; WEST 1997, 389 f.; BUCHHOLZ 2010, 21–26).

τὴν δ' ἑτέρην πόλιν ἀμφί: 'around the other city' (cf. 490–491a n.), literally 'on both sides ...'; on the accent of ἀμφί in anastrophe, SCHW. 2.436 f. n. 1. — λαῶν: 497n.

510 1st VH ≈ 17.214, 20.46, Hes. *Th.* 186, 'Hes.' *Sc.* 60; VH = *Od.* 3.150; ≈ 8.506; VE = 14.337. — **shining:** Elsewhere in the *Iliad*, the inflectable VB formula *teúchesi lampómenoi* is used 2× in reference to Achilleus' arms (17.214 of Hektor in Achilleus' first armor, 20.46 of Achilleus himself; a variant at 19.398 [see *ad loc.*]). The motif of shining armor – of the shield also at 522 – elsewhere in the *Iliad* often prepares for major achievements by the wearer (16.70b–72a n., 19.374–383n.); here it matches both the imagery and the material used for the shield (BECKER 1995, 116).

δίχα ... ἥνδανε βουλή: interpreted in various ways, with linguistic criteria tending to support interpretation (a): (a) by analogy with *Od.* 3.150 and 8.506 (τρίχα ... ἥνδανε βουλή), as well as with formulations containing δίχα + θυμός (*Il.* 20.32, 21.386, 'Hes.' *fr.* 204.95 M.-W.), as an expression of two different preferences and thus of differences in opinion among the besiegers: to fight, conquer and take everything *vs.* to extort at least half the possessions; this might provide a link to the dominant motif in the action of the *Iliad*, 'discord within the besieging army' (schol. bT; *LfgrE s.v.* δίχα; LEAF p. 608; CERRI; MARG [1957] 1971, 32 n. 42; ANDERSEN 1976, 9; TAPLIN [1980] 2001, 350; ALDEN

---

509 εἵατ(ο): 504n.
510 σφισιν: = αὐτοῖς (R 14.1), *sc.* the besiegers.

2000, 63–65; PRIMAVESI 2002, 205 f.; ELMER 2013, 42–44, 244 n. 44, with a juxtaposition of ἀνδάνειν [individual preference] *vs.* ἐπαινεῖν [consensus within the community]; on the etymology of ἀνδάνω, 1.24n.); (b) an expression of the fact that it was agreed to issue the besieged citizens an ultimatum with two choices, which they do not want to accept, see 513a: either payment of ransom or destruction of the city; on this, 511n. (LA ROCHE; FAESI; AH; EDWARDS; SCHADEWALDT [1938] 1965, 483 n. 1).

511 2nd VH ≈ 22.120. — Over the course of the action of the *Iliad*, several possibilities for how the siege of a city can end are portrayed: with an unconditional retreat by the besiegers (see the Achaian discussion in Books 2 and 9 [esp. 2.110 ff., 9.393 ff.] regarding a return home), with the destruction of the city (see e.g. the allusions to Achilleus' raids in the vicinity of Troy), or with ransoming via possessions being handed over; this occurs in Agamemnon's demands in the treaty between Achaians and Trojans at 3.284–291 (payment of ransom or fight to the end; later only partially accepted by the Trojans: 7.363 f., 7.389 ff.; thus rejected entirely by the Achaians: 7.400 ff.) and in Hektor's thoughts at 22.111–121 about a final offer to Achilleus (payment of reparations instead of battle; see also RICHARDSON on *Il.* 22.114–118; DE JONG on *Il.* 22.114–121).

ἄνδιχα: a distributive compound ἀνά + δίχα (RISCH 367): 'in two equal parts, half and half' (*sc.* for the besiegers and the citizens).

512 = 22.121 (where likely interpolated, see DE JONG *ad loc.*). — **κτῆσιν ὅσην ... ἐντὸς ἔεργεν:** 'all possessions that ...', expands on πάντα (511) (LA ROCHE; DE JONG on *Il.* 22.121; *LfgrE s.v.* ὅσ(σ)ος 839 f.36 ff.; cf. 2.845n.). – ἐντὸς ἔεργεν is an inflectable VE formula (6× *Il.*, 1× *Od.*, 2× Hes.). — **ἐπήρατον:** 'desirable, popular', signals the effect on the observer (BECKER 1995, 117), perhaps also from the point of view of the besiegers (*LfgrE*).

513 The phrase *lóchōi hypethōréssonto* initiates the description of an 'ambush' (*lóchos*, the verb *lochḗsai* at 520; on the term, 24.779n.), which forms a contrast to fighting in the open field (*emáchonto máchēn*, 533). In Homeric epic, the *lóchos* (termed a *dólos* 'trickery' at 526, from the point of view of those attacked) frequently has a negative connotation, on the one hand, and is also mentioned as a military tactic employed by the best among the warriors, on the other, see 1.227 f., 13.277 (1.226–227n., 6.178–195n.; *LfgrE s.v.* λοχάω; EDWARDS 1985, 18–41; DUÉ/EBBOTT 2010, 33–49, 69–87). The elements of the theme[P] 'ambush' contain (DUÉ/EBBOTT *loc. cit.* 70): (1) selection of the participants (mention of the defenders staying behind [514 f. women, children, the elderly] suggests

---

511 ἠὲ ... ἠ(έ): 'either ... or'. — διαπραθέειν: inf. of the thematic aor. of δια-πέρθω ('destroy'); on the form, R 16.4, R 8. — ἠ' ἄνδιχα: on the elision, R 5.1. — δάσασθαι: aor. of δατέομαι 'distribute'.
512 πτολίεθρον: epic vocabulary, an expansion of πόλις/πτόλις (on the πτ-, R 9.2). — ἔ(ϝ)εργεν: impf. of ἐέργω/εἴργω, 'enclosed', i.e. 'hid, contained'.
513 οἳ δ(έ): *sc.* the citizens under siege. — λόχῳ: final dat. 'for an ambush'.

all men able to bear arms [519 Greek *laói*], led by two gods [516]); **(2)** planning and arming (513b); **(3)** selection of the location (520 f.); **(4)** concealment and waiting (522–524); **(5)** surprise attack (525–529); (6) return; the latter is lacking here, since the scene transitions to an open battle, with the attackers hastening to the scene and the outcome remaining open (530–540).

οὔ πω πείθοντο: 'did not yet give in' (*LfgrE s.v.* πείθω 1097.23 ff.), i.e. did not yet consider concessions (Leaf). — **ὑπεθωρήσσοντο:** 'secretly armed themselves', the compound only here; on the preverb ὑπο- expressing secrecy, cf. esp. ὑποκλοπέομαι (*LfgrE s.v.*), additional examples in Schw. 2.524; see also 319n. (ὑπὸ ... ἁρπάσῃ). θωρήσσομαι denotes not only the external act of putting on armor, but also the mental preparation for battle as well as actually going into battle (*LfgrE*).

514–515 The elderly and children protecting the city recalls Hektor's instructions at 8.518 ff. (where the Trojan warriors spend the night outside in the field); the women and old men recall the *teichoscopia* in Book 3 (3.146 ff., 3.384: Helen at the Skaian Gate together with the elders and women of Troy) and point forward to Book 22, where Hektor falls before the eyes of his relatives (22.25 ff., 22.405 ff., 22.460 ff.: Andromache and the elderly parents on the wall). The fate of women, children and the elderly in the case of a conquest is a repeated theme (e.g. at 6.450 ff., 22.62 ff., 24.730 ff.): Edwards; on the formulaic language, 514n.

514 From caesura A 4 ≈ 4.238, 5.688, 6.366, 24.730. — **ἄλοχοι ... καὶ νήπια τέκνα:** an inflectable formula expanded with the epithet φίλαι (5× *Il.*: 2.136n.), which is commonly used in the context of the absence of the husband/father and the risk faced by women and children (24.729b–730n.). ἄλοχοί τε φίλαι is an inflectable formula after caesura A 4 (8× *Il.*, 1× *Od.*; of which 6× followed by an additional kinship term: 6.366n.), νήπια τέκνα is a VE formula (11× *Il.*, 3× *Od.*: 2.311n., where also on νήπιος 'small, child-like, inexperienced'; in addition, Briand 2011, 198 ff.).

515 with age upon them: i.e. the group of men who are no longer active warriors due to their age; on Nestor, cf. 4.313–316 (*LfgrE s.v.* γῆρας).

ἐφεσταότες: The part. actually refers in the first instance to fem. ἄλοχοι and neut. τέκνα, whereas the masc. encompasses the entire group consisting also of boys and elderly men (differently at 2.136 f., see *ad loc.*): Monro (1882) 1891, 157; Chantr. 2.21.

516–519 Ares and Athene are the only gods depicted on the shield (cf. 535–538n.). Their presence is doubly highlighted (517–519): (a) optically, on the pictorial plane, with the narrator[P] having the figures made entirely from gold (517n.)

514 ῥ': = ἄρα (R 24.1).
515 ῥύατ(ο): 3rd pers. pl. impf. of ῥῦμαι/ἔρυμαι 'watch over, guard'; on the ending, R 16.2. — ἐφεσταότες: = ἐφεστῶτες, perf. part. of ἐφ-ίσταμαι (cf. R 6). — μετά: adverbial, 'among them'. — ἀνέρες: = ἄνδρες; initial syllable metrically lengthened (R 10.1). — ἔχε: 'held (firmly)'; on the unaugmented form, R 16.1.

and over life-size (518n.), and thus clearly distinguishable from the other figures; (b) linguistically, by their description being separated from that of other figures via dual forms introduced by *ámphō* 'both' (CHANTR. 2.26; AUBRIOT 2001, 23), as well as via various word plays[P] such as the anaphoric echo of *ámphō* and *amphís* (VB 517/519), polyptoton of the adjective 'golden' and a *figura etymologica* (517 with n.).

516 ≈ 5.592; 1st VH ≈ 14.134, 14.384, *h.Ap.* 514; VB = *Il.* 13.795, 23.114, *Od.* 10.103. — **Ares led them, and Pallas Athene:** Whereas in the action of the *Iliad* the two support opposing parties and are direct adversaries in battle (5.826 ff., 20.69), here they are united in an undertaking and jointly lead the men (as Ares at 5.591 f. leads the Trojans into battle together with the war goddess Enyo [CG 12]), since *both* are equally considered 'stewards of battle', see e.g. 4.439, 5.428–430, 13.127 f., 17.398 f., 20.358 f. (ERBSE 1986, 162): Ares is associated exclusively with the bloody and destructive aspects of war (CG 6; *HE s.v.* Ares; WATHELET 1992, 118 f. and 126–128; cf. his epithets: *LfgrE s.v.* Ἄρης), while Athene is also considered the 'protector of cities' (epithet *erysíptolis*), even if this function scarcely makes an appearance in the action of the *Iliad* (6.86–101n.; CG 8), in contrast to her tactical guidance at various points in the conflict, see e.g. 4.73–140, 15.121–141 (ERBSE 1986, 129, 143 f., 153 f.; WATHELET 1995, 167–169, 172). – Other gods also lead warring parties into battle in the *Iliad*: Poseidon leads the Achaians (14.384), and Apollo the Trojans (15.260 f., 15.307, 15.355 ff.); on this motif, 14.384n. (where also for parallels in Ancient Near Eastern literature).

οἳ δ' ἴσαν: *sc.* citizens-at-arms who lay the ambush, likewise at 520 οἳ δ' … ἵκανον, 522 τοί γ' ἵζοντ(ο) and 523 τοῖσι δ' … . On very short sentences in the narrator-text[P], see HIGBIE 1990, 97–99. — **ἦρχε δ' ἄρά σφιν:** The sing. in the predicate perhaps indicates that the two gods are considered a unit, likewise at 5.592 (ἦρχε … Ἄρης καὶ πότνι' Ἐνυώ), 7.386 (ἠνώγει Πρίαμός τε καὶ ἄλλοι Τρῶες): LEAF; on the accent (likewise at 520), WEST 1998, XVIII. — **Παλλὰς Ἀθήνη:** 217–218n.

517 gold: Generally speaking, gold is a characteristic attribute of gods (205–206n.), see also the golden armor of Zeus and Poseidon at 8.43 = 13.25 (on dress as an indicator of status/identity in general, TZAMALI 1996, 295; FOLEY 1999, 259 f.); elsewhere only Aphrodite is termed 'golden' (3.64n.: "an expression of Aphrodite's beauty"). Here the description 'golden' also recalls the material used in making the shield, see 475 (BECKER 1995, 118).

517–519 χρυσείω … ἔσθην, | καλὼ … μεγάλω … θεώ … | … ἀριζήλω: duals; ἔσθην is the dual of the plpf. of ἕννυμαι, 'were wrapped in, wore'.
517 δὲ (ϝ)είματα (ϝ)έσθην: on the hiatus (twice), R 4.3.

χρυσείω … χρύσεια: on the form, 418n. — **εἵματα ἔσθην:** a frequently attested *figura etymologica* related to the root (ϝ)εσ- (cf. Latin *ves-tis*, English. *vest*), including as an inflectable VE formula (5× *Il.*, 12× *Od.*, 1× *h.Ven.*): *LfgrE s.v.* εἷμα; on the mid. perf. stem (originally an old root pres.?), CHANTR. 1.297; NUSSBAUM 1998, 141.

518 1st VH ≈ *Od.* 9.426, 13.289, 14.7, 15.418, 16.158, 18.68. — **divinities:** indicates that the figures depicted are clearly recognizable as gods (BECKER 1995, 119); beauty and especially being larger than life-size are characteristic of the appearance of gods, see e.g. the epiphanies of Aphrodite at *h.Ven.* 173 f. and of Demeter at *h.Cer.* 188 f., 275 (for additional examples in post-Homeric texts, RICHARDSON on *h.Cer.* 188–211 and on 275 ff.; FAULKNER on *h.Ven.* 173–175; on differences in size as a means of highlighting deities in pictorial art, FITTSCHEN 1973, 13).

σὺν τεύχεσιν: 269–270n. — **ὥς τε θεώ περ:** with a causal connotation, i.e. substantiating καλὼ καὶ μεγάλω (3.381n.; AH; RUIJGH 575 f.; on ὥς τε, 318b n.).

519 ἀμφίς: 502–503n.; here it means either 'both sides', i.e. essentially 'on both sides, both' (cautiously, EDWARDS; SCHW. 2.439) or 'all around' (AH; *LfgrE*; undecided, CHANTR. 2.89). — **ἀριζήλω:** 219n. — **λαοί:** 497n. — **ὑπ' ὀλίζονες ἦσαν:** adverbial ὑπό 'underneath', i.e. 'under them'; probably in actual spatial terms with regard to a difference in size, similar to ὑπῆσαν at 11.681 of foals with their mothers, i.e. 'were ⟨depicted⟩ underneath on a smaller scale' (AH; LEAF; *LfgrE s.v.* ὀλίγος; CHANTR. 2.85 and 2.139; LEUMANN 1950, 72; RENGAKOS 1993, 120; FRITZ 2005, 351). – The comparative ὀλίζων (< *ὀλίγjων) is not attested again until the post-Homeric period (esp. in Alexandrian poets and Attic inscriptions): *DELG*, BEEKES and LSJ *s.v.* ὀλίγος.

520–529 The besieged are trying to supply themselves with more food via a cattle raid (cf. Hektor's argument based on the shortage of supplies in a city under siege at 287 ff.) and/or to cut off the food supplies of the besiegers. On the use of cattle (production of meat and hides) and sheep (wool, milk and meat) in Homeric society, and on cattle farming as an indicator of wealth, 2.403n. and 2.449n.; RICHTER 1968, 15, 44–55; for a list of examples of cattle raids in early epic, *LfgrE s.v.* βοῦς 90.21 ff.; see also 509–540n.; for pictorial representations of cattle raids, FITTSCHEN 1973, 12 f.

520 ≈ 23.138; 1st VH to ὅθι: = 10.526; ≈ 4.210, 5.780, *Od.* 15.101; to ἵκανον: ≈ *Il.* 6.297, 7.186. — **οἳ δ(έ):** 516n. — **εἶκε:** either a secondary impf. from the root of ἔοικα, i.e. 'where it seemed fitting' (AH; LEAF; EDWARDS on 520–522; CERRI; EBELING *s.v.* εἴκω; SCHW. 2.144) or an impf. of εἴκω ('yield') in an impersonal construction, 'where there was space for, i.e. the opportunity', as at Sappho *fr.* 31.8 Voigt (WILLCOCK; *LfgrE s.v.* εἴκω; BEKKER 1863,

---

518 τε: 'epic τε' (R 24.11). — περ: stresses the preceding word (R 24.10), 'just as gods', i.e. 'since they are indeed gods'.
520 ὅθι: '⟨to the spot⟩ where' (likewise 521). — σφισιν: = αὐτοῖς (R 14.1).

137; Sʜɪᴘᴘ [1953] 1972, 299; Tᴢᴀᴍᴀʟɪ 1996, 178; cautiously, Sᴄʜᴡ. 1.745 n. 2; undecided, Cʜᴀɴᴛʀ. 1.310 n. 1; *LfgrE s.v.* ἔοικα 622.68 ff.; for older bibliography, AH, *Anh.* p. 164).

521 1st VH ≈ 2.861. — **watering place:** i.e. a location that provides an especially advantageous opportunity to the attackers, since the herdsmen are distracted when watering the animals (Eʟʟɪɢᴇʀ 1975, 37).

ἐν ποταμῷ: 'by the river'; a VB formula (4× *Il.*, in the *Od.* 3× after caesura A 3). — ὅθι τ(ε): a reference beyond the scene to the generally applicable (Rᴜɪᴊɢʜ 472). — ἀρδμός: likewise at *Od.* 13.247; a term for a natural watering place for animals, derived from the verb ἄρδω 'to water', cf. *h.Ap.* 263 ἀρδόμενοι, *Il.* 21.346 νεοαρδής 'freshly watered' (*DELG s.v.* ἄρδω). — βοτοῖσιν: The Homeric *hapax*[P] βοτά, in post-Homeric texts a word from poetic language esp. for sheep (in contrast to θηρία), is here employed as a collective term for grazing livestock (524, 528 f.: sheep and cattle); it is related to the root of βόσκω 'feed, graze' (*DELG s.v.* βόσκω; cf. 2.287n. and 3.89n. on the epithets ἱππόβοτος 'horse-nourishing' and πουλυβότειρα 'feeding many'). — πάντεσσι βοτοῖσιν echoes VE formulae with epithet + βροτοῖσιν (e.g. δειλοῖσι βρ. at 24.525n., πάντεσσι/πᾶσι βρ. at *Od.* 13.397/15.255): Eᴅᴡᴀʀᴅꜱ.

522 ἔνθ᾽ ἄρα τοί γ(ε): picks up οἳ δ᾽ ὅτε δή at 520, as well as τοῖσι at 523 (516n.). — εἰλυμένοι αἴθοπι χαλκῷ: a variation of the VE formula κεκορυθμένος/-οι αἴθοπι χαλκῷ (9× *Il.*, 1× *Od.*). εἰλυμένοι is the perf. mid.-pass. part. of ε(ἰ)λύω, i.e. 'encased, wrapped in' (cf. Latin *volvo*: Cʜᴀɴᴛʀ. 1.131), χαλκός designates the armor (349n.), cf. 14.383 ἕσσαντο περὶ χροΐ νώροπα χαλκόν; the meaning of αἶθοψ is disputed ('ember-colored'?, 'shining, sparkling'?: 24.641n.).

523 2nd VH ≈ 24.799. — **two men to watch:** They are meant to report the arrival of the herds (524) in order for the attack to happen unexpectedly and as fast as lightning (526–529), cf. the use of look-outs at *Od.* 16.365–370. The moment of surprise during raids on livestock is elsewhere (11.671–683a) realized via attacking at night; for variations of the motif 'attack to raid livestock', see Dᴜᴇ́/ Eʙʙᴏᴛᴛ 2010, 82–84.

τοῖσι δ᾽ ἔπειτ᾽ ...: In Homeric epic, ἔπειτα can describe both temporal sequences and logical consequences: 'then, since (thus)' (19.112–113n., 16.667–668n.). — λαῶν: 497n.; either dependent on ἀπάνευθε, 'away from, apart from the warriors' (AH; Fᴀᴇꜱɪ), or an attribute of σκοποί (Wɪʟʟᴄᴏᴄᴋ; *LfgrE s.vv.* ἀπάνευθε and σκοπός); undecided, Lᴇᴀꜰ; Lᴀ Rᴏᴄʜᴇ.

---

521 ποταμῷ, ὅθι: on the hiatus, R. 5.6. — τ(ε): 'epic τε' (R 24.11). — ἔην: = ἦν (R 16.6). — πάντεσσι βοτοῖσιν: on the declension, R 11.3 and R 11.2.
522 τοί: anaphoric demonstrative pronoun (R 14.3).
523 τοῖσι: dat. of advantage; anaphoric demonstrative (R 17). — ἀπάνευθε: 'apart, separately'. — εἴατο: 504n.

524 δέγμενοι: durative 'expectant, waiting', rather than δεχόμενος, which does not fit in a hexameter (2.137n.). – **ἕλικας βοῦς:** a VE formula (3× *Il.*, 4× *Od.*, 2× Hes., 1× *h.Merc.*; also 5× early epic after caesura B 1), frequently expanded via the epithet εἰλίποδας ('shambling': on which, 6.424n.). ἕλιξ is a distinctive epithet[P] of cattle, probably related to the root of εἰλέω/ ἑλίσσω, similar to the noun ἕλικες (a term for jewellery: 401n.), perhaps the abbreviated form of a compound *ἑλικό-κραιρος on analogy with ὀρθό-κραιρος at 573n. (*DELG* and BEEKES *s.v.* ἕλιξ; BECHTEL 1914, 121; similarly RISCH 162); in this case, it would mean 'with crooked horns', cf. *h.Merc.* 191 f. βοῦς ... | ... κεράεσσιν ἑλικτάς (HAINSWORTH on *Il.* 9.466–469 and 12.293; WEST on *Od.* 1.92; *LfgrE s.v.* ἕλιξ II; RICHTER 1968, 47 f.).

525–534 The verses are probably to be understood as a combination of descriptions of images with explanatory passages of narrative content, which explicate the intermediary steps in the action not depicted on the shield (PRIMAVESI 2002, 197 f., 202–204); this interpretation is supported by the frequency of aorist predicates and participles (otherwise comparatively rare in shield descriptions; προγένοντο, προνόησαν, ἐπέδραμον, ἐπύθοντο, μετεκίαθον, ἵκοντο and προϊδόντες, βάντες, στησάμενοι), as well as by the repeated references to the rapid succession of events (τάχα, ὦκα δ᾽ ἔπειτα, ὡς οὖν ... αὐτίκ᾽, αἶψα): cf. 478–608n. section **B.3.**, 509–540n., 530n., 531–532n.

525 2nd VH = *Od.* 17.214. – **οἳ δέ:** refers in the first instance to μῆλα (neut.) and βοῦς (usually fem. in the pl.) (schol. bT; AH; LEAF; but τά at 527 [see *ad loc.*]), but perhaps also already includes the herdsmen, mentioned in the same verse, who walk behind the animals (CERRI; cf. 515n.; differently, *LfgrE s.v.* ἕπομαι 656.22 ff.: referring to σκοποί [i.e. they came to report], ἅμα 'immediately'). – **προγένοντο:** γίγνομαι meaning 'come' is always used in the aor. (*LfgrE s.v.* γίγνομαι 151.71 ff.); on the prefix προ-, cf. 'Hes.' *Sc.* 345, *h.Bacch.* 6 f. and esp. *Il.* 4.382 πρὸ ὁδοῦ ἐγένοντο (with KIRK *ad loc.* and CHANTR. 2.130), i.e. approximately 'advance, approach'; cf. the similarly phrased τάχα ... ἄγχι γένοντο at 8.117, 23.447.

526 pipes: The *sýrinx* (so-called Pan-flute), made from several wooden or reed tubes, is considered an invention of Hermes; in post-Homeric literature, it occurs especially as the instrument of Hermes' son Pan (*LfgrE s.v.* σῦριγξ with bibliography; *BNP s.v.* Pan; WEST 1992, 109–112). Hermes – *inter alia*, the protector of herdsmen and their animals (cf. 14.490 f., Hes. *Th.* 444, *h.Merc.* 491–498, 567 ff.: 14.491n.; ALLEN/HALLIDAY/SIKES on *h.Merc.* 568; VERGADOS on *h.Merc.* 491–492) – made them for himself (*h.Merc.* 511 f.) after handing his first instrument, the lyre, to Apollo as reparation for stealing his cattle (*h.Merc.* 490):

---

524 δέγμενοι ⟨εἰς τότε⟩, ὁππότε ... ἰδοίατο: 'waiting for the time when they would see'; ἰδοίατο is opt. as an indication of indirect speech, 3rd pers. pl. aor. mid. (on the ending, R 16.2, on the middle, R 23). – ὁππότε: on the -ππ-, R 9.1. – μῆλα (ϝ)ιδοίατο: on the prosody, R 4.3. – καὶ (ϝ)ἕλικας: on the prosody, R 4.4.

526 τι: acc. of respect (R 19.1), strengthens οὐ: 'not in any respect, in no way, not at all'.

CG 17; *LfgrE s.v.* Ἑρμείας 710.3 ff.; VERGADOS on *h.Merc.* 511–512. – The seemingly bucolic image of the flute-playing, unsuspecting herdsmen provides a strong contrast to the lightning-fast surprise attack and their violent deaths (527, 529); on the motif of helpless herdsmen in similes, 161–164n.

τερπόμενοι σύριγξι: τέρπομαι with instrumental dat. 'amusing themselves with Pan-pipes', i.e. to be understood as an actual activity in the sense 'playing the Pan-pipe' (rather than as an expression of a mood), similarly at 9.186, *h.Merc.* 506 (LATACZ 1966, 192, 196, 207; cf. on δίσκοισιν τέρποντο at 2.774n.).

527 οἳ μέν: the citizens carrying out the attack, in contrast to the besiegers οἳ δ᾽ at 530; on the swift change of subjects designated with οἵ in 520–534 (516n., 525n.), see AUBRIOT 1999, 18 f. (mixing of the camps as first impression). – **τὰ προϊδόντες:** 'spying them from afar' (*LfgrE s.v.* ἰδεῖν), with neut. pl. for animals as objects of prey, similarly at 11.244 f. (CHANTR. 2.21). – **ἐπέδραμον, ὦκα:** For various formulations marking speed during an attack from ambush, see DUÉ/EBBOTT 2010, 75 f.

528 τάμνοντ᾽ ἀμφί: 'segregate from two sides, from all around, for oneself', similar are περιταμνόμενος of a raid on livestock at *Od.* 11.402 ≈ 24.112 and ἀπετάμνετο at *h.Merc.* 74 (*LfgrE s.vv.* ἀμφί 663.54 and τάμνω 302.61 ff.; on the mid., cf. LSJ *s.v.* ἀποτέμνω: 'with a view of appropriating'). – **βοῶν ἀγέλας:** a formulaic phrase before caesurae C 1 (likewise at 11.678, 15.323, *Od.* 12.299; with the words in reverse order and separated, *Il.* 11.696, 18.573, *h.Merc.* 288) and B 1 (*Od.* 12.129). – **πώεα καλά:** a VE formula, in addition to the present passage also at *Od.* 11.402, 12.129, 24.112, in all cases expanded to οἰῶν π. κ. (see 529). πῶυ ('herd'), etymologically related to ποιμήν, is almost always combined with gen. οἰῶν or μήλων (*LfgrE s.v.* πῶυ).

529 VE = *h.Merc.* 286. – **ἀργεννέων οἰῶν:** The formulaic phrase is elsewhere at VE (οἰῶν ἀργεννάων 588; ἀργεννῆς ὀίεσσιν 6.424, *Od.* 17.472) or in hyperbaton (*Il.* 3.198); on the spellings ὀίων and οἰῶν, G 43; WEST 1998, XXIV. On the color adj. ἀργεννός ('bright, whitish, shimmering'; from the same root as ἄργυρος, Latin *argentum* 'silver') and on the colors of the coats of sheep (in the *Iliad* generally white), 3.141n., 24.621n. – **μηλοβοτῆρας:** 'herdsman'; this form of the *nomen agentis* occurs only here and at *h.Merc.* 286, later texts use μηλοβότης. On the suffix -τήρ, RISCH 28–30; CHANTRAINE 1933, 322 f.

530 But the other army: The reference is to the besiegers, who had not thus far noticed the expedition of the besieged. The situation mentioned at 531 perhaps refers to the consultation regarding the action going forward in 510–512 (see *ad loc.*; AH on 531 ['a war council' (transl.)]; LEAF; EDWARDS on 530–532), but it remains unclear whether this is an assembly of all the individuals involved in the siege or a consultation among the leaders (gap^P).

---

529 ἀργεννέων: on the synizesis, R 7; on the declension, R 11.1. – κτεῖνον δ᾽ ἔπι: 'also killed' (cf. R 20.2).

οἳ δ’ ὡς οὖν ἐπύθοντο: ὡς οὖν is usually combined with a verb of perception (here ἐπύθοντο) and frequently links (esp. where the subject changes) the preceding action with a new storyline (REYNEN 1958, 70 ff., *ad loc.* 74 f.; DE JONG [1987] 2004, 105 f. and 266 n. 12, 267 n. 17). – πυθέσθαι designating an immediate acoustic perception can be accompanied by an acc. object, as here (likewise 15.379 κτύπον, *Od.* 10.147 ἐνοπήν), elsewhere often by a gen. object (*LfgrE s.v.* πεύθομαι, πυνθάνομαι 1205.11 ff. as well as 1204.16 ff.). — **πολὺν κέλαδον:** likewise at 9.547; it denotes the loud 'noise, uproar' that emanates from numerous sources (humans and animals), of the noise of battle elsewhere πολὺς ὀρυμαγδός (KAIMIO 1977, 32, 80; cf. 493n.).

531–532 sat: The participants in the assembly were seated, in accord with the custom of Homeric assemblies, while the speakers addressed them standing up and sometimes stepping forward into the middle (506n., 19.77n.); on the order of events in an assembly and the place of assembly (also of a besieging army, e.g. of the Achaians, 7.382, 11.807 f.), 1.54n. — **behind ... horses:** on horses and chariots, 224n.

εἰράων: only here and at Hes. *Th.* 804 (where also at VB: †εἰρέας ἀθανάτων); the etymology of the word is uncertain, but since antiquity it has been linked to Ionic-epic εἴρω/εἴρομαι and interpreted as 'place of speaking, assembly place', i.e. equated with ἀγορή, ἐκκλησίη (schol. A and D; FRISK and *DELG* and BEEKES *s.v.* *εἴρη; RISCH 11). But the interpretation of εἰράων προπάροιθε as 'in front of the places for speaking' is problematic, since there were no speaker's podiums in Homeric assemblies (LEAF); perhaps it describes the position of a figure in a *pictorial* representation more generally: the participants lined up before the background of the place of assembly (FAESI: 'in the foreground' [transl.]; AH: 'in front of it, along', the pl. 'of individual sections of the ἀγορά' [transl.; with reference to *Od.* 8.16]) or in front of rows of seats (suggestion by LATACZ: perhaps related to εἴρω derived from the root *ser-, Latin *serere*?). — **αὐτίκ’ ... | ... αἶψα:** In the apodosis after a temporal clause, αὐτίκα marks the beginning of a new, spontaneous action, which here concludes with αἶψα δ’ ἵκοντο (*LfgrE s.v.* αὐτίκα 1606, 47 ff.; ERREN 1970, 35 ff.; BONIFAZI 2012, 273–275). — **ἐφ’ ἵππων | βάντες ἀερσιπόδων:** ἀερσίπους is a generic epithet[P] of horses (another 2× *Il.* at VB) and means 'lifting the feet', i.e. 'fast' (3.327n.). In Homer, the plural and dual of ἵππος often denote the team of horses together with the chariot (*LfgrE s.v.* 1211.57 ff., 1216.43 ff.), e.g. here and in other passages with ἵππων + ἐπιβαίνω (5.46, 5.328, 16.343, 'Hes.' *Sc.* 286; cf. ἐπιβαίνω + ὀχέων 5.221, etc., δίφρου 8.44, etc.); even in this context, an epithet for 'fast' can sometimes stand, perhaps as a kind of brachylogy for 'mount the chariot drawn by swift-footed horses' (7.17 ἵππων ἐπιάλμενον ὠκειάων, 8.128 f. ἵππων | ὠκυπόδων ἐπέβησε, *Od.* 18.263 ἵππων τ’ ὠκυπόδων ἐπιβήτορας, *h.Hom.* 33.18 ταχέων ἐπιβήτορες ἵππων): *LfgrE s.vv.* βαίνω 18.5 ff. and ἵππος 1216.43 ff.; FRITZ 2005, 160. — **μετεκίαθον:** 'walked/drove behind, fol-

---

532 ἵκοντο: here used absolutely: 'they arrived'.

lowed after, pursued'; a compound of the defective verb ἔκιον with the expansion -αθ- (perhaps with the function of an aor.: 16.685n.).

533–539 ἐμάχοντο μάχην ... | βάλλον ... | [4 verses] | ὡμίλεον ... ἠδ' ἐμάχοντο: a framing via a general formulation for 'to fight', in between are expressions describing mass fighting, which also occur elsewhere in battle descriptions in Homeric epic: fighting at a distance with missiles (βάλλω: 16.24n.) and close combat in battle lines (ὁμιλέω: 194n.; see also *LfgrE* s.v. ὁμιλαδόν); on the description of mass fighting, individual combat and different battle phases in the *Iliad*, 3.15–37n., 6.1–72n.; RAAFLAUB 2011, 14–16.

533 ≈ *Od.* 9.54. — **στησάμενοι ... μάχην:** μάχην is an internal acc. with μάχοντο, like μάχην ἐμάχοντο (12.175, 15.414, 15.673); στησάμενοι is interpreted syntactically in various ways: (a) intransitive and absolute, 'line up' (LA ROCHE; PORZIG 1942, 94), with a natural order of the sequence of motion rushing to the spot (αἶψα δ' ἵκοντο) – lining up (στησάμενοι δ(έ)) – fighting (ἐμάχοντο μ.); (b) transitive, since the aor. mid. of ἵσταμαι is generally used transitively (but see περιστήσαντο at 2.410n.): (b1) with μάχην as the obj. (ἀπὸ κοινοῦ with both verbs), 'draw up, establish battle-lines' (AH on *Od.* 9.54; LEAF; WILLCOCK; EDWARDS; CHANTR. 2.176 n. 1; *LfgrE* s.v. ἵστημι 1246.70 f.); (b2) with ἵππους to be supplied as obj., 'set up the teams of horses' (VAN LEEUWEN; CERRI), although this is elsewhere phrased in the active in early epic (ἵ. στῆσε/-σαν). — **ποταμοῖο παρ' ὄχθας:** a phrase at VE (παρ'/ἐπ': 4.487, *Od.* 6.97, 'Hes.' *frr.* 13.1, 343.12 M.-W.); without ποταμοῖο: 5× *Il.*, 1× *Od.*) and 1× at VB (*Il.* 11.499 ὄχθας πὰρ ποταμοῖο).

534 = *Od.* 9.55. — **bronze-headed:** The adj. *chalkḗrēs* refers to the lance-head ('fitted with bronze [head]': 6.3n.), perhaps also to the spear-butt at the end of the shaft (cf. *LfgrE* s.v. σαυρωτήρ).

The metrical structure of the verse – all spondees except in the 4th *metron* – is rarely encountered in Homeric epic (9× *Il.*, 7× *Od.*: DEE 2004, 483) and is here striking after two purely dactylic verses: the rhythm perhaps emphasizes the weight of the battle after the hasty deployment. — **χαλκήρεσιν ἐγχείῃσιν:** likewise at 20.258, *Od.* 9.55, 11.40 (VE with ἐγχείῃσιν/ἐγχειάων in total 7× *Il.*, 2× *Od.*); on the metrical system of the noun-epithet formulae designating 'lance/spear', 6.3n.; BAKKER (1991) 2005; *LfgrE* s.v. χαλκήρης; also 16.318n.

535–538 535 ≈ 'Hes.' *Sc.* 156 (ἐθύνεον); 536–538 = 'Hes.' *Sc.* 157–159. — WEST and other scholars follow Düntzer in athetizing the verses, probably rightly so, as interpolations from the pseudo-Hesiodic *Scutum* (*app. crit.*; WILLCOCK; EDWARDS; WEST 2001, 12 n. 28 [among the 'rhetorical expansions']; 2011, 353); the following reasons have been put forward (for detailed discussion, see SOLMSEN 1965; LYNN-GEORGE 1978; BLÖSSNER 1991, 72 f.): (a) although monstrous figures serve an apotropaic function also on other shields in the *Iliad* (thus the Gorgo and others at 5.740–742, 11.36 f.), and although Achilleus'

---

534 βάλλον: 'pelted', durative/iterative impf. — ἐγχείῃσιν: on the declension, R 11.1.

shield will terrify observers, this effect is ascribed especially to its extraordinary luster (19.12–19n., 19.374–383n.); the present vivid description is particularly characteristic of the pseudo-Hesiodic shield of Herakles, while similar aspects are absent from the shield of Achilleus (SCHADEWALDT [1938] 1965, 361 f.;
SOLMSEN 1965, 2 f.; TAPLIN [1980] 2001, 351: 'This primitive conception of battle
is not typical of the *Iliad*'); (b) the way in which the personifications act in battle is without parallel in the *Iliad* but not in 'Hes.' *Sc.* (where see 246 ff.) (535n.,
536–537n.; LYNN-GEORGE 1978, 399 ff.; *contra* ERBSE 1986, 28; AUBRIOT 1999,
19–21; CLARKE 1999, 234 n. 6; ALDEN 2000, 61 f. n. 33, 67; PALMISCIANO 2010,
55 f.); (c) idiosyncracies of interpretation arise from 539 f. (539–540n.).

535 Eris, Kydoimos and Ker are personifications of different phases of violent
confrontations, namely 'strife, attack' (cf. 3.7n.), 'thick of battle' and 'death': (1)
Eris, goddess of strife and sister of Ares, is also depicted on the *aegis* (5.740) and
appears elsewhere in the *Iliad* in anthropomorphic form; she is predominantly
an agent causing fighting (cf. Hes. *Th.* 228: Eris as the mother of fighting and
killing), sometimes acting in conjunction with other deities (see esp. 4.440–
443 [beside Ares and Athene, Deimos and Phobos at 4.439 f.], 5.517 f., 11.3–12,
20.48): CG 30 f. and 38; (2) in early epic, the noun *kydoimós* designates the
turmoil, confusion and panic of the crowd in battle (217–218n.); (3) *kēr* means
'death, doom' and is here thus a kind of death demon – Hes. *Th.* 211 lists Ker
in addition to Móros and Thánatos as offspring of the 'night'; elsewhere in the
Iliad, pl. *kéres* is usually used as a term for 'creatures bringing death or taking
the dead with them [...] and not having a defined form' (2.301–302n. with bibliography, 2.384n.; CG 29; *LfgrE s.v.* κήρ 1406.59 ff.; DIETRICH 1965, 243–248; also
WEST on Hes. *Th.* 217; on the somewhat differently designed personification
of *móira*, 119n.). In early epic, Kydoimos and Ker act as persons, and likely in
concrete shape, only here and at 'Hes.' *Sc.* 156 ff.; in contrast, the abstracts
depicted on the *aegis* (*Il.* 5.739 f.) and on Agamemnon's shield (11.37), *déimos,
phóbos, alkḗ* and *iokḗ* ('fear', 'terror', 'defense' and 'attack'), are not embedded
in a storyline (CG 31).

ἐν δ' ... ἐν δὲ ... ὁμίλεον, ἐν δ(έ): In descriptions of objects in the *Iliad*, the formulation
ἐν δέ + verb serves to enumerate depictions on objects ('on it', i.e. on the object: 481n.,
483n.), likewise at 'Hes.' *Sc.* 154 f. (ἐν δὲ Προΐωξίς τε ... τέτυκτο, | ἐν δ' ...); in the Homeric
shield description, the relevant activity performed by Hephaistos is mentioned (478–
608n. section **B.1.b.**). In the present passage, the formulation thus initially suggests the
interpretation 'on it, he made ...', whereas in the continuation, battle action follows in
an atypical manner (i.e. 'on it ⟨was shown how they⟩ ... fought'; this formulation causes
the action of the production process to merge in the mind of the audience with that
of the scene described (SOLMSEN 1965, 3 f.; LYNN-GEORGE 1978, 401 f.; BECKER 1995,
122; differently, AH and *LfgrE s.v.* ὁμιλέω: ἐν δὲ ... ὁμίλεον in the sense ἐν τοῖσι ὁμίλεον

'among, i.e. among them [*sc.* the warriors on both sides] fought ...'). – ὁμίλεον (rather than 'Hes.' *Sc.* 156: ἐθύνεον 'they charged') denotes mass fighting (533–539n.); as at 539, the verb is here used absolutely, in early epic also with dat. or the prepositions μετά, ἐν or περί (*LfgrE s.v.* ὁμιλέω). – **ὀλοή:** 'bringing destruction' (related to ὄλλυμι), usually in direct speech (character language[P]), frequently in reference to destructive forces, with κήρ also at 13.665, more frequently with μοῖρα (9× early epic): 24.39n.; *LfgrE.*

536–537 The basic information '*all* involved without exception are in the power of Ker' is skilfully developed in a triple anaphora (on which, 24.10–12n.): Greek 3× *állon* ('one ..., another ..., | another') comprises all categories of warriors, both living – wounded and unscathed – and dead. — **dragged:** The formulation 'dragged by the feet' evokes associations with scenes in which warriors pull at the feet of slain opponents in order to capture the body and especially the armor, see 540 (e.g. 4.463 ff., 11.257 f., 13.383 f., 14.477, 16.762 f., 17.288 f., 18.155 f., 22.396 ff.: 155n., 539–540n.). In other passages in Homeric epic, multiple Keres 'carry' (*phérein*) or 'lead' (*ágein*) the dead away (2.302, 2.834, 8.528, 9.410 f., 11.332, *Od.* 14.207). An unusual aspect of the present passage is that the death demon also seizes living, unwounded warriors, a sign that they are destined to die; cf. the graphic description at 'Hes.' *Sc.* 252–257 (LYNN-GEORGE 1978, 400 with n. 15).

νεούτατον ... ἄουτον: The repetition of part of a compound in an antithetical juxtaposition of an affirmative and a negated term is elsewhere especially common in gnomes (for examples from the *Odyssey*, FEHLING 1969, 251–253). νε-ούτατος ('newly wounded', elsewhere only at 13.539, 'Hes.' *Sc.* 253) and ἄ-ουτος ('unwounded'; elsewhere ἀν-ούτατος at *Il.* 4.540 and ἀνουτητεί at 22.371 ['without wounding']) are derived from οὐτά(ζ)ω ('strike, wound' [in close battle], with the athematic root aor. οὖτα: 6.64n.); the word formation ἄουτος is unusual: ἄ- rather than ἄν- (an initial digamma for οὐτα- cannot be detected elsewhere in early epic: CHANTR. 1.125) and the word stem -ουτ- rather than -ουτατ- (*DELG s.v.* οὐτάω). — **τεθνηῶτα:** on the form, G 95; CHANTR. 1.430 f. — **κατὰ μόθον:** 158b–160n. — **εἶλκε ποδοῖϊν:** ≈ 14.477 (see *ad loc.* for the formulaic phrase), with gen. of the body part grasped, like ποδῶν 155 f., ποδός 11.258, 13.383, 17.289; on the gen./dat. dual ending -οιϊν, 14.228n.

538 strong red: Elsewhere in early epic, blood is usually described as black and only rarely as red (*LfgrE s.v.* αἷμα 306.30 ff.; NEAL 2006, 296). The color term *daphoineós* ('red, brown-red'), frequently used of terrifying animals (snake, lion, jackal: *LfgrE s.v.*), reinforces Ker's gruesome appearance (cf. HANDSCHUR 1970, 122–124), which at 'Hes.' *Sc.* 249–252 is further intensified via the motif of blood-thirstiness. In the *Iliad*, it is usually the god Ares who is associated with

---

537 τεθνηῶτα: = τεθνεῶτα (on metrical grounds, without shortening in the internal hiatus: R 3). — κατὰ (μ)μόθον: on the prosody, M 4.6.

bloodshed and blood-thirstiness on the battlefield, cf. his epithet *miaiphónos* 'stained with slaughter' (5.31, 5.455, 5.844, 21.402) and the formulaic verse at 5.289, 20.78, 22.267, as well as 7.329 f.

ἀμφ' ὤμοισι: a formula after caesura A 3 (8× *Il.*, 7× *Od.*, 3× 'Hes.' *Sc.*, 3× *h.Merc.*). — δαφοινεόν: a less common form of δαφοινός, expanded for metrical reasons (CHANTR. 1.96), a derivation from φοιν- (see the adj. φοινός, φοινήεις), the etymology of which, although unclear, has been associated since antiquity with φόνος (16.159n.); a connection with φοῖνιξ 'red' is more likely. The prefix δα- (rather than δια-, Aeolic ζα-) is interpreted as a semantic intensification: 'through and through, very much' (CHANTR. 1.169; *DELG s.vv.* φοινός, 1 φοῖνιξ; FRISK *s.v.* δα-).

539–540 These two verses seamlessly continue from 533 f.: the description of open battle continues, and the statement 'like living men' recalls that this is the description of an image (HEFFERNAN 1993, 19; BECKER 1995, 122 f.). Although such references are rare in the Homeric description of the shield, see also 518, 548 f., 591, cf. 418n. on Hephaistos' golden servants (on such references in post-Homeric literature, see RUSSO 1965, 25, 122 [on 189]; BECKER 1995, 122 n. 226). If these two verses follow from the passage 535–538, a change in subject should probably be assumed between 535 and 539 f. ('they joined together, fought', *homíleon/hōmíleon*) on both contextual and linguistic grounds, since it is unlikely that Eris, Kydoimos and Ker fight over bodies 'like living men' rather than the warriors themselves doing so, see below (EDWARDS on 535–538; LYNN-GEORGE 1978, 402–404 [*contra* SOLMSEN 1965, 5 f., who includes 539 f. in the interpolation]). What is more, an anticlimax would arise in the final verses of the image after 536 f. (suggestion by FÜHRER). — **dragged away:** The battle for the dead in order to steal or retrieve the body is a typical motif of battle descriptions in the *Iliad* (e.g. at 4.491 ff., 5.573, 11.257 f., 16.762 f., 16.781 f., 17.713; for additional examples, 536–537n.), esp. in the previous two Books after the killings of Sarpedon, a Trojan ally (16.563–683, esp. 16.633 ff.), Kebriones (16.751 ff.) and particularly Patroklos (17.1–18.238): 155n., 16.496n., 16.762–763n., 16.781–782n.; *LfgrE s.vv.* ἕλκω 554.52 ff. and ἐρύω 724.17 ff. The image with the unnamed warriors thus reflects the battle descriptions in the *Iliad* and recalls the fighting over Patroklos' body in particular (cf. MARG [1957] 1971, 33; ANDERSEN 1976, 11; ALDEN 2000, 67).

ὡμίλεον ... | ... ἀλλήλων ἔρυον: in reference to both armies, as at 534: they shoot at each other (βάλλον δ᾽ ἀλλήλους), start fighting hand-to-hand and drag away each oth-

---

539 ὡμίλεον: on the synizesis, R 7. — ὥς τε ζωοὶ βροτοί: 'like living men', refers to both predicates; on the 'epic τε', R 24.11. — ἠδ(έ): 'and' (R 24.4).
540 κατατεθνηῶτας: = κατατεθνεῶτας (537n.).

er's dead (533–539n.; Lynn-George 1978, 402f. with n. 29). – **ὥς τε:** 318b n. – **ζωοὶ βροτοί:** the phrase is also at *Od.* 23.185/187, *h.Ap.* 364, in each case with the antithesis god – human being (elsewhere also the focus of the use of the term βροτός [+ ἀνήρ]: 85n., 362n.). But here βροτός is simply the generic term 'human being', with emphasis on ζωός: the warriors depicted represent *living* humans, cf. 418 (*LfgrE s.vv.* βροτός 102.75 f. and ζωός; Heffernan 1993, 19). – **κατατεθνηῶτας:** an epithet of νεκρός/νέκυς, always at VE (173n.) with the exception of 16.526, 16.565; it emphasizes the finality of death. The separation of the words is comparable to 6.71 (see *ad loc.*).

541–572 The 'city at war' is followed by another passage of life during peacetime. The three kinds of agricultural labor, plowing, harvesting and the grape harvest, were associated with particular seasons by numerous interpreters: reaping as an image of summer, since the heliacal rise of the Pleiades in mid-May signals the beginning of reaping (486n.) according to Hes. *Op.* 383 f.; grape harvesting as an image of fall, since the harvest starts with the heliacal rising of Arcturus at the beginning of September according to Hes. *Op.* 609–614 (AH and Cerri on 541–572; Leaf p. 609; Taplin [1980] 2001, 351–353; West on Hes. *Op.* 381–617; West 2011, 353). But the image of plowing cannot be linked unequivocally to a season, since it took place multiple times between the harvest and the next seeding (541n.): according to Hesiod, it is meant to take place during the cosmic setting of the Pleiades, Hyades and Orion from the beginning of November onward (*Op.* 384 and 615–617: 486n.; West on Hes. *Op.* 381–617), as well as in the spring and summer (*Op.* 462f.) – it is thus interpreted as an image of November (West 2011, 353) or of the spring (Leaf p. 609; Cerri on 541–572; Taplin [1980] 2001, 351; Fittschen 1973, 14: 'spring or winter' [transl.]). But rather than seasons, the three images likely depict the labors – naturally seasonal – of the agricultural year (Wirbelauer 1996, 150 f.) that are representative of the production of the staples 'bread and wine', i.e. preparation of the soil, bringing in the harvest and the grape harvest as images of the cultivation of grains and wine (in contrast to animal husbandry, which is the focus of 573–589); on 'bread and wine' as a universal paraphrase for 'nourishment', see 19.161n.; cf. the meals for the laborers depicted at 545 f., 560, also Odysseus' report at *Od.* 9.107–111, 9.131–135 of the way of life of the Cyclopes and Athene's description of Ithaka at 13.244–246 (Lentini 2006, 151 with n. 1; on the significance of grain and viticulture, Richter 1968, 107–109, 127; *BNP s.vv.* Nutrition, Grain, Wine; also 14.122–124a n.). On the interpretation of all agricultural scenes (including those with animal herds) against the background of I-E depictions of wealth, Allen 2007 (with older bibliography).

541–549 Depiction of a field being plowed: 541–542a/548–549a nature of the soil, with concluding commentary at 549b; 542b–547 actions of the person plowing (Edwards; Becker 1995, 124–130). The narrative flow of the description of plowing is altered in comparison with preceding images: there quick changes in action and contextual bustling in attack and battle, here calm, uniformly recurring action, supported linguistically by iterative/frequentative verb forms (543, 546), an iterative temporal clause ('whenever' at 544), repeated expressions for 'turn' (543, 544, 546) and the phrase 'hither and tither', i.e. 'back and forth' (543): 543n., 544–546n. – Homer elsewhere mentions plowing only in similes[P]; these instances focus on the physical exertion that requires strength and endurance (13.703–708 [esp. 705], *Od.* 18.364–375), with the exhausted plowman longing for refreshment in the evening (13.31–34), a circumstance only implied here in the drink offered at regular intervals (cf. FRÄNKEL 1921, 46; REINHARDT 1961, 402; NOACK-HILGERS 2001, 175).

541 VE = *Od.* 2.328, 23.311. — **a soft field:** A harvested (grain) field remained fallow for at least one year (i.e. after the harvest starting in May/June until the sowing that started in November of the subsequent year, in a so-called 'crop rotation system'), but was repeatedly plowed until the next sowing (LEAF; EDWARDS; *LfgrE s.v.* νειός; WEST on Hes. *Op.* 462–463 and *Th.* 971; RICHTER 1968, 101; NOACK-HILGERS 2001, 163, 165, 183 ff.; cf. *BNP s.v.* Agriculture).

ἐν δ' ἐτίθει: = 550, 561, 607 (also 3× *Il.*); a variant of describing Hephaistos' actions via the formula ἐν δ(ὲ) ‿ – (object) – – ‿ (ποίησε/ποίκιλλε) in 573, 587, 590, similarly at 490 (478n.); cf. 14.179 τίθει δ' ἔνι δαίδαλα πολλά (in reference to a garment made by Athene, see *ad loc.*). The impf. ἐτίθει (beside aor. ἔτευξε, ποίησε) is likely used for metrical reasons, like ποίκιλλε at 590 (DE JONG 2011, 12 n. 22; cf. 1.437n., 24.266–274n.; differently PERCEAU 2002, 114: durative/descriptive for the sake of varying the temporal rhythm; on this, cf. PRIMAVESI 2002, 196 n. 45; HOEKSTRA on *Od.* 14.13). — **νειόν:** a designation for a harvested field, generally used in the context of plowing, as here, cf. 10.353, 13.703, *Od.* 5.127, 8.124, 13.32, Hes. *Op.* 462–464, *Th.* 971 (*LfgrE s.v.* νειός: 'fallow field'; RICHTER 1968, 94, 100); probably related etymologically to νειόθεν/νειόθι '[from] below' and νείατος 'lowermost': FRISK, *DELG*, BEEKES *s.v.* — **πίειραν:** 342n. — **ἄρουραν:** a general term for farmland (from the same root as ἀρόω [ἀροτῆρες at 542], Latin *arare*): *LfgrE*; RICHTER 1968, 93.

542 many plowmen: The many plowmen in the field are perhaps occupied with different stages of the work in accord with 544–547 (BECKER 1995, 125); on several plowmen plowing a large field concurrently, see RICHTER 1968, 102 f.; NOACK-HILGERS 2001, 199, 202 f.; on the appearance of ancient plows, SCHIERING 1968, 147–152; WEST on Hes. *Op.* 427.

τρίπολον: also νειῷ ἔνι τριπόλῳ at *Od.* 5.127, Hes. *Th.* 971. τρί-πολος likely means 'plowed three times' (EDWARDS; *LfgrE s.v.*; RICHTER 1968, 101; NOACK-HILGERS 2001, 176–182; dif-

---

541 ἐν: adverbial, 'on it'. — μαλακήν: 'soft', i.e. easily broken.

ferently HAINSWORTH on *Od.* 5.127: 'furrowed three times', with a ritual reference); the second element, like πολέω (Hes. *Op.* 462: during the plowing of the field, see WEST *ad loc.*), is related to *kʷelh₁-, the root of πέλω/πέλομαι 'move about' (FRISK, *DELG*, BEEKES *s.v.* πέλομαι; cf. 370–371n.; *LIV* 386). – On emphasis via an accumulation of epithets with progressive enjambment[P], 130–131n.

543 ζεύγεα … ἐλάστρεον: Homeric *hapax legomena*[P] ('they urged on the yoked teams'); ἐλαστρέω is a frequentative related to ἐλαύνω (*LfgrE*; the formation is not entirely clear: SCHW. 1.706; RISCH 310). — **δινεύοντες:** 'turning' (cf. 494n.); always used intransitively, it here denotes the turn at the edge of the field, cf. 544–547 (*LfgrE*). — **ἔνθα καὶ ἔνθα:** 'back and forth'; a formulaic phrase, usually at VE (10× *Il.*, 11× *Od.*, 1× Hes., 1× *h.Merc.*), as here, or before caesura B 2 (16× early epic).

544–546 ὁπότε … ἱκοίατο …, | … | δόσκεν … στρέψασκον: Both the aor. of the iterative opt. and the aor. stems with iterative suffix signal the completion of a process repeated multiple times (SCHW. 2.278; on the generally unaugmented σκ- forms, see G 60, 24.12a n. with bibliography): reaching the edge of the field, refreshment, turning the plow.

544 VE = 13.707. — **στρέψαντες:** The active is here used 'quasi-intransitive', the yoked teams (543) are to be supplied as the obj. (*LfgrE s.v.* στρέφω 238.56 ff.; cf. CHANTR. 2.172); the participles δινεύοντες and στρέψαντες at 543 f. reinforce the notion of the back and forth as a kind of circular movement (cf. post-Homeric βουστροφηδόν of the direction of writing). On the process, *LfgrE s.v.* στρέφω 239.28 ff.: 'the τέλσον is the starting point on one side of the field, στρέψαι denotes the turning on the opposite side, see 546'; similarly WILLCOCK on 544: 'στρέψαντες i.e. having gone down and back'. — **τέλσον:** a technical term, attested only here, at 547 and 13.707 (plowing simile), denoting the field edge where the furrow ends and the plowman turns (*LfgrE s.v.*: 'turning place' [transl.]); the etymology is unclear (FRISK *s.v.*): either like τρί-πολος (542n.) and περι-τέλλομαι ('move about') related to the I-E root *kʷelh₁- 'execute a turn' (SCHW. 1.285, 1.516; EDWARDS; JANKO on 13.703–707; cautiously *DELG s.v.*; on the root, *LIV* 386–388), or related to an I-E root *kʷels- 'draw furrows' (BEEKES *s.v.*; older bibliography in FRISK; on the root, *LIV* 388 f.).

545 ≈ *Od.* 3.51; 2nd VH = 3.46; ≈ *h.Cer.* 206. — Wine – usually mixed with water – is also offered as refreshment elsewhere (6.261n., 19.161n.; RICHTER 1968, 127), but is also regarded with reserve (6.264–268n.); on the vessel shape of the *dépas*, 24.101n.

ἐν χερσί: often combined elsewhere with forms of τίθημι in formulaic phrases denoting the handing over of an object (24.101n.); in the same position in the verse as here is ἐν

---

543 ζεύγεα … ἐλάστρεον: on the uncontracted forms, R 6; on the unaugmented form ἐλάστρεον, R 16.1. — καὶ ἔνθα: on the correption, R 5.5.

544 οἵ: on the anaphoric demonstrative function of ὅ, ἥ, τό, R 17. — ἱκοίατο: 3rd pers. pl. aor. opt. of ἱκάνω; on the ending, R 16.2. — ἀρούρης: on the -η- after -ρ-, R 2.

545 τοῖσι: on the declension, R 11.2. — δ(έ): apodotic δέ (R 24.3).

χερσὶ τίθει (5× *Il.*, 4× *Od.*, cf. also 23.152 ἐν χερσὶ ... | θῆκεν), in the present passage with the contextually appropriate iterative δόσκεν (derived from τίθημι is only τίθεσκεν, attested at 'Hes.' *fr.* 67a, b M.-W.). On the dat. of obtained place of rest (with and without ἐν), SCHW. 2.155 f.; CHANTR. 2.79 f. — **μελιηδέος οἴνου:** an inflectable formula at VE (gen.: 1× *Il.*, 1× *Od.*, 1× *h.Cer.*; acc.: 1× *Il.*, 4× *Od.*, 1× *h.Hom.*) and after caesura B 1 (2× acc.); on the epithet (literally 'sweet as honey, honeyed', thus 'delicious, invigorating'), 6.258n. The disregarding of ϝ in οἴνου is due to inflection of the formula (CHANTR. 1.123; RUIJGH [1985] 1996, 231 f.; WEST 2001, 250; cf. M 14, FOR 23).

546 ὄγμους: a verbal noun related to ἄγω (FRISK, *DELG* and BEEKES s.v.); an agricultural technical term, it here (and at *h.Cer.* 455) denotes the track created in the field by plowing (a furrow or piled-up earth?), as well as the row of cut grain lying on the ground that has been cut in one pass ('swath': *Il.* 11.68, 18.552, 18.557): *LfgrE*; RICHTER 1968, 103 n. 743, 120 with n. 903.

547 The intention of the plowmen of reaching the edge of the field as soon as possible (since a refreshing drink awaits them there) is a narrative element within the description, perhaps analogous with similes that mention demanding physical labor and the laborers' desire for refreshment, e.g. at 11.86–89 (wood cutters), *Od.* 13.31–34 (plowman); see also 541–549n., end.

νειοῖο βαθείης: βαθύς can designate vertical or horizontal depth, here of the fallow field as the depth underground into which the plow cuts, cf. 10.353 and μαλακήν 541 (*LfgrE*: 'deeply plowed'; cf. 2.147–148n. on βάθυ λήϊον; on νειός, 541n.).

548–549 2nd VH of 549 ≈ *h.Merc.* 196; VE ≈ *h.Cer.* 240. — a return to the texture of the soil (541–549n.), with a fluid transition from the appearance of a real field to the artwork on the shield: color differences on the ground (real behind the plowman and 'at the back' on the image), similarities with a plowed field (illusionistic effect), reference to the material metal, effect of the creation on the observer (EDWARDS; BECKER 1995, 126–130, esp. 130; PURVES 2010, 134). — **darkened:** This optical impression can be explained via the effects of light on the relief surface of the plowed ground; some scholars understand this as a reference to the combination of gold with other metal alloys and associate it with the material *kýanos* (on which, 564n.; AH; EDWARDS; cf. 474–475n.).

---

546 δόσκεν ... στρέψασκον: iterative (-σκ-: R 16.5). — τοί: anaphoric demonstrative pronoun (R 14.3); like οἵ in 544, refers to the ἀροτῆρες, here after their refreshment. — ἀν' ὄγμους: 'along the furrows', i.e. they return along the furrows already drawn.

547 νειοῖο: on the declension, R 11.2. — βαθείης: on the -η- after -ι-, R 2.

548 μελαίνετ' ὄπισθεν: = μελαίνετο ὄπισθεν, 'blackened behind' (*sc.* behind the plowmen), i.e. the soil broken by the plow is darker. — ἀρηρομένη: perf. pass. part. of ἀρόω 'plow'. — δὲ (ϝ)ε(ϝ)ῴκει: on the prosody, R 4.3.

549 περ: concessive (R 24.10). — ἐοῦσα: = οὖσα (R 16.6). — θαῦμα: predicative. — τέτυκτο: plpf. pass. of τεύχω, 'was made, created'.

ἦ δὲ … | … τὸ δή: The change in gender signals the transition from the object depicted (ἡ νειός, ἄρουρα) to the artwork (BECKER 1995, 128). — χρυσείη: on the form, 418n. — περὶ θαῦμα τέτυκτο: περί is adverbial, 'exceedingly, very much' (SCHW. 2.423 f.; CHANTR. 2.125; on the accent [variant πέρι], SCHW. *loc. cit.* n. 4; WEST 1998, XIX), cf. 17.279 ≈ *Od.* 11.550 and esp. 8.281. – θαῦμα τέτυκτο is a variation of the VE formula θαῦμα ἰδέσθαι (83n., 377n.; PRIER 1989, 158 f.; cf. θαυμάσσεται, ὅς κεν ἴδηται: 466–467n.), which comments on the completed work with regard to the production process (DE JONG 2011, 7; cf. τεῦξε 478n.).

550–556a A portrayal of a field in which different steps of the grain harvest are being carried out (cf. Hes. *Op.* 479–482): harvesters cut with sickles, 'sheaf-binders' tie the sheaves together with special bindings (made from straw or rushes), boys gather up the stalks lying on the ground (CERRI; WEST on Hes. *Op.* 480; RICHTER 1968, 119–121). – Elsewhere in the *Iliad*, reaping occurs as a metaphor in the context of death in battle: at 11.67–71 in a simile[P] for mowing down an opponent, and at 19.220–227 in Odysseus' warning against sending the Greek troops into battle without prior refreshment (19.221–224n.; AUBRIOT 1999, 23–25; see also 552n. on literal echoes). Reaping is mentioned in the *Odyssey* together with other tasks in the field as paid labor (*Od.* 18.357 ff., esp. 366–380: Odysseus suggests a competition in reaping, plowing or fighting in battle).

550 precinct of a king (*témenos basiléion*): The term *témenos* denotes a delimited piece of land that either has been demarcated as the sacred precinct of a deity (e.g. at 8.48, 23.148) or has come into the possession of a ruler (here *basiléus*: 556b–557n.), be it as an inheritance or as a reward for special achievements (attested already in Mycenaean texts, as the term for the holdings of a ruler and a dignitary: *DMic s.v. te-me-no*); in the *Iliad*, this is granted to heroes such as Meleagros (9.578), Bellerophon, Glaukos and Sarpedon (6.194, 12.313), Aineias (20.184) and Iphition (20.391), in the *Odyssey* to Alkinoös (6.293) and Odysseus (17.299). On the term *témenos* and its etymology, 6.194n.; *LfgrE s.v.* τέμενος with bibliography; GUIZZI 2010. Land-holdings can consist of farmland, as here, and can also comprise orchards, vineyards and pasture (14.122–124a n.). A number of scholars thus contemplate counting the vineyard and pastures of the subsequent images among the holdings of the 'royal estate' (EDWARDS; GUIZZI *loc. cit.* 89).

ἐν δ' ἐτίθει: 541n. — βασιλήϊον: thus most editors, following several mss. and papyri, on analogy with 556, with an indication of ownership as 20.391 τέμενος πατρώϊον or with a gen. (*Od.* 6.293, 17.299) and like equivalent phrases in Mycenaean texts (*LfgrE s.v.* τέμενος 391.37 ff.). βαθὺ λήϊον ('deep grainfield') is also transmitted (this expression also at 2.147 [see *ad loc.*], 11.560, 'Hes.' *Sc.* 288): *app. crit.*; LEAF; QUATTORDIO MORESCHINI 1972, 245 f.; VAN DER VALK 1964, 134 f., by contrast, argues in favor of the reading βαθὺ λήϊον. — **ἔριθοι:** here denotes hired male harvesters (see also 559 f.); (συν-)έριθος is elsewhere a term for female help-meets in a variety of areas. Similar to the θῆτες, these are likely free wage-laborers (male or female), cf. Hes. *Op.* 602 f. (LSJ and *LfgrE s.v.*; RICHTER 1968, 19; NDOYE 2010, 172; cf. schol. bT on 560).

551 2nd VH = 'Hes.' *Sc.* 292; ≈ *Il.* 23.114, *Od.* 3.463, Hes. *Th.* 675. — **reaping hooks:** on the shape of sickles and sickle-knives for the harvesting of hay and grain, SCHIERING 1968, 155–158.

ἤμων: ἀμάω is also used absolutely at 24.451, Hes. *Op.* 39; the additional verse 551a (see *app. crit.*), transmitted by schol. T on 483–606, which adds an object with ἤμων, appears to have been inserted because of its reference to Athens (cf. HT 5; EDWARDS; BOLLING 1925, 182).

552–554 Despite the fact that purely dactylic hexameters are the most common verse scheme in the *Iliad* and *Odyssey* (DEE 2004, 1–95), the present three verses with their uniform rhythm and repetition of certain words and sounds (δράγματα δ' ἄλλα ... | ἄλλα δ' ἀμαλλοδετῆρες ἐν ἐλλεδανοῖσι δέοντο | ... ἀμαλλοδετῆρες) may evoke associations with the uniform rhythm of work during reaping.

552 δράγματα: derived from the verb δράσσομαι 'hold onto (with one's hand)' (cf. 13.393, 16.486), thus literally 'handful', denotes the number of stalks that can be grasped with one hand in order to cut them with the sickle (cf. Hes. *Op.* 480 ἀμήσεις ... περὶ χειρὸς ἐέργων and *Il.* 11.69 τὰ δὲ δράγματα ταρφέα πίπτει) or to tie them together for transport (553; cf. the denominative δραγμεύω at 555): *LfgrE*; RICHTER 1968, 119; FRISK, *DELG*, BEEKES *s.v.* δράσσομαι. — **μετ' ὄγμον:** 546n.; 'along the swath' (AH; EDWARDS; WILLCOCK). — **ἐπήτριμα πῖπτον ἔραζε:** ἐπήτριμος means 'in rows', at 211 of signal fires, 19.226 f. ἐπήτριμοι ... | πίπτουσιν of falling warriors echoing falling stalks (reaping as a metaphor for killing on the battlefield: 19.226n.). πῖπτον ἔραζε is an inflectable VE formula (12.156, 17.633 and *Od.* 22.280 on missiles). On the accent of πῖπτον, WEST 1998, XXI.

553 ἀμαλλοδετῆρες: 'sheaf-binders', a rarely attested *nomen agentis* derived from ἄμαλλα ('sheaf') and δέω (RICHTER 1968, 120 n. 905; on the suffix, 529n.). — **ἐλλεδανοῖσι:** a term for the bindings used for tying up sheaves, and attested only in the combination ἐν ἐλλεδανοῖσι + δέω/δέομαι (also at *h.Cer.* 456, 'Hes.' *Sc.* 291), perhaps a derivation from εἰλέω 'twist, turn' with an Aeolic pronunciation (FRISK and *DELG s.v.* ἐλλεδανοί; on the suffix, RISCH 106).

554 three: a typical number[P] (cf. 1.53n.), cf. the common motifs with threes at 155n., 24.454–456n. (for a list of groups of three, BLOM 1936, 17–20). Here it perhaps serves to depict a typified reality.

---

551 ἤμων: 3rd pers. pl. impf. of ἀμάω 'reap'.
554 ἐφέστασαν: 'stood by', 3rd pers. pl. plpf. of ἐφ-ίσταμαι. — αὐτάρ: 'but' (R 24.1).

555 δραγμεύοντες: a *hapax legomenon*[P], denotes the gathering of stalks into bundles (552n.). — **ἀγκαλίδεσσι:** also at 22.503; ἀγκαλίς means '(bent) arm', a metrically convenient derivation in -ίδ- related to ἀγκάλη, which is common in post-Homeric texts but has a prosodic structure (– ◡ –) that does not suit the hexameter (MEIER 1975, 53).

556a ἀσπερχὲς πάρεχον: 'ceaselessly handed (*sc.* the gathered-up stalks to the sheaf-binders)'; on ἀσπερχές (literally 'with zeal, vigorously'), 16.61–62n.

556b–557 The 'king', *basileús*, standing nearby in quiet joy is probably a contrasting figure to the *basileús* as warlord in the action of the *Iliad*, perhaps in particular to Achilleus (see the periphrastic denomination[P] for Achilleus at 1.331, 16.211), with a life dominated by toil and misery (see Thetis on her son at 442 f.: 62n.) and who had considered such a peaceful life on his estate for himself – albeit only briefly (9.399 f., but see Achilleus' longing for it at *Od.* 11.489 ff., after he has entered the underworld): GÄRTNER 1976, 61 f.; TAPLIN (1980) 2001, 352. — **king:** The owner of the *témenos*, who supervises the harvest, here bears the title *basileús*, which in Homeric epic is employed for all 'local and regional leaders', as well as for members of governing bodies (1.9n. with bibliography; also WEILER 2001, 53 ff.; SHEAR 2004, 69 ff.; CARLIER 2006; HORN 2014, 36–41). In contrast to the simile at 11.68 ('a wealthy man's field'), the landowner (of a *témenos*) here is thus a figure of authority with a political function; he is marked as such via his *sképtron* (see below and 505n.; EDWARDS; *LfgrE s.v.* βασιλεύς 45.54 ff.; CARLIER 1984, 143 n. 22; 2006, 102 n. 8; GUIZZI 2010, 83–85). In Homeric society, all social strata, including kings and their kin, are involved in agricultural labor (cf. 24.29n.). — **in silence | ... staff:** The silence of the king who carries a *sképtron* – an insignia of power, on one hand (2.101–108n.; *LfgrE s.v.* σκῆπτρον 144.53 ff.), and the mark of the speaker in assemblies, on the other (505n.) – i.e. the explicit absence of speech (e.g. in the shape of instructions) makes everything clear: nothing disturbs the practiced workflow, and the 'king' is standing in the midst of the laborers in silent contentment (PINAULT 1994, 513 f.; BECKER 1995, 132). This is a remarkable contrast with other scenes on the shield pertaining to the human sphere (478–608n. section **B.1.b.**), where loud noises such as music and song (493, 495, 569–572), shouting (502, 530) or roaring animals (575, 580) are mentioned repeatedly (WILLE 2001, 85 f.).

βασιλεύς ... | σκῆπτρον ἔχων: a more pregnant variant of the VB formula σκηπτοῦχος βασιλεύς (1.279n.); cf. ἔστη σκῆπτρον ἔχων in the assembly at 2.101, 2.279. — **γηθόσυνος**

---

555 ἀγκαλίδεσσι: on the declension, R 11.3.
556 πάρεχον: on the unaugmented form, R 16.1.
557 κῆρ: acc. of respect (R 19.1).

κῆρ: VE = 4.272, 4.326. Like the verb γηθέω, the adj. expresses 'an intensive sensation of glad satisfaction and contentment' (LATACZ 1966, 154, 233 [transl.]); on κῆρ, 19.57n. (on the VE formula ἀχνυμένος κ.). — **σιωπῇ:** 'silently, quietly', 'with the situational aspect of quietness' (*LfgrE s.v.* σιωπῇ [transl.], but cf. *loc. cit. s.vv.* σιγάω and σιγῇ: more commonly 'with the situational aspect of withholding information' [transl.]).

558–560 preparations for a meal, in that a group of men is occupied with the preparation of meat (558–559a) and a group of women prepares a dish of grain (559b–560); this corresponds to the common division of labor between men (meat) and women (bread), e.g. when serving (*Od.* 1.139 ff., 4.55 f./65 f., 15.138 ff.) or during preparations for a sacrificial meal (3.421–463): WICKERT-MICKNAT 1982, 52 f.; RUNDIN 1996, 190; cf. 24.625–626n.; *HE s.v.* 'Food'; on the individual steps of meat preparation, BRUNS 1970, 46–49. In the case of large feasts, a sacrifice for the gods is always included (cf. the type-scenes 'sacrifice' [1.447–468n., 2.410–431n.] and 'meal' [24.621–628n.]; *HE s.v.* 'Feasting'; HITCH 2009, 43), and some formulations do indeed evoke associations with ritual acts (WATKINS 1978, esp. 10; on this, see nn. on the individual verses). In the present description, particular emphasis is on the aspect 'a plentiful meal' (see the adjectives 'great' and 'abundant' at 559 f.), perhaps in reference to the wealth (cf. 559n.) and generosity (cf. *Il.* 9.69 ff., *Od.* 17.416 ff.: STEIN-HÖLKESKAMP 1989, 39; RUNDIN *loc. cit.* 181 ff.; cf. SCHEID-TISSINIER 1994, 253–255) of the 'king'. The description of the action reveals nothing specific regarding the meal itself (BECKER 1995, 132: 'The words merely describe the action that is suggested by the image, without turning it into a story'). The connection between the preparation of the meat and the grain is thus a matter of dispute (560n.), as is whether the various dishes are meant for different groups of people: on the basis of the image of the king among the laborers (556 f.), it should probably be assumed that (a) a joint feast is being prepared, with meat consumed by *everyone* involved in the harvest, rather than that (b) the slaughtered ox is meant exclusively for the king, while the laborers are served *only* the dish of grain set before them at 560; in favor of (a): LEAF; EDWARDS on 560; BRUNS *loc. cit.* 57; TAPLIN (1980) 2001, 352 n. 23; in favor of (b): WILLCOCK; KIRK 1976, 12 (like the similes, the description of the shield portrays simple, everyday life in contrast to the heroic world of the *Iliad*, but in the present scene 'the heroic attitude momentarily reasserts itself'); RUNDIN *loc. cit.* 190 ff.; on the two Greek terms for 'meal', 558n. and 560n.

558 VE = *Od.* 2.322. — **under a tree:** i.e. in the shade, cf. 5.693, *h.Cer.* 100 (TAPLIN [1981] 2001, 352), a detail with bucolic effect. *drys* can denote 'tree' in general or 'oak' specifically (cf. the term *dry-tómos* 'tree-feller' already attested in Mycenaean texts [*Il.* 11.86, 16.633, 23.315: MYC] and the proverbial saying 'oak and stone' [22.126, *Od.* 19.163, Hes. *Th.* 35 with WEST *ad loc.*]); in the second case, it is perhaps thought of as marked as such in the depiction by its imposing size, cf. its distinctive epithets[P] *hypsíkomos* 'lofty and leafy' (2× *Il.*, 4× *Od.*, 2× Hes.) and *hypsikárēnos* 'with a tall crown' (1× *Il.*, 1× *h.Ven.*): LfgrE *s.v.* δρῦς; *BNP s.v.* Oak. — **heralds:** The heralds (*kérykes*) employed by kings are, in a manner of speaking, 'the «personal assistants» of the heroic world' (HAINSWORTH on *Il.* 9.174–177) with a variety of duties in different areas, including in the context of meals (9.174, *Od.* 1.109, 1.146, 7.163, etc.) and the slaughter of sacrificial animals (e.g. *Il.* 3.118 ff., 19.169 ff.); on the function of heralds in general, 1.321n., 1.334n. — **feast:** *dais* (literally 'share' in the joint meal) is a term for a celebratory communal meal (1.5n.) and frequently signals hospitality that creates a community and is designed to fortify the status of the host (2.404–409n., 24.802n. [each with bibliography]; *LfgrE s.v.* δαίς; SCHEID-TISSINIER 1994, 268–274; RUNDIN 1996, 186–205).

πένοντο: 'were busy doing', frequently of preparations for meals (1.318a n.; *LfgrE s.v.* πένομαι).

559 1st VH ≈ *Od.* 2.56, 17.535. — **ox:** In Homeric epic, cattle are a sign of their owner's wealth (2.449n.), they are valuable and are sacrificed only on special occasions (1.66n., 2.402n., 24.125n.) or are slaughtered on the occasion of a special meal, e.g. at the end of a day of fighting (7.466 ff., 8.505 ff./545 ff., 23.30 ff. [Patroklos' funeral feast], *Od.* 9.45 f.) or to host special guests (*Il.* 6.174, 7.314 ff., *Od.* 3.421 ff., etc.): *LfgrE s.v.* βοῦς 88.46 ff.; *BNP s.vv.* Cattle and Meat, consumption of; RICHTER 1968, 44–53). – on the emphasis on the quality of livestock, 24.125n.

ἱερεύσαντες … ἄμφεπον: an abbreviated version of the sequence '(1) slaughtering, (2) skinning, (3) preparing', see esp. 7.314/316 (24.622n.): ἱερεύω means both 'sacrifice' and 'slaughter', since a festive meal involving the consumption of meat is always combined with a sacrificial act (6.173–174n., 24.125n.; *LfgrE s.v.* 1137.34 ff.; cf. 558–560n.); ἀμφ-έπω ('be occupied with': 348n.) is also used in the context of the preparation of meat at 11.776, 23.167, 24.622, *Od.* 8.61, 19.421. — **αἱ δὲ γυναῖκες:** 495b–496n.

560 The term *álphita* used here for the dish of cereal denotes flour or groats of barley or other types of grain (see below *s.v.* ἄλφιτα) that is used as the basis for the making of porridge or flatbread and considered a staple food (*Od.* 2.290, 19.197, 20.108, 20.119): WEST on *Od.* 2.290; RICHTER 1968, 108, 114 f.; on the different species of grain cultivated in antiquity and on their use, *BNP s.v.* Grain; DALBY 2003, 45–47, 162 f. It is also added to other foods (*Od.* 10.234 [Kirke's potion], 14.77), used as an ingredient in drinks (*Il.* 11.631–641, *Od.* 10.518–520 = 11.26–28) or burned as a sacrificial offering (*Od.* 14.429, *h.Ap.* 491, 509). The present formulation can be interpreted in various ways (BRUNS 1970, 56 f.): either the women sprinkle ground or kibbled grain into a liquid not described here in order to turn it into gruel or porridge (schol. T and D; AH; STENGEL 1910, 66 f.; RICHTER *loc. cit.* 114 f.; RUNDIN 1996, 190), much as at *Il.* 11.640, *Od.* 10.520 = 11.28 (although this is a type of mixed drink), or they sprinkle it on the meat, as Eumaios does at *Od.* 14.77, 14.429 (LEAF; FAESI; VAN LEEUWEN; EDWARDS; BRUNS *loc. cit.* 57; TAPLIN [1980] 2001, 352 n. 23) – although women are never involved in cooking meat elsewhere in Homeric epic (558–560n.). In any case, the use of products from the grain harvest completes the cycle with regard to the preceding reaping scene. — **to eat:** The term *deípnon* designates a meal taken during the day, e.g. as refreshment during work (11.86, *Od.* 9.311, 15.500), prior to going into battle (*Il.* 2.381, 8.53, 19.171, 19.275, 19.346) or before a journey (*Od.* 15.77), cf. esp. *Od.* 15.495–507 (where *deípnon* designates the sailors' food during work, *dais* the meal provided by Telemachos as part of their payment): 2.381n.; BRUNS 1970, 57 f.; RUNDIN 1996, 185.

δεῖπνον ἐρίθοισιν: predicative, 'as a meal for the hired harvesters' (SCHW. 2.153); on ἐρίθοισιν, 550n. — λεύκ' ἄλφιτα πολλὰ πάλυνον: a variation of the inflectable VE formula (ἐπὶ δ᾽) ἄλφιτα λευκὰ πάλυνε/-ον (11.640, *Od.* 10.520, 11.28, 14.77, cf. ἐπί τ᾽ ἄλφιτα λευκὰ θύοντες 2× *h.Ap.*); by reversing the noun and attribute (rather than πολλ᾽ ἄλφιτα λευκὰ πάλυνον), the addition πολλά, i.e. the large amount, is emphasized. — ἄλφιτα: a term for ground grain, like ἀλείατα (see *Od.* 20.108); the difference between ἄλφιτα and ἀλείατα is evaluated in various ways: either coarse meal (groats) *vs.* fine meal (*LfgrE s.v.* ἄλφιτα), or 'barley flour' *vs.* 'wheat flour' (RUSSO on *Od.* 20.108; RICHTER 1968, 114, with reference to the epithet λευκός used with ἄλφιτα [8× early epic of 18 examples overall], like κρῖ λευκόν 'barley' [8× early epic]; *contra* WEST on *Od.* 2.290: restriction of ἄλφιτα to '*barley* groats' is 'almost certainly post-homeric'). The term for barley grains used in a ritual context is οὐλαί, οὐλοχύται (1.458n.). On the etymology of ἄλφιτα, see BEEKES and *ChronEG* 9 *s.v.* ἄλφι. — πάλυνον: 'sprinkle', in early epic usually of ἄλφιτα (see above on the VE formula ἄλφιτα λευκὰ π. and *Od.* 14.429 ἀλφίτου ἀκτῇ), also at *Il.* 10.7 (simile) of snow in the fields; probably derived from πάλη 'meal, dust' (*LfgrE s.v.*; FRISK *s.v.*; *DELG s.v.* 2 πάλη).

561–572 a depiction of a vineyard; on its layout with stakes, ditches and an enclosure, see RICHTER 1968, 107, 130 f.; on viticulture, *loc. cit.* 127–133; *BNP s.v.* Wine. The static description of the structure (561–565) is followed by a transitional verse – which evokes the idea of a wine harvest – and a description of a lively scene full of movement, with music, song and dance accompanying the harvesting (567–572): BECKER 1995, 133–137; for additional dancing scenes, 494n. (on the wedding, 493 ff.). In this, the third image of agriculture, the idealization of labor is the most pronounced: with music, carrying the harvest-baskets becomes easy and is done with a spring in the step. The description speaks to various senses, with the narrator conveying optical *and* acoustic impressions: (a) specifications of color and material evoke a chiaroscuro effect

(562–565; cf. 548 f.); (b) the different timbres of the lyre and of human voices are described as 'light' or 'sweet' and 'gentle' and as loud cries (567–572n.); (c) the description of the rhythm of the dance is underlined with onomatopoetic elements (571–572n.). The emphasis is on the aesthetics, with stress on the perceptible qualities 'beautiful' (optically and acoustically: 562, 570), 'honeyed' (568), 'gentle' (571). In contrast, the descriptions of Alkinoös' orchard and vineyard in the *Odyssey* stress their productivity (*Od.* 7.112–132).

561–562 on the series of epithets and enjambment, 130–131n.; on 'beautiful' (*kālós*) at VB, 490–491a n.

ἐν δ' ἐτίθει: 541n. — **σταφυλῇσι ... | ... βότρυες:** denotes the grape on the vine and the grape cluster; βότρυες is a Homeric *hapax*[P] (but see βοτρυδόν at 2.89). On σταφυλή, cf. *Od.* 7.121, 24.343 and the compounds πολυστάφυλος ('rich in grapes': 2.507n.) and ἐριστάφυλος ('with large grapes'): RICHTER 1968, 129 with n. 993, 131 n. 1005. — **ἀλωήν:** 57n. — **χρυσείην:** on the form, 418n. — **ἀνά:** adverbial, here 'everywhere on top', *sc.* on the vineyard made of gold (i.e. on all the vines in the vineyard, cf. *Od.* 24.343): SCHW. 2.422; CHANTR. 2.90.

563 ἑστήκει δὲ κάμαξι ... ἀργυρέῃσιν: ἀλωή is to be supplied as the grammatical subject: the golden vineyard 'stood there with silver stakes' (*sc.* for the vines); the uprightness of the stakes (and vines) is transferred to the vineyard as a whole (LEAF; *LfgrE s.v.* ἵστημι 1240.58 ff.; RICHTER 1968, 131). — **διαμπερές:** 'from one end to the other, through and through' (19.272n.), i.e. throughout the entire vineyard.

564 field-ditch: The 'ditch' is an irrigation ditch dug around the plantation and used to conduct spring water (cf. 21.257 f., *Od.* 7.129 f.). Its dark color on the golden background is linguistically distinct from the black of the grapes (*mélanes* at 561, see also *meláinet'* at 548 of the plowed field): The adjective *kýaneos*, already attested in Mycenaean texts (*DMic s.v. ku-wa-ni-jo-qe*), is derived from the noun *kýanos* (*DMic s.v. ku-wa-no*: 'lapis lazuli' or 'enamel'?; on the suffix of material adjectives, 24.21n.), which is associated etymologically with Hittite *kuwanna* (designation for a precious stone or for copper?), as well as with other terms from I-E languages that denote materials from which a blue color can be extracted (e.g. azurite, smalt); the literal meaning is unclear (*DELG*, *ChronEG* 3 and 6 *s.v.* κύανος). In the *Iliad*, *kýanos* is linked with the color adj. *mélas* ('black'), is used in the description of the decoration of Agamemnon's arms (11.24/35) and is mentioned together with a variety of metals among the building materials for the palace of Alkinoös (*Od.* 7.87). Homeric *kýanos* is in-

---

561 ἐν: 541n. — σταφυλῇσι: on the declension, R 11.1. — βρίθουσαν: part. of βρίθω (+ dat.) 'be heavily laden (with)'.
564 κυανέην: on the -η- after -ε-, R 2. — ἀμφὶ ... περὶ ... ἔλασσεν: on the so-called tmesis, R 20.2; on the -σσ-, R 9.1.

terpreted as the seemingly black alloy 'niello', made from silver, copper, lead and sulfur, or as an imitation of lapis lazuli in the shape of enamel or goldstone (blue goldstone, blue aventurine glass) inlays (EDWARDS p. 203; HAINSWORTH on *Il.* 11.24; *LfgrE* s.v. κύανος with bibliography; FITTSCHEN 1973, 5 f.; IRWIN 1974, 79–84; SHEAR 2004, 59; somewhat differently, GIUMLIA-MAIR/CRADDOCK 1993, 19 ff.: *Corinthium aes*; on this, 474–475n.). In the present passage, the adj. *kyáneos* perhaps denotes, like the adj. 'gold' and 'silver' (562 f.), both the color and the material, similar to the figures on Agamemnon's corselet and shield (snakes, 11.26/39) and on Herakles' shield (snakes and *Kēres*, 'Hes.' *Sc.* 167, 249); elsewhere in early epic, it is used as a color term 'dark, bluish black' (cf. *Il.* 4.277/282, 24.93 f.), esp. of hair, garments and clouds (often appearing menacing: 16.66n.): IRWIN *loc. cit.* 84–108; DÜRBECK 1977, 141–144.

ἀμφὶ ... περί: adverbial; either 'on both sides' (of the vines) and 'all around' (the vineyard) (AH; cf. FRITZ 2005, 73) or a variation for metrical reasons (CHANTR. 2.129) with no difference in meaning (FEHLING 1969, 195). — κάπετον ... ἕρκος: κάπετος means 'ditch' (cf. 24.797n.) and is related to the root of σκάπτω (FRISK, *DELG* s.v. σκάπτω); ἕρκος denotes the protective 'enclosure' (1.283b–284n.) surrounding the entire vineyard, as a delimitation of the garden from nature (RICHTER 1968, 105–107, 130 f.). — ἔλασσεν: ἐλαύνω is a technical term for forging, on the one hand, see 12.295 f. (*LfgrE* s.v. 518.38 ff.), and is used in agriculture of the drawing of lines such as furrows, ditches or fences by driving in stakes, on the other (*LfgrE* s.v. 518.64 ff.).

565 of tin: The metal, shining brightly when freshly polished, is also used elsewhere beside other metals for color effects: 'white' shield bosses from tin beside 'black' *kýanos* on Agamemnon's shield (11.34 f.), tin next to gold on Achilleus' shield (574: patterns on hides), gold and tin decorations on Agamemnon's corselet (11.25) and as fittings on a chariot (23.503), 'glossy' tin on a valuable bronze corselet (23.561); on tin as a material, also 474–475n. and 613n. (on Achilleus' greaves).

κασσιτέρου: on the juxtaposition of material adjectives and the gen. of material (likewise in the case of Agamemnon's shield at 11.24 ff.), SCHW. 2.128 f. — ἀταρπιτὸς ... ἐπ' αὐτήν: ἀταρπιτός is a by-form of ἀταρπός ('footpath, trail'), probably formed on analogy with ἀμαξιτός (related to ἄμαξα), perhaps related to τραπέω 'press, tread (grapes)' (*DELG*, BEEKES s.v. ἀταρπός); at 17.743, it designates a mountain trail used to transport wood, at *Od.* 14.1 and 17.234 the path leading to Eumaios' remote farm, while at *h.Ap.* 227 it is used beside κέλευθος (*LfgrE* s.v. ἀταρπός; BECKER 1937, 35); ἐπ' αὐτήν refers contextually to ἀλωή, but can be interpreted in different ways: either 'across, through it', i.e. a 'trail' within the vineyard (AH; FAESI; *LfgrE* s.v. ἀταρπός; similarly FRITZ 2005, 136 f.) or 'toward it', as with verbs of movement, i.e. an access path (La Roche; Chantr. 2.110; Becker 1995, 135; cf. schol. A on the reading ἐς αὐτήν).

566 νίσοντο: literally 'return' (related to νέομαι), here 'walk back and forth' (*LfgrE*); probably a reduplicated pres. stem (νῖσ- < *ni-ns-) rather than a desiderative (*ni-ns-se-): *LIV* 454 f.; Beekes s.v. νέομαι; Giannakis 1997, 207–209; on the spelling νισ- vs. νισσ-, West 1998, XXXIII. — **φορῆες:** 'bearers', a Homeric *hapax*[P] (on the formation, Risch 157; Perpillou 1973, 85, 349 f.). In this verse, which interprets the layout of the vineyard, it denotes the harvesters in general (see the iterative temporal clause ὅτε τρυγόῳεν; on this, Becker 1995, 135: 'The description has generalized the depicted action into a habitual activity of the characters depicted'). They are perhaps depicted in the subsequent scene as παρθενικαὶ δὲ καὶ ἠίθεοι (567; cf. the sequence φορῆες … φέρον at 568) or these young people are simply helpers in addition to the vintners, similar to ἀμαλλοδοτῆρες vs. παῖδες at 554/555 (AH; undecided, *LfgrE* s.v. φορεύς; somewhat differently Cerri: φορῆες ['carriers' (transl.)] are παρθενικαὶ and ἠίθεοι, but the subj. of τρυγόῳεν is indeterminate, i.e. in general the 'harvesters' [transl.]). — **τρυγόῳεν:** from τρυγάω 'harvest' (likewise at *Od.* 7.124 grapes, at 'Hes.' *Sc.* 292 vines), in the iterative opt. (Schw. 2.649; Chantr. 2.260; on the epic diectasis, G 48).

567–572 Rather than the description of the harvest proper, a dancing scene follows, dominated by terms for music, qualities of tone (the lyre's bright sound that carries, the boys' delicate voices, loud cries) and the conjunction of sounds and movement, by means of which the narrator[P] achieves a very high degree of *enárgeia* (on which, 478–608n. section **B.3.**): 571–572n.; Kaimio 1977, 81, 101; on the properties of singing voices, West 1992, 42–45. In 570 f., the narrator[P] links with this in an imagined acoustic sphere an aesthetic qualification of the items beyond the optical he presents (Becker 1995, 136 f.; see also 571–572n. s.v. λεπταλέη).

567 VE ≈ *h.Cer.* 24. — **παρθενικαὶ … ἠίθεοι:** a half-verse variant beside the briefer ἠ. καὶ παρθένοι (593: dancers) and παρθένος ἠίθεός τε (22.127 f.: lovers), cf. the indications of age at *Od.* 11.38 f.; the term encompasses youths of both sexes of marriageable age (Wickert-Micknat 1982, 104 f., 114). — **ἀταλὰ φρονέοντες:** The meaning and etymology of the adj. ἀταλός are unclear: either 'child-like' or 'delicate' (likewise at 20.222 πώλοισιν, *Od.* 11.39 παρθενικαί), with the context sometimes adding an aspect of playfulness (*LfgrE* s.v. ἀταλός; Moussy 1972, 159 f.; on the uncertain etymology, *DELG* and Beekes s.v.). The phrase ἀταλὰ φρονέων (likewise at Hes. *Th.* 989 of a child), much like ἀταλάφρονα (*Il.* 6.400 of Astyanax), means approximately 'cheerful, blithe, carefree' (6.400n.; *LfgrE* s.v. φρονέω 1042.51 ff.; somewhat differently *h.Cer.* 24 of Hekate, see Richardson *ad loc.*: 'with youthful spirit'). It underlines the exuberance, the light,

---

566 τῇ: with the function of a relative pronoun, locative dat. without preposition (R 14.5, R 19.2): 'on which'.
567 ἠίθεοι ἀταλά: on the hiatus, R 5.6.

playful aspects of the youths' dancing, cf. ἀταλότατα παίζει in the hexameter on the Dipylon oinochoe, dedicated to the best of the dancers (508n.; on this, HEUBECK 1979, 117 f.; HENRICHS 1996, 32–35).

568 1st VH = *Od.* 9.247; 2nd VH ≈ *Od.* 9.94; VE = *Il.* 9.186. — **μελιηδέα καρπόν:** a variant, appropriate to the grape harvest, of the formula μελιηδέα οἶνον (545n.); καρπός can refer to the wine itself: 3.246 (see *ad loc.*), *h.Hom.* 7.41.

569 The motif of the singer performing a song with the lyre (*phórminx:* 495a n.) while surrounded by dancers also occurs in the *Odyssey:* see Demodokos' appearance at 8.261–264, where he performs the song of Ares and Aphrodite (266 ff.); for additional examples of a singer performing with a lyre (esp. *Il.* 9.186–194, Achilleus), 495a n., 604b–605a n.

τοῖσιν δ' ἐν μέσσοισι: 507n. — **φόρμιγγι λιγείῃ:** an inflectable VE formula (dat./acc.: 2× *Il.*, 6× *Od.*, 1× *h.Ap.*); λιγύς denotes a bright, piercing sound, in the *Odyssey* also in reference to the singing of female voices (1.248n.; KAIMIO 1977, 44).

570 1st VH = 'Hes.' *Sc.* 202; 2nd VH ≈ *h.Merc.* 54, 502. — **Linos:** Linos is a designation for a song, on the one hand, and in post-Homeric sources also the name of a mythical figure associated with music in a variety of ways, on the other (schol. T and b; Eust. 1163.53 ff.): (a) he was considered the son of a Muse (among others, Urania) and Apollo and, due to his untimely death, was mourned by singers at feasts with a song in which his name was called out repeatedly ('Hes.' *fr.* 305 M.-W.), likely a reference to the call *aílinon* recurring in the song (Pind. *fr.* 128c.6; subsequently usually a mourning cry in tragedy, see LSJ *s.v.* αἴλινος); (b) according to Herodotus (2.79), a mourning song corresponding to the Greek Linos song was performed in Phoenicia, on Cyprus and in Egypt; (c) he was also considered a gifted poet and singer (sometimes thought to be the first poet overall) and was claimed by Thebes as a local hero who had been killed by Apollo and mourned by the Muses (Paus. 9.29.6–9); (d) he was credited with cosmological poetry (on the sources, see WEST 1983, 56–67). 'Linos' is generally interpreted as a song named for the original ritual cry (of mourning?) *aílinon*, with the hero as its personification (cf. the similar situation with Hymenaios at 493n. and Thamyris at 2.595n.); the origin remains unclear (originally a Phoenician cry of mourning for a god of vegetation?): *KlP s.v.* Linos; *BNP s.vv.* Linus and Ailinos; FRISK and *DELG s.v.* λίνος; REINER 1938, 109–113; ARNOULD 1990, 219–221; GRANDOLINI 1996, 61–63; WEST 1997, 262 (Linos is 'a periodically dying nature-figure of «Aegean» type'; STEPHENS 2002/2003, 16–21). The character of the Linos song in the present passage cannot be determined clearly: the context – especially the description of the dance at 567/571 f. – suggests of

---

569 μέσσοισι: on the -σσ-, R 9.1.

its own accord a cheerful song, with the scholia thus interpreting the Linos here as a song sung by the winemakers for entertainment (schol. b and T on 569–570; cf. WEGNER 1968, 32; WEST 1992, 28 f.; *BNP* s.v. Work songs). This forms a marked contrast to the mourning character ascribed to the song in numerous sources (see above); it is thus interpreted as a mourning song here as well, an expression of a melancholy popular mood in the face of dying vege- tation during the fall (HÄUSSLER 1974, 9–11; LYNN-GEORGE 1988, 192; cautiously LEAF *ad loc.* and on 572; EDWARDS; undecided, *LfgrE* s.vv. ἰυγμός, λίνος). This ambivalence perhaps also corresponds to the character of the occasion: 'This divergence may reflect the dual nature of the cult and its ritual, death and re- turn, lamentation and joy' (ALEXIOU [1974] 2002, 57, 218 n. 19; on associations with death in images of agriculture, see AUBRIOT 1999, 25–27). On other song types in the *Iliad*, 493n.

ἱμερόεν: 'exciting desire' (related to ἵμερος 'desire'), here an adverbial acc., describing the effects on the ear; elsewhere an epithet, in a musical context of ἀοιδή (VE formula 2× *Od.*, 1× Hes., 1× *h.Ven.*), as here, and of the sound of the φόρμιγξ (*h.Ap.* 185), also of χορός (603 and a further 5× early epic): *LfgrE* s.v. ἱμερόεις; KAIMIO 1977, 57; KLOSS 1994, 57 f. — κιθάριζε: likewise at 'Hes.' *Sc.* 202 and 10× *h.Hom.* (a term common in post-Ho- meric texts for playing the lyre: LSJ s.v.), a metrical-prosodic variant of φορμίζω (3× *Od.*, 1× *h.Ap.*): *LfgrE* s.v. φορμίζω. — λίνον: internal acc. (song type), similar to παιήονα (1.473) *et al.* (schol. A, T; *LfgrE* s.v. ἀείδω 157.56 ff.). — ὑπό: adverbial, here 'with it', i.e. with (the accompaniment of) the kithara, cf. the *iterata* (CHANTR. 2.138 f.: 'at the same time' [transl.]; *LfgrE* s.v. ἀείδω 156.45 ff.; CALAME [1977] 1997, 80 f.; GRANDOLINI 1996, 62). — καλὸν ἄειδε: a variable VE formula (1× *Il.*, 2× *Od.*, 3× *h.Merc.*); usually with adverbial καλόν, probably here as well (where καλόν might also be an attribute with λίνον) by analogy with ἱμερόεν (AH; LEAF; KAIMIO 1977, 55 with n. 113; GRANDOLINI 1996, 38 f.; cautiously *LfgrE* s.v. καλός 1312.1 f.).

571–572 with singing … | …kept time to the music: The youths with their filled baskets move in a circular dance around the boy singing 'in their midst' (569; cf. *Od.* 8.262–264); on the dance moves, TÖLLE 1964, 61–63, 66; KURZ 1966, 138 f.; see also 494n. Their dancing is accompanied by singing, which is de- scribed with two terms: (a) *molpḗ* in Homeric epic usually denotes a song ac- companying dancing (on this, cf. esp. *Od.* 1.152, 4.17–19, 23.143–147): *LfgrE* s.vv. μολπή, μέλπω; WEST on *Od.* 1.152; WEGNER 1968, 42 f.; CINGANO 1993, 349–353); (b) *iygmós* (a Homeric *hapax*[P]; in tragedy a term for a cry of mourning) is de- rived from the verb *iýzō* 'shout, howl, jeer' (likely an onomatopoetic formation related to an interjection; cf. 17.66 and *Od.* 15.162, where it designates cries de- signed to deter predators): *LfgrE* s.v. ἰύζω; TICHY 1983, 169); if Linos is inter-

---

571 τοί: anaphoric demonstrative pronoun (R 14.3). — δὲ (ῥ)ρήσσοντες: on the prosody, M 4.6.

preted as a song of mourning (570n.), *iygmós* can be interpreted as a term for the chorus-like *aílinon* cry (AH; CALAME [1977] 1997, 81 with n. 218; GRANDOLINI 1996, 62 f.); on antiphonal songs (response songs) in early Greek and Ancient Near Eastern literature, see WEST 1997, 42 f.

λεπταλέη: 'thin, delicate', of the boy's high voice (EDWARDS; KAIMIO 1977, 48, 191; WEST 1992, 45, 388); an expansion of λεπτός not attested again until Hellenistic epic (*DELG*, BEEKES *s.v.* λέπω; KRAPP 1964, 236), where it is employed (esp. in Callimachus) as a term to denote the aesthetic qualities of music and poetry (STEPHENS 2002/2003, 13–16). – **ῥήσσοντες ... | ... σκαίροντες:** an imitation of rhythmic movements by verbal echoes in the 2nd VH (*LfgrE s.v.* σκαίρω: '«responsion» of the part. with 571 and repetition of the sound οντ' [transl.]): Ionic ῥήσσω (Attic ῥάττω) means 'push, beat', of dancers 'beat (the time)'; an etymological connection, e.g. with ἀράσσω ('hit, beat') or ῥήγνυμι ('break'), is uncertain (FRISK, *DELG*, BEEKES *s.v.* ῥάσσω; *LfgrE s.v.* ῥήσσω). In the present passage, the part. likely means 'stomping (in time)'; cf. the imitation of the Homeric passage at Apoll. Rhod. 1.538 f. (φόρμιγγος ... ὁμαρτῇ | ... πέδον ῥήσσωσι πόδεσσι; on this, RENGAKOS 1993, 123; 1994, 137), in a comparable context also at *h.Ap.* 516 f. (φόρμιγγ' ἐν χείρεσσιν ἔχων, ἐρατὸν κιθαρίζων, | ... οἳ δὲ ῥήσσοντες ἕποντο). σκαίρω means 'leap, spring', likewise at *Od.* 10.412 (calves leap around their mothers): *LfgrE.* Post-Homeric texts use e.g. πηδάω in its place (NAEREBOUT 1997, 281; BIERL 2001, 151 n. 118). – **ἁμαρτή:** an instrumental of a verbal adj. ossified into an adv. meaning 'at the same time, concurrently', it consists of ἅμα + ἀρ- (cf. ἀραρίσκω), likewise at 5.656, 21.162, *Od.* 22.81 (FRISK and BEEKES *s.v.* ἁμαρτή; *DELG s.v.* ἁμαρεῖν; SCHW. 1.550). It is also transmitted with an initial ὁμ- in papyri and mss. (see *app. crit.*), but Aristarchus appears to have read ἁμαρτή (schol. A and T on 5.656; WACKERNAGEL 1916, 70 f.; RENGAKOS 1993, 123; on ὁμ-, WEST 1998, XXX; cf. 24.438n. *s.v.* ἁμαρτέων).

573–589 The peaceful mood in the images with agricultural labor is replaced by two images of animal herds conveying mixed emotions: an unsuspecting herd of cattle, accompanied by herdsmen and dogs, is on its way to the pasture (573–578) but has been overtaken by raw violence – two lions snatch the bull, while herdsmen and dogs remain powerless (579–586); sheep are grazing calmly (587–589). Like the images of agricultural labor, these two are linked to the seasons, namely winter, since the cattle apparently spend some time (the night?) inside the compound (575), while there are shelters on the sheep pasture (589): TAPLIN [1980] 2001, 353; ALDEN 2000, 70 f.; differently schol. T on 587–588 (sheep in the meadow are appropriate for spring). But here too this assignment does not necessarily follow from the description (cf. 541–572n. and EDWARDS on 573–589); the introductory verb form *poíēse* (573/587) introduces a new set of images (478–608n. section **B.1.b.**), with herds of cattle and sheep representing large and small livestock, see also the animal raids at 524, 528 f. On animal husbandry (esp. cattle, sheep and goats) in Homeric epic generally, RICHTER 1968, 32–64; *BNP s.v.* Husbandry.

The change of introductory verb from ἐν δ᾽ ἐτίθει (541/550/561) to ἐν δ᾽ ... ποίησε (573/587) and the similar structure of the introductory verses 587/590 with the subj. περικλυτὸς Ἀμφιγυήεις lend certain similarities to the final three images (WIRBELAUER 1996, 151 f.).

573–586 A depiction of a herd of cattle on their way to pasture (on the scene, cf. 520–529, esp. 525 f.): some static (573 f., 579–580a), some with dynamic movement and accentuated by sound (575 ff., 580b ff.), with intensification of the acoustic effects (575 f., 580 f.) and the drama. References to an image are missing, with the exception of 574 ('made from gold and tin') and 577 ('golden herdsmen'); in the words of the person doing the describing, it turns into a 'story, and is fully dramatized' (BECKER 1995, 138–141 [quotation p. 140]; similarly EDWARDS on 582–586: 'a steady progression of time during these scenes'): cattle noisily flock to a meadow (575) along the river (576), lions grab a bull (579–581) and begin to feed (582 f.), the herdsmen drive forward the dogs (583 f.), who do not dare attack but instead approach barking and then retreat (585 f.); the passage is thus longer than any lion simile in the *Iliad* or the *Odyssey* (LONSDALE 1990, 143). On connections with the action of the *Iliad*, 579–586n.; on depictions of lions attacking animal herds in Geometric and Ancient Near Eastern art, see BUCHHOLZ *et al.* 1973, 13–18 (esp. 18), 28–30; GIULIANI 2003, 46 ff.; D'ACUNTO 2010, 175–179.

573 1st VH ≈ 490, 587; 2nd VH = 8.321, *Od.* 12.348, *h.Merc.* 220. — **oxen:** on the significance of cattle, 520–529n., 559n.

ἀγέλην ... βοῶν: a formulaic phrase, usually continued by a formulaic phrase with πῶυ and οἰῶν or μήλων (528n.); here, see 587 f. — **ὀρθοκραιράων:** 'with straight horns', a rare epithet with βοῶν (see *iterata*) and νεῶν (see 3 [with n.], 19.344): RICHTER 1968, 45 n. 292.

574 of gold and of tin: Cow-hides in Homeric epic are usually described as dark in color (*aíthōn* ['brown'], *pammélas* ['deep black'], *oínops* ['wine-colored': dark red? reddish brown?]), sometimes also as shining brightly (*argós*; on which, *LfgrE s.v.* ἀργός 1206.61 ff.; RICHARDSON on *Il.* 23.30): RICHTER 1968, 47; on the color effect of metals, 565n.

χρυσοῖο ... κασσιτέρου: 565n. — τετεύχατο: 478n., 548–549n.

575 The herd of cattle is on its way from the 'manure' to the pasture: *kópros* means literally 'dung, manure', thus at *Od.* 9.329 f., 17.297 f.; here (and at *Od.* 10.411) it denotes the stables or yard where the manure was stored until it could be put to use (RICHTER 1968, 104).

---

573 ἐν: 541n.— ὀρθοκραιράων: on the declension, R 11.1.
574 τετεύχατο: on the ending, R 16.2.
575 ἐπεσσεύοντο: on the -σσ-, R 9.1. — νομόνδε: 'to the meadow', on the suffix, R 15.3.

μυκηθμῷ: likewise at *Od.* 12.265, derived from μυκάομαι 'bellow, moo' (580n.).

576 a verse with peculiarities of sound and language: (1) pure dactyls, (2) an accumulation of -ᾰ- und -ŏ-, (3) the structure of the 1st and 2nd VH correspond, due to (3a) words with similar sounds and identical metrical structure in corresponding positions in the verse, each with an increasing number of syllables (on problems in transmission, see below), (3b) anaphora of παρ(ά), (3c) chiasmus of noun and attribute; the 1st VH suggests via on-omatopoeia the murmuring of the river, the 2nd VH movement in the depiction, whereby by means of the dimensions of 'sound and movement' it continues the expansion of the initially static image begun at 575 (EDWARDS on 573–576; BASSETT [1938] 2003, 156 f.; for additional examples of onomatopoeia in Homer, EDWARDS, Introd. 57 f.). — **κελάδοντα:** of rivers and winds 'noisy, resounding' (cf. 310n.; used as the name of a river at 7.133); derived from the noun κέλαδος (*DELG* and BEEKES *s.v.* κέλαδος). — **ῥαδαλόν:** The word is transmitted in numerous variants (see *app. crit.* and WEST 2001a, 133–135); the most likely of which are: (1) ῥοδανόν, the main reading of the mss. and of three papyri, the sound of which exactly matches the equivalent in the 1st VH; at the same time, ῥοδανός is not attested elsewhere and is considered a by-form of ῥαδινός 'pliant, slender' (23.583 of a whip), thus of reeds approximately 'swaying' (LEAF; CERRI; *LfgrE s.vv.* ῥοδανός [with bibliography] and ῥαδινός; on the uncertain etymology, *DELG* and BEEKES *s.v.* ῥαδινός); (2) Zenodotus' reading ῥαδαλόν (schol. A and bT; inserted into the text by WEST; *contra* NARDELLI 2001, section V. *ad loc.*); the term is also attested in the Hellenistic poet Nicaenetus (*fr.* 1.4) and is explained as 'easily movable, easily shivering' by the scholia (WEST *loc. cit.* 134: ['waving'] 'This seems therefore to be a real word, perhaps Ionic'; differently VAN DER VALK 1964, 44–46 [an invention by Zenodotus]). — **δονακῆα:** 'reed thicket', attested only here and in Oppian (*Halieutica* 4.507); derived from δόναξ 'reed' (schol. D; *LfgrE*).

577 χρύσειοι: 418n. — **ἐστιχόωντο:** 'walked, marched up'; derivation from either στείχω or στίχες is possible (2.92n.; *LfgrE s.v.* στιχάομαι).

578 2nd VH = *Od.* 17.62, 20.145; ≈ 2.11, *h.Merc.* 194. — **dogs:** Dogs are also presented in similes[P] in the *Iliad* as hunting or herding animals (RICHTER 1968, 80–83; BUCHHOLZ *et al.* 1973, 108–114); speed is among their prime qualities, see 283, 584 (for examples and additional bibliography, 3.26n., where also on dog epithets).

τέσσερες: on the spelling with -ε-, WEST 1998, XXX. — **ἀργοί:** as a dog epithet, means 'swift', sometimes specified by πόδας, as here (283n.).

579–586 In Homeric epic, the loss of cattle in raids (520–520n.) and particularly in attacks by predators is considered a great risk in animal husbandry; these

---

576 πάρ: = παρά (R 20.1). — παρὰ (ρ)ραδαλόν: on the prosody, M 4.6.
577 ἐστιχόωντο: on the epic diectasis, R 8. — βόεσσιν: on the declension, R 11.3.
578 σφι: = αὐτοῖς (R 14.1). — πόδας: acc. of respect (R 19.1).

are also common motifs in similes. The present scene thus recalls not only the besieged city with cattle raids by the besieged, but also the many similes in the battle descriptions in Books 15–17, see esp. the linguistic echoes at 582 f. (583n.) and reminiscences of motifs at 585 f. (see *ad loc.*): AUBRIOT 1999, 29–31; ALDEN 2000, 70–72 (*contra* LONSDALE 1990, 121 f.): cattle snatched by lions serve as a comparison for dying warriors (16.487–491n.); the attempts by the herdsmen to defend their herds, or at least to snatch away the already-killed animals from the lions, illustrates *inter alia* the battle for the arms and/or body of the fallen warrior, see 17.109 ff. and 17.657 ff. (Menelaos), where the lion is driven away by man and dog, on the one hand, and 161 f. (Hektor with Patroklos), 17.61–69 (Menelaos with Euphorbos), where the lion initially has the advantage, on the other (3.26n; EDWARDS; RICHTER 1968, 37; LONSDALE *loc. cit.* 39–70, 103–107; ALDEN *loc. cit.* 69 f.; on herdsmen in similes[P], 161–164n.).

579 lions: In similes in the context of battle, lions symbolize especially the courage and aggression of a warrior; pairs of lions working together are also found at 5.554 ff., 10.297, 13.198 ff., and two animals fighting one another at 16.756 ff. (3.23n., 16.756–761n., 24.41b–44n.).

σμερδαλέω ...: σμερδαλέος ('gruesome, terrible', always at VB) can refer to a visual or – when used as an adv. – an acoustic impression (cf. 19.41n.), of an animal also at 2.309 (δράκων): *LfgrE s.v.*; on Zenodotus' variant with a specification of color/material with the adj. κυάνεος instead of σμερδαλέος (on analogy with 574, 577), see WEST 2001, 250. – **ἐν πρώτῃσι βόεσσιν:** 'among the foremost cattle', cf. the expression πρώτῃσι καὶ ὑστατίῃσι βόεσσιν in the lion simile at 15.630–636 (esp. 634): *LfgrE s.v.* πρῶτος.

580 ἐρύγμηλον ... μακρὰ μεμυκώς: onomatopoetic terms intensifying μυκηθμῷ at 575: ἐρύγ-μηλος is a *hapax legomenon*[P], aurally (ε-υ-) tailored to the VE ('The sound of the word is important here, anticipating μεμυκώς': EDWARDS on 579–580). It is related to the root of ἐρεύγομαι ('regurgitate, bellow') with aor. ἐρυγεῖν (20.403–406: 'bellow'; cf. Latin *erugare* and *rugire*), from which ἐρυγμός and hence in turn ἐρύγμ-ηλος (RISCH 109); whether the different meanings can be assigned to *one* root is unclear (FRISK, *DELG* and BEEKES *s.v.* ἐρεύγομαι 2; JANDA 2014, 477–483). – μεμυκώς is an onomatopoetic perf., see also 21.237 (TICHY 1983, 63; cf. βεβρυχώς 16.486n.); intensified via the adv. μακρά ('widely [audible], loud') likewise at 2.224, cf. also inflectable formula μακρὸν ἀΰσας (VE 14× *Il.*: 3.81n.; KAIMIO 1977, 27 f.; on additional terms for the bellowing of cattle, KRAPP 1964, 153–155).

---

579 σμερδαλέω ... λέοντε: duals.
580 ἐρύγμηλον(ν) ἐχέτην: on the prosody, M 4.6. — ἐχέτην: 3rd pers. dual impf. act., 'held onto, held in their grasp'; on the unaugmented form, R 16.1.

581 μετεκίαθον: 'pursued', cf. 531–532n.; the object τόν (the main transmission beside τώ, τούς) points to the main objective of the dogs and herdsmen, namely to avoid the loss of the animal. — **αἰζηοί:** as an adj., means 'vigorous, strong', as a noun '(young) man' (2.660n.); cf. κύνες θαλεροί τ' αἰζηοί in hunting similes (3.26, 11.414, 17.282).

582 2nd VH = 17.389; ≈ *Od.* 22.364. — **ἀναρρήξαντε:** the compound in early epic also at 7.461 (obj. τεῖχος), 20.63 (obj. γαῖαν), with the subj. in each case being Poseidon; a powerful expression that, together with the graphic formulation at 583a, illustrates the brutality of the attack. — **βοὸς ... βοείην:** a *figura etymologica* with a material adj. related to βοῦς (RISCH 131–133), literally 'from cowhide', also the nominalized 'cowhide' (*sc.* δορή or ῥινός): *LfgrE*; FEHLING 1969, 159: 'strongly pleonastic' [transl.]).

583 ἔγκατα καὶ μέλαν αἷμα λαφύσσετον: ἔγκατα is a term for the entrails of cattle, cf. the formulaic 2nd VH αἷμα καὶ ἔγκατα πάντα λαφύσσει in lion similes for Agamemnon and Menelaos (11.176, 17.64) in contrast to the formulation ἔντερα χαλκὸς ἄφυσσε (2nd VH of 14.517) in a battle scene (LONSDALE 1990, 139). λαφύσσω, in early epic only here and in the formulaic verse mentioned above, means 'slurp up, devour'; the primary ending -τον rather than -την for the impf. (see 580) is likely used for metrical reasons – similar to 10.361, 10.364, 13.346 (likewise before caesura C 2) (SCHW. 1.667; CHANTR. 1.474; JANKO on 13.346).

584 dogs: 578n.

αὔτως: 'just so (without achieving anything), in vain', see 585 f. (schol. A and T; *LfgrE s.v.* 1684.19 ff.). — **ἐνδίεσαν:** δίεσαν is an impf. from the athematic pres. stem δίημι (CHANTR. 1.293; HACKSTEIN 2002, 135). Used transitively, it usually means 'hunt, chase off' (δίεμαι 162n.; GARCÍA-RAMÓN 1991, 108: 'make flee, hunt' [transl.]). Two interpretations are feasible in the present passage: (a) 'they hunted them' (*sc.* the lions), with ταχέας κύνας as the obj. of the part. ὀτρύνοντες (see the punctuation in WEST: a comma after ἐνδίεσαν; MAZON: '[...] chase them and urge on their swift dogs' [transl.]); (b) ταχέας κύνας is an obj. ἀπὸ κοινοῦ of the predicate and of the part., in which case ἐν-δίεσαν 'they sent in their dogs in a rush, set their dogs on' (schol. D: ἐνεκελεύοντο, παρορμῶντες ἐπέβαλλον; *LfgrE s.v.* δί(ημι); LA ROCHE; LEAF; EDWARDS; GARCÍA-RAMÓN *loc. cit.*: 'make run' [transl.]; undecided, VAN LEEUWEN); the latter interpretation perhaps better fits both the compound in ἐν- and the situation (the herdsmen vainly set the dogs on the lions, who are *not* chased off). — **ταχέας κύνας:** a phrase after caesurae B 1 (3× *Il.*) and B 2 (1× *Il.*, 2× *Od.*): 3.26n.

585–586 Dogs recoiling from a wild animal are also described in similes: 15.271–276 (hunt: lion ≈ Hektor) and similarly esp. at 17.61–67 (guarding livestock: lion ≈ Menelaos), where it illustrates the fear of the Trojans who cannot prevent Menelaos from initially getting hold of the arms of the slain Euphorbos (on

---

581 εἵλκετο: 'was dragged along' (*sc.* by the lions). — ἠδ(έ): 'and' (R 24.4).
582 τώ ... ἀναρρήξαντε: duals, aor. part. of ἀνα-ρήγνυμι 'tear open'.
583 λαφύσσετον: 3rd pers. dual, here impf. (↑).

this, EDWARDS *ad loc.*), cf. 17.725–729 during the rescue of Patroklos' body (dogs [≈ Trojans] retreat from boars [≈ the two Aiantes]). But in different similes, the herdsmen and dogs, united in fighting, manage to chase wild animals (esp. lions) away from the herds or the stockyard (with noise at 10.183–186, with weapons and fire at 11.548–555, with noise and weapons at 17.109–112, with weapons and fire at 17.657–664; also 12.299–306): KRAPP 1964, 151 f.; RICHTER 1968, 81; BUCHHOLZ *et al.* 1973, 109 f.; see also 579–586n.

585 δακέειν μὲν ἀπετρωπῶντο λεόντων: τρωπάω is a poetic by-form of τρέπω, in the mid.-pass. (+ gen.) the compound means 'turn away (from)' (*LfgrE*); the preceding inf. δακέειν contains the contextual qualification 'as concerns biting' (AH, LEAF and WILLCOCK; similarly CHANTR. 2.302), i.e. although they do not turn to retreat (thus τρωπᾶσθαι at e.g. 11.568, 15.666, 16.95), they also do not attack with all their might (see 586).

586 ἱστάμενοι δὲ μάλ' ἐγγύς: cf. the VB formula στῆ δὲ μάλ' ἐγγὺς ἰών (6× *Il.*, in battle situations, each time introducing an attack). — **ὑλάκτεον:** a *hapax*[P] in the *Iliad* (see also the *v.l.* ὑλαγμός at 21.575), an expansion of ὑλάω used more commonly in post-Homeric texts; both verbs occur together in the simile at *Od.* 20.13–16: Odysseus' heart was 'barking' (ὑλάκτει: 20.13/16) like a mother-dog (ὑλάει: 20.15) defending her pups (SCHW. 1.706; PORZIG 1942, 239; TICHY 1983, 167).

587–589 A description of a sheep pasture that is distinct from other scenes on the shield: it is uncommonly short, and movement, sounds and explicit mentions of human beings are absent (the latter are present only indirectly via the circumstances mentioned at 589). The three verses illustrate an atmosphere, and the impression of a pictorial work of art comes to the fore: (1) the introductory verse deviates from all previous ones by emphasizing the artist rather than the depiction (BECKER 1995, 142); (2) 588 contains three visually impressive characteristics (beautiful, large, shimmering white); and (3) 589 shows the buildings visible on the pasturage. With its peaceful mood, this description provides a strong contrast to the drama of the preceding scene, a moment of calm between two images dominated by action, sound and movement (EDWARDS; MARG [1957] 1971, 32; BECKER 1995, 141 f.).

587 ≈ 590; 1st VH ≈ 490, 573; 2nd VH = 1.607, 18.383, 18.393, 18.462, *Od.* 8.300, 8.349, 8.357, Hes. *Th.* 571, 579, 'Hes.' *fr.* 209.3 M.-W. — **περικλυτὸς Ἀμφιγυήεις:** 383n.

588 1st VH = *h.Ap.* 280; VE ≈ *Il.* 6.424, *Od.* 17.472. — **sheepflocks:** Sheep are comparatively rare in battle similes in the *Iliad* (*LfgrE s.v.* ὄϊς 611.47 ff.); like cattle

---

585 ἤτοι ... μέν: 'but'. — δακέειν: aor. inf. (R 16.4). — λεόντων: pl. rather than dual (R 18.1).
586 ἐκ ... ἀλέοντο: 'evaded'; on the so-called tmesis, R 20.2.
587 ἐν: 541n.
588 μέγαν: with νομόν.

(520–529n., 559n.), they are a sign of wealth (*LfgrE loc. cit.* 610.36 ff.; cf. also 573–589n.). On sheep-rearing and the use of sheep (esp. to supply wool and milk), see RICHTER 1968, 53–59, 62–64; *BNP s.v.* Sheep.

ἐν καλῇ βήσσῃ: a variation of the VB formula οὔρεος ἐν βήσσῃσ(ιν) (5× *Il.*, 3× Hes., 1× *h.Merc.*) denoting a valley in the cultivated countryside in contrast to a gorge in the wilderness (*LfgrE s.v.* βῆσσα). — οἰῶν ἀργεννάων: 529n.; on formulaic expressions for 'cattle and sheep', 573n.

589 σταθμούς ... κλισίας ... σηκούς: a sketch of a pasturage, where only the final two terms are unequivocal in meaning: κλισίαι denotes huts for the herdsmen (cf. *Od.* 14.45 ff., 14.194, 14.404 ff., 15.301, etc. [Eumaios' hut]; *h.Ven.* 75, 173), σηκοί pens for the sheep (cf. *Od.* 9.219–227, 9.438 f. [for segregating lambs and ewes] and *Il.* 8.131 σηκασθῆναι): *LfgrE s.vv.*; KNOX 1971, 30. σταθμός, a general term for an animal farm ('shelter, stables, farm-stead'), is here either an equivalent element in a tripartite enumeration (stables, huts and pens), and the verse as a whole is in apposition to νομόν 'pasture' (AH; RICHTER 1968, 25; KIRK on 5.140), or it is the general term for the two subsequent subcategories (LEAF; *LfgrE s.v.* σταθμός: 'shepherd's compound', containing 'herdsmen's huts' and 'animal pens'; similarly FAESI; KNOX 1971, 30: 'A pastoral establishment [...] consists of a κλισίη [...], a yard or αὐλή adjoining it in which animals are kept loose or in pens, and [...] a fenced pasture too. The whole grouping is referred to as σταθμός/-οί'; cf. schol. A, bT). — **κατηρεφέας:** a verb-noun compound (κατά, ἐρέφω) meaning 'roofed', here an epithet of κλισίας (cf. 24.450 of Achilleus' κλισίη: καθύπερθεν ἔρεψαν), in contrast to the open pens (σηκούς), also of 'caves' formed by overhanging trees (*Od.* 9.183, 13.349, Hes. *Th.* 594, 777): *LfgrE s.v.* κατηρεφής; CERRI; cf. the compounds with ἀμφ- (1.45n.: 'closed on both sides'), ὑψ- (19.333n.: 'with a high roof') and ἐπ- ('roofing, covering'). These compounds with -ηρεφής frequently occur in the same verse position as here, elsewhere almost always with a final syllable that is 'long by position' (1.45n.); the present metrical idiosyncracy (a short in the *longum*, likewise at *Il.* 1.45, *h.Merc.* 23) can thus be explained via modification of the formula (M 14). On the verse structure, see also CHANTR. 1.104 (short within the *longum* '[...] at the caesura or before punctuation' [transl.]) and 14.175n. (a break in sense after the *longum* in the 5th foot, after a 'difficult' word). — **ἰδέ:** 'and'; a metrical variant of ἠδέ (2.511n.).

590–606 The motif 'dance' completes the cycle of images in the sphere of human life, cf. the echoes of the first image of the wedding celebration in the dancing vocabulary *orchēstéres/órchéont'* (494/594), *edíneon/edíneuon* (494/606), and the mention of the audience's receptive stance (496a/603–604a: 603–604a n.). The choral dance (*choreía*) is part of a communal ceremony, a ritual commonly tied to divine cults, that plays a central role in the life of a community and offers the opportunity for encounters and for the consolidation of a sense of group identity (BURKERT [1977] 1985, 102 f.; SHAPIRO *et al.* 2004, 342; for gen-

---

589 κατηρεφέας: on the prosody, ↑.

eral bibliography on dance, 494n.). The final image, which according to the general ekphrasis structure can be considered the shield's climax (KAKRIDIS [1963] 1971, 123; TAPLIN [1980] 2001, 353), the circular dance, is noteworthy in comparison to what preceded it in a number of aspects: the description is (a) the longest of all, (b) the only one that contains mythological characters (in the context of the model from mythical times: 591 f.), (c) offers – on analogy with similes[P] in the *Iliad* that involve scenes from non-wartime, peaceful daily life – a comparison from the realm of art, namely the potter's craft (600 f.), and (d) shows a markedly dense presence of art via different actors, with the result that links are established between the creation of Hephaistos that is described (590) and the work of other artists: the handiwork of the mythical artist Daidalos (592) and the potter mentioned by way of comparison (601), and in addition, the art of dancing as performed by circle-dancers 'with well-practiced feet' (599b) and acrobats (605b), and thus implicitly music (*molpḗ* 606; on the singer, 604b–605a n.). The narrator here focuses on what is visually perceptible (595–598 equipment and 594/599 f./606 positioning and movement of the dancers), while being rather restrained in the mention of sound (as in the preceding description of the sheep pasture: 587–589n.); he mentions the effect of the dance performance on the audience (603 f.) and portrays this all as the unbiased enjoyment of art (*terpómenoi* 604a): 600–601n., 603–604a n.; EDWARDS; CERRI on 603; BECKER 1995, 143–147; SIMON 1995, 132 f.; AUBRIOT 1999, 39 ff.; MOOG 2001, 8 f.). – In his choice of a circular dance, the narrator might have been animated by the desire to visualize order and beauty in the interaction of all involved, characterized by perfection and harmony, and in addition may have been inspired by contemporary vase paintings in Geometric art with bands of dancers (593–602n., 594n.; MOOG 2001, 12–14; see also CARRUESCO 2016, esp. 70–91).

590 ≈ 587. — The final two images of the sphere of human life are linked by being introduced via virtually identical verses (573–589n.). – The noun *chorós* means both 'dance' (thus at 603 as an action noun) and 'dancing ground' (*Od.* 8.260 ff.); in the present passage, the analogy with the remaining introductory verses that provide information on the scene (with the exception of 573: 478–608n. section **B.1.b.**) suggests the meaning 'dancing-ground', esp. the echoes of 587 (*nomós* 'pasturage'), as does the continuation of the description at 593 f. 'There ... were dancing' (*entha ... | ŏrchéont'*, cf. 550 f.): schol. A, bT; EDWARDS on 590–592; CERRI; *LfgrE s.v.* χορός 1243.14 ff.; MARG (1957) 1971, 37 n. 50; ELLIGER 1975, 33 n. 8; PRIESS 1977, 137 n. 2; BECKER 1995, 143; GRANDOLINI 1996,

---

590 ἐν: 541n.— ποίκιλλε: on the unaugmented form, R 16.1.

65; favoring the meaning 'dance' and the resulting interpretation (a depiction of dance or a type of dance): SCHADEWALDT (1938) 1965, 484 f. n. 1; FITTSCHEN 1973, 15 f.; SIMON 1995, 131 f.; undecided, FRONTISI-DUCROUX (1975) 2000, 136 f. and 147; MORRIS 1992, 14 f. When the entire description (esp. 595–606) is taken into acount, the meaning of *chorós* broadens beyond the dancing-ground to include both actors and activity (ambiguity introduced deliberately by the narrator: POSTLETHWAITE 1998, 94 f.; CAVALLERO 2003, 192–196).

ἐν ... ποίκιλλε: an 'intensive' variant of the metrically equivalent ἐν ... ποίησε (490, 573, 587), with a Homeric *hapax*[P] (*LfgrE s.v.* ποικίλλω; on the impf., cf. ἐτίθει 541n.). ποικίλλω is a denominative of ποικίλος ('rich in forms, manifold'), like δαιδάλλω (479) from δαίδαλο-, cf. Δαίδαλος 592 (TICHY 1983, 302); it refers to the artisan's skill, perhaps also to the design of the circular dance in the manner of a decorative band (EDWARDS on 590–592; BECKER 1995, 144), and offers, together with the subsequent reference to Daidalos, a linguistic variation of the qualification of Hephaistos' work so far in Book 18 (MORRIS 1992, 13; cf. 379n. on δαιδαλ-).

591 2nd VH ≈ 6.210, 13.433, 24.774, *Od.* 11.460, 11.499, 12.189, 13.256, 13.260. — **like that which once:** Commentators already in antiquity noted that this formulation is not designed to characterize the work of the god as a *mimesis* of human works; rather, it points to a mythical model (schol. A on 591–592: *parádeigma*; on the term, NÜNLIST 1998, 262), the mention of which evokes a specific idea for the audience (BECKER 1995, 144 f.). — **Knosos:** In antiquity, Crete was considered the origin of dance, and the Cretans themselves excellent dancers (16.617n.; LEAF on 590; CERRI on 590–606, section 3); for depictions of dancers in Minoan art, BURKERT (1977) 1985, 34; LONSDALE 1995, 279 ff.; for an archaeologically attested circular space in Minoan Knossos and its interpretation as a dancing-ground, WARREN 1984, esp. 318 f. and 323; on Crete and the role of Knossos (Mycenaean *ko-no-so*) in general, 2.645–652n., 2.646n. The allusion to Knossos and the connection with dance and acrobats (605b) notwithstanding, there is no reference in the description of the dance that follows to the Minoan tradition of bull-leaping; rather, the narrator's visual models – actual circle-dances of the time aside – appear to be Geometric vase paintings of circle-dances (605b–606n.; FITTSCHEN 1973, 16 f. with n. 79; see also 593–602n.).

οἷον: emphasizes – in contrast to the formulation with the relative pronoun ὅς (thus at 24.758) – the quality (τῷ ἵκελον ≈ τοῖον), i.e. 'of the sort, like that which' (RUIJGH 525 f.). — Κνωσῷ: on the spelling with *one* -σ-, WEST 1998, XXXII. — εὐρείῃ: a generic

---

591 τῷ: on the demonstrative function of ὅ, ἥ, τό, R 17. — τῷ (ϝ)ίκελον(ν), οἷον: on the prosody, R 4.4 and M 4.6 (note also the caesura). — ἐνί: = ἐν (R 20.1). — Κνωσῷ εὐρείῃ: on the bridging of hiatus by non-syllabic ι (*Knōsóy eureíē*), M 12.2; likewise 592 καλλιπλοκάμῳ Ἀριάδνῃ (*kalliplokámōj Ariádnē*). — εὐρείῃ: on the -η after -ι-, R 2.

epithet[P] of regions (frequently Crete or Lycia: each 7× early epic), in the case of cities (mostly Troy: 9× early epic; Knossos only here) likely in reference to the surrounding countryside; at VE 5× *Il.*, 8× *Od.* (6.173–174n.).

592 Daidalos ... Ariadne: a four-word verse (on which, 1.75n.); it contains the only mention of mythical characters in the shield description, namely as part of an unusual comparison in which – in contrast to elsewhere in the *Iliad* – the gaze is directed from the lived experience of the audience to the heroic world (WIRBELAUER 1996, 153): the names, in combination with the subsequent depiction of a group of young male and female dancers, evoke associations with the myth of the labyrinth; the young Athenian men and women who were saved from the Minotaur were thought to have learned a special dance under Daidalos' direction, the so-called 'crane dance', the performance of which is linked to initiation rites (schol. D on 590 and bT on 591–592; FRONTISI-DUCROUX [1975] 2000, 145–147; CALAME [1977] 1997, 53–58, 123–127; 1990, 118–121; GRANDOLINI 1996, 64–66; POSTLETHWAITE 1998, 99–102; SHAPIRO *et al.* 2004, 308–310). This creates a mythical reference for the dance performance described; this aside, the dancing scene is described in a generalizing manner, similar to all preceding scenes: a choral dance with circle- and line-dances, acrobats, the joy of the audience (see also CALAME 1990, 118: details such as daggers [597 f.] and two acrobats [605] do not fit, strictly speaking, with the 'crane dance'). – Although the story of the labyrinth is not mentioned explicitly in Homeric epic, altogether there are quite a few references to the myth of Theseus and Ariadne in early epic (on the myth of Theseus in the *Iliad*, 3.144n.): according to Hes. *Th.* 947 f., Ariadne is a daughter of Minos, the king of Crete, and the wife of Dionysos; *Od.* 11.321–325 mentions her abduction by Theseus and her death at the hands of Artemis on the island of Dia at Dionysos' behest. A more detailed portrayal of the version known from Geometric vase paintings and subsequently especially from post-Homeric texts, in which Ariadne helps Theseus overcome the Minotaur, is attested for the historian Pherecydes (*FGrHist* 3 F 148 = *fr.* 148 Fowler), as well as possibly for the *Cypria* (in an excursus by Nestor, see Proclus, *Chrest.* § 4 West; on this, WEST 2013, 98, 110); it is entirely unclear whether Ariadne is identical with a 'mistress of the labyrinth' recorded on a Linear B tablet from Knossos (on this, *DMic s.v. po-ti-ni-ja*; BURKERT [1977] 1985, 23 and 354 n. 24). For the different variants of the myth of Ariadne and their transmission, *LfgrE s.v.* Ἀριάδνη; *HE*, *LIMC* and *BNP s.v.* Ariadne; CALAME 1990, 98–116. – Daidalos, according to post-Homeric texts an Athenian inventor, architect, artist and craftsman who built the labyrinth, is mentioned in early epic only here (for discussion regarding the 'Daidaleion' of unknown purpose recorded on a Linear B tablet from Knossos, see *DMic s.v. da-da-re-jo-de*); at the same time, the terms from the word-family *daidal-*, etymologically related to his name, are used repeatedly in the context of elaborately decorated craft objects, esp. those made by Hephaistos, including the shield at 479, 483 and 19.380, the helmet at 612, the arms overall at 19.13 and 19.19 (379n. and 19.13n. with bibliography; *HE* s.v. Daidalos; *BNP* s.v. Daedalus).

ἤσκησεν: means 'work diligently (on)'; used especially of elaborate work by specialists in a variety of crafts, e.g. at 14.179 for Athene's textile work, at 14.240 of Hephaistos' metalwork, also at e.g. 4.110, 23.743, *Od.* 23.198 (14.179n.). — **καλλιπλοκάμῳ**: 407n. — Ἀριάδνη: Derivation of the name from ἀρι + ἁδνός (interpreted as Cretan for ἁγνός, i.e. 'very sacred') is hardly plausible (*DELG* s.v. ἁδνόν; *LfgrE* and BEEKES s.v. Ἀριάδνη); in Zenodotus, the name is Ἀριήδη (schol. AT; RENGAKOS 1993, 85; WACHTER 2001, 182 f. *ad* CHA 11c).

593–602 The group of dancers comprises youths of both sexes (as at 567 f.; men and women at *Od.* 23.146 f.) who are of marriageable age (593n.; CALAME [1977] 1997, 26) – according to ancient explanations (schol. bT on 591–592 and Eust. 1166.16 ff.), an indication of the connection to the dance in the myth of Theseus (592n.). The mixed-sex nature of the group is visualized in dress and different accessories, described in the structurally exactly equivalent verses 595 f. and 597 f. The young men and women hold one another by the hands (594n.) and alternately form up for circular and line dances (600–602: see *ad locc.*; schol. bT on 602), although it remains unclear whether they dance segregated by gender (as on the pseudo-Hesiodic shield at 'Hes.' *Sc.* 280 ff., as well as in numerous additional sources) or whether the groups mingle (as at Lucian, *de saltatione* 12 f.): TÖLLE 1964, 54 ff.; CALAME (1977) 1997, 25–28 (with n. 29). 86; GRANDOLINI 1996, 64–66; HENRICHS 1996, 19–21; SHAPIRO et al. 2004, 302; for vase paintings of dancing groups including both sexes, see also WEGNER 1968, 60 ff.; FITTSCHEN 1973, 15 f. with fig. 6 and pl. X; WICKERT-MICKNAT 1982, 24–29; D'ACUNTO 2010, 181–188; for additional bibliography on dance, 494n., 594n.

593 2nd VH = *h.Ven.* 119 (dance of young women). — The dancing group is comprised of young people of marriageable age, as is indicated particularly by the adj. *alphesíboiai*: it means literally 'bringing oxen' (see below; cf. the female name Peri-boia), in reference to the bride price provided by the chosen suitor (implying the wedding motif): FAULKNER on *h.Ven.* 119; OLSON on *h.Ven.* 117–120; on the exchange of gifts on the occasion of young women's marriages (bride price and dowry) in Homeric society, 16.177–178n.; RICHARDSON on *Il.* 22.49–51; cf. 6.394n. (*s.v.* πολύδωρος); on cattle as valuable property, 520–529n., 559n.

---

593 ἔνθα: 'there', i.e. on the dancing-ground depicted. — παρθένοι ἀλφεσίβοιαι: on the correption, R 5.5.

ἠίθεοι καὶ παρθενικαί: 567n. — ἀλφεσίβοιαι: a compound with an initial element related to ἀλφεῖν ('bring, yield') and a final element -βοια related to βοῦς (on the formation, Risch 192; Beekes *s.v.*; Tronci 2000, 287 ff., esp. 294 f.).

594 ≈ *h.Ap.* 196 (dance of goddesses); 2nd VH ≈ *Il.* 21.489, 24.671. — **holding:** Male and especially female dancers holding one another by the hand are also found in pictorial representations (Wegner 1968, 49 ff. and pl. Ib, IIIb, VId; D'Acunto 2010, 181–188, esp. 182 and 188). Since the gesture occurs also in the context of male control over women (bibliography see 33n.), some scholars link the dance of the clearly marriageable young people (593n.) to courtship and marriage (Lonsdale 1995, 276 f.; D'Acunto 2010, 182 f.); for other uses of the gesture, see 24.361n. (with bibliography).

ὠρχέοντ(o): a general term for dancing (likewise at *Od.* 8.371, 8.378, 14.465, Hes. *Th.* 4), cf. the *nomen agentis* ὀρχηστήρ at 494; more specific are the terms ἐδίνευον (606) denoting turning (494n.), θρέξασκον running (in various formations: 599/602), ῥήσσοντες ... σκαίροντες (571 f.) stomping and jumping: *LfgrE s.v.* ὀρχέομαι; Kurz 1966, 137–139; Wegner 1968, 40–44; for a collection of Greek vocabulary related to dance, Naerebout 1997, 274–289 (esp. 279 ff. on dance-steps); on the movements in circle-dancing, Tölle 1964, 61 f. — ἐπὶ καρπῷ χεῖρας: a formulaic expression (see *iterata* as well as the VE formula χεῖρ' ἐπὶ καρπῷ 4× *Il.*, 2× *Od.*) specifying the part of the body designated by χείρ ('arm' or 'hand'; *LfgrE s.v.* χείρ 1161.63 ff.).

595 λεπτάς: 'slender, delicate', in early epic frequently denoting the special qualities of textiles (*LfgrE*); this use is attested already in Mycenaean (*DMic s.v.* re-po-to). — ὀθόνας ... χιτῶνας: ὀθόναι, a *plurale tantum*, is perhaps an Egyptian loan word; it means 'cloth' and here designates female dress analogous to the young men's χιτών (*LfgrE s.v.* ὀθόναι; Beekes *s.v.* ὀθόνη; Lorimer 1950, 390 with n. 3; cf. 3.141n.; on χιτῶνας, 25n.).

596 olive oil: The practice of treating woolen or linen textiles with oil to impart a sheen (see *Od.* 7.105–107) is attested already in the Mycenaean period (6.295n.; Shelmerdine 1995, 101 f. and 105 n. 4). On the enormous value of beautiful textiles in Homeric society, 6.90–91n.; Taplin (1980) 2001, 353–356 (esp. on the *Iliad*).

εἵατ(o): formation by analogy with εἷμαι (*Od.* 19.72, 23.115) for the perf. stem in εἱ- of ἕννυμαι (cf. also ἕσθην 517 [see *ad loc.*]; for the same form from ἧμαι, 523): Schw. 1.767 n. 4; Chantr. 1.297. — ἐϋννήτους: an epithet of textiles ('well spun', transferred from the yarn to the garments made from it: 24.580n.). — ἦκα: 'a little, gently', positive of ἥκιστα, with psilosis (3.155n.).

---

594 ὠρχέοντ(o): on the synizesis, R 7.
595 ἔχον: on the unaugmented form, R 16.1.
596 εἵατ(o): 3rd pers. pl. plpf. (≈ impf.) of ἕννυμαι, 'were clothed in, wore' (on the ending, R 16.2).

597–598 2nd VH of 598 ≈ 480. — **knives:** The young men's daggers are probably not indications of a weapon dance but primarily the visual counterpart of the women's wreaths (see also SHAPIRO *et al.* 2004, 314 f.: 'Weapons serve to emphasize the social standing of the dancer' [transl.]); mention of them provides an opportunity for referring to the smithing materials gold and silver (EDWARDS; TÖLLE 1964, 77; BECKER 1995, 154; depiction of armed dancers in Geometric representations in WEGNER 1968, 64 f. and pl. Va; FITTSCHEN 1973, 16 n. 77 and pl. Xb). — **sword-belts:** 479b–480n.

μαχαίρας: 'knife, dagger'; in early epic, it is not used as a weapon in battle but rather, in addition to the present passage, in cult actions (by Agamemnon at 3.271 and 19.252, by Cretans at *h.Ap.* 535) and as a surgical instrument (3.271n.; MARTIN 1983, 89 f.). Ancient scholars considered 597 f. suspect, since weapon dances required swords (on this, see above), which are never called μάχαιρα by Homer, and since the verses were missing in Aristophanes' text (HT 11) (schol. A), but the latter can be explained as a copying error (due to the similarities between the 1st VH in 595/597 and VB in 596/598): EDWARDS, following APTHORP 1980, 80, 118 n. 139; differently CERRI (perhaps an interpolation by a rhapsode). — χρυσείας: 418n.

599 ὀτὲ μὲν θρέξασκον: continued at 602 by ἄλλοτε δ᾽ αὖ θρέξασκον ('soon ..., soon ...'), like 11.64 f. (likewise iterative) and 20.49 f., conversely ἄλλοτε μὲν ... ὀτὲ δέ 11.566/568; together with the repeated iterative, it stresses the multiple changes in the two formations over the course of the dance (on the aor. iterative, cf. 544–546n.; on adverbial τέ, SCHW. 2.649 n. 2; CHANTR. 2.360 f.). In early epic, the sigmatic aor. stem θρεξα- occurs only here and at 13.409 (ἐπιθρέξαντος), elsewhere the aor. is rendered by the root δραμ-, as is common also in Attic (CHANTR. 1.324, 415; KÖLLIGAN 2007, 188 f.) — ἐπισταμένοισι: 'skillful, masterful', elsewhere of people ('well-versed'), here in enallage (*LfgrE*).

600–601 1st VH of 600 = 15.362; ≈ 3.381, 20.444; 2nd VH of 600 ≈ *Od.* 5.234. — The comparison[P] with the turning of a potter's wheel being examined by the potter visualizes the dancers' circular, nimble, uniform running as a controlled movement in a circular dance (BECKER 1995, 146); emphasis is on the dancers' movement (see 2nd VH 601: 'to see if it will run' [*théēsin*]), underlined linguistically by picking up *thréxaskon* from 599 ('they ran') with the etymologically

---

597 ῥ(α): on the avoidance of hiatus, R 24.1, cf. R 5.1.

598 ἐξ ... τελαμώνων: 'starting from ... straps', i.e. 'on ... straps'.

599 οἵ: anaphoric demonstrative (R 17), refers to ἠίθεοι and παρθένοι. — θρέξασκον: iterative form (-σκ-: R 16.5) of the sigmatic aor. of τρέχω. — ἐπισταμένοισι: on the declension, R 11.2. — πόδεσσιν: on the declension, R 11.3.

600 ῥεῖα: adv., 'easily'. — παλάμῃσιν: on the declension, R 11.1.

601 πειρήσεται: short-vowel subjunc. of the mid. aor. (Attic pass. deponent); on the form, R 16.3; on the subjunc. in the comparative clause, 207–209n. — αἰ: = εἰ (R 22.1). — κε: = ἄν (R 24.5). — θέῃσιν: 3rd pers. sing. subjunc. (R 16.3).

related *trochón* at 600 ('wheel'): cf. word play[P]; on word repetition in simile and narrative, Edwards Introd. 27 f. and 31. The comparison with the potter's wheel matches both the illustration of fast, controlled, smooth circular movements in the dance and the scene of creating the shield as a whole with regard to the making of an artwork by the artist (potter/Hephaistos; on the ekphrasis, see also 478–608n. section **B.4.**); for additional comparisons from the sphere of crafts, Moulton 1977, 91 n. 8; cf. 16.211–217n.; on ancient potter's wheels, Müller 1974, 99–105; *BNP s.v.* Pottery, production of.

ὡς ὅτε τις: a formulaic phrase before caesura B 1 (6× *Il.*, 2× *Od.*, 1× 'Hes.'; cf. the VB formula ὡς δ' ὅτε τις: 7× *Il.*, 3× *Od.*), in the present passage with wide separation of τις ... | ... κεραμεύς; on ὡς ὅτε, 207n. – τροχὸν ... | ... πειρήσεται, αἴ κε θέῃσιν: πειράω/-ομαι only here with acc. obj. (elsewhere gen.: Leaf; Schw. 2.105), with αἴ κε (+ subjunc.) as an indirect question: 'tests the wheel to see if it runs' (Monro [1882] 1891, 267; cf. Wakker 1994, 370 f.; on the subjunc. ending -ῃσιν [without ι *subscr.*], West 1998, XXXI). – τροχός, here the term for the potter's wheel, is from the root of τρέχω (see the word play[P] with θρέξασκον at 599 and 23.517/520) and is used elsewhere in the *Iliad* to denote chariot wheels (6.42, 23.394, 23.517), in the *Odyssey* for disks of wax or tallow (*LfgrE s.v.* τροχός; on the verbs τρέχω and θέω, Létoublon 1985, 194–199; Kölligan 2007, 186–190, 195 f.). – ἄρμενον: aor. part. related to the root of ἀραρίσκω ('fitting' < *'attached': *LIV* 269 f. with n. 4); it is probably to be taken with ἐν παλάμῃσιν, as at *Od.* 5.234 and *h.Merc.* 110: 'fitted to the hands', i.e. a wheel that fits well in the hands and that the potter tests by running it through them to see how well it turns (Leaf; *LfgrE s.vv.* ἀραρίσκω 1180.48 ff. and παλάμη ['using tools ... , that «fit the hand»'; Müller 1974, 101; a different interpretation, Eckstein 1974, 27: τροχὸς ἄρμενος of the potter's wheel that is either well 'made', i.e. assembled [thus Cerri following schol. A on 600–601 and D on 600: 'well put together', i.e. uniform on all sides, ensuring a smooth rotation], or one that is well 'fitted' to the base [i.e. that sits comfortably on a axle, allowing it to rotate smoothly and quickly]; in this case, ἐν παλάμῃσιν would have to refer as an adverbial addition to πειρήσεται at 601). – κεραμεύς: a Homeric *hapax*[P] (see also 9.469 ἐκ κεράμων of drinking cups), elsewhere in early epic at Hes. *Op.* 25 (κεραμεὺς κεραμεῖ); an occupational term for potters attested already in the Mycenaean period (MYC; *DMic s.v.* ke-ra-me-u; Eckstein 1974, 26 f. n. 163).

602 αὖ: marks the return to 599; on the visualization via αὖ(τε), Bonifazi 2012, 218–229. – ἐπὶ στίχας: 'in rows' (cf. 2.687 [see *ad loc.*], 3.113); στίχες usually denotes facing lines, in Homeric epic, aside from the present passage, of battle formations in particular (*LfgrE s.v.* στιχός; cf. 16.173n.). – ἀλλήλοισιν: 'toward one another', dat. of destination (cf. Schw. 2.139; Chantr. 2.68).

603–604a The expression *himeróenta chorón* ('the charming dance') and the participle *terpómenoi* ('enjoying') render the emotions sparked by observing a dance performance, fascination (*hímeros*) and joyful pleasure (*térpsis*) in the aesthetic interplay of music and movement (see also *Od.* 1.421 f. = 18.304 f.); on the fascinating effects of music, song and/or dance, see esp. 17.518–520, also *Il.* 18.570 (Linos song), *Od.* 18.194, 18.403, 23.144 f., Hes. *Th.* 7 f., 104, 'Hes.' *Sc.* 201–203, 280, *h.Merc.* 451 f., 481, *h.Ven.* 13. The verb *térpomai* serves *inter alia* to denote aesthetic pleasure and is frequently used in the context of the audience of a singer's performance (e.g. 1.473 f., *Od.* 8.44 f., 8.91, 8.367 f., 8.429, 17.605 f., etc., *h.Ap.* 149 f., 169 f.): LfgrE s.v. τέρπω; LATACZ 1966, 204 f., 208 ff.; KLOSS 1994, 57 f.; cf. PEPONI 2012, 98–107 (on the effects of Hermes' musical performance at *h.Merc.* 420 ff.). Together with 496, this reference to the audience's receptive status forms a frame surrounding the earthly scenes on the shield: here pleasure, in the first scene amazement (*thaúmazon*) at the wedding processions accompanied by dance (495b–496n.; CAVALLERO 2003, 192).

603 VE ≈ 24.712, 'Hes.' *fr.* 75.7 M.-W. — The chiastic arrangement of the parts of the sentence perhaps reflects the arrangement of the audience described: the subj. πολλὸς ὅμιλος, distributed at VB and VE, frames the obj. ἱμερόεντα χορόν in the verse middle. — **ἱμερόεντα:** 570n.

604–606 = *Od.* 4.17–19 (wedding in the house of Menelaos); 604 = *Od.* 13.27 (Demodokos).

604b–605a Whether the sentence 'and among them a divine singer | sang and played the lyre' (transl. VERITY; *metá de sphin emélpeto théios aoidós | phormízōn*), contained in some modern editions and translations, is part of the *Iliad*, is disputed. The history of its transmission is problematic: it is absent from all mss. and papyri of the *Iliad*, as well as from the ancient commentaries; it is transmitted in the *iteratum* in the *Odyssey* (4.17b–18a), as well as in Athenaeus' remark that *Od.* 4.17–19 is an interpolation from the present passage of the *hoplopoiia* (*Deipnosophistae* 180a–181d); accordingly, Aristarchus would have inserted the *Iliad* verses into the passage in the *Odyssey*, while at the same time 'removing the singer from the Cretan dance' (181c–d; cf. schol. MᵇT on *Od.* 4.17 PONTANI: the three verses [*sc.* 4.17–19] are interpolated by Aristarchus). A number of editors (among them LEAF, VAN LEEUWEN, ALLEN, MAZON, WEST) and scholars consider the sentence un-Homeric in the present passage; it is thought to have been interpolated – like the additional verse 606a, transmitted in only *one* papyrus – since a mention of accompanying music in the dancing scene was missed (*app. crit.*; LEAF; CERRI; JANKO Introd. 28; VERITY 439; LUDWICH 1884, 439–441, 536 f. and 1885, 479 f.; WEST 1967, 132–135; APTHORP 1980, 160–165; ALDEN 2000, 54 n. 20; WEST 2001, 250–252; cautiously EDWARDS on 604–606; SBARDELLA 2010, 65–71; additional bibliography on the discus-

---

603 πολλός: = πολύς (R 12.2). — περιΐσταθ': = περιΐστατο.
604a τερπόμενοι: *constructio ad sensum*, refers to πολλὸς ... ὅμιλος.

sion in ERBSE on 604–606; PONTANI on *Od.* 4.17; POSTLETHWAITE 1998, 93–97; on the textual criticism, also REVERMANN 1998, 32–37). At the same time, WOLF ([1795] 1985, 208 f. with n. 49) and numerous scholars following him included the sentence in the text of the *Iliad* on the basis of the passage in Athenaeus and defended it as authentic on contextual grounds: (a) an absence of musical accompaniment from dancing is odd, given the parallels at 494 f. and 569 f., as well as the additional dancing scenes in the *Odyssey* (esp. 8.251–265), the Homeric hymns (*h.Ap.* 189–203) and the pseudo-Hesiodic *Scutum* (201–206); on this, EDWARDS: *Il.* 18.604 f. and *Od.* 4.17–19 may represent an abbreviated and a longer version of the same, standardized description of a dance; somewhat differently, REVERMANN 1998: acceptance of a non-reconstructable lacuna that mentioned the musical accompaniment; (b) the immortalization of the singer on the shield, and thus of the poet himself in the *Iliad*, similar to the characters[P] of Phemios and Demodokos in the *Odyssey*, is particularly appropriate in the present passage (SCHADEWALDT [1938] 1965, 367; [1938] 1966, 163 f. n. 3; MARG [1957] 1971, 17, 36 f.; VAN DER VALK 1964, 527–530; FORDERER 1965, esp. 24, 26 f.; RITOÓK 1971, 201–207; USENER 1990, 125–127; WIRBELAUER 1996, 153 f.; DALBY 1998, 210 f. n. 41; MOOG 2001, 10, 14 f.; FRONTISI-DUCROUX 2002, 483; CAVALLERO 2003, 197–201; cautiously TAPLIN [1980] 2001, 354; POSTLETHWAITE 1998, 97 ff.). The extent to which the depiction of singers in the *Odyssey* allows for conclusions regarding the profession of the actual narrator is disputed; see DE JONG on *Od.* p. 191 f. (bibliography n. 2); BIERL 2012a, 118 f. (bibliography n. 30); also SCHUOL 2006 (esp. 141); KRUMMEN 2008 (esp. 33 f.). It remains dubious whether a self-referential mention of the singer is appropriate in this description of a scene where the attention is focused on the appearance and movement of the dancers. — **lyre:** 495a n., 569n.

ἐμέλπετο: 571–572n. — θεῖος ἀοιδός: an inflectable VE formula (nom., acc.: 11× *Od.*), ἀοιδός in the *Il.* only at 24.720 (mourning singer, see *ad loc.*). — φορμίζων: also at *Od.* 1.155, 4.18, 8.266, *h.Ap.* 182 (always the nom. sing. pres. part.), κιθαρίζω is more common (570n.).

605b–606 [604b–605] acrobats | led: The term *kybistētéres* denotes solo dancers performing acrobatic interludes, perhaps leaps (as in Geometric vase painting with acrobats) or somersaults and other turning movements (606; cf. the acrobatic performance with a ball at *Od.* 8.372–379). In a sarcastic speech in the *Iliad*, Patroklos employs terms from the word family *kybist-* when he compares Kebriones' headlong fall from the chariot with a diver's plunge (16.745–750;

605b–606 δοιὼ ... κυβιστητῆρε ... | ... ἐξάρχοντες ἐδίνευον: two duals in combination with plural forms (R 18.1). — μέσσους: on the -σσ-, R 9.1.

see also the fish leaping from the burning river at 21.353–355): CERRI; TÖLLE 1964, 63 f.; KURZ 1966, 22; WEGNER 1968, 43, 65–68 with pl. III b and VI d; FITTSCHEN 1973, 17. The function of the two acrobatic dancers in the present scene is described via the participle *exárchontes*: they 'lead' this dance song (*molpḗ*: 571–572n.), i.e. appear as the group's 'lead dancers' like the two exceptional dancers at the court of Alkinoös at *Od.* 8.370–380 (on this, BIERL 2012, 128 f.; on the pictorial representation of a 'lead dancer', HENRICHS 1996, 38–40; WACHTER 2001, 45 f. *ad* COR 17b). The word family *(ex-)arch-* is used *inter alia* to describe the actions of individuals striking up or leading certain types of songs (cf. also the term *chorēgós* e.g. in Alcman's choral lyric): songs of lament and mourning (*góoi* and *thrḗnoi*: 51 [with n.], 316n. [with n.], 22.430, 23.17, 24.721, 24.747, 24.761), dance songs and other songs (*molpḗ, aoidḗ, chorós*: *Od.* 4.19, 'Hes.' *Sc.* 205, *h.Hom.* 27.18), in post-Homeric texts also dithyramb and paian (Archilochus *fr.* 120 f. West): CALAME (1977) 1997, 43 ff.; ZIMMERMANN 1992, 20; HENRICHS *loc. cit.* 40–44; BIERL 2001, 344 n. 110.

κατ' αὐτούς | ... κατὰ μέσσους: 'among them', is further specified by κατὰ μέσσους 'in their midst' (AH; EDWARDS; CHANTR. 2.114; on κατὰ μέσσους, 507n.; on the anaphora, FEHLING 1969, 197). At the same time, the spatial arrangement of the dancers remains vague (ELLIGER 1975, 35; CALAME [1977] 1997, 36: spectators in the outer circle, chorus dancers in the inner circle, acrobats in the center). — **ἐδίνευον**: 494n.

607–608 [606–607] 2nd VH of 607 = 21.195; ≈ 23.827, 'Hes.' *fr.* 204.56 M.-W.; 1st VH of 608 ≈ 6.118 (see *ad loc.*), 20.275; 2nd VH of 608 ≈ 6× *Od.*, 1× *h.Cer.* — Okeanos is considered the origin of all things, on the one hand (14.246 with n.), and is the circular stream at the outermost edges of the earth, on the other (399n., 402n.). In an analogous manner on the shield, as a stream (*potamós*; cf. 'Hes.' *Sc.* 314–317) it frames the images of earthly scenes and, as decoration on the outer edge of the shield, it leads back to the actual shield and thus the remainder of the arms (on the shield edge, 479b–480n.; on pictorial representations of Okeanos and I-E conceptions of it as a snake, *LfgrE s.v.* Ὠκεανός). Linguistic echoes of the first image on the shield (2nd VH 607: 486/489) complete the circle of the ekphrasis (see also 2nd VH 608/609: 478): in conjunction with the cosmic phenomena of earth, sky, sea and heavenly bodies mentioned at the outset of the creative process (483 ff.), iconographically this represents an overall picture of the world (BECKER 1995, 147 f.; PURVES 2010, 48–53).

ἐν δ' ἐτίθει: 541n. — **μέγα σθένος Ὠκεανοῖο**: on the formulaic expression μέγα σθένος + gen. of a personal name, 486n. — **ἄντυγα**: 479b–480n. — **σάκεος**: 458n. — **πύκα**

---

607 ἐν: adverbial, 'on it'. — ποταμοῖο ... Ὠκεανοῖο: on the declension, R 11.2.
608 ἄντυγα πάρ: παρ' ἄντυγα (R 20.1–2).

ποιητοῖο: a VE formula (also 6× *Od.*, 1× *h.Cer.*, of which 6× with τέγεος), an intensification of εὐποίητος (of armor parts, 16.106, 16.636); it highlights the conclusion of the production of the shield via alliteration (π-) and sound repetition (πυμα-/πυκα-), and refers back to the introduction via ποίει (478/482: 478n.). The verbal adj. (εὐ-)ποιητός is a epithet of parts of buildings, armor and artifacts (*LfgrE s.v.*; cf. the artist signatures ἐποίει/ἐποίησε); πύκα is an adv. related to πυκ(ι)νός ('dense, compact, solid'; also metaphorically of mental processes): 14.216–217n.

608a–d The harbor and the fish mentioned in the four additional verses transmitted in a papyrus – evidently an interpolation based on 'Hes.' *Sc.* 207–209a/211b–213 – disrupt both the ring-composition-like conclusion of the shield-making (see above) and the continuation at 608/609 (WEST 1967, 135 f.; APTHORP 1980, 161).

609–617 [608–616] Hephaistos forges the remaining defensive arms: corselet, helmet and greaves. After they are complete, Thetis immediately departs from Olympos with the arms.

A change in narrative[P] pace: in contrast to the making of the shield (130 verses), the production of the remaining arms, their delivery and Thetis' departure are mentioned only briefly (5/2/2 verses; cf. her arrival at 369–423). This illustrates the haste with which the action is now driven forward, supported by the catalogue-like list using the verb *teúxe* (609 and the triple anaphora of *teúxe ... hoi* ['he made for him'] at VB of 610/611/613; on the anaphora of the predicate, FEHLING 1969, 193 f., 212); the absence of additional detailed descriptions of smith-work also renders the images on the shield more intense (EDWARDS). This custom creation for Achilleus is characterized in general by its elaboration (612a) and especially by the particular gleam of the metals used (610, 613, 617: 610n., 611–612n., 613n.); Achilleus in his armor will thus shine forth in a stunning manner among the other Greeks (19.397 f. [see *ad loc.*]: comparison with the sun god); on the function and effect of the gleam of armor (heroic attribute, intimidation of enemies), 16.70b–72a n., 19.17n., 19.374–383n.

609 [608] 1st VH = *Od.* 8.276, Hes. *Th.* 585, *h.Merc.* 52; ≈ 349 (see *ad loc.*); 2nd VH = 478 (see *ad loc.*).

610 [609] 2nd VH = *h.Ven.* 86. — **corselet:** on the nature of metal corselets (a cuirass made from two cast plates or scale armor) based on archaeological finds, 3.332n.; SHEAR 2000, 46–48; BUCHHOLZ 2010, 214–226 (esp. 226). — **shining:** The arming scene and Achilleus' *aristeia* also stress the luster emanating from

---

609 αὐτάρ: 'but' (R 24.2).
610 ἄρα (ϝ)οι: on the prosody, R 4.3. — οἱ: = αὐτῷ (R 14.1), i.e. for Achilleus; likewise 611, 613.

his appearance (esp. 19.397 f.) and particularly from his bronze corselet (cf. 22.134 f. with DE JONG *ad loc.*; 609–617n.).

φαεινότερον πυρὸς αὐγῆς: an expressive/intensive, hyperbolic comparison, in which the characteristic 'shining' is portrayed to the highest degree of perfection vis-à-vis the object of comparison, which serves as a scale (on the stylistic means and the Greek comparative, MEID 1967, 239–242; TZAMALI 1996, 186 f., 365 f.; for a collection of examples of more common comparisons 'like fire', *LfgrE s.v.* πῦρ 1655.43 ff., 1657.20 ff.; a list of epithets with θώρηξ in TRÜMPY 1950, 10). – πυρὸς αὐγῆς is an inflectable VE formula (2× gen., 3× dat.: 9.206, *Od.* 6.305, 23.89, *h.Ven.* 86); on αὐγή (mostly the glow of fire or of the sun), GRAZ 1965, 308–315; HANDSCHUR 1970, 63–66; CIANI 1974, 11–14.

611–612 [610–611] 2nd VH of 611 (from caesura C 1) = 13.188, *Od.* 22.102, 'Hes.' *Sc.* 137; ≈ *Od.* 18.378; 612 ≈ *Il.* 9.187. – For the archaeological evidence for various types of helmets (made from bronze), the nature of the crest (made from horsehair) and its impressive effect and protective function, 3.337n., 6.469n.; SHEAR 2000, 57–59; BUCHHOLZ *et al.* 2010. – **lovely:** 490–491a n. – **gold:** The special furnishing of the crest makes the bearer stand out from the crowd (BUCHHOLZ 2012, 196 f.); on the attribute 'golden' and the decoration of Achilleus' crest with golden hair or threads, 19.383n.; HANDSCHUR 1970, 142 f.

κόρυθα βριαρήν: an inflectable noun-epithet formula in various positions in the verse (6× *Il.*); βριαρή is an epithet with different terms for 'helmet', and based on its meaning ('massive, heavy') it likely indicates a helmet made of metal (bronze) or with metal parts (16.413n., 19.380b–381a n.). For different terms denoting 'helmet' (κόρυς, τρυφάλεια [458n.], πήληξ, κυνέη [literally 'dogskin']), 3.316n., 16.70b–72a n. – **καλήν, δαιδαλέην:** 379n., 390n. – **ἐπὶ ... ἧκεν:** 'he set on top of it' (*LfgrE s.v.* ἵημι 1154.63 f.; FRITZ 2005, 171); cf. on the crest at 19.383 (Ἥφαιστος ἵει ...).

χρύσεον: on the metrical-prosodic variants with material adjectives in -ε(ι)ος, 24.21n.

613 [612] leg-armor: Greaves (made from leather or in addition reinforced with bronze) appear to have been part of a warrior's basic equipment since the Mycenaean period (1.17n.; for the archaeological evidence, CATLING 1977; BUCHHOLZ 2010, 213 f.). Homeric epic does not provide any indication of their composition and appearance: silver (3.331n.: ankle protectors?, buttons?) and bronze (7.41) are mentioned as metals used. Tin greaves are not attested anywhere and contribute to the exclusiveness of Achilleus' new equipment (also mentioned at 21.592). Since the soft metal is not easily justified for employment for protective armor (easily shaped and fitted for greaves? used in the form of a plating or as decoration?), perhaps a poetic usage is to be considered: after

---

611 βριαρήν: on the -η- after -ρ-, R 2.
612 ἐπὶ ... ἧκεν: on the so-called tmesis, R 20.2. – χρύσεον: on the synizesis, R 7.

the stunningly impressive shield, the especially shiny corselet (610) and the crest with golden hair (612), Achilleus' greaves must be extraordinary in appearance; the use of tin, elsewhere employed for color effects in combination with other metals (cf. 565n.), is meant to evoke a bright gleam – especially long-lived in comparison with silver (609–617n.; EDWARDS; FORBES 1967, 28; CATLING *loc. cit.* 144; SHEAR 2000, 188 n. 322; FRANZ 2002, 62 f. with n. 278; on the ancient use of tin in general, *BNP s.v.* Tin).

ἑανοῦ κασσιτέροιο: ἑανός is elsewhere an epithet of textiles of especially high quality (5.734 = 8.385: Athene lets her 'colorful' πέπλος ἑ. slip to the ground; 352 ≈ 23.254: Patroklos' remains are wrapped in a cloth, a ἑ. λίς), but its etymology and meaning are unknown ('gleaming' or 'soft', i.e. 'supple, pliable'?: 352–353n.). The choice of words in the present passage perhaps highlights the exclusiveness of the easily shaped metal, the optical effects of which are elsewhere in early epic characterized by λευκός (11.34 f.) and φαεινός (23.561).

614 2nd VH ≈ Hes. *Op.* 70, 'Hes.' *Sc.* 219. – **ὅπλα:** in early epic usually with the meaning 'tools, equipment' (409n.), in the sense 'arms' only here and, following from it, at 19.21 (see *ad loc.*), as well as at 10.252, 10.272, Hes. *Th.* 853 (Zeus' thunder and lightning); here it perhaps echoes 409/412 (ὅπλα τε πάντα) (battle gear beside a smith's equipment: SOMMER 1977, 100 f.). – **κάμε:** κάμνω used transitively means 'make something with effort, laboriously (i.e. carefully, artfully)'; it denotes Hephaistos' smith-work (cf. the phrase Ἥφαιστος κάμε τεύχων at 2.101, 8.195, 19.368 [where also of Achilleus' arms], as well as 7.220) and other craftwork (*LfgrE s.v.* κάμνω; ECKSTEIN 1974, 6 f.). – **κλυτὸς Ἀμφιγυήεις:** an abbreviated variant of the formula περι-/ἀγα-κλυτὸς Ἀ. (on which, 383n.).

615 [614] mother: She had stayed behind with Charis (468n.). – 'A periphrastic denomination[P] by means of a 'paidonymic' [...] is rare [...] and probably serves for emphasis', elsewhere of a mother only at *Od.* 17.554 in the case of Penelope (2.260n.). In the present passage, the denomination is also significant in that the narrator[P] uses it, as in the preceding and following scenes, to highlight the mother-son relationship (see also 19.4) and to direct attention to Achilleus, who is the designated recipient of the arms (EDWARDS; cf. 436n., 437–443 [56–62n.], 19.4n., 19.20n.).

616–617 [615–616] 617 ≈ 137 (Thetis' promise). – The beginning and end of Thetis' visit to Hephaistos are designed differently (609–617n.): Thetis' departure is mentioned only briefly, with no indication of gratitude or leave-taking; this reflects the haste of her actions, driven by her arrangement with Achilleus (136 f.: 'at dawn') (schol. A and bT). The type-scene[P] 'arrival' begins and is con-

---

615 μητρός: dependent on προπάροιθεν. — Ἀχιλλῆος: on the declension, R 11.3.
616 ἴρηξ ὥς: = ὡς ἴρηξ. — Οὐλύμπου: initial syllable metrically lengthened (R 10.1).

tinued at 19.3 ff. (19.1–39n., 19.3n.). — **like a hawk:** In Homeric epic, bird comparisons[P] both generally and with a falcon (*írēx*) in particular, which is considered the fastest of the birds (15.237 f., see also at 13.62 'with quick wings', 13.819 'swifter than hawks', *Od.* 13.86 f.), predominantly signify great speed of movement (2.764n., 19.350–351a n., 24.345n.). The present passage thus illustrates in the linguistically briefest form the extraordinarily swift and easy directional change of location of the goddess, laden with the armor, from Olympos to the Myrmidon encampment of ships (19.3), where her son is (19.4 f.) (on the narrative pace, cf. 19.114–119n.). Comparisons of warriors and deities with birds of prey also serve to illustrate their speed *and* aggressiveness simultaneously (on the *írēx*, see 13.62–64 [Poseidon], 16.582 f. [Patroklos], 21.494 f. [Hera]): 16.582–583n.; the comparison here thus perhaps also indicates a change in Thetis' demeanor (from the care-worn mother of Book 18 to the arms-bearing preparer of battle, see 19.8–11, 19.34–38; cf. 19.6b n.): SCOTT 1974, 115; TSAGARAKIS 1982, 136 f.; PATZER 1996, 149 f.; JOHANSSON 2012, 177; cf. BANNERT 1988, 67: 'A fulcrum for the action of the fourth day of battle' [transl.]); for additional comparisons in the case of divine journeys, 24.80–82n. — **Olympos:** 186n. — **armor:** on its luster, 610n.

ἴρηξ: denotes a bird of prey, usually interpreted as a term encompassing different species of falcons (also hawks and others: 16.582n.); the etymology is unclear (perhaps related to ἵεμαι [cf. Attic ἱέραξ] or a substrate word): *LfgrE*; BEEKES. — ἆλτο: on the accent, WEST 1998, XX. — Οὐλύμπου νιφόεντος: Hes. *Th.* 953 (ἐν …) is similar; the VE formula νιφόεντος Ὀλύμπου (4× Hes., 1× *h.Hom.*) and the formula before caesura C 2 Ὄλυμπον ἀγάννιφον (186n.) are more common. On the mountain epithet νιφόεις 'snow-covered, snowy', 14.227n. — μαρμαίροντα: means 'sparkling, glittering', usually of light reflecting (dawn at 19.1 f.) on metal (χαλκός: 13.801, 16.664, 18.131, 23.27; χρυσός: 13.22): 3.397n.

Bibliographic Abbreviations

1 Works cited without year of publication (standard works)

AH   *Homers* Ilias. Erklärt von K.F. Ameis und C. Hentze, Leipzig and Berlin [1]1868–
1884 (Books 1–6 by Ameis, rev. by Hentze; 7–24 by Hentze); most recent editions: vol. 1.1 (Books 1–3) [7]1913, rev. by P. Cauer; vol. 1.2 (4–6) [6]1908; vol. 1.3
(7–9) [5]1907; vol. 1.4 (10–12) [5]1906; vol. 2.1 (13–15) [4]1905; vol. 2.2 (16–18) [4]1908;
vol. 2.3 (19–21) [4]1905; vol. 2.4 (22–24) [4]1906. (Reprint Amsterdam 1965.)

AH, *Anh.*   *Anhang zu Homers* Ilias. Schulausgabe von K.F. Ameis, Leipzig [1]1868– 1886
(commentary on Books 1–6 by Ameis, rev. by Hentze; 7–24 by Hentze); cited
in this volume: Heft 6 (on *Il.* 16–18) [2]1900.

AH on *Od.*   *Homers* Odyssee. Erklärt von K.F. Ameis und C. Hentze, Leipzig and Berlin
[1]1856–1860; cited in this volume: vol. 1.1 (Books 1–6), rev. by P. Cauer, [13]1920.

AH, *Anh.* on *Od.*   *Anhang zu Homers* Odyssee. Schulausgabe von K.F. Ameis, Leipzig [1]1867;
cited in this volume: Heft 1 (on *Od.* 1–6), rev. by C. Hentze, [3]1883.

Allen   Allen, T.W. *Homeri* Ilias. Oxford 1931. (3 vols.)

Allen/Halliday/   Allen, T.W., W.R. Halliday and E.E. Sikes (eds.). *The Homeric Hymns.* Oxford
Sikes   1936. (Reprint Amsterdam 1980.)

ArchHom   *Archaeologia Homerica. Die Denkmäler und das frühgriechische Epos.* Edited
by F. Matz and H.-G. Buchholz under the authority of the DAI. Göttingen
1967–.

Autenrieth/Kaegi   Autenrieth, G. and A. Kaegi. *Wörterbuch zu den Homerischen Gedichten.*
Stuttgart and Leipzig [14]1999 (= reprint of [13]1920, with a Preface by J. Latacz
and an Introduction by A. Willi; Leipzig [1]1873).

Beekes   Beekes, R. *Etymological Dictionary of Greek*, with the assistance of L. van
Beek. Leiden Etymological Dictionary Series 10. Leiden and Boston 2010. (2
vols.)

BNP   *Brill's New Pauly*, ed. by H. Cancik and H. Schneider, trans. by C.F. Salazar,
Leiden 2002–2011. (German original: *Der Neue Pauly. Enzyklopädie der
Antike*, ed. by H. Cancik and H. Schneider. Stuttgart and Weimar 1996–2003.)

CAD   The Assyrian Dictionary of the Oriental Institute of the University of Chicago
(CAD), ed. by M.T. Roth et al. Chicago 1956–.

Cerri   *Omero* Iliade *libro XVIII. Lo Scudo di Achille.* Introduzione, traduzione e commento di G. Cerri. Classici 6. Rome 2010.

ChronEG   *Chronique d'étymologie grecque*, ed. by A. Blanc, C. de Lamberterie and J.-L.
Perpillou, appears annually in: *RPh* 70ff., 1996ff. (also in: DELG); cited in
this volume: ChronEG 1, *RPh* 70, 1996, 103–138; ChronEG 3, *RPh* 72, 1998,
117–142; ChronEG 5, *RPh* 74, 2000, 257–286; ChronEG 6, *RPh* 75, 2001, 131–162;
ChronEG 9, *RPh* 78, 2004, 155–179.

CG   Graf, F. 'Cast of Characters of the *Iliad*: Gods.' In *Prolegomena*, pp. 122–139.

CH   Stoevesandt, M. 'Cast of Characters of the *Iliad*: Human Beings.' In *Prolegomena*, pp. 140–150.

Chantr.   Chantraine, P. *Grammaire homérique*[6]. Paris [6]1986–1988 ([1]1942–1953). (2 vols.)

https://doi.org/10.1515/9783110572889-007

COM	Latacz, J. 'Introduction: Commenting on Homer. From the Beginnings to this Commentary.' In *Prolegomena*, pp. 1–26.
Cunliffe	Cunliffe, R.J. *A Lexicon of the Homeric Dialect*. Expanded Edition with a New Preface by J.H. Dee. Norman 2012 (¹1924).
DELG	Chantraine, P. *Dictionnaire étymologique de la langue grecque. Histoire des mots*. Nouvelle édition avec, en supplément, les Chroniques d'étymologie grecque (1–10). Paris 2009 (¹1968–1980).
Denniston	Denniston, J.D. *The Greek Particles*². Oxford ²1954 (¹1934).
DMic	Aura Jorro, F. *Diccionario Micénico*. Madrid 1985–1993. (2 vols.)
Ebeling	Ebeling, H. *Lexicon Homericum*. Leipzig 1885. (Reprint Hildesheim 1987; 2 vols.)
Edwards	Edwards, M.W. *The Iliad. A Commentary, vol. V: Books 17–20*. Cambridge 1991.
Faesi	*Homers* Iliade. Erklärt von J.U. Faesi. Leipzig ⁴1864–1865 (¹1851–1852).
Faulkner	Faulkner, A. (ed.) *The Homeric Hymn to Aphrodite*. Introduction, Text, and Commentary. Oxford 2008.
Fernández-Galiano	Fernández-Galiano, M. In *A Commentary on Homer's* Odyssey, *vol. III: Books XVII–XXIV*. Oxford 1992. (Original Italian ed. 1986.)
FOR	Latacz, J. 'Formularity and Orality.' In *Prolegomena*, pp. 39–64.
Frisk	Frisk, H. *Griechisches etymologisches Wörterbuch*. Heidelberg 1960– 1972. (3 vols.)
G	Wachter, R. 'Grammar of Homeric Greek.' In *Prolegomena*, pp. 65–115.
Graziosi/Haubold	*Homer* Iliad *Book VI*, ed. by B. Graziosi and J. Haubold. Cambridge Greek and Latin Classics. Cambridge 2010.
Hainsworth on *Il*. 9–12	Hainsworth, J.B. *The Iliad. A Commentary, vol. III: Books 9–12*. Cambridge 1993.
Hainsworth on *Od*. 5–8	Hainsworth, J.B. In *A Commentary on Homer's* Odyssey, *vol. I: Books I–VIII*. Oxford 1988. (Original Italian ed. 1982.)
HE	*The Homer Encyclopedia*, ed. by M. Finkelberg. Chichester 2011. (3 vols.)
Heubeck on *Od*. 9–12	Heubeck, A. In *A Commentary on Homer's* Odyssey, *vol. II: Books IX–XVI*. Oxford 1989. (Original Italian ed. 1983.)
Heubeck on *Od*. 23–24	Heubeck, A. In *A Commentary on Homer's* Odyssey, *vol. III: Books XVII–XXIV*. Oxford 1992. (Original Italian ed. 1986.)
Hoekstra	Hoekstra, A. In *A Commentary on Homer's* Odyssey, *vol. II: Books IX–XVI*. Oxford 1989. (Original Italian ed. 1984.)
HT	West, M.L. 'History of the Text.' In *Prolegomena*, pp. 27–38.
HTN	Latacz, J. (ed.). *Homer. Tradition und Neuerung*. Wege der Forschung 463. Darmstadt 1979.
Janko	Janko, R. *The Iliad. A Commentary, vol. IV: Books 13–16*. Cambridge 1992.
de Jong on *Od*.	de Jong, I.J.F. *A Narratological Commentary on the* Odyssey. Cambridge 2001.
de Jong on *Il*. 22	*Homer* Iliad *Book XXII*, ed. by I.J.F. de Jong. Cambridge Greek and Latin Classics. Cambridge 2012.
von Kamptz	Kamptz, H. von. *Homerische Personennamen. Sprachwissenschaftliche und historische Klassifikation*. Göttingen and Zurich 1982. (Originally diss. Jena 1958.)
K.-G.	Kühner, R. and B. Gerth. *Ausführliche Grammatik der griechischen Sprache. Zweiter Teil: Satzlehre*. Hanover 1898–1904. (Reprint Hanover 1992; 2 vols.)

Kidd	*Aratus* Phaenomena, ed. with Introduction, Translation and Commentary by D. Kidd. Cambridge Classical Texts and Commentaries 34. Cambridge 1997.
Kirk	Kirk, G.S. *The* Iliad. *A Commentary, vol. I: Books 1–4*. Cambridge 1985; *vol. II: Books 5–8*. Cambridge 1990.
KlP	*Der Kleine Pauly. Lexikon der Antike in fünf Bänden*, ed. by K. Ziegler and W. Sontheimer. Stuttgart and Munich 1964–1975. (Reprint Munich 1979; 5 vols.)
Lattimore	*The* Iliad *of Homer*. Transl. by R. Lattimore, introduction and notes by R. P. Martin. Chicago and London 2011 ([1]1951).
Leaf	*The* Iliad[2]. Ed. with Apparatus Criticus, Prolegomena, Notes, and Appendices by W. Leaf. London 1900–1902 ([1]1886–1888). (2 vols.)
van Leeuwen	Ilias. Cum prolegomenis, notis criticis, commentariis exegeticis ed. J. van Leeuwen. Leiden 1912–1913. (2 vols.)
LfgrE	*Lexikon des frühgriechischen Epos*. Founded by Bruno Snell. Prepared under the authority of the Academy of Sciences in Göttingen and edited by the Thesaurus Linguae Graecae. Göttingen 1955–2010.
LIMC	*Lexicon Iconographicum Mythologiae Classicae*, ed. by H.C. Ackermann and J.R. Gisler. Zurich etc. 1981–1999. (18 vols.)
LIV	*Lexikon der indogermanischen Verben. Die Wurzeln und ihre Primärstammbildungen*. Ed. by M. Kümmel, Th. Zehnder, R. Lipp, B. Schirmer under the direction of H. Rix and with the collaboration of many others. Second, expanded and improved edition ed. by M. Kümmel and H. Rix. Wiesbaden 2001 ([1]1998).
LSJ	Liddell, H.R., R. Scott and H.S. Jones. *A Greek-English Lexicon*[9]. Oxford 1940. (Reprint with revised supplement 1996.)
M	Nünlist, R. 'Homeric Meter.' In *Prolegomena*, pp. 116–121.
Mazon	*Homère*, Iliade, Tome 4: *Chants 19–24*. Texte établi et traduit par P. Mazon avec la collaboration de P. Chantraine *et al*. Paris 1947.
MHV	Parry, M. *The Making of Homeric Verse. The Collected Papers of Milman Parry*. Edited by Adam Parry. New York and Oxford 1971. (Reprint 1987.)
MYC	Wachter, R. 'Homeric – Mycenaean Word Index.' In *Prolegomena*, pp. 236–258.
NTHS	Bierl, A. 'New Trends in Homeric Scholarship.' In *Prolegomena*, pp. 177–203.
Olson on *h.Ven.*	Olson, S.D. (ed.). *The Homeric Hymn to Aphrodite and Related Texts: Text, Translation and Commentary*. Texte und Kommentare 39. Berlin and Boston 2012.
P (superscript)	Nünlist, R. and I. de Jong. 'Homeric Poetics in Keywords.' In *Prolegomena*, pp. 164–176.
Prolegomena	*Homer's* Iliad. *The Basel Commentary: Prolegomena*, ed. by A. Bierl and J. Latacz. Berlin and Boston 2015.
RE	*Paulys Real-Encyclopädie der Classischen Altertumswissenschaft*. New edition, ed. by G. Wissowa with the cooperation of numerous specialists. Stuttgart 1894–2000.
Richardson on *Il.* 21–24	Richardson, N.J. *The* Iliad. *A Commentary, vol. VI: Books 21–24*. Cambridge 1993.
Richardson on *h.Cer.*	Richardson, N.J. *The Homeric Hymn to Demeter*. Oxford 1974.
Risch	Risch, E. *Wortbildung der homerischen Sprache*[2]. Berlin and New York 1974 ([1]1937).

Ruijgh	Ruijgh, C.J. Autour de 'te épique'. Études sur la syntaxe grecque. Amsterdam 1971.
Russo	Russo, J. In *A Commentary on Homer's* Odyssey, *vol. III: Books XVII–XXIV.* Oxford 1992. (Original Italian ed. 1985.)
Schadewaldt	*Homer* Ilias, neue Übertragung von W. Schadewaldt. Frankfurt am Main 1975.
Schw.	Schwyzer, E., A. Debrunner, D.J. Georgacas and F. and S. Radt. *Griechische Grammatik*. Handbuch der Altertumswissenschaft 2.1.1–4. Munich 1939–1994. (4 vols.)
STR	Latacz, J. 'The Structure of the *Iliad*.' In *Prolegomena*, pp. 151–163.
ThesCRA	*Thesaurus Cultus et Rituum Antiquorum*, ed. by the Fondation pour le Lexicon Iconographicum Mythologiae Classicae (LIMC) and the J. Paul Getty Museum. Los Angeles 2004–2014. (8 vols. and one index vol.)
Thompson	Thompson, S. *Motif-Index of Folk-Literature: A Classification of Narrative Elements in Folktales, Ballads, Myths, Fables, Mediaeval Romances, Exempla, Fabliaux, Jest-Books and Local Legends²*. Copenhagen 1955–1958 (¹1932–1936). (6 vols.)
Vergados on *h.Merc.*	Vergados, A. (ed.) *The Homeric Hymn to Hermes*. Introduction, Text and Commentary. Texte und Kommentare 41. Berlin and Boston 2013.
Verity	*Homer, The* Iliad. Transl. by A. Verity with an Introduction and Notes by B. Graziosi. Oxford 2011.
Wathelet	Wathelet, P. *Dictionnaire des Troyens de l'*Iliade. Université de Liège. Bibliothèque de la Faculté de Philosophie et Lettres. Documenta et Instrumenta 1. Liège 1988. (2 vols.)
West on Hes. *Op.*	*Hesiod*, Works and Days. Ed. with Prolegomena and Commentary by M.L. West. Oxford 1978.
West on Hes. *Th.*	*Hesiod*, Theogony. Ed. with Prolegomena and Commentary by M.L. West. Oxford 1966.
West on *Od.* 1–4	West, S. In *A Commentary on Homer's* Odyssey, *vol. I: Books I–VIII.* Oxford 1988. (Original Italian ed. 1981.)
Willcock	*Homer*, Iliad. Ed. with Introduction and Commentary by M.M. Willcock. London 1978–1984. (2 vols.)

2 Editions of ancient authors and texts*

Archilochus (West)
  in *Iambi et elegi graeci ante Alexandrum cantati²*, vol. 1, ed. M.L. West. Oxford 1989 (¹1971).
Callinus (West)
  in *Iambi et elegi graeci ante Alexandrum cantati²*, vol. 2, ed. M.L. West. Oxford 1992 (¹1972).
CEG
  Hansen, P.A. *Carmina epigraphica Graeca*. Texte und Kommentare 12 and 15. Berlin and New York 1983–1989. (2 vols.)

---

* Included are editions only of works for which different editions offer differing verse, paragraph or fragment numbers.

Certamen (West)

in *Homeric Hymns, Homeric Apocrypha, Lives of Homer*, ed. and transl. by M.L. West. Loeb Classical Library 496. Cambridge, Mass. and London 2003.

'Epic Cycle' (West) or (Davies)

- in *Epicorum Graecorum Fragmenta*, ed. M. Davies. Göttingen 1988;
- and in *Greek Epic Fragments from the Seventh to the Fifth Centuries BC*, ed. and transl. by M.L. West. Loeb Classical Library 497. Cambridge, Mass. and London 2003.

Eumelus, fragments (West)

in *Greek Epic Fragments from the Seventh to the Fifth Centuries BC*, ed. and transl. by M.L. West. Loeb Classical Library 497. Cambridge, Mass. and London 2003.

'Hesiod', fragments (M.-W.)

in *Hesiodi* Theogonia, Opera et dies, Scutum, ed. F. Solmsen; *Fragmenta selecta*³, edd. R. Merkelbach et M.L. West. Oxford 1990 (¹1970).

Pherecydes (*FGrHist*/Fowler)

- No. 3 in *Die Fragmente der griechischen Historiker (FGrHist)*, by F. Jacoby, vol. 1². Leiden 1957 (¹1923); also in *Brill's New Jacoby*, ed. by I. Worthington (http://referenceworks.brill-online.com/search?s.q=Pherekydes&s.f.s2_parent=s.f.book.brill-s-new-jacoby, retrieved 30.05.2018);
- and in *Early Greek Mythography*, ed. R.L. Fowler, vol. 1: Texts. Oxford 2000.

Proclus (West)

in *Greek Epic Fragments. From the Seventh to the Fifth Century BC*. ed. and transl. by M.L. West. Loeb Classical Library 497. Cambridge, Mass. and London 2003.

Sappho (Voigt)

in *Sappho et Alcaeus. Fragmenta*, ed. E.-M. Voigt. Amsterdam 1971.

Scholia on the *Iliad* (Erbse)

Scholia graeca in Homeri Iliadem (scholia vetera), rec. H. Erbse. Berlin 1969–1988. (7 vols.)

Scholia on the *Iliad* (van Thiel)

Scholia D in Iliadem secundum codices manu scriptos. Proecdosis aucta et correctior 2014, ed. H. van Thiel. Elektronische Schriftenreihe der Universitäts- und Stadtbibliothek Köln 7. http://kups.ub.uni-koeln.de/5586/ (retrieved 30.05.2018).

Scholia on the *Odyssey* (Pontani)

Scholia graeca in Odysseam, ed. F. Pontani. Pleiadi 6. Rome 2007–.

Tyrtaeus (West)

in *Iambi et elegi graeci ante Alexandrum cantati*², vol. 2, ed. M.L. West. Oxford 1992 (¹1972).

3 Articles and monographs

Journal abbreviations follow l'Année Philologique.

Ahrens 1937   Ahrens, E. *Gnomen in griechischer Dichtung (Homer, Hesiod, Aeschylus)*. Halle.

Albracht (1886) 2005 Albracht, F. *Battle and Battle Description in Homer: A Contribution to the History of War*, transl. by P. Jones, M. Willcock and G. Wright. London. (German original: *Kampf und Kampfschilderung bei Homer. Ein Beitrag zu den Kriegsaltertümern*. Beilage zum Jahresbericht der Königlichen Landesschule Pforta. Naumburg an der Saale 1886.)

Alden 2000   Alden, M. *Homer Beside Himself: Para-Narratives in the* Iliad. Oxford.
Alden 2005   Alden, M. 'Lions in Paradise: Lion Similes in the *Iliad* and the Lion Cubs of *Il.*
                    18.318–22.' *CQ* 55: 335–342.
Alexiou (1974) 2002 Alexiou, M. *The Ritual Lament in Greek Tradition*². Greek Studies. Lanham
                    etc. (¹1974).
Aliffi 2002   Aliffi, M.L. 'Le espressioni dell'agente e dello strumento nei processi di
                    «morte violenta».' In Montanari 2002, 409–423.
Allan 2003   Allan, R.J. *The Middle Voice in Ancient Greek; A Study in Polysemy*. Amster-
                    dam Studies in Classical Philology 11. Amsterdam.
Allan 2009   Allan, R. 'Orale elementen in de Homerische grammatica. Intonatie-eenheid
                    en enjambement.' *Lampas* 42: 136–151.
Allan 2010   Allan, R.J. 'The *infinitivus pro imperativo* in Ancient Greek: The Imperatival
                    Infinitive as an Expression of Proper Procedural Action.' *Mnemosyne* 63:
                    203–228.
Allan 2013   Allan, R.J. 'Exploring Modality's Semantic Space: Grammaticalization, Sub-
                    jectification and the Case of ὀφείλω.' *Glotta* 89: 1–46.
Allen 2007   Allen, N.J. 'The Shield of Achilles and Indo-European Tradition.' *CFG, Estu-
                    dios griegos e indoeuropeos* 17: 33–44.
Aloni 1979   Aloni, A. 'Sistemi formulari e intenzione poetica. Note a Omero, *Iliade* XVIII
                    2, 4, 5.' *RIL* 113: 220–230.
Andersen 1976   Andersen, Ø. 'Some Thoughts on the Shield of Achilles.' *SO* 51: 5–18.
Andersen 1990   Andersen, Ø. 'The Making of the Past in the *Iliad*.' *HSCPh* 93: 25–45.
Andronikos 1968   Andronikos, M. 'Totenkult.' *ArchHom.* chap. W. Göttingen.
Anghelina 2007   Anghelina, C. 'On Some Adverbs with Variable Endings in Ancient Greek.'
                    Glotta 83: 1–12.
Antonaccio 1995   Antonaccio, C.M. 'Lefkandi and Homer.' In *Homer's World: Fiction, Tradition,
                    Reality*, ed. by Ø. Andersen and M. Dickie, pp. 5–27. Papers from the Norwe-
                    gian Institute at Athens 3. Bergen.
Anziferowa 1983   Anziferowa, G.M. 'Über eine Gruppe homerischer Nasalpraesentia.' *Eirene*
                    20: 5–32.
Apthorp 1980   Apthorp, M.J. *The Manuscript Evidence for Interpolation in Homer*. Bibliothek
                    der Klassischen Altertumswissenschaften, N.F. 2.71. Heidelberg.
Apthorp 1995   Apthorp, M.J. 'Did Homer Give His Nereids Names? A Note on the Ancient
                    Manuscript Evidence.' *Acta Classica* 38: 89–92.
Apthorp 1996   Apthorp, M.J. '*Iliad* 18.200–201: Genuine or Interpolated?' *ZPE* 111: 141–148.
Arend 1933   Arend, W. *Die typischen Scenen bei Homer*. Problemata 7. Berlin.
Arnould 1990   Arnould, D. *Le rire et les larmes dans la littérature grecque d'Homère à Platon*.
                    Collection d'études anciennes, Série grecque 119. Paris.
Arpaia 2010   Arpaia, M. 'Bibliografia sullo scudo di Achille (1945–2008).' In D'Acunto and
                    Palmisciano 2010, 233–245.
Aubriot 1999   Aubriot, D. 'Imago Iliadis. Le Bouclier d' Achille et la poésie de l'*Iliade*.'
                    Kernos 12: 9–56.
Aubriot 2001   Aubriot, D. 'Humanité et divinité dans l'*Iliade* à travers le personnage
                    d'Achille.' In *Dieux, héros et médecins grecs. Hommage à Fernand Robert*, ed.
                    by M. Woronoff, S. Follet and J. Jouanna, pp. 7–27. Besançon.
Aubriot-Sévin 1992 Aubriot-Sévin, D. *Prière et conceptions religieuses en Grèce ancienne jusqu' à
                    la fin du Ve siècle av. J.-C.* Lyon etc.

Bakker 1988   Bakker, E.J. *Linguistics and Formulas in Homer: Scalarity and the Description of the Particle 'per'*. Amsterdam and Philadelphia.

Bakker (1991) 2005   Bakker, E.J. 'Peripheral and Nuclear Semantics.' In Bakker 2005, 1–21. (First published as 'Peripheral and Nuclear Semantics in Homeric Diction: The case of Dative Expressions of «Spear».' *Mnemosyne* 44 [1991] 63–84.)

Bakker 1997   Bakker, E.J. *Poetry in Speech: Orality and Homeric Discourse*. Myth and Poetics. Ithaca and London.

Bakker (1997) 2005   Bakker, E.J. 'Storytelling in the Future.' In Bakker 2005, 92–113. (First published in *Written Voices, Spoken Signs: Tradition, Performance, and the Epic Text*, ed. by E.J. Bakker and A. Kahane, pp. 11–36. Cambridge, Mass. 1997.)

Bakker (1999) 2005   Bakker, E.J. 'The Poetics of Deixis.' In Bakker 2005, 71–91. (First published as 'Homeric οὗτος and the Poetics of Deixis.' *CPh* 94 [1999] 1–19.)

Bakker 2005   Bakker, E.J. *Pointing at the Past: From Formula to Performance in Homeric Poetics*. Hellenic Studies 12. Cambridge, Mass. and London.

Balensiefen 1955   Balensiefen, E. *Die Zeitgestaltung in Homers Ilias*. Tübingen.

Bannert 1987   Bannert, H. 'Versammlungsszenen bei Homer.' In Bremer *et al.* 1987, 15–29.

Bannert 1988   Bannert, H. *Formen des Wiederholens bei Homer. Beispiele für eine Poetik des Epos*. Wiener Studien, Beiheft 13. Vienna.

Barck 1976   Barck, C. *Wort und Tat bei Homer*. Spudasmata 34. Hildesheim and New York.

Barth 1989   Barth, H.-L. 'Achill und das Schicksal des Patroklos. Zum angeblichen Widerspruch zwischen Hom. P 410f. und Σ 9–11.' *Hermes* 117: 1–24.

Basset 1979   Basset, L. *Les emplois périphrastiques du verb grec μέλλειν*. Lyon.

Basset 2006   Basset, L. 'La préfiguration dans l'épopée homérique de l'article défini du grec classique.' In *Word Classes and Related Topics in Ancient Greek (Proceedings of the Conference on 'Greek Syntax and Word Classes', Madrid, 18.–21. Juni 2003)*, ed. by E. Crespo, J. de la Villa and A.R. Revuelta, pp. 105–120. Bibliothèque des cahiers de l'Institut de linguistique de Louvain 117. Louvain-La-Neuve.

Bassett 1919   Bassett, S.E. 'Versus tetracolos.' *CPh* 14: 216–233.

Bassett (1938) 2003   Bassett, S.E. *The Poetry of Homer*[2]. Ed. with an introduction by B. Heiden. Sather Classical Lectures 15. Lanham etc. ([1]1938).

Bechert 1964   Bechert, J. *Die Diathesen von ἰδεῖν und ὁρᾶν bei Homer*. Munich.

Bechtel 1914   Bechtel, F. *Lexilogus zu Homer. Etymologie und Stammbildung homerischer Wörter*. Halle.

Beck 2005   Beck, D. *Homeric Conversation*. Hellenic Studies 14. Cambridge, Mass. and London.

Beck 2012   Beck, D. *Speech Presentation in Homeric Epic*. Austin.

Beck 1986   Beck, W. 'Choice and Context: Metrical Doublets for Hera.' *AJPh* 107: 480–488.

Becker 1995   Becker, A.S. *The Shield of Achilles and the Poetics of Ekphrasis*. Greek Studies: Interdisciplinary Approaches. Lanham.

Becker 1937   Becker, O. *Das Bild des Weges und verwandte Vorstellungen im frühgriechischen Denken*. Hermes Einzelschriften 4. Berlin.

Beekes/Cuypers 2003   Beekes, R.S.P. and M. Cuypers. 'ΝΕΚΥΣ, ΑΝΤΙΚΡΥ, and Metrical Lengthening in Homer.' *Mnemosyne* 56: 485–491.

Bekker 1863   Bekker, I. *Homerische Blätter*, vol. 1. Bonn.

Bekker 1872   Bekker, I. *Homerische Blätter*, vol. 2. Bonn.
Benveniste 1969   Benveniste, E. *Le vocabulaire des institutions indo-européennes. Vol. 2: pouvoir, droit, religion*. Paris.
Bergren 1975   Bergren, A.L.T. *The Etymology and Usage of ΠΕΙΡΑΡ in Early Greek Poetry: A Study in the Interrelationship of Metrics, Linguistics and Poetics*. American Classical Studies 2. New York.
Bernsdorff 1992   Bernsdorff, H. *Zur Rolle des Aussehens im homerischen Menschenbild*. Hypomnemata 97. Göttingen.
Bertolín Cebrián 1996 Bertolín Cebrián, R. *Die Verben des Denkens bei Homer*. Innsbrucker Beiträge zur Kulturwissenschaft, Sonderheft 97. Innsbruck.
Bielefeld 1968   Bielefeld, E. 'Schmuck.' *ArchHom* chap. C. Göttingen.
Bierl 2001   Bierl, A. *Der Chor in der Alten Komödie. Ritual und Performativität*. Beiträge zur Altertumskunde 126. Munich and Leipzig.
Bierl 2004   Bierl, A. '«Turn on the Light!» Epiphany, the God-Like Hero Odysseus, and the Golden Lamp of Athena in Homer's *Odyssey* (Especially 19.1–43).' *ICS* 29 (Divine Epiphanies in the Ancient World): 43–61.
Bierl 2012   Bierl, A. 'Orality, Fluid Textualization and Interweaving Themes. Some Remarks on the *Doloneia*: Magical Horses from Night to Light and Death to Life.' In Montanari *et al.* 2012, pp. 133–174.
Bierl 2012a   Bierl, A. 'Demodokos' Song of Ares and Aphrodite in Homer's *Odyssey* (8.266–366): An Epyllion? Agonistic Performativity and Cultural Metapoetics.' In *Brill's Companion to Greek and Latin Epyllion and its Reception*, ed. by M. Baumbach and S. Bär, pp. 111–134. Leiden and Boston.
Binder 1964   Binder, G. *Die Aussetzung des Königskindes. Kyros und Romulus*. Beiträge zur Klassischen Philologie 10. Meisenheim am Glan.
Blanc 2008   Blanc, A. *Les contraintes métriques dans la poésie homérique. L'emploi des thèmes nominaux sigmatiques dans l'hexamètre dactylique*. Collection linguistique publ. par la société de linguistique de Paris 94. Leuven and Paris.
Blanck 1974   Blanck, I. *Studien zum griechischen Halsschmuck der archaischen und klassischen Zeit*. Cologne.
Blom 1936   Blom, J.W.S. *De typische getallen bij Homeros en Herodotos, I: Triaden, hebdomaden en enneaden*. Nijmegen.
Blome 1991   Blome, P. 'Die dunklen Jahrhunderte – aufgehellt.' In *Zweihundert Jahre Homerforschung. Rückblick und Ausblick*, ed. by J. Latacz, pp. 45–60. Colloquium Rauricum 2. Stuttgart and Leipzig.
Blößner 1991   Blößner, N. *Die singulären Iterata der Ilias. Bücher 16–20*. Beiträge zur Altertumskunde 13. Stuttgart.
Boegehold 1999   Boegehold, A.L. *When A Gesture Was Expected: A Selection of Examples from Archaic and Classical Greek Literature*. Princeton.
Böhme 1929   Böhme, J. *Die Seele und das Ich im homerischen Epos*. Leipzig and Berlin.
Bolling 1925   Bolling, G.M. *The External Evidence for Interpolation in Homer*. Oxford.
Bolling 1953   Bolling, G.M. 'Three Puzzles in the Language of the *Iliad*.' *Language* 29: 293–296.
Bonifazi 2012   Bonifazi, A. *Homer's Versicolored Fabric: The Evocative Power of Ancient Greek Epic Word-Making*. Hellenic Studies 50. Washington.
Bonnafé 1984   Bonnafé, A. *Poésie, nature et sacré, vol. 1: Homère, Hésiode et le sentiment grec de la nature*. Collection de la maison de l'orient méditerranéen 15.3. Lyon.

Borchhardt 1977   Borchhardt, H. 'Frühgriechische Schildformen.' In *ArchHom* chap. E 1 ('Kriegswesen, Teil 1: Schutzwaffen und Wehrbauten'), pp. 1–56. Göttingen.

Bouvier 2002   Bouvier, D. *Le sceptre et la lyre. L'*Iliade *ou les héros de la mémoire.* Collection HOROS. Grenoble.

Bowra 1952   Bowra, C.M. *Heroic Poetry.* London.

Braswell 1971   Braswell, B.K. 'Mythological Innovation in the *Iliad*.' *CQ* 21: 16–26.

Bremer 1976   Bremer, D. *Licht und Dunkel in der frühgriechischen Dichtung. Interpretationen zur Vorgeschichte der Lichtmetaphysik.* Archiv für Begriffsgeschichte Supplementheft 1. Bonn.

Bremer *et al.* 1987   Bremer, J.M., I.J.F. de Jong and J. Kalff (eds.). *Homer: Beyond Oral Poetry. Recent Trends in Homeric Interpretation.* Amsterdam.

Bremer 1987   Bremer, J.M. 'The So-Called «Götterapparat» in *Iliad* XX–XXII.' In Bremer *et al.* 1987, pp. 31–46.

Bremmer 1983   Bremmer, J.N. *The Early Greek Concept of the Soul.* Princeton.

Briand 2011   Briand, M. 'À propos de νήπιος dans l'*Iliade* et l'*Odyssée*: ambiguïtés et variations auctoriales, entre récit et performativité.' In *Vox poetae. Manifestations auctoriales dans l'épopée gréco-latine. Actes du colloque organisé les 13 et 14 novembre 2008 par l'Université Lyon 3*, ed. by E. Raymond, pp. 195–213. Paris.

Brommer 1942   Brommer, F. 'Gefässformen bei Homer.' *Hermes* 1977: 356–373.

Brommer 1978   Brommer, F. *Hephaistos. Der Schmiedegott in der antiken Kunst.* Mainz.

Brümmer 1985   Brümmer, E. 'Griechische Truhenbehälter.' *JDAI* 100: 1–168.

Bruns 1970   Bruns, G. 'Küchenwesen und Mahlzeiten.' *ArchHom* chap. Q. Göttingen.

Bryce 2006   Bryce, T. *The Trojans and Their Neighbours.* London and New York.

Buchan 2012   Buchan, M. *Perfidity and Passion: Reintroducing the* Iliad. Madison.

Buchholz 1871   Buchholz, E. *Die homerischen Realien, Bd. 1, Abt. 1: Die homerische Kosmographie und Geographie.* Leipzig.

Buchholz *et al.* 1973   Buchholz, H.-G., G. Jöhrens and I. Maull. 'Jagd und Fischfang.' *ArchHom* chap. J. Göttingen.

Buchholz 2010   Buchholz, H.G. 'Kriegswesen, Teil 3: Ergänzungen und Zusammenfassung.' *ArchHom* chap. E 3. Göttingen.

Buchholz 2012   Buchholz, H.-G. 'Erkennungs-, Rang- und Würdezeichen.' *ArchHom* chap. D. Göttingen.

Buchholz *et al.* 2010   Buchholz, H.-G., H. Matthäus and M. Wiener. 'Helme mit Berücksichtigung eines unbekannten altägäischen Bronzehelms.' In Buchholz 2010, pp. 135–209.

Burgess 1997   Burgess, J.S. 'Beyond Neo-Analysis: Problems with the Vengeance Theory.' *AJPh* 118: 1–19.

Burgess 2001   Burgess, J.S. *The Tradition of the Trojan War in Homer and the Epic Cycle.* Baltimore and London.

Burgess 2006   Burgess, J.S. 'Neoanalysis, Orality, and Intertextuality: An Examination of Homeric Motif Transference.' *Oral Tradition* 21: 148–189.

Burgess 2009   Burgess, J.S. *The Death and Afterlife of Achilles.* Baltimore.

Burgess 2012   Burgess, J.S. 'Intertextuality without Text in Early Greek Epic.' In *Relative Chronology in Early Greek Epic Poetry*, ed. by Ø. Andersen and D.T.T. Haug, pp. 168–183. Cambridge.

Burkert (1960) 2001   Burkert, W. 'Das Lied von Ares und Aphrodite. Zum Verhältnis von *Odyssee* und *Ilias*.' In Burkert 2001, pp. 105–116. (First published in *RhM* 103 [1960] 130–144.)

Burkert (1977) 1985   Burkert, W. *Greek Religion*. Transl. by J. Raffan. Cambridge, Mass. (German original: *Griechische Religion der archaischen und klassischen Epoche*. Stuttgart 1977.)

Burkert (1981) 2001   Burkert, W. 'ΘΕΩΝ ΟΠΙΝ ΟΥΚ ΑΛΕΓΟΝΤΕΣ. Götterfurcht und Leumannsches Missverständnis.' In Burkert 2001, pp. 95–104. (First published in *MH* 38 [1981] 195–204.)

Burkert 1994   Burkert, W. Review of D.D. Hughes. *Human Sacrifice in Ancient Greece*. London and New York 1991. *Gnomon* 66: 97–100.

Burkert 2001   Burkert, W. *Kleine Schriften 1: Homerica*, ed. by C. Riedweg *et al*. Hypomnemata, Supplement 2. Göttingen.

Butterworth 1986   Butterworth, J. 'Homer and Hesiod.' In *Studies in Honour of T.B.L. Webster*, vol. 1, ed. by J.H. Betts, J.T. Hooker and J.R. Green, pp. 33–45. Bristol.

Buttmann (1818) 1825   Buttmann, Ph. *Lexilogus, oder Beiträge zur griechischen Wort-Erklärung, hauptsächlich für Homer und Hesiod²*, vol. 1. Berlin (¹1818).

Byre 1992   Byre, C.S. 'Narration, Description, and Theme in the Shield of Achilles.' *CJ* 88: 33–42.

Cairns 1993   Cairns, D.L. *Aidōs: The Psychology and Ethics of Honour and Shame in Ancient Greek Literature*. Oxford.

Cairns 2001   Cairns, D.L. (ed.). *Oxford Readings in Homer's Iliad*. Oxford.

Cairns 2003   Cairns, D.L. 'Ethics, Ethology, Terminology: Iliadic Anger and the Cross-Cultural Study of Emotion.' In *Ancient Anger: Perspectives from Homer to Galen*, ed. by S. Braund and G.W. Most, pp. 11–49. Yale Classical Studies 32. Cambridge.

Cairns 2012   Cairns, D.L. 'Atē in the Homeric poems.' In *Papers of the Langford Latin Seminar 15, 2012*, ed. by F. Cairns, pp. 1–52. ARCA 51. Prenton.

Calame (1977) 1997   Calame, C. *Choruses of Young Women in Ancient Greece: Their Morphology, Religious Role and Social Function*, transl. by D. Collins and J. Orion. Greek Studies: Interdisciplinary Approaches. Lanham 1997. (French original: *Les choeurs de jeunes filles en Grèce archaïque, vol. 1: Morphologie, fonction religieuse et sociale*. Filologia e critica 20. Rome.)

Calame 1990   Calame, C. *Thésée et l'imaginaire athénien. Légende et culte en Grèce antique*. Lausanne.

Camerotto 2009   Camerotto, A. *Fare gli eroi. Le storie, le imprese, le virtù: compositione e racconto nell'epica greca arcaica*. Padua.

Canciani 1984   Canciani, F. 'Bildkunst, Teil 2.' *ArchHom* chap. N 2. Göttingen.

Cantarella 2005   Cantarella, E. 'Violence privée et procès.' In *La violence dans les mondes grec et romain. Actes du colloque international (Paris, 2–4 mai 2002)*, ed. by J.-M. Bertrand, pp. 339–347. Paris.

Carlier 1984   Carlier, P. *La royauté en Grèce avant Alexandre*. Études et travaux publiés par le groupe de recherche d'histoire romaine de l'université des sciences humaines de Strasbourg 6. Strasbourg.

Carlier 2006   Carlier, P. 'Ἄναξ and βασιλεύς in the Homeric Poems.' In *Ancient Greece: From the Mycenaean Palaces to the Age of Homer*, ed. by S. Deger-Jalkotzy and I.S. Lemos, pp. 101–109. Edinburgh Leventis Studies 3. Edinburgh.

Carruesco 2016   Carruesco, J. 'Choral Performance and Geometric Patterns in Epic Poetry and Iconographic Representations.' In *The Look of Lyric: Greek Song and the Visual*,

	ed. by V. Cazzato and A. Lardinois, pp. 69–107. Studies in Archaic and Classical Greek Song 1. Leiden and Boston.
Carter/Morris 1995	Carter, J.B. and S.P. Morris (eds.). *The Ages of Homer: A Tribute to Emily Townsend Vermeule*. Austin.
Casewitz 1992	Casewitz, M. 'Sur le consept de «peuple»' In *La langue et les textes en grec ancien. Actes du colloque Pierre Chantraine (Grenoble, 5.–8.9.1989)*, ed. by F. Létoublon, pp. 193–199. Amsterdam.
Casson 1971	Casson L. *Ships and Seamanship in the Ancient World*. Princeton. (Reprint with addenda and corrigenda Baltimore and London 1995.)
Catling 1977	Catling H.W. 'Beinschienen.' In *ArchHom* chap. E 1 ('Kriegswesen, Teil 1: Schutzwaffen und Wehrbauten'), pp. 143–161. Göttingen.
Cauer (1895) 1923	Cauer, P. *Grundfragen der Homerkritik*[3], vol. 2. Leipzig ([1]1895).
Cavallero 2003	Cavallero, P. 'La danse du bouclier d'Achille (*Iliade* 18: 590–606). Questions textuelles.' *Gaia* 7: 189–203.
Chantraine 1933	Chantraine, P. *La formation des noms en grec ancien*. Collection linguistique 38. Paris.
Christensen 2010	Christensen, J.P. 'First-Person Futures in Homer.' *AJPh* 131: 543–571.
Ciani 1974	Ciani, M.G. *ΦΑΟΣ e termini affini nella poesia greca. Introduzione a una fenomenologia della luce*. Università di Padova, Pubblicazioni della facoltà di lettere e filosofia 51. Florence.
Cingano 1993	Cingano, E. 'Indizi di esecuzione corale in Stesicoro.' In *Traduzione e innovazione nella cultura greca da Omero all'età ellenistica, Scritti in onore di Bruno Gentili*, vol. 1, ed. by R. Pretagostini, pp. 347–361. Rome.
Clark 2010	Clark, M. 'Pouludamas and Hektor.' In *Approaches to Homer's* Iliad *and* Odyssey, ed. by K. Myrsiades, pp. 127–147. American University Studies 19.38. New York etc.
Clarke 1995	Clarke, M. 'Between Lions and Men: Images of the Hero in the *Iliad*.' *GRBS* 36: 137–159.
Clarke 1999	Clarke, M. *Flesh and Spirit in the Songs of Homer: A Study of Words and Myths*. Oxford Classical Monographs. Oxford.
Clarke 2006	Clarke, M. 'Achilles, Byrhtnoth, and Cú Chulainn: Continuity and Analogy from Homer to the Medieval North.' In Clarke *et al.* 2006, pp. 243–271.
Clarke et al. 2006	Clarke, M.J., B.G.F. Currie and R.O.A.M. Lyne. *Epic Interactions: Perspectives on Homer, Vergil, and the Epic Tradition Presented to Jasper Griffin by Former Pupils*. Oxford.
Classen (1851–1857) 1867	Classen, J. *Beobachtungen über den Homerischen Sprachgebrauch*, Frankfurt am Main. (Originally published as five individual studies that appeared in the Frankfurter Gymnasialprogramme in 1854–57 and a Lübecker Programm in 1851.)
Collobert 2011	Collobert, C. *Parier sur le temps. La quête héroïque d'immortalité dans l'épopée homérique*. Collection d'études anciennes 143. Paris.
Combellack 1981	Combellack, F.M. 'The Wish without Desire.' *AJP* 102: 115–119.
Constantinidou 2010	Constantinidou, S. 'The Light Imagery of Divine Manifestation in Homer.' In *Light and Darkness in Ancient Greek Myth and Religion*, ed. by M. Christopoulos, E.D. Karakantza and O. Levaniouk, pp. 91–109. Lanham etc.
Corlu 1966	Corlu, A. *Recherches sur les mots relatifs à l'idée de prière, d'Homère aux tragiques*. Paris.

Crielaard 1995   Crielaard, J.P. 'Homer, History and Archaeology: Some Remarks on the Date of the Homeric World.' In *Homeric Questions: Essays in Philology, Ancient History and Archaeology, Including the Papers of a Conference Organized by the Netherlands Institute at Athens (15.5.1993)*, ed. by J.P. Crielaard, pp. 201–288. Amsterdam.

Crotty 1994   Crotty, K. *The Poetics of Supplication: Homer's* Iliad *and* Odyssey. Myth and Poetics. Ithaca and London.

Currie 2006   Currie, B. 'Homer and the Early Epic Tradition.' In Clarke *et al.* 2006, pp. 1–45.

Currie 2012   Currie, B. 'The *Iliad*, *Gilgamesh*, and Neoanalysis.' In Montanari *et al.* 2012, pp. 543–580.

Cuypers 2005   Cuypers, M. 'Interactional Particles and Narrative Voice in Apollonius and Homer.' In *Beginning from Apollo: Studies in Apollonius Rhodius and the Argonautic Tradition*, ed. by A. Harder and M. Cuypers, pp. 35–69. Caeculus 6. Leuven etc.

D'Acunto 2010   D'Acunto, M. 'Efesto e le sue creazioni del XVIII libro dell'*Iliade*.' In D'Acunto/Palmisciano 2010, pp. 145–198.

D'Acunto/Palmisciano 2010   *Lo scudo di Achille nell'Iliade: esperienze ermeneutiche a confronto. Atti della giornata di studi, Napoli, 12 maggio 2008*, ed. by M. D'Acunto and R. Palmisciano. Aion 31.2009. Pisa and Rome.

Dalby 1998   Dalby, A. 'Homer's Enemies: Lyric and Epic in the Seventh Century.' In *Archaic Greece: New Approaches and New Evidence*, ed. by N. Fisher and H. van Wees, pp. 195–211. London and Swansea.

Dalby 2003   Dalby, A. *Food in the Ancient World from A–Z*. London and New York.

Danek 1998   Danek, G. *Epos und Zitat. Studien zu den Quellen der* Odyssee. Weiner Studien Beiheft 22. Vienna.

Davies 2006   Davies, M. '«Self-Consolation» in the *Iliad*.' *CQ* 56: 582–587.

Davies 2016   Davies, M. *The* Aethiopis: *Neo-Neoanalysis Reanalyzed*. Hellenic Studies 71. Cambridge, Mass. and London.

Dee 2004   Dee, H.J. *Repertorium Homericae Poiesis Hexametricum. A Repertory of the Hexameter Patterns in the* Iliad *and the* Odyssey. *Pars II: Repertorium Versuum Forma Dispositum*. Alpha-Omega A 238.2. Hildesheim etc.

Delcourt (1957) 1982   Delcourt, M. *Héphaistos ou la légende du magicien*. Preceded by *La magie d'Héphaistos* by A. Green. Paris. (¹1957).

Dentice 2012   Dentice di Accadia Ammone, S. *Omero e i suoi oratori. Tecniche di persuasione nell'*Iliade. Beiträge zur Altertumskunde 302. Berlin and Boston.

Deppert-Lippitz 1985   Deppert-Lippitz, B. *Griechischer Goldschmuck*. Kulturgeschichte der antiken Welt 27. Mainz.

Derderian 2001   Derderian, K. *Leaving Words to Remember: Greek Mourning and the Advent of Literacy*. Mnemosyne Supplements 209. Leiden etc.

Despini 1996   Despini, A. *Ancient Gold Jewellery*. Athens.

Detienne 1967   Detienne, M. *Les maîtres de vérité dans la Grèce archaique*. Paris.

Detienne/Vernant (1974) 1978   Detienne, M. and J.P. Vernant. *Les ruses de l'intelligence. La mètis des Grecs²*. Paris (¹1974).

Di Benedetto (1994) 1998   Di Benedetto, V. *Nel laboratorio di Omero²*. Turin (¹1994).

Dicks 1970   Dicks, D.R. *Early Greek Astronomy to Aristotle*. Ithaca. (Reprint 1985.)

Dickson 1995   Dickson, K. *Nestor: Poetic Memory in Greek Epic*. New York and London.

Diels (1914) 1924   Diels, H. *Antike Technik. Sieben Vorträge³*. Leipzig and Berlin (¹1914).

Dietrich 1965   Dietrich, B.C. *Death, Fate and the Gods: The Development of a Religious Idea in Greek Popular Belief and in Homer*. University of London Classical Studies 3. London.

Dihle 1970   Dihle, A. *Homer-Probleme*. Opladen.

Dubel 1995   Dubel, S. 'L'arme et la lyre: Remarques sur le sens du bouclier d'Achille dans l'*Iliade*.' *Ktema* 20: 245–257.

Duckworth 1933   Duckworth, G.E. *Foreshadowing and Suspense in the Epic of Homer, Apollonius, and Vergil*. Princeton.

Dué/Ebbott 2010   Dué, C. and M. Ebbott. Iliad *10 and the Poetics of Ambush: A Multitext Edition with Essays and Commentary*. Hellenic Studies 39. Cambridge, Mass. and London.

Düntzer (1864) 1979   Düntzer, H. 'Über den Einfluß des Metrums auf den homerischen Ausdruck.' In *HTN*, pp. 88–108. (Slightly abridged; first published in *JbbClassPhil* 10 [1864] 673–694; also in H. Düntzer. *Homerische Abhandlungen*, pp. 517–549. Leipzig 1872.)

Durante 1976   Durante, M. *Sulla preistoria della tradizione poetica greca. Parte seconda: Risultanze della comparazione indoeuropea*. Incunabula Graeca 64. Rome.

Dürbeck 1977   Dürbeck, H. *Zur Charakteristik der griechischen Farbenbezeichnungen*. Bonn.

Eckstein 1974   Eckstein, F. 'Handwerk, Teil 1: Die Aussagen des frühgriechischen Epos.' *ArchHom* chap. L 1. Göttingen.

Edgeworth 1983   Edgeworth, R.J. 'Terms for «Brown» in Ancient Greek.' *Glotta* 61: 31–40.

Edwards 1984   Edwards, A.T. 'Aristos Achaiōn: Heroic Death and Dramatic Structure in the *Iliad*.' *QUCC* 46: 61–80.

Edwards 1985   Edwards, A.T. *Achilles in the* Odyssey: *Ideologies of Heroism in the Homeric Epic*. Beiträge zur Klassischen Philologie 171. Königstein/Ts.

Edwards 1968   Edwards, M.W. 'Some Stylistic Notes on *Iliad* XVIII.' *AJPh* 89: 257–283.

Edwards 1970   Edwards, M.W. 'Homeric Speech Introductions.' *HSCPh* 74: 1–36.

Edwards 1975   Edwards, M.W. 'Type-Scenes and Homeric Hospitality.' *TAPhA* 105: 51–72.

Edwards 1980   Edwards, M.W. 'The Structure of Homeric Catalogues.' *TAPhA* 110: 81–105.

Edwards 1986   Edwards, M.W. 'The Conventions of a Homeric Funeral.' In *Studies in Honour of T.B.L. Webster*, vol. 1, ed. by J.H. Betts *et al.*, pp. 84–92. Bristol.

Edwards 1987   Edwards, M.W. *Homer: Poet of the* Iliad. Baltimore and London.

Edwards 1992   Edwards, M.W. 'Character and Style: Achilles in *Iliad* 18.' In *De Gustibus: Essays for Alain Renoir*, ed. by J.M. Foley, pp. 168–184. New York and London.

Eichner 1985   Eichner, H. 'Das Problem des Ansatzes eines urindogermanischen Numerus «Kollektiv» («Komprehensiv»).' In *Grammatische Kategorien. Funktion und Geschichte. Akten der VII. Fachtagung der Indogermanischen Gesellschaft, Berlin 20.–25. Februar 1983*, ed. by B. Schlerath and V. Rittner, pp. 134–169. Wiesbaden.

Eisen/von Möllendorff 2013   Eisen, U.E. and P. von Möllendorff. 'Zur Einführung.' In *Über die Grenze. Metalepse in Text- und Bildmedien des Altertums*, ed. by U.E. Eisen and P. von Möllendorff, pp. 1–9. Narratologia 39. Berlin and Boston.

Eles 2002   Eles, P. von *Guerriero e sacerdote. Autorità e comunità nel'età del ferro a Verucchio. La Tomba del Trono*, ed. by P. von Eles, contributions by C. Bendi *et al.* Quaderni di archeologia dell'Emilia Romagna 6. Firenze.

Ellendt (1861) 1979   Ellendt, J.E. 'Einiges über den Einfluß des Metrums auf den Gebrauch von Wortformen und Wortverbindungen im Homer.' In *HTN*, pp. 60–87. (First published as Programm Königsberg 1861; also in J.E. Ellendt. *Drei Homerische Abhandlungen*, pp. 1–34. Leipzig 1864.)

Elliger 1975   Elliger, W. *Die Darstellung der Landschaft in der griechischen Dichtung.* Untersuchungen zur antiken Literatur und Geschichte 15. Berlin and New York.

Elmer 2013   Elmer, D.F. *The Poetics of Consent: Collective Decision Making and the* Iliad. Baltimore.

Erbse (1978) 1979   Erbse, H. 'Hektor in der *Ilias*.' In H. Erbse. *Ausgewählte Schriften zur Klassischen Philologie*, pp. 1–18. Berlin. (First published in *Kyklos. Griechisches und Byzantinisches. Rudolf Keydell zum 90. Geburtstag*, ed. by H.G. Beck et al., pp. 1–19. Berlin and New York 1978.)

Erbse 1986   Erbse, H. *Untersuchungen zur Funktion der Götter im homerischen Epos.* Untersuchungen zur antiken Literatur und Geschichte 24. Berlin and New York.

van Erp 2012   van Erp Taalman Kip, A.M. 'On Defining a Homeric Idiom.' *Mnemosyne* 65: 539–551.

Erren 1970   Erren, M. 'αὐτίκα «sogleich» als Signal der einsetzenden Handlung in *Ilias* und *Odyssee*.' *Poetica* 3: 24–58.

Fantuzzi 2012   Fantuzzi, M. *Achilles in Love: Intertextual Studies.* Oxford.

Faraone 1987   Faraone, C.A. 'Hephaestus the Magician and Near Eastern Parallels for Alcinous' Watchdogs.' *GRBS* 28: 257–280.

Fehling 1969   Fehling, D. *Die Wiederholungsfiguren und ihr Gebrauch bei den Griechen vor Gorgias.* Berlin.

Fenik 1968   Fenik, B. *Typical Battle Scenes in the Iliad: Studies in the Narrative Techniques of Homeric Battle Descriptions.* Hermes Einzelschriften 21. Wiesbaden.

Fenik 1974   Fenik, B. *Studies in the* Odyssey. Hermes Einzelschriften 30. Wiesbaden.

Fingerle 1939   Fingerle, A. *Typik der Homerischen Reden.* Munich.

Finkelberg 1988   Finkelberg, M. 'A Note on Some Metrical Irregularities in Homer.' *CPh* 83: 206–211.

Finkelberg 2004   Finkelberg, M. '«She turns about the same spot and watches for Orion»: Ancient Criticism and Exegesis of *Od*. 5.274 = *Il*. 18.488.' *GRBS* 44: 231–244.

Fittschen 1973   Fittschen, K. 'Bildkunst, Teil 1: Der Schild des Achilleus.' *ArchHom* chap. N 1. Göttingen.

Floyd 1990   Floyd, E.D. 'The Sources of Greek Ἴστωρ «Judge, Witness».' *Glotta* 68: 157–166.

Foley 1991   Foley, J.M. *Immanent Art: From Structure to Meaning in Traditional Oral Epic.* Bloomington and Indianapolis.

Foley 1999   Foley, J.M. *Homer's Traditional Art.* University Park.

Foltiny 1980   Foltiny, S. 'Schwert, Dolch und Messer.' In *ArchHom* chap. E 2 ('Kriegswesen Teil 2: Angriffswaffen'), pp. 231–274. Göttingen.

Forbes 1967   Forbes, R.J. 'Bergbau, Steinbruchtätigkeit und Hüttenwesen.' *ArchHom* chap. K. Göttingen.

Ford 1992   Ford, A. *Homer: The Poetry of the Past.* Ithaca and London.

Forderer 1965   Forderer, M. 'Der Sänger in der homerischen Schildbeschreibung. Ein Beitrag zur Textkritik.' In *Synusia. Festgabe für Wolfgang Schadewaldt zum 15. März 1965*, ed. by H. Flashar and K. Gaiser, pp. 23–28. Pfullingen.

Forssman 1980   Forssman, B. 'Ein unbekanntes Lautgesetz in der homerischen Sprache?' In *Lautgeschichte und Etymologie. Akten der 6. Fachtagung der Indogerma-*

nischen Gesellschaft, Wien, 24.–29. September 1978, ed. by M. Mayrhofer, M. Peters and O.E. Pfeiffer, pp. 180–198. Wiesbaden.

Fowler 1991 Fowler, D.P. 'Narrate and Describe: the Problem of Ekphrasis.' *JRS* 81: 25–35.

Francis 2009 Francis, J.A. 'Metal Maidens, Achilles' Shield, and Pandora: The Beginnings of «Ekphrasis».' *AJPh* 130: 1–23.

Francis 2012 Francis, J.A. 'Living Images in the Ekphrasis of Homer and Hesiod.' In *Papers of the Langford Latin Seminar 15, 2012*, ed. by F. Cairns, pp. 113–141. ARCA 51. Prenton.

Fränkel 1921 Fränkel, H. *Die homerischen Gleichnisse*. Göttingen. (= ²1977: unaltered reprint with an afterword and bibliography, ed. by E. Heitsch; abridged English translation in de Jong 1999, vol. 3, pp. 301–321 [= Fränkel 1921, pp. 16–35] and Wright/Jones 1997, pp. 103–123 [= Fränkel 1921, pp. 98–114].)

Franz 2002 Franz, J.P. *Krieger, Bauern, Bürger. Untersuchungen zu den Hopliten der archaischen und klassischen Zeit*. Europäische Hochschulschriften 3.925. Frankfurt am Main.

Frazer 1989 Frazer, R.M. 'The Return of Achilleus as a Climactic Parallel to Patroklos' Entering Battle.' *Hermes* 117: 381–390.

Freeman 1999 Freeman, P. 'Homeric κασσίτερος.' *Glotta* 75: 222–225.

Friedrich 1975 Friedrich, R. *Stilwandel im homerischen Epos. Studien zur Poetik und Theorie der epischen Gattung*. Bibliothek der Klassischen Altertumswissenschaften, N.F. 2.55. Heidelberg.

Friedrich 2007 Friedrich, R. *Formular Economy in Homer: The Poetics of the Breaches*. Hermes Einzelschriften 100. Stuttgart.

Fritz 2005 Fritz, M.A. *Die trikasuellen Lokalpartikeln bei Homer. Syntax und Semantik*. Historische Sprachforschung Ergänzungsheft 44. Göttingen.

Frontisi-Ducroux (1975) 2000 Frontisi-Ducroux, F. *Dédale. Mythologie de l'artisan en Grèce ancienne²*. Paris (¹1975).

Frontisi-Ducroux 1986 Frontisi-Ducroux, F. *La cithare d'Achille. Essai sur la poétique de l'*Iliade. Biblioteca di QUCC 1. Rome.

Frontisi-Ducroux 2002 Frontisi-Ducroux, F. '«Avec son diaphragme visionnaire: ΙΔΥΙΗΣΙ ΠΡΑΠΙΔΕΣΣΙ», *Iliade* XVIII, 481. À propos du bouclier d'Achille.' *REG* 115: 463–484.

Führer 1967 Führer, R. *Formproblem-Untersuchungen zu den Reden in der frühgriechischen Lyrik*. Zetemata 44. Munich.

Fulkerson 2013 Fulkerson, L. *No Regrets: Remorse in Classical Antiquity*. Oxford.

Gaertner 2001 Gaertner, J.F. 'The Homeric Catalogues and Their Function in Epic Narrative.' *Hermes* 129: 298–305.

Gagarin 2008 Gagarin, M. *Writing Greek Law*. Cambridge.

Gagliardi 2007 Gagliardi, P. *I due volti della gloria. I lamenti funebri omerici tra poesia e antropologia*. Bari.

Galinsky 1972 Galinsky, G.K. The Herakles Theme: *The Adaptations of the Hero in Literature from Homer to the Twentieth Century*. Oxford.

Garcia 2013 Garcia Jr., L.F. *Homeric Durability: Telling Time in the* Iliad. Hellenic Studies 58. Cambridge, Mass. and London.

García-Ramón 1991 García-Ramón, J.-L. 'Étymologie historique et synchronie homérique: δίε/ομαι, διερός, διιπετής, διαίνω, δῑνέω et I.E. *dieh₁/*dih₁- «se hâter».' *RPh* 65: 105–117.

Garland (1982) 1984   Garland, R.S.J. 'γέρας θανόντων: an Investigation into the Claims of the Homeric Dead.' *Ancient Society* 15–17 (1984–1986) 5–22. (First published in *BICS* 29 [1982] 69–80.)

Gärtner 1976   Gärtner, H.A. 'Beobachtungen zum Schild des Achilleus.' In *Studien zum antiken Epos*, ed. by H. Görgemanns and E.A. Schmidt, pp. 46–65. Meisenham am Glan.

Germain 1954   Germain, G. *La mystique des nombres dans l'épopée homérique et sa préhistoire*. Paris.

Giannakis 1997   Giannakis, G.K. *Studies in the Syntax and Semantics for the Reduplicated Presents of Homeric Greek and Indo-European*. Innsbrucker Beiträge zur Sprachwissenschaft 90. Innsbruck.

Gigante/Bonino 1973   Digante, M. and F. Bonino. *Omero. Dieghesis*. Naples.

Giuliani 2003   Giuliani, L. *Bild und Mythos. Geschichte der Bilderzählung in der griechischen Kunst*. Munich.

Giumlia-Mair/Craddock 1993   Giumlia-Mair, A.R. and P.T. Craddock. *Corinthium aes. Das schwarze Gold der Alchimisten*. Antike Welt 24 Sondernummer 1. Mainz.

Graf 1990   Graf, F. 'Religionen und Technik in den frühen Hochkulturen des vorderen Orients und des Mittelmeerraumes.' In *Technik und Religion*, ed. by A. Stöcklein and M. Rassem, pp. 65–84. Dusseldorf.

Graf 1995   Graf, F. 'Ekphrasis: Die Entstehung der Gattung in der Antike.' In *Beschreibungskunst – Kunstbeschreibung. Ekphrasis von der Antike bis zur Gegenwart*, ed. by G. Boehm and H. Pfotenhauer, pp. 143–155. Munich.

Grandolini 1996   Grandolini, S. *Canti e aedi nei poemi omerici. Edizione e commento*. Testi e commenti 12. Pisa and Rome.

Gray 1954   Gray, D.H.F. 'Metal-Working in Homer.' *JHS* 74: 1–15.

Graz 1965   Graz, L. *Le feu dans l'Iliade et l'Odyssée. ΠΥΡ: champ d'emploi et signification*. Études et commentaires 60. Paris.

Grethlein 2006   Grethlein, J. *Das Geschichtsbild der* Ilias. *Eine Untersuchung aus phänomenologischer und narratologischer Perspektive*. Hypomnemata 163. Göttingen.

Grethlein 2007   Grethlein, J. 'The Poetics of the Bath in the *Iliad*.' *HSCPh* 103: 25–49.

Grethlein 2008   Grethlein, J. 'Memory and Material Objects in the *Iliad* and the *Odyssey*.' *JHS* 128: 27–51.

Griffin 1977   Griffin, J. 'The Epic Cycle and the Uniqueness of Homer.' *JHS* 97: 39–53. (Also in Cairns 2001, pp. 365–384; Nagy 2001, vol. 2, 97–111.)

Griffin 1980   Griffin, J. *Homer on Life and Death*. Oxford.

Griffin 1986   Griffin, J. 'Homeric Words and Speakers.' *JHS* 106: 36–57.

Grimm 1962   Grimm, J. 'Die Partikel ἄρα im frühen griechischen Epos.' *Glotta* 40: 3–41.

Gschnitzer 1983   Gschnitzer, F. 'Der Rat in der Volksversammlung. Ein Beitrag des homerischen Epos zur griechischen Verfassungsgeschichte.' In *Festschrift für Robert Muth*, ed. by P. Händel and W. Meid, pp. 151–163. Innsbruck.

Guilleux 2001   Guilleux, N. 'Le *i* bref de datif singulier athématique: les règles d'une élision homérique et tragique.' *RPh* 75: 65–82.

Guizzi 2010   Guizzi, F. 'Ho visto un re … . La regalità nello scudo di Achille.' In D'Acunto/Palmisciano 2010, pp. 83–95.

Gundert 1983   Gundert, B. *τέλος und τελεῖν bei Homer*. Kiel.

Hackstein 2002   Hackstein, O. *Die Sprachform der homerischen Epen. Faktoren morphologis-cher Variabilität in literarischen Frühformen: Tradition, Sprachwandel, Spra-chliche Anachronismen.* Serta Graeca 15. Wiesbaden.

Hagel 2008   Hagel, S. 'Die Sänger aus musikarchäologischer Perspektive.' In *Homer. Der Mythos von Troia in Dichtung und Kunst (Katalog zur gleichnamigen Ausstel-lung: Basel 16.3.–17.8.2008, Mannheim 13.9.2008–18.1.2009)*, ed. by J. Latacz et al., pp. 106–111. Munich.

Hammer 2002   Hammer, D. *The* Iliad *as Politics: The Performance of Political Thought.* Okla-homa Series in Classical Culture 28. Norman.

Hampe 1952   Hampe, R. *Die Gleichnisse Homers und die Bildkunst seiner Zeit.* Die Gestalt 22. Tübingen.

Handschur 1970   Handschur, E. *Die Farb- und Glanzwörter bei Homer und Hesiod, in den ho-merischen Hymnen und den Fragmenten des epischen Kyklos.* Dissertationen der Universität Wien 39. Vienna.

Hannah 1994   Hannah, R. 'The Constellations on Achilles' Shield (*Iliad* 18.485–489).' *Elec-tronAnt* 2.4, 1994.

Hardie 1985   Hardie, P.R. 'Imago mundi: Cosmological and Ideological Aspects of the Shield of Achilles.' *JHS* 55: 11–31.

Haslam 1976   Haslam, M.W. 'Homeric Words and Homeric Metre: Two Doublets Examined (λείβω/εἴβω, γαῖα/αἶα).' *Glotta* 54: 201–211.

Haubold 2000   Haubold, J. *Homer's People: Epic Poetry and Social Formation.* Cambridge Classical Studies. Cambridge.

Haubold 2005   Haubold, J. 'The Homeric Polis.' In *The Imaginary Polis: Symposium January 7–10, 2004*, ed. by M.H. Hansen, pp. 25–48. Acts of the Copenhagen Polis Centre 7; Historisk-filosofiske Meddelelser 91. Copenhagen.

Häußler 1974   Häußler, R. 'λίνος ante Λίνον?' *RhM* 117: 1–14.

Hawke 2008   Hawke, J.G. 'Number and Numeracy in Early Greek Literature.' *SyllClass* 19: 1–76.

Heath 1992   Heath, J. 'The Legacy of Peleus: Death and Divine Gifts in the *Iliad*.' *Hermes* 120: 387–400.

Heath 2005   Heath, J. *The Talking Greeks: Speech, Animals, and the Other in Homer, Aeschylus, and Plato.* Cambridge.

Hebel 1970   Hebel, V. *Untersuchungen zur Form und Funktion der Wiedererzählungen in Ilias und Odyssee.* Heidelberg.

Heffernan 1993   Heffernan, J.A.W. *Museum of Words: The Poetics of Ekphrasis from Homer to Ashbery.* Chicago and London.

Heiden 2008   Heiden, B. *Homer's Cosmic Fabrication: Choice and Design in the* Iliad. Oxford and New York.

Heitsch 2006   Heitsch, E. *Altes und Neues zur* Ilias. *Überlegungen zur Genese des Werkes.* Abhandlungen der Akademie der Wissenschaften und der Literatur Mainz, Geistes- und sozialwissenschaftliche Klasse 2006.3. Mainz and Stuttgart.

Helbig (1884) 1887   Helbig, W. *Das homerische Epos aus den Denkmälern erläutert. Archäologi-sche Untersuchungen*². Leipzig (¹1884).

Henrichs 1996   Henrichs, A. *"Warum soll ich tanzen?" Dionysisches im Chor der griechischen Tragödie.* Lectio Teubneriana 4. Stuttgart and Leipzig.

Hentze 1902   Hentze, C. 'Die Formen der Begrüssung in den homerischen Gedichten.' *Philologus* 61: 321–355.

Hentze 1904   Hentze, C. 'Die Monologe in den homerischen Epen.' *Philologus* 63: 12–30.
Hermary/Leguilloux 2004   Hermary, A., M. Leguilloux *et al.* 'Les sacrifices dans le monde grec.' In *ThesCRA* 1: 59–134.
Heubeck 1979   Heubeck, A. 'Schrift.' *ArchHom* chap. X. Göttingen.
Higbie 1990   Higbie, C. *Measure and Music: Enjambement and Sentence Structure in the* Iliad. Oxford.
Higgins (1961) 1980   Higgins, R. *Greek and Roman Jewellery*². London (¹1961).
Himmelmann 1969   Himmelmann, N. *Über bildende Kunst in der homerischen Gesellschaft.* Abhandlungen der Akademie der Wissenschaften und der Literatur Mainz, Geistes- und sozialwissenschaftliche Klasse 1969.7. Mainz.
Hirschberger 2008   Hirschberger, M. 'Die Parteiungen der Götter in der *Ilias*. Antike Auslegung und Hintergründe in Kult und epischer Tradition.' *WS* 121: 5–28.
Hitch 2009   Hitch, S. *King of Sacrifice: Ritual and Royal Authority in the* Iliad. Hellenic Studies 25. Cambridge, Mass. and London.
Hoekstra 1965   Hoekstra, A. *Homeric Modification of Formulaic Prototypes: Studies in the Development of Greek Epic Diction.* Verhandelingen der Koninklijke Nederlandse Akademie van Wetenschappen. Afdeling Letterkunde, N.R. 71.1. Amsterdam.
Hogan 1981   Hogan, J.C. 'Eris in Homer.' *GB* 10: 21–58.
Hohendahl-Zoetelief 1980   Hohendahl-Zoetelief, I.M. *Manners in Homeric Epic.* Mnemosyne Supplements 63. Leiden.
Hölkeskamp 1997   Hölkeskamp, K.-J. '*Agorai* bei Homer.' In *Volk und Verfassung im vorhellenistischen Griechenland. Beiträge auf dem Symposum zu Ehren von Karl-Wilhelm Welwei (Bochum, 1.–2. März 1996),* ed. by W. Eder and K.-J. Hölkeskamp, pp. 1–19. Stuttgart.
Hölkeskamp 2002   Hölkeskamp, K.-J. 'Ptolis und Agore: Homer and the Archaeology of the City-State.' In Montanari 2002, pp. 297–333.
Holmes 2008   Holmes, P. 'The Greek and Etruscan Salpinx.' In *Studien zur Musikarchäologie VI. Herausforderungen und Ziele der Musikarchäologie, Vorträge des 5. Symposiums der Internationalen Studiengruppe Musikarchäologie im Ethnologischen Museum der Staatlichen Museen zu Berlin, 19.–23. September 2006,* ed. by A.A. Both et al., pp. 241–260. Orient-Archäologie 22. Rahden/Westfalen
Hölscher 1939   Hölscher, U. *Untersuchungen zur Form der* Odyssee. *Szenenwechsel und gleichzeitige Handlungen.* Hermes Einzelschriften 6. Berlin.
Hölscher 1955   Hölscher, U. Review of W. Schadewaldt. *Von Homers Welt und Werk. Aufsätze und Auslegungen zur homerischen Frage*². Stuttgart 1951. *Gnomon* 27: 385–399.
Holst-Warhaft 1992   Holst-Warhaft, G. *Dangerous Voices: Women's Laments and Greek Literature.* London and New York.
Hommel 1969   Hommel, H. 'Die Gerichtsszene auf dem Schild des Achilleus. Zur Pflege des Rechts in homerischer Zeit.' In *Politeia und Res publica. Beiträge zum Verständnis von Politik, Recht und Staat in der Antike,* ed. by P. Steinmetz, pp. 11–38. Palingenesia 4. Wiesbaden.
Horn 2014   Horn, F. *Held und Heldentum bei Homer. Das homerische Heldenkonzept und seine poetische Verwendung.* Classica Monacensia 47. Tübingen.
Hubbard 1981   Hubbard, T.K. 'Antithetical Simile Pairs in Homer.' *GB* 10: 59–67.
Hubbard 1992   Hubbard, T.K. 'Nature and Art in the Shield of Achilles.' *Arion* 2: 16–41.

Huber 2001   Huber, I. *Die Ikonographie der Trauer in der Griechischen Kunst*. Peleus 10. Mannheim and Möhnesee.

Hughes 1991   Hughes, D.D. *Human Sacrifice in Ancient Greece*. London and New York.

Hunger/Pingree 1999   Hunger, H. and D. Pingree. *Astral Sciences in Mesopotamia*. Handbuch der Orientalistik 1.44. Leiden etc.

Hunzinger 1994   Hunzinger, C. 'Le plaisir esthétique dans l'épopée archaïque: les mots de la famille de θαῦμα.' *BAGB* 1994: 4–30.

Huys 1995   Huys, M. *The Tale of the Hero Who Was Exposed at Birth in Euripidean Tragedy: A Study of Motifs*. Symbolae Series A 20. Leuven.

Iakovides 1977   Iakovides, S. 'Vormykenische und mykenische Wehrbauten.' In *ArchHom* chap. E 1 ('Kriegswesen Teil 1: Schutzwaffen und Wehrbauten'), pp. 161–221. Göttingen.

Irwin 1974   Irwin, E. *Colour Terms in Greek Poetry*. Toronto.

Jablonka/Rose 2004   Jablonka, P. and C.B. Rose. 'Late Bronze Age Troy: A Response to Frank Kolb.' *AJA* 108: 615–630.

Jahn 1987   Jahn, T. *Zum Wortfeld 'Seele–Geist' in der Sprache Homers*. Zetemata 83. Munich.

Janda 2014   Janda, M. *Purpurnes Meer. Sprache und Kultur der homerischen Welt*. Innsbrucker Beiträge zur Sprachwissenschaft, N.F. 7. Innsbruck.

Janik 2000   Janik, J. 'ΔΙΚΗ in the Works of Homer.' *Eos* 87: 5–31.

Janko 1979   Janko, R. 'The Etymology of σχερός and ἐπισχερώ: a Homeric Misunderstanding.' *Glotta* 57: 20–23.

Jankuhn 1969   Jankuhn, H. *Die passive Bedeutung medialer Formen untersucht an der Sprache Homers*. Ergänzungshefte zur ZVS 21. Göttingen.

Johansson 2012   Johansson, K. *The Birds in the* Iliad: *Identities, Interactions and Functions*. Gothenburg Studies in History 2. Gothenburg.

de Jong (1985) 2001   Jong, I.J.F. de. '*Iliad* I.366–92: A Mirror Story.' In Cairns 2001, 478–495. (Revised version; originally published in *Arethusa* 18 [1985] 5–22.)

de Jong (1987) 2004   Jong, I.J.F. de. *Narrators and Focalizers: The Presentation of the Story in the* Iliad². Amsterdam (¹1987).

de Jong 1999   Jong, I.J.F. de (ed.) *Homer: Critical Assessments. Vol. 3: Literary Interpretation; vol. 4: Homer's Art*. London and New York.

de Jong 2007   Jong, I.J.F. de. 'Homer.' In *Time in Ancient Greek Literature: Studies in Ancient Greek Narrative*, vol. 2, ed. by I.J.F. de Jong and R. Nünlist, pp. 17–37. Mnemosyne Supplements 291. Leiden and Boston.

de Jong 2009   Jong, I.J.F. de. 'Metalepsis in Ancient Greek Literature.' In *Narratology and Interpretation: The Content of Narrative Form in Ancient Literature*, ed. by J. Grethlein and A. Rengakos, pp. 87–115. Trends in Classics Supplementary volume 4. Berlin and New York.

de Jong 2011   Jong, I.J.F. de. 'The Shield of Achilles: From Metalepsis to Mise en Abyme.' *Ramus* 40: 1–13.

de Jong/Nünlist 2004   Jong, I.J.F. de and R. Nünlist. 'From Bird's Eye View to Close-up: The Standpoint of the Narrator in the Homeric Epics.' In *Antike Literatur in neuer Deutung, Festschrift für Joachim Latacz anlässlich seines 70. Geburtstages*, ed. by A. Bierl *et al.*, pp. 63–83. Leipzig.

Kaimio 1977   Kaimio, M. *Characterization of Sound in Early Greek Literature*. Commentationes Humanarum Litterarum 53. Helsinki.

Kakridis 1949   Kakridis, J.T. *Homeric Researches*. Acta Reg. Societatis Humaniorum Litterarum Lundensis 45. Lund.

Kakridis (1963) 1971   Kakridis, J.T. 'Imagined Ecphrases.' In J.T. Kakrides. *Homer Revisited*, pp. 108–124. Publications of the New Society of Letters at Lund 64. Lund. (German original: 'Erdichtete Ekphrasen. Ein Beitrag zur homerischen Schildbeschreibung.' *WS* 76 [1963] 7–26.)

Kakridis 1961   Kakridis, P.J. 'Achilleus' Rüstung.' *Hermes* 89: 288–297.

Karageorghis 1968   Karageorghis, V. 'Die Elfenbein-Throne von Salamis, Zypern.' In Laser 1968, pp. 99–103.

Karageorghis 1976   Karageorghis, V. 'Θρόνος ἀργυρόηλος.' *Kadmos* 15: 176.

Karsai 1998   Karsai G. 'Achilles and the Community.' In *Epik durch die Jahrhunderte. Internationale Konferenz Szeged 2.–4. Oktober 1997*, ed. by I. Tar, pp. 38–58. Acta antiqua et archaeologica 27. Szeged.

Keil 1998   Keil, D. *Lexikalische Raritäten im Homer. Ihre Bedeutung für den Prozeß der Literarisierung des griechischen Epos*. Bochumer Altertumswissenschaftliches Colloquium 35. Trier.

Kelly 2007   Kelly, A. *A Referential Commentary and Lexicon to* Iliad *VIII*. Oxford Classical Monographs. Oxford.

Kelly 2007a   Kelly, A. 'ΑΨΟΡΡΟΟΥ ΩΚΕΑΝΟΙΟ: a Babylonian Reminiscence?' *CQ* 57: 280–335.

Kelly 2008   Kelly, A. 'The Babylonian Captivity of Homer: The Case of the ΔΙΟΣ ΑΠΑΤΗ.' *RhM* 151: 259–304.

Kelly 2012   Kelly, A. 'The Mourning of Thetis: «Allusion» and the Future in the *Iliad*.' In Montanari *et al.* 2012, pp. 221–265.

Kemmer 1903   Kemmer, E. *Die polare Ausdrucksweise in der griechischen Literatur*. Beiträge zur historischen Syntax der griechischen Sprache 15. Wurzburg.

Kim 2000   Kim, J. *The Pity of Achilles: Oral Style and the Unity of the* Iliad. Greek Studies: Interdisciplinary Approaches. Lanham etc.

Kirk 1976   Kirk, G.S. *Homer and the Oral Tradition*. Cambridge etc.

Kitts 2008   Kitts, M. 'Funeral Sacrifices and Ritual Leitmotifs in *Iliad* 23.' In *Transformations in Sacrificial Practices. From Antiquity to Modern Times. Proceedings of an International Colloquium, Heidelberg, 12–14, July 2006*, ed. by E. Stavrianopoulou, A. Michaels and C. Ambos, pp. 217–240. Performanzen/Performances 15. Berlin.

Kloss 1994   Kloss, G. *Untersuchungen zum Wortfeld 'Verlangen/Begehren' im frühgriechischen Epos*. Hypomnemata 105. Göttingen.

Knox 1971   Knox, M.O. 'Huts and Farm Buildings in Homer.' *CQ* 21: 27–31.

Kokolakis 1980   Kokolakis, M.M. 'Homeric Animism.' *Museum philologum Londiniense* 4: 89–113.

Kölligan 2007   Kölligan, D. *Suppletion und Defektivität im griechischen Verbum*. Münchner Forschungen zur historischen Sprachwissenschaft 6. Bremen.

Kopp 1939   Kopp, J.V. *Das physikalische Weltbild der frühen griechischen Dichtung. Ein Beitrag zum Verständnis der vorsokratischen Physik*. Fribourg.

Köstler (1946) 1950   Köstler, R. 'Die Gerichtsszene auf dem Achilleusschild.' In R. Köstler. *Homerisches Recht. Gesammelte Aufsätze*, pp. 65–77. Vienna. (First published in *AAWW* 83 [1946] 213–227.)

Krafft 1963	Krafft, F. *Vergleichende Untersuchungen zu Homer und Hesiod*. Hypomnemata 6. Göttingen.
Krapp 1964	Krapp, H.J. *Die akustischen Phänomene in der* Ilias. Munich.
Krischer 1971	Krischer, T. *Formale Konventionen der homerischen Epik*. Zetemata 56. Munich.
Krischer 1981	Krischer, T. 'σιγᾶν und σιωπᾶν.' *Glotta* 59: 93–107.
Krischer 1994	Krischer, T. 'Patroklos, Antilochos und die Ilias.' *Mnemosyne* 47: 152–165.
Krummen 2008	Krummen, E. '«Jenen sang seine Lieder der ruhmvolle Sänger ...». Moderne Erzähltheorie und die Funktion der Sängerszenen in der *Odyssee*.' *A&A* 54: 11–41.
Kullmann 1956	Kullmann, W. *Das Wirken der Götter in der* Ilias. *Untersuchungen zur Frage der Entstehung des homerischen 'Götterapparats'*. Deutsche Akademie der Wissenschaften zu Berlin. Schriften der Sektion für Altertumswissenschaft 1. Berlin.
Kullmann 1960	Kullmann, W. *Die Quellen der Ilias (Troischer Sagenkreis)*. Hermes Einzelschriften 14. Wiesbaden.
Kullmann (1977) 1992	Kullmann, W. Review of A. Dihle 1970. In Kullmann 1992, pp. 198–215. (First published in *Gnomon* 49 [1977] 529–543.)
Kullmann 1985	Kullmann, W. 'Gods and Men in the *Iliad* and the *Odyssey*.' *HSCPh* 89: 1–23.
Kullmann (1991) 1992	Kullmann, W. 'Ergebnisse der motivgeschichtlichen Forschung zu Homer (Neoanalyse).' In Kullmann 1992, pp. 100–134. (Original, shorter version in Latacz 1991a, pp. 425–455.)
Kullmann 1992	Kullmann, W. *Homerische Motive. Beiträge zur Entstehung, Eigenart und Wirkung von* Ilias *und* Odyssee, ed. by R.J. Müller. Stuttgart.
Kullmann (1999) 2002	Kullmann, W. 'Die Darstellung verborgener Gedanken in der antiken Literatur. Vortrag gehalten anläßlich eines Symposions zum 65. Geburtstag von Joachim Latacz am 17. Mai 1999.' In Kullmann 2002, pp. 177–205.
Kullmann 2002	Kullmann, W. *Realität, Imaginationen und Theorie. Kleine Schriften zu Epos und Tragödie in der Antike*, ed. by A. Rengakos. Stuttgart.
Kunze 1931	Kunze, E. *Kretische Bronzereliefs*. Stuttgart.
Kurz 1966	Kurz, G. *Darstellungsformen menschlicher Bewegung in der* Ilias. Bibliothek der Klassischen Altertumswissenschaften, N.F. 2.11. Heidelberg.
Landels 1999	Landels, J.G. *Music in Ancient Greece and Rome*. London and New York.
Lardinois 2000	Lardinois, A. 'Characterization through Gnomai in Homer's *Iliad*.' *Mnemosyne* 53: 641–661.
La Roche 1869	La Roche, J. *Homerische Untersuchungen*. Leipzig.
La Roche 1897	La Roche, J. 'Die Stellung des attributiven und appositiven Adjectives bei Homer.' *WS* 19: 161–188.
Laser 1968	Laser, S. 'Hausrat.' *ArchHom* chap. P. Göttingen.
Laser 1983	Laser, S. 'Medizin und Körperpflege.' *ArchHom* chap. S. Göttingen.
Laser 1987	Laser, S. 'Sport und Spiel.' *ArchHom* chap. T. Göttingen.
Latacz 1966	Latacz, J. *Zum Wortfeld 'Freude' in der Sprache Homers*. Bibliothek der Klassischen Altertumswissenschaften N.F. 2.17. Heidelberg.
Latacz 1977	Latacz, J. *Kampfparänese, Kampfdarstellung und Kampfwirklichkeit in der Ilias, bei Kallinos und Tyrtaios*. Zetemata 66. Munich.
Latacz (1985) 1996	Latacz, J. *Homer: His Art and His World*, transl. by J.P. Holoka. Ann Arbor. (German original: *Homer. Der erste Dichter des Abendlands*⁴. Dusseldorf 2003 [Munich and Zurich ¹1985].)

Latacz 1991	Latacz, J. (ed.). *Homer. Die Dichtung und ihre Deutung*. Wege der Forschung 634. Darmstadt.
Latacz 1991a	Latacz, J. (ed.). *Zweihundert Jahre Homerforschung. Rückblick und Ausblick*. Colloquium Rauricum 2. Stuttgart and Leipzig.
Latacz (1995) 2014	Latacz, J. 'Achilleus. Wandlungen eines europäischen Heldenbildes.' In Latacz 2014, pp. 267–364. (First published as Lectio Teubneriana 3. Stuttgart and Leipzig ¹1995, ²1997.)
Latacz (2001) 2004	Latacz, J. *Troy and Homer: Towards a Solution of an Old Mystery*, transl. by K. Windle and R. Ireland. Oxford. (German original: *Troia und Homer. Der Weg zur Lösung eines alten Rätsels*. Munich and Zurich ³2004 (Munich and Berlin ¹2001, most recent ed. Leipzig ⁶2010.))
Latacz (2001) 2010	Latacz, J. *Troia und Homer. Der Weg zur Lösung eines alten Rätsels*⁶, Leipzig 2010 (Munich and Berlin ¹2001).
Latacz 2002	Latacz, J. 'Troia – Wilios – Wilusa: Drei Namen für ein Territorium.' In *Mauerschau. Festschrift für Manfred Korfmann*, ed. by R. Aslan *et al.*, pp. 1103–1222. Remshalden-Grunbach.
Latacz 2008	Latacz, J. 'Der Beginn von Schriftlichkeit und Literatur.' In *Homer. Der Mythos von Troia in Dichtung und Kunst (Katalog zur gleichnamigen Ausstellung: Basel 16.3.–17.8.2008, Mannheim 13.9.2008–18.1.2009)*, ed. by J. Latacz et al., pp. 62–69. Munich. (Also in Latacz 2014, pp. 117–134.)
Latacz (2011) 2014	Latacz, J. 'Strukturiertes Gedächtnis. Zur Überlieferung der Troia-Geschichte durch die «Dunklen Jahrhunderte».' In Latacz 2014, pp. 469–511. (First published in *Der Orient und die Anfänge Europas. Kulturelle Beziehungen von der Späten Bronzezeit bis zur Frühen Eisenzeit*, ed. by H. Matthäus, N. Oettinger and S. Schröder, pp. 135–166. Wiesbaden.)
Latacz 2014	Latacz, J. *Homers* Ilias. *Studien zu Dichter, Werk und Rezeption (Kleine Schriften II)*, ed. by T. Greub *et al.* Beiträge zur Altertumskunde 327. Berlin and Boston.
Lateiner 1995	Lateiner, D. *Sardonic Smile: Nonverbal Behaviour in Homeric Epic*. Ann Arbor.
Lehrs (1833) 1882	Lehrs, K. *De Aristarchi studiis Homericis*³. Leipzig (¹1833).
Lentini 2006	Lentini, G. *Il 'padre di Telemaco'. Odisseo tra* Iliade *e* Odissea. Pisa.
Lesky 1947	Lesky, A. *Thalatta. Der Weg der Griechen zum Meer*. Vienna.
Lesky (1956) 1966	Lesky, A. 'Peleus und Thetis im frühen Epos.' In A. Lesky. *Gesammelte Schriften. Aufsätze und Reden zu antiker und deutscher Dichtung und Kultur*, ed. by W. Kraus, pp. 401–409. Bern and Munich. (First published in *SIFC* 27–28 [1956] 216–226.)
Lessing 1766	Lessing, G.E. 'Laokoon: oder Über die Grenzen der Malerei und Poesie.' In G.E. Lessing. *Werke und Briefe in zwölf Bänden, vol. 5.2: Werke 1766–1769*, ed. by W. Barner, pp. 11–206. Frankfurt am Main 1990. (English transl. of chapters 16–19 in de Jong 1999 vol. 4, 301–316.)
Létoublon 1985	Létoublon, F. *Il allait, pareil à la nuit. Les verbes de mouvement en grec: supplétisme et aspect verbal*. Études et commentaires 98. Paris.
Létoublon 1999	Létoublon, F. 'L'indescriptible bouclier.' In *Euphrosyne. Studies in Ancient Epic and Its Legacy in Honor of D.N. Maronitis*, ed. by J.N. Kazazis and A. Rengakos, pp. 211–220. Stuttgart.

Létoublon 2001	Létoublon, F. 'Le discours et le dialogue intérieur chez Homère.' In *Eranos. Proceedings of the 9th International Symposium on the Odyssey (2–7 September 2000)*, ed. by M. Païsi-Apostolopoulou, pp. 247–272. Ithaka.
Létoublon 2011	Létoublon, F. 'Speech and Gesture in Ritual: The Rituals of Supplication and Prayer in Homer.' In *Ritual Dynamics in the Ancient Mediterranean: Agency, Emotion, Gender, Representation*, ed. by A. Chaniotis, pp. 291–311. HABES 49. Stuttgart.
Leukart 1994	Leukart, A. *Die frühgriechischen Nomina auf -tās und -ās. Untersuchungen zu ihrer Herkunft und Ausbreitung (unter Vergleich mit den Nomina auf -eús)*. Mykenische Studien 12. Vienna. (Originally diss. Zurich 1973.)
Leumann 1950	Leumann, M. *Homerische Wörter*. Schweizerische Beiträge zur Altertumswissenschaft 3. Basel. (Reprint Darmstadt 1993.)
Levet 1976	Levet, J.-P. *Le vrai et le faux dans la pensée grecque archaïque. Étude de vocabulaire, vol. 1: Présentation générale. Le vrai et le faux dans les épopées homériques*. Paris.
Lloyd-Jones 1971	Lloyd-Jones, H. *The Justice of Zeus*. Berkeley etc.
Lohmann 1970	Lohmann, D. *Die Komposition der Reden in der* Ilias. Untersuchungen zur antiken Literatur und Geschichte 6. Berlin and New York. (Excerpt in English transl.: 'The «Inner Composition» of the Speeches in the *Iliad*.' In Wright/Jones 1997, pp. 71–102.)
Longo 2010	Longo, F. 'L' ΑΓΟΡΗ di Omero. Rappresentazione poetica e documentazione archeologica.' In D'Acunto/Palmisciano 2010, pp. 199–223.
Lonsdale 1990	Lonsdale, S.H. *Creatures of Speech: Lion, Herding, and Hunting Similes in the* Iliad. Beiträge zur Altertumskunde 5. Stuttgart.
Lonsdale 1990a	Lonsdale, S.H. 'Simile and Ecphrasis in Homer and Virgil: The Poet as Craftsman and Choreographer.' *Vergilius* 36: 7–30.
Lonsdale 1995	Lonsdale, S.H. 'A Dancing Floor for Ariadne (*Iliad* 18.590–592). Aspects of Ritual Movement in Homer and Minoan Religion.' In Carter/Morris 1995, pp. 273–284.
Lord (1967) 1994	Lord, M.L. 'Withdrawal and Return. An Epic Story Pattern in the Homeric Hymn to Demeter and in the Homeric Poems.' In *The Homeric Hymn to Demeter. Translation, Commentary, and Interpretive Essays*, ed. by H.P. Foley, pp. 181–189. Princeton. (First published in *ClJ* 62 [1967] 241–248.)
Lorenz 1984	Lorenz, B. 'Notizen zur Verwendung der Zahl «Zwölf» in der Literatur.' *Literaturwissenschaftliches Jahrbuch* 25: 271–279.
Lorimer 1950	Lorimer, H.L. *Homer and the Monuments*. London.
Louden 1993	Louden, B. 'Pivotal Contrafactuals in Homeric Epic.' *ClAnt* 12: 181–198.
Louden 2006	Louden, B. *The* Iliad: *Structure, Myth, and Meaning*. Baltimore.
Lowenstam 1993	Lowenstam, S. *The Scepter and the Spear: Studies on Forms of Repetition in the Homeric Poems*. Lanham.
Ludwich 1884	Ludwich, A. *Aristarchs homerische Textkritik*, vol. 1. Leipzig.
Ludwich 1885	Ludwich, A. *Aristarchs homerische Textkritik*, vol. 2. Leipzig.
Lührs 1992	Lührs, D. *Untersuchungen zu den Athetesen Aristarchs in der Ilias und zu ihrer Behandlung im Corpus der exegetischen Scholien*. Beiträge zur Altertumswissenschaft 11. Hildesheim etc.
Luther 1935	Luther, W. *'Wahrheit' und 'Lüge' im ältesten Griechentum*. Borna and Leipzig.

Lynn-George 1978 Lynn-George, J.M. 'The Relationship of Σ 535–540 and *Scutum* 156–160 Re-Examined.' *Hermes* 106: 396–405.

Lynn-George 1988 Lynn-George, M. *Epos, Word, Narrative and the* Iliad. Hampshire and London.

Maass 1978 Maass, M. *Die geometrischen Dreifüsse von Olympia*. Olympische Forschungen 10. Berlin.

MacDowell 1978 MacDowell, D.M. *The Law in Classical Athens*. London.

Mackie 1996 Mackie, H. *Talking Trojan: Speech and Community in the* Iliad. Greek Studies: Interdisciplinary Approaches. Lanham etc.

Mader 1970 Mader, B. *Untersuchungen zum Tempusgebrauch bei Homer (Futurum und Desiderativum)*. Hamburg.

Maehler 2000 Maehler, H. 'Beobachtungen zum Gebrauch des Satz-Asyndetons bei Bakchylides und Pindar.' In *Poesia e religione in Grecia. Studi in onore di G.A. Privitera*, ed. by M.C. Fera and S. Grandolini, pp. 421–430. Naples. (2 vols.)

Malten 1912 Malten, L. 'Hephaistos.' *RE* 8.1: 311–366.

Mannsperger 1995 Mannsperger, B. 'Die Funktion des Grabens am Schiffslager der Achäer.' *Studia Troica* 5: 343–356.

Mannsperger 1998 Mannsperger, B. 'Die Mauer am Schiffslager der Achaier.' *Studia Troica* 8: 287–304.

March 1987 March, J.R. *The Creative Poet: Studies on the Treatment of Myths in Greek Poetry*. BICS Supplements 4. London.

Marg (1957) 1971 Marg W. *Homer über die Dichtung. Der Schild des Achilleus*². Orbis antiquus 11. Münster (¹1957). (Abridged version in Latacz 1991, pp. 200–226.)

Markoe 1985 Markoe, G. *Phoenician Bronze and Silver Bowls from Cyprus and the Mediterranean*. University of California Publications, Classical Studies 26. Berkeley etc.

Maronitis 2004 Maronitis, D.N. *Homeric Megathemes. War – Homilia – Homecoming*. Greek Studies: Interdisciplinary Approaches. Lanham etc.

Martin 1983 Martin, R.P. *Healing, Sacrifice and Battle: Amechania and Related Concepts in Early Greek Poetry*. Innsbrucker Beiträge zur Sprachwissenschaft 41. Innsbruck.

Martin 1989 Martin, R.P. *The Language of Heroes: Speech and Performance in the* Iliad. Myth and Poetics. Ithaca and London.

Martin 2000 Martin, R. 'Wrapping Homer Up: Cohesion, Discourse, and Deviation in the *Iliad*.' In *Intratextuality: Greek and Roman Textual Relations*, ed. by A. Sharrock and H. Morales, pp. 43–65. Oxford.

Martínez García 1996 Martínez García, F.J. *Los nombres en -υ del griego*. Europäische Hochschulschriften 21.166. Frankfurt am Main.

Masciadri 2008 Masciadri, V. *Eine Insel im Meer der Geschichten. Untersuchungen zu Mythen aus Lemnos*. Potsdamer altertumswissenschaftliche Beiträge 18. Stuttgart.

Mawet 1979 Mawet, F. *Recherches sur les oppositions fonctionnelles dans le vocabulaire homérique de la douleur (autour de πῆμα - ἄλγος)*. Académie Royale de Belgique, mémoires de la classe des lettres, 2ᵉ série 63.4. Brussels.

Meid 1967 Meid, W. 'Zum Aequativ der keltischen Sprachen, besonders des Irischen.' In *Beiträge zur Indogermanistik und Keltologie, Julius Pokorny zum 80. Geburtstag gewidmet*, ed. by W. Meid, pp. 223–242. Innsbruck.

Meier 1975 Meier, M. *-ιδ-. Zur Geschichte eines griechischen Nominalsuffixes*. Ergänzungshefte zur Zeitschrift für vergleichende Sprachforschung 23. Göttingen.

Meier-Brügger 1989   Meier-Brügger, M. 'Griech. θυμός und seine Sippe.' *MH* 46: 243–246.

Meier-Brügger 1990   Meier-Brügger, M. 'Zu griechisch κυλλός.' *HSF* 103: 30–32.

Mills 2000   Mills, S. 'Achilles, Patroclus and Parental Care in Some Homeric Similes.' *G&R* 47: 3–18.

Minchin 1995   Minchin, E. 'Ring-Patterns and Ring-Composition: Some Observations on the Framing of Stories in Homer.' *Helios* 22: 23–35.

Minchin 1996   Minchin, E. 'Lists and Catalogues in the Homeric Poems.' In *Voice into Text: Orality and Literacy in Ancient Greece*, ed. by I. Worthington, pp. 3–20. Mnemosyne Supplements 157. Leiden etc.

Minchin 1999   Minchin, E. 'Describing and Narrating in Homer's *Iliad*.' In *Signs of Orality: The Oral Tradition and its Influence in the Greek and Roman World*, ed. by E.A. Mackay, pp. 49–64. Mnemosyne Supplements 188. Leiden.

Minchin 2001   Minchin, E. *Homer and the Resources of Memory: Some Applications of Cognitive Theory to the* Iliad *and the* Odyssey. Oxford.

Minchin 2007   Minchin, E. *Homeric Voices: Discourse, Memory, Gender*. Oxford.

Monro (1882) 1891   Monro, D.B. *A Grammar of the Homeric Dialect*². Oxford (¹1882).

Montanari 2002   Montanari, F. (ed.). *Omero. Tremila anni dopo. Atti del congresso di Genova, 6.–8.7.2000*. Storia e letteratura 210. Rome.

Montanari *et al.* 2012   Montanari, F., A. Rengakos and C. Tsagalis (eds.). *Homeric Contexts: Neoanalysis and the Interpretaion of Oral Poetry*. Trends in Classics Supplementary volume 12. Berlin and Boston.

Monteil 1963   Monteil, P. *La phrase relative en grec ancien. Sa formation, son développement, sa structure des origines à la fin du Ve siècle a.C.* Études et commentaires 47. Paris.

Moog 2001   Moog-Grünewald, M. 'Der Sänger im Schild – oder: Über den Grund ekphrastischen Schreibens.' In *Behext von Bildern? Ursachen, Funktionen und Perspektiven der textuellen Faszination durch Bilder*, ed. by H.J. Drügh and M. Moog-Grünewald, pp. 1–9. Neues Forum für Allgemeine und Vergleichende Literaturwissenschaft 12. Heidelberg.

Morris 1992   Morris, S.P. *Daidalos and the Origins of Greek Art*. Princeton.

Morrison 1992   Morrison, J.V. *Homeric Misdirection: False Predictions in the* Iliad. Michigan Monographs in Classical Antiquity. Ann Arbor.

Moulton 1977   Moulton, C. *Similes in the Homeric Poems*. Hypomnemata 49. Göttingen.

Moussy 1972   Moussy, C. 'Ἀταλός, ἀτάλλω, ἀτιτάλλω.' In *Mélanges de linguistique et de philologie grecques offerts à Pierre Chantraine*, ed. by A. Ernout, pp. 157–168. Études et commentaires 79. Paris.

Muellner 1976   Muellner, L.C. *The Meaning of Homeric* εὔχομαι *Through its Formulas*. Innsbrucker Beiträge zur Sprachwissenschaft 13. Innsbruck.

Müller 1974   Müller, D. *Handwerk und Sprache. Die sprachlichen Bilder aus dem Bereich des Handwerks in der griechischen Literatur bis 400 v.Chr.* Beiträge zur Klassischen Philologie 51. Meisenheim am Glan.

Müller 1968   Müller, F. *Darstellung und poetische Funktion der Gegenstände in der* Odyssee. Marburg/Lahn.

Murnaghan 1997   Murnaghan, S. 'Equal Honor and Future Glory: The Plan of Zeus in the *Iliad*.' In *Classical Closure: Reading the End in Greek and Latin Literature*, ed. by D.H. Roberts, F.M. Dunn and D. Fowler, pp. 23–42. Princeton.

Mutzbauer 1893   Mutzbauer, C. *Die Grundlagen der griechischen Tempuslehre und der ho-*

merische Tempusgebrauch. Ein Beitrag zur historischen Syntax der griechischen Sprache. Strasbourg 1893.

Naerebout 1997   Naerebout, F.G. *Attractive Performances. Ancient Greek Dance: Three Preliminary Studies.* Amsterdam.

Nagler 1974   Nagler, M.N. *Spontaneity and Tradition: A Study in the Oral Art of Homer.* Berkeley etc.

Nagy (1979) 1999   Nagy, G. *The Best of the Achaeans: Concepts of the Hero in Archaic Greek Poetry*[2]. Baltimore and London ([1]1979).

Nagy 1990   Nagy, G. *Greek Mythology and Poetics.* Ithaca and London.

Nagy 1996   Nagy, G. *Poetry as Performance: Homer and Beyond.* Cambridge.

Nagy (1997) 2003   Nagy, G. 'The Shield of Achilles: Ends of the *Iliad* and Beginnings of the Polis.' In G. Nagy. *Homeric Responses*, pp. 72–87. Austin. (First published in *New Light on a Dark Age: Exploring the Culture of Geometric Greece*, ed. by S. Langdon, pp. 194–207. Columbia, MO and London 1997.)

Nagy 2001   Nagy, G. (ed.). *Greek Literature. Vol. 1: The Oral Traditional Background of Ancient Greek Literature; vol. 2: Homer and Hesiod as Prototypes of Greek Literature.* New York and London.

Naiden 2006   Naiden, F.S. *Ancient Supplication.* Oxford.

Nappi 2002   Nappi, M.P. 'Note sull'uso di Αἴαντε nell'*Iliade*.' *RCCM* 44: 211–235.

Nardelli 2001   Nardelli, J.-F. Review of M.L. West (ed.). *Homerus Ilias volumen alterum, rhapsodiae XIII–XXIV.* Munich and Leipzig 2000. *BMCR* 2001.06.21.

Ndoye 2010   Ndoye, M. *Groupes sociaux et idéologie du travail dans les mondes homérique et hésiodique.* Besançon.

Neal 2006   Neal, T. *The Wounded Hero: Non-Fatal Injury in Homer's* Iliad. Sapheneia 11. Bern etc.

Nesselrath 1992   Nesselrath, H.-G. *Ungeschehenes Geschehen. 'Beinahe-Episoden' im griechischen und römischen Epos von Homer bis zur Spätantike.* Stuttgart.

Nickau 1977   Nickau, K. *Untersuchungen zur textkritischen Methode des Zenodotos von Ephesos.* Untersuchungen zur antiken Literatur und Geschichte 16. Berlin and New York.

Nicolai 1993   Nicolai, W. 'Gefolgschaftsverweigerung als politisches Druckmittel in der *Ilias*.' In *Anfänge politischen Denkens in der Antike. Die nahöstlichen Kulturen und die Griechen*, ed. by K. Raaflaub *et al.*, pp. 317–341. Schriften des Historischen Kollegs, Kolloquien 24. Munich.

Noack-Hilgers 2001   Noack-Hilgers, B. 'Die Kunst des Pflügens. Von Homer über Cato zu Palladius.' In *Landwirtschaft im Imperium Romanum*, ed. by P. Herz and G. Waldherr, pp. 157–203. Pharos 14. St. Katharinen.

Nowag 1983   Nowag, W. *Raub und Beute in der archaischen Zeit der Griechen.* Frankfurt am Main.

Nünlist 1998   Nünlist, R. *Poetologische Bildersprache in der frühgriechischen Dichtung.* Beiträge zur Altertumskunde 101. Stuttgart and Leipzig.

Nünlist 2002   Nünlist, R. 'Some Clarifying Remarks on «Focalization».' In Montanari 2002, pp. 445–453.

Nünlist 2003   Nünlist, R. 'The Homeric Scholia on Focalization.' *Mnemosyne* 56: 61–71.

Nünlist 2009   Nünlist, R. *The Ancient Critic at Work: Terms and Concepts of Literary Criticism in Greek Scholia.* Cambridge.

Nünlist 2009a   Nünlist, R. 'The Motif of the Exiled Killer.' In *Antike Mythen. Transforma-*

tionen und Konstruktionen, ed. by C. Walde and U. Dill, pp. 628–644. Berlin and New York.

Nussbaum 1998   Nussbaum, A.J. *Two Studies in Greek and Homeric Linguistics.* Hypomnemata 120. Göttingen.

Nussbaum 2002   Nussbaum, A.J. 'Homeric OPHAI (*Od.* 14.343) and OMEITAI (*Il.* 9.274): Two of a Kind?' *ColbyQ* 38: 175–196.

Onians 1951   Onians, R.B. *The Origins of European Thought about the Body, the Mind, the Soul, the World, Time, and Fate: New Interpretations of Greek, Roman and Kindred Evidence, also of Some Basic Jewish and Christian Beliefs.* Cambridge. (Reprint 1988.)

van Otterlo 1948   van Otterlo, W.A.A. *De ringcompositie als opbouwprincipe in de epische gedichten van Homerus.* Verhandelingen der Koninklijke Nederlandsche Akad. van Wetenschappen, Afd. Letterkunde 51.1. Amsterdam.

Otto 2012   Otto, B. 'Der Thron als Würdezeichen.' In Buchholz 2012, pp. 20–83.

Otto 2009   Otto, N. *Enargeia. Untersuchungen zur Charakteristik alexandrinischer Dichtung.* Hermes Einzelschriften 102. Stuttgart.

Owen 1946   Owen, E.T. *The Story of the* Iliad. London.

Pagani 2008   Pagani, L. 'Il codice eroico e il guerriero di fronte alla morte.' In *Eroi nell'*Iliade. *Personaggi e strutture narrative*, ed. by L. Pagani with a foreword by F. Montanari, pp. 327–418. Pleiadi 8. Rome.

Palmer 1963   Palmer, L.R. *The Interpretation of Mycenaean Greek Texts.* Oxford.

Palmisciano 2010   Palmisciano, R. 'Il primato della poesia nello scudo di Achille.' In D'Acunto/Palmisciano 2010, pp. 47–64.

Papadopoulou 2011   Papadopoulou, Z.D. 'Typical occasions for musical activities in cults. Private activities.' In *ThesCRA* 6: 414–423.

Parry (1928) 1971   Parry, M. 'The Traditional Epithet in Homer.' In *MHV*, pp. 1–190. (French original: *L'Épithète traditionnelle dans Homère. Essai sur un problème de style homérique.* Paris 1928.)

Pattoni 1998   Pattoni, M.P. 'ὤ μοι ἐγώ, (τί πάθω;). Una formula omerica e i suoi contesti.' *Aevum antiquum* 11: 5–49.

Patzer 1972   Patzer, H. *Dichterische Kunst und poetisches Handwerk im homerischen Epos.* Sitzungsberichte der wissenschaftlichen Gesellschaft an der J.W. Goethe-Universität Frankfurt a.M. 10.1. Wiesbaden. (Abridged English transl. in de Jong 1999, vol. 4, pp. 155–183 [= Patzer 1972, pp. 10–40].)

Patzer 1996   Patzer, H. *Die Formgesetze des homerischen Epos.* Schriften der wissenschaftlichen Gesellschaft an der J.W. Goethe-Universität Frankfurt a.M., Geisteswissenschaftliche Reihe 12. Stuttgart.

Pelliccia 1995   Pelliccia, H. *Mind, Body, and Speech in Homer and Pindar.* Hypomnemata 107. Göttingen.

Pelloso 2012   Pelloso, C. *Themis e dike in Omero. Ai primordi del diritto dei Greci.* Classica Philosophica et Iuridica, Saggi 1. Alessandria.

Peponi 2012   Peponi, A.-E. *Frontiers of Pleasure: Models of Aesthetic Response in Archaic and Classical Greek Thought.* Oxford.

Perceau 2002   Perceau, S. *La parole vive. Communiquer en catalogue dans l'épopée homérique.* Bibliothèque d' études classiques 30. Louvain etc.

Perceau 2015   Perceau, S. 'Visualisation, oralisation, dramatisation: La poétique des listes de noms dans l'épopée homérique'. In Πολυφόρβη Γαίη. *Mélanges de littéra-*

ture et linguistique offerts à Françoise Létoublon*, ed. by F. Dell'Oro and O. Lagacherie, pp. 117–132. Gaia 1. Grenoble.

Perpillou 1972   Perpillou, J.-L. 'La signification du verbe εὔχομαι dans l'épopée.' In *Mélanges de linguistique et de philologie grecque offerts à Pierre Chantraine*, ed. by A. Ernout, pp. 169–182. Études et commentaires 79. Paris.

Perpillou 1973   Perpillou, J.-L. *Les substantives grecs en -εύς*. Études et commentaires 80. Paris.

Peters 1980   Peters, M. *Untersuchungen zur Vertretung der indogermanischen Laryngale im Griechischen*. SAWW 377.8. Vienna.

Petersmann 1973   Petersmann, G. 'Die monologische Totenklage der *Ilias*.' *RhM* 116: 3–16.

Pflüger 1942   Pflüger, H.H. 'Die Gerichtsszene auf dem Schild des Achilleus.' *Hermes* 77: 140–148.

Phillips 1980   Phillips, J.H. 'The Constellations on Achilles' Shield (*Iliad* 18.485–489).' *LMC* 5: 179–180.

Pinault 1994   Pinault, G.-J. 'Les deux formes du silence homérique et l'origine du verbe σιωπάω.' In *Mélanges François Kerlouégan*, ed. by D. Conso, N. Fick and B. Poulle, pp. 501–526. Annales littéraires de l'Université de Besançon. Paris.

Pizzani 2000   Pizzani, U. 'Qualche osservazione sulla terminologia «teratologica» in Omero.' In *Poesia e religione in Grecia. Studi in onore di G. Aurelio Privitera*, ed. by M. Cannatà Fera and S. Grandolini, pp. 527–539. Naples. (2 vols.)

Porzig 1942   Porzig, W. *Die Namen für Satzinhalte im Griechischen und im Indogermanischen*. Untersuchungen zur indogermanischen Sprach- und Kulturwissenschaft 10. Berlin.

Postlethwaite 1998   Postlethwaite, N. 'Hephaistos' θεῖος ἀοιδός and the Cretan Dance.' *Eranos* 96: 92–104.

Pötscher 2001   Pötscher, W. 'Charis und Aphrodite (Hom. *Il.* 18.382f. *Od.* 8.266ff.).' *WS* 114: 9–24.

Powell 1988   Powell, B.B. 'The Dipylon Oinochoe and the Spread of Literacy in Eighth-Century Athens.' *Kadmos* 27: 65–86.

Pralon 1995   Pralon, D. 'L'honneur du vaincu. L'altercation entre Hector et Poulydamas *Iliade* XVIII 243–313.' *Ktema* 20: 233–244.

Preisshofen 1977   Preisshofen, F. *Untersuchungen zur Darstellung des Greisenalters in der frühgriechischen Dichtung*. Hermes Einzelschriften 34. Wiesbaden.

Prier 1989   Prier, R.A. *Thauma idesthai: The Phenomenology of Sight and Appearance in Archaic Greek*. Tallahassee.

Priess 1977   Priess, K.A. *Der mythologische Stoff in der Ilias*. Mainz.

Primavesi 2002   Primavesi, O. 'Bild und Zeit. Lessings Poetik des natürlichen Zeichens und die Homerische Ekphrasis.' In *Klassische Philologie inter disciplinas. Aktuelle Konzepte zu Gegenstand und Methode eines Grundlagenfaches*, ed. by J.P. Schwindt, pp. 187–211. Bibliothek der Klassischen Altertumswissenschaften, N.F. 2.110. Heidelberg.

Primmer 1970   Primmer, A. 'Homerische Gerichtsszenen.' *WS* 83 (N.F. 4): 5–13.

Pritchett 1991   Pritchett, W.K. *The Greek State at War*, Part V. Berkeley etc.

Pucci (1982) 1998   Pucci, P. 'The Proem of the *Odyssey*.' In Pucci 1998a, pp. 11–29. (First published in *Arethusa* 15 [1982] 39–62.)

Pucci 1998   Pucci, P. 'Honor and Glory in the *Iliad*.' In Pucci 1998a, pp. 179–230.

Pucci 1998a   Pucci, P. *The Song of the Sirens: Essays on Homer*. Lanham etc.
Purves 2010   Purves, A.C. *Space and Time in Ancient Greek Narrative*. Cambridge.
Quattordio Moreschini 1972   Quattordio Moreschini, A. 'A proposito di un passo dell'*Iliade*: Σ 550 ss.' *SSL* 12: 244–250.
Raaflaub 1993   Raaflaub, K.A. 'Homer to Solon: The Rise of the Polis. The Written Sources.' In *The Ancient Greek City-State: Symposion on the Occasion of the 250th Anniversary of The Royal Danish Academy of Sciences and Letters (1.–4.7.1992)*, ed. by M.H. Hansen, pp. 41–105. Copenhagen.
Raaflaub 2005   Raaflaub, K. 'Homerische Krieger, Protohopliten und die Polis. Schritte zur Lösung alter Probleme.' In *Krieg – Gesellschaft – Institutionen. Beiträge zu einer vergleichenden Kriegsgeschichte*, ed. by B. Meißner, O. Schmitt and M. Sommer, pp. 229–266. Berlin.
Raaflaub 2011   Raaflaub, K. 'Riding on Homer's Chariot: The Search for a Historical «Epic Society».' *Antichthon* 45: 1–34.
Radt 2006   Radt, S. *Strabons* Geographika, *Bd. 5 (Buch I–IV: Kommentar)*. Mit Übersetzung und Kommentar hrsg. von S. Radt. Göttingen.
Ramelli 1996   Ramelli, I. 'Il significato arcaico di στεφανόω come «adornare»: un' ipotesi interpretativa.' *Aevum Antiquum* 9: 243–248.
Ready 2011   Ready, J.L. *Character, Narrator, and Simile in the* Iliad. Cambridge.
Redfield (1975) 1994   Redfield, J.M. *Nature and Culture in the* Iliad: *The Tragedy of Hector*². Durham and London (Chicago ¹1975).
Reece 1993   Reece, S. *The Stranger's Welcome: Oral Theory and the Aesthetics of the Homeric Hospitality Scene*. Michigan Monographs in Classical Antiquity. Ann Arbor.
Reece 2009   Reece, S. *Homer's Winged Words: The Evolution of Early Greek Epic Diction in the Light of Oral Theory*. Mnemosyne Supplements 313. Leiden and Boston.
Reichel 1990   Reichel, M. 'Retardationstechniken in der *Ilias*.' In *Der Übergang von der Mündlichkeit zur Literatur bei den Griechen*, ed. by W. Kullmann and M. Reichel, pp. 125–151. ScriptOralia 30. Tübingen.
Reichel 1994   Reichel, M. *Fernbeziehungen in der* Ilias. ScriptOralia 62. Tübingen.
Reiner 1938   Reiner, E. *Die rituelle Totenklage der Griechen*. Tübinger Beiträge zur Altertumswissenschaft 30. Stuttgart and Berlin.
Reinhardt 1961   Reinhardt, K. *Die Ilias und ihr Dichter*, ed. by U. Hölscher. Göttingen.
Renehan 1982   Renehan, R. *Greek Lexicographical Notes: A Critical Supplement to the Greek-English Lexicon of Liddell-Scott-Jones, Second Series*. Hypomnemata 74. Göttingen.
Rengakos 1993   Rengakos, A. *Der Homertext und die hellenistischen Dichter*. Hermes Einzelschriften 64. Stuttgart.
Rengakos 1994   Rengakos, A. *Apollonios Rhodios und die antike Homererklärung*. Zetemata 92. Munich.
Rengakos 1995   Rengakos, A. 'Zeit und Gleichzeitigkeit in den homerischen Epen.' *A&A* 41: 1–33.
Revermann 1998   Revermann, M. 'The Text of *Iliad* 18.603–6 and the Presence of an ΑΟΙΔΟΣ on the Shield of Achilles.' *CQ* 48: 29–38.
Reynen 1958   Reynen, H. 'Die Partikel οὖν bei Homer.' *Glotta* 37: 67–102.
Reynen 1983   Reynen, H. *ΕΥΧΕΣΘΑΙ und seine Derivate bei Homer*. Bonn.

Richardson 1990   Richardson, S. *The Homeric Narrator*. Nashville.

Richter 1968   Richter, W. 'Die Landwirtschaft im homerischen Zeitalter.' Mit einem Beitrag 'Landwirtschaftliche Geräte' von W. Schiering. *ArchHom* chap. H. Göttingen.

Rijksbaron (1984) 2002   Rijksbaron, A. *The Syntax and Semantics of the Verb in Classical Greek. An Introduction³*. Amsterdam (¹1984).

Rijksbaron 1988   Rijksbaron, A. 'The Discourse Function of the Imperfect.' In *In the Footsteps of Raphael Kühner (Proceedings of the International Colloquium in Commemoration of the 150th Anniversary of the Publication of Raphael Kühner's 'Ausführliche Grammatik der Griechischen Sprache, II. Theil: Syntaxe', Amsterdam 1986)*, ed. by A. Rijksbaron, H.A. Mulder and G.C. Wakker, pp. 237–254. Amsterdam.

Rinon 2008   Rinon, Y. *Homer and the Dual Model of the Tragic*. Ann Arbor.

Ritoók 1971   Ritoók, Zs. 'Anmerkungen zu Homer.' *AAntHung* 19: 201–215.

Rix (1976) 1992   Rix, H. *Historische Grammatik des Griechischen. Laut- und Formenlehre²*. Darmstadt (¹1976).

Robert 1901   Robert, C. *Studien zur Ilias*. Berlin.

Robert 1950   Robert, F. *Homère*. Paris.

Rocchi 1979   Rocchi, M. 'Contributi allo studio delle Charites (I).' *StudClas* 18: 5–16.

Roisman1984   Roisman, H. *Loyalty in Early Greek Epic and Tragedy*. Beiträge zur Klassischen Philologie 155. Königstein/Ts.

Rollinger 1996   Rollinger, R. 'Altorientalische Motivik in der frühgriechischen Literatur am Beispiel der homerischen Epen. Elemente des Kampfes in der *Ilias* und in der altorientalischen Literatur (nebst Überlegungen zur Präsenz altorientalischer Wanderpriester im früharchaischen Griechenland).' In *Wege zur Genese griechischer Identität. Die Bedeutung der früharchaischen Zeit*, ed. by C. Ulf, pp. 156–210. Berlin.

de Romilly 1997   Romilly, J. de. *Hector*. Paris.

Rosén 1984   Rosén, H.B. *Strukturalgrammatische Beiträge zum Verständnis Homers*. Munich.

Roth (1970–1974) 1990   Roth, C.P. *'Mixed Aorists' in Homeric Greek*. New York and London. (Earlier versions of chap. 2–5 were previously published: chap. 2 as 'Some «Mixed Aorists» in Homer.' *Glotta* 48 [1970] 155–163; chap. 3 as 'More Homeric «Mixed Aorists».' *Glotta* 52 [1974] 1–10; chap. 4–5 as 'Thematic S-Aorists in Homer.' *HSCPh* 77: 181–186.)

Rougier-Blanc 2005   Rougier-Blanc, S. *Les maisons homériques. Vocabulaire architectural et sémantique du bâti*. Études d'Archéologie Classique 13. Nancy and Paris.

Ruijgh 1957   Ruijgh, C.J. *L'élément achéen dans la langue épique*. Assen.

Ruijgh (1985) 1996   Ruijgh, C.J. 'Le mycénien et Homère.' In Ruijgh 1996, pp. 221–268. (First published in *BCILL* 26 [1985] 143–190.)

Ruijgh (1985a) 1996   Ruijgh, C.J. Review of L. Basset. *Les emplois périphrastiques du verbe grec* μέλλειν. Lyon 1979. In Ruijgh 1996, pp. 596–606. (First published in *Lingua* 65 [1985] 323–333.)

Ruijgh 1996   Ruijgh, C.J. *Scripta minora ad linguam Graecam pertinentia*, vol. 2, ed. by A. Rijksbaron and F.M.J. Waanders. Amsterdam.

Rundin 1996   Rundin, J. 'A Politics of Eating: Feasting in Early Greek Society.' *AJPh* 117: 179–215.

Russo 1965   Russo C.F. *Hesiodi* Scutum. Introduzione, testo critico e commento con tra-
                    duzione e indici. Biblioteca di studi superiori 9. Florence.

Rutherford 1982   Rutherford, R.B. 'Tragic Form and Feeling in the *Iliad*.' *JHS* 102: 145–160.

Rutherford (1996) 2013   Rutherford, R. *Homer²*. Greece & Rome. New Surveys in the Classics 26.
                    Cambridge (¹1996).

Ruzé 1997   Ruzé, F. *Délibération et pouvoir dans la cité grecque de Nestor à Socrate*. His-
                    toire ancienne et médiévale 43. Paris.

Sabbadini 1967   Sabbadini, E. 'Ricerche di lessicografi sui termini omerici ΑΗΤΟΣ – ΑΙΗΤΟΣ
                    – ΑΗΤΗΣ.' *Rivista di studi classici* 15: 78–84.

Sacks 1987   Sacks, R. *The Traditional Phrase in Homer: Two Studies in Form, Meaning and
                    Interpretation*. Columbia Studies in the Classical Tradition 14. Leiden etc.

Sammons 2010   Sammons, B. *The Art and Rhetoric of the Homeric Catalogue*. Oxford.

Sarischoulis 2008   Sarischoulis, E. *Schicksal, Götter und Handlungsfreiheit in den Epen Homers*.
                    Palingenesia 92. Stuttgart.

Sbardella 2010   Sbardella, L. '*Erga charienta*: Il cantore e l'artigiano nello scudo di Achille.'
                    In D'Acunto/Palmisciano 2010, pp. 65–81.

Schadewaldt (1936) 1997   Schadewaldt, W. 'Achilles' Decision.' In Wright/Jones 1997, pp. 143–
                    169. (German original: 'Die Entscheidung des Achilleus.' *Die Antike* 12 [1936]
                    173–201; also in Schadewaldt 1965, pp. 234–267.)

Schadewaldt (1938) 1965   Schadewaldt, W. 'Der Schild des Achilleus.' In Schadewaldt 1965,
                    pp. 352–374. (First published in *Neue Jahrbücher für Antike und deutsche
                    Bildung* 1 [1938] 65–82; abridged version in Latacz 1991, pp. 173–199.)

Schadewaldt (1938) 1966   Schadewaldt, W. *Iliasstudien³*. Berlin (Leipzig ¹1938). (Reprint
                    Darmstadt 1987.)

Schadewaldt (1952) 1965   Schadewaldt, W. 'Einblick in die Erfindung der *Ilias. Ilias* und *Mem-
                    nonis*.' In Schadewaldt 1965, 155–202. (First published in *Varia variorum.
                    Festgabe für Karl Reinhardt dargebracht von Schülern und Freunden zum 14.
                    Februar 1951*, pp. 13–48. Münster etc.)

Schadewaldt (1956) 1970   Schadewaldt, W. 'Hektor in der *Ilias*.' In W. Schadewaldt. *Hellas und
                    Hesperien. Gesammelte Schriften zur Antike und zur neueren Literatur in
                    zwei Bänden². Vol. 1: Zur Antike*, ed. by R. Thurow and E. Zinn, pp. 21–38.
                    Zurich and Stuttgart. (First published in *WS* 69 [1956 = Festschrift Albin
                    Lesky] 5–25.)

Schadewaldt 1965   Schadewaldt, W. *Von Homers Welt und Werk. Aufsätze und Auslegungen zur
                    homerischen Frage⁴*. Stuttgart (¹1944).

Schäfer 1990   Schäfer, M. *Der Götterstreit in der* Ilias. Beiträge zur Altertumskunde 15.
                    Stuttgart.

Scheid-Tissinier 1994   Scheid-Tissinier, E. *Les usages du don chez Homère. Vocabulaire et pra-
                    tiques*. Travaux et mémoires. Études anciennes 11. Nancy.

Scheid-Tissinier 1994a   Scheid-Tissinier, E. 'À propos du rôle et de la fonction de l'ἵστωρ.' *RPh*
                    68: 187–208.

Scheid-Tissinier 2011   Scheid-Tissinier, E. 'Que disent les Anciens?' In *Débats antiques (Travaux
                    de la Maison René-Ginouvès, 13)*, ed. by M.-J. Werlings and F. Schulz,
                    pp. 55–64. Paris.

Schein 1984   Schein, S.L. *The Mortal Hero: An Introduction to Homer's* Iliad. Berkeley etc.

Schein 2002   Schein, S.L. 'Mythological allusion in the *Odyssey*.' In Montanari 2002,
                    pp. 85–101.

Scherer 1953	Scherer, A. *Gestirnnamen bei den indogermanischen Völkern*. Forschungen zum Wortschatz der idg. Sprachen 1. Heidelberg.
Schiering 1968	Schiering, W. 'Landwirtschaftliche Geräte.' In Richter 1968, pp. 147–158.
Schmid 1950	Schmid, S. *-εος und -ειος bei den griechischen Stoffadjektiven*. Zurich.
Schmidt 1981	Schmidt, E.G. 'Himmel – Meer – Erde im frühgriechischen Epos und im Alten Orient.' *Philologus* 125: 1–24.
Schmidt 1976	Schmidt, M. *Die Erklärungen zum Weltbild Homers und zur Kultur der Heroenzeit in den bT-Scholien zur* Ilias. Zetemata 62. Munich.
Schmidt 1983/84	Schmidt, M. 'Hephaistos lebt. Untersuchungen zur Frage der Behandlung behinderter Kinder in der Antike.' *Hephaistos* 5/6: 133–161.
Schmidt 2006	Schmidt, M. 'Some Remarks on the Semantics of ἄναξ in Homer.' In *Ancient Greece: From the Mycenaean Palaces to the Age of Homer*, ed. by S. Deger-Jalkotzy and I.S. Lemos, pp. 439–447. Edinburgh Leventis Studies 3. Edinburgh.
Schmitt 1990	Schmitt, A. *Selbständigkeit und Abhängigkeit menschlichen Handelns bei Homer. Hermeneutische Untersuchung zur Psychologie Homers*. AbhMainz 1990.5. Mainz and Stuttgart.
Schmitt 2011	Schmitt, A. 'Anschauung und Anschaulichkeit in der Erkenntnis- und Literaturtheorie bei Aristoteles.' In *Anschaulichkeit in Kunst und Literatur. Wege bildlicher Visualisierung in der europäischen Geschichte*, ed. by G. Radke-Uhlmann and A. Schmitt, pp. 91–151. Colloquium Rauricum 11. Berlin and Boston.
Schmitt 1967	Schmitt, R. *Dichtung und Dichtersprache in indogermanischer Zeit*. Wiesbaden.
Schmitt Pantel *et al.* 2004	Schmitt Pantel, P. *et al.* 'Le banquet en Grèce.' In *ThesCRA* 2: 218–250.
Schnapp-Gourbeillon 1981	Schnapp-Gourbeillon, A. *Lions, héros, masques. Les représentations de l'animal chez Homère*. Textes à l'appui. Histoire classique. Paris.
Schnaufer 1970	Schnaufer, A. *Frühgriechischer Totenglaube. Untersuchungen zum Totenglauben der mykenischen und homerischen Zeit*. Tübingen.
Schofield (1986) 2001	Schofield, M. '*Euboulia* in the *Iliad*.' In Cairns 2001, pp. 220–259. (First published in *CQ* 36 [1986] 6–31; also in M. Schofield. *Saving the City: Philosopher-Kings and Other Classical Paradigms*, pp. 3–30. London and New York 1999.)
Schubert 2000	Schubert, P. *Noms d'agent et invective: entre phénomène linguistique et interprétation du récit dans les poèmes homériques*. Hypomnemata 133. Göttingen.
Schulz 2011	Schulz, F. *Die homerischen Räte und die spartanische Gerusie*. Syssitia 1. Dusseldorf.
Schulze 1892	Schulze, W. *Quaestiones epicae*. Gütersloh.
Schuol 2006	Schuol, M. 'Sänger und Gesang in der *Odyssee*.' In *Geschichte und Fiktion in der homerischen* Odyssee, ed. by A. Luther, pp. 139–162. Zetemata 125. Munich.
Scodel 1999	Scodel, R. *Credible Impossibilities: Conventions and Strategies of Verisimilitude in Homer and Greek Tragedy*. Beiträge zur Altertumskunde 122. Stuttgart and Leipzig.
Scodel 2008	Scodel, R. *Epic Facework: Self-Presentation and Social Interaction in Homer*. Swansea.

Scott 1974	Scott, W.C. *The Oral Nature of the Homeric Simile*. Mnemosyne Supplements 28. Leiden.
Scott 2009	Scott, W.C. *The Artistry of the Homeric Simile*. Hanover, N.H. and London.
Scully 1984	Scully, S. 'The Language of Achilles: The ΟΧΘΗΣΑΣ Formulas.' *TAPhA* 114: 11–27.
Scully 1986	Scully, S.P. 'Studies of Narrative and Speech in the *Iliad*.' *Arethusa* 19: 135–153.
Scully 1990	Scully, S. *Homer and the Sacred City*. Myth and Poetics. Ithaca and London.
Scully 2003	Scully, S. 'Reading the Shield of Achilles: Terror, Anger, Delight.' *HSCPh* 101: 29–47.
Seaford 1994	Seaford, R. *Reciprocity and Ritual: Homer and Tragedy in the Developing City-State*. Oxford.
Seeck 1998	Seeck, G.A. 'Homerisches Erzählen und das Problem der Gleichzeitigkeit.' *Hermes* 126: 131–144.
Segal 1971	Segal, C. *The Theme of the Mutilation of the Corpse in the* Iliad. Mnemosyne Supplements 17. Leiden.
Sellschopp 1934	Sellschopp, I. *Stilistische Untersuchungen zu Hesiod*. Hamburg. (Reprint Darmstadt 1967.)
Shapiro *et al.* 2004	Shapiro, H.A. *et al.* 'Dance.' In *ThesCRA* 2: 300–343.
Shear 2000	Shear, I.M. *Tales of Heroes: The Origins of the Homeric Texts*. New York and Athens.
Shear 2004	Shear, I.M. *Kingship in the Mycenaean World and Its Reflections in the Oral Tradition*. Philadelphia.
Shelmerdine 1995	Shelmerdine, C.W. 'Shining and Fragrant Cloth in Homeric Epic.' In Carter/Morris 1995, pp. 99–107.
Shipp (1953) 1972	Shipp, G.P. *Studies in the Language of Homer*². Cambridge Classical Studies. Cambridge (¹1953).
Shive 1987	Shive, D. *Naming Achilles*. New York and Oxford.
Simon 1995	Simon, E. 'Der Schild des Achilleus.' In *Beschreibungskunst – Kunstbeschreibung. Ekphrasis von der Antike bis zur Gegenwart*, ed. by G. Boehm and H. Pfotenhauer (Bild und Text), pp. 123–141. Munich.
Singor 1991	Singor, H. 'Nine against Troy. On Epic φάλαγγες, πρόμαχοι, and an Old Structure in the Story of the *Iliad*.' *Mnemosyne* 44: 17–62.
Slaten 1993	Slaten, H. 'The Circulation of Bodies in the *Iliad*.' *New Literary History* 24: 339–361.
Slatkin (1991) 2011	Slatkin, L.M. *The Power of Thetis and Selected Essays*. Cambridge, Mass. and London. (Originally published as *The Power of Thetis: Allusion and Interpretation in the* Iliad. Berkeley etc. 1991.)
Smith 2011	Smith, A.C. 'Marriage in the Greek World.' In *ThesCRA* 6: 83–94.
Smith 1979	Smith, P.M. 'Notes on the Text of the Fifth Homeric Hymn.' *HSCPh* 83: 29–50.
Snell (1964) 1966	Snell, B. 'ἅλιος.' In B. Snell. *Gesammelte Schriften*, pp. 65–67. Göttingen. (First published in *Festschrift für Eugen von Mercklin*, ed. by E. Homann-Wedeking and B. Segall, pp. 172–173. Waldsassen 1964.)
Snell 1978	Snell, B. *Der Weg zum Denken und zur Wahrheit. Studien zur frühgriechischen Sprache*. Hypomnemata 57. Göttingen.
Snodgrass 1998	Snodgrass, A. *Homer and the Artists: Text and Picture in Early Greek Art*. Cambridge.

Solmsen 1901   Solmsen, F. *Untersuchungen zur griechischen Laut- und Verslehre.* Strasbourg.

Solmsen 1965   Solmsen, F. '*Ilias* Σ 535–540.' *Hermes* 93: 1–6.

Sommer 1977   Sommer, F. *Schriften aus dem Nachlass,* ed. by B. Forssman. MSS, NF Beiheft 1. Munich.

Sommerstein/Bayliss 2013 Sommerstein, A.H. and A.J. Bayliss. *Oaths and State in Ancient Greece,* with Contributions by L.A. Kozak and I.C. Torrance. Beiträge zur Altertumskunde 306. Berlin and Boston.

Spatafora 1997   Spatafora, G. 'Esigenza fisiologica e funzione terapeutica del lamento nei poemi omerici. Studio sul significato di κλαίω, γοάω, στένω, οἰμώζω/κωκύω, ὀδύρομαι.' *AC* 66: 1–23.

Squire 2011   Squire, M. *The* Iliad *in a Nutshell: Visualizing Epic on the Tabulae Iliacae.* Oxford.

Stallmach 1968   Stallmach, J. *Ate. Zur Frage des Selbst- und Weltverständnisses des frühgriechischen Menschen.* Beiträge zur Klassischen Philologie 18. Meisenheim am Glan.

Stanley 1993   Stanley, K. *The Shield of Homer: Narrative Structure in the* Iliad. Princeton.

Stansbury-O'Donnell 1995 Stansbury-O'Donnell, M.D. 'Reading Pictorial Narrative: The Law Court Scene of the Shield of Achilles.' In Carter/Morris 1995, pp. 315–334.

Stein-Hölkeskamp 1989 Stein-Hölkeskamp, E. *Adelskultur und Polisgesellschaft. Studien zum griechischen Adel in archaischer und klassischer Zeit.* Stuttgart.

Stengel 1910   Stengel, P. *Opferbräuche der Griechen.* Leipzig and Berlin.

Stephens 1983   Stephens, L. 'The Origins of a Homeric Pecularity: μή plus Aorist Imperative.' *TAPA* 113: 69–78.

Stephens 2002/2003 Stephens, S.A. 'Linus Song.' *Hermathena* 173/174: 13–28.

Steuernagel 1998   Steuernagel, D. *Menschenopfer und Mord am Altar. Griechische Mythen in etruskischen Gräbern.* Palilia 3. Wiesbaden.

Stoevesandt 2004 Stoevesandt, M. *Feinde – Gegner – Opfer. Zur Darstellung der Troianer in den Kampfszenen der* Ilias. Schweizerische Beiträge zur Altertumswissenschaft 30. Basel.

Stubbings 1962   Stubbings, F.H. 'Food and Agriculture.' In Wace/Stubbings 1962, pp. 523–530.

Stubbings 1962a   Stubbings, F.H. 'Crafts and Industries.' In Wace/Stubbings 1962, pp. 531–538.

Sullivan 1987   Sullivan, S.D. 'πραπίδες in Homer.' *Glotta* 65: 182–193.

Sullivan 1989   Sullivan, S.D. 'The Physic Term *Noos* in Homer and the Homeric Hymns.' *SFIC* 82: 152–195.

Sullivan 1995   Sullivan, S.D. *Psychological and Ethical Ideas: What Early Greeks Say.* Mnemosyne Supplements 144. Leiden etc.

Szemerényi 1962   Szemerényi, O. 'Principles of Etymological Research in the Indo-European Languages.' In *II. Fachtagung für Indogermanische und Allgemeine Sprachwissenschaft, Innsbruck 10.-15. Oktober 1961,* pp. 175–212. Innsbrucker Beiträge zur Kulturwissenschaft, Sonderh. 15. Innsbruck.

Szlezák 2004   Szlezák, T.A. '*Ilias* und Gilgamesch-Epos.' In *Troia. Von Homer bis heute,* ed. by H. Hofmann, pp. 11–33. Tübingen.

Tabachovitz 1951 Tabachovitz, D. *Homerische εἰ-Sätze. Eine sprachpsychologische Studie.* Lund.

Taplin (1980) 2001   Taplin, O. 'The Shield of Achilles within the *Iliad*.' In Cairns 2001, pp. 342–
                        364. (First published in *G&R* 27 [1980] 1–21; also in Latacz 1991, pp. 227–
                        253.)
Taplin 1992   Taplin, O. *Homeric Soundings: The Shaping of the* Iliad. Oxford.
Tausend 2001   Tausend, K. 'Zur Bedeutung von E-U-KE-TO in mykenischer Zeit.' *Dike* 4:
                        5–11.
Thalmann 1984   Thalmann, W.G. *Conventions of Form and Thought in Early Greek Epic Poetry*.
                        Baltimore and London.
Thomas 2002   Thomas, B.M. 'Constraints and Contradictions: Whiteness and Femininity
                        in Ancient Greece.' In *Women's Dress in the Ancient Greek World*, ed. by L.
                        Llewellyn-Jones, pp. 1–16. Swansea.
Thompson 1998   Thompson, R. 'Instrumentals, Datives, Locatives and Ablatives: The -φι Case
                        Form in Mycenaean and Homer.' *PCPS* 44: 219–250.
Thür 1996   Thür, G. 'Oaths and Dispute Settlement in Ancient Greek Law.' In *Greek Law
                        in its Political Setting*, ed. by L. Foxhall and A.D.E. Lewis, pp. 57–72. Oxford.
Thür 2007   Thür G. 'Der Reinigungseid im archaischen griechischen Rechtsstreit und
                        seine Parallelen im Alten Orient.' In *Rechtsgeschichte und Interkulturalität.
                        Zum Verhältnis des östlichen Mittelmeerraums und 'Europas' im Altertum*, ed.
                        by R. Rollinger *et al.*, pp. 179–195. Philippika 19. Wiesbaden.
Tichy 1981   Tichy, E. 'Beobachtungen zur homerischen Synizese.' *MSS* 40: 187–222.
Tichy 1983   Tichy, E. *Onomatopoetische Verbalbildungen des Griechischen*. SAWW 409.
                        Vienna.
Tölle 1964   Tölle, R. *Frühgriechische Reigentänze*. Waldsassen.
Treu 1955   Treu, M. *Von Homer zur Lyrik. Wandlungen des griechischen Weltbildes im
                        Spiegel der Sprache*. Zetemata 12. Munich.
Tronci 2000   Tronci, L. 'Eredità indoeuropea e innovazione nel greco omerico: l'elemento
                        -ι° come «marca» caratterizzante di primi membri di composto.' *SSL* 38: 275–
                        311.
Trümpy 1950   Trümpy, H. *Kriegerische Fachausdrücke im griechischen Epos. Untersuchun-
                        gen zum Wortschatze Homers*. Basel.
Tsagalis 2004   Tsagalis, C. *Epic Grief: Personal Laments in Homer's* Iliad. Untersuchungen
                        zur antiken Literatur und Geschichte 70. Berlin and New York.
Tsagalis 2008   Tsagalis, C. *The Oral Palimpsest: Exploring Intertextuality in the Homeric
                        Epics*. Hellenic Studies 29. Washington.
Tsagalis 2010   Tsagalis, C. 'The Dynamic Hypertext: Lists and Catalogues in the Homeric
                        Epics.' *Trends in Classics* 2: 323–347.
Tsagalis 2011   Tsagalis, C. 'Towards an Oral, Intertextual Neoanalysis.' *Trends in Classics* 3:
                        209–244.
Tsagalis 2012   Tsagalis, C. *From Listeners to Viewers: Space in the* Iliad. Hellenic Studies 53.
                        Cambridge, Mass. and London.
Tsagarakis 1977   Tsagarakis, O. *Nature and Background of Major Concepts of Divine Power in
                        Homer*. Amsterdam.
Tsagarakis 1982   Tsagarakis, O. *Form and Content in Homer*. Hermes Einzelschriften 46. Wies-
                        baden.
Tucker 1990   Tucker, E.F. *The Creation of Morphological Regularity: Early Greek Verbs in
                        -éō, -áō, -óō, -úō and -íō*. Historische Sprachforschung, Ergänzungsh. 35. Göt-
                        tingen.

Turkeltaub 2007   Turkeltaub, D. 'Perceiving Iliadic Gods.' *HSCPh* 103: 51–81.

Tzamali 1996   Tzamali, E. *Syntax und Stil bei Sappho*. MSS, N.F. Beiheft 16. Dettelbach.

Tzamali 1997   Tzamali, E. 'Positive Aussage plus negierte Gegenaussage im Griechischen. Teil I: Die ältere griechische Dichtung.' *MSS* 57: 129–167.

Ulf 1990   Ulf, C. *Die homerische Gesellschaft. Materialien zur analytischen Beschreibung und historischen Lokalisierung*. Vestigia. Beiträge zur Alten Geschichte 43. Munich.

Usener 1990   Usener, K. *Beobachtungen zum Verhältnis der* Odyssee *zur* Ilias. ScriptOralia 21. Tübingen.

van der Valk 1964   Valk, M. van der. *Researches on the Text and Scholia of the* Iliad, vol. 2. Leiden.

Veneri 1984   Veneri, A. 'Tra storia e archeologia: Il ἱερὸς κύκλος in Omero, Σ 504.' *SMEA* 25: 349–356.

Voigt 1934   Voigt, C. *Überlegung und Entscheidung. Studien zur Selbstauffassung des Menschen bei Homer*. Pan-Bücherei. Philosophie 16. Berlin.

Wace/Stubbings 1962   Wace, A.J.B. and F.H. Stubbings (eds.). *A Companion to Homer*. London and New York.

Wachter 1990   Wachter, R. 'Nereiden und Neoanalyse: Ein Blick hinter die *Ilias*.' In *WJA* 16: 17–31.

Wachter 2001   Wachter, R. *Non-Attic Greek Vase Inscriptions*. Oxford.

Wachter 2007   Wachter, R. 'Greek Dialects and Epic Poetry: Did Homer have to be an Ionian?' In *ΦΩΝΗΣ ΧΑΡΑΚΤΗΡ ΕΘΝΙΚΟΣ. Actes du Ve congrès international de dialectologie greque (Athènes 28–30 septembre 2006)*, ed. by M.B. Hatzopoulos, pp. 317–328. ΜΕΛΕΤΗΜΑΤΑ 52. Athens.

Wachter 2008   Wachter, R. Review of *Homeri* Ilias. Recensuit / testimonia congessit M.L. West, 2 vols. Stuttgart and Leipzig 1998–2000 and of West 2001. *Kratylos* 53: 116–122.

Wachter 2012   Wachter, R. 'The Other View: Focus on Linguistic Innovations in the Homeric Epics.' In *Relative Chronology in Early Greek Epic Poetry*, ed. by Ø. Andersen and D.T.T. Haug, pp. 65–79. Cambridge.

Wackernagel (1878) 1979   Wackernagel, J. 'Die epische Zerdehnung.' In Wackernagel 1979, pp. 1512–1565. (First published in *BKIS* 4 [1878] 259–312.)

Wackernagel (1881) 1953   Wackernagel, J. 'Zum Zahlwort.' In Wackernagel 1953, pp. 204–235. (First published in *KZ* 25 [1881] 260–291.)

Wackernagel (1887) 1979   Wackernagel, J. Review of K.F. Johansson. *De derivatis verbis contractis linguae Graecae quaestiones*. Uppsala 1886. In Wackernagel 1979, pp. 1799–1811. (First published in *Philologischer Anzeiger* 17 [1887] 229–241.)

Wackernagel (1914) 1953   Wackernagel, J. 'Akzentstudien III: Zum homerischen Akzent.' In Wackernagel 1953, pp. 1154–1187. (First published in *GN* [1914] 97–130.)

Wackernagel 1916   Wackernagel, J. *Sprachliche Untersuchungen zu Homer*. Forschungen zur griechischen und lateinischen Grammatik 4. Göttingen. (Reprint 1970.)

Wackernagel (1920/24) 2009   Wackernagel, J. *Lectures on Syntax with Special Reference to Greek, Latin, and Germanic*, edited with notes and bibliography by D. Langslow. Oxford. (German Original: *Vorlesungen über Syntax mit besonderer Berücksichtigung von Griechisch, Lateinisch und Deutsch. Erste Reihe²*. Basel 1926 [¹1920]; *Zweite Reihe²*. Basel 1928 [¹1924].)

Wackernagel (1925) 1953   Wackernagel, J. 'Griechische Miszellen.' In Wackernagel 1953, pp. 844–875. (First published in *Glotta* 14 [1925] 36–67.)

Wackernagel 1953   Wackernagel, J. *Kleine Schriften*, vols. 1–2, ed. by the Academy of Sciences in Göttingen. Göttingen.

Wackernagel 1979   Wackernagel, J. *Kleine Schriften*, vol. 3, ed. by B. Forssman. Göttingen.

Wagner-Hasel 2000   Wagner-Hasel, B. 'Die Reglementierung von Traueraufwand und die Tradierung des Nachruhms der Toten in Griechenland.' In *Frauenwelten in der Antike. Geschlechterordnung und weibliche Lebenspraxis*, ed. by T. Späth and B. Wagner-Hasel, pp. 81–102. Stuttgart and Weimar.

Wakker 1994   Wakker, G.C. *Conditions and Conditionals: An Investigation of Ancient Greek.* Amsterdam.

Walsh 2005   Walsh, T.R. *Fighting Words and Feuding Words: Anger and the Homeric Poems.* Lanham etc.

Waltz 1933   Waltz, P. 'L'exagération numérique dans l'*Iliade* et dans l'*Odyssée*.' *REHom* 3: 3–38.

Warren 1984   Warren, P. 'Circular Platforms at Minoan Knossos.' *ABSA* 79: 307–323.

Wathelet 1992   Wathelet, P. 'Arès chez Homère ou le dieu mal aimé.' *LEC* 60: 113–128.

Wathelet 1995   Wathelet, P. 'Athéna chez Homère ou le triomphe de la déesse.' *Kernos* 8: 167–185.

Wathelet 2000   Whatelet, P. 'Dieux et enchantements dans l'épopée Homérique.' In *La Magie. Actes du colloque international de Montpellier (25.–27.3.1999)*, vol. 2, ed. by A. Moreau *et al.*, pp. 169–184. Montpellier.

Watkins (1976) 1994   Watkins, C. 'Towards Proto-Indo-European Syntax: Problems and Pseudo-Problems.' In C. Watkins. *Selected Writings, vol. 1: Language and Linguistics*, ed. by L. Oliver, pp. 242–263. Innsbrucker Beiträge zur Sprachwissenschaft 80. Innsbruck. (First published in *Papers from the Parasession on Diachronic Syntax*, ed. by S. Steever *et al.*, pp. 305–326. Chicago 1976.)

Watkins 1978   Watkins, C. '«Let us now praise famous grains».' *PAPhS* 122: 9–17.

Webb 2009   Webb, R. *Ekphrasis, Imagination and Persuasion in Ancient Rhetorical Theory and Practice.* Farnham.

van Wees 1988   Wees, H. van. 'Kings in Combat. Battles and Heroes in the *Iliad*.' *CQ* 38: 1–24.

van Wees 1992   Wees, H. van. *Status Warriors. War, Violence and Society in Homer and History.* Amsterdam.

van Wees 1996   Wees, H. van. 'Heroes, Knights and Nutters: Warrior Mentality in Homer.' In *Battle in Antiquity*, ed. by A.B. Lloyd, pp. 1–86. London.

van Wees 2005   Wees, H. van. 'Clothes, Class and Gender in Homer.' In *Body Language in the Greek and Roman Worlds*, ed. by D. Cairns, pp. 1–36. Swansea.

Wegner 1968   Wegner, M. 'Musik und Tanz.' *ArchHom* chap. U. Göttingen.

Weiler 2001   Weiler, G. *Domos Theiou Basileos. Herrschaftsformen und Herrschaftsarchitektur in den Siedlungen der Dark Ages.* Beiträge zur Altertumskunde 136. Leipzig.

Wenskus 1990   Wenskus, O. *Astronomische Zeitangaben von Homer bis Theophrast.* Hermes Einzelschriften 55. Stuttgart.

West 1983   West, M.L. *The Orphic Poems.* Oxford..

West 1992   West, M.L. *Ancient Greek Music.* Oxford.

West (1995) 2011   West, M.L. 'The Date of the *Iliad*.' In M.L. West. *Hellenica: Selected Papers on Greek Literature and Thought. Vol. 1: Epic*, pp. 188–208. Oxford. (First published in *MH* 52 [1995] 203–219.)

West 1997	West, M.L. *The East Face of Helicon: West Asiatic Elements in Greek Poetry and Myth*. Oxford.
West 1998	West, M.L. 'Praefatio.' In *Homeri* Ilias. Recensuit / testimonia congessit M.L.West, vol. 1, pp. V–XXXVII. Stuttgart and Leipzig.
West 2001	West, M.L. *Studies in the Text and Transmission of the* Iliad. Munich and Leipzig.
West 2001a	West, M.L. 'Some Homeric Words.' *Glotta* 77: 118–135.
West (2001) 2011	West, M.L. 'The Fragmentary Homeric Hymn to Dionysos.' In M.L. West. *Hellenica: Selected Papers on Greek Literature and Thought. Vol. 1: Epic*, pp. 313–328. Oxford. (First published in *ZPE* 134 [2001] 1–11.)
West 2003	West, M.L. '*Iliad* and *Aethiopis*.' *CQ* 53: 1–14.
West 2003a	West, M.L. *Homeric Hymns, Homeric Apocrypha, Lives of Homer*, ed. and transl. by M.L. West. Loeb Classical Library 496. Cambridge, Mass. and London.
West 2007	West, M.L. *Indo-European Poetry and Myth*. Oxford.
West 2011	West, M.L. *The Making of the* Iliad: *Disquisition and Analytical Commentary*. Oxford.
West 2013	West, M.L. *The Epic Cycle: A Commentary on the Lost Troy Epics*. Oxford.
West 1967	West, S. (ed.). *The Ptolemaic Papyri of Homer*. Papyrologica Coloniensia 3. Cologne and Opladen.
Westbrook 1992	Westbrook, R. 'The Trial Scene in the *Iliad*.' *HSCPh* 94: 53–76.
White 2002	White, H. 'Notes on Greek Lexicography.' *Myrtia* 17: 327–330.
Whitman 1958	Whitman, C.H. *Homer and the Heroic Tradition*. Cambridge, Mass..
Wickert-Micknat 1982	Wickert-Micknat, G. 'Die Frau.' *ArchHom* chap. R. Göttingen.
Wickert-Micknat 1983	Wickert-Micknat, G. *Unfreiheit im Zeitalter der homerischen Epen*. Forschungen zur antiken Sklaverei 16. Wiesbaden.
Wilamowitz 1916	Wilamowitz-Moellendorff, U. von. *Die* Ilias *und Homer*. Berlin.
Willcock (1964) 2001	Willcock, M.M. 'Mythological Paradeigma in the *Iliad*.' In Cairns 2001, pp. 435–455. (First published in *CQ* 14 [1964] 141–154; also in de Jong 1999, vol. 3, pp. 385–402.)
Willcock 1977	Willcock, M.M. 'Ad hoc Invention in the *Iliad*.' *HSCPh* 81: 41–53.
Willcock 1997	Willcock, M.M. 'Neoanalysis.' In *A New Companion to Homer*, ed. by I. Morris and B. Powell, pp. 174–189. Mnemosyne Supplements 163. Leiden etc.
Wille 2001	Wille, G. *Akroasis. Der akustische Sinnesbereich in der griechischen Literatur bis zum Ende der klassischen Zeit*. Tübinger phänomenologische Bibliothek. Tübingen. (2 vols.; originally Habilitationsschrift Tübingen 1958.)
Willemsen 1957	Willemsen, F. *Dreifusskessel von Olympia. Alte und neue Funde*. Olympische Forschungen 3. Berlin.
Willenbrock (1944) 1969	Willenbrock, H. *Die poetische Bedeutung der Gegenstände in Homers* Ilias. Marburg/Lahn. (Originally diss. Marburg 1944.).
Willetts 1977	Willetts, R.F. 'Homeric doors.' *LCM* 2: 93–100.
Willi 1999	Willi, A. 'Zur Verwendung und Etymologie von griechisch ἐρι-.' *HSF* 112: 86–100.
Willi 2008	Willi, A. 'Genitive-Problems: Mycenaean -*Ca-o, Co-jo, -Co* vs. later Greek -ᾱο, -οιο, -ου.' *Glotta* 84: 239–272.
Wilson 2002	Wilson, D.F. *Ransom, Revenge, and Heroic Identity in the* Iliad. Cambridge.
Wilson 1987	Wilson, J.R. 'Non-temporal οὐκέτι/μηκέτι.' *Glotta* 65: 194–198.

Wirbelauer 1996 — Wirbelauer, E. 'Der Schild des Achilleus (*Il.* 18.478–609). Überlegungen zur inneren Struktur und zum Aufbau der «Stadt im Frieden».' In *Vergangenheit und Lebenswelt. Soziale Kommunikation, Traditionsbildung und historisches Bewußtsein*, ed. by H.-J. Gehrke and A. Möller, pp. 143–178. ScriptOralia 90. Tübingen.

Wolf (1795) 1985 — Wolf, F.A. *Prolegomena to Homer*, translated with Introduction and Notes by A. Grafton, G.W. Most and J.E.G. Zetzel. Princeton. (Latin original *Prolegomena ad Homerum sive de operum Homericorum prisca et genuina forma variisque mutationibus et probabili ratione emendandi*. Halle 1795.)

Wolff 1946 — Wolff, H.J. 'The Origin of Judicial Litigation among the Greeks.' *Traditio* 4: 31–87.

Wolff 1961 — Wolff, H.J. 'Der Ursprung des gerichtlichen Rechtsstreits bei den Griechen.' In H.J. Wolff. *Beiträge zur Rechtsgeschichte Altgriechenlands und des hellenistisch-römischen Ägypten*, pp. 1–90. Forschungen zum römischen Recht 13. Weimar. (German version of Wolff 1946 with appendices.)

Worthen 1988 — Worthen, T. 'The Idea of «Sky» in Archaic Greek Poetry. ἐν δὲ τὰ τείρεα πάντα, τά τ᾽ οὐρανός ἐστεφάνωται *Iliad* 18.485.' *Glotta* 66: 1–19.

Wright/Jones 1997 — Wright, G.M. and P.V. Jones. *Homer: German Scholarship in Translation*. Oxford.

Wyatt 1969 — Wyatt Jr., W.F. *Metrical Lengthening in Homer*. Incunabula Graeca 35. Rome.

Zanker 1994 — Zanker, G. The Heart of Achilles: Characterization and Personal Ethics in the Iliad. Ann Arbor.

Zimmermann 1992 — Zimmermann, B. *Dithyrambos. Geschichte einer Gattung*. Hypomnemata 98. Göttingen.

Lightning Source UK Ltd.
Milton Keynes UK
UKHW012006210722
406211UK00002B/40